THE GOLDEN FLEECE FOUND!

Basil C. Hill

TRAFFORD
PUBLISHING™

Note for Librarians: A cataloguing record for this book is available from Library and Archives Canada at www.collectionscanada.ca/amicus/index-e.html
ISBN 1-4120-4319-0

PUBLISHING™

Offices in Canada, USA, Ireland and UK

This book was published *on-demand* in cooperation with Trafford Publishing. On-demand publishing is a unique process and service of making a book available for retail sale to the public taking advantage of on-demand manufacturing and Internet marketing. On-demand publishing includes promotions, retail sales, manufacturing, order fulfilment, accounting and collecting royalties on behalf of the author.

Book sales for North America and international:
Trafford Publishing, 6E–2333 Government St.,
Victoria, BC v8t 4p4 CANADA
phone 250 383 6864 (toll-free 1 888 232 4444)
fax 250 383 6804; email to orders@trafford.com
Book sales in Europe:
Trafford Publishing (uk) Limited, 9 Park End Street, 2nd Floor
Oxford, UK oxi 1hh UNITED KINGDOM
phone 44 (0)1865 722 113 (local rate 0845 230 9601)
facsimile 44 (0)1865 722 868; info.uk@trafford.com
Order online at:
trafford.com/04-2126

10 9 8 7 6 5

ABOUT THE AUTHOR

Tired of the nightly terror attacks called "Nightmares and Night Terrors," the writer decided to open his eyes during one such encounter. To understand what he had seen, he visited all manner of strange places and read every type of mystical and religious book available, searching for answers. His theory then was that there were either two spiritual worlds, or one spiritual world inhabited by at least two opposing groups.

Frustrated with the lack of understanding of spiritual matters after twenty years of digging, the writer visited a Benny Hinn crusade as a cynical reporter and skeptic. An unusual supernatural experience, a trip to Israel, and an encounter similar to what Saul experienced on the road to Damascus brought the sought-after answers and much more.

At one of Israel's ancient holy sites, a bright light knocked him down and began a conversation. The writer asked: "Why me? I am tired of games, half-truths and esoteric riddles. If you are who I perceive you are, please tell me why there is so much confusion among your children? Are we all in endless cycles of lies and delusions?"

This response came from within a bright light: "Here Son, receive these keys to my ancient schematic that had been published a long time ago. In it you will see that I had foreseen all of the shortcomings of my flocks. That is why I have decreed that all have erred and come short. Those who postulate that they do not err, I want you to highlight all of their errors. Do not compromise my word: I chasten those that I love."

The writer retorted: "How will men know that you have sent me?"

The reply: "In the outer pillars of the Temple of Solomon I have published two names. To those two human pillars I have given letters of restoration. Translate the names: Jachin and Boaz."

BOOK INTRODUCTION

I grew up as a disinherited spiritual orphan. My mother, "Wisdom" was a stranger to me. I became a spiritual hermit and survived on discards from garbage cans called rebellion, and addiction to carnal pursuits. Occasionally, I foraged on the leftovers of religion and philosophy. As I walked in the footsteps of Don Quixote searching for windmills, I found new and formidable giants. A part sponsorship of an archeological expedition occasioned the building of a museum that got me hooked on archeology. On a trip to Israel I discovered the ultimate artifact: the stone that David used to destroy Goliath. That dramatic "Damascus encounter" transformed my interest into spiritual archeology. I am now very blessed and comfortably reunited with my mother and "Omnipotent Father." In this book I will share my experiences and my inheritance.

There are mythological tales from every corner of the globe. Some are verbal dictates passed down from generation to generation. Others are allegorical stories about the movement of stars and the behaviour of orbs and other celestial beings. Others, like the story of "Jason and the Argonauts" are esoteric parables. According to legend, a golden lamb or fleece was stranded on a rock in the centre of a turbulent sea. Rocks converged on all sides upon any object or vessel that pursued the golden prize. In addition to that, a seven-headed monster guarded it. Finally, one named Jason arrived and miraculously overcame all obstacles to fetch "The Golden Fleece." This book releases powerful apocalyptical data concealed beneath the allegorical tale of "Jason and the Argonauts."

Events of religious significance have coded precedents in the Old Testament. The Golden Fleece is the key that reveals them and unlocks apocalyptic messages for Jews, Muslims, Christians and all nations (natural and adopted) out of the loins of Abraham. By accentuating the precision of the Hebrew language, "Lost Tribes of Israel" are traced. Also, there are at least 100 fresh revelations released by divine inspiration to usher in the next move of God—*The Season of Sheaves* for *The Church without Spot or Wrinkle*. *The Golden Fleece Found!* is a complete non-fiction deliverance manual: the spirit level to test all major doctrines is unveiled in the format of a suspense novel. It is also a book of wisdom, prophecy, and guidance for churches and nations. The redemptive purposes of the three flocks that Jacob envisioned at Padan-aram (Jews, Christians and Muslims) are revealed as per prophecies in Isaiah 60 and 62.

In order to facilitate the advent of the new season of restoration, a comprehensive dossier of the spiritual world and its key players (ignored and misunderstood for years) is also included. By using the tri-dimensional blueprint for the Temple of Solomon, we were able to find our spiritual temple's outer courts, inner courts, Holy of Holies, and the altars of them all. Finally, there is an oasis of wisdom for millions of seekers, Carl Sagan followers, and fans of *The Da Vinci Code* and *The Celestine Prophecy*. In addition to adjusting esoteric thermometers, *The Golden Fleece Found!* provides "missing insights," solutions to world enigmas, and offers relief to those seeking respite from the spiritual wilderness.

ACKNOWLEDGEMENTS

Special thanks to Vren for the artwork and especially the years of inspiration and encouragement. Special thanks to Ray and Ceil, Roger and Des for the endless hospitality and encouragement for the past 10 years. Special thanks to Sister Chiddick, Alex, Alec, Marion, Mrs. Benjamin, and Mark1 for proofreading and editing services. Special thanks to my covenant partners T.B.N, The China Revival Church and The India Evangelical Church for standing in the gap and for my consistent prayer coverage for years. Special thanks to those who have helped and would prefer to remain incognito in Israel, Ukraine, Dubai, Syria, America and Rome. Thanks to those friends in Australia, Paris, Germany, Switzerland, Spain, Barbados (especially Roger, Des, Alec and Michele) and Trinidad (especially Mario, Ingrid, Leston and Manuel). Special thanks to Gregory, Wingrove, Aziz, Francis, Ramez, Joseph, Theo, the Shaw family and Mrs. Richards in Antigua and in Barbuda. I give thanks to all at Zionway Ministries—especially Brothers Charles, Niron, Carl, Manuel, Bertram, Lance, Stanford, Noyce, Sister Lou and Brother and Sister Irish. Special thanks to the dedicated staff at the Bibliotheque Nationale, the Smithsonian Institute and National Geographic. Special thanks to Doctor Knight, and all those members of the diplomatic corps who have helped with this project. To my family, friends and in-laws, I would never have endured without your encouragement and endless assistance.

CONTENTS

PROLOGUE

EVE OF THE APOCALYPSE

A young Hebrew lad by the name of Daniel recorded some prophecies over 2500 years ago. Those predictions have since been documented in the Tanakh and Gentile translations called Bibles. The related events have unfurled with unprecedented precision in the regatta called world history.

His depiction of Western Civilizations (evolving from the Roman Empire) as toes of an allegorical beast, rampaging over feudal Europe has also proved to be historically accurate. Within the last fifty years, archaeological finds from the oceans of antiquity have not only confirmed his prophecies, but also triggered a deafening silence from Daniel's skeptics.

Another Hebrew named John the Revealer foretold events over 2000 years ago in a book translated as Revelation. He had apparently forewarned us about the Russian nuclear reactor disaster and also the Persian Gulf War. Since John was the last known Hebrew prophet that spoke corporately to Jews and Gentiles alike, we have scrutinized his prophecies for events past and those yet to come.

According to Daniel 9:2 (repeated in detail in Matthew 24:34-50), a series of events that have already begun to manifest will be completed before the passing of a generation. It stands to reason that since all of Daniel's prophecies have been fulfilled and John is on target so far, the ones left should be pretty imminent. The remaining ones were anticipated to occur within either a seventy-year period that began in 1948 (1948+70=2018) or seven Jubilee years from 1948 (1948+350=2298). Out of both computations we have possible years 2018 through to 2298. John prophesied in 98 C.E. If Jeshua was the true light and John was His last witness, then the Jewish people should have had 18 esoteric years* of darkness. Afterwards, they would have had to await the 1st Jubilee as per Leviticus 25:2, Leviticus 25:8-10 and Jeremiah 3:14-18 for the "dawn of the light" to return. Or is it the shadows of sunset- 98+1800 =1898? A Jubilee year is 50 years according to Leviticus 25: 1898+50=1948. Thus the process of Israel becoming a nation could not have been completed before 1948. The remaining six (listed below) can be summed up with eight frightening words: *We are on the eve of The Apocalypse!*

1. A conglomeration of ten ethnic groups and seven organizations would emerge from the ashes of the fragmented Roman Empire to form a confederation.

2. A people from the Orient would have an army in the hundreds of millions.

3. Israel would be summoned from the Diaspora to become a nation.

4. The Temple of Solomon would be rebuilt.

5. The nations of Iraq/Iran (formerly Babylon) will be attacked on all sides, and then destroyed: Jeremiah 50 & 51.

6.   A person of severe influence will emerge on the forefront of world affairs. First, he will appear as a peacemaker with solutions to a major impasse, and then unveil his "Jekyll and Hyde" personality.

*Master's Footnote: Time, Times, and Half Time. The beats (whether fractional or whole) are exponential: $1/2 = 100$, $1 = 1000$.

The consensus among the world's most erudite thinkers is that the earth is expected to undergo very serious physical and/ or spiritual changes within the next 200 years. For the first time in history, Christians, Muslims, and Hindus are studying the prophecies of John while secular leaders are searching Nostradamus' vague poetic parables for new insights. Although those computations might be new revelations to many, hopefully this book will bridge the canyon between the wisdom of the wise-hearted and that of the willing-hearted.

CHAPTER 1. ALTAR AT THE BASE OF JACOB'S LADDER

CHAPTER 1A. SEED IN A HAYSTACK

Are explorers past and present driven by a common motivating factor? Every time I pose that question the responses differ. The reply most often received is that people are propelled by a burning desire to know. In many cases, mine included, accidental occurrences and chance encounters were sparks that ignited the discovery processes. Over twenty years ago, a dozen men and women of different ethnic, religious and philosophical backgrounds gathered in a television studio to discuss various historical chance encounters. I, an amateur archaeologist, was blessed to be among the panelists. We were asked to retrieve fragments (figuratively) of civilizations that had survived major catastrophes and to document the nature of the threads that made the fabric of amalgamation possible. Our task was to reconstruct past cultural bridges. The theme of the series was *Reconstructing Babel*. We elaborated on many things people today take for granted that may have caused tremendous friction initially: culture and language assimilation, congruency of speech, language comprehension, diversity of dress and moral codes of conduct.

It is safe to say that the assemblage consisted of the marginally religious to the esoterically learned, religiously curious, academics, stoics, agnostics and atheists. Though a bit odd, the panel bonded exceeding well socially and educationally, primarily through those shows and the ensuing lectures. I made sure that members of the clique were afforded first viewer rights of my numerous archaeological finds. At the end of the series, we wondered aloud whether or not humankind was following a carefully laid out script. I have deliberately omitted the name of the country for security purposes. The media feedback and public responses to our lectures were so tremendous that radio and television became wired, literally and figuratively, whenever any of us were panelists. The topics were intellectually provocative.

On another occasion, four of us were requested to evaluate the results of a survey sponsored by an educational institution. Who, among a select group of persons, had the greatest positive effects on humankind's improvement of spiritual well-being and elevation of wisdom? The names were Moses, Gandhi, Buddha, Mohammed, Zoroaster, Solomon, and Jesus or Jeshua. What we did not know was that the institution had sent out similar surveys and those names were the ones that kept resurfacing.

On a later radio show, an elderly man with a thick accent uttered and I quote, "Adam and Solomon were messengers on similar missions. One was entrusted with a schematic. One lost it; one retrieved it only to lose it again. Find the thief and you won't find the plan. However if you retrieve the plan, you will find the thief. For over two thousand years the wisest among our civilizations have been trying to solve that riddle. The person who does will find the Golden Fleece, in which are the "world's most valued secrets."

My reaction was one of bewilderment. Here was an unknown person giving me an imprecise riddle with no clues. I simply dismissed his statements until months later when the same caller volunteered the following clues: (1) an ancient garden that existed on earth. In that garden supposedly there was a tree that was capable of cross-pollinating just about everything. I was about to hang up when he shouted, "The Tree of Life." That caught my attention! "That tree illuminated and transformed a special foundation stone. The stone was metamorphic, iridescent, and 'had seven eyes,'" he explained. So according to my unknown seer, (2) clue was a special stone and (3) a special branch out of that tree was grafted and planted all over the world. Until I found that "branch," I would never advance my barometer of knowledge beyond 33 degrees. He definitely caught my attention! (4) The last clue he gave me was that there was a 'Mother of Books' produced from the same tree. Seemingly, its pages were filled with lost history, solutions to oft-sought enigmas, and the world's most pursued archaeological leads. Having mentioned archaeological research, which is one of my greatest passions, I yearned for, yet received no more of his calls.

The year 1998 brought a major breakthrough for me. Whilst in Israel, I found a huge olive tree growing out of a slab of stone. Inscribed on the slab were the words of King Solomon. Proverbs 3:13 "Happy is the man that findeth *Wisdom*, and the man that getteth *Understanding.*" Verse 15, She is more precious than rubies. Verse 18, She is a "Tree of Life" to them that findeth her and happy is every one that retaineth her. Those verses reminded me of passages in Isaiah 11:1 that puzzled me for years: a *Branch* from which sprang understanding and wisdom.

I became a fanatic for information on King Solomon. From his seed, the Ethiopian branch flowed into the family of Ras Tafari Makonnen and the Hebrew branch ended with the only woman reported so precisely in the Holy Koran—Miriam, mother of Isa, Jeshua or Jesus. The biggest surprise of all the findings was that most people who responded across all ethnic and religious persuasions considered his distant seed, Jeshua or Jesus as He is called, to have had the greatest impact on the following categories of teaching: *Spiritual Advancement, Wisdom and Morality*. Across diverse ethnic, cultural and religious backgrounds, that Hebrew carpenter with no known formal educational background topped all polls consistently as the world's most influential and erudite philosopher, magi, teacher, and mirror of pious living.

It was my original intention to publish an angry account fifteen years ago. I had been frustrated with the lack of knowledge possessed by people who called themselves followers of Christ (Christians/Believers) about the person Jeshua. Christian bookstores had very little background information on their pillars. To correct that shortage of data, members of my academic team decided to collect as much missing information (good or bad) we could find on the people considered as *Christian Pillars*: Jeshua, Saul of Tarsus, Titus, James the Elder, Barnabas etc. However, only a minimal amount of personal information on them was readily available. Facts are that Muslim bookstores accessed more knowledge and research material than their Christian counterparts did fifteen years ago.

Among my treasured works was a dissertation by an Oriental youth on "Sayings of a Hebrew Carpenter" by Jeshua of Galilee. At one meeting of the select panel, an exposé was presented entitled "Pearls of Picturesque Speech" by an Imam containing some real pearls of wisdom. They were the utterances by Jeshua in the Christian gospels. I was amazed at the respect the Holy Koran has for Isa or Jeshua. I found excerpts from the New Testament Gospels. Amazingly, many "Pearls" consisted of some of the finest interpretations of the Hebrew Laws by the same Jeshua available in all major spoken and written languages. Also among the "Pearls" were perennially prophetic words of the late Emperor Haile Selassie's speech before the United Nations, which have become the theme of one of Bob Marley's hit songs, "War." The opening lines will be used as subliminal lyrics in this literary sonata: "Until the philosophy that one race is superior and another inferior is finally destroyed, there will always be war."

The fruits of different members of the original panel's investigations, cumulative years of traveling to all corners of the globe and our candid sharing of experiences (some unpleasant, many frightening), could have been the basis for any number of really exciting books. Those, together with more than twenty years in search of "unbiased truth, wisdom, knowledge, and understanding," have caused me to agree with scriptures I found in the Torah and the Tanakh (Hebrew Bible)—Ecclesiastes 7:20 "For there is *not* a just man upon the earth, that doeth good and sinneth not;" also from the Tanakh, Romans 3:23 "All have sinned, and come short of the glory of God."

CHAPTER 1B. THE PRICE OF WISDOM

In my many years as a researcher and investigative reporter into unknown and little known sciences, I have had many supernatural encounters. Had I made a transcript of them in this book, the size would have been prohibitive. So I decided to reverse the order. Publish the findings first—then the roads traveled, or better termed—as roads where the brave dared to tread. Without flattering myself—those who listened to my talk shows might conclude that I am somewhat qualified to discuss the positive and negative aspects of sciences where the rules of such are unknown. I have witnessed too many cases of people who have been magnetized by the glorified term, "The human need to know" that lost their lives stalking their presumed "right to know." Others ended up "Basket Cases," captured and bound by forces that twenty years ago I would have termed "unexplainable." My appraisal:

BETWEEN THE BOUNDARY OF SUCCESS ON ONE SIDE AND FAILURE ON THE OTHER, THERE IS THE LONG FENCE OF PERSISTENCE, BUILT ON THE WALL OF ENDURING FAITH.

Wisdom is neither cheap nor easy. All wisdom is pricey. Purity of wisdom (absolute truth) comes with obedience, abstinence, and purity of mind, body and spirit (or soul, body and spirit). Coveted or incongruent wisdom—part truth or untruth—comes with the penalty of darkness—bondage for disobedience—the price for impurity. Some felonies in the realm of darkness are death and the following sicknesses: physical, mental, spiritual, and financial.

Isn't the term "right to know" misconstrued and presumptuous? One has to seek wisdom. All except one type can be purchased, found, acquired or stolen. True and pure wisdom cannot be bought. It comes from one source. Proverbs 9:10, "*The fear of the Lord is the beginning of wisdom.*" That Source bestows the gift and power of true wisdom, only upon those "chosen" to find *ultimate truth and wisdom.*

There is a very subtle and deadly game played by "mental thieves" that sap other persons' energies and if possible their wisdom by osmosis. Not by investigating, not by studying, but like parrots and monkeys they "peek" and "copy" everything "novel and fresh." Since every bit of wisdom has strict instructions for usage (benefits for proper usage and penalties for misuse), acquiring wisdom without its schematic is dangerous (Ecclesiastes 10:10-14). There are specific "spirit-types" that specialize in such.

Every seer, wise or learned person knows that the birthplace or origin of all wisdom is the spiritual realm. What many people may not know, is that the point of contact or bridge between the spiritual (unrevealed) and carnal (tangible) or bridge between the invisible (un-revealed) and the manifest (revealed) is an altar. There are physical and spiritual bridges. Also there are visible altars and invisible ones. All altars are conduits of either positive or negative energies. I might add that there are places set apart with honest intent to worship and to pay homage to the *Creator of the Universe*. Similarly other altars are established (knowingly or un-knowingly) at physical places where spiritual infractions (especially blood related) have been committed contrary to consecrated laws of *The Creator*. In Genesis 4:10 and 11, that place where Cain slew his brother became an accursed altar.

ALTARS ARE SPIRITUAL BATTLEFIELDS THAT ARE AFFORDED NEITHER VACATIONS NOR SABBATHS.

This book will index case histories of the perennial battles that raged over time for the con-trol of mighty power bases by overpowering altars of persons, institutions or both persons and the custodians of institutions. For all intents and purposes, documented bridges of wisdom or podiums of collective thought processes will be referred to as "Altars." An intangible altar can be likened to "The Ladder of Jacob" and will be treated with the same respect. Once an altar has been constructed, it should be scrutinized for damage, spiritual energies and the identi-ties of the custodians. After 25 years of digging, we concluded that the works and messages of Moses, Noah, Abraham, Isaiah, Jeremiah, Nehemiah, Elijah and Elisha have corroborating messages confirmed by miraculous signs and wonders from God. The Torah—the compila-tion of 66 holy books—bore their records.

The more than 600 laws in the Hebrew Pentateuch—reproduced in the Old Testament of the Occidental Bibles in French, German, Italian, Chinese, Czech, Polish, Dutch, Romanian, Greek, Spanish and Portuguese—many mentioned by Messenger Mohammed (since found in the Koran) are among the world's best known catalogued bridges of wisdom. God's indivisible laws are utterances from "The Oracle" of His highest altar. The author's assignment is to find and reveal the identity of the chief custodian of God's highest altar.

Numberless polls worldwide show that the greatest expounder of those laws was in fact a carpenter of Nazareth, a Hebrew Master Magi. His source of wisdom was the Oracle of the most coveted altar of the priesthood of Melchizedek placed within the most guarded sanctuary on earth. Two cherubim, whose wings touched from wall to wall in King Solomon's Temple, protected that sacred altar. There is or was no might on earth or in the universe that could gain entry to such a guarded sanctuary unless that being was pure, pious and predestined. A veil covered that altar. A veil also covered the *Most Holy Altar* of the last temple built in Jerusalem. Even though those veils were made of perishable materials, as long as the custodians lived in an absolute state of purity and obedience, no one could or would dare to enter the place called the *Holy of Holies*.

A Jewish historian recalled with awe what he reported as one of the most unusual, un-natural and frightening sequences of events that occurred on the "day the veil was ripped from the top to the bottom." Josephus Flavius witnessed the strange occurrences on the day that Jeshua—referred to as a Nazarene rabble-rouser by the Roman establishment—was crucified as per state custom. Jeshua was accorded the punishment set aside for insurrectionists. "At the time of His approximate death, the skies suddenly darkened and there was a violent earth-quake." Those events by themselves were frightening because of their suddenness and their severity. However what followed amazed the zealots, the Priests and ordinary folks. "There was a great noise like thunder as the whole of Jerusalem shook violently. The *Sacred Veil* of the temple in Jerusalem was ripped at that very instant from top to bottom with such precision as if by a giant invisible knife."

I froze when I first got that revelation. It was a very profound discovery. The subsequent transformation of my life from one of happenstance to utmost obedience and discipline was not easy. Had it not been ordained, this task would have been impossible. However, with the price I had to pay, honestly I am not sure I could have persevered without the careful and timely supernatural revelations and miracles that I was allowed to witness.

The challenge to explore the spiritual/supernatural world is unmatched in its range, potential error and danger. Bridges that cross those boundaries will always challenge people's imaginations. Of all the revered entities from the other side, only one (so far) has dictated delicate and precise instructions as to how to cross that bridge. That one has not only orally dictated a schematic but also gave us a flawless sequence of events thousands of years before they occurred. Those events though previewed and published thousands of years ago, have proved to be accurate to this day. That one, the God of Abraham, Isaac and Jacob has been proven to be the most accurate, most powerful, most consistent, and most reliable. He has given us a glimpse of the afterlife and some of the key figures in the supernatural world also.

Those opinions are worldwide opinions and also my investigation team's points of view.

Few researchers will admit publicly that as soon as you attempt to explore the supernatural world, you are immediately confronted. The forces that tackle you seek declarations of intent. I challenge any person to prove that he/she can successfully navigate spiritual passages through untold worlds without the map of Jason. Without a full understanding of the schematic, many explorers have ended up like the predecessors of Jason, smashed to pieces on the rock-piles of chaos.

CHAPTER 1C. ALTARS OF JUDAISM, CHRISTENDOM AND ISLAM

Over twenty countries were visited while compiling the critical data for this treatise. In the Torah, we have found God's blueprint for man to be *His temple* on earth. The Gospels not only give insights into spiritual battles against the human temple, but also confirm over 300 prophecies of the Torah. When the need arises to quote a different language text, notations will be made accordingly. Utterances from Moses, an undisputed chosen vessel to receive and transport The Logos, were taken mainly from English (King James) sources. References from the Holy Koran are from English translations. Given that Prophet Mohammed urged his followers to confirm the Torah, and Saul of Tarsus and Jeshua taught extensively from it, we will use it as a source document since all of its records and accounts of prophets, patriarchs, and laws of the universe are harmonious.

Ethnicity is based on the ability of a select group of people to maintain unbroken geopolitical and genealogical bridges for generations of years. The ones whose customs, languages and histories survive, they become an ethnic block. This book will never utter such idiocy as a yellow race, white race, or black race; since such groundless allegations could be answerable in courts of law. Accordingly, we will try to use the continental name of the Americas.

ALTARS TRANSMIT, EMIT OR ENGULF SPIRITUAL ENERGY!

The preceding pronouncement is based on evidence from twenty-plus years of painstaking investigations along with data from the discourse of Moses. Altars are spiritual bridges from darkness to light or from light to darkness—Isaiah 42:6-7. That statement needs clarification.

Unlearned persons have assumed that darkness was a type of pigmentation. On the contrary, absence from physical light causes loss of pigmentation (what a paradox). Revealed wisdom is light; unrevealed is darkness. True light is preordained and directed to selected persons, places or things. The other types often usurp and engulf the unlit. They assist rather than overturn darkness. True light comes from the source of creation or supreme order—*Genesis 1:2-4*.

We will spend some time examining the first utterances made on this earth: the first words, the first laws. Moses' first book profiled that the world was enveloped in darkness prior to God's command that light manifest itself. God did not tell the darkness to reappear. The fact that God allowed interruption periods for His light meant that any time His light was hid, darkness would reappear. Darkness emboldens characteristics of suppression, encroachment, chaos, negativity, concealment, and the natural inclination to disobey God's word. Darkness is the primary domain of "Chaos;" all unknown principles (good and bad) are stored there. Those seeds are important to recognize since as we examine nations, families, organizations, and personal situations we can perform self-analyses as we progress.

Surveys after surveys confirm that Solomon was among the wisest of men that ever lived: Biblical attestation—1st Kings 4:29-34. Millions of people worldwide attempt a sort of educational osmosis by fashioning an esoteric reconstruction of his elaborate temple. Over eons, myth gave rise to hope that a flash, a flicker or a figment of his natural altar might enlighten them. The main shortcomings with successive generations were their pursuit of the "Created Altar" rather than *"The Source"* of the one, true, matchless Oracle or The Creator of the altar. 1 Kings 4:29, Solomon's "wisdom and understanding" were "spiritual gifts from God."

Every institution used as a vehicle for dispensing wisdom or power also has a national or institutional altar. Absence of declaration of intent and purpose has caused many esoteric explorers to be engulfed by chaos, the chaotic energy of serpentine darkness. As we unravel the damage, theft or usurping plans of the "master thief," many emotions will be invoked. Guilt, sorrow, pain, hurt, doubt, distrust and anger are prerequisites for penitence. So the chain is as follows: revelation to (penitence or indifference), then correction, absolution or consequence. Circumstances sometimes dictate that correction be in the form of retrieval or restitution— other times, reparation. Hence, the purposes for sharing these evaluations by paid researchers and 25 years of evidence gathered is to disclose the principal causes of hate, mistrust, much pain, hurt, anger and intolerance. My greatest hope is that some person, family, nation, and institution will benefit from these painstaking revelations.

God gave instructions to His Patriarchs to select and to erect tangible altars. Initially they were always of stone, "made without human hands" placed at sites to commemorate special events or spiritual victories. The sequel to this will have maps showing the locations of those ancient altars. Readers can then deduce for themselves whether the perennial conflicts on those sites are natural or spiritual. Over time, altars sustained natural and spiritual assaults. This book urges all three flocks of Judaism, Christianity and Islam to examine their altars for physical and spiritual cracks, fractures and theft.

Source material surveys and the revelations of Prophet Mohammed's vision were the lynch pins for me to discover that which lured millions of people over the years to pursue—yet fail to find—the elusive "Fleece." I was also secretly looking for reasons that different shadows engulfed Christianity, Islam and Judaism. I felt that the answers were wedged between the altars of Abraham, Isaac, Ishmael, Jacob, Esau, and the ruins of the Temple of Solomon. Those differences have been sources of major bloody conflicts for centuries. I will commence with a few bold statements and then supply the supportive evidence as the book progresses:

1) Jews worldwide seem to have an unrivalled respect for the sanctity and accuracy of the "written" Hebrew word of God. While we were examining Holy Books, we noticed a common problem with translators that were not of the "Chosen Covenant Seed." Inadvertently, blockages either natural or supernatural occurred. Attempted resolution to those blockages usually led to institutionalized "New Ways" or "New Paths" to God. It became necessary to examine "every known and penned doctrine critically" to see if God had a scripted "preferred way" or if in fact there was "One True Way." Are there many ways? Are there many tributaries that get us there? If so, then why is there religious intolerance?

2) The person painted and portrayed artistically as Jesus in most Occidental Christian churches—from the 15th century to our present times—is different in appearance from the Hebrew Carpenter, descendant of David, son of Miriam of the tribe of Judah. His genealogy, hinted in Psalm 87 is a case in point why *The All Wise God* admonished us that "We should make no graven image of the things above or below." All have come short or have shortcomings. So much so that to Hebrew, Muslim and African scholars, the parading of a European looking Jesus—whose Hebrew/Christian followers suffered degradation and death at the hands of Gentile Rome during its most vicious anti-Semitic and anti-Christian campaigns—is sacrilegious, shameful and or brazen denial.

3) The three monotheistic religions from the loins of Abraham (Judaism, Christianity, and Islam) proclaim, point to and name the same Messiah. All three state that He was born, or will be born of a Hebrew virgin. All "followers" of the three have erred!

4) The Koran isn't vague in identifying by name the "Special Master" or anointed one, previously pointed out by the Hebrew prophet Isaiah in Isaiah 9:6 as "Wonder or Miracle Worker, Counselor, Prince of Peace, Everlasting 'Firstfruit' and the Torah translation—"Might of God." Koran translations state that "He" was not only God's messenger, but also His servant, God's witness, His prophet and His sign for the coming hour of judgment: Sura 43, 61. His name is given as Yasu, Isa or Jesus son of Miriam. In the Holy Koran not only is He the fruit of a miraculous conception but also it states that God sent Jesus with resurrection power and with the Gospel to confirm the Law (previously sent by Moses) with *signs* and *miracles*.

   By universal consensus, the best expounder of the Hebrew Law (barring none) is Jeshua (Yasu) or Jesus the Nazarene, son of Miriam (Mary). Another erudite scholar was a former Pharisee, Saul or Paul of Tarsus who studied under the great Gamaliel. He had the amazing ability to simplify the Gospel teachings and make them palatable to the ordinary folk of His day. James the first elder of the Jerusalem flock, and Titus (his successor) have written inspired letters also. Strange as it seems, even though all four taught from the Torah, many Jews study neither the history nor the teachings of Jeshua, Titus, James and Saul of Tarsus. However to date, Jeshua has, and had the greatest positive impact on religious, secular and Jewish history.

5) The Torah and the Tanakh categorically affirm that Jeshua would arrive on a set date and depart by the date predestined. Many Jews assume that the calculation is wrong.

6) All three monotheistic faiths have the same proclamation about God's chosen vessel. In spite of that, followers of all three faiths, have different interpretations of their own proclamations.

In the Holy Koran, we find Jeshua referred to as the one with "Rhu Allah" or "Spirit of God." In the Torah in Isaiah 9:6 ...He will be *called* or he will have the title of "Mighty God." In the Holy Bible—John 1:1-14 and John 1:41..."We have found the "Messias" (the Christ). Those three holy books identified Him as the special "child (is) born" of God through a virgin woman. The fact that Isaiah's prophecy said *"is born,"* instead of *"will be born,"* hints that the sign was prenatal and concealed before it was established. Hence Mohammed like Daniel, like John (while on the isle of Patmos) was told to "Seal the vision until the appropriate time." The Tanakh, The Koran and The Bible point to a special "Cornerstone" chosen by God. God's word concerning the mystical cornerstone states: "made without human hands," and that He would have a supernatural entrance and exit.

Zealous followers of Messenger Mohammed believe that a physical black stone in Mecca is the Sign, and that the prophet was not just sent to seal—but he was "The Seal." However the Koran is clear—Jeshua is "The Witness." Muslim brothers, members of our analytical team for years, had severe difficulty when we encountered the fact that among Prophet Mohammed's mentors were Christians and Jews. We were troubled also when the following questions were presented to us:

a) Did God ever abandon the Hebrews or the remnant that inhabited *His holy hill* of Psalm 122:1-9? Since a Jewish remnant that dwelt in Jerusalem (especially from 1948) became spiritual guardians of His holy hill and attempted to maintain the customs and language, why can't they claim fruits of "The Covenant?"

b) Is God a covenant keeper or a covenant breaker?

c) What documents did Prophet Mohammed's mentors peruse to learn of God's promises to father Abraham? Why aren't the revelations to Prophet Mohammed highlighted and separated? Which suras are injections from the selected schools of thought?

d) To which of Abraham's seed had "*The Covenant*" been given?

e) Which of Abraham's seed fulfilled God's plan for a Theocracy?

f) Why are there conflicting opinions about "the person" identified by Prophet Mohammed as the *"Sign and the Witness"* and the "viewpoints" of Muslim translators?

g) Why are God's redemptive plans for all humankind—Jews, Arabs, Christians, and Gentiles, (Isaiah 9:6) the most mistranslated of all Hebrew tests?

h) I have heard Rastafarians and Muslim seed of Abraham lecturing recently on the topic of "Returning Messiahs." Brothers, be careful! God does not contradict His word. By inference, both schools of thought confirm that the Messiah had come. However, both schools of thought imply—through a veiled doctrine of "Reincarnation"—that He returned as their source and only prophet. Since both philosophies contradict each other, it is obvious that at least one of those groups is in error. Psalm 2 is specific. God decreed absolute honour, trust and truth to only one "Son." Acts 1:11 must be scrutinized: "Ye men of Galilee, why stand ye gazing up to heaven? This same Jesus, which is taken up from you into heaven, shall so come in like manner as ye have seen him go into heaven."

i) There is a popular saying that goes like this: "Some are born great; others achieve greatness and still others have greatness thrust upon them." However in the eyes of God, greatness and righteousness are achieved through His approved and acceptable sacrifice only.

The higher the calling, the greater the sacrifice has to be. On that account, who among men, so far, made the ultimate sacrifice (as per Psalm 22 and Isaiah 53) for all? Whose disciples were willing to bear the ultimate sacrifice also?

I have scrutinized known and many unknown exegeses of religious icons and found that zealous followers often published data different from the actual revelations of the sources. In those cases whereby a person had a mystical experience inside *The Sanctified Veil,*" the experience was so awesome that as he or she tried to convey the esoteric experience exoterically, much was lost. The results in most cases were inaccurate transpositions and later vehicles for creating exposed/usurped altars and flawed doctrines by untrained followers. I found more emphasis placed on the experiences rather than the preparation, the sanctification, and 'the sacrifice' acceptable for entry. Very rarely did I encounter clear guidelines for preservation and protection from the "Chief Thief." I have inserted the word "Sanctified" deliberately. I have known of instances whereby either the personage or the domain of the veil was tarnished and the encounter was far from pleasant.

Moses on the other hand dedicated his writings towards the preparation, cleansing and identification of "The Path or The Way" through the "Most Holy Veil." I was extremely impressed with his presentation. It was unbiased, historically correct and spiritually rigid. Mohammed's dissertation—unlike that of Moses—did not catalogue the successes or failures of adepts that were called to teach and expound on their experiences. As a result, his teachings were subject to constant debates from philosophical schools of thought, namely, the Kharijites, the Ismailiya (Secret Seveners), the Mutazilites and the Asherites. Without specific notations, is there any way to distinguish between "revelations of the prophet" and the opinions of those sects? For instance: Prophet Mohammed did not record any Suras himself. In Sura 2, 128 the prayer of exhortation asking God to "Make us Muslims" is the same insertion in footnote C-48 listed below Sura 121. That note gives the impression that Suras 2, 122-141 reflect the authors' opinions. Since there are Suras without specific references to authorship in the Holy Koran, we have no way of telling which of the 114 chapters or Suras in the Holy Koran are specific revelations to Prophet Mohammed or which are editorial inserts. Some adepts insist that the prophet's words are extracted and placed in "The Hadith." Since God's pattern is to proclaim *directly* to His prophets and then to confirm the same messages through other prophets with signs and wonders, corroborations and miracles are necessary before we can imply that God replaced His Torah—Sura 3, 19: "The religion before Allah is Islam." Since Jeshua and Mohammed, both referred to the Torah as the "Book," our diligent staff compared early Hebrew and Arabic versions. They deduced that those interpretations accurately portrayed the cosmology of the people and their regions. However the original Hebrew texts offered the true flavour of the religious customs and gave more precise and unambiguous interpretations of the scriptures and their meanings. The Holy Koran gives explicit instructions that Muslims study the Torah and the Tanakh. We will list a few of those translated Suras:

1. "We gave Moses the Book and followed him up with a succession of Messengers; we gave Jesus the son of Mary clear signs and strengthened him." Sura 2, 87.

2. "O Jesus son of Mary! Recount my favour to thee and to thy mother. Behold I strengthened

thee with the holy spirit so that thou didst speak to the people in infancy and in maturity. Behold I taught thee The Book of Wisdom, The Law and the Gospel:" Sura 5, 110

3. "To thee (Jesus son of Mary mentioned in Sura 5, 46) we sent the Scripture in truth, confirming the scripture that came before it:" Sura 5, 48. The Koran was not yet written when those were dictated. So "The Law" or "Book" consists of the records of: a) Successes and failures of spiritual heirs of God's covenant partners, b) God's decrees to Moses and the first priesthood, c) His promises for obedience, and d) His punishments for breaches. They are all documented in the Torah. God promised us a new permanent priesthood and a New Covenant; therefore the testator must bear witness to the law.

CHAPTER 1D. INSIDE THE SANCTIFIED VEIL

In times past, God used judges, kings, priests and prophets as messengers. Up to the day that God gave John admonishing instructions on the isle of Patmos (through to this day) His pattern has been consistent. The special prophet that God would choose to be His "New Covenant Witness" and "Chosen Shepherd," according to Isaiah 42:1-7, would be the everlasting sacrifice for all—Arabs, Chinese, Gentiles, Jews, Indians, Pakistanis etc. **God does not send prophets to begin new ministries.** Prophets report from God to "His Body Temple." Hence, John the Harbinger or John the Baptist introduced Jeshua's *all- inclusive restorative* ministry.

Another sign of God's prophets being "chosen," is that they are given the coveted gift to foretell events. Historical confirmation of those events is "the" prime prerequisite to be considered a true prophet of God. Therefore the offices of missionaries, messengers and prophets are ministries sent out from a particular home base unto "the dispersed."

There are many doctrines worldwide, allegedly founded by "prophets of God." God is specific—all are to be grafted into the "Chosen Branch," singular. This disquisition will recreate God's laws of double-reference and specificity. Afterwards, all followers, persons and organizations can retrace individual paths back to each base altar to correct, mend, adjust, rebuild or to repair spiritual damage. Satan is an altar thief. If he cannot steal it, he will damage it. If he cannot damage it, he will tarnish it. What he can't tarnish, he will covet. With that in mind, I made a conscious effort to study all Holy Books for prior prophecies, historical confirmations, manifestations of *God's Laws of Specificity* and *Double-Reference*, and also for His detailed instructions through the "*Path or Way.*"

The Torah and another holy book, *The Tanakh*, are the only known sources and accessible exegeses that not only pass, but also surpass the aforementioned litmus tests. In addition, they offer step-by-step, detailed instructions through the "*Path or Way.*" Additionally, those volumes also displayed the names, places and events surrounding the persons that either successfully negotiated *The Way*, or failed, and the reasons why. The Bible, a Gentile translation of the Tanakh, is a detailed account of messengers' successes and rewards, or failures and sudden demise. "Bibles," which are the Occident's best translations of the Torah, plus witnesses' testimonies, confirm what chosen prophets Moses, Zechariah, Nehemiah, Ezekiel, Micah, David, Daniel, Isaiah and others foretold. Tanakhs/Bibles confirm the Old Testament and the Torah bears witness in code and prophecies to the New Testament. The Bible's 66 books written by some 40 messengers over 3000 years is a spiritual manual containing correlating prophecies. Jeshua was emphatic: "He was sent to confirm (not to change) the Law."

In recent months, with discoveries of original texts, much is made of the pinpoint precision of since-evolved events and most importantly the name, mission and the forecasted first instances that the Chief adept (Messiah) would visit and exit. With my able assistants I accessed a certain classified library. We stumbled upon authored evidence of fiery debates between Roman and Greek thinkers wrestling with the interpretation and the understanding of "The Logos" the same way scholars of Islam and followers of Prophet Mohammed juggled and wrestled for the ascendancy of their opinions.

What has been mislabeled as the first church of the 1st century was actually a school of philosophy founded by a Simone, a former sorcerer of the Roman province of Samaria. Justin Martyr studied the gospels (in Greek) in Carthage and Cyrene. He was so impressed with the fervor of the zealots (called Believers then), in preferring death to renouncing the "Reformed Hebrew Doctrine," that he became a secret convert through the churches in North Africa that were subsequently forced underground. Romans were given special privileges of appealing before they were put to death. Some Roman citizens, inspired by the clarity of the appeals in Latin, later converted and attended the first European Christian church in Lyon 177 C.E.

It is noteworthy that Rome as a nation initially encouraged openness of thought and philosophy. To the Roman gentry, Christianity originated from an assumed inferior civilization that dared to teach: "The apex of wisdom could be reached through its way, which was truth and life." Christianity therefore challenged the philosophical fabric and "exalted status" of Roman society and was therefore illegal and "sacrilegious." Henceforth, anyone espousing such dogma, anyone having literature supporting such, was a state heretic and therefore eligible for punishment by death.

Roman martyrs acquired their "Faiths" under very trying circumstances and were willing to undergo public ridicule, torture and death—rather than reject their faith, namely—Tertullian, Origen, Eusubius, and Justin *Martyr*. The latter died in 165 C.E., and was the 1st Roman to be *martyred* for Christendom; *hence the origin of the name for all later martyrs.* We thoroughly scrutinized Justin's "Apologies" and his "Dialogue:" two famous Christian pieces in Latin. As we examined the early doctrinal debates, it became obvious why men like Barnabas, James the Elder and Saul of Tarsus had no problem elaborating on the so-called difficult issues. They were able to provide the correct Hebrew Scriptures for edification. They knew "The Word." Years later we unanimously concluded that those Hebrew companions of Jeshua—selected en masse to enter *The Veil*—were chosen to be "*Oracles of the Veil.*" That attestation can be found in Romans 3:2 "To the Jews were committed the Oracles of God." That text could have inspired Iraneus, Polycarp, Augustine and Justin. They spent much time in the 2nd and 3rd centuries trying to persuade the isolated and doctrinally deficient church in Rome to seek guidance and to link with the Christian churches in Asia and Africa. The idea was shelved because of inherent Roman myths of intellectual superiority and pride. There were also fears and suspicions that all Romans were traitors that would hand over Christians to be tortured and killed.

Noetus and Praxeas, both prominent Romans contributed to sacrilegious teachings in Rome of yore. Noetus was a Roman convert. At the beginning of the 3rd century he had established himself as a seasoned debater. He became so famous that "Noetics" the philosophical doctrine is named after him. Since the legendary Noetus, the alleged Firstfruit Roman "Christian" philosopher opined "The Trinity," we will examine the doctrine. His main legacy, which fueled the Trinitarian debate, was his theory that Christ was God the Father who was born, punished and died.

Who in the world could or would dare punish God? Can God, who is all, be reduced or be changed? Malachi 3:6, "I am the Lord, I change not." Since Micah, Daniel, Isaiah and David, among others, had given earlier prophecies about the birth of a special *Son*, should not His ethnogenic surname be "Ben-God," by paternal planting and authority? John 20:31, "These are written that ye might believe that Jesus is the Christ, the *Son of God*." While Jeshua was on earth He took pains to explain to His disciples, the spiritual nature of God the eternal "Spirit Father" in John 5:19-24. John 5:43, spells out clearly: "I am come in my Father's name." We will also examine the words: "There is one God, and one mediator between God and men, the *man* Christ Jesus," in 1ˢᵗ Timothy 2:5. In John 5, Jeshua taught that He would fulfill His predestined call to be the "Firstfruit" of the Resurrection, also confirmed in the Holy Koran, as Sura 19, 33—"Peace is upon me the day of my birth, and the day of my death, and the day of my being raised up alive."

Praxeas was another proponent who not only echoed the same sentiments as Noetus but also documented his views and shared them with the new teachers of the state-approved philosophical schools in Rome. Tertullian, one of Rome's Church Fathers and martyrs criticized the arguments of Praxeas with these words: "He replaced prophecy with heresy." In the last chapter we will examine in detail major doctrinal differences between the Romans' sponsored state religion in the 3ʳᵈ and 4ᵗʰ centuries, and the founding Jerusalem church with its first century Asian and African branches. Wisdom from within "The Veil" can only be received inside "The Veil." At the end, we will examine the doctrine of the Trinity and ask:

1. Since the God of Moses, Jacob, Isaac, Jeshua and Mohammed and Esau is omnipresent, all wise, all-knowing, all-powerful, changeless, and limit-less, what forms could God be, other than the immeasurable forms of invisible and spirit? In actual fact, electricity is a force but it does not speak, prophesy or work miracles. We will also examine the words of Jeshua in John 14:28 "My Father is *greater* than I."

2. How many Christians comprehend the doctrine and spiritual implications of the Trinity?

3. Is it a doctrine of "Roman" origin widely accepted by most Christian churches?

4. Is the "Doctrine of the Trinity," Scriptural? Did any of Jeshua's disciples teach it?

5. The early Hebrew Believers understood the harmony or "one-ness" between "His Chosen Firstfruit" and God (the invisible, omnipresent Holy Spirit-Father).

6. Was the Trinity the main reason that followers of Mohammed chose to build their own religion around their language, on their own "Ethnic Foundation stone," and an unwavering truism that God is: Creator of all, including His sons from the "Firstfruit" to the last fruits?

Here are some other questions for every person of every nation, tongue and creed:

a.) Did later Roman Gentiles receive sufficient teachings to understand God's precepts?

b.) Could the Romans of the 3ʳᵈ to 4ᵗʰ centuries who were outside of the Sanctified Veil understand all of its deep mysteries?

c.) Could anyone other than a "Master" teach that every spirit needs an earthly or carnal vehicle to manifest in or through? Shouldn't the Most Holy Spirit (1ˢᵗ Corinthians 2:12) of necessity, select the "Most Holy" vehicle as Redeemer and Oracle?

d.) Since God is without limit and is *The Most Holy Spirit*, is there any being, place or thing big enough to hold all of God?

e.) Israel's prophets were able to describe God's *immutability*. Malachi 3:6, *I am the Lord, I change not!* Does the Trinity challenge God's word?

f.) Does the presence of God in or with a particular person, place or thing transform His omnipresent nature?

Jeshua and His witnesses taught extensively that the way to God's heart is through repentance, love and humility. A doctrine that attempts to humanize or to limit the immeasurable Spirit God, or to restrict God—for oneself, to or for a particular prophet, icon, faith, race or nation—contradicts the nature of God and the essence of His spirit being. In Isaiah 45:18, "For thus said the Lord that created the heavens; God himself that formed the earth and made it; he hath established it, he created it not in vain, he formed it to be inhabited: I am the Lord; and there is none else." Hence God gave all the provisions for the New Covenant to Jeremiah in Jeremiah 31:31-36. Hopefully the answers to the above will be found in the last chapters.

CHAPTER 1E. THE ORACLES OF GOD

To the Jews were committed "The Oracles of God! It is written, "Were committed." God gave His word and His contract personally to the ancient Hebrews. The same way that the Torah evolved into the Tanakh, His preserved word progressed from ancient Aramaic into this prophetic oracular medium called the Hebrew language (Isaiah 43:1-12). The opening statement seals a covenant contract agreement. The people selected to preserve and protect the sanctity of *His Word* from contamination would become a nation in the land where God had concealed His most powerful altars. They would be rewarded if they performed their tasks in an exemplary manner and be punished if they failed. By deduction, the Messiah would be born, and would minister from and upon the land chosen by God. Of all teachers, whose lives we scrutinized, Jeshua is the only known shepherd to do the following: a) have all of His chosen followers drawn "within the veil" b) overcome the devil c) heal the sick d) perform miracles d) fulfill 300 prior prophecies. Besides those, He was able to receive and to manifest the Most Holy Oracle of the Living God.

Panels of Rabbis and serious Jewish law professors in Israel are currently studying recently found parchments that are believed to contain actual accounts of Jeshua's witnesses. I have met Jews in Israel that have had access to translations of the Qumran Scrolls. Some have become messianic Jews and are actively working behind the scenes with messianic Palestinians and messianic Arabs to live and to teach that "The only way to peace is through the 'Prince of Peace.'" Isaiah 45:17, "Israel shall be saved in the Lord with an everlasting salvation: ye shall not be ashamed nor confounded" like the idols' makers of verses 14&15.

One professor confided to me that—except for linguistic imperfections—the Hebrew/Greek *original* texts, especially those of Paul, John, James, Luke and Simon are "scripturally" enlightening, historically accurate, and comprise some of the most beautiful elaborations of the "Logion or Logos." For all intents and purposes, of the reports we studied and examined so far (and we analyzed many), we are more than inclined to agree with that assessment. The

Hebrew language is insightful, pure and precise. Each letter, word, clause, punctuation mark, placement of clause and sentence is clearly designated. Their texts are "mega- dimensional." *No one can translate a perfect language into an imperfect message medium.* There must be inaccuracies. As the book proceeds, the flaws that I encountered will be noted.

A strange thing happened over the years of this Odyssey. At the beginning I was an agnostic. There were issues I hoped to have resolved by questioning erudite zealots. In every instance I ended up with more questions than answers. I made a secret promise that should I find the answers to my many questions plus the most often unanswered ones, I would publish my findings. I will pen some of the most asked questions—the answers to which I decided to seek:

1. Why did Christianity (a monotheistic religion) have hundreds of so-called variants?

2. Why do most churches behave like teen fans competing for the attention of their icons?

3. Why and when did Jewish people cease to offer the same sacrifices as the Levites did?

Is it coincidental or a deliberate act of God that from the day Jesus died until this day: a) the sacred veil that ripped at the exact time of Jesus' death has never been repaired? b) The sacrifices of bulls and goats ended? c) The "Last Temple" was destroyed and never rebuilt?

4. What caused every seed of Judah and Israel to receive double portions of slavery and why was there no Jubilee celebration on the land of Israel for almost 2000 years?

5. How does the dispersion of Jews worldwide affect the selection of Sabbath days? When they were in one place in the same time zone, all the Sabbaths coincided. Today, when it is Saturday in Israel, it is Friday in some countries and Sunday in others. Would there be a time when the "Letter of the Law" allowed flexibility, or are those believers in the Diaspora out of covenant and replaced, as some Gentiles teach?

Questions 5, 6, and 7 came from the Eberite regions.

5. Who is the Anointed One or Messiah as per prophecy?

6. What happened to the Hamitic Hebrews of antiquity in the Torah? Did the Hamitc seed of Abram: Jews, Arabs and Ethiopians get wiped out? Where are they?

7. In Genesis 14:13, Abram was referred to as a Hebrew. Are all his seed Hebrews?

The process of reconstructing the original canvas of humankind from the current ethnic mosaic can be likened to the two inks in a computer printer. Usually, there are black ink cartridges and multi-coloured ink cartridges. I have learned that the base ink is necessary for the multi-coloured ink to manifest. I will also highlight the ethnicity of a few key players of antiquity, to attempt to find out whether or not all people originated from one human source river, and like coloured ink, human tributaries are fed from a source pool, or mother gene. I will attempt to be as unambiguous as possible.

CHAPTER 1F. THE WORLD'S MOST SOUGHT-AFTER SECRETS!

This book contains first glimpse information on most things that people wanted to ask; yet knew not to whom or to what should their questions be directed. Where can one verify such data? There is one answer: "soon to be revealed storerooms of wisdom." Other accessible storerooms are *Solomon's Temple*, archaeology, history, astronomy (not astrology) and messages coded in Hebrew over 2000 years ago. The versatility of computers offers us new research tools. By selecting letters of the Torah and the Tanakh according to congruent patterns of numerical sequencing, correlating New Testament messages are popping up. Without exaggeration, this book contains over 100 of the world's most sought-after secrets.

The books of Daniel and John "The Revealer" should be studied together. Both warn of perennial pursuits by spirits entrenched under altars of nations. Those spirits would congregate in the form of a *beast* (Daniel 2:31-45) that would strengthen through war, blood and the sweat of rebellious seeds of Israel and Judah. The prophet Daniel characterized the nations that would be formed out of the ashes of the Babylonian Empire. The rise and fall of Empires: Medo-Persia, Greece and Rome were all foreseen. Even the Colonial wars and the maximum 430-year dominance of certain "captor nations" were also noted. God used His prophets to detail the symptoms of the "End Times." Sad to say, the season of destruction at the feet of the allegorical "beast," whose ten toes constituted mixtures of clay and iron is imminent—Daniel 2:44. Political antagonists are being put in place for a plot that had been forecasted—a living drama that will unfold before the departure of this generation—"*The Apocalypse.*" Though not widely discussed by the secular media, an assigned code name has been derived for the final "*Head Beast over the Occident.*" It is the French word "Bahomet."

The empires that carried the unicorn's scepter, like a baton in the relay of world history were: Babylon, Medo-Persia and Rome. All of them subjugated God's people and benefited from unrighteous mammon. The Gentile nation of Rome and its branches rule "The West." Deuteronomy 28:23 reads "The heaven is made of brass and the earth that is under thee shall be iron." Wherever Israel, Judah, and the so-called "Lost Tribes" live, their livelihoods would be adversely influenced by the seeds of nations in the "beast, whose feet were mixtures of iron and clay" for a prescribed maximum period of years. Scriptures are Daniel 2:34-35, Genesis 15:13 and Revelation 17:11-14. Let us check our arithmetic. A generation of years is 70 years, so 1948 + 70 = 2018. 1898+350= 2248. Computations as per God's indelible word: 1776+430 (2206) must fall within the period of years 2018 to 2248 and the date 2206 does. 1776 +400=2176. The nation that carries the "Torch of the Unicorn" must build its house with unjust gain and shed innocent blood until either 2176 or no later than 2206. The 7000 years to redemption according to the Hebrew calendar and by Kabbalists is 2204.

Asaph, a Davidic worship leader prophesied the history of Israel (in Psalm 78 from verses 5 to 64) thousands of years in advance. Zoroaster, a Persian seer released a premonitory word about the birth of the "Chosen" from a virgin. That utterance enabled followers (the Magi) to find the child at His birth, thousands of years later. Chinese Magi coded those and other "revelations" in their alphabet. Those seeds, mostly lost, were preserved in esoteric symbols through the calligraphy of the earliest Chinese alphabet. The natives of Australia interpreted the messages of the heavens (etched by David in Psalm 19) thousands of years before David was born. This book will not cover the antediluvian or unrevealed epoch on Earth, when the Logos was mimicked through ritual ceremonies. To this day, there remain tangible altars from the period called prehistory. Those energies, like antennae, are still connected to Fellers and their roots.

During the pre-Babel Epoch, heads and wings of birds were used to convey the "abode of the exalted" and serpents or snakes were carved or drawn to depict the dwellers and the domain of the damned. The attempt to portray man's bridge to the other side of death is a grim reminder that without a true guide through the tunnel of wisdom, chaos will engulf the unlearned. So many civilizations, scratching in the dark became victims of chaos. In my next book, "Noah's Flood—*the evidence*," I will mention at least two areas where so-called "Lost Tribes" are located. I will allude to isolated fragmented landmasses where translations of so-called primitive art reveal the existence of a prehistoric language from intelligent people of yesteryear. I will also show that the tendency for seed of esoterically enlightened ancient civilizations to inhabit concise geographical areas on earth (that align with stellar maps) was not accidental. The oral accounts of all pre-deluge events passed on by their ancestors will be analyzed meticulously and critically.

Prior to the arrival of human beings (with their gifts of choice), all the mechanisms of the giant universal clock were obedient to an invisible law/force. After the arrival of humankind, all preserved etchings found so far, indicate that our ability to survive is directly dependent upon orderly sustainable systems and harmonious relationships with others. Absence of those (checks and balances) ferment a primitive and oft-detrimental system of survival based on "temporary and limited" might.

God then chose a humble family from around the incessant tributaries of the Tigris and Euphrates. According to legend, now confirmed by history, a few "then righteous, though un-known and insignificant" people were given a set of laws from the *Creator of the Universe*. They were promised that as long as any of their seed remained faithful to that covenant, they would be blessed for being witnesses. They would multiply and become a mighty nation, and their seed would live to see the manifestation of all that was promised. They were selected to re-produce through an unbreakable seed promise to God. That promise in the form of a "Hybrid Seed" would survive capture, theft, deceit, lying, immorality, death, and destruction. A nation of nations would emerge from the loins of Patriarch Abraham. From his seeds would emerge a "Seed of seeds." That seed would even conquer death and have the ability to proliferate spiritu-ally. Sura 19 in the Holy Koran from verses 1 to 33, begin with the prayer of Zechariah, the father of John the Harbinger. The verses also include Jeshua's birth and the hope through His resurrection. Can it happen? Did it happen? Preserved writings forecasted that those events would come to pass. Many witnesses wrought mighty miracles in the name of the one who uttered those words. Now some 5000 years later, we must take both microscopic and macro-scopic views of those prophecies.

That nation and their seed were chosen to be corporate "Oracles of God" and covenanted to do just that, forever. They messed up big time, not once, but many times and often. If one examines the collective behaviour of survivors of that covenant, and compare the attributes of the "Covenant Keeper," Jeremiah could not describe the marriage relationship better. Take it from me—a person who owned a bar for many years—that is expert analysis. I spent hours listening to lament from husbands of unfaithful wives and vice versa. To all that are being blessed because of that covenant, that "Have had enough of Religion," you should find this book edifying. In the temple built by Solomon, *the Oracle* was also part and parcel of *the fin-ished work*. Since the first and last person on a building site is a carpenter, a carpenter must be the initiator and finisher of our (faith) works. God compared himself to a faithful husband: You can mess with any husband on the block, those of your friends and of your enemies. You cannot mess with God. The history of the Jewish people is a true case and point.

CHAPTER 1G. MOMMA MIA, LOOK WHAT WE INHERITED!

Careful scrutiny of the spheres around us reveals major differences in their compositions, orbital paths, cycles and roles in the universal order of things. The planets either look like places that may have resembled our earth but somehow died, or those that have the potential to be earth-like. What then is our purpose on Earth and why was this planet chosen? If in fact it is a quarantine area, then it has been strategically located, adequately equipped with enough food, water, minerals, energy and land for all. Any other location in our solar system would make our earth both too close to the sun or too cold and inhabitable for sustainable development. The mixture of two parts hydrogen to one part oxygen is not only the only one of billions of combinations that produce water, but the uniqueness of its properties makes possible the invisible storage in vapor above, and effortless transporting by the wind. Those cost-effective means of international distribution enable the world's most precious commodity (water) to be funneled freely through inter-connected reservoirs called oceans.

Job described the rain cycle (hydrological cycle) in detail over 3500 years ago and Solomon over 2000 years prior to the births of Perrault and Mariotte. However the latter two were given credit for "discovering" the rain cycle. Job 36:27, "He maketh small drops of water; they pour down rain according to the vapor thereof." Ecclesiastes 1:7, "All the rivers flow into the sea; yet the sea is not full; unto the place from which the rivers come, thither they return again." Verse 28…"Which the clouds do drop and distil upon man abundantly."

The choice of the preservative salt is the perfect mineral for retarding evaporation and enhancing marine life. Both storerooms (sea and air) help rather than hinder space, and travel is made possible on or through them rather than around them. Grass, a sustainable commodity for most indigenous herbivores is miraculously supplied. Genesis 1:12, Moses wrote, "The earth brought forth grass." Every island and every continent that is warm enough produce grass. Had the computation for electromagnetism been off by the slightest percentage, matter would not solidify and we would have quite a difficult time surviving in a primordial soup.

Our earth for the most part is a large incubation chamber: in seed/out fruit. The air we breathe has an interesting combination. Plants breathe in carbon dioxide during the daytime and exhale oxygen; we humans breathe a mixture of oxygen with a spattering of nitrogen (pollutants excluded). Fire, an essential source of energy is added to the array of unlimited "sustainables"—all for simple prices of gratitude, tolerance, obedience and reverence. Evidence suggests that there is an everlasting blueprint with unambiguous guidelines for survival, adequate distribution and sharing. Since ethnological science has documented and published DNA evidence to show that everyone on earth is ancestrally related, then we should be "our brothers' keepers!"

A bit of deviation is necessary at this point to paraphrase two questions posed by a member of our research team. In one of my lectures I used the term "First Will and Testament" to define the Code. It was my intention to use that name for my thesis. However the queries put forth were these: "If your code is a First Will and Testament, then someone extremely wealthy had to die to leave such a will? Who in heaven or earth could have been so wealthy, unselfish and generous?" Here is a saying that has been accepted universally as a truism: "Nothing is free." Everything has a price! This Odyssey is no exception. It was a project compiled by a select group of people from varying ethnic backgrounds that diligently looked for and found "The Schematic of Life."

THERE IS A FIRST WILL AND TESTAMENT WITH CONDITIONS FOR ESCAPING EARTH CYCLES OF LIFE AND DEATH. ANY OBEDIENT HEIR CAN SURPASS THE BOUNDS OF THE UNIVERSE WHERE THERE IS

NEITHER DEATH NOR PAIN!

Let us conduct an experiment to eliminate all doubters. Take a large tablecloth and place it on a flat surface. With your fingers, gently push the corners towards the middle (the way tectonic plates formed most mountain ranges) until folds and wrinkles appear. Imagine for whatever reason our planet dissipates. The magnetic alignments caused by contoured orbital paths could allow another celestial body to lock into earth's original position. Trapped nitrogen, carbon dioxide and other gases might begin the process of transforming another planet into a new spherical mass, the way our embryonic earth was billions of years ago. If you were selecting people to populate that new planet, would you choose those that have been purged from selfishness, greed, murder, rape etc., or would you say whosoever will, may come? Most people are choosy about the neighborhoods they elect to live in and place restrictive hedges when they can. So it is logical to assume that we would be most discriminating. Maybe our earth is such a quarantine station for such purposes. Unlike shards from Babel, this manual outlines the conditions for selection and the conditions for rejection. Though a solvent for removing spiritual plaque from the soul, it is only applicable to those willing to use it wisely.

I hasten to comment that teams of researchers associated with this project have applied the principles outlined in these chapters with remarkable effect. So far, hundreds of formerly sick and dying people can attest to them being remarkably healed as a result of the findings. Since the same principles are outlined herein, I pray the same positive effects on as many of my readers as possible.

CHAPTER 1H. MOST IMPORTANT CLUES OVERLOOKED!

Over 50% of the people considered the "Movers and Shakers" of all modern civilizations have scrutinized the ruins of Solomon's Temple looking for "*WISDOM OF THE AGES.*" Many have studied an invented science built on "Masonry," that elevated the collective wisdom of the Occident a mere 30 out of a possible 360 degrees. For two thousand years, men have searched for and have *not* found the Master Mason. The irony of that exercise is that all known accounts specifically identified Hiram Abiff as a "worker in brass," and that "all the stones were uncut." The building had palm, cedar, pomegranate, almug, fir and olive trees, for lumber. The obvious question is that if the only stones were uncut foundation stones, then why search an invented science centered on Masonry when 90 percent of the material was made of wood; why not Carpentry? The promised Master Builder would be a bridge between the natural and the spiritual. He would have to build a spiritual temple on earth. Zechariah 3:8…"For behold I will bring forth my servant The Branch." Zechariah 6:12, "Behold the *man* whose name is The Branch." In both instances the word "Branch" is capitalized. The next and obvious probing question is whose child, that of a *widow* or *the virgin*?

KEYS

Here are clues that emerge by decoding the name Hiram Abiff: Miriam and Abib (Firstfruit). One of the gates of the Old City of Jerusalem is blocked. A directional gate is blocked in the oft-recited legend, also. The word "Jubilee" not only unlocked the old riddle but also proclaimed a "New Season" that only the true Messiah could usher in. Since none of Solomon's wives were virgins, the virgin that God chooses (Isaiah 7:14) to birth His seed of redemption would have to produce a pure Firstfruit for all Hebrew feasts. At this juncture I will share a thought that plagued me for years. As an archaeology student/convert, I secretly thought (as people in those professions are wont to fantasize) that no transcript was ever made as to the whereabouts of the "tree of life." All records report that God removed it. Every time I read that someone extracted healing properties from a plant, I imagined that original tree was concealed somewhere, pollinating others. For years I dreamt of finding a shoot, a root, a remnant, a graft or even a fossil. I prayed for and received not one but all five of the aforementioned.

Isaiah 28:16, "Behold I lay in Zion for a foundation stone, a tried stone, a precious cornerstone, a sure foundation." The foundation stone was preconceived and then laid. The first worker on a building site (preparing the formwork) and the last one (doing the finished work) is usually a carpenter. It stands to reason that the One chosen as "author and finisher," of our spiritual works on earth must be one skilled in spiritual and physical carpentry. 1st Kings 5:17, "The King commanded, and they brought great stones costly stones, to lay the foundation of the house." Verse 18, "Solomon's builders and Hiram's builders did hew them, and the stonesquarers: so they prepared timber and stones to build the house." Therefore, the person chosen by God to build a specific spiritual house, according to His deliberate design, was, is and always will be in total harmony with the will of God. Solomon's Temple had 10 times more timber in the construction than stone.

I have found the "Builder's Son." He is not a Ma-son. He is Son (of) Man. He is a spiritual and physical "Carpenter." In the Torah, the identities of the builders are coded. However there was a "Chief Builder." 2nd Kings 12:11, "They gave the money …into the hands of them that did the work, that had oversight of the house of the Lord; they laid it out to the carpenters and builders that wrought upon the house of the Lord." Mark 6:3, "Is not this the "Carpenter" the son of Mary, the brother of James and Jude and Joses and Simon?"

Since the wives of covenant seeds represent spiritual houses on earth, let us examine the name of the temple builder for clues. Solomon's builder was Hiram. The plans for the Melchizedek Priesthood were concealed in the loins of his builder. Decoding the name "Hiram," the female Hebrew name of Miriam surfaces. Miriam the mother of Jesus had both the genes of Judah and Levi in her loins. Her first fruit must lay the foundation stone. Concealed in the rubble of the Temple of Solomon is the complete schematic, to be revealed for the first time for all to see and know. Another surprise—millions missed the important clue. How could we assume that the builder was dead and that his son was the "seed of a widow?" Didn't the builder himself give us the sign through Isaiah the prophet? Isaiah 7:14, Therefore the Lord himself will give you a sign; Behold, a "virgin" shall conceive and bear a son and shall call His name (God with us is the translation of Immanuel). It does not take a rocket scientist to figure that the virgin would know the identity of the Father, because it is written that she would call her son, "God manifest in our presence." It is obvious that God was revealing to us that He is the builder and that He gave the blueprint to His Son to build His spiritual house on earth.

CHAPTER 1I. TIME, A MASTER'S KEY

Libraries of Antiquity bore witness: "Masters kept precise time." Why did God choose 1998, during the first Jubilee celebrations in Israel (foretold in Zechariah 8:22-23) to impart this wisdom? God's seasons are calculable. There were many dark days and years in my life before the true light would shine. Like Saul, I had a Damascus encounter. Since then I have been called to bear witness to that "Day, Light, Rest, and new song in my spirit."

Earth is settled in a strategic orbit not too far or too close to the sun. The cycles of the following orbs: Sun, Moon, Mercury, Venus, Jupiter, Saturn were completed before the Sabbath or birth of Saturn's regulatory day (Sabbath day or Satur(n)day). The rest day ushers in the light day. We get varying notes on a musical scale from the positions of those orbital masses in relation to the earth. In the universe, three different types of light are assigned regulatory functions. Of the three, the sun has the primary role. God also promised to unveil a more powerful universal light force. It stands to reason that the "Day of Revelation" must be preceded by preordained darkness. Dictionaries give over 60 definitions for the one-syllable word *"light;"* however it would take a complete "Master's Day" to confirm that "special light"—Colossians 1:12-13. Spiritual carpentry reveals that a day of revelation from the *Master of Masters* is 1000 years or 14 generations. From Abraham to the male covenant-seed David (14 generations); from David to the Babylonian captivity (14 generations); from the Babylonian captivity add 14 generations and you arrive at a very significant "Day of redemption—the birth of Jesus."

The exact times that the Messiah would arrive and when He would be cut off were foreordained in Daniel 9:24-26. There would be an interruption, a period of darkness before the new light arrives. In other words "the carpenter" would lay *the foundation stone.* Then he must return to complete the "finished work." According to the prophet Daniel in the 7[th,] 8th and 9th chapters of his book, at that time not only would a New Covenant that would include Jews and Gentiles be given, but also all old sacrifices would cease. Earlier in the outline, I challenged readers to pay attention to God's prescribed time for His special pronouncements. Satan knows those seasons—so on the eve of those appointed times, he attacks either covenant seed or the land from which those pronouncements must emanate. Daniel 9:25 "Know therefore and understand that from the going forth of the commandment to restore and to build Jerusalem unto the Messiah the Prince shall be seven weeks and threescore and two weeks, 69 weeks—490-70 = 420 years. Daniel had just returned to Jerusalem with the Jews at the end of the 70 years of desolation prophesied by Jeremiah in Jeremiah 29:10. There must have been major significance attached to that "Day" since Jeremiah penned the prophecy of a *New Covenant* in Jeremiah 31:31. It reads: "Behold the days come, saith the Lord, that I will make a new covenant with the *house of Israel* and with the *house of Judah*," both tribes. Daniel was one of the young Hebrew captives during the Babylonian captivity. It lasted from Nebuchadnezzar's conquest of Judah—606 B.C.E. through Darius' reign to the third year of Cyrus who liberated the Jews and sent them to rebuild their Holy City in 536 B.C.E. Persian rule over Babylon ended in 490 B.C. just after *The Battle of Marathon.* As we formerly heralded, the Babylonian captivity signaled a period of darkness or "rest" point prior to a very important 14-generation "Third Day." Between the last stanzas there was a rest, the equivalent "post Egyptian-bondage" years of God's silence for over 480 years preceding the erection of Solomon's Temple.

The following statement might not be fully comprehensible until this book has been read completely. Whenever the "Promise" manifests or "becomes flesh" in the third "Yowme" or "Day," a new light will come forth. In the "Beginning was the Logos or Word." Next was the process to harmony or disharmony then 360 degrees right back to His original purpose. His *Word* never returns void! Three epochs or stages it takes from darkness to light: (1.) Bondage or subjugation, unrevealed or darkness, (2.) Wilderness or transition, and (3.) Place of promise "Promised Land" or Shabbath period of rest. When the process is confirmed, a double portion of obedience, "perfect seven or double three and double rest" is achieved. There is no mystery concerning the number seven, the number represents completion of God's major cycles. If we check the notes in a scale we find C, D, EF, (small rest between E and F) F, then G, A, BC (small rest between B and C). The first century found the Occident in darkness. The second century was the Occident's transition period. This third century is a period of unprecedented revelations. Many previously concealed things shall surface! Since the seed of promise given to Abraham took 99 years (three birth spasms) before it was sown, then the first travail of the *Seed* is 33 years. As we progress on this journey, the "Master's Number (33)" in the Occident, will take on much more significance. Hopefully, the discovery of the *Golden Fleece* will unlock sufficient wisdom for humankind to escape out of the wildernesses of: "Fabricated Religious Sciences, Misinformation, Ignorance, Darkness, Poverty, Racial Prejudice and Arrogance."

Here is an esoteric exercise for people who read Hebrew. In the book of Zechariah in the Tanakh, please find the ninth chapter and then circle every ninth word in the entire chapter to see what message is revealed. Examine also Isaiah 11:11-16, and await the fulfillment of every prophecy within the next twenty years. Here is another important insight. The persons, the events, the name of the Messiah and His disciples, the names of His kin, and the miracles He would perform have been meticulously preserved and embedded in the Torah thousands of years ago in binary code. God's chosen and true prophets take glad tidings, admonishing, and/or restorative messages from God to His children. Priests lead flocks either to God or away from God. Since Jeshua is the only priest known to make intercession for all of humankind, and the only prophet to receive accolades form the following prophets: Moses, Isaiah, Micah, Hosea, Daniel, Exekiel, Jeremiah, Zoroaster, Mohammed, worship leader Asaph, and kings—David and Solomon, we need to hear His counsel. Collectively, they prophesied—Jesus' birth, His power, His might, His resurrection, and/or His all-inclusive restorative anointing for Christians, Gentiles, Jews, and Muslims. Rejecting the word of the king of kings, prophet of prophets and the priest of priests, is the same as rejecting the combined counsel of all of God's prophets and more seriously, rejecting God's word. Hear the words of Jeshua: "I AM THE WAY, THE TRUTH AND THE LIFE; NO ONE COMES TO THE FATHER BUT THROUGH ME."

CHAPTER 2. THE FORBIDDEN FILES

CHAPTER 2A. THE DAWN OF AQUARIUS

I was like most people, intellectually curious. There were so many questions and so few answers. I was not born in a computer age where one could put questions on the Internet, find an invisible college professor and fire away. The disadvantage of being born prior to 1948 is that first you had to find—before you could confront—your guru. There were neither many gurus nor was access to the few, bereft of ritualistic overtones.

RESEARCH

The maze called research, though interesting and unpredictable, was very tedious. There were known institutions of learning; there were wise and "otherwise" people. Then there were those like myself that dedicated their lives to the pursuit, acquisition, understanding and dispensing of wisdom.

WISDOM

The quality and quantity of wisdom that was available to King Solomon, as referenced by fragments from the Library of Alexandria, were reservoirs compared to our collective droplets. Unfortunately, there isn't one central reference section in any library or through the Internet for that matter labeled "Absolute Wisdom."

The search for ultimate wisdom has left trails of blood, frustration, secrecy, madness and few scattered pockets of enlightenment. However to apply a broad category to our overall progress or lack thereof for the past two thousand-year underdevelopment of Western Civilization, there is only one realistic assessment: marginally wise. Since collectively we are wisdom-deficient, it stands to reason that we must find wisdom-filled persons, places or media. King Solomon, regarded as 'Ultra-Wise' by many, gave us this lead: "Fear of the Lord is the beginning of wisdom." In other words, seek the maker of this giant clock (the universe) that holds all matter and time—from future to past. He conceals the future and releases measured amounts faithfully. At the end of every millisecond, the preceding time frame is stored in a perpetual storeroom called "Past." That *Great Architect of the Universe* is the "Source of all wisdom."

If all that we retrieved were disclosed, would any publishing company in the world publish them? How would one reveal the sources, since most of the categories of wisdom are classified, esoteric, deliberately hidden, believed destroyed, controlled, or are guarded from the plebs? Where would one store the rest? One would have to create a "Forbidden Files" library. Sometime in the future, by divine decree, then and only then should there be gradual release. That is exactly where we are right now:

WHAT A TASK THAT WAS AND STILL IS. ANYONE THAT UNDERTAKES SUCH A TASK AND LIVES TO COMPLETE IT, HAS TO FACE THAT ULTIMATE DECISION.

Most scientific pundits agree that the sighting of Pluto in 1948 was the light that revealed the "Age of Aquarius." Many ancient astronomical almanacs point to the birth of a "new stellar year." I have discovered etchings of ancient astronomers referring to the same period as the "age of the fifth sun." My beliefs are cemented in the prophecies of Joel and Nehemiah. We are beginning to reap the fruits of the "Day of Enlightenment."

CHAPTER 2B. DOOR BEFORE THE BEGINNING

The first truism that must be enshrined in anyone who is serious about analyzing any structure is the nature of its foundation. Most mighty institutions/buildings did not begin so mightily. There were the usual struggles to establish proper foundations, then to maintain, then to establish whatever is regarded now as a Mount Olympus. What if persons were able to find major scrap heaps, the discarded remains from which could be traced the trials and errors of many considered-infallible institutions? Before every play is unveiled, before every movie is made, there were many rehearsals. In rusty vaults worldwide lay heaps of discarded plans, first drafts, much research and even untidy and unfinished work. Much wisdom and secrets are concealed in those musty files.

In essence, we know Pythagoras' Theorem, but wouldn't it be nice to find all his scrap papers? According to his friend, mentor, biographer and thousands of papyri of ancient Egypt, there is evidence showing that the Priest-class of Egyptian antiquity used his identical calculations for their esoteric formulae. Students and followers of Thales, Pythagoras, Herodotus and Strabo call those early configurations algebra, mathematics and theorems hundreds of years later.

Ancient records reveal that thousands of years ago, God planned a Theocracy for 12 tribes of mostly burnt-skinned people on a self-sufficient landmass—2nd Samuel 7:10. If they remained steadfast, they would be the most blessed nation on earth in spiritual and material wealth. Disobedience would bring alienation, subjugation to their enemies and their seed and roles' reversal: seed of kings would become slaves and vice-versa—Psalm 78:61. Only monuments and shadows of their mighty past remain. What we refer to as Greek sciences and mathematics, actually existed in Egypt and other parts of Africa—mainly in the Nubian Kingdom—3000 years prior to the birth of Greece. Much of that wisdom was used to build the Sphinx, other pyramids and obelisks. Etched in stone in those monuments are accurate measurements and movements of the cosmos. I will highlight the fact that the so-called mythology (eschatology is a better word) of Stone Age people reflects a deeper understanding of the hidden mysteries of *The Creator* or *Great Architect of the Universe*. In my lectures, I often use them as teaching aids.

Fifteen years ago this search for residual foundational scrap started as an intellectual exercise. Even though now I can say, "What a heck of a trip that was," I would never recommend unsupervised snooping around the secret storerooms of:

1. History.

2. Religion

3. Education

4. Countries and Cultures.

Here are some facts that may or may not startle you. Whoever the most educated person in the Occident is, he or she utilizes a maximum of 11 percent of his or her full potential. In Eastern cultures and in select circles of the Occident, "the Wisest" are called Masters. He or she who is a master has acquired 29-30 degrees out of life's circle of wisdom. If that person is extremely prominent: a doctor, a judge or the holder of the highest academic degrees, many societies will award an additional 3 degrees. 33° is still a long way from 360°.

Millions assume that success is measured by the results of the major *sprint events* of the "Olympics of Life" called *Intellect, Money and Power*. Those 100 and 200 and 400-meter dashes respectively are naturally the most glamorous. However, in the pentathlon called "Achievement," other events—*Right Attitude and Spiritual or Mental Correctness"*—are more important, and chalk up more cumulative end points than the heavily glamorized sprints. Hence the saying: "The race is not for the swift." Since a circle has 360 degrees, then a true circle of wisdom should naturally encompass the equivalent number of degrees. During this study, we encountered books by allegedly godly men that consistently cast dispersions on all the inhabitants south of the Mediterranean Sea. We also encountered records of richer kings and kingdoms in that region than any other place on earth. Most or all of them were connected to a God-given ancient "prophetic decree." As the book progresses, the decree will be listed along with benefits for compliance and the consequences of infringement.

King Solomon, an Afro-Semitic magi and Israel's third king, had access to 360 degrees of wisdom potential. Where did he acquire such wisdom—from his knowledge of Stone Masonry? Definitely not! He acquired higher degrees-potential from The Great Architect of the Universe. Wisdom dictates that whoever builds God's spiritual house on earth as per the blueprint given to Solomon, then that house should possess the power, wisdom and might of the great Architect. It also is logical to assume that the greatest thief would target that house the most. Since the universe is considered to be the greatest architectural structure known and its builder or builders regarded by the wisest on earth as "The Most Wise," then the Chief Architect must be omniscient and omnipotent. The Chief must know every aspect of the "Universal All." Anyone pursuing the apex of wisdom must aspire to know and learn from the Chief. Ponder this also: once anything is revealed, it is measurable and calculable. For a person to possess complete wisdom, that person must possess knowledge of both the revealed and the unrevealed. No one can possess that magnitude of wisdom potential by pursuit only. He or she must to be selected by the chief *Architect* who is incalculable, immeasurable and therefore *unrevealed*.

The dynastic period of ancient Egypt can be described in this manner. Simply put, the bottom of Jacob's ladder is equivalent to the apex of wisdom that humankind could achieve on its own. During that period, finite man tried desperately to apply natural measures to supernatural principles. Early, pre-Christian Greece and Rome made similar errors. They attempted to comprehend and replicate the architectural mastery of the Chief by strengthening the vehicles of mind and body with natural principles only. Moreover, the wisdom of Egypt, Greece and Rome had not peaked sufficiently to discern that the mind was in fact a highway to the spiritual realm. That is why educational disciplines – legacies of "Western Civilizations," – offer fallible philosophical attempts to fill the large spiritual and mental black holes in the constellation called "the mind." What was left in the wake of those misdirected adventures will be described in great detail within this discourse.

CHAPTER 2C. ISRAEL, A COVENANTED LAND/PEOPLE

Israel is the most unique piece of real estate on earth. Every extraterrestrial (Numbers 13:33 and Jeremiah 4:16-17) that has ever traversed this earth knows that and so does every news director and major magazine editor. Successive progenitors of that nation of Semitic, Japhethic and Hamitic Hebrews were the first in history not only to *pursue and find* the apex of wisdom but have pledged to protect it, teach it, live it and to sow it *forever*. That covenant promise was not made to some mortal president of a finite country, but with the Great Architect himself. That covenant was signed in blood in human terms with everlasting implications. Curses would follow any covenant breaker or his seed and supernatural blessings to any covenant keeper and his seed, natural or grafted. Deuteronomy Chapter 28 is self-explanatory. The contents of that chapter have Satan obsessed with the eradication of the land Israel and also Abraham's covenant seed. That Covenant has saved this generation of brazenly disobedient people from total annihilation.

Israel is unique in that all her founding patriarchs, plus her chosen seed heirs spoke to and received prophetic utterances from the All Wise, All Knowing and All Powerful God. Those proclamations were first documented and then confirmed by history, archaeology and living witnesses. Those witnesses were not always Jews. Many of the non-Jewish (Gentile) witnesses (especially their seed) were hostile to Israel and her people. Their testimonies however, which have been borne out with historical and archaeological evidences, correspond with and confirm the data in The Torah and The Tanakh.

The interesting thing about her witnesses is not only the fact that most of their prophetic utterances have been fulfilled, but spiritually related events in Israel's history have happened more than once. Events prior and prophesied have happened two or more times. Their history seems to possess an echo effect. Over 2500 years ago Asaph forecasted Israel's entire spiritual history in Psalm 78. At that time, did anyone understand the profundity of the suffering that would befall the nation for forsaking *The Tabernacle of Shiloh?* In verse 60 of Psalm 78, Israel was forewarned 490 years in advance that their *habitual rebellion* would cause them to "Reject the Promised Lawgiver" and the price they would pay for that misdeed. I will elaborate on some of those events as we progress.

The Oracle of the Ancient Hebrews cannot be compared with any other. He is mega-dimensional. That Oracle not only has the power to proclaim things prophetically, but also the unique ability to cause like events to occur twice (or several times) so as to negate any insinuations of accidental occurrences. Many of the so-called oracles of antiquity have become inaccurate and defunct. They have caused no superhuman events to occur nor have they had corroborating prophets. Human hands had constructed many. Since those oracles have come from and or are confined to this earth, they are finite and fallible.

The Oracle of Abraham, Isaac, and Jacob predates the earth, is incorruptible, superhuman and has manifested itself in soul, body, spirit, thing, word, deed, and document—among other things. I bear witness what history, archaeology and the results of this elaborate research reveal collectively: the Oracle of Abraham/Moses/Isaac/David/Jeshua is the most complete and "only known" source of true and complete wisdom—evidenced and found on earth—so far. It can be stated as forcefully as possible that this *source* of wisdom is all powerful, all wise, all knowing, has *personalities*, possesses the capacity to think, speak, prophesy, build and destroy. Over the years, we have been taught that we possess mind, soul and body. We humans possess soul, body and spirit wrapped into one frame. Unlike us with limited tri-dimensional capabilities, that source Oracle is limitless. There is no parallel as to clarity and accuracy. That Oracle always kept a succession of sojourners as witnesses. Collectively they bore witness to a reservoir of limitless wisdom and truth. That wisdom cannot be achieved by natural means. Cleansing, forgiveness, confession, piety, and Agape lead to "The One Source" of ultimate truth. Only then can we achieve everlasting peace, wisdom, happiness and joy. Through God's progressive generational purging processes, the select oracle-witness must overcome the collective failures of: (1) the judges of Israel, (2) the kings of Israel, (3) the kings of Judah, and the Levitical priesthood. Imagine the disrespect out of competing spiritual midget-oracles: not even a confirming echo? Every major Hebrew prophet had forewarned Israel that whenever that "Day" or period of enlightenment arrived and none of "Her Chosen" was in a state of readiness, God would punish them first and then select substitutes. During such a spiritual vacuum, Omri, an *army chief* (not of the seed of Judah or of Levi) defended Israel's throne for about *22 years*. Additionally, he constructed an edifice in Israel—1st Kings 15:23-24.

The most revered of the ancient tribes of Israel were Judah and Levi. The only remnant of the Tribe of Levi found to date, are the Jews of Konhan East India and the Hamitic Lemba tribes in South Africa. Their celebrations, songs, burials and festivities refer back to the Aaronic times. DNA research confirms their lineage. Judah was given a promise of invincibility as long as "she" remained faithful and obedient. All of Israel's natural enemies would be defeated at the hands of the seed of Israel and the seed of Judah. Levi was granted temporary custody of the spiritual matters until the advent of the Everlasting Melchizedek Priesthood.

As a result of generations of Jews living under Rome's subjugation, the "Learned and Wise" of Israel were removed with spiritual surgery. It was Mohammed's tenure in the region that blocked the "coded" game plan from being fully implemented. The Western world was heading down an abyss of false doctrines, replacement theology, replacement ethnology and also a demonic system known to many only by the code name "Bahomet." Mohammed *was a successful army chief. He ministered for about 22 years.*

SOME INTERPRET THE INSIGNIA OR SYMBOL OF THE TRIBE OF JUDAH AS THE HEAD OF A MAN; OTHERS SEE THE SYMBOL AS THE HEAD OF A LION BECAUSE OF THE BROAD NOSE AND BUSHY HAIR.

2nd Samuel 7:10 is the only place where God promised a *specific location* for a nation that He had selected for His purposes. "I will appoint a place for my people Israel and *will plant* them, that they may *dwell in a place of their own and move no more...*"

2D. THE WORLD'S MOST PROPHESIED EVENT!

The most powerful and revered ancient writings recovered from all aver the world bear witness in stone (often mislabeled as *Phallic Worship*), symbolism, eschatology, sacred dance and astronomical observations, to the same event. They pointed to a time, when the stars would announce the birth of a pious, humble, sinless teacher on earth. Though the mother was always portrayed in human terms, to the father was bestowed supernatural reference. Over 300 prophecies of that man in the Torah advised us that He would be of the lineage of King David, be born to a virgin woman, be a sign, and would be called: "Wonder or Wonderful, Counselor, Prince of Peace, Everlasting First fruit and (Mighty God) or Might of God." Simply translated it was that a man would be born to a virgin woman and would be the chosen teacher to usher in new dimensions of wisdom. The prophet Isaiah foreknew. In Isaiah 53, He would be the

"Repairer of the Breach" and be rejected by His kin when He came. Moses and David prophesied that He would be smitten. David described in detail how He would die—Psalm 22, and Isaiah did also: Isaiah 50:6 and Isaiah 53. Isaiah in particular told us that He would come as a sacrificial lamb to be slain for our transgressions. In clefts or rock in Solomon's Temple are all the clues as to the identity of that man. Academics of numerous ethnic and religious backgrounds refer to Him as the greatest teacher that ever lived. Earliest Muslims used Him as "the ultimate example" of pious living. In the Torah in numerically coded sequences are the names of His mother, His name Jeshua, His disciples and the women that found His empty tomb. That knowledge cannot be concealed any longer. Most of the prophecies concerning Him have been fulfilled.

The Prophet Isaiah wrote 66 chapters, most of them foretelling future events of Israel's history. He prophesied the Messiah's birth, purpose, rejection, suffering and ministry. Just about all of those events have already been fulfilled. Isaiah had prophesied every major event in the restorative ministry of Jesus. Computers are now proving that detailed events of the New Testament had been coded in Hebrew in the Torah.

John, one of Jeshua's disciples had accurately scripted the events of the 21st century as they are unfolding today. Those prophecies were recorded some two thousand years ago. The prophet Daniel also wrote a detailed account of European history thousands of years before Europe was born. One of England's Kings by the name of James commissioned the compiling of Hebrew sacred writings containing 66 books called the King James Bible. Despite the hostility that existed between Euro-Gentiles and 1st Century Hebrews, the first five books' translations correspond for the most part with the original Torah.

The Holy Koran has references to Jeshua being strengthened with Ruh Allah or Spirit of God and affirms that Moses brought the Law; Jesus brought the Gospel and the evidences, His teachings, miracles and grace of His life. Sura 2:253, "Those messengers we endowed with gifts, some above others: To some of them Allah spoke; others he raised to degrees; To Jesus the son of Mary we gave clear Signs and strengthened him with the Holy Spirit."

Every time someone offers fresh revelations on the true ethnicity of Jeshua, apologists proclaim that they are unimportant. Why then if it is so unimportant would an entire nation go to the length and breadth of the realm of deception to conceal, disguise, and ultimately change His identity—especially when they were specifically ordered not to make any graven images? The world needs to know that the last 360-degree "Master" to have walked on this earth was the Afro-Semitic Nazarene called Jeshua in Hebrew, Iasu or Isa in Arabic and Jesus in many other languages. That conclusion was arrived at after examining esoteric shards. This discourse will release hundreds of revelations including fresh ones about His ethnicity and spiritual prowess, as evidenced by Psalm 87, Psalm 110, and Micah 5:2.

When Jeshua was on earth, members of the Sanhedrin (with their limited understanding of esoteric matters) should have been so excited to be with such a great master. As is the nature of carnally minded men, the competition for the spotlight (which plagues many an institution of learning today) did what it does best: attempt to covet and then attempt to hinder all that they could not covet. God Almighty dispenses *Wisdom Pearls* to those "Chosen" to be His End-*times' Oracles*, performing the functions of "Kings and Priests." Hence it is written: "Many are called; few are chosen."

CHAPTER 2E. SURVIVING ON 10%

Let us take a cursory look at our (Western Civilization's) underdevelopment over the past two thousand years. Important findings:

1. The scientific community has determined that we utilize approximately **10 percent** of our total cranial capacity. So we can conclude that my previous references to our collective underdevelopment are within 1 percentage point of published scientific figures.

2. Inhabitants of major population centers, and people of every culture are functioning on the ruins of former civilizations (that rose and fell); we can deduce that all have come short. All have suffered from a "Wilderness Syndrome," or are subject to the "Cycle of Babel."

3. Everyone alive on this earth has the same DNA family history. To put it bluntly, the world's worst enemies were once part of the same tribe at some time in our prehistory. There were only two ethnic groups of people: a) Always migratory, wandering, hunting, changing, intermarrying over time and b) The other always inhabited the same landmasses, maintained the same customs and probably speak the same language at their festivities that their ancestors did after the last great geological catastrophe. Both groups have the same DNA molecular structure. Both groups' family trees originated from the same ancestral root.

4. We intellectuals are quick to judge and generalize. Fullness of education comprises utilizing one's full potential: physically, mentally and spiritually, plus the acquisition of data on things known, things past and things concealed. Persons functioning 90 percent deficiently are not qualified to make certain generalizations and judgments without adding: "In our opinion."

5. Since history is the record of past people, places and things, then prehistory can be classified as a fatal misconception, an arrogant perception, or an assortment of falsely documented data. Barring the above, we are left to assume that prehistory is some unknown discipline, a form of prejudicial understanding or unqualified assessment—in my humble opinion.

6. We write on paper in the Steel Age and store a modern form of hieroglyphic in electronic computer chips. People wrote on stone during the Stone Age to secure ceremonial and esoteric information. Such writings were from people whose mathematical computations and understanding of astronomy far surpassed anything achieved by our current and modern civilizations. Our classification of those people as primitive falls into the same categories of assessments as the above, in my opinion. Those brief examples are put on the front burner to prepare the mind to be ready to receive fresh revelations. Since so much of our mental space is dedicated to maintaining statistics, rehashing data or engaging in instant playback, I will not encroach on the area of the brain where the 11 percent or less of accumulated data is stored. The reason is that at the end, one can compare these new findings with previous assessments and upgrade, reject, add or subtract as one sees fit.

NO ONE PUTS NEW WINE INTO OLD WINESKINS!

There will be times, when the accepted philosophy of an institution differs drastically from the unearthed data. Whenever that happens, let us classify into which category the inconsistencies fall: human error, presumption, manipulation, arrogance, demonic infiltration, deception, or none of the above. The differences should then be carefully documented. Hopefully each reader will determine not so much the cause, but may understand why the "Cycle of Babel" eventually catches up with anything built askew. It is written, "Thou shall know the truth and the truth shall set you free!"

There is enough data on Babel to write two hundred books. Please understand that a lot of precautionary measures had to be undertaken prior to the commencement of this project. It is not my intention to embarrass any institution by these disclosures. However, look at what is happening. This new generation, looking for answers, is being led to believe that information accessible on a CD-ROM is infallible. For example, as a child we were told to drink lots of milk. Milk was good for all? Facts are that most of our health problems originate from animal foods. Some people are lactose intolerant. The teaching point here is that philosophies of fallible men and women need to be reviewed and updated regularly. Therefore from time to time, we must find credible theses as tributaries necessary to replenish our educational reservoirs with fresh wisdom. The chapter entitled "Acceptable Myths with Contrary Data" will document "Babel Slants" and then enclose often-sought, yet verifiable data. This book must cover most of the major highways used by humankind, which have serious engineering flaws. I am speaking figuratively of course. People need to be warned, not alarmed. To be forewarned is to be forearmed. Such juicy areas as "Demonic Infiltration" require entire books.

2F. WHO IS THAT IN THE MIRROR?

Are we who we say we really are? Did our parents know their roots? On our passports, a country of origin is listed. On landing cards we are asked to state our nationalities. Some indicate: American, Australian, Arabic, British, African, Canadian, Dutch, German, Israeli, Japanese, French, Spanish, Swiss, Danish, Turkish, Greek, Scandinavian, Indian, Pakistani, etc., and we usually do so proudly when we insert the title and why not? The titles reflect the most recent dominant cultures that inhabit the countries where we reside or resided. Books about discoveries and conquests verify such. Behind every cultural door are vast piles of hidden debris of civilizations that inhabited the lands we call home. Those early people looked different from the way we look now; many were called by different names. Those trailblazers fused our ancestral and genetic makeup and influenced two very rarely studied areas called "personalities" and "traits.

England—though named after the Angles—was once inhabited by Normans, Saxons and Visigoths—hence the name Anglo-terra, "Anglo-land" or England. Their earliest people, a large-nosed, brown people were called Hittite. Most British maintain the large ears and noses of their Hittite ancestors. Over time, as polar ice melted, those wandering Hittites settled in colder regions. As they intermarried or were conquered by Visigoths, Vandals, Normans and Saxons, their seed assumed the identities of the dominant civilizations. Climatic conditions did the rest. Carefully examine the noses and ears of the dwellers of the most remote people on the British and Scottish mainland. Their ears, noses, hairs and voice patterns reflect a more Hamitic base. Today, black people who take winter vacations return so much lighter. Melanin-depleted people (or white people as is more popularly referenced) return well tanned after a few weeks in the sun.

So after many hundreds of years, we began to assume that non-melanin people originated in cold countries and melanin-rich or extremely tanned people originated in tropical countries. If the criterion for "white" classification is permanent residence in a very cold country, then Eskimos should be lily white or as pale as ghosts. However they are people with melanin. Why is that so? Even though they have dwelt in cold countries for centuries, they have had less than seven genetic movements. In the chapter on "Accepted Myths/Contrary Evidence," other details will follow; consequently, I will not cause unnecessary duplication. The original inhabitants of Europe were called Hittite and Germani. Germans kept their ancestral name and they have retained not only their original lands, but also the ears, noses, speech patterns of quote: *"OTHER RACIAL TYPES,"* whatever that means.

America is the home of one of the largest and culturally rich *indigenous groups*. They had extended an invitation to some homeless immigrants a few hundred years ago and gave them permission to hunt and kill a few buffalo for food. It is amazing how little things change. Immigrants have been arriving ever since. Our children and grandchildren continue to hunt and kill to survive. The habits (iniquities) of the parents fall on the children up to the third and fourth generation. Some are still killing buffalo "b---fellow" and blood fellows.

It is very important to unearth the curses of the past. Most importantly it must be stated in no uncertain terms, the passage from darkness to light must be undergone in three separate stages. The Biblical teaching points were Egypt, The wildernesses of Sin/Paran/Zin/Shur, and the Promised Land. Observe the animals of the jungle. The young are extremely vulnerable to predators that capitalize on their weaknesses. Similarly the same applies in the spiritual. This book will identify the Chief perpetrator, expose his strategies and publish his files for all to read. When that is finished, the world's partially educated and spiritually unskilled warriors would be foolish to continue underestimating such a formidable foe.

CHAPTER 3. WORLD'S OLDEST SURVIVING LANDMASS!

CHAPTER 3A. CONCEALED LEGACIES OF AFRICA

Museums the world over are stocked with artifacts from former civilizations. Some were "*Discovered.*" Several were retrieved from diving expeditions; others from purchases, gifts, and archaeological excavations. Easter Island and a Caribbean island that I am actively studying are remnant masses. I have seen structures and monuments made by ancient occupants. As a diver and amateur archaeologist I find landmasses that survive large-scale cataclysms fascinating. Some lands even ride the waves of time: they rise and fall again and again.

Africa is the oldest surviving landmass and the only continent to have had its name changed not once but many times. Over the ages, Africa had been called Gondwanaland, Pangaea, Itiopi, Tamar-i and Ta Nisi (ancient Zoan). It has been ravaged by fire, winds, water, and at the expense of every greedy and powerful nation past and present. Its physical and political landscape changes as fast as the average computer window. In Isaiah 18:1-2, Isaiah recorded that her ancient civilizations sent ambassadors by sea.

Africa is an archaeological and historical paradox in that it challenges probability odds as to why it hasn't disappeared totally. It has shrunk from the largest at one time to the world's second largest continent. It is now approximately 12,000,000 square miles with a population of 1 billion plus people. It has over 95% of the world's chrome reserves, 85% to 90% of world's platinum and 70% of the world's Tantalite. It has also 100% of the known Tanzanite reserves, 70% of the world's cobalt, 70% of the world's natural gas reserves, and 55% of the world's gold reserves, 2/3rd of which are concentrated in three countries: Algeria, South Africa and Zimbabwe. Nigeria is the world's 7th largest oil producer. Africa has snow, waterfalls, deserts, rivers, caves, volcanoes, beaches, forests, mountains, and almost every type of tropical beast and tropical bird. Africa is also self sufficient in every mineral, every metal and is targeted by every demonic force imaginable. The greatest and most influential teachers and prophets that ever lived were born on some part of a land or nation physically connected to Africa. The list includes Hebrew prophets from Moses to Micah, Jeshua, His disciples and Prophet Mohammed. Others, including God's chosen redeemers Moses and David, married African women. Today, there are 100 plus major language branches that give rise to over 6800 different variations currently spoken on the continent. Those do not include over 42,000 dialects that are known and spoken on the land also. Many are linguistic shards from former civilizations. Africa, home to some of the world's earliest universities (Grand Lodges) greatest architects of yore (whose feats have yet to be paralleled) is a country at least one and a half times the size of the United States. There isn't a person alive today that does not have a genetic or ancestral link with someone that was born on or lived on that land called "Mother or Cradle of Civilization."

From about 850 B.C. to 650 B.C., the Ethiopian Empire covered the entire Mediterranean, south to the Nile Valley. From around 700 C.E. to approximately 1300 C.E., the Moors out of North Africa controlled from Southern France, Spain and Libya to the river Niger in the south. That mix is reflected in the features of many French and what people refer to as Latinized Spanish today. The Moors also introduced chess, checkers, fine architecture and an unprecedented wealth of medicinal and astronomical knowledge previously unknown in Europe. After their surrender in 1492, several of their former kings were either killed or they were shipped across the Atlantic as slaves—Deuteronomy 28: 36-41. Nahum 3:10 "They cast lots for her honourable men and all her great men were bound in chains." Most of the so-called "Lost Tribes of Israel" reside in countries that encircle the Euphrates. Inhabitants of Kashmir, India, Pakistan and Afghanistan, are remnants of the 10 northern tribes. Confirmation can be found in Esther 2:6, and Esther 1:1.

A Scottish missionary named Reverend Wilson—and others before him—encountered an isolated Jewish community along the coast of Mahrashtra (in India) approximately 25 miles south of Bombay called Bene Israel or Children of Israel. Kohanim is the Hebrew name for a member of the Aaronic priestly clan. The capital of Nagaland in E. India is Kohima and the coastal town where the seed of that Hebrew remnant were discovered is called Konhan. Those links I found particularly interesting since Indians, people of the Caribbean and Africans were shipped to North and South America as bondservants on identical sugar plantations. God promised to ignore their cries from the cane fields (Jeremiah 6:20) until they stopped visiting "temples" Jeremiah 7:4 and *abandoned false religions*, Jeremiah 7:8.

The remnant of another ancient Hebrew community was found in Ethiopia (as per prophecy of Amos). The Falasha, as they are called, practiced the strictest observances of the Hebrew law. They taught from the Torah. Remnants of the tribes of Simeon and Judah in the south were either transshipped as slaves across the Atlantic or married seed of Ethiopians and other Africans. Some returned to Israel to work as missionaries after the civil war in Ethiopia. Others are carrying on their original roles of protecting the land. London professors of Jewish Studies—Tudor Parfait and Hillel Avidan have access to DNA analyses showing that the Lemba Tribes on the north of South Africa are remnant seed of the Aaronic priests.

Let us examine the words that God spoke through Amos. To God, the Ethiopians and the Hebrews are the same. Amos 9:7, "*Are ye not as children of the Ethiopians unto me, O children of Israel?*" Some were shipped through Joppa and Gorè to islands of the sea of Gentile nations, divided according to Gentile tongues: Genesis 10:4-6. Others have returned to their prophetic calling, living in a thriving desert metropolis called Dimona. Why does God have Amos remind the children of Israel that they and the Ethiopians are the same? Let us seek the evidence. Esther 1:1, From India to Ethiopia were 120 provinces where the people had been mixing and intermarrying to such a degree that the king had no way of telling who were Jews or not. Also the fact that Paul, Simon and many other Jews spoke Greek exposes why the Hebrew word "Javan" in Joel 3:6 should not have been translated as land of Greeks but the ancient city in Southern Arabia. Their seed began The Atlantic Slave Trade. As a result of that mistranslation, some researchers assumed that the isles in the Aegean Sea might have been the islands where "*Lost Tribes of Israel*" are concealed. However, Moses` prophetic warning in Deuteronomy 28:49 dispels that notion since most Biblical Jews understood Greek. It was recorded for posterity: "A nation whose tongue thou shalt *not* understand."

God always conceals a remnant. God also prophesied through Malachi the prophet. Malachi 2:11, "Judah hath profaned the holiness of the Lord, which he loved and married the daughter of a strange god. Verse 12, The Lord will cut off the man that does this, the *master* and *the scholar."* Verses 13 to 17 are particularly relevant. However in Malachi 3:1-4, God promised to send an uncompromising messenger, the same as prophesied by Isaiah, in Isaiah 53:11-12. Through Him alone is the salvation of Israel and Africa—among others. Malachi 3:4, "Then shall the offering of Judah and Jerusalem be pleasant unto the Lord as in the days of old." The cedars from Hiram were shipped from Joppa. Was it the same Joppa where Peter was told in a vision not to refer to melanin-deficient people (called Gentiles then) as unclean? To be sure, we will examine in detail the type of lumber used on Solomon's Temple and also the stonework. The *carpentry* and *masonry* of Solomon's Temple are the most important principles as models for building—character, family, institution, or nation. Some of the allegedly Lost Tribes of the North married Berbers, Arabs, Persians, Medes, Tibetans; some are called Libyans, Assyrians, Turks, and Iranians etc. Most of their seed, ignorant of the identity and covenant of their forefathers, have adopted strange religions and have become sworn enemies of their former kin. Incidentally David's daughter Abigail married Jether the Ishmaelite. It is written: "In the latter times, brother will rise against brother." It is happening as we read.

History makes reference to a warrior Queen that invaded Egypt and ruled from the Nile to the Euphrates. Her headquarters was the Syrian City of Palmyra. All the major historians described her Hamitic features—"large black eyes, dark complexion with pearl white teeth and extremely beautiful." Yet, modern painters portray her the way that Syrians appear today (forgetting that the ancient Syrians did not have the influx of Berbers in their ancestry in those times). Those that paint ancient Hebrews do the same thing. They reflect their current features, neglecting the fact that current ethnic landscapes changed drastically within the past two thousand years.

Beneficiaries of that source tributary of Africa, on the lake of natural sustenance (people, cultures, land and energy) appear to have an ignoble death wish for the land. Why are news media so obsessed with wishing away that segment of Africa north of the Sahara? Israel and Egypt—which are, and always were connected to Africa—are now located on a mythical land-mass called Middle-East.

3B. ACCIDENTAL OCCURRENCE OR SUBTLE DECEPTION?

A Flemish cartographer named Geradus Mercador (1512 to 1594) began the process of pre-senting lands in the north latitudes larger than those in the south latitudes. Since then, every mapmaker (except one) shows Africa smaller than the United States. The Northern Hemi-sphere is usually shown bigger than the Southern Hemisphere. The grid lines from 10 to 20 degrees north latitude are consistent with the measurements of the grids for the Southern Hemisphere and Africa. However from 20 to 30 degrees north where America begins, the grid lines even though equal in degrees, miraculously grow from 10 to 20 percent in imagined surface area. From 50 to 60 degrees north latitude they grow even bigger. A mystifying en-largement process occurs right before our very eyes.

Yesteryear's greatest institutions of learning: Grand Lodge of Thebes, Luxor, Ta-Merry, Waat, Tanis or Ta-Nisi (ancient Zoan) and the University of Timbuktu were built in Africa and demolished before writing and reading were introduced in Europe. Around the middle of the 1st century, while Europe was wrestling with feudal wars, science flourished around the Muslim dominated Northern Africa and Mediterranean countries. Some of the most renown scientists were: Abu Ali Hasan Ibn Al Haitham, Ali Ibn Rabban Al-Tabari, Al-Faraghani, Abu Al Nasr Al Farabi, Abu Hamid Ibn Muhammad Al-Tusi Al-Ghazali, Muhammad Bin

Musa Al-Khawarizmi and innumerable others.

East is a specific geographical direction; so are west, north and south. Take out a compass and figure out what part of the continent, Africa, is the geographical idiocy referred to as Middle and East. In later chapters the contents of a few ancient vaults will be revealed. Questions beg to be asked:

a)   What caused that self-sufficient land with such a rich and powerful heritage to sink perpetually into despair?

b)   What caused a land that was so fertile to have constant bouts with drought?

c)   What caused the land to receive no vacation from pestilence, war or bloodshed?

Jeremiah 4:16 and 17 described the powerful spirits that would be obsessed with enslaving *all* cities of *Judah* and the way they behaved like fences around a city. Jeremiah 4:4, Jeremiah 5:18-19 and Jeremiah 6:20 are among numberless prophecies.

Are we to assume that all the inhabitants of Africa are remnants of Judah? Definitely not! With the slave hunters combing the north and west coasts, the lands south of the Sahara should have been safe for a while. However, while the human hunters went south, the land hunters—the same Europeans—went after the entire land. Africa was carved up and forced labour was used on nearly all of the colonies. By the time the various colonies gained their independence, few could lay claim to being of successive generations of indigenous people. Within the past 50 years, most of the immigrant populations (in 90 percent of the former colonies) have been remnants exhausted from civil wars, Indian traders and business people, and seed of the same 10 northern tribes referenced in Esther 1:1.

Bearing in mind that we utilize only 10 percent of our mental capacities, should we assume that everything we believe is true? There are things that we have stored permanently in our subconscious files—we hope they are true; yet they cannot be supported by logic, evidence, or history. We pass them unto our children and many of those things produce discomfort when attempts are made to separate facts from fiction. People tend to hatch belief systems based on ingrained perceptions without examining "who or what" constituted those beliefs. Since education consists mainly of the sum of things known, plus the experiences of yesteryear, it stands to reason that our ability—to access, effectively utilize, dispense, and acquire wisdom accurately—is of primary importance. Naturally we need to examine the foundations of what we call institutions of learning: the factories of our educational systems.

Greece, falsely credited with being the architectural planners and foundation builders of Western Civilizations, was in a state of institutionalized "dunce-ness" at the very time that such credit was attributed to her. China already had writers and philosophers long before Greece did. Anaximander, Anaximenes, Eudoxus, Thales, and other pioneering Greek intellectuals were educated in the Egyptian mystery schools. Long afterwards they established their esoteric centers chiefly in Asia Minor because their country was initially intolerant "to those higher forms of learning." Socrates was poisoned for teaching. He was condemned to death in 399 B.C., for corrupting young Athenian minds and was forced to drink hemlock. According to Greek legendary accounts, Eudoxus was the founder of one of Greece's earliest "Mystery Schools." Scores of his first students in turn became some of Greece's great teachers. Archaeological records seem to infer that the site of that ancient academy where Plato allegedly studied was near Knidos. Greek legends also infer that Eudoxus had to become an initiate of the Egyptian Mystery Schools in order to access the teachings and wisdom first-hand. According to Jambilicus who wrote the biography of Pythagoras (Life of Pythagoras), "The Theorems of Lines (as geometry was called) are of Egyptian origin." Pythagoras (a former student of Thales) spent over twenty years furthering his studies in Egypt. Thales had been initiated into the Mystery Schools in Egypt and was one of the first Greek students. What we call *square root* of Greek origin actually was used in Egypt under the name of a *double remen* and Noah used *the cubit* in his measurements for the Ark. The cubit was also used in Egyptian mathematics under the name of *the royal*. Those can be verified by examining a 16th century B.C. papyrus stored in the Museum of Turin. A copy is also on display at the Louvre in Paris.

The researches of Caveing, Diop, and Gillings offer data to contradict and negate previously "accepted" myths. The existence of the Rind Papyrus plus the *words* of the Greek Pioneers should have been enough to negate the myth that the Greeks invented those sciences but many kept repeating the idiocy. In spite of evidence to the contrary their myths survived. Although more documentation exists in masterpieces by J. A. Rogers and Herodotus to refute those allegations, recognized institutions of learning in the Occident print the foolishness today *in textbooks* as if they were factual.

When the Library of Alexandria was at its peak, during the Egyptian Dynastic periods, Greeks attended Egypt's courtyard lectures. When they attempted to bring the newfound wisdom back home to Greece, many were banished and ostracized. Known researches: J.A. Rogers and Cheikh Anta Diop documented such. Not a few Greek students partially translated and trans-shipped some of Egypt's philosophy. As in every case when students copy each other's works, they inadvertently copy errors also. Similarly, what Egypt stored in stone, the Greeks institutionalized. However, certain data that they did not understand were recorded for posterity in legends known as Greek mythology. One of the most noteworthy is the story of "Jason and the Argonauts." The Rosetta stone's discovery reminded us of the educational vacuum that existed prior to its translation. Hopefully these volumes will raise the Occident's esoteric and spiritual barometers.

During the peak of Egypt's dynastic civilizations, institutions of learning consisted of temples, universities, museums and esoteric centers. They were under one roof called Grand Lodges. Teachers were the Priest Kings. They performed priestly functions, definitely not according to the Order of Melchizedek. I will not get into the period where the priesthood became polluted. I will mention however their gravest error, an error repeated daily—by persons in pursuit of higher mental elevation, by churches, and most institutions of wisdom and power. Their unguarded altars were overpowered. Egyptian priest Imhotep, builder of Egypt's first pyramid, performed surgical operations on the human torso and the brain at least 1500 years before the birth of Greece's so-called founders of medicine.

The first fruit from any *Master* with knowledge above 33° is foreknowledge of the formula to achieve "God's redemptive plan for all humankind." Moreover, God would not allow any seed of Abraham to be without knowledge of His "redemption plan," because He made that promise to *Abraham and all of his seed*. The fact that there are people, not of the seed manifesting "fruits of the promise" and people of the "seed" functioning without "fruits of the promise" necessitates open and intelligent debate. Whereas those without the fruits would document their opinions, *True Masters* would reflect God's wisdom emanating out of fresh revelations from His unfailing word. For example:

a.   The direct bloodline through which the promised seed would germinate is through Isaac, through David, through David's seed. Some of us are called to teach. Few of us are chosen to teach "wisdom" above "33 degrees."

b.   God our Creator is *Love*. To be an oracle of God to reveal the above, one must also manifest Agape—love from God, and love for all. No true oracle of God (who is Love) can harbour hate and "unforgiveness."

c.   The redemptive plan of God as prophesied through Isaiah must be fulfilled on the foundation of the *above*. Jews, Muslims, Christians and Gentiles are to be included or "grafted" through the special "chosen" human *Branch*.

d.   When the Branch, the Light become manifest, He would lead us *into all truth*. He would have *Oracle Power* echoing only the words of the Master. Persons that are serious in their pursuit of true wisdom, knowledge and understanding—the apex of education—must first *find* that *Master* and His *teachings* before they can find that wisdom. Millions have pursued and failed to find the "*Wisdom of Solomon*." His hidden legacy is finally here.

e.   Let this foundation seed be sown in our minds that "Three is the number of days (epochs) for the *Chosen Light or Luminary* to manifest."

CHAPTER 4. DIFFERENT CONCEPTS OF TIME!

CHAPTER 4A. THE MOST ANCIENT CONCEPT OF TIME

The first thing we need is a proper understanding of different concepts of time. Time had a commencement point. Scientists have determined that light travels at 300,000 km per second. I might add that "light speed" is attained in our gravity-enriched atmosphere. Since things that travel have varying speeds, it is logical that time is no exception. Conception speed differs from average and maximum attained speed. In this chapter we want to look at time from its prime or ancient first movement.

The principles of time computation appear to have been of primary concern to all civilizations except this current Western Civilization. Ancient teachers would *knock* such terms into the minds of their students as: "Time, Times, and Half Time." Our present perception and method of computing time is obviously different from those of the ancients. To transpose ancient time into modern times, first we need to understand the mechanism from which our time emanates.

Members of our research team were tickled pink when we were interviewing African Americans in the sixties. They would ask you, "Do you know what time it is?" We would look at our watches and they would say laughingly, "No Maaan, It is happening time!" The inability of our so-called wise people to comprehend the times or seasons have caused such oft-repeated idiocies as "prehistory" and "primitive" to be part of our vocabularies.

The educational void, under which Europe developed, took approximately 1600 years for gaps—or better yet, canyons—to be filled. Christian churches today have affixed a constant value of 24 hours to the Hebrew word "yowme" (period of revelation) and as such unwisely calculate that this current world is 6000 years old. If that is so, how do they explain China's 9000-year unbroken history? Ponder this also! According to documented data, Adam lived to be 930 years and Noah lived to be 950 years old (350 of those years were after the Flood). So if Christendom's reckoning is correct, from whence came the 1500 skilled workers that built the Pyramid of Cheops 4650 years ago? Where did they derive accounts of eons of inundations of the Nile River? The name of the architect (Khufu or Cheops) and the size of his work force are inscribed in hieroglyphic on one of the slabs. As a result of the miscalculation of time by unlearned people, a lot of false alarms have been issued regarding the "Day of Doom." Inaccurately translated data and lack of understanding of God's wisdom have turned millions into skeptics. They have heard the cries of: "Wolf!" too often.

The spread of Christianity to the Occident needs thorough and careful scrutiny. While the Antioch and African 1st branches of the Messiah's church spread as far as Russia, Rome's 3rd tier was built on the mythical foundation that they received all teachings first hand from Jesus' disciples. As such, all of Rome's teachings and computations were accepted without thorough scrutiny.

Alexandria, the debate and intellectual center of Europe and Asia Minor from 323 B.C. to 30 C.E. approximately, encouraged different philosophical and intellectual schools of thought. The fruits of their spirited debates were tributaries, which in turn fed the reservoirs of knowledge in the Occident. By the end of the first 200 years of Christendom, nearly all the wise and educated Christian teachers in and around Rome were either burnt or martyred and their learning tools and centres destroyed. Why were the Mystery Schools in Greece and Rome not destroyed initially like they did to the properties of Jews and Christians?

1. For the most part they existed prior to the Christian sect's rise to prominence. 2. Their views were much more radical. 3. In many instances, Gnosticism, Pantheism, Occult sciences and doctrines considered food for the mind, were discussed and taught. Verbal exchanges, dialogues and spirited debates were encouraged—since all the *Mystery Schools* tried to emulate the Library of Alexandria with its open courtyard debate systems and its reputation as "The Learning Oasis" of yore.

Two of Rome's most notable students that established similar types of "Mystery Schools" in the second century (C.E.) were Justin Martyr and Titus Flavius Clemens. Titus Flavius Clemens was a theologian of Greek ancestry who headed a liberal school. In that school, Gnosticism and Pantheism were analyzed to ascertain if in fact Christianity was a new doctrine or a Jewish spin of ancient Greek thought processes. Romans that studied in Carthage or Alexandria could return and open advanced schools of learning as long as their institutions fostered or encouraged open debates. Philo Judaeus was the first official translator of Hebrew Scriptures into Greek. Pantheism, named after Pantheus and philosophy (named after Philo?) were popular disciplines. Justin Martyr began using his position of eminence to teach Christian doctrines, relying on his great debating style to draw intellectual lines in the sand among Christianity, mysticism and mythology. As soon as word of his teachings reached the authorities, he was beheaded in 165 C.E. making him the *first known Roman Christian martyr*. Since Bishops in Crete, Carthage and Asia Minor were driven underground during the great persecution, any good news would have been welcome. They learned that Latin translations of the Christian texts, plus the zeal of the martyrs, were encouraging other Romans to come to Cartage and Asia Minor to pursue the truth. Some came and told of the polluting of the teachings through the liberal schools in Rome.

Polycarp, Bishop of Smyrna, made a secret journey to Rome before the end of the second century and found out that a church headed by an Anicetus was appealing to local customs and introducing doctrines that were spiritually compromising. He reported to the head church in Antioch, that Rome—the new center of wealth, power and military might—was polluting the gospels. Polycrates also confirmed his findings and together they sent letters to the churches in Ephesus, Crete, Carthage and Smyrna. The Roman authorities soon learnt of their campaign and like Justin Martyr, both Polycarp and Polycrates were martyred. The teachings that they identified and condemned will be listed in detail in later chapters. Confirmation can be had in Constantine's letters as he invited Bishops of Rome's Empire to attend the first Council of Nicea in 325 C.E. It was the Christian convert Emperor Theodosius1-the Great, after unifying both provinces—Rome of the East and Rome of the West—issued a decree in 395 C.E. to eliminate *"Arian heresies" and paganism from all Roman provinces*. The second *Council of Nicea of 787 C.E. ordered graven images restored in all Roman churches*. Three popes that questioned the decree died suddenly—two were assassinated and one died under very strange circumstances.

As we progress we shall begin to understand more about civilizations that survived a season of jubilees (7X70) years. Civilizations that pursued the times and those that understood the times appear to have been the ones that have survived the times. The Trojans did not understand the times; neither did the Saxons, Visigoths, Berbers, or the Vandals etc.

CHAPTER 4B. BEGINNING OF DAYS

Let us contrast the levels of understanding between the tongues of a nation that *knew the times* as opposed to one that *pursued the times*. The Hebrew word BÂQAR means to break forth or to reveal. BÔQER means dawn. Each time those words are translated from Hebrew to English the word "Day" is used. Genesis 1:5 is the first noted incidence of the translation. There is no specific time affixed; simply, "The evening and the morning were the first day."

Note carefully it *did not say from* the evening to the morning. It is noted: "The evening and the morning," in other words the door to the unrevealed and the first fruit of all revealed (Alpha and Omega). To the most learned, receive insight into the identity of The Ancient of Days: Daniel 7:13-14.

In the natural, the Electro-magnetic spectrum (Light) contains wave frequencies or energy bands all with varying forms of light. The spiritual also has its days. All that was first revealed was the first day: first word/life, first wisdom, first light, first gamma rays, first radio waves, first x-rays, first infrared lights, and first ultra violet rays. There are also feast and commemorative days of major importance: Pentecost, Advent, Judgment, Purim, and Shabbat. In the book of Job we encountered a number of specific days: Day of Darkness, Day of Battle and Day of Wrath. The entire redemptive package was wrapped into the Light spectra called day. "The rest" lay in the *womb of the unrevealed* or darkness. Through that womb, *God travails in threes*. Hence the original place of birth is called *day of birth*.

God revealed His purposes and a physical image of His invisible spirit whole, His Glory—hence, He is the entire "*Light of the Universe.*" Before "*The Word*" was manifest, or revealed, or became flesh, "*The Word*" was part and parcel of the All, or God. Hence, in the beginning, the Logos was with God and the Logos was God. Why? There was not yet any manifestation of the invisible word. Since the word cannot return void, the moment the word was spoken, it became matter; it was confirmed. The living word came alive and became light and life. Out of the Occident's dark beginnings, one of the world's most carnal civilizations' grappled with interpreting spiritual things. Romans 8:7, "The carnal mind is enmity towards God."

Specific amounts of released energy or revealed wisdom within a set time is a day. Each time a specific season of revelation unfolds we call it a new day or a day of new beginnings. Everything made was placed in a domain called future and then separated by time. Someone please explain to my simple mind why is it that we are able to arrive at a fixed time frame of 24 hours as the only reference for day, with so many options available.

There is an entire discourse on another type of day called "The Papyrus of Ani," or "The Book of the Coming forth by Day." That book, listed among Egypt's funerary texts, documents events from both sides of the spiritual divide. The absence of guidelines or classification of beings caused "curious people" heavy damage on user-unfriendly spiritual highways. On the other hand, for decades, China published books on the Laws of Opposites, or principles of Yin and Yang. Those books highlight the failures of the occidental educational institutions to teach contrasting principles or "Laws of Opposites." As a result, millions of young people are reaping the consequences of generations of inaccuracy. Since each action has an equal and opposite reaction, then each law (documented or not) has benefits (known or unknown) for the obedient, and punishments (known or unknown) for the transgressors. Judges have lectured many persons, including myself, with the words—"Ignorance is no excuse to the law."

CHAPTER 4C. THOSE THAT KNEW THE TIMES

King Solomon is often regarded as one of the wisest men that ever lived. Solomon, who had extra degrees of wisdom potential, built a physical structure based on true spiritual principles. Cemented in clefts of rock of that structure were the benefits and consequences of positive and negative behaviour. Approximately 2000 years later, a Nazarene blood relative was the first teacher to navigate the narrow road to true wisdom—spelling out, in simple parables, the consequences and/or benefits of success or failure. Jeshua as he was called, built a spiritual structure centered on people, showing the method of transposition of principles from the adamic to the spiritual. The fact that there are some 360 prophecies prerecorded by ancient Hebrew prophets foretelling the time and the nature of His mission is remarkable enough. In over 100 Muslim verses, Isa Ibn Miriam (Jesus son of Mary) is revered. Now that computers are available as research tools, we are finding every detail of Jeshua's legacy foretold in code in Hebrew versions of the Bible, the Tanakh. As many numerical sequences are selected, more and more revelations keep popping out, providing spiritual food for a new generation of books.

Countless Muslim and Jewish researchers are baffled over those revelations. Some are waiting and are trying to conceal the findings. Others are wondering out loud whether or not Prophet Mohammed was sent to rescue the lost sheep and if the zeal of his followers overshadowed his mission. Fortunately, those Jews and Arabs that are discovering Jeshua's teachings are experiencing an intimate personal relationship with God, and are becoming "Believers."

At the beginning of the 1st century, while Rome practiced state censorship, Muslim nations flourished because of state-assisted incentives to pursue knowledge and wisdom critically. Now Satan has switched spirits. Muslim nations are encouraging censorship and some are reacting violently to doctrinal scrutiny. Towards the end of 1998, intolerant extremists on both sides viciously attacked "Charismatic Jews and Arabs" living in Israel. The silence of the international press on such a high profile event was deafening. How can one find truth without scrutiny?

Surveys' results: the greatest spiritual teacher—barring none, was Jeshua or Jesus, as Westerners call Him, "a carpenter from Nazareth." His unprecedented clarity in explaining complex scripture is legendary. The laws of consequence He described in graphic perennial classics called parables: The Prodigal Son, the Good Samaritan, the Kinsman Redeemer and the Sower of the Vineyard—among others. In Matthew 5, Jeshua was the first to teach on Personality Syndrome Correctness called "Beatitudes." He was the first and last known 360-degree, wisdom-filled teacher to release tools on becoming a "Perpetual Overcomer" by expounding on the *Laws of: Consequence, Immunity,* and *Spiritual Resistance.* He was the first to reveal the path of hidden mysteries to ultimate wisdom, truth and righteousness for all humankind, regardless of race, creed or country of origin. Those Laws were first taught to a chosen twelve to expand the office of the Melchizedek priesthood. As a result, lots of Orthodox Jews today still harbour generational anger on the point that a Hebrew scholar would take this guarded wisdom to the Gentiles. They forgot that the prescribed paths of His restorative ministry were foretold. Our research team examined His life on earth in detail. Surprisingly, in addition to the accounts of witnesses who met Him personally, Jesus is lauded in at least 15 Suras in the Holy Koran. Detailed accounts of Jesus' earthly life, His piety, His fairness, His unselfish love and His teachings have been documented in the Tanakh and the New Testament segment of the Holy Bible. The prophecies relating to His identity, His mission, and His lineage are documented in the Torah or "Old Testament" segment of the Holy Bible. His entire restorative package has been prophetically etched in clefts of rock in the structure of Solomon's Temple.

I have met scholars who criticized the clannishness of the ancient Hebrews. They argued that the Hamitic\Semitic\Japhethic Hebrews only mingled with and intermarried Ethiopians and other tribes, except during periods of captivity. They inferred that there were doctrines of superiority. Let me point out early in this discourse, that the Gentiles were not despised because they were the only non-coloured people in the region at the time. The countries which they came from worshipped gods of wood and stone; they had unguarded altars, coveted altars and initial generational curses that God did not want mingled with His chosen seed—Leviticus 19:19. If those allegations were true, would God have included the Gentiles in His plan of restitution prophesied by Isaiah? Isaiah 11:10—that "root" from the stem of Jesse shall the Gentiles seek. There is no evidence found anywhere to concretize the myth that ancient Hebrews practiced racial prejudice as we know it today. There is evidence that they were "religiously clannish" and that is a horse of a different colour.

4D. UNDERSTANDING THE CLOCK, THE SCHEMATIC

I am wearing a watch at the moment that gives me the seasons, hours, minutes, seconds, years, and has compass readings and so forh. Man built it. It has its rules. I have to insert batteries every so often. It is very accurate; however once in a while when the battery needs changing it loses time. The universe is a giant clock. It gives minutes, history, seasons, astronomy, archaeology, sunrises, sunsets, does not lose time and it has been accurate for generations of years. It has in itself the other 90 percent of wisdom that us humans know nothing about and are too proud to admit. The main criterion for establishing non-accidental phenomena is that "As long as persons or things replicate identical patterns of behaviour, movements or shapes, those parallels cannot be accidental." By these criteria established by the masters of today and yesteryear, the universe was created by the most intelligent being or beings: Genesis 1:1 and Isaiah 45:12.

Solomon, considered by many so-called masters as "ultra-wise," advised us in Proverbs 3:19 that the Lord founded the earth by *Wisdom* and established the heavens by *Understanding*. Isaiah11:2 documents the seven ministering spirits of God. Since logic and other established principles dictate that every thing of repetitive motion has a prime mover, the universe has a *Chief Architect*. Ponder the fact that we adore persons who make the Halls of Fame in sports and persons who win awards. Then for Pete's sake, why not the maker of the rain cycle, the perpetual motions of the heavens and the sustainable quarantine station called "earth." In my opinion, He is the fairest being I have ever known or would ever want to know. I will endorse the name of God Almighty or Almighty God. The Hebrew seer Isaiah, who accurately foretold Israel's history through to the end times, told us who made this giant clock. God promised us, through Isaiah, a master technician to fix everything that could go wrong—Isaiah 40:12 and Isaiah 40:11. Isaiah 42:1-9 accurately forecast the role of the repairer to be manifest—since confirmed in Matthew 12:18-21. Since God's word declared that the heavens were created and stretched out, which is harder to believe? Events past that someone did, or events that would take place three thousand years in advance by someone who invented a gizmo and would brag how accurately it would perform?

Allegedly, the Library of Alexandria was one of the most complete libraries of all times. The main library was available to the Masters of those times only. Alexandria was unique in that the city was a major thoroughfare and the library's open courtyard sessions and debates were available for all to attend and to learn by osmosis. It was by those processes that many of the Great thinkers of early Greece acquired their teachings and subsequent initiations: Thales of Miletus, Herodotus, and Pythagoras among others. What the early Greeks did not understand, was enshrined in an intangible storeroom called Greek mythology. It was theorized that within time, some bright seed or seeds would spring up and decipher the data for the benefit of humankind. According to Aristotle, Egyptian priests invented the "mathematikai technai."

Rome did an intellectual reshuffle. State-controlled religion transformed their educational elite into paranoid plebs. Roman architects of Western Civilization diverted from the openness practiced by the Greeks. They began to control and to confine knowledge by fear and autocratic means. It is amazing how "religion" influenced the state to sanction book burnings and to outlaw the keeping of books on science and religion. Mass confiscation, destruction, theft and burnings were the order of the day during the rise of European civilizations. The West had been re-educated on a 2nd foundation of civilizations that were spiritually prejudiced and intellectually confused. Thank heaven that records from the 7th to the 12 centuries of Muslim scientists survived. Very accurate translations of the Hebrew and Greek teachings of Jeshua in Arabic and some of the finest maps and data on planetary systems have been preserved in nations occupied by the Arabic seed of Abraham.

Let us take a look at one of the early doors in mythology. Everyone probably read or heard of the story of Jason and the Argonauts. If Williamson is William's son, and Jacobson is the son of Jacob; take an educated guess as to the identity of Jason, or better yet—whose son is Jason. That is correct—Son of Jehovah or Jah. The one whose story is told by the constellations in Astronomy (not the imitation science of astrology) and the only one referenced in all eschatology records at the ancient Library of Alexandria. It was stated that the chosen person would to be the first to penetrate the labyrinth (life/death cycle) and would defeat the host of the damned. That "Light of God" would be ordained to redeem the lost by His everlasting sacrifice and by surpassing the 360-degree cycle of Hades. Some visitors to ancient libraries tried to initiate the resurrection rite. Others tried to imitate it. All the languages and customs found of people that existed before a major global catastrophe, referenced a stellar season or constellation—yet to be born. Those Egyptologists and archeologists who understood the times all concur that the esoteric symbolism and ceremonial dances of "un-evolved people" were their ways of concealing the hidden messages until the "Day of Revelation. In the storeroom called Greek mythology, we are told that the only one who could fetch that Golden Fleece was Jason. All the other secret libraries went underground when news of the burning of Alexandria reached them.

Under the cloak of a clandestine occult *triangle of blood,* called the Atlantic Slave Trade, an organization known as the Grail Seekers intimated that they had found the Fleece. They advised all to cease their pursuit of it. I did not plan to include anything on that matter in this book. However I might as well mention a bit since many books had been written about other copycat groups also called Grail Seekers. Hopefully this discourse will clarify the issue once and for all. That door, in which the foundation scraps are, could fill at least two books. However as we cover the secrets behind the Atlantic Slave Trade, some of that data will be enclosed. The rest will be assigned to sequels of this discourse.

CHAPTER 4E. JA AND SON CLOCKWORKS UNLIMITED

Let us take an imaginary trip, from the construction of a mechanical clock through to the establishment of its brand name, then on to the building of its head office. Workmanship, materials, plans or blueprints, office workers (especially the repair staff) were put in place before production began. Before the ascension to corporate giant, with worldwide marketing, many clock makers had humble beginnings. Let us use a simple analogy of Mo and Son. Their primitive workshop had carpentry tools mainly; since almost all the early clocks were wooden. Mo was an expert builder/carpenter; he taught his son well. Mo passed on to his son, all knowledge pertaining to building and fixing clocks. All the scraps and all the discarded data were stored in the storeroom before "the beginning." Except for occasional researchers and curious folks, the old building is fit to become a museum.

Usually, when prototypes are produced, names and dates of construction are etched for posterity. However Mo, his son, the plans, the materials, and the priesthood existed before the date of construction. Let us insert Ja or "Jah" and Son. Ja, His Son and at least one other worker (Psalm 110 and John 17:2-5) existed before this giant clock or universe was built. The priest in Psalm 110:4 is Melchizedek, the forerunner of the everlasting priesthood.

Let us examine the threefold principle—thought, plan, and action—in Isaiah 42:1, 5, and 6. The door before the first chime or "Big Bang" has some of the world's most sought-after secrets—things known, unknown, visible, and not yet manifest—obviously invisible. A schematic emanating from the maker of this clock must have access to the "unrevealed." The big question—how would "The Establishment" react to the revelations? "Is there or was there such a schematic?" If such a schematic were found, those volumes would have to be filled with prophecy; files classified "enigma" would have to be relabeled as "solved." With the revelation of such a schematic, people of the world would be able to break the cycles of poverty and ignorance. People would not have to be functionally literate anymore. Hollywood might have to stop calling demons and devils "extraterrestrials and "space aliens." Some educational books would have to be reclassified as "misinformation," especially those on Evolution. Understandably, denial of its existence could be predicated on the following assumptions: a) this perfectly repetitious mechanism was accidentally made; b) there was no such schematic; 3) there are other reasons. Isaiah 44:6 and Isaiah 44:24 are clues. "I am the Lord that maketh all things; that stretcheth forth the heavens alone; that spreadeth abroad the earth by myself." Verse 26 gave an insight into the harmony between himself and His Son. He would confirm everything that the Son said.

Years ago, when a team of researchers began revealing bits and pieces of information about evidence from civilizations that existed earlier than a global deluge, an avalanche of protest ensued. Retrieved files are now stored in vaults, museums and secret locations for security purposes, I assume. Even though researchers were led to believe that no such records survived, it should have been obvious that their fragments are not the only ones in existence. Millions will know by the end of this book that other fragments survived and that more evidence is readily available. From that evidence, "The Missing Insight" alluded to for centuries is now found and documented in "The Golden Fleece Found!" However, for restitution and repairs to be made, this light must be accessible. Why should anyone remain under bondage to these categories of "Pharaohs:" religious confusion, racial confusion, financial confusion, historical confusion, spiritual confusion, and mental and physical confusion?

The schematic has a primordial code—a code of interrelated principles if you may. Ja and

His son completed their clock before the date etched thereon. By the time the date was placed on the first clock, their work was finished. Isaiah 42:5, "Thus saith God the Lord, he that created the heavens and stretched them out; he that spread forth the earth, and that which cometh out of it; he that giveth breath unto the people upon it, and spirit to them that walk therein." Job 26:7, "He stretcheth out the north over the empty place and hangeth the earth in space." Isaiah 46:9-10, "I am God, and there is none like me, declaring the end from the beginning, and from ancient times the things that are not yet done." More scriptures—Daniel 2:20-22—"Blessed be the name of God forever and ever for wisdom and might are his and He changeth the times and the seasons…He giveth wisdom to the wise, and knowledge to them that know understanding. He revealeth the deep and secret things. He knoweth what is in the darkness, and the light dwelleth with Him." Let us refer to specific words of Jeshua as told by a chief witness John. John 17:5, "O Father Glorify thou me with thine own self with the glory I had with thee *before the world was.*"

For an explanation of the aforementioned statement please refer to the chapter Mystery of Mysteries. In our mythical factory, they twisted springs as hard as they could and designed prototypes to estimate the many things that could go wrong. They not only acquired spare parts but also built schematics with subtle notations. Follow instructions and the clock will give eons of wonderful service. Obey and benefit, disobey and pay!

The hand that commutes time in seconds beholds the glory of most clocks—next, the minute hand, and then the hour hand. In the heavens the stars rotate in groups called constellations. It takes roughly 26,000 years to make a complete rotation/stellar day. A "day" in the life of a constellation is 26,000 of our modern years approximately. Since the stages of darkness to light are threefold. It takes a threefold process of revelation "yowme" from darkness to light. In Egypt, it took three deliverance days before the spiritual bondage broke. It would make more sense to use "epoch" or "age" for days of yore. The six (days) or epochs that Moses referenced in Genesis 1, were they 24-hour days, stellar days or epochs?

THE WAYS FOR GOD'S DECREED REVELATIONS OR BIRTH SPASMS ARE THREEFOLD: CONCEALMENT OR BONDAGE, WILDERNESS OR TRANSITION AND MANIFESTATION OR PROMISES.

Stored in hieroglyphic, (clefts of rock in Egypt) is at least 52,000 years (or two stellar days) of prehistory. Genesis 1:14, "Let there be lights in the firmament of the heaven to divide the day from the night; and let them (lights) be for signs and for seasons, and for days and for years," not just days. Those epochs were recorded by co-relating the movements of the belt stars of Orion with calculable inundations of the Nile. The structures in The Valley of the Kings are more than stone monuments. They are non-perishable Stone Age storerooms of wisdom. The alignment of the Temples of Uxmal with those of Luxor and Gizeh with the esoteric centers of Tibet and Llasha are not accidental. Before the ancient land (of which a few Caribbean islands are residual masses) sunk, the inhabitants built their sacred sites according to precise formulae. Remember and forget not that in the beginning there were no islands.

Stored in three bank vaults are artifacts and findings from those former civilizations to be included in future publications. All their holy places were strategically aligned so that "initiates" could celebrate and pay homage while facing the same focal point simultaneously. In fact the side work for the pyramids of Uxmal and others in Central America revealed errors in early Greek computations as they initially omitted the base value zero. In 141C.E. Ptolemy issued his erroneous thesis on the position of the earth as it relates to the other orbital masses.

Imperial Rome accepted his views; they were not to be challenged. So those views were accepted as infallible for 1400 years.

There are seven major orbs that participate in a dance of dominance around the earth. The sun and moon play the roles of second and hour hand or hour and day hands, as you prefer to reference. The sun group's cycle around us takes about one week. The seven orbs complete their dance or rotational day in one of what we call (since Roman times) modern weeks.

The moon has its own cycle, which influences the fluctuating tides of lakes, seas and oceans. Her cycles last between 28 to 31 days—roughly one month. Mankind did not always use such complex time scales. Seconds and minutes are phenomena of modern timepieces. During the time that Jeshua lived in Israel, there was no such thing as an hour. The days were divided into eight "Watch" periods of three hours' duration from sunrise to sunset as follows:

Night Watches

First watch = Sunset to 9.00 P.M.

Second watch = 9.00 P.M to midnight.

Third watch = Midnight to 3.00 A.M.

Fourth watch = 3.00 A.M to Sunrise.

Day Watches

First Watch = Sunrise to 9.00 A.M

Second Watch = 9.00 A.M to Noon.

Third Watch = Noon to 3.00 P.M.

Fourth Watch = 3.00 P.M till Sunset.

CHAPTER 4F. FUTURE

When the "Universal Clock" was completed, all components were put in place and stored in the domain of the unrevealed called "Future." Picture a window on a computer monitor. From the beginning to our "now," is relegated to a reference point called "Past." Now to the end of time is in a window called "Future." Ecclesiastes 3:15 "That which hath been is now; that which is to be hath already been and God requireth that which is past." There is no fixed reference called present. It is an ever-changing variable. It is a reference point relevant to a specific place. Everyone reading this book tells him/herself that he/she is in the present although realistically they are not reading this page at the same time. That is why it had been so difficult to find out which came first, the chicken or the egg. If all dimensions of time were placed on a progressive line, eventually the line would curve back to the conceptual point. At point A, both the chicken and the egg coexisted. However, forward or backward from the starting point, either the chicken or the egg existed separately. Every time an event from the future comes to past, it creates a transitory or "present phase" to capture the events of that specific reference point. Daniel was suspended above the bridge of time: Daniel 7:13-14.

Let us look at the construction of the clock first. Picture a slinky with three springs you can compress for children to play with. Compress them; they merge into one. Release them. They twang into different directions. I will repeat this for emphasis. Let us call one spring the future, one the past, one the present. With your imagination compress all three into one so that they fit into each other like the universe in the beginning. Since then, whenever the future races to the past, at whichever point the two references intersect, we call that present. The Sun, Moon, Mars, Mercury, Venus, Jupiter and Saturn are main icons in this clock.

No perfectly repetitious rotations can be considered accidental. To be calculable, our constellations must have boundaries, known or unknown—whether we can see them or not. We cannot see the horizon; we feel we know where it is. Each orb has a dominant regulatory function that triggers a new epoch. On any day of the week the above named orbs perform a dance of dominance—a follow-the-leader dance. By their pre-programmed rotations, a particular orb is dominant on each separate day. On Sunday, the sun is the dominant orb. Monday it is the moon; Thursday (Thor's day} reveals the dominance of Jupiter. Friday is Freyer's day or Venus' day and Saturn leads Saturdays. Since neither 360 nor 365 can be evenly divided into whole numbers by 7, it is impossible on the Roman calendar to have a specific date fall on the same day every year. The Roman calendar synchronizes with the Hebrew calendar only once every fifty years. Bearing that in mind, it would appear to be an exercise of immense frivolity to commemorate any particular event of Hebrew antiquity on a particular day on a modern Roman calendar. As is recorded in Esther 1:13, "Wise men knew the times." For instance, the feasts of—Passover, Unleavened Bread and Pentecost were (and still are) Hebrew feasts celebrated on the 14th 15th and 16th of the First Month "Abib" of the Hebrew Calendar. To assume that because the 16th of Abib fell on a Sunday in April over 2000 years ago it would fall on a Sunday every year after that is shifting the emphasis from the event, to the day and entirely miss the significance in the future. Some symbolically commemorate Jesus' Resurrection on Easter Sunday. So they commemorate Advent on the preceding Friday by counting backwards. Should there be any surprise that they cannot arrive at the "three days" Jesus laid in the tomb if they attempt to marry Advent to a Friday (Good Friday) every year?

Every possible day from the first of the sequences to the last of the sequences was stored in the window called future. There is no factory in outer space making days; it races from the future into the past and new days are released into each present situation. The path to God is a progressive 360-degree path. Nothing is wrong with commemorating specific days for Shabbats, or making mangers or even sanctifying specific dates, as long as the focus progresses from a past creation to a future manifestation. Hence the Hebrew feasts were for times and seasons—Weeks, Jubilee, Passover, Pentecost, and Firstfruits—until their future manifestation through the Ancient of Days.

The constellations decreed the time first—Psalm 19. The heavens declared the glory or message of the Creator. Put another way, there is a schematic in the heavens. Ancient wise men were trained to receive wisdom from the heavenly schematic. Just like Mo and his son who envisioned every nick and bump in the primordial model, Ja and His Son, not only envisioned, but they—unlike later computer builders—computed all blunders and enclosed mechanisms for fixing them. The main wrecker Satan, functions like a computer virus that uses evil beings, spirits and minds. Similarly there are spiritual viruses sent by evil minds. Each person needs that "spiritual antivirus" package that the maker has sent to protect His most holy treasures.

Until the arrival of humankind, every aspect of the clock was running at obedient speed. Having already decided on giving humankind his free will, all tests showed the inclination towards disobedience and rebellion was such that humankind had to be assigned the last epoch. Hence our advent on earth is not at the beginning as some would like to assume but towards the end or fifth epoch. Archaeological etchings of the *"Solar Mythos"* refer to our times as the *Age of the Fifth Sun.*

Ancient clocks were built with keyholes. The makers designed special keys to wind the gizmos. Man is made with spiritual keyholes called altars. Ancient Greece, with its limited spiritual knowledge, stated (and many have followed the fallacy) that man is composed of body, mind and soul. Correction, man (and woman) is made with soul, body and spirit. Souls, inner beings or personalities are all synonyms. The passage is through the mind; the core is the heart. The body is a vehicle for carrying spirit or spirits (whether good or bad). The composition of the group determines your personality/personalities. So a person with a wicked personality has what type of spirit? Thank you for your correct response.

We are tri-dimensional beings. A car has a body, engine components and inner space. Here is a question for all intelligent beings. When selecting a car, especially a used one picked for longevity, what is most important dynamic we look for? Then why do we not examine a person's ability to handle the bumpy road of life before we covenant with them? If a person is impatient, irritable or moody in a restaurant because the meal is a few minutes late and flies in a fit of rage for that, I care not how attractive the person looks; can that time bomb cement a healthy relationship? If you own a pet parrot and build a cage outside for it—if you spread corn, apples and sunflower seeds in it—instantly birds of the air will invade the cage and steal your pet's food. Any altar (worth stealing) not protected or guarded is vigorously pursued until it is invaded. That is the world's number one truism in a nutshell. Naturally I have to include a chapter on how to reclaim altars. Most computer operating systems keep tracking harmful invaders and keep issuing countermeasures. I will show the corrective plans that Ja and Son have included over time and the ingenious programme they have used to trap the wrecker. Remember an altar in this book's context is a place where spirits communicate or travel to or through. Altars are powerful spiritual magnets. Therefore, altars attract and magnetize the highest and most potent spiritual forces.

Agape is God-approved attraction on an altar of obedience. Whereas Lust is a carnally magnetized attraction; conversely hate is the fusion of negative energies. Both "Lust and Hate" enlarge themselves over altars of disobedience. *Lust is one of the world's oldest spirits.* In Genesis 6:2 and 3, Spirits of lust *followed* pre-terrestrial beings from their heavenly abode to *magnetize and invade* the altars of *"the daughters of men."* The primary reason that prostitutes, their "johns" and "cross-sexuals" look so drained—is not at all obvious. The personalities that have changed them have been on earth for a long time. Their overworked "sin-meters" reflect their spiritual histories. Many have been in beings of different genders previously; hence "cross-sexual" beings display contrary "traits."

CHAPTER 5. IDENTIFYING AND RECLAIMING ALTARS

5A. STOLEN TREASURES

Archaeologists call the earliest period of yesteryear "The Stellar Mythos." The ancient astronomers of that epoch measured distances and computed the times by observing the movements of the cosmos or constellations. During that first epoch or age, the attention grabber sent spiritual viruses through the doorway of Astronomy. Those ancient intangible altars became corrupted and transformed over time into an esoteric science called Astrology. To the created instead of the Creator was homage paid.

The same pattern continued with the second epoch "The Lunar mythos." The Moon was the focal reference for time, and ceremonies. The corrupted ceremonies left wide open doors to unguarded altars called—obeah, voodoo, occultism, and witchcraft. Those have hatched eggs over time; today they are referred to as palm reading and psychic networks.

During the third epoch (the Solar Mythos), the "Fellers" influenced the "Wise and Learned" so that homage shifted from the spiritual "Light of the Universe" to the carnal light-substitute, the sun. Things created were sought after with vigour, and those altars were constantly invaded. Even the priesthood that was assigned to guard those altars was corrupted and usurped, compounding and compromising many situations (hence the cloaks of secrecy that became the hallmarks of the esoteric). Whenever I am referring to the priesthood enshrined to Abraham and his seed, I will call it by either name—Aaronic or Levitical (father or son)—priesthood. Whenever I use the New Covenant reference I will call it by its proper name "Melchizedek Priesthood." We are approaching the end of the fifth epoch. In the end times, seed of Levi and Judah will be "Lost" custodians of usurped altars.

Today we have other doctrines of demons called New Age (new light) supposedly trying to fill the voids created by spiritual bastardy. Any light that cannot be manifest (that has to be hid) cannot be the true light. Crystal power, Tarot, and Ouija are names of what manifested through those altars. At this juncture I need to reference some factual data. Each orb has unique characteristics and laws relevant to its domain. Everyone born on earth and every earthly thing are subject to the laws of gravity. However if an earthling leaves earth and crosses another threshold, his/her capabilities are magnified. The Messiah's covenant allows us to surpass boundaries and to step beyond hemispheres by faith. Hence, there are spiritual parallels between Neil Armstrong's famous leap and Zaccaeus' climb. Whenever we traverse planetary dimensions (physically or spiritually), we are outside the laws of our natural realm and become magnified beyond the norm. Those were the principles to which the ambitious brethren at Babel aspired—to build a structure beyond the gravitational boundaries and laws of the earth. They were confounded. Unfortunately the legacy of the Fellers did not perish at Babel. Since mere mortals acquire so much power when we visit another dimension, can you imagine what happens when Ja and His Son come into our presence? I have documented cases where formerly physically disabled people began to walk and formerly deaf began to hear. Even during weekly services (some televised) thousands witness the healing power of God. However, with Ja or His Son, it is not the breach in dimensional boundaries that give them such awesome powers. I used the illustration in the previous sentence to educate untrained minds as to the behavior of other external beings (altar usurpers). Whenever they attack persons with spiritual openings (through nightmares) or *while attempting to pray*, they overpower them.

When this book is released, movie makers and comic books and will stop calling spiritual viruses by the names of monsters/space villains, and label them by their correct names—evil spirits, demons, devils, thrones, and principalities—Ephesians 6:12. Vaults will be opened and many so-called secrets will jump out of closets. If more people could understand and perceive the daily happenings in the spiritual domain, humans would not be so careless with their bodies (spiritual vehicles). I have witnessed things (demonic beings) scream and flee in terror at the approach of Jah and His Son. That simply confirmed what has been documented about them—as children would say—"They are awesome."

CHAPTER 5B. THE IMPORTANCE OF CODES

There are no civilizations that have progressed from ancient to current times without the existence of a "Moral Code." The Code is a country's declaration over its highest altar. Do not tell me about a constitution—that is not a moral code. During the reign of the pharaonic dynasties, Ancient Egypt had their "Papyrus of Ani or Book of Going forth by Day." The Shang, Zhou, Qin, Tang, Han, Manchu, Sung, Yuan and Ming dynasties of China established their country on the moral code and principles of Yin and Yang. Examining the back doors of history, our research team found one of the oldest codes "The Code of Hamurabi," which outlined the moral high ground of all the ancient Grand Lodges. It can be described as a very long version of the Ten Commandments. Approximately 300 laws were inscribed. Even though the document is about 4000 years old, it had laws on social issues from restitution for social ills to punishment for moral infractions.

Today, most of us have replaced our moral code of ethics with a constitution. It never worked and it never will work. A constitution does not call its citizens to defend its spiritual altars: just its physical borders and personal rights of its nationals. Only proper moral codes and corporate spiritual strengths (from upright spiritual leaders)) defend national altars from spiritual nuclear attacks. As soon as generations of iniquity create spiritual imbalance to the point where the scales hit bottom, immediately those civilization are taken down. Nineveh, Troy, Sodom, Gomorra, Endor and Pompeii are some examples to note.

At this point I have to vent a little anger at Israel, North Africa and all the Arab nations. Descendants of Abraham, get your act together! I will spell out God's messages to you in one brief paragraph. I am speaking mainly to the Muslim Arabs, the Hebrews, the Africans and Arab Christians. Your countries' solutions are not political. Not only has the Living God given you a code but also the promise and fulfillment—an everlasting covenant. Are you foolish enough to follow the paths of civilizations that have pursued Babel policies, knowing the ultimate outcome? You are behaving like a dysfunctional family. Instead of sitting down to discuss your problems with your just and righteous father, you are allowing untrained strangers to meddle in your family affairs. You are allowing demonic forces to interfere in your destinies—Jeremiah 4:16-17, and Daniel 2:34-45.

God's Old Covenant was sealed with the blood of an unblemished lamb. That covenant, witnessed by an Aaronic priest, *was unto their generations.* It is obvious that something "New" has happened. Since the destruction of the Jerusalem temple in the first century, priests (not of Levi) are being ordained inside and outside Israel. Jews and Gentiles are receiving "gifts of atonement." Did God cease from punishing people for coming into His holy place, or did the prophecies of Isaiah 53, Psalm 22 and 69, and Micah 5:2 come to fruition through a specific seed of Levi and Judah?

The Everlasting Priesthood requires an *Everlasting Covenant* and an *Everlasting Sacrifice.* Since the ancient sacrifices ceased, it meant that the altar from which the Everlasting Priesthood emanated, had to have been pre-foundational and incorruptible. Psalm 110:4, "Thou art a priest forever after the order of Melchizedek." God also promised a theocracy. Blessed is the nation whose God is the Lord. God also promised "The Decree" in Psalm 2:7-12. That Son was preordained to take the broken pieces and to repair them as a potter remoulds his clay. That Son was foretold by Isaiah 53:1-12. Here are more questions:

1.) Who was that generous kinsman redeemer? Who was the innocent man that God promised Isaiah he would send to suffer for Jews, Arabs, Christians, and Gentiles—Moses, Jesus or Mohammed?

2.) Which of the prophets was born to a virgin as per prior prophecy—Moses, Abraham, Jesus or Mohammed? Who is the King referred to in Psalm 2—ruling from Zion, when all the Davidic line ruled from Judah?

3.) Who is that king that God referred to through David as His Son (capitalized)?

4.) Since God promised a spiritual house on earth, whose ministry fulfilled the prophetic blueprint outlined in the physical temple that Solomon built—Jeshua or Mohammed?

5.) Which philosophy is the best for peace among all the seed of Abraham—Jacob/Esau/Isaac/Ishmael? An eye for an eye and a tooth for a tooth, martyrdom and a Jihad, or forgive your enemies; do good to them that hate you? Love the Lord with thy whole heart, mind and strength and thou shall love thy neighbor as thyself?

Satan has concentrated his largest army of demonic forces: Amalek, Sanballat, Philistia and her hosts, around locations where the seed of all of Israel's 12 tribes live. He targets Israel, Pakistan, India, Africa, and the Gulf regions by interfering in politics, blocking spiritual visions and causing spiritual deafness. First of all, you need to go back to your spiritual foundations.

Israel, I am starting with you first. You will not have peace unless you put a stop to the moral filth that is being imported from Russia immediately. Imagine Hebrew women posing in the nude and indulging in all forms of imported pagan immorality especially in Tel Aviv?

Daughters of Abraham, for the sake of the covenant that you have foolishly forgotten, your wars are spiritual. How can you expect your highly moral God to help you if you compromise your spiritual principles? Have you forgotten your history? God asked Elijah whether it was Baal or God that was prospering the crops of your ancestors. I will use my prophetic voice to ask you a similar question: "Is it your perceived wisdom, your good looks, your business, your bank account or the stock market that is prospering you or is it your Covenant Partner God Almighty?"

GULF REGIONS: God has and is prospering you because of His promise to Abraham and because of your promise to make the Lord your God over your nations. Remember that Abraham was an Eberite. This book will reveal how his seed became Africans, Jews, Arabs, Indians, Caribbean people, Pakistanis, Surinamese, Brazilians and Americans. However the seed of Isaac merged both offices of Kings and Priests. That seed had a double purpose—that of establishing both a physical altar on Jerusalem and a spiritual one "Zion" on the confirmation of *The Law* for all the natural and "wild olive" grafts: Indonesians, Arabs, Africans, Chinese, Japanese, Indians, Pakistanis, Greeks, Romans and their Gentiles' seed.

God first promised Israel that theocracy but instead, Israel asked for a king like other nations. They got a Benjamite called Saul and are suffering up to today for that foolishness. Arab nations got the theocracy that God promised. Can a theocracy bring peace? Can a theocracy heal your sick? God wants a personal relationship with all of His children. He wants to invite all inside the Holy of Holies, which Mohammed craved for. You all can go into the Holy of Holies and have that personal relationship with our all wise, All-knowing God. A priest has to make atonement on behalf of self and his repentant flock. Isaiah prophesied that the special intercessor *Immanuel* (God with us) would bring the peace and happiness that you seek.

There needs to be holy convocations with Africans, Arabs and Jews, first with their spiritual leaders, and then with their political leaders. According to the promises of their fathers, they have only two options: a) to choose God's prophetic purposes for His people so that their dwelling places can be the most blessed and greatest civilization on earth from the northernmost to the southernmost tip of the continent of Africa, or b) to continue to reject them. How do we solve the problems? They are all spiritual. The second thing necessary is a twenty-one day fast between all serious Muslims, Jews and Christians (those who are physically and spiritually able). It can be an abstinence fast wholly or partially; it can be water fast, a liquid fast or a prayer fast asking the God of Abraham, Isaac and Jacob who keeps covenant to intervene. The issues are not as complicated as they are made out to be. It is amazing that the entire host of hell knows God's preference for their regions, and so do their (known and unknown) agencies. Picture the spiritual Aliyah after obedience.

CHAPTER 5C. SPIRITUAL PROBLEMS, SPIRITUAL SOLUTIONS ONLY!

The second to last time I went to Jerusalem, I was with a delegation of almost 2000 persons. Numerous had prophetic gifts, and others had their ears and eyes of understanding opened (they could see and hear in the spiritual realm). I am not talking about any mumbo-jumbo; I mean those who can hear the God of Abraham, Isaac, and Jacob. Most of them were Holy Spirit-filled. We went to fulfill promises recorded in Zechariah. 8:22-23, made over two thousand years ago. I was on my way to David's tomb when a vendor stopped me.

"How do you explain that all these people come to pray for peace; we are three different people, all with different beliefs? There will be no peace, he exclaimed!" We were there in August 1998. Without batting an eyelid, I replied: "Many times when true light is about to shine forth, it has to break through some obstacles. Usually, large obstacles cast what appear to be three shadows. When that light moves into its rightful place, Glory be to God, no devil, no demonic force can or will stop it."

I left in deep thought and continued on my journey. After I left David's tomb, I witnessed an occurrence similar in nature to the one that Saul experienced on the road to Damascus. Whenever those occur, fright, awe and humility take full control. "Signs and Wonders follow." In due time that event will either be confirmed, or else I will be ridiculed for equating my experience to that of Saul.

On a different matter—it is a documented fact that spirits connect to humans through blood. The spirits of anger will attract the spirits of antagonism, which usually party with the spirits of violence, which usually cause blood to be spilled so that all can take a drink. God is spirit. He decreed first to Moses and then to Abraham our great Patriarch that He would accept in lieu of His everlasting sacrifice, blood of the most obedient of His creatures. The blood of a lamb without blemish would be accepted as a "Promise of things to come." Abraham was willing to offer his firstborn son. God substituted a lamb (first time). The first sacrifice substitution was made. For a promise to become a will and testament, someone has to die. Whoever the Messiah is, He must die for His sheep to complete *the second passing of the law.* That multi-ethnic person of Psalm 87 must be ethnically all-inclusive, entirely righteous, humble, tolerant, and peaceful.

The irony of this whole thing is that before the arrival of the Roman forces in 1099, Jerusalem was a city in harmony, full of religious tolerance. The three branches traded and lived in harmony. Within the twinkling of an eye, a nation that previously scoffed at the God of Moses, Abraham, Isaac and Jacob, first carried away the sacred things in 70 C.E. Then in 1099, their national altars were strengthened with blood and murder of God's people the second time. Backed by official church silence, those so-called zealots, without repenting of their ancestral and generational curses, installed *Replacement Theology* and *Intolerant Ethnology* on foundations of blood and falsehoods. Even though all such were prophesied by Isaiah, Asaph, David, Moses, Jeremiah, Ezekiel, Daniel and John, only K.C. Price and Reverend Billy Graham are known to have addressed such issues as racial misinformation within churches, on international platforms.

In the year 2000 the head of the Catholic Church went to Jerusalem and repented for *some* sins of his organization. Say what you may about that very courageous act of humility, it had serious positive spiritual consequences. It was during the first Jubilee celebrated in Israel in 2000 years. The organization is usually very secretive about its internal policies. Since a few of our researchers are Catholics, we will list the generational transgressions so that whoever the successor might be to this Pope, the provisions of 2nd Peter 2:20 and Matthew 12:43 might not become applicable. To receive a complete pardon, *all transgressions* must be confessed first before forgiveness can be sought—Proverbs 28:13.

Historical records in Rome and Israel can verify what is recorded in Paul's writings that it was he Paul who was in Rome twice in prison and used that opportunity to bring the Gospel. At the beginning of the Protestant reformation, Martin Luther found 100 erroneous teachings. Since the institution teaches that it is infallible, nothing was ever done about the findings. I will list serious infractions as per our 25 years of research.

Richard Andrews and Paul Schellenger were not the first to pursue the mystery of Rennes-le-Chateau. They investigated the movement of a body from Jerusalem to the south of France. However they unearthed much more details than their predecessors did. Did they succumb to the temptation that many researchers find themselves in? I have known fellow reporters that have coined stories around partial evidence, only to be embarrassed later. Did my literary brothers get sufficiently close and then arrive at their own conclusions? Had they supplied the evidence and then let the audiences decide, perhaps a simple thing like a feminine article might have given them a much deeper meaning. Instead of assuming that somehow God could have died and was buried in France, they might have realized that the people that transshipped the body, referred to Jesus' mother as "Mother of God." When that is translated in Latin, then there is no need to speculate anymore. On the tomb in question are these words in Latin: *MATRI DEUM.* I hate to disappoint you, but the word for mother (in Latin) is "mater." In

Latin, the word for God is "Deus," a masculine noun. The dative case changes the word to "matri." The archaic conjugational use of the "Gerund"—Deum, gives us a literal translation of—here lies "God's-Most-Holy Mother." The defense rests its case.

1. Since women are made to germinate earth-born seed, there are no prior references in the Torah to the effect that Mary (mother of Jesus) would receive a special position in heaven and that she would be "Raptured." She—like Sarah and Rebecca—died, and was buried in Jerusalem.

2. Jerusalem (near the Pool of Shilom) is the original place (original tomb) where Mary the mother of Jesus was buried. There were many letters from the early "Church Fathers" who were concerned that Mary's body might in fact be desecrated, according to a specific sordid ritual held by a European based organization.

3. If those men were correct in their scrutiny, it might be possible that the Templars moved the body for that reason. I will touch on such in a later chapter.

4. John the Harbinger introduced the Good News. His first requirements were *to repent* and *to be baptized*. How can a child that has not learned to talk repent of sins?

5. Paul and Titus were the two that had full authority to bring the Gospel to the Gentiles. Paul proclaimed a curse on any person who had the nerve to present *any other Gospel*. Jeshua echoed the same sentiments: "Not one tittle should be changed or omitted." Deciding which sins are unimportant, which sins are important, and trivializing sins by terming them "venial," is arrogance beyond explanation—Matthew 5:17-20.

6. The doctrine of infallibility is an invented, added, and seriously false doctrine—Galatians 1:8. All, not some, have sinned and come short.

7. From the date of the infamous fire, which burnt Rome in 64 C.E. (July), subsequent live shows at the Roman Coliseum and Jerusalem's fall after the siege (70 C.E.), Simon (Peter) was nowhere near Rome; otherwise he would have been a main course on a lion's menu. Paul had to reserve his anger for Simon Bar Jona about the matter of the circumcision until he encountered Simon at Antioch. The head of the Jerusalem church, James, presided over and resolved the dispute. Refer to Paul's letter to the Galatians (Galatians 2:11-14). James exercised his authority to dispatch "Chief among the brethren—Judas Barsabas and Silas," to notify all churches of the resolutions—Acts 15:22-32. Who then is the Roman Peter, the first Pope? Simon's previously presumptuous position (on the matter of circumcision without first consulting Elder James) created the first spiritual crack in the Jerusalem church's altar. Incidentally, Simon Bar Jona was never called Peter when he was alive.

Since Satan has stolen, solidified and strengthened a large altar under the city of Rome, repentance during "Jubilee" (as per Leviticus 25) is very important. For spiritual eggs to be removed and uprooted, they must be exposed first. John warned of those dangers, and the plight that might befall that institution, if all entrenched errors are not removed permanently—Revelation 18: 5-7. Here is direct evidence that when altars are left unguarded they become invaded and the curse goes unto the offspring of persons, families, or institutions. The anger against God's people began under Nero and progressed through to Titus' siege and carnage in Jerusalem in 70 C.E., up to this day. Constantine, Charlemagne, Justinian, later Emperors, annexed the faith and rebuilt it on Rome's bloody foundations. They later established dual headquarters in Byzantium and Rome. With each move, the most evil spirit in the demonic realm, Leviathan, moved in a snakelike manner all over Europe, strengthened by the blood of thousands of Christians' martyrs and Jews. In her wake followed the Grail Seekers with their esoteric maps. Some were searching for Atlantis. Others were searching for the "Philosopher's Stone." Some searched for and found "Lost Tribes." Also, Jews were offered as human sacrifices by occultists (who killed them ritually during days of High Energy) as Adolph and many others did. They allowed Satan to use their human altars for such purposes. There are cities in Europe where the spiritual eggs of that serpent-like spirit are hatching at unprecedented proportions, feeding on the blood of aborted babies—her speciality (Caviar in the spiritual abode) waiting for their appointed times. In Isaiah 13:9-12 those events were first prophesied. Daniel foresaw the countries from which the events would occur. There will be many reading this who have benefited from the riches of unrighteous mammon. Millions of people on both sides of the Atlantic worked without pay for over 400 years, as prophetically noted in Genesis 15:13. Think of the Inca gold adorning church steeples and resting in the vaults of empires. That is why Prophet Joel, writing shortly after Jehovah's great victory at the hands of Jehoshaphat, (Joel 2:24 and 25) previewed how it would be done. Jehoshaphat was anointed King in 936 B.C.E.

Persons/places/institutions that allowed their altars to be invaded, have unregulated highways to and from the spiritual divide. Satan's 24-hour satellites influence their directions and destinations. Those pirates must be overcome by spiritual violence after repentance or face the horrors seen by John at Patmos. Revelation 9:20-21, also Revelation 18:4-6 are scriptures' references. Some churches are finding that their memberships are falling drastically; people are falling asleep mentally, physically and spiritually. Look at your foundation doors, check your gates and examine the gatekeepers! Since most breast cancers can be detected and risks reduced by thorough and repeated self-examinations, we need frequent self scrutiny also. We have been forewarned about extensive proliferation of spiritual viruses in Romans 3:23, "For all have sinned, and come short of the Glory of God."

CHAPTER 5D. THE LESS IS BLESSED OF THE GREATER

The ant is not the smallest creature; by far it is not the largest. Oomph for oomph it is one of the strongest creatures around. The sun is not the largest orb in the universe but, in my humble opinion, its role can be counted among the most significant. The 1st law of all the High Centres of learning is transposed into a Primordial Code that my research team finally decoded: *AS ABOVE, SO BELOW!*

There is a symbiotic relationship between the things above and the things below. If I only touch this beyond reference, this book will never end. If you examine the major orbs that feature in our solar system, they resemble either an earth that has been spent, or an earth yet to be formed. In other words, in the planetary symphony, if a catastrophe (man-made or natural) were to blow up this earth, another orb would probably lock into earth's former position, and trapped gases might begin to unleash until they arrive at a place where our genus (Homo Sapiens) could live. Scientists are welcome to test my theory. The fragmented particles might behave like items put in a recycle file on your computer. Our wise Creator has selected Earth. Let us not go over our sequence of deductions where we arrived at a chief architect and settled for God Almighty. As other chapters unfold you will see that to have been sound analysis. Homo-Sapiens Sapiens did not inhabit earth in the beginning.

The Pentateuch, one of the most precious documents left on earth, its contents translated into *The Five Books of Moses*, confirms this. The number of times the entire clock will spin before the alarm rings is coded in Moses' 1st book. Mathematicians, you can figure out how many generations of years existed in the beginning of the heavens and the earth. Genesis 1: 1-25 records celestial time as generations. Figure out how many years elapsed since Moses wrote, subtract it from total time allotted, (first compute Moses time into present time) and there you go. For all you folks who have been adding celestial time sequentially into present time, notice even Moses put the words "Generations" in Genesis 2:4, "These are *the generations* of the heavens and the earth." Before I move on, let me highlight another common error I have noticed. I have encountered persons who simply add the years of the male siblings of Adam's family up to the time of Noah and assume that there were only male siblings in those genera-tions. So to all that used such formulae, your computations are erroneous! Please remember that ancient Israel was a patriarchal society and as such only males and their seed were docu-mented. Refer to Genesis 1:27, "Male and *female* created he them." That is also the reason that so many people could not discern from whence Cain got his wife. She was of the seed (male and female) from verse 27. It was not unusual to marry within a family clan: refer to the paral-lels with Isaac and his wife. Deciphering Genesis 2:4, we get—"These are the generations of the heavens and of the earth, when they were created 'in the day' that the Lord God made the earth and the heavens."

Isn't the hour cycle preceded by the minute cycle, and the week cycle preceded by the day cycle? It would be logical to deduce that at least a season of stellar years was completed before the solar epoch could have been ushered in. Since Israel is fitted into God's prophetic time-piece, we need to mirror her events daily for alarm chimes.

The ancient Israelites, though among the smallest of nations at the time of their rise and fall, were like ants to the giant nations in those times. There are certain things about their nation that have tri-dimensional meanings. Their struggles equate to historical struggles, re-ligious struggles, and personal/spiritual struggles. To put it bluntly, if you duplicate Israel's victories, whether you refer to a church, human being, family or country, you will achieve the same victories. If you repeat their errors, without a doubt, whether you are an icon, imaginary super star, church, country, religious or political leader, sooner or later, you will be punished.

It is difficult to create a spiritual scenario that has not happened to ancient Israel. They have, and are visited by the fiercest demonic forces (Isaiah 14:8-9). They have fought them, overcome them and at times been temporarily defeated by them. Sometimes they remember their winning combinations; many times they forget their teacher. For this statement I will not put my opinion. I will release one of the greatest secrets of this age. The victory belongs to (him/her or institution) whoever perfects the (spiritual) fighting techniques of David.

Israel is the second hand of our clock. It ticks; the minute hand (the temple/church altars tack) then the hour hand or all nations tock. Israel is not accidentally in the news daily. Ar-chaeologists (for the most part) agree that a whole generational sequence, (cycle) of celestial time was unleashed before Homo-Sapiens Sapiens was introduced on the earth. In any system where perpetual motion is required, an entity is usually inserted to trigger the counter-force. That is explained partially in the principles of Yin and Yang. Hence the truism: For each action there is an equal and opposite reaction. No engine goes rrrrrrr all the time; it has to have its interruption or rest-cycles. Our societies teach us to go all the time; no wonder our civilizations burn out so quickly. We need to be taught the important principle of fasting. Here are other reasons why more wisdom can be gained by studying the underside of the pendulum:

1. It is not as crowded. We have to be pure in soul, mind and spirit. Hopefully, the experiences that we gain will allow us to overcome temptations.

2. So much more wisdom can be obtained from *The Creator* or His victorious warrior, David's spiritual successor. Refer to the prophetic references in Psalm 110:1-6. First the special king would rule the heathen. He would also be a priest *forever* and *rule from Zion*. That successor according to prophecy would *overcome death* and sit at God's right hand.

CHAPTER 5E. INSIGHT INTO THE MIND!

No forensic scientist or doctor has ever found a mind in a person. The mind is a "spiritual highway." We do not have to open each package of unsolicited mental information. It is our doorway to all choices or our free will—a gift from our Creator. Smoke enough cigarettes, within time your insides will look and behave like chimneys. Harbour enough misfits around your house because you like the way they dress and talk; sooner or later you get hurt. There is a wise saying: "A person is known by the company he/she keeps"—so in the natural, more so in the spiritual.

In the mind is stored—our free will, memory, intellect, emotion, and passageway to our souls. The computer design was not given to man to be used as a satanic altar, but to show how the vehicle functions. The C.P.U or the microprocessor is the inner being of the computer. Other computers—human/spiritual beings and pre-arranged programmes (thoughts/vibes)—can access it. Our minds are steps to our individual altars; so are our eyes and mouths. Saul of Tarsus, one of the most eminent Rabbinical scholars, expounded in a letter to Jews, who were in Rome, that individuals are constantly exposed to a war between the forces of the carnal world and those of the spiritual world. The battle is waged primarily on the spiritual battlefield of the mind. When we sleep, we rest all of our carnal capabilities and the spiritual highway is open to traffic from both domains. Read Proverbs 3:24. Our spiritual state before we surrendered to sleep determines our journeys. Unresolved conflicts continue. If we are attacked, choked, or frightened during sleep, those are indications that our spiritual temples are not up to par. There is an evil spirit called a night terror—Psalm 91:5. Persons who use hallucinogens intending to receive "induced highs" actually venture into highways, the way drunk drivers do, and fall (many times) very low indeed. While that drunk driver thinks he or she is cool, every other driver, including law enforcement officers, can spot his/her erratic behaviour. In the spiritual, your condition determines your journey. If your life is cluttered with spiritual debris—and most often it will be—(since mostly the spiritually untrained and disobedient venture into that induced-high domain) you are immediately affronted. Evil spirits love company and most likely they will invite you back to stay longer and longer until they exchange places with your rightful spirits.

Touching accursed things and ingesting them as substitutes for God's real things, invoke the wrath of God. There are many conduits, ways and passages to spiritual "High Ways." The ones from the satanic divide open very strange spiritual doors. There are actually drug-invoked genies. I hate to burst some bubbles here but in the Orient, cocaine had been used on certain ancient altars in the past. I know people have been surprised and scared out of their wits when demonic "forces" affronted them. Here is the best advice money can buy. No counterfeit can match or come near any original thing. The same way the body craves for goodies, the spirit craves for spiritual foods. The author of this book has sampled every possible type of spiritual junk-food available. I will share a wonderful secret with you. This book offers to each reader the ability to take the best spiritual laxative available "repentance for spiritual cleansing." When you find the only spiritual manna, the bread from the tree of life, which has a special already built-in spiritual wine, there is no drunk or high even close in comparison.

5F. CORRECTIONAL INSTITUTES/ LARGE DESERTS!

I counseled ex-drug addicts. When a person is under the prophetic anointing, especially while fasting, it is possible to receive insights into the spiritual world and to get answers to things unknown. We were interceding for a nation that was having political upheavals. That occasioned a "Jericho March." We marched by a prison compound where the majority of inmates had decided to seek forgiveness (for their sins) weeks earlier and to be "Born again." Suddenly, squeals and grunts (like those of pigs growling) pierced the morning silence. The Spirit of the Lord revealed that "hog-like" spirits were feasting in a gutter leading from the compound. Later on the same day, as I entered the compound, I inquired as to which room was located in the vicinity of the waste pipe. I was told that it was the prisoners' bathroom. I was scheduled to teach that day. However, before the commencement of the teaching programme, I asked all those that were masturbating the night before to repent and to come for prayers. Someone asked "How is it that every time you come in here you can tell us what happened the night before." I explained how the "Gift of Discernment" works. They confessed that a new prison officer was watching a porno channel and that he left it on all night, to give the inmates a treat.

Here were prisoners trying desperately to walk the straight path. They requested and received permission to have a 24-hour Christian programme installed in the main hall, which incidentally faces all the cells. Out of the blue, a new officer arrived and did what no person ever did: he changed the Christian station. Was it a mere co-incidence? I believe not. Pastors beware! Prisons are spiritually dry places. Satan does not surrender turf easily. Deserts are where Philistines' spirits are strongest, unless you have received the Davidic anointing. Deserts are strongholds for spiritual serpents.

I am saddened when I hear seed of Judah glorifying correctional institutes in their music. When a person is presented before a judge and he/she is sentenced, in actuality, the society had just placed a curse on that person. Jails are strongholds for entrenched spirits of jealousy, hate, lesbianism, masturbation, homosexuality and murder. They are there by the troop loads. God's surgical decree in Genesis 2:18 is final. Lesbianism and Homosexuality are ancient and brazen spirits that challenge the foundations that God laid in Genesis 1:27, Genesis 2:18, and Genesis 2:21-23. They defy and defile. In Leviticus 20:13 and Romans 1:26, the owner's manual and schematic decreed punishments for those sins.

In the archives of the most spiritually attacked country on earth, Israel, the writings of the prophet Samuel give an insight into the personality or the inner being of the person we call King David. In one of the most widely read books, the King James Bible, the exploits that I am referring to are chronicled in 1st Samuel 17:34-51. That was not an imaginary battle that took place between David and Goliath. David took on the best desert warrior and decapitated him. David was a man who realized that most distressful persons have demon spirits in or working through them. It is said, "A man is known by the company he keeps." Samuel gave us an insight into David's true character by describing the men that David used to hang out with in 2nd Samuel 23:8-39.

I searched innumerable libraries. Several adored works of philosophy I found borrowed. Countless were recycled expressions, *thought processes* of people who lived in civilizations that succumbed to the curses of Babel. Those that flirted with alternate ways to achieve higher spiritual understanding, never ventured beyond cosmetic spirituality. There were others that gave detailed analyses of negative spirituality. The plights of those adepts were always bizarre and unhappy. Conversely, Moses' first books offered great fruits of wisdom, ranging from "peeks at the pre-Edenic world" to mathematical computations. They also previewed in code, the history of every nation and of every religious institution (in the Book of Judges). They gave us the blueprint for every generational blessing and curse (Deuteronomy 27-28).

In a nutshell, Moses' books highlight the covenant faithfulness of God, verses the failures of His covenant partner's seed. Remember that God gave to man, dominion over the earth and that God is a God of order. He is a covenant keeper. Pay close attention to God's system of doing things. First He establishes a thing with His patriarchs and then confirms it with a specific generational numbered seed. A promise was made first to the Patriarch Abraham. Since man had been causing all provided altars to be corrupted, *God chose multiples of seven generations of righteous seed for His redemptive purposes.* In the chapter previewing the antichrist, I will chronicle Satan's plan, patiently executed by extraterrestrial forces over generations.

CHAPTER 6. THOSE THAT SOUGHT, AND FAILED TO FIND THE FLEECE!

The human body is a geocentric (earth-positioned) vehicle. It carries disobedient or obedient seed. It can transform a carnal person into a refined spirit being. Unlike most vehicles, if the owner maintains prolonged obedience and if prior generations of kindred were obedient also, it *will* provide trouble-free operations and exceed the manufacturer's warranty—Exodus 34:6-7. The *mind* is the gearbox for both the body and the *soul*. Soul or compartment for intellect/will/emotion and spirit or spirits, is the least understood of the three main components. The decisions of the mind trigger actions that influence the soul. Cumulative actions over time shape the primary altar-component—personality or spirit. Unfortunately we pay most attention to the least important of the three—the *casing/shell/body*.

Trials and trails by occupants of past civilizations met spiritual dead-ends. Wise people that lived and studied the "Times" have found treatises from "The Ancients," documenting man's search for the "One Way" through Hades, one way through the cycle of life and death, and one true way through the labyrinth of the spiritual cosmos. Since the futile pursuit of that path had left many "Babels," a decision was taken by the "Intelligencia" of yesteryear to relegate all such exploits, manuscripts and discussions, to a world called *"The Esoteric."* Very shortly I will recap their collective exploits for: a) those who would like to know... b) those that have some knowledge, and c) those that do not care one way or another.

CHAPTER 6A. MANY DEAD-ENDS

THE ORIENT. The first masters of the Orient knew that the season was not yet due for the "Passage or Way" of the transmigration of souls to be brought to light. They preserved in code the formula for computing that season. The one predestined to be the *First Fruit* was depicted in the unfolding of the stellar map called Astronomy. That one would leave the great beyond and come among us to show us "The Way, Truth and The Wisdom." In the meantime their people were taught (physical and mental) principles of preservation for their vehicles until that time when they would receive the truth. They preserved those predictive messages in the symbols of their earliest alphabet. In fact, hidden within the characters was a message about a nation yet to be formed, "Chosen" to covenant with God. The *Promised Master* would be born through the seed of a distant people (the Jews). That great event would occur when a constellation called Aries would emerge from the womb of Virgo. At that appointed time, Serpens (another constellation) would drift towards Aries on a collision course as if to engulf it. *Their Luminaries* calculated the season by using the aforementioned astronomical computations. *Confucius* is dead. None of their seers achieved the rite of passage for five reasons: a) They did not know. b) They were not chosen to know. c) The appointed time had not yet arrived. d) They were not of the seed of Isaac, so they were not selected to "roll away the stone" and e) The Kinsman Redeemer must be of the seed of Naomi and Boaz.

Africa (like Sarah) bore special seed; she had a long barren period before her appointed time.

India, Pakistan, and the Kashmir Mountain regions.

There are more seed of "Lost Tribes" of Israel living in those regions than in any other location. Esther 1:1 gives a preview. Until the seed of Abraham reconnect with the Prince of Peace, they will know no peace. *Buddha* is dead. However if one examines the teachings of Buddha it would be discovered that Buddha had advised his followers: a) To abstain from sinful living b) that the Messiah was yet to come and c) that He would lead the *world* to all truth. Those who obeyed His word would be saved (from the cycles of life and death). Books by former Buddhist monks that have found the Messiah, Jeshua, expound on and confirm this. Thongsouay Sakdarak is one of many.

EGYPT. Pre and Post-Dynastic Egypt experimented with and failed to comprehend the *"Mystery of Transmigration of Souls"* through a carnal approach and literal application to esoteric principles. Residual references are in the "Papyrus of Ani." Those spiritual legacies are preserved as museums display their dead mummies and statues—Isaiah 45:14-17.

Persia (Iraq/Iran). Fragments of the ancient Babylonian Empire and seed of Joseph, Isaac and Esau (Edom) dwell in a physical and spiritual desert metropolis. *Zoroaster*, a Persian seer prophesied that "The Chosen One" would be born of a virgin. Zoroaster is dead. In addition to that, we have found no prognostications about an unusual birth of Hussain Ali Bahauallah—a Persian, born in 1817. He performed no miracles. In 1863 he founded the Bahai faith. He died in 1892. Hagar the mother of Esau was the spiritual womb of most desert-born religions. She received one source "Refreshing" and was told to return to Sarah. Accordingly, all religions born in desert regions, which have one source prophet only and are stagnant, must return to the Sarah religion to be nourished again. Otherwise, their prophetic plight is either that of Isaiah 60:6 and 7, or that of Jeremiah 50 and 51. Also, whereas the wives of the chosen patriarchs prophetically reflect the religions of their seed, similarly, the relationship between them and their spouses would generally mirror the spiritual relationships between their seed and God. According to this ancient schematic, adherents of desert religions would yearn for a personal relationship with their father. A seed of Isaac would be comfortable with the memory of the Old Temple. The commemoration of their feasts on holy days would be more important to them than the closeness to their father. Some seed of Mary should receive continual mentoring from the Father and mature with signs and wonders.

GREECE attempted to find the path through *mind* and *body* only. Since they understood *neither* the dimensions of the mental thoroughfare nor the fact that other passengers had access to its use, the Greeks and their seed left a lot of unguarded altars—"incongruent, everchanging and oft-conflicting" Philosophies.

THE AMERICAS: South, Central and North—their earliest occupants applied literal translations to the "Priestly Sacrifices." First and foremost, only a select minority was permitted inside the "Veiled Sanctuaries of Higher Wisdom." Like China, Africa, Haiti, and India, they left millions of unguarded altars/ passageways to and from the spiritual world.

CUMULATIVE ASSESSMENT:

I watched a show once, whereby clues were given to a puzzle. A grand prize was promised to the first person that got the correct answers. During the show there were many anxious and eager participants; unfortunately their acumen did not match their zeal. So the kind- hearted host kept assisting the willing-hearted participants. As I studied the civilizations that survived "The Times," many seemed to have been rewarded, at least for their "pursuits" of the "Way," confirming somewhat the words "Those that hunger and thirst for righteousness shall be filled." Cumulative evidence now suggests that coded alphabets and cosmological ceremonies of civilizations classified as "Ancient and Esoteric," bear witness to an eschatological pursuit of "The Resurrection of the dead." At least their seed reaped and are reaping fruits for their persistence.

CHAPTER 6B. BEHOLD THE FLEECE!

Between 780 B.C. E and 750 B.C.E. God called Prophet Isaiah to be a "Spiritual Watchman" during the reigns of four of Judah's kings: Uzziah, Jotham, Ahaz, and Hezekiah. In 1947 the Dead Sea Scrolls were found. One scroll contained a pre-Masoretic (well-preserved 2000-year) text in Hebrew by the same Prophet Isaiah. Hebrew scholars attest to its accuracy. In addition to those manuscripts, preserved writings in Assyria confirm the veracity of Isaiah's predictions especially with regards to the fall of the Babylonian Empire. Scrutiny of the prophecies of Isaiah revealed not only the foretelling of the Messiah to come, but His mission, how He would die, and the importance of His death as a sacrifice for the sins of all.

God Almighty is Spirit. Spirits gain access to persons through body fluids. Hence we may discern the symbiotic relationships between blood, body fluids and occult related activities in one spiritual mirror, and those of our Holy God and unblemished blood in the other. Only unblemished blood was, and is permitted on God's altars. Body fluids spilled deliberately and in disobedience to any of God's laws are transgressions against "His Highest Altar." Punishment immediate or delayed is predestined. The ram caught in the thicket was given as a sacrifice for Abraham's son. The first spiritually acceptable substitution was made: "Firstborn Son" for "Unblemished Lamb." Isaac carried the wood for that sacrifice to Mt. Moriah.

According to God's Law of Double-Reference, that substitution had to be done better. David chronicled a contract, a promise by *The Creator* who can do anything but fail, fib or forget. It is known simply as Psalm 23. The scripture reference comparing the Messiah to a sheep to be led to slaughter is Isaiah 53. God demands the best. God never violates His laws. The bigger the sacrifice, the greater the reward. Sow the best? The Creator promised to send a perfect shepherd to those obedient like sheep. The most obedient animals on earth are sheep. Examine the lives of everyone who ever lived on earth. Who can be considered a perfect example of obedience? Conduct your own surveys! Who was willing to lay down his life for all of his followers: Jews, Arabs, Christians and Gentiles? The Creator ordained a lamb without blemish to be His "Special Sacrifice." One righteous seed-multiple of seven generations of Isaac, must take a better sacrifice to Mt. Moriah—Psalm 2.

A student of Gamaliel wrote a letter of instruction from his prison in Rome addressed to all the Jews that were seeking spiritual illumination in 61 C.E. Gamaliel was an eminent doctor of rabbinical law. The grandson of Hillel, he was reputed to be the first of only seven rabbis to be that highly educated. The former student, Saul of Tarsus an erudite Pharisee himself, received a miraculous conversion and was transformed from a murdering zealot to one of the greatest expounders of the Hebrew Laws. In his letter to the Hebrew brethren (or Hebrews 8 in the New Testament*) he expertly explained the better sacrifice for the promised spiritually joined offices of King and Priest. Jeremiah detailed the promise of a New Covenant with both houses of Levi and Judah—Jeremiah 31:31-32. In verse 32 Jeremiah contrasted the unbreakable "New Covenant" with the old one that the Israelites broke repeatedly.

*The Dead Sea Scrolls will affirm that "Hebrews" is on the same scroll with Paul's other letters.

The philosophy of Jesus the Galilean can be summed up in one sentence. If anyone loves his Creator unselfishly with complete soul, body and spirit, seeks His wisdom and loves his/her neighbor as self, that person will overcome sickness, poverty and spiritual death. We in the Occident, in an attempt to prove that we have better philosophers than those in the Orient, pack our educational books with Greek, French, British, and American noetics. Not to be outgunned, disciples of Oriental philosophical schools of thought retorted, "Since your icons brought you philosophy, which you are using as your moral codes, ours have brought us religion." Here is a word of caution. Anyone that erects an altar in his/her house, school, church, temple or nation is issuing a spiritual statement: "**I am bonded to the message and to the spiritual messenger/custodian of that altar.**"

A territory automatically becomes fair game for the entire spiritual world as soon as blemished blood is spilled on or within the proximity of its assigned altar. Blood that is spiritually blemished through disobedience, blood sins or generational curses, will weaken and vanquish any altar eventually. Incense and candles cannot repel demonic forces—on the contrary, they attract them. Since time began, there was only one human, "The True Light," whose *golden light* illuminates the world—1st John 2:7-11.

His blood was sinless and pure enough to bond eternally with God. As God's "Golden Light" touched *The Lamb*, Ja-son, Son of Jah or Immanuel, Prince of Peace became the "Golden Fleece or Lamb *slain* for the sins of the world—Colossians 1:12-13. 1st John 2:8, "The darkness is past, and the true light now shineth." Verse 9, "He that saith he is in the light, and hateth his brother, is in darkness even until now." Any prophet, pope, bishop, priest, pastor, person, pimp, prostitute or "plebe" that wants the intimate presence of God, first must confess and remove all blemished body fluids. False utterances stain saliva!

I will reprint the actual prophecy of that made 1000 years before the fact. Psalm 68:18, "Thou hast ascended on high, thou hast led captivity captive: thou hast received gifts for men; yea for the rebellious also, that the Lord God might dwell among them." That revealing Wisdom/Light/Truth, though challenged by every evil being is inextinguishable. Isaiah 53 prefaced Him as a lamb led to the slaughter. Isaiah 49:5-7 first predicted the rejection by His seed and then the hope for the "Wild Olive." God did not say redeemers; He quoted one redeemer/servant/seed of David. Isaiah 49:6, "It is a light thing that thou should be my servant to raise up the tribes of Jacob and to restore the preserved of Israel: I will give thee for a light to the Gentiles, that thou mayest be my salvation to the ends of the earth." If God's only redeemer is Hebrew, yet all-nations' inclusive, then from whence are the origins of the conflicting messages allegedly from all-excluding ethnic prophets?

CHAPTER 6C. SEED PROPHECIES THAT ECHO

God offered specific covenant gifts and made everlasting promises to nations in Abraham's loins. Since his seed became Ethiopians, Jews, Arabs, Indians, Americans, Brazilians, South Americans, Africans, Pakistanis and Caribbean people, we need to see to which seed were everlasting promises made. In the Torah, the words for Eberite and Hebrew are the same, "Ibriy." In Genesis 14:3, Abraham was called a Hebrew. Whether his seed—parading as other people from other nations—know it or not, certain of the promises apply to them regardless of their knowledge or lack thereof. In 1st Chronicles 9:3, after the Babylonian captivity, those returnees that eventually dwelt in Jerusalem were the Levites, the children of Israel, Judah, Benjamin, Ephraim and Manasseh. Many of their seed spread across Jordan and neighbouring Arabic nations. In Joshua 17, *Manasseh, firstborn of Joseph and almost all his seed settled in what is called Jordan today.* In Deuteronomy 27 and 28 are stipulations for all of Abraham's seed. In Isaiah 41:8, God picked out His "Covenant Choice Seed." Here in a nutshell are promises to *all* of Abraham's seed: (1) Birth of a New Everlasting Priesthood. (2) Word or Oracle Power (Genesis 15:1, (3) Shield or supernatural protection, (4) Great Reward, (5) Seed as stars of heaven—Genesis 15:5. (6) Land, (7) Trials and enslavement up to 400-year periods, Genesis 15:13. (8) Eventual Triumph/Victory and (9) Divine *Judgment* to their *unjust oppressors.*

EVERY SEED NATION OF ABRAHAM THAT REJECTED THE PRINCE OF PEACE KNOWS NO PEACE.

The seed "Israel" preserved and protected the *covenanted code, language* and *land.* Their *Aliyah* is a *spiritual statement* that they are "standing in the gap" for those that are lost and dispersed. Therefore they automatically inherit *more responsibilities,* which bring great rewards or blessings if they are steadfast, pure and holy. Conversely severe punishments would follow if they became lax, disobedient or "Paganistic." Since Israel is the only nation on earth whose code was given by God personally, her national altars bear witness to a blood covenant with the All Wise, All Knowing God. God, being spirit, decreed that an unblemished lamb would act as surrogate. Those familiar with ancient Italian and Jewish customs should understand this. As two people stood, arms locked, both would nick flesh and exchange blood. The message was unmistakable. The two would become one. Abraham was willing to offer his firstborn son and "yoke all his seed to God." That was accepted until another and better sacrifice as per Jeremiah 31:31, the "Eternal Sacrifice" was made. God became a tag team partner to people that vowed to overcome the kingdom and armies of Satan.

The fifth book of Moses is called Deuteronomy or "Deuteronomion" from two Greek words: "deuteros nomos" or second rendition of the law. Traditionally, it became necessary to have a first presentation of the law, then a second—for clarity and emphasis. There are churches and temples that perform such rites literally to this day. They have a first and second reading of the Word or Law. Figuratively that means whatever the Lord God enshrines, he will bring it again for those that blinked. He proves by His Law of Double-Reference that what he says or does is no accident. In other words, God would not present any philosophy or teaching unless he made a first presentation, spelled out the conditions, rewards or punishments for implementation or rejection, and then *confirmed His word.*

Moses brought down the physical law, the "Ten Commandments." Moses broke them in anger. God gave him The Law a *second time.* When The Law or "Golden Fleece" manifests, it *will be a broken* (contrite) sacrifice. It took David two attempts before he could return the Ark of the Lord. He was successful on the *second attempt.* The one designated to usher in the presence of "God with us" must not do it the first time. Isaiah 7:14 prefaced the name Immanuel or "God with us." *The same messenger* must finish the work the second time around (Acts 1:11).

THE LIVING LAW OR WORD HAS COME, HAS BEEN "BROKEN" AND WILL RETURN A SECOND TIME: HENCE THE CONFIRMING REFERENCE, "GOD OF THE SECOND CHANCE."

David, while he was king, offered sacrifices to God. Instead of being killed for doing so, David was actually blessed. That was the exclusive function of the Aaronic Priests until the final "Melchizedek Priesthood" is transformed from an esoteric inference in Psalm 110 to a factual corroboration. A former student of Gamaliel elaborated on the transformation of "The Holy Office" in a letter indexed for posterity in Hebrews "Chapter 7."

Melchizedek of Genesis 14:18, King of the most High God and priest forever, did not have an earthly office. See chapter "Beyond the Boundaries" also Hebrews 7:1-28. His entrance and exit doors remained open. They were open before the beginning and they will exist after the final filming of the human script. Abraham paid tithes. He sowed into that ministry. His descendants that worship the most High God are still being blessed of that ministry. If Abraham did not sow into the New Priesthood, would his seed be included in the New Covenant? Those who teach that the Jews did not renew their Covenant (since the promise with the Levites was unto their generations) need to be reminded of three important things: 1) Jesus had the lineages of both Levi and Judah in His veins. 2) Abraham sowed into the ministry of Melchizedek. 3) In John's vision on the isle of Patmos, remnants *of all tribes were included* in the redemption package.

In Moses 2nd book (The Exodus from Egypt) Exodus 19:10, the people were not sanctified sufficiently after the "First Wash." They had to be washed a *second time* (that one for the iniquities of parents and ancestors). In Exodus 19:6, Moses recorded God's most important promise ever made to anyone: You shall be unto me a "Kingdom of Priests and a Holy Nation." Verse 5 has the conditions: "If you will *obey my voice* and *keep my Covenant.*" In other words GOD'S EARTHLY ALTARS ARE FOR YOU TO SAFEGUARD AT ALL TIMES.

Here is a question for all of my Hebrew friends: "Will you continue to allow your altars to be harassed by the spirits of Amalek, Philistia, Sanballat, and Tobiah?" You have been forewarned by Moses in his second book. In Exodus 17:15, Moses erected a spiritual war banner with the consecrated inscription "Jehovah-Nissi." Verse 16, "The Lord hath sworn that He will war with Amalek from 'generation to generation.'" Let us back up for a moment. The Creator God established an altar in the heavens as a primary teaching and praise medium. David spelled that out clearly in Psalm 19. Is there any other option available to seed of Abraham other than total unconditional obedience to all of God's laws in order to receive His redemptive package, promises and full provisions?

CHAPTER 6D. BEYOND REASONABLE DOUBT.

Manna (physical bread) lasted *40 years* in the wilderness. The prescribed duration of spiritual bread (both kingly and priestly food) also must be *40 years.* Isaac waited *40 years* before God's ordained time to meet Rebekah. Solomon reigned in Jerusalem over all Israel 40 years. When the messianic seed arrived, it would have been planted in the regions of Canaan to germinate *40 years.* The predestined obedient path of God through His Covenant Promise is for a seed that is able to reverse the curse that God placed on the earth in Genesis 4:12. That seed must comply with all of God's laws. So we will examine God's Law of *Double Reference* to see which seed of Abraham was totally obedient to all (not some) of the requirements.

King David ruled 40 years providing kingly food for *33 years in Jerusalem* and *7 years in Hebron.* John the Harbinger (called John the Baptist) brought reformation around the region of *Hebron for 7 years.* He bore witness of the *Spiritual Manna* to come (Priestly Bread). Incidentally, Jeshua son of Miriam (who had both the lineages Judah and Levi) brought "Reformation" and "Spiritual Manna" around *Jerusalem 33 years.* David began by shepherding his "father's sheep." First he had to overcome the spirit of "rejection" from his own blood kin. When the prophet was sent to the household of Jesse, the father of David, neither his kin nor Samuel considered David for selection. God told Samuel that He would not accept any of the eight sons he presented. Only then did the prophet reluctantly ask Jesse, "Is there yet another son?" Then the delayed reaction, "Oh by the way, there is another one minding the sheep." David then overcame "Lion and Bear" spirit types when they attacked "lost sheep." In other words, he had a heart of compassion for the lost. David introduced higher worship and higher praises in the Psalms. He, as a king, besought and received the presence of the Lord into an earthly house. He redeemed Israel and her altars. As a king, he offered holy sacrifice to the Lord, a role allocated exclusively to priests. He invited and received confirmation that God would abide in an earthly house with His people. Therefore any true ministry, path or way to God for any seed of Jacob and Esau to be "Chosen," must pass the 40-year redemptive test, must fulfill "all prior prophecies," must be all-inclusive, and must have miraculous signs, wonders and healings. The Promised Seed must redo those steps better—Malachi 3:1 and 4 and Zechariah 9:9. Since the lamb was ordained to be without blemish, His mother must be a virgin. Isaiah 7:14, "Behold, a virgin shall conceive and bear a son." That special Son (Psalm 2) is from the "Perfect Father." The religious folks must also *reject Him.* Isaiah 53:3, He will be despised and rejected. The child would not come until both *Israel and Judah, be without kings.* "Before the child (Imman-u-el) shall know to refuse the evil and choose the good, the land that thou abhorrest shall be *forsaken of both* her *kings."* That warning (in Isaiah 7:15-16) should have been sufficient.

Just imagine that after 400-plus years of silence from God, when *Israel and Judah* had neither a king nor a prophet, John the Harbinger arrived with messages of repentance and imminent news of *great things to come.* Contrary to Satan's wishes, there must have been great expectancy. King Herod would not have gone through the trouble of attempting to kill all the Hebrew lads two years and under had the birth of Jeshua been a secret. Unfortunately many were expecting a king for an earthly office with definable powers. Jesus' restorative ministering anointing transforms the physically and spiritually hungry: sick get healed, deaf hear, dumb speak, blind see, lame walk, fishers of meat become fishers of spirit and former prostitutes become proselytes. Prophet Isaiah also spoke forth that Gentile nations would be grafted into the True Olive. Those utterances are in Isaiah 11:10 and Isaiah 11:1-3. Jesus' ministry was foretold in Isaiah 9:6-7. Prophet Zechariah forewarned that the end of the bloodline of David would coincide with the Messiah's season. Here is serious evidence. Joseph, the surrogate father of Jesus had David's bloodline in him. His eventual wife Mary was of dual lineage. Joseph was a trained carpenter. He cared for Jesus as for his own sons. He taught "the child" physical and spiritual carpentry. Joseph had both spiritual and physical carpentry skills in his genes. All of Jesus' earthly brothers and sisters served in Jesus' ministry. None bore children. To all still awaiting the Messiah, the end of dual Judaic and Levitical bloodlines, without any more physical fruits, is evidence that the Messiah arrived and is scheduled to return. Let us assume that Jesus' brothers and sisters knew something of special significance. All of them ministered to Jesus. Every aspect of Jeshua's ministry fulfilled prior prophecies. To be fair, the ancient Hebrews could not go to a bookstore and get those prophecies on one scroll. They had to study under the priesthood, which was in a similar state to that of many religious institutions today: routinely ritualistic because of weak custodians and satanically inspired impersonators.

Later in this book, as we examine our purposes on earth, hopefully we can appreciate the complete wisdom of our Creator. He foresaw all of our failings and put restitution plans in place. The writings of the prophet Zechariah should be studied in detail. The most accessible source is the Pentateuch or Old Testament for many in the west. Zechariah 9:9 previewed Jesus' ride on the donkey on Palm Sunday. In Isaiah 42:6, the "New Covenant" witness was previewed. Zechariah 11:12 foretold the price of Jesus' betrayal—30 pieces of silver. The prophet Daniel gave us the precise time in code that the Messiah would come, how long He would stay and when He would leave. Prophecies about Israel's plight for rejecting the Messiah are in Psalm 78:60, Ezekiel 21:10, and Isaiah 53:1-12.

The Roman calendar was not yet invented at the time of Daniel. Daniel 9:25 showed us the exact time that the Messiah would appear. Along with the above, let us scrutinize two profound prophecies in Psalm 118. In verse 22 "The stone which the builders refused *is become* the head stone of the corner." Also in verse 27, "God is the Lord, which hath showed us light (revelation): Bind *the sacrifice* with cords, even unto the horns of the altar." In the two aforementioned prophecies God did not state, "The stone will become" nor "has become," He established that the stone "is become head," after first being rejected by His own. Here is another fragment that surfaced to the top of our evidence list. God referenced His sacrifice that He wanted *fastened to the altar*. His words: "Bind the Sacrifice." The ultimate destination of that Special Sacrifice is in the nostrils of God. There would be everlasting bonding to God. Jeshua's consecrated name is "Immanuel" which could have been translated, "Way to God." English translators have used "God with us."

CHAPTER 6E. OTHER PROPHETS AND MESSENGERS SPOKE!

The constellations proclaim the Messiah. Demonic spirits admit the Lordship of Jeshua and tremble at His name. The Holy Koran affirms Jeshua birth and supernatural exit. Michael or Micah prophesied approximately 70 years during the reigns of Judah's kings: Ahaz, Jotham and Hezekiah. In Micah 5:2, he prophesied even Jesus' birthplace: "But thou Bethlehem Ephratah though thou be little among the thousands of Judah, yet shall he come forth unto me that is to be ruler in Israel whose goings forth have been of old, from everlasting." Here a person, who had been of old, would have been concealed from us on earth until the designated time when the person's entrance would be announced in Bethlehem. Matthew 1:20 confirmed that an angel of the Lord made the announcement.

Mary the mother of "Jeshua," or "Isa," is the only lady *revered* or even written about in the Holy Koran not just once but over 20 times. The Koran also explains why God chose her: "She guarded her chastity" and "His mother was a faithful woman." Other Koran quotes are—"One of the Devout..." and "God chose her above all women." Also, Jesus' birth and unusual power gifts are recorded in the Holy Koran. Sura 19, 19—the angels announce to Miriam: "I am only a messenger from thy Lord (to announce) to thee the gift of a holy son."

Two thousand years before Jesus' birth, the Spirit of God spoke through David giving every detail of Jesus' death including the first words Jesus would utter on the cross. Psalm 22:1, "My God, my God why hast thou forsaken me?" Verse 7 portrayed in advance, what would have been the behaviour of the mockers while His disciples fled: "All they that see me laugh me to scorn: they shoot the lip, they shake the head. Verse 8, "He trusted in the Lord that he would deliver him. Let him deliver him seeing that he delighted in him." Verses 14 and 15 described His agony. The amazing thing about those verses is not only the fact that King David etched them 4000 years ago, but also that such graphic detailed events had been given and encoded precisely in the Hebrew texts of the Torah. Verse 16 reads, "They pierced my hands and my feet." Next in sequential occurrences, God gave us the spiritual behaviour of the assembly, mocking and behaving like dogs when they see blood. In actuality there were doglike spirits waiting as usual whenever there was shed blood. Little did they know that the eternal trap was put in place for them. The *Power of Purim* was about to be confirmed the second time. Psalm 22:18 speaks, "They part my garments among them and cast lots upon my vesture." David did not say parted. Prophetically he spoke. It is not unusual for God to speak through "His Anointed." After all, Satan and his evil band can have people pay large sums of money for *lateral* information through the mouths of psychics. *Satan does not know the future;* neither can he or his minions read your minds. That is why they throw so many pitches tempting you constantly to see which spiritual balls you like to hit. They have a very organized network with simultaneous access to *information* on *unrepented sins*.

Every December, certain magazines publish 100 predictions for the next year. Rule number one: treat any so-called spiritual pronouncements made outside of God's Holy Hill and outside of His spiritual network of continuity with skepticism. Whether those dictates have to do with visions received to set up new religions, or about events, yet to happen, God already promised us that the gates of hell will not prevail against His spiritual network. God could not spend centuries pruning His vineyard and then hand it over to neophytes. If He did, then Satan would have permanent bragging rights over God. Satan already promised to exalt his network of lies, false teachings and minions on earth. To come into a domain assigned to man and overthrow it, first you have to deceive, brainwash, and or destroy man.

Here is a summary of the tabloid premonitions over the last ten years. Less than half of 1% had been fulfilled. If a certain evil spirit knows that one of his spirit partners had planted AIDS and cancer in a famous person that had been dwelling heavily in iniquity, that spirit can make an educated guess. The information can be relayed through one of its altars. What if the infected person wants to change his/her way of life? Suppose that magazine is used as a conduit and published the person's name on their speculative lists? What if that person repented before the Lord with humility and a repentant heart for his/her sins first, then of his/her iniquities, then of the curses of at least four generations? God in His mercy would most likely release His powerful anointing. That anointing would then shatter every yoke. Instantly the person could be healed and Satan would be exposed. He is a killer, liar, thief, counterfeiter and destroyer.

There have been instances whereby persons with known or unknown linkages to the "Tribes of Levi and Judah," fulfill the generational requirements for certain gifts. In other words they might be the firstborn of seven generations of that seed. There would be covenant potential in them. God commences the nourishing of His chosen before they are born; then increases their gifts as they progress in Him—Jeremiah 1:5. If augural gifts began to manifest at birth, then God would signal His intent to enlarge or to disuse such gifts. Satan would pounce on the person's potential with sinful enticements. God does not bestow gifts and remove them. In such cases, those persons either did not yet ripen or were snatched before reaching their prophetic potential in God. Their foretelling would hit and miss. Satan would then use those persons' occasional hits to give himself credibility. God already gave such persons admonishing scriptures in Isaiah 8:18-19. In addition, Leviticus 19:31 warns us: "Regard not them that have familiar spirits neither seek after wizards to be defiled by them." More importantly, there is no neutral side in the spiritual world. Thank God for His *Power of Purim*. I have seen many that have returned to their rightful redemptive purposes. Transformation from disobedience to obedience is so great when you treasure the new spiritual gifts that God bestows upon you. Naturally the chief thief (the one that used to kick you around) will behave like a jilted lover trying anything and everything to pull you down. The rewards for ignoring him are immeasurable. I should know. I have been there; for that purpose God has chosen me to bring these evidences to you. I am a modern day witness of His delivering powers, His miracle powers and His saving grace. The hand that welcomed me into the Most Holy Veil was that of the *Conquering Lion of the Tribe of Judah*, Jeshua.

CHAPTER 7. VICTORY OVER SICKNESS AND DEATH

CHAPTER 7A. SPIRITUAL ROOTS

Ancient Hebrew customs forbade the touching of the dead or touching anything to do with death. Those were some of the most sacrilegious acts persons could commit. Dead things were spiritually unclean. According to tradition, the biggest curses would follow. The Levites had elaborate rituals for cleaning such transgressions. While Jeshua was on earth he not only constantly touched the sick and the dead but also healed them and brought them back to life. At His trial, had they charged Him with *touching the dead,* the detractors might have had a valid charge to lay on Him. However there would be a major problem: that of finding any evidence since in all cases the dead returned to life.

There has been only one prior case in recorded history whereby anyone was able to ask God for any of His disciples to receive the gifts of the victories over sicknesses and death. Prophet Elijah was able to pass on those gifts of God to his successor Elisha. Jesus not only did that, but so much more. 2000 years after His exit, disciples of Jesus, especially formerly extremely sinful ones like me, can walk in His promises and achieve the same for suffering people. Adepts of all faiths concur that Jeshua had a highly unusual ministry. The most unusual aspect of His ministry is that Jeshua not only broke the cycles of life and death, but also *was, and is* able to physically touch and to transfer the power of His ministry. Those adherents that seek earnestly and sincerely the truth, can access His wisdom and power to do the following:

1. Continue His good works.

2. Present the gospel or *Good News* in truth and sincerity.

3. Destroy the kingdom of darkness' lies, sicknesses and untimely deaths.

I should add—most of the demons that Jesus cast out—they had already inflicted sicknesses or serious infirmities on persons. Since I have been called to this ministry, about half of the cases that I deal with, relate to—allegedly incurable diseases: AIDS, cancer, paralysis etc. There was a case in Jerusalem involving an Icelandic lady with a faulty lung. She also used a pacemaker. She came to ask me and my friend to pray for her. After the prayers, she fell. I noticed that she coughed up a metal object that hit the wall and dropped to the ground. A lady nearby, who was apparently a nurse, screamed: "She is dead; her pacemaker fell out." All that was said after that was, "Stand up in Jesus' name!" She confirmed that she had had pains in her lungs and her heart. She reported that she felt a tug in the heart area; then something stopped. Afterwards she felt ease. An Oriental male ran over and asked in broken English, "Could you pray for me also?"

I am inserting this information to show that if all seed of Abraham (natural or adopted) were as spiritually strong as they are supposed to be, people would not be running to the satanic imposters. Fact is that in my travels I have found some churches that are receiving the restorative anointing. God bless Atlanta Georgia! Numerous churches there are experiencing the strong presence of the Spirit of God.

I had just left a country because of exhaustion. I popped into a church service in time to hear Satan bragging through a youngster (that he had held hostage) that his time is ripe to increase spiritual pressure, especially on young people. His taste was being refined for young blood. The computer was going to be one of his mightiest weapons for the upcoming millennium. I was a visitor in the church and was fuming at the utter disrespect. I could take it no longer; so I went up to the pastor who informed me that the demon had refused to shut up. He also reasoned that any attempt at deliverance would take all night. He had to travel early in the morning. He was visiting, so he would get the local pastor to find more information on the youth. As soon as the youngster faced my direction, the evil spirit that was in him exclaimed, "Oh that's you, you trouble maker?" There is one name that demons are terrified of. I claimed Jesus' name and authority that He gave to all of His "called apostles" then whispered, "In Jesus' name shut up!" A lady who was scampering to exit the church asked me, "What did you say to that thing?" I told her just like Caleb said, that there is no ground that cannot be taken for the Lord. *Jesus reclaimed man's full authority on the earth.*

I then inquired of some lads who mentioned that they were his classmates, "How much gusto do you all have?" "We want to help our friend," they all replied. Dear God, Bless them and seal them. "Out of the mouth of babes and sucklings I will ordain praise." I offered to give the embattled youngster a ride. The spirit intervened: "I am not going anywhere with you!" In Jesus' name I ordered him to be quiet. I will state unequivocally: "No other name has the authority nor commands the fear in evil spirits like the name "Jeshua or Jesus." The events that followed should be etched in their minds forever. *"The authority in Jesus' name is the arrow of righteousness from the bow of God's throne."*

I arranged for his friends to drive him home and to stop first at a playing field. I joined them and we began to pray first. At a specific point, the boy's schoolmates recited what Catholics and Anglicans call a confession; Pentecostals and "Charismatics" refer to as a sinner's prayer. We did a second wash for the iniquities or habitual serious sins of ourselves, our parents, our parents' parents going all the way back on both sides of our families. Having no recollection of what they all did, we confessed every known sin. We confessed that we had sins we had no recollection of, we confessed our intentional and unintentional sins, the sins of our minds, hearts, mouths, bodies and the most neglected ones, sins of our attitudes. We confessed sins of dishonesty: cheating, lying, slander, theft and covetousness. We confessed sins of impurity and spelled out each one: masturbation, fornication, rape, paedophilia, incest, lust, homosexuality, lesbianism, abortions/murders, occult and witchcraft-related sins.

We confessed sins of "unforgiveness," prejudicially judging others, sins of hate, rebellion and impatience. We confessed sins of addiction, sins of desecrating our altars and those of our communities and countries. We added sins of not tithing correctly and bad judgment. In other words, we did sanctify today (first wash) and tomorrow (second wash) as in Exodus 19:10. We asked God to cleanse first, then to hallow the ground where we stood. In anticipation of his response, we removed our shoes. We renounced Satan and all his works, hexes, gifts and ungodly soul ties. At that point God began to be impatient. Normally it is the person that is possessed or a weak "Believer" that becomes impatient. The word of God was confirmed that day: He is the same yesterday, today and forevermore.

Never exceed your anointing; beware of pride and vanity. Humble yourselves. The same awesome power of God—that quaked the mountain in Moses' presence, was in the Ark, descended on the tabernacle in the wilderness, and sent Jeshua—will let you know how puny we are. Next, we held hands symbolically representing a chain. I asked all to hold tight. As soon as I took authority in the name of the one everlasting "High Priest," the name that explodes with *Resurrection Power*, the name with *Purim Power*, the name that causes all demons to tremble, "Jeshua, God with us," Boom! Two, not one, of the youngsters started hyperventilating and frothing at the mouths. I then called upon the redeeming power of Jeshua. "Satan has defied you and disrespected your altar tonight." As soon as I proclaimed, "Almighty God this battle is yours," the one in which Satan was arrogantly bragging half an hour before began to bring up horrible smelly stuff. "Since you bestowed all that was lost on the Redeemer of humankind, please forgive the custodians for allowing this invasion, and deal mercilessly with these 'intruders.'"

As soon as the word "intruders" had been uttered, I immediately loved wrestling. I had previously watched wrestling and hated it. The other kid was hurled upside down. Just as I thought he was going to land on his head, he landed on his feet staggering, emitting a trail of the most horrible gook. That first emission even fools experienced pastors sometimes. Manifestation does not necessarily mean that some or all have left. Very rarely today do we encounter one intruding demon possessing anyone. Ask Almighty God through His Son, to reveal the extent of the contamination. Take authority against all curses and all links. I asked all present for us to agree on the type of fast we would undertake on behalf of the embattled. Since many had never fasted in their lives, we agreed on a three day liquid fast. We returned three days later to pursue every spiritual root. The first seven days after a three day cleansing is the most important time for the redeemed, during which time he/she must thank Jeshua for His complete redemption package and renounce Satan and all of his works.

Follow through is very important after deliverance for these reasons. 1. Matthew, a former tax collector and disciple of Jeshua, gave us an everlasting warning—Matthew 12:43. I will write out the scripture: "When the unclean spirit is gone out of a person, he walketh through dry places, seeking rest, and findeth none." He searches deserts where the bones are dry, deserts where the altars are baked in iniquity, in short—any spiritual *wilderness*. Flash back to high school. The bully (the young kid that manifests the spirit of domination) always followed its prey. The bully has to know that if it returns it will be whipped again and again. In deliverance, the bully returns with seven meaner bullies—Matthew 12:45, "Then goeth he, and taketh with himself seven other spirits more wicked than himself, and they enter in and dwell there: and the last state of the man is worse than the first." After deliverance, ejected spirits stalk the person they previously held captive, relentlessly. Those persons have to be obedient and permanently bonded to God's laws: no exceptions whatsoever. 2nd Peter 2:20 reminds us that the final stages would be much worse than the first. That is why it is very important that you exercise the authority that Jesus left for all of His witnesses. If you have *the gift of prophecy*, then speak confusion into their navigational systems. Forbid them to find other dry places and shatter their tag team ability to seek help among their kind.

MATTHEW 12: 43 AND 2ND PETER 2:20 CONFIRM THAT EXPELLED DEMONS WILL MAKE EVERY ATTEMPT TO REGAIN ENTRY AND TO ADD REINFORCEMENTS.

2. If there are lingering spirits or spiritual eggs, the person's lifestyle either chases them or encourages them. News about expelled demons is headline news in "All Demon Network."

Every demon would be trying to recapture the treasured prize, a refurbished virgin altar. There are so many teaching aids that The Creator has given us to learn how to get away from the *Big Fish* and its belly. The animals in the wild as they fight for survival, seek security in numbers among the stronger ones. Predators specialize in stalking the young and vulnerable. So it is in the natural; so it is in the spiritual also. Try to nurture persons beyond the crucial 40-day period by teaching them how to rebuild and to repair spiritual damage.

The promise given to Abraham was ordained to be an everlasting will and covenant. From Abraham's seed through David, first someone had to die as surrogate for that promise engraved in righteous blood to be an everlasting covenant. Here is bad news for Satan. That everlasting testament always did and always will have living witnesses. *The Will* also had to be recorded; so it had to manifest (become flesh) then revert back to the author to be vetted. It is now on the righteous altar of the living God as everlasting testimony. Human flesh has rebuilt a righteous altar to God on the "E^ts of Life." The Architect sent the plans to rebuild and reclaim every captured spiritual ground. That season prophesied by Joel is here! As a result, the clouds of Ezekiel 47 are full of fresh spiritual pollen straining to be released. I bear witness.

CHAPTER 7B. IMPORTANT SYMPTOMS

Since deliverance ministries are relatively new in so many churches, I will give details for the anointed of God only. I will use Biblical language to prevent some curious and disrespectful person from ending up like the sons of Sceva in Acts 19:14. If you have recited the sinners' prayer in earnest and have sought forgiveness from your sins and those of your progenitors, you are not only saved but also bonded to God. If you sincerely asked God to break every hex and generational curse on your life and accepted His one ordained everlasting sacrifice, unless you fall back into sinful living, you will be freed from *all* evil influences. If you have done the aforementioned, you should *not* have nightmares, temper tantrums, addictions, fears and phobias. You should not be accident-prone anymore. If you have done the cleansings and you are a person, a pastor or member of a church, *not* experiencing the full presence of God at this moment, you are either a bench warmer—James 1:5/James 1:26-27, in a type of wilderness—Revelation 3:16, or in bondage to spirits or abominations—Revelation 2:20.

a) *BOUND IN A TYPE OF BABYLON:* a spiritual state where God's presence is blocked because of current or former generation curses from habitual and unrepented sins (Exodus 34:6-7). Those include messing with voodoo, Ouija boards, tarot cards, or *possessing* certain rings, amulets or *covenants* emanating from satanic altars, or three different types of sins with decreed death sentences.

b) *HARBOURING ABOMINATIONS:* those are sins that involve the human body, which can or do cause evil spirits to enter knowingly or unknowingly. I am not going to pull punches here. This is very serious stuff. See subcategories of *addiction* and *domination* below. If you are a pastor, a priest, a man or a woman of God that ministers on an altar of the Lord, you cannot engage in masturbation, adultery, fornication, homosexuality, or touch anything "accursed." If you are doing any of those, or you wear a guard or ring that had been given you for "protection" even as a child, you are spiritually oppressed, depressed or possessed! Those rings have been prepared over satanic altars and are conduits for satanic spiritual energies. Exodus 28:43 states "an everlasting statute" *with a death sentence attached.*

Some congregations foolishly teach the idiocy "SECURITY OF BELIEVERS." Please read these scriptures over and over again: 2nd Peter 2:20 and Romans 2:12...For as many as have *sinned in the law* will be *judged by the law*. In Paul's letter to the Galatian brethren, he warned Christians that if in fact they commit sins, they *crucify the saviour all over again*. In his letter to the Colossian brethren he was explicit in Colossians 3:25...he that doeth wrong shall receive for the wrong, which he hath done: and there is no respect of persons (pimp, drug pusher, prostitute, pastor, pope or peasant). No one is exempt or infallible.

The most demons I have cast out at a given time had been lodged in "saved" people that were hiding behind cloaks of self-righteousness while secretly engaging in sinful living. Satan always sends his most powerful demons for persons that have positions of authority in churches. Those spirits are strong enough to sit in churches, weaken worship and negate effective message sermons to such an extent that people *often* sleep during the services. They decrease churches' memberships drastically and rapidly. In many such instances there is discord in the church; personal and church family members are constantly in and out of trouble especially with addictive substances and sexually related sins.

Do not assume that all persons who sleep in churches do so because the pastors have lost the anointing. A person might be really tired, especially after a long drive or a work shift. If the church is anointed and persons are demonized, demons will either put the persons to sleep or try to make them so uncomfortable that the persons would want to leave the service. When a church is fully anointed, no demon or evil spirit can stay quiet during the service. The person will scream, vomit, burp loudly or run as fast as possible from the holy fire. A church or temple is ordained to be "The House of the Lord." If a person constantly sleeps in church, at least one serious problem is evident. I will do a brief profile of evil spirits by categories.

Main Categories of Evil Spirits

1. There is the category of *Oppression*. Those spirits constantly stalk and adversely affect circumstances and spiritual climates around persons. Such persons become serial blunderers: they often say the wrong things. They keep making the wrong decisions. They are in constant hard luck situations. They keep misplacing or forgetting things, especially money and keys. People who find themselves in that category should never take unusual risks in dangerous situations or with money. They are prone to accidents, losses and sicknesses. There are accidents actually caused by the spirits of oppression. Those spirits try to persuade them always that their circumstances would change with some sudden avalanche of new wealth. On the contrary, the spirits that are trying to influence them are the very ones oppressing them, hoping to lead them to the next categories.

2. There is the category of *Depression*. Those are mind binding or mood altering spirits. There are six main channels that create openings in that category: Low self-esteem, fear, "unforgiveness," jealousy, hate and hopelessness (inability to handle severe personal losses).

3. There is the category of *Possession*. Those are spirits that have manipulated persons into three strikes of transgressions. Replacement spirits (Psalm 51:10), death-inducing spirits enter through deliberate releases of blood or seminal fluids whereby the nuclei of treasured life are exchanged disobediently. Those spirits enter the blood stream and lodge close to one or more of the body's vital organs. Persons in the above category often have sudden mood changes or unprovoked temper tantrums. Their eyes appear glazed.

Oft-times they are restless, encounter night terrors, and say or do "strange" things. Their stomachs usually growl uncontrollably. Those intruding personalities or evil spirits have a threefold mission:

a) Completely change the personality of the person by supplanting the original "Right Spirit" given at birth with other "wrong" personality or personalities. If pregnant mothers crave for highly unusual things like soap or dirt, they need prayers. In Romans 1, Paul described the "wrong spirits" of homosexuality, lesbianism and adultery. Spirits of "homosexuality and lesbianism are penned in Romans 1:26 and Leviticus 20:13. Other examples are severe drug and alcohol addictions.

b) Create an incubation factory by allowing the ingestion of body fluids and body wastes, or the proliferation of as many like spirits as possible.

c) Acquire more borrowed time on earth by creating openings for other categories. Any spirit in the category of possession that delivers the ultimate prize (a lost soul unto death) has the distinction in the "Ghoulish abode" of becoming a *generational spirit* with the license to oppress and hopefully possess future offspring of the victim or victims.

4. There is the category of *Infirmity*. Most sicknesses, even some accidental ones, have spiritual roots. Roots sometimes go back as far as four generations—Exodus 34:6-7. Prostrate cancer is manifesting strongly in many sons and grandsons that have had spiritual openings large enough to receive inherited generational curses. Habitual adulterers find themselves afflicted similarly. Fibroids, breast cancer and lots of female complications also have their spiritual roots. For those that are active, or intend to get active in the ministries of *Healing and Deliverance*—just do what our first teacher did: take authority in the name of the "Firstfruit" Son of God, Jeshua. Command the spirits of infirmity to go!

Addiction is a powerful *subcategory* that opens the way for "Possession" or "infirmity." A unique feature of the human body is the ability of the brain to transfer messages of urges and needs. Many of our urges and needs are spiritually motivated. Since spirits magnetize over altars, any substance that has been used in an occult or satanic ceremony is accessible as a spiritual conduit. Certain mind enhancing drugs, tobacco and liquid spirits are used in occult ceremonies. Any person that has spiritual openings and uses a substance that had been prepared ritualistically or over satanic altars is fair game for spirits of addiction. Spirits of "Addiction" are able to proliferate easily. Those spirits control the person's mind (will or intellect) first, with the intent to lock on to a vital organ. They generate *insatiable cravings* whether for: a) drugs, tobacco, liquor, stolen goods then hopefully enough b) (Blood or semen) via homosexuality, lesbianism, masturbation, paedophilia, rape, adultery, murder, fornication or abortion. Addiction and lust are group spirits. Once they *penetrate*, they proliferate and control more than one area of the body simultaneously. Given the slightest chance, they will open the person to spirits of *oppression, possession and or infirmity.*

There is another subcategory of spirits that is *difficult to detect* without considerable experience in deliverance ministries. Those in the category of *Domination* are comfortably controlling either minds or bodies. They love attention: the more they dominate, the happier they are. First, they aim to control minds. If they get both minds and bodies—even better for them. Those spirits do not go after the average Joe or Jane. They search for highly charismatic persons that are able to wield strong influences on others. Those types of persons are uncomfortable unless they are in authority, or in positions of influence. In that subcategory is "Vanity." Vanity persuades persons that *they* make the situation—not the other way around.

That category also has the ability to propel their "likeable persons" into highly successful or high profile situations where mental or sexual influences can be exerted en masse. Subtle antagonisms are the hallmarks of large-scale bondage in that subcategory that (given the slightest chance) will entice psychological, spiritual or physical death (abortion included). Persons oppressed by "domination" overuse their "gifts of persuasion." They love to have the final say. I have seen that spirit latch on to pride, and then piggyback into houses of worship.

Evil spirits move in large groups. Their ability to summon help to strengthen their troops is something to be mindful of; as soon as general cleansing takes place, cut off their ability to communicate with other spirits immediately. If at all possible take the person to a place where the spiritual energy is strongly positive. Evil Spirits increase their resistance at established strongholds. The same is true for opposite situations. Unless you have had lots of experience in *Deliverance Ministries,* do not conduct deliverance sessions at brothels, jails, insane asylums, and Turkish or Roman baths. Displaced and wayward former disciples need to repent first and seek spiritual help immediately with their deliverance before reclaiming God's redemptive purposes for their lives and then read the chapter with the testimony of a former witch. I wish I had the knowledge listed above when I was in the music industry. Many of my friends were lost because of lack of wisdom. Satan has taken too many young and talented artists and musicians' lives.

CHAPTER 7C. REGAINING AND RETAINING YOUR RIGHT SPIRIT!

If you pick up a glass or a vase made of clay marked "*FRAGILE, or HANDLE WITH CARE,*" and dropped it, chances are that you wrecked it. We are earthen vessels designed with a temporary engine that was never ours. It was lent to us for a time. Every time we disobey the instructions of the manufacturer, we tarnish and fracture the merchandise. In Psalm 51, the great king had a reality check. Not only had he seduced a man's wife but also had arranged the man's untimely death. In verses 7 -10, David, bound with guilt and a sudden realization as to what happened to him, cried out to his Maker in anguish and sorrow: "*1. Purge me, 2. Wash me, 3. Return my joy and gladness, 4. Blot out all mine iniquities 5. Remove my sins from before me 6. Create in me a clean heart and 7 Renew a right spirit within me.*"

There were 12 tribes of Israel. One of the tribes turned its back in the midst of its enemies and fled. Jesus had 12 disciples. One turned and slid back (hence the term backslid) into sin. Matthias got his portion. Saul of Tarsus reminded Jews in Rome, and the few Roman converts, of the prophetic utterances of Isaiah in Romans 15:12. Isaiah (Isaiah 11 from verse 10) prophesied that at the end of Jesse's bloodline (David's father) that the Messiah would come and usher in the Gentiles en masse. He stressed that He would come not once, but twice. As is customary with God, He confirms His word. Accidents cannot replicate identically. Isaiah 11:11, "It shall come to pass in that day, that the Lord shall set his hand *again, the second time…*" the prophet not only uses the pregnant word "again" but cements it with the term "a second time." In the 53rd chapter of Isaiah, the most important aspect of the Messiah's restorative ministry is stated: *HE CAME TO RESTORE THE BREACHES.*

Here is a step-by-step approach to your process of spiritual renewal or restoration. Most important is the process for maintaining your vessel after it had been reclaimed and sterilized.

First and foremost, commence studying the *Gifts of the Holy Spirit* and the *Fruits of the Holy Spirit*. Pray for the *Power of the Holy Spirit* that was unleashed at Pentecost. The Holy Spirit is available to do greater works today. Keep in mind "It is not by might or by power but by my Spirit," saith the Lord. You must acquire a complete Bible with an Old and New Testament. You must have tremendous faith. Ephesians 6:12 outlines the tools.

The method of preparation is in Psalm 24:4. I am giving the Biblical references first. So based on that commandment, go to Exodus 19:10 and 11. Do not duplicate Uzzah's error. The first instruction recorded as the *Firstfruit* words of John the Harbinger (the Baptist), and Jesus when He began His first sermon: "*Repent*," of all sins known and unknown. Deuteronomy 27 in addition to Exodus 20:1-17 should be fully studied and understood. Do not attempt to enter into the presence of our Holy God to intercede or to offer sacrifice while (spiritually) unclean. Anytime that is done, the altar, whatever it is, gets contaminated. The symbolism of burning all the flesh of the old sacrifices can be translated another way: "Do not put new wine into old skins!" Spell out and confess the different categories of sins for *self and all participants*. This is not a recitation or ritual; it is a prerequisite for spiritual sterilization.

If you have had problems with your attitude, homosexuality, jealousy, "unforgiveness," masturbation, fornication, adultery, addiction, rape, theft, abortion, hate or murder, spell them out. The second category of sins is called Iniquity. When you get into confessing the second category of sins: "Iniquities," confess of self and of parents up to the third and fourth generations on both sides of the family. Since you do not know what they committed, confess all, including the horrible ones listed in Deuteronomy 27. Proverbs 28:13, "*He that covereth his sins shall not prosper.*" Any person that feels he or she is too anointed or clean to say those prayers, stop immediately and leave. Already a spirit of pride surfaced and all that would happen is that spirit would hamper the deliverance process. The word of God says—if you sin in one, you sin in all. Romans 3:23, "All have sinned and come short..." No person on earth is ever clean enough to enter the "Most Holy Veil." Whenever permission is sought to enter, *all must confess first and seek forgiveness—in order to be cleansed.*

The presence of the Lord is so powerful. The most spiritual magnet needs a spotless altar to connect to. That is why whenever altars are rebuilt and become spotless again, most sicknesses, most demonic forces either leave immediately or in heavy compound cases, begin the process of deliverance immediately. Most cases need follow-up work. In all cases, the (formerly bound) person must renounce old and ancient covenants that are not of God. Seek the assistance of experienced ministries in compound situations. There might be ungodly soul covenants with persons, amulets or buried figurines that need to be broken, destroyed or removed. The gift of discernment is a powerful tool. Moses laid the foundation of inviting and receiving God to leave His place of perfection or "Rest" to come down and bless His people, after they had been spiritually washed *THREE TIMES*. Notice how occult practitioners have copied the processes and turned them into demonic rituals.

Customers have to go regularly to get their *washes* (called baths in occult circles) for a *sum* each time. There are many persons that have prophetic callings on their lives that Satan has snatched. They honestly believe that they are assisting persons through the services they are providing. Beware: Satan is playing a deadly chess game with you. Like chess, he sacrifices a few pawns to catch bigger bait to strengthen his kingdom. That is why so many of them have to sniff snuff, gargle with liquor, sprinkle with incense, bury things and plant things to strengthen his altars. By the way, they are all evil, whether you believe it or not. Their assignments are to deceive and to entice you to be evil. Their boss is deceptively evil.

CONSECRATED JEWISH FEASTS

I spent a bit of time going over the meanings and commemorative dates of the consecrated Jewish feasts: Firstfruits, Trumpets, Unleavened Bread, Passover, Pentecost, Tabernacles and Purim. As I analyzed the dates (on the Hebrew calendar) and how Jesus, not only perfected, fulfilled and figuratively became them, the parallels between the ancient dates and His confirmation of the seasons could not have been coincidental. I had a problem however finding the parallel in Jesus' ministry between the praise and worship and the music catalyst at a Hebrew feast or in the Torah. It was David, the sons of Korah, and Asaph that laid the foundation for music being the harmonious usher for the presence of God in the congregation. The Psalmists used dancing, singing and the playing of trumpets, harps, cymbals etc.—Psalm 21, 27, 34, 40, 65, 66, 81, 95, 96, 100, 103 to107, 134, 135, 136, and 144 to 150. Palms were used in the praise and worship on a Sunday while Jeshua rode into Jerusalem on a donkey. An old prophecy was fulfilled and a new one began. Zechariah 9:9, "Rejoice, rejoice people of Zion! Shout for joy, you people of Jerusalem! Look, your King is coming to you! He comes triumphant and victorious but humble and riding on a donkey." Jesus laid the prophetic foundation for any church functioning with the anointing of "King and Priest:" to usher in the presence of God with joyful singing and praises on the 1st day of the week in commemoration of the feast of "Firstfruits." I bear witness and many others that are active in *Deliverance Ministries* confirm—during worship, after corporate repentance, praise is a powerful tool to usher in the anointing. Hence it is written: "He inhabits the praises of the righteous." For heaven's sake, get rid of your egos. The humbler you are the greater the anointing for deliverance. It is not by might or by power but by God's Spirit.

Initially I had difficulty understanding the significance of the three days that Jesus spent in His tomb. I then realized that it took three days of *darkness* for the "Promise of Deliverance" to burst forth out of Egypt. The *three days* Jeshua spent in the grave were documented as Passover, Unleavened bread and Firstfruits which occurred and fell on (14th, 15th, and 16th) Thursdays, Fridays and Saturdays, only during Jubilee years. Since the birth of modern calendars, researchers in the Occident have messed up computations by assuming that specific events were fixed to specific days on their calendars. They ignored the fact that incongruence exists between the ancient time systems and our modern ones. For instance, very rarely did Passover fall on a Friday. Do not forget that the months on the Roman calendars only synchronize to the Hebrew calendars every fifty years. That is why *the feast or the event* was sacred *not the particular day* on which the feast fell.

CHAPTER 7D. TRAINING FOR THE WISE-HEARTED

All types of organizations prepare training materials. Some have manuals, reference guides, props and case studies documented for posterity. Here is a case study: a quick reference for pastors and deliverance teams. First I will outline the spiritual foundation, mainly for churches that have arrived at their spiritual *Promised Lands and for those desirous of getting there.* The remainder will be spiritually coded in another chapter.

    A. Football and Chess as Teaching Tools. God is so good that he has given us teaching aids in so many things; some we use for recreation without seeing the deeper meanings: for example—American Football. Disguise your plays, for Pete's sake. Do not become predictable. The aim is to get across the goal line. Since Satan cannot read your mind or the mind of our Creator, he has no authority to halt your game. Guard the prize (your soul) against interception. We have three chances in each drive to the finish line before we lose "possession." The word "possession" is serious business. It is a spiritual battle of life and death; not a chance game. If you commit any three types of "blood sins," unless you have "praying relatives" with an army of angels warding those demons off you, you will either be oppressed, depressed, possessed—or all three. Try to recover the ball immediately while there is still time remaining "on the clock." It is an all or nothing game; no priest can change the score. It matters not what they have told you or what you have read on that matter. The word of God states that nothing should be added or subtracted from His word. A catechism is a desecration of God's word for several reasons:

1.   It violates God's word by changing His word: "Nothing should be added or subtracted."

2.   It robs you of the knowledge of God since over 40 books of sound teachings are eliminated. Teachings of God must corroborate all spiritual messages of ancient Israel. Even Hagar was told to go back to her mistress. So all "Hagar" temples must return to the one true shepherd. If your temple, church, tabernacle or your life does not line up with those noted as "chosen" in Israel's history: David, Daniel, Elijah etc., obviously you have not arrived at that place of promise within "The Veil." Humans that allow the devil to use them and their institutions to impede God's purposes—their semiconductors are wired to his channels of sin, disobedience and/or erroneous teachings.

If your attitude does not pass the litmus test of Matthew 5, you do have at least one spiritual problem. It is the last quarter. You are one yard short; you have one play left. The best defensive linebacker the game has ever seen—Satan is on the line of scrimmage with his "Doomsday Defense." Every quarterback who has ever been sent previously has been butt-kicked. The good ones have retired. With so much at stake, whom would the owner teach every aspect of the game and release formations the devil wishes that he knew? Fact is that the elementary defense plays taught in spiritual high school are the same ones Satan reuses and gains all of his successes with. He forces fumbles and turnovers because he is a brilliant tactician and great at the mind game. Here is the best news you will ever hear.

THE GREATEST COACH IN HISTORY IS ON THE SIDELINES; HE SEES ALL THE WEAKNESSES IN SATAN'S DEFENSES.

Here are bigger secrets: He can read Satan's mind and Satan cannot read His. He is the owner of the franchise's son. Trust me, if you mess up and do not make amends before the game is over, your contract will be cancelled. There will be no next season.

B.   Chess. The game of chess gives us a subliminal peek into the workings of the kingdom of Satan. There are millions of pawns that Satan will sacrifice to get his "Bishops." It is important to pray for those that preach and teach the word endlessly. Those that have crusades, TV Ministries and teaching facilities need strengthening prayers daily, even hourly. A true "Bishop" that eats, sleeps, lives, and teaches the word with power and might is the spiritual equivalent of a squadron of fighter bombers loaded with "M.O.A.B's" and nuclear warheads.

C.   English cricket and American baseball. The fielding teams mimic Satan's armies while we are wrestling with temptations. We, the batters, need our spiritual helmets and bats. I will list some rebuilding guidelines. I will start by assuming that a particular pastor or church is not yet functioning with the power and gifts of the Holy Spirit. It might be that your wilderness situation is a result of you not yet arriving at your "place of promise." Do not be embarrassed. We have been there. Pastors, if either you or your church is in the wilderness, first climb up like Caleb and Joshua did. Next, bring your institution to the point of spiritual renewal. That is a foundation requirement if you want to receive the breakthroughs from sicknesses, oppression, depression, fear, spiritual drought and poverty. Do not attempt to get involved in deliverance unless all persons participating have been cleansed as per chapters 7 and 8 of this manual. Otherwise there would be more contamination for the suffering persons. I will list as much information as possible so that weak, wounded or lukewarm shepherds can get confidential assistance so that you can improve on your batting techniques.

CHAPTER 7E. GUIDANCE TO PLACES OF TRANSFORMATION.

There is a new school of thought that is being promoted by Satan (a new doctrine of the devil) as to the gender of God. I even visited a church where the minister, to avoid being labeled a sexist, greeted God as "Father/mother God." An action must occur first before a reaction can be created. A positive entity must first create the action. I do not want to get into a silly gender-debate. God, through His word, advised us that He is our Father. Whether you noticed it or not, females were grafted from the original "E^ts" and placed into the first garden to bear human fruit. When the earth is reconstructed will we need more fruit?

GOD IS ABOVE GENDER! SINCE HE HAS ALL ATTRIBUTES, THIS ULTRA-POSITIVE FIRST ATTRIBUTE IS HYPERPOSITIVE! OK?

This book had been predestined to coincide with an unprecedented time in history when the Gospel would reach the whole world on what Ezekiel described as a flying scroll—Ezekiel 2:9. That preview of satellites beaming broadcasts by cable was also foreseen in Zechariah 5:2-11. Naturally philistine spirits are trying to hinder the "Power" that destroys yokes. Their yokes on cities, families, sleeping temples, synagogues, churches and people will be defeated as "Jehovah Sabaoth" raises up more like David. How in blazes can armies defeat their enemies if they are not teaching their soldiers how to fight? How can armies win battles when their soldiers have very little or no battle experience? How can they defeat sickness, poverty and spiritual ennui if they are not studying the fighting manual and not eating the correct spiritual foods?

There is what started out to be a small 24-hour Gospel TV station in California that used to do a telecast called "Praise the Lord." True to the character of the enemy, as the prophet recorded in Nehemiah 2:9, he sent Tobiah and Sanballat spirits to stop the rebuilding of that television temple. True to God's word, there is really nothing wrong with the composition of the stones. Faulty spiritual workmanship and happy-go-lucky guardians of the altar allowed Satan the first knockdown. Since that TV station has followed the path of Israel's history to the T, and chronicled David's life, I was not shocked to hear that they are having constant battles with "The Spirit of Amalek." The station has come up with an inexpensive way of building satellites. Rather than hustle them, they used them for broadcasting the "Good News." By the time this book is published I will prophesy that they will be all over the world. T.B.N is the name and by the time I conclude this book, I will list their addresses and where you can track their progress. Their coming into being had been prophesied previously by Isaiah. He called their satellite ministry a flying scroll.

What can be done if a person desires complete spiritual transformation? Here are four easy steps toward complete spiritual transformation:

1. Make sure that before you reconnect with any former hell-raisers, that you are receiving good counseling and are attending Holy Spirit-filled churches. Those are churches that "have arrived in their "Promised Lands" spiritually. By their fruits we will know them. Miraculous signs and wonders are taking place in their churches. One must be able to see formerly sick people being healed instantly. Other gifts (not just the ability to speak in tongues) begin to manifest. *Gifts* and *Fruits* are two separate things. Satan will, on occasion, use one of your former friends to attempt to pull you down as he used Sanballat and Tobiah in the book of Nehemiah. He uses friends that are weak spiritually, but strong carnally and "persuasively."

2. Immediately change your lifestyle and the people you used to hang out with, unless those persons are serious about undergoing spiritual transformation also. It is very difficult to attempt to change, if you and someone were living in an unholy union and want to continue doing so after transformation. To attempt transformation together without professional help is forbidden for three reasons: a) A blind person that is seeing for the first time cannot ask a visually challenged person, "Where is so and so?" (b) It is a double prize for the satanic kingdom to grab back; (c) there are too many memories of habits that engulfed you both. Many times persons that overcame spirits of homosexuality, fornication, adultery or addiction (group spirits) receive calls or visits shortly thereafter from friends either still bound or formerly bound purporting to be changed. Treat all such with caution. Some can be wolves in sheep's clothing. Stay close to your counselor until it is time to proclaim your full deliverance, "The Good News." Do not get into any spiritually compromising situations. The sick cannot help the weak.

3. Purchase a Bible or a Tanakh that has the Old and the New Testament. Find out if the town where you reside has 24-hour T.B.N satellite programming; if not, write to them or call 1-888-WANT TBN (1-888-926-8826). 1-714-731-1000 is their 24-hour number with volunteers always ready to pray with and for someone. If you or someone you know is extremely depressed or even suicidal, *CALL THAT 24-HOUR PRAYER NUMBER.* They are very experienced. Call that number first for prayers and get the address of the nearest Holy Spirit-filled church in your area.

4. Contact helpful ministries that have powerful outreach teaching and study programmes:
    World Changers Ministries, 2500 Burdette Road, College Park, Georgia U.S.A. 1-770-996-0450. London 1-44-121-326-9889; www.creflodollarministries. org;
    T.D. Jakes: The Potter's House is listed as 1-800-BISHOP 2 in the U.S.A.
    Victory Outreach Center,
    P.O. Box 277, Hemel, Hempstead, Herts HP2D7 England.
    Leading the Way Ministries; www.leadingtheway.org
    P. O. Box 121, Oxted, Surrey, RH89BP, England.
    Exalted Word Broadcast Ministries 515 Jersey Avenue South, Golden Valley Minnesota 55426 U.S.A. Email: randy@stwc.com;
    Life in the Word Ministries: www.joycemeyer.org;
    Urgent Deliverance prayers: In the U.S.A. call 1-888-BLM-INFO.

If you and all members of your family are attending a powerful church (spiritually) that is teaching the gospel, may God bless you! I must add that I am addressing worst-case scenario situations, people who have been seriously and viciously wounded spiritually. Referencing ancient Israel, they could do nothing against the Pharaoh spirits until God granted them a deliverer. They were still spiritually weak in the wilderness. They were terribly afraid of Pharaoh's armies. Only after they got to the *Promised Land* did a Joshua and a Caleb arise out of the heap. If you refer to the prophetic word as to shortcomings of today's churches (as per John's vision) it will become obvious why God did not say, "Some have sinned" but that "All have sinned and come short of His Glory." This carpenter's spirit level is for strengthening both shepherds and sheep. "The spirits of the prophets are subject to the prophets."

CHAPTER 8. HEALTHY TABERNACLES.

CHAPTER 8A. GUIDE FOR SHEPHERDS!

I have yet to be at a funeral where the person who died was bad. They all somehow "Made it right, just in time." No one but Satan himself could have written that line. Yes we hope they made it. Here is an eternal rule for judge, pimp, pope, prostitute, pastor, drunkard, beggar or big shot: Your score towards the end of the game is what counts! In this life or death game, the winners take all. How your inner beings lived, so they will die. Only at the time of death do many people realize that bodies are temporary vehicles that eventually rot and stink very fast. At funerals, family members and friends reflect on the things they thought were so important in life and realize that in a fleeting moment it is all gone. How many use the death of a friend or loved one as a wake-up call? Most persons leave funerals and go right back to their lives of problematic priorities. If a person functioned in 90 percent error-mode while alive (unless they died to foolishness and were spiritually reborn) they messed up big time.

PURGATORY IS A PLACE IN HELL WITH A NO EXIT SIGN!

Purgatory means everlasting purging! Some have told our research team that their myth of purgatory was hinged on this gospel. I will give all the details so that you can see why I called the foundation mythical. John 5:28-29 reads, "For the hour is coming in which all that are in the graves shall hear his voice, and shall come forth; they that have done good, unto the resurrection of life; they that have done evil, unto the resurrection of damnation." You see why prophets are not liked? We are called by God to speak His mind. Hebrews 12:6 advises us that God chastens those that He loves and scourges every son He receives. David, even though he was king, *danced in the streets* before the Ark of the Lord. Jesus picked fishermen, tax collectors; He ate with publicans. He did not turn up His air-conditioned nose at prostitutes or down-and-out people. He did not snub the Samaritan woman. He did not stay in His own neighborhood preaching to His own kind. God help those preachers that are puffed up because of one or more of *YOUR* gifts—read 1st Corinthians 4:6, 19 and Colossians 2:18.

Of all the Kings that ruled Israel and Judah, after Solomon and David, only one who ruled Israel—Jehu, and four that ruled Judah—Hezekiah, Josiah, Jehohash, and Jehoshaphat, were, for the most part, obedient and pleased God enough to receive a passing grade. Ancient and current Israel had only brief periods of relative prosperity and peace from her enemies. It is logical that persons and institutions that parallel Israel's checkered history are infected similarly. Let us start off with a few hard, no-nonsense details:

1. We are not as intelligent as we think we are.

2. We are not as important as we think we are.

3. Since total wisdom consists of all there is to know and all that can be known, our spiritual and intellectual wildernesses are light years away from all of our promised plateaus.

4. Blind sheep have difficulty finding their way in wildernesses.

5. Blind and lost sheep have little or no chance of surviving without a skilled shepherd.

6. There are wild beasts in every wilderness.

7. Hungry, thirsty, blind and lost sheep are easy prey for lions and bears.

8. It is a horrible experience being torn to pieces by a lion or a bear, especially when one cannot see from which direction the next chomp is coming from.

CHAPTER 8B. THE SPIRIT LEVEL

If your church assembly does the following, it is perfect in the sight of God. You are in the spiritual *Promised Land* and you need to pray daily for all other assemblies to climb up to your standards:

1. Spiritually, you measure up to the spiritual/historical successes of ancient Israel, and

2. At least seven times per year, you and your entire assembly come before the Lord—praying, fasting and commemorating the spiritual aspects of all Israel's sacred festivals and feasts. Israel's ancient and sacred festivals are:
    THE PASSOVER.
    Leviticus 23:5, 14th of the 1st month of the Hebrew year, Abib (March/April).
    THE FEAST OF THE UNLEAVENED BREAD.
    Leviticus 23: 6-8, day after Passover for seven days. 15th of Abib.
    THE FEAST OF WEEKS or PENTECOST (Firstfruits or Harvest).
    Leviticus 23:15-21, sixth of Sivan, (May/June) 49 days from 22nd of April.
    THE FEAST OF TRUMPETS.
    Leviticus 23:23-25, 1st of Tishri (7th month on the Hebrew calendar, September/October on the Roman calendar).
    DAY OF ATONEMENT.
    Leviticus 23:26-32, 10th day of Tishri (September/October on the Roman calendar, 7th month on the Hebrew calendar) usually a day of fasting and atonement.
    FEAST OF TABERNACLES OR BOOTHS.
    Leviticus 23:33-43, 15th-23rd Tishri (7th month on the Hebrew calendar, September/October on the Roman calendar) usually seven days following the *Day of Atonement*.
    FEAST OF PURIM.
    14th/15th Adar (March/April: Esther 9:20-22 & 26-28).

3. Your church board is elected by God and not by men. In other words, when it is necessary to appoint elders and ministries, you pray, fast and seek the wisdom of the Lord in your selection processes. After three days, fast and place the names of candidates in concealed ballots. Put on blindfolds and ask God to select the ones that He wants. That is scriptural my friends. "In all your ways acknowledge Him and He will direct your paths." Many sincere and holy persons that God wants on His Church Boards are daily washing the pastors' cars and taking their children to schools. Lots of them are caretakers of the buildings and are landscaping the church grounds. They teach and encourage the flock by their

exemplary lives. Other members who believe and spread the belief that they are anointed to receive positions of influence overtake such. Remove your own carnal opinions and commit to memory the fact that God's original plan was to establish a Theocracy.

4. All members of your congregation fulfill the provisions of Malachi 3:10.

5. You have a team of intercessors (selected by God) thoroughly and regularly cleansed (spiritually). Intercessory ministry is not a circus; it is the most serious ministry in the church. People who can pray and know how to pray must pray daily, especially for the pastors, elders, your community, nation, and for the peace of Jerusalem. The numbers on the intercessory teams are determined by the size of your congregation. Some have twelve members, others have 50. Refer to Exodus 18:14-26 for guidance on such matters.

6. Your congregation *must* institute a monthly prayer chain, covering elders, intercessors, kingdom purposes, and other ministries that have outreach outposts in dangerous countries. That day is a holy day of prayer and fasting. On the day that you begin the chain, have all persons, pastors, elders, and flock seek forgiveness for sins known and unknown. First read Exodus 19:10-11 and also Genesis 35:2 on spiritual cleansing. Ask the Spirit of the Lord to strengthen the church and ask for fresh revelations. I am more convinced than ever that God has to purge this generation totally for His Theocracy to be established. Pray for all the seed of Esau and Jacob. Pray for peace to prevail in their lands. Prayer for the physical and spiritual restoration of Jerusalem (Psalm 122:6) should be a priority since both destines are inseparable. Pray for wisdom and divine revelation from God for all Arab nations, Africa, India, Pakistan, China, Japan, Russia, Europe, Poland, Central, North and South America, Australia, Scandinavia and all islands of the sea. Pray for the restoration of communities' altars. Pray for the restoration of your countries' altars. Many use this occasion to pray for: a) corporate repentance b) cleansing of the entire congregation, c) setting up mighty armies to march spiritually against certain entrenched principalities and d) to weaken and eventually knock down their foundations. Those you do only when your assembly is restored to its rightful place of spiritual prominence. You cannot fight Philistines if you have not yet overcome lion and bear spirits.

7. Be a part of or plan a local convocation annually.

8. Partake in one or more international convocations.

9. Seek supreme guidance while setting up those ministries outlined in 1st Corinthians 12.

10. Your church must have the spiritual shape of the *Bride of Christ*. Since God has given us teaching aids, no horse-like church or serpent-like church and no giraffe-shaped church will qualify as a church without spot or wrinkle. If your assembly has one elder functioning as pastor, worship leader, teacher, bus driver, and elder, then the tail and the head have the same spiritual shape.

Moses followed God and led the congregation out of the wilderness. Joshua and Caleb followed God and led the congregation into the Promised Land. John announced Jesus' ministry. Jeshua was the foundation stone. 12 disciples were pillars. Another set led by Saul, Philip, Silas and John Mark, were missionaries. God sets the boundaries and limits His anointing for each office. A person trying to fit his body into all those different positions is functioning like a serpent. Then that institution will have a serpent shape spiritually. If one or two persons function as heads, and there are only ushers and worship ministries, no junior pastors, no helps, no intercessors or shoulders, and no hands or outreach ministries—then that church has a giraffe shape, spiritually. Do not confuse zeal with pride. It is about God, not about you: so be very careful with His bride. God is a jealous God.

I am going to take the liberty to list one church that impressed me very much with its numerous ministries, especially with the way that they trained their young people to get involved in ministry work. You can contact them by mail, email or telephone. If you are serious about climbing to higher levels in the Lord, I believe that they have lots of material in their bookstores that can assist you. They also have outreach teaching ministries and convocations. I experienced a mighty move of God on the day that I visited them. As I got out of my vehicle and stepped unto their parking lot (the outer gates of a tabernacle) I felt the presence of the Lord very strong indeed. I told an aircraft engineer friend and his family who were with me that day: "Something serious is being cooked inside spiritually." I was not disappointed. The anointing was so heavy after the pastor stepped unto the "Inner Court" while the choir "tore up" the heavenlies. After 5 minutes, he had to stop to allow the Spirit of the living God to take over. Imagine a pack of dominoes lined up close together and someone blows on one. A spiritual breeze that I am so familiar with blew in that congregation and bodies were falling like dominoes. The pastor didn't even get to touch one. I am talking about the day when I sneaked into World Changers Ministries in Atlanta Georgia, pastored by Dr. Creflo Dollar. I do not think I have seen a corporation so well organized. God, please continue to bless him, his personal family and his spiritual family!

Your church cannot be an isolated church. There is neither discrimination nor sin in heaven. There will be neither discrimination nor sin in the redeemed earth. If you believe that your church is so anointed that you are more correct than anyone else is, that you do not attend any convocations but your own because your self-righteous flock might be tarnished, then:

YOU MIGHT HAVE VERY STRONG RELIGIOUS SPIRITS UNDER THE ALTARS OF YOUR ASSEMBLY.

Forsake not the assembling of the righteous. If you assume that only your church is righteous, then you are presumptuous and you are judging: Matthew 7:1. Does your church assist some charitable organization other than your own and some other missionary outreach with either materials or financing? The kingdom of God is based on sowing and reaping (Matthew 4: 4). Only sowing among your own kind is selfishness. Outreach ministries, whether with printed material, witnessing or preparing labourers for the harvest are ministries that need the most prayers worldwide. The entire body of Christ needs to pray against the spirits of "Amalek," antichrist, anger, persecution and death at least once monthly. If you are in a country that is under bondage and your assembly is serious about reclaiming your national altars, go over the provisions in this chapter and then list your country's situation as "special prayer requests" with the international ministries given in this segment. Those outreach ministries will highlight your plight so that when their members get the priority lists, they will pray for your situations. Inquire about international convocations. If you are financially strapped because of the part of the world that you are in, do not be embarrassed. If God wants you to attend, he will minister to someone to sow that particular seed. Persons ministering in a modern day "Babylon" need to increase their fasting and prayer times.

King David was appointed and anointed to unite the northern and southern kingdoms of Israel. Denominational churches that have their own schools of higher learning need to be watchful of the move of the second hand in God's universal and spiritual clock. Pay attention to the harmonic relationships between God, His kingdom and His redemptive purposes. Observe His seasons and synchronize every faulty mechanism accordingly. Be vigilant and abstain from criticizing sheep. The time is soon approaching when obedient vineyards will merge under the Kinsman Redeemer spiritually.

Seek the wisdom of the Lord: Daniel 10:1-21, Nehemiah 8:1 to18 and Joel 1:13-14. Take into account that it is not your vineyard. Beware of the prophecies of Matthew 7:21-23. God instructed Luke to record an event in Luke 2:41-49. In Mary's loins, every New Testament church was metaphysically represented. Any church that pays more attention to customs, rituals, in short—carnal things, as opposed to *The Word*, will lose the presence of "The Living Word," and have to go back to Jerusalem (the foundation) to find it. Going about the business of your Father (God) should be the main priority of all churches. Learn, live, teach and be *The Word*; then share and sow *The Word*.

CHAPTER 8C. IS THERE A SPECIAL DAY FOR THE LORD?

Every Sunday, Crystal Cathedral sends greetings worldwide: "This is the day the lord hath made, let us rejoice and be glad in it." May God continue to bless you Dr. Shula! Every day is the Lord's Day. From the wisdom of Psalm 19:1-2 and Psalm 24:1, we must honour and pay homage to God daily. During the tenure of the Levitical priesthood, the sixth day, Saturday was observed as the Sabbath day. Today, millions of worshippers keep the same traditions. According to the tradition of the Torah, Saturday is the Sabbath Day and Sunday is the first day, "First Fruits." In Exodus 31:13 The Levites were given these instructions: "My Sabbaths (plural) ye shall keep: for it is a sign between you and me throughout *your generations.*" There are many Sabbaths: *Purim, Jubilee, Firstfruits, and Pentecost.* Why stipulate "your generations?" Obviously, God in His wisdom foreknew that the world's populations would live in different time zones. During the rotation of the orbs, Saturdays and Sundays exist simultaneously. If you are in a part of the world where you elect to consecrate Saturday as your Sabbath, so be it. If you elect to consecrate the first day of the week as both your Firstfruit and your Sabbath day, so be it. After all, it was God that gave Leviticus 23:39's decree: "The first day shall be a Sabbath."

In the days of the Levites, there was one congregation in one time zone. If you want to be legalistic, buy your own bulls and goats and kill them on your altars. You should not be in the Holy Sanctuary unless you have proof that you are of Levitical lineage (1 Chronicles 23:31, 32). In Hosea 2:11, God prophesied that He would cause Israel's feast days, her new moons and her *Sabbaths to cease.* One-issue congregations love to stir up arguments with sheep of different persuasions. God foresaw those and forewarned us not to do such. Romans 14:5, "One man esteemeth *one day above another:* another esteemeth every day alike." Let every man be persuaded in his own mind. Verse 6: "He that regardeth the day, regardeth it unto the Lord." Stop helping Satan to do his work by sowing divisions among God's people. Spend your quality time witnessing to *"The Lost"* instead.

Let us see what the early church decreed about such—Colossians 2:16, "Let no man therefore judge you in meat, in drink or in respect of an holy *day* or of the new moon, or the *Sabbath days.*" Verse 17 needs special scrutiny. It tells us that the Sabbath is a shadow of things to come: Christ became the manifestation of the real Sabbath. Verse 18, "Let no man beguile you…

intruding into things he hath not seen vainly puffed up by his fleshy mind." In other words, if you were spiritual, you would not dabble in "fleshy arguments."

Here are three reasons. a) In Exodus 35: 2, when the Sabbath ordinance was given, it was to the Levites *unto their generations*. b) It was *not* one of the *everlasting ordinances* and c) the law did not specify the first six. "Six days shall work be done." Note there was no mention of which six. It is not written six consecutive days. The emphasis was on the event, the Sabbath, and not the day. Do not get into foolish chronological arguments on such. Whether you count by Roman numerals and rest the seventh sequential day or you work six and rest one, then observe it. In other words, the amount of time you spend gathering what you think is important must not exceed the Lord's apportioned hallowed time. Once it is for righteousness sake, Christ is the end of the Law. Hence he who was "Shabbat" broke and ate the corn on the Sabbath.

The first of thy Firstfruits belongs to the Lord. Leviticus 23:10, the feast of *Firstfruits* was ordained to be observed when they came into "The Land of Promise." It was echoed again in Exodus 40:2. On the *first day* of the first month shalt thou *set up the tabernacle*. God afforded Moses a prophetic peek at the day He wants His tabernacles commemorated. Follow the preview of the breaking of the middle wall. Leviticus 23:15, "Count unto you the *morrow after the Sabbath* from the 'Day' ye brought forth *the sheaf*." In Mark 16:9, the *firstfruit* of the "resurrection" occurred on the *first day*. Thrice, God gave Moses specific instructions that when the Israelites came into their "*Land of Promise*," He wanted Sunday **celebrated forever** as the "New Feast Day:" Leviticus 23:15, 21 and Exodus 40:2. That was confirmed when the first church received the outpouring of the Holy Spirit on Sunday (Acts 2:1-4). In the early churches, they celebrated on Sundays (1st Corinthians 16:1-2, John 20:19-26, and Acts 20:6-12) because they confirmed Exodus 40:2, that the "True" tabernacle was finished. If you are celebrating the letter of the law instead of the spirit of the law, you are in the old tabernacle with the old sacrifices, which did cease.

Why is it that from 1948 to date, "*a remnant*" in Israel (Pentecostal in spirit) celebrates their *Firstfruits'* days on Sundays? Simply, they were obedient to the decree of Leviticus 23:39, and also they built on the foundation of the Jerusalem church. Observe the church at Corinth—1st Corinthians 16:2—those awaiting Paul's ministering for the offering of the Firstfruits to the Lord: "Upon the *first day* of the week..." Sunday was for worshiping the Lord with tithes and offerings. The days were divided into four segments. Each six-hour segment was called "a watch." For tithing the formula is *First* of ten. Prayer and praise days, the formula: *First* of seven. God ordained for himself and accepted *The Better Sacrifice* (Isaiah 53:10) that Paul so brilliantly elaborated on in his letter to the early Hebrew congregation (Hebrews 12:24). The everlasting sacrifice, the Lord's "Chosen Firstfruit," is now commemorated to celebrate the fulfillment of Purim, Jubilee, Passover, Unleavened Bread and Pentecost. I would like to advise you very subtly, that, in the eyes of God, the spirit of the law—Pentecost, has eclipsed the letter of the law. In the final analysis, it is the spirit of Pentecost that will usher in the spiritual—Passover, Unleavned bread, Purim, Jubilee, Booths, and Advent.

Genesis 17:11, the foreskin or first part of the flesh (seed of man or circumcision) was sacrificed as a type and shadow of the "Spiritual Circumcision" required of the Lord in Psalm 50:5; then asked of the Lord in Psalm 50:13 and answered in Hebrews 10:4. A better sacrifice by a better priesthood was commemorated on a *better feast day*. Hence the early churches celebrated the Pentecostal experiences, worshiped, served communion and preached on Sundays. Acts 2:1 recorded, "When the *Day* of *Pentecost* was come." Acts 20:7, "Upon the *first day of the week*, when the disciples came together to break bread, Paul preached unto them."

1st Corinthians 16:2, Paul ordered the churches in Galatia to meet and provide for the needy during their meetings "Upon the *first day of the week.*" In Hebrews Chapters 8, 9 and 10, Paul explains to the entire congregation the *better tabernacle, the better sacrifice*, the *"Better Covenant"* and hence the *"Better Feast Day"* in Acts 20:7. In Hebrews 10:9, it is recorded, "He taketh away the first testament." So if God took away the first testament why would you want to celebrate it (partially) unless you wanted the yoke of the *Letter of the Law?*

I must admit that I have encountered people that are yoked to the letter of the law in my travels; they suffer from spiritual blindness. Is there a message by inference that they have not arrived at "the promised plateau?" Notice how so many scriptures that are simple and clear become incoherent to them? Instead of receiving enlightenment, they offer their (out-of-context) interpretations of completely different scriptures to justify *legalism.* Refer to 1st Timothy 6:3-6 and 2nd Timothy 3:5, "a form of godliness."

The first thing God did was to send "His Spirit" to move away the negative energies of the earth. The message is everlasting. Without God's Spirit moving in anything on this earth, that thing is engulfed by "chaos." If your assembly is still wrestling with such, it is obvious that it has not comprehended the depth of the Hebrew word "Yowme" in Genesis 1:2. Simply put, energy is a force. Earth is the domain of "negative energy and gravity." Noah removed the covering of the ark on the first day—Genesis 8:13. Therefore the day that God's "Power" was returned to man is worth celebrating. As for me, like Noah, Jeshua and His apostles, I am celebrating the "Day" that the "Ark" was revealed—the first day. Next we will examine how God protected branches of His church against the gates of hell.

CHAPTER 8D. BOAST NOT AGAINST THE BRANCHES!

Can you imagine a blossom, a sheaf or a leaf boasting against the trunk of a tree because of its assumed position of prominence on the tree? God prophesied that His church would be grafted. He told us that the root would be of Davidic lineage. So the root was planted in Jerusalem. A branch from that root spread from Jerusalem, through Asia, Northern Africa, then to Rome and beyond its territories. Even though spiritual parasites attacked the lumber, it survived and spread over many lands. Solomon's influence and fame spread far and wide, even though he was far from perfect. Rebekah made substitutions; yet God allowed her seed to flourish with character blemishes. God's law of double-reference is such that the Messiah's house will have spiritual parasites and termites in the lumber also.

After the reign of Constantine, a form of Christianity flourished with the assistance of the most powerful nation in the world at that time, Rome. Corporate vows of poverty, confession, communion, and the *Power of Purim* were the main tools; it lasted seventeen centuries. Then came the season of: "The Just...living by faith" and that ushered in the branches of the organized *Protestant Reformers.* Through the "Power of Praise" came the leaves, the *Pentecostal Movement.* Unfortunately there are inherited parasites, insects, spots and wrinkles.

The church survived, not because it was built on a foundation of some sorcerer named Simone Paeter, but because it was rooted in a tested and proven foundation stone, Jeshua. The spiritual termites came, not through the foundation, but through the grafts and the inherited weaknesses of Solomon when he built the physical prototype. It followed the proliferation path of the seed of Isaac from the womb of Rebekah also. Deceit, theft and many other faults were in Jacob, but God allowed His imperfections because of promises to Abraham and his son Isaac. Likewise looting, deceit, and other transgressions were in those branches of the church; however because of the Covenant of God and His Son, the church had to survive.

Any woman prominently featured in any of Israel's ancient holy books was a prophetic prototype of a future church. Hagar, the servant would mirror a church formed after God had selected His chosen bride. That expression of His body would be in desert regions. The message from the angel was not to form a new religion otherwise the angel would have said:

Leave thy mistress and God will establish you. In Genesis 16:9, the angel said: "Return to thy mistress and submit thyself under her hands." Rebekah's deceit in changing the features and complexion of Jacob would be duplicated in a major church out of the seed of Jacob. It came to pass that a branch of the early Christian church got grafted and transplanted to Rome. Even though God specifically forbade the making of any graven images, the Roman branch changed Jesus' features and pigmentation. Just as Rebekah did, they hid the ethnicity of the Hebrew Messiah. They substituted the features of a relative of a Roman painter who was used as the model for His paintings. God did not interfere with Rebekah's deception then. He has waited some 2000 years for all the dots to be filled in before sending an admonishing prophet to reveal the imperfections. *God cannot be fooled.*

God's Holiest Altar is a solemn place where either the Spirit of God is, or strong evil spirits invade and control. Beware of being demoted for spewing condemning words on God's holy altars—Matthew 7:1. Great shepherds have been rebuked and replaced for doing such in the past. Here are a few examples of some that used God's altar to criticize or to judge His people. God's anger is kindled immediately whenever an exalting self-righteous spirit rises in the person that attempts to take God's place in *His Tabernacle.* The spiritual demotion is certain. In some cases, spiritual or physical replacement follows. Joshua and Caleb replaced Moses and Aaron. Eliakim replaced Shebna in Isaiah 22; Elisha replaced Elijah (after Elijah accused the brethren of abandonment). That sin blocks the anointing, cracks the altars and allows *diseases* to enter the churches. In the book of Acts, no profane hand touched the Lord's anointed before the transgressions of Ananias and Sapphira. After their deliberately disobedient acts, the disciples began to receive *"stripes."* In Isaiah 53, stripes are equated with diseases. As we crack and widen church altars, we crucify Christ all over again. Public transgressions must be cancelled publicly. Repent and rebuke such!

Some churches that celebrate Advent as the main feast day are still awaiting the fulfillment of the Pentecostal experience. Be wise, grieve *Not* the Holy Spirit; fast and seek God's wisdom. Without that power and the wisdom that follows, many of your shepherds and flocks will continue in adultery until the day that I have asked God to reveal all imposters. Some Pentecostal churches are in bondage to sin also. The same warning applies to you.

CHAPTER 8E. INSIDE THE REALM OF NOTHING!
DOMAIN OF THE UNSEEN/UNKNOWN!

This might surprise you; there isn't such thing as "Nothing." Just because something is not known to or by a person, or not visible, does not mean it doesn't exist. Here is a simple exercise. Close one of your hands. Make a fist. Open and look inside. What is in there? Nothing might be visible, however if you took a microscope and looked on the same hand, you would see clusters of bacteria and germs. People, who sneeze, cough and blow their noses in public need to cover their mouths and noses and to wash their hands before eating. I must compliment the Muslims, Jehovah's Witnesses and Seventh Day Adventists for their stringent teachings on cleanliness. Wouldn't it be wonderful if all of God's children would learn to clean themselves generationally, mentally, physically, and spiritually?

Inside the realm of nothing are billions of things. So in the natural, so it is more so in the spiritual. Let us go into a rarely disturbed storeroom. "Traits" can be hereditary. Many blood diseases are inherited. There are numerous spiritually induced ailments, habits and "traits." There was a case recently of a male who looked and behaved in an effeminate manner. He had female *urges*, and even frequented the ladies room. He was convinced that there was a lady trapped in his body. He was almost right. He had female type spirits camping inside. His grandmother adored him as a child. The baby was cute. Grandma left all that she had for the little boy when she died. *All means all.* Physical assets and her spiritual liabilities (traits) also she left him. In such a case the *Familial Spirits* that inhabited the grandmother left her at her death and waited patiently for their chances to invade. Grandma, in that instance died with unrepentant sins. The term "Three strikes" not only applies to baseball but it is a teaching point so graciously elaborated on in Mark 4:37- 41. It would have been a different case altogether had the lad not fallen thrice or if he had lived a spotless life. The mother over-sheltered the very pretty boy growing up. Female-inclined spirits followed him and persuaded the parents to send him to an overseas college. The parents sent him large amounts of monies and the spirits even picked his roommate. Over time, his hands drooped; his voice shrieked; his stance and walk became very effeminate. *Feminine traits developed to such an extent that his gender became questionable.*

I visited another one in a hospital dying of AIDS. After the cleansing and repentance, the demons left him. He had lost his ability to speak; so I asked the Lord if he could signal his obedience by squeezing his belly button so many times for yes. He was a member a legislative branch in a certain country. Without going over the cleansing processes again, the demons came out. I pray to God that he does not succumb again. The last time I saw him, he had climbed from about 70 pounds back to a robust masculine looking man of 190 pounds. Almighty Father, please preserve and strengthen him.

Women and men whose sexual urges run counter-clockwise should be able to trace the sources easily. Usually it was a first opportunity transfer of body fluids in disobedience to one of God's Holy laws punishable by death. There was either a direct exchange with someone that had the "traits" or by someone with spiritual openings, immediately after a second or third generation passage, just after a grandparent (of a different gender) died.

Grounds for those swift transfers include three strikes of atrocities along with transfers of unrepented sins of parents. Those abominations include indulgence in witchcraft, sorcery, adultery, incest, abortion, fornication, rejection, "unforgiveness," homosexuality, lesbianism, and rape. Rape and adultery during pregnancy are very dangerous and expose the unborn child to serious spiritual complications. Tons of so-called crib deaths are demonic attacks that mothers had been too weak spiritually to fend off. Victims in the last category that find themselves in those predicaments, need to find a church, knowledgeable in deliverance ministering, to pray for the repairing of all spiritual damage immediately.

I had a case recently where the first three openings were pounced upon so quickly. There was a person in a leadership position in a church. The person and her spouse had broken up.

I do not know what is meant by the term "broken up" when the word of God declares that "two" shall become one flesh. At birth the mother gave her baby a ring from one of Satan's publicity-seeking agents. The ring, supposedly could ward off bad luck. If it could ward off bad luck, why not ward of Satan from their personal altars. Remember the game of Chess? Satan will sacrifice a few pawns to get a king or a Bishop. In the mind of this formerly religiously-confused person, a suitor was seen who appeared to be a good replacement for the spouse. Temptation led to masturbation (strike two) and then, "What the heck, we will get married anyway." I did not ask the Spirit of the Lord, what the last strike was regarded as, whether fornication or adultery. That was one of those cases whereby the religious person had asked me to assist with prayer for a close friend. I, Caleb, was supposed to be the support to that person, who would have been a Joshua. I make no exceptions: whenever I pray with anyone, we must humble ourselves before the Lord and then spiritually cleanse all concerned. If you are going to be offended, do not call me to pray for or with you. God's word says that all have sinned and fallen short. If you offend in one, you sin in all. Lo and behold the quantity of demons that manifested and left the Elder baffled me. When I finally approached the person we went to intercede for, the nightmares that she was having were related to generational and personal blemishes. Nothing except generational curses, (which were in the realm of oppression) surfaced. They only became noticeable in the so-called hard luck she was experiencing. She has now become Holy Spirit-filled and is a spiritual intercessor in the same church as the Elder.

Ironically, I had a later appointment that day to deal with a severe cancer case and had intended to ask that Elder to be my backup. I got so angry with Satan. I asked the Lord to stand with me as I treated the next case as Elijah did against the "Prophets of Baal." I made two phone calls first to get assistance. Both were busy. I really needed an intercessor. According to procedures in the scriptures, wisdom dictates that you go into battle with at least two. In an emergency, use this scripture, "I will never leave you or forsake you!" I did that as I claimed Jesus' authority and proceeded to acquire one of the great victories for Jehovah Sabaoth. That victory was especially sweet for several reasons:

1.   It was the day that Christians commemorate Jesus' death, the Day of the Passover when God remembers His greatest victories.

2.   Just after I made the second phone call, an impish mischievous-looking evil spirit appeared outside the phone booth with a message from its disrespectful boss: "You think because of what just happened you are tough? You really think you are hot stuff? We have 50,000 waiting for you at the next battlefield!" One thing I must say is that they know the scriptures. However they dare not quote the scriptures the way they are written! They are very good at misquoting and twisting scriptures to attempt to fool the altar-damaged. That is the reason I am so concerned that Satan has used those False-Christ Spirits and "False Prophets" mentioned in 1st Corinthians 15:15 and 2nd Corinthians 11:13.

It is written that one shall chase a thousand, and two shall put ten thousand to flight. If you are a young warrior, stay within the ranks of the Roman numeral format. When I ask my God for 10 million, as long as I am willing and confident enough to face the counter-attacks that will undoubtedly result and to overcome them, then God will strengthen me. So I told the little imp, "Go tell Satan that he had better have, not 50,000 but one million. I will not battle him for anything less." I started warming up with warring prayers. The righteous indignation swelled within me.

I began to increase speed on the highway. Twice I escaped serious accidents. The imp was running in front of my vehicle, appearing and disappearing as if purposing to distract me. I stopped. "Tell me," I inquired, "If you and your gang were so confident with your 50,000 and I challenged you to up the battle force to 1 million, why are you trying to wreck me before the battle even begins? Wouldn't you all like to get a piece of me? Loudly I proclaimed, "One million or nothing!" I slowed down to a crawl and looked up to my boss and had a private inaudible conversation. What did I say? "Heavenly Father, this victory is yours. This is the deal, all or nothing. I want one million of his best, including those that have the worship leader in bondage!" The rest of the conversation I will not print. That was either the easiest or the second easiest victory I witnessed for my Boss. Within five minutes after cleansing, the destruction and spiritual carnage were awesome.

Ask the lord to cancel unresolved conflicts. Always take full authority, and negate the destructive capabilities of all surrounding evil spirits, in addition to those entrenched in the embattled. Also cut off their abilities to communicate with, and to get assistance from their sources. I sent legions to witness. Why not? The scripture says, "Every knee shall bow, and every tongue shall confess that Jesus is Lord;" so I took full authority in the one name that terrifies all demons and commanded them to proclaim Jeshua's Lordship forever.

Two days earlier, the worship leader's church had a "Going Home" service for her. The last thing they told her: "Prepare to meet your maker with courage." I have no problem with that, but since we are assured three score and ten, I promised my Boss (above) that testimony to bring her congregation higher in faith. Within one week, her weight was restored; all the cancer was gone. She not only got back her job but received a promotion also. Imagine the talk in the streets. The person that was written off—she walked into church the next Sunday. Silence reigned. Were they seeing an apparition? While they were still gaping, she took the microphone from the pastor and sang a sweet song for her Lord. I was told there was not a dry eye in the congregation. Father, please strengthen her in the name of your precious Son and Redeemer. Those that teach about "Purgatory for the Dead" and "Security of the Believer" need to fast and seek the wisdom of the lord. Read John's "Book of Revelation" to see which one of the churches you fit into. After you have read John 5:29-32, call all of your elders and do the same exercise after serious cleansing. Every promise is conditional.

There is no such thing as bad luck or hard luck. Luck is an abbreviation for Lucifer. He has the right and he uses it well, to block:

1.   Your access to the Father because of unrighteousness as per Psalm 1:5.

2.   Your blessings as per Zechariah 3:1.

3.   Your health by inflicting you with sicknesses—Exodus 23:25, Matthew 4:23, and Job 2:7.

4.   Your prosperity because of your sins and your parents/ grandparents sins, going back four generations—Exodus 34:7. In fact before you begin, read Proverbs 28:13.

Pastors/Elders I am going to forewarn you. It is inevitable that one day while praying for a person or persons that demons or evil spirits will manifest. It must happen as long as you are sanctified and you are living a sinless life. On the other hand, if you are living a secretly sinful life, one day while pretending on the pulpit, your secret demons will manifest. It will happen. You know why? God is sick and tired of persons desecrating His altars. The habits you display identify the type of spirit or spirits that control you. Every one of your ungodly habits are not only seen (Psalm 139:7-12) and known by God, but to His prophets as well and they manifest in your eyes and in your "Personalities and Traits."

Every time you look into the eyes of a prophet of God, he or she discerns your *filthy habits*. I will call a solemn prayer and fast worldwide to purge God's altars. I will allow a specific period after the publication of this manual. God, I am asking you for a spiritual fireball, an anointing so powerful to root out imposters and double-minded hypocrites: "*You are on borrowed time, so you better repent and seek spiritual assistance from your habitual and presumptuous sins as in Psalm 19:9-13*." I have already inserted some 24-hour numbers where you can get professional help. Should God allow the heavens to open up to permit you a peek into the spiritual domain by witnessing deliverances, here are some ground rules: 1) The process you can speak about. 2) You are to secure the same respect for the person's privacy as a banker does for your private business. 3) The Testimony is for the relieved person to give; it is not to be forced. A testimony can be as brief as, "Thank you God. I was seriously lost and Jesus' sacrifice set me free." That seals your healing and your deliverance my friends. The scriptures proclaim:

"YOU ARE REDEEMED BY THE BLOOD OF THE LAMB AND THE WORDS OF YOUR TESTIMONY. LET THE REDEEMED OF THE LORD SAY SO."

Do not be ashamed when you give your testimony. Many of the toughest pastors on the battlefields had been "Sauls," transformed to Pauls, myself included. Rejoice; be not ashamed when you receive your victory; then you can declare like I do, "I bear witness!" Joel 2:28, "I will pour out my spirit on all flesh." Set up private offices where your deliverance teams can be isolated. Have all participants fast first. Most types come out only with prayer and fasting. Treat all situations as "These types." When you dig deep enough you never know what will surface, especially in the ancestral and generational curses' categories. Some you can see like AIDS. Most look healthy on the outside. You can't tell a book by its cover unless your "Gift of Discernment" is fully developed. Pastors, set those ground rules in place immediately.

All disclosures and conversations released within deliverance sessions must be washed away immediately with the past sins. Under no circumstances can any pastor, member of your deliverance team—or congregation for that matter—discuss what took place during a deliverance session except in general terms *only*. One may share the experience with another member of the team that may have been absent: otherwise woe, serious woe to you. That is very important. There is now no condemnation to those that are in Christ Jesus.

CHAPTER 9. FOUNDATION OF THE LEANING TOWER!

As tempted as I am to include the symbiotic relationship between *The Leaning Tower of Pisa* and the spiritual Odyssey of its home nation, wisdom and space constraints have overruled such. Instead I will document the spiritual blueprint of a much earlier and even more enigmatic structure in this volume—first the nation.

CHAPTER 9A. A MIRROR CALLED ISRAEL

The country called Israel sits on a mantelpiece (the tip of North Africa) like a mirror on an old piece of furniture. In that mirror, the lives of people, parents, countries and institutions can be found. In spite of everything, our ancestors survived eras. Thank God for the living evidence in survival called Israel. The country is a schematic, a tri-dimensional mirror. In her you can find triumphs and defeats for self, institution and your nation. Behind the little medicine cabinet at the back is where all the goodies are. Many natural mirrors sit on termite-infested furniture. People look into their mirrors daily. How many see the termites? Similarly, it matters not what your name, rank or country of origin is; like Israel, before God called you, in your vessel dwelt strange personalities. There will be perennial battles for the ultimate control of your turf. They will always feel that because they once invaded your dwelling places, they have legal rights to be there. They will challenge you until the end.

I get very nervous when I hear extremists on both sides of the Palestinian/Israeli conflict trying to bend religion as a basis for their arguments. 3500 years ago when Moses documented his now famous thesis, he had no idea what would transpire today. So when God ordained that Hagar's prayer for help should be answered because of the lad Ishmael, it meant that *Hagar's womb held no "spiritual brides" for posterity.* Ishmael was not authorized to carry messianic seed. Recently in Palestinian journals, writers were playing into Satan's hands by arguing that if Jehovah gave Israel the right to occupy the land, then Allah gave them their right. Abraham insisted on buying the land (the field and the cave) to bury Sarah. Nevertheless, there is one God of Abraham, Isaac, Moses (or Musa) and He is the same God that Prophet Mohammed sought for guidance. The same God granted Prophet Mohammed the fulfillment of his promise for a theocracy. To invent a national god by whatever name to justify a position and to challenge Jehovah (or Allah who by the way is the same God) on that premise is a certain recipe for disaster. I have included my advice as to the proper way that the conflict should be settled: *Get Satan out of the conflict and negotiations.* I will explain in detail later on.

East, west, north and south are specific geographic directions. Since east and west, north and south are directional opposites, where is Middle East in relation to west? Why are most countries in the Middle East in the north latitudes and west longitudes? Take Israel as an example. Israel lies between 31 to 33 degrees north and 34.5 to 35.5 degrees west approximately. Israel and Egypt are situated on the northeastern tip of the continent of Africa, a country that is almost twice the size of the United States of America. Occidental news networks insist on referencing those regions as belonging to the Middle East unless the situation is Muslim-related and negative, then they will say: North African regions.

*THERE IS NO GEOGRAPHICAL POINT CALLED **MIDDLE** EAST.*

Most of the cartographers, historians and most of the "Ologists" have concealed that fact. At one time, every continent on earth was connected to Africa. In other words, before the continents began sliding away on conveyor belt types of foundations. After the original mass called Pangaea settled, the plates continued their slow withdrawal processes until we arrived at our Fifth Yowme or (fifth tectonic epoch). Place a tablecloth on a flat surface and then afterwards push slowly towards the middle; watch peaks and valleys appear. Note the consistency of The Creator. People on earth are the same. At one time before the melting of polar ice, we all looked alike and lived in the same neighborhood. People drifted away into far lands, married into strange cultures and served other gods. That parallels the history of Israel: one family into a mixed multitude, from captivity into a nation of promise. Today we have arrived at a tangible place of promise called country, denomination or family. Those are locations of promise. We can use the schematic to gauge our journeys. Are we in bondage (mind/body/spirit), wilderness, outside the tabernacle, in the Promised Land, or finally into the Holy of Holies? Let's face it, many will die and have already died in wildernesses. Right spirits are already stolen. God already foreknew that and spoke it through His servants. Job 4:21, "They die even without wisdom." Proverbs 10:21, "The lips of the righteous feed many but fools die for want of wisdom."

CHAPTER 9B. TEACHING TOOLS

People seem to be obsessed with *seeking after false gods*: cocaine, the right man, the right woman, the right secure future, the right neighborhood and the right *"Ology, Osophy and or Ism."* Whoever you are, whatever you have adapted as your moral code, examine the foundation; examine its ancestral altar. Does it gel with God's schematic? Does your spiritual structure fit *plumb* to the chief cornerstone?

RELATIONSHIPS MIRROR.

Let us focus on our individual paths. Israel's *Judges* of antiquity represent the different types of relationships that were supposed to lead us to happiness. There were many one-night stands and altar defilers. Led astray in ignorance, consciously or not, and driven by ancestral and generational blindness, conquerors were really the blind leading the blind. This is not the time for throwing blame. Just as Israel survived captivity and genocide, other generations have survived the barrages of war and famine. The northern and the southern kingdoms were carried away for four hundred years as prophesied. The southern kingdoms scattered around Masada and Qumran fled and were absorbed into the Ethiopian, Nubian and other southern countries. True to prophecies, they were enslaved and shipped to The Caribbean, Brazil, Suriname and America as per Deuteronomy 29:28 and Deuteronomy 30:1-3 among others. There are some deep concealed things that I will not touch on here, but later on. Seed of Judah and others (ignorant of their mighty past) search bars, brothels, and sample many mates trying to find their missing ribs. The same way modern hotels re-programme their door locks, unless you are "spiritually born-again," You will sniff like dogs and die in frustration looking for your missing bones.

A lot of us—the scattered of *The Occident*—call ourselves Americans, Europeans etc., are really enslaved in a land of spiritual captivity. Israel became a nation in 1948. Pluto was officially recognized in 1948 as the newest "Revealed Light," hence the term, "New Age." The first Jubilee for the new nation was 1998. Enter the "Shabbat or Dawn of the Age of Wisdom or Aquarian Age." Everyone alive from 1998 is in a position to break the dreaded yokes that have been ignored, concealed or inflicted. If your altars have been conduits for the armies of darkness, heed this urgent warning. In 1967, after the Six-Day War, we saw an outpouring not only of the Spirit of God but also a period of unprecedented disrespect for the human temple. The kingdom of darkness had progressed in conceit and cockiness from its years of uninterrupted expansion, especially with the help of agenda-controlled mass media and weak spiritual teachers. Naturally, when the Internet was born Satan unleashed his army of demons using the speed and ease of the computer to disperse his confusion and filth.

MIRRORS FOR HUSBANDS.

The kings who ruled Israel represent the types of husbands out there. You can examine them all. Every married man that exists or has ever lived matches either a king or Judge that ruled Israel. Some turned their backs on their families. Some served other gods: sports, gambling, booze, drugs, money and harlotry. Then there are the ones like David. They are gorgeous, attractive, basically good and caring, have their faults but take good care of home. However you can only count on their presence in personal family matters, on occasions such as births or deaths of offspring. Like David, they rally all family members only at weddings, baptisms, national festivities and funerals.

MIRROR OF THE PERFECT HUSBAND.

There were and are the fortunate few. They repair and strengthen all family altars. They are caring spiritual pillars and are always contented. They can take five barley loaves with two fishes and set up a livelihood to feed family and many others with plenty left over. They are not egotistical or self-righteous but worship their Father in heaven. They love their wives the way Jesus loves His flock. They love their family the way Jeshua loves His disciples and flock. They follow Jesus' example of rebuking those that need rebuke. They live and lead by example. They become the best teachers, prophets and providers. Jesus healed the sick, lame and blind. Perfect husbands will teach their families to abstain from watching things that deliver spiritual blindness. They will teach them to eat the right foods and to live clean spiritual lives, so that their spiritual temples may become spotless and healthy.

MIRROR FOR EVERY MAJOR DOCTRINE?

Whenever God sends inspired writings, they must be able to confirm truths, shatter myths and offer fresh revelations. If this discourse is one such, then as we progress, we will mirror major doctrines to see what God is revealing. I need to state a principle without giving any (what could be called) esoteric secrets to people who jump on God-ordained wisdom to advance their demonic domain. Humankind's perception of carnal things is usually tri-dimensionally computed through length, width, and height. To represent anything spherical (well rounded on all sides and balanced) on a flat surface, we use a tri-dimensional formation called a pyramid.

"The Holy Trinity" appears to be an attempt (not necessarily accurate) to explain that concept carnally. That would be fine if the God of Abraham, Isaac, Moses and Mohammed could be restricted to any dimension. Is God limited? Is God only tri-dimensional or is He omni-dimensional? The problem with the Trinitarian doctrine is that it subtly tries to calculate and sectionalize an incalculable God who has such magnitude and limitless power. Iraneus and all the early "Church Fathers" rebuked the theory and challenged it in its infancy. Here are some other labels from early erudite Christians: "Heresy," "Doctrine of demons" and "a borrowed pagan doctrine." Except for two possible references (from Latin to English only and not in the Hebrew or Greek texts) did we find any witness of Jeshua referencing anything that could be classified as such. Is there any precedent in the Tanakh? In one of the final chapters, we will examine the doctrine of the Trinity from a spiritual, not an emotional perspective. From this schematic, all spiritual doctrines can be mirrored also.

SPIRITUAL MIRROR.

Whenever persons are lost, inadvertently they become disoriented. In some instances, a compass might help. There is a more powerful compass than our physical one. People tend to ignore the spiritual ingredient in our equation of balance. Much emphasis is placed on finances, gyms, diets, and tangible things. Some even wonder why, with their lovely jobs, money and "good looks" they are not happy. Many of those types take pills to wake up, pills to sleep, pills to relax, and their moods are determined by variables like the performances of stock markets. Movies are entertaining. However if we mirror our lives after movie stars and their fictional story characters, we are in deep trouble: numerous actors/actresses receive regular therapies. Facts are that we live in unbalanced societies. A false god does not a happy person make. I care not if the calf is as fat as Mount Everest and the gold is 2400 carat, a golden calf is a golden calf. We may be happy for a while, but then we go through the cycle of round and round the mulberry wilderness. Our selfishly isolationist pursuit of carnal joy is temporary, superficial and incomplete. How many times people ask, "What happened to 'So and so' that seemed so happy? They had everything; what could have caused such a fine family to break up? What could have caused such a solid person to lose it?" Satan and his armies specialize in breaking down our walls, our families and our altars. Some reading this might be saying, "I am OK and I am very happy." However, in every game of chess there are two players. One must win and the other has to lose. If you can see tomorrow, or next year, know for sure what's in your body or what spirit or spirits control you, then you are all right. If not, someone has to win and someone has to lose.

MIRROR OF A PERFECT WIFE!

I can picture the men right now saying what about the women: what about them? We need to read the entire Book of Esther; study the qualities of Naomi. Most men are looking for a lovely garden, well watered with flowers, orchids, fruits, birds and bees. The best gardens are the ones that you reconstruct together. There is a before and after reconstruction phase. Behind the rubble of many women are fine temples with blessed vineyards, flowering gardens, and most importantly altars that can be rebuilt most beautifully with the help of "The Perfect Potter." Men, search for the altars first with your spiritual eyes. I operated a bar for years. I have heard the lament of dejected men, as their search for "The Ark" netted an arch (shaped like a lobster); they sounded pitiful. The scripture says, "Seek ye first the Kingdom of God and His righteousness and everything else will be added thereafter." What stage of Israel's history are you? We should be at a point of self-scrutiny and introspection, not condemnation. Some are even saying that is not fair. Oh no? Show me a fairer, consistent system? It is not my fault that you did not use the gauge. It has been there for a long time. You might be suffering from emotional or spiritual disorientation. At this juncture, you are to discern: what caused it and why you got disoriented. I can answer that with the word, "Disobedience:" (of self), your parents, your grand parents, and your great grand parents before that. The spiritual energies that follow cause constant restlessness in lives, sleep and attitudes. Spiritually untrained minds often say—such a person has hard luck, is accident-prone or sickness-prone. It boils down to where you are spiritually and why. I do not need to fill these pages with sweet sounding hypotheses; all we have to do is to make charts of our lives, those of our ancestors, and then use the history of the ancient Israelites as our guides. The best charts I have found are prophetic warnings etched over 3500 years ago translated as Deuteronomy chapters 27 and 28. Let's be fair: a perfect wife should have a perfect husband. This book outlines to you, your spouse and all in your family, the tested and proven "Way to Perfection."

MIRROR OF OUR FOUNDATIONS.

Let us gauge from the present to the past—when you and/or your parents were standing on preserved altars—through to the gradual and subtle shifting foundation, until the altars had been damaged either by you, you parents, or your parents' parents. Now pay close attention. You might say that the altars in your family have never been corrupted or stolen. Do you know what transpired over 280 years ago in both your ancestral backgrounds? Exodus 34:7 tells us that the iniquities (gross injustices and habitual sins) of the parents fall unto the children and children's children (up) to the third and fourth generations.

By deduction, we already established that everyone in our families within the past 300 years had been in 90 percent error mode. Our guards had been inattentive, drunk, weak or absent. There are persons reading this that are already in the process of passing on traits to their offspring. By the habits they display, their traits are discernible. In an epoch where most people are not able to see the thief but he can see us, those types of behaviour translate into carelessness of the highest order. If none of the aforementioned infractions have occurred in the spiritual mosaic of your families' history, see which of the following categories you fit into:

1. Your altars are so heavily guarded for 24 hours that you are untouchable. In over twenty years of research, I am inclined to believe there are only two places on earth, where many of the assumed stolen or destroyed volumes of antiquity are. One is known; however the other one is spiritually guarded by generations (remnants of Lost Tribes) who fast and pray daily. They will not be reconciled until the end of time, fulfilling a prophecy, "…Those not of my flock." If you are one of the aforementioned, may God continue to bless you!

2. Your altars are already stolen. You are in bondage. Deliverance is needed.

3. You are in a constant spiritual battle, but you, your parents, and your children after you are winning and will win. Like Israel you await the Promised Zion.

4. You are an Amalek, a Jebusite, or a Perizzite. God and men/women of God know your secret enclaves. Your script, like that of Judas, had been written long ago. It makes no sense for me to ask God to help your souls, so I will not waste my prayers. Some time in the future, I will look over the great divide, when I see you in your place of damnation

and everlasting torment. It would be the like watching a horror movie with one exception.

Your torture will not end! The persons that fit category 4 are totally demonized. They have sold their souls to crooked brokers that offer no refunds. They have made blood covenants and really need serious confidential help. Since the spirits that control them have multiple personalities, they must be serious about getting help. Call one of the 24-hour ministries that have experience in "cult deliverance" and let them handle such cases.

5. You are in a wilderness. ***This book is dedicated to you.***

CHAPTER 9C. FROM THE TILT TO THE SHIFT!

There was a time in the recent past (of persons reading this) when either they or their parents had certain codes of conduct about what their mouths did or emitted, what their minds dwelt on, what their bodies did or did not do and or what their eyes looked at. Those principles (codes of conduct) pulled many people through tough times when technically they should have starved to death. By the grace of God, they and their families forged a decent living. God wasn't simply a "swear-word" in the house, but a redeemer to respect and to worship. Those people knew who they were and where they came from. Their parents, like ancient Israel, encouraged them with such words: Remember and forget not. Every family had a Code of Ethics or a shortened form of The Code of Hamurabi, The Ten Commandments, Apostles Creed, Muslim Creed or things very similar and appropriate. Parents taught and used them to strengthen families' altars.

Years ago, a child (overhearing adults talk about what is acceptable to society) asked another, "Who is society?" In those days children dared not ask grown people about the business of grown-ups. The other child replied. "Those are the children of the slaves, the railroad workers and the poor migrants that have grown up and have replaced the Indians." Why so asked another? The first one replied, "They all want to be chiefs." Somewhere in the words of the previous sentences lie the foundations to most of the problems in America and the roots of perennial defilement to the majority of our nation's altars.

There were once Spartans, Trojans, Romans, Visigoths, Saxons, Normans and Celts etc., etc. America is not mentioned prophetically in any of Moses' books except in code: Ten toes of the beast in the book of Daniel and a fierce nation from the north that will invade and make Iraq/Iran a desolate waste with smart bombs: Jeremiah 50 and 51. Believe it or not, the historic paths of all the major nations on earth today have already been foretold. The script has already been written. Babylon was once *the only super power*. So were Persia, Russia, Rome, England, France, Spain, Holland and Germany. Is it coincidental that all super powers enslaved seed of Abraham and worked them without pay for hundreds of years?

HERE IS A SERIOUS WARNING TO THE STATE OF ISRAEL. ANY AGREEMENT PUT TOGETHER BY A LEAGUE, WHICH COMPRISES SEVEN INTERNATIONAL ORGANIZATIONS AND TEN NATIONS, WILL SPELL SERIOUS DOOM.

Refer first to Daniel 2:44—after that, verse 34—and then Revelation 17:7. No religion which does not link to the promises of *Abraham and his seed* has an altar worth stealing. Their altars already belong to "The Thief." That is as diplomatic as I can put it. Have no fear: at the appointed time, all darkness/disobedience will disappear on the decreed "Day."

There needs to be graphic illumination about some ancient altars:

1.   THE ALTARS OF INDIAN ANTIQUITY.

2.   THE ALTARS OF IMMIGRANT DISCOVERY.

3.   THE ALTARS OF SLAVERY.

As we glide through the archives of history, we should observe that one of Satan's success-ful weapons has been to separate us from our past. God kept instructing all of His prophets to keep His observances, to put His festivities into remembrance and to forget not the past. Since God kept reminding us not to forget our past and we glibly state "the more things change the more they remain the same," the solution is simple. Document our victories, extract the formu-lae used for our successes, scrutinize our losses and eliminate causes ranging from continuous family tragedies to poverty.

The material selected for our educational systems and for our libraries need to be exam-ined and upgraded closely to see if there has been deliberate or accidental tampering. Errors that keep repeating themselves over and over again cannot be accidental.

CHAPTER 10. ANCIENT ALTARS FROM WHENCE THE BREACHES?

CHAPTER 10A. THE GRAIL SEEKERS

New stones are made from aggregates daily. Naturally *formed stones* are ancient. In the Occident, cities were built with old stones and some old buildings are constructed with recycled stones. Since the ancient Babylonian Empire was destroyed, all the nations that sprang from its loins have similar traits. Let us examine the American altars of Antiquity. There was an ancient America before the birth of modern America. There is also an ancient landmass called Africa whose northern coasts were the centers of much trade, commerce, and pyramid buildings, out of whose loins Israel and most Arab nations were born.

Ask most American children and they will tell you that in 2001, America was 225 years old. Yet, if you go to the Appalachian Mountain regions or any location where original people are confined, Lunar or Stellar epochs come into play. Native American calendars reflect the years of their modern "Egyptian" captivity. Early missionaries had documented the prayers of Native American converts that held hands and prayed to Jehovah Sabaoth during the Lenten season of 1836 as their villages were unjustly burned. 40 days later Mexican General Lopez (Santa Anna) came in like a whirlwind and massacred all, including their main adversary, Davy Crockett, at Fort Alamo on March 6th, 1836. Today an adverse weather pattern and a city in California "Santa Anna" are named after Lopez.

Let us separate America into two tribes: indigenous and immigrant. The indigenous society was part of what we call *hunter/gatherer*. Their societies were structured differently. The *priestly class* was responsible for the altars, sacred ceremonies and remained separated from the rest. The calligraphers reported to the magi and only they (wrote/etched) the sacrosanct data. When Moses departed and stayed too long, the people were ignorant of what was required for altar bonding. The untrained neophytes desecrated the altars and *built golden calves*. Spirits of theft, deception, ingratitude, rape and murder invaded improperly guarded altars. Hence we must scrutinize the altars of America for invasions also.

The first immigrants to America (an impoverished people) were offered a place to stay. They were given permission to kill a few buffalo. They introduced those same spirits on an altar called "Discovery." Each wave of immigrants brought friction and conflicts. The railroad immigrants invented a prophet. He had no lineage with David and no lineage with Abraham. He did not go up into a mountain to receive his commandments. *His were sent down.* That prophet was polygamous. His devotees first reported that their source tablets or "Laws" were in one type of metal. Years after, some of their members or groups of members disputed the source material. A conclusion could not be arrived at as to the metallic structure of the tablets. So the group split into two factions: those that held that the original tablets were in brass and those that held that the original tablets were in gold. God gave us an insight into the nature of the deceiver. "He has come to rob, kill and to destroy." Whenever the name of Jesus is mentioned or attached to any church, automatically one is to assume that it is a Christian church. In 1ˢᵗ John 2:18 and 19 a false "antichrist" spirit is described. This schematic is designed to draw a spiritual line in the desert to give all adepts the same choices Joshua gave to the ancient congregation. Choose one way or the next. Spirits easily glue to corrupted altars. Altars that do not gel with the history of Israel nor that fit the schematic in the womb of Rebekah, you can discern to whom they belong.

CHAPTER 10B. HALLOWED EVE

Enter the Grail Seekers! That group will be touched on lightly in this chapter. They, like most secret groups, have a foundational riddle. Their riddle is a coded message held under their foundation door. They were to pursue the Holy Lance that slaughtered the "Sacrificial Lamb." They linked with other brethren that embraced the "Right by Might Doctrine." According to their secret oaths: "They must desire to be appointed to all positions of leadership and power;" in other words, "Us before them." "Us-a-crats" wrestle with "Them-o-crats" the same way that the lion and the unicorn wrestle for the crown or pinnacle of power. The spirit that propels the unicorn, highlighted by Daniel, is always able to justify its spiritual feasts, called wars. It is even able to beguile Christians into believing that if people can be classified as evil or inferior, their demise is justifiable. I will list the plight of some powerful nations of yesteryear that reaped the punishments from a righteous God that does not discriminate against any of His children.

The gentry of the "Grail Seekers" were directed to search for and inhabit lands with "High Spiritual Energies" and to subdue them. Special maps showing "Ley-lines" were printed and distributed to their members only. They were to trade among their overseas brethren in establishing their kind as "Man" and the other kinds as three fifths of a man. By that classification, when America's Declaration of Independence was written proclaiming, "All men equal," provisions were already made as to who they considered as men. Anyone considered a traitor to the cause should be put to death. Anyone of "Their kind" that crossed the border whether by marriage, fair wage or trade, was a traitor and therefore an "Infidel." Their European counterparts used the same premise to obtain a decree from Pope Fernan Martins 5ᵗʰ in the early 16ᵗʰ century (1513) to expel the Jews "Back to Africa" where they came from. Several of their members had large sugar plantations. History records that they needed cheap labour. A remnant of ancient Israelites, (mainly of the tribes of Simeon and Judah) fled to the south when Jerusalem was invaded in the 1st century and settled in Coastal Africa. Those, disobedient of their decrees not to forget their past and their God, ended up enslaved for 430 years. Hundreds of thousands ended up into the nets of the seed from which their ancestors had previously escaped years earlier. The prophecy that many will be held captive in the west was therefore fulfilled. The abundance of blood and sexual liquids available—under the guise of "slavery"—enlarged the altars of occultism. Thrones and Dominions accompanied the spirits of adultery, sorcery, fornication, rape and murder in those times. Those are now heavily concealed under numerous altars in America.

During the 24-Hour period called Halloween, stores (some serious and know what they are doing) others simply following marketing trends, sell altar-enhancing objects. During those seasons, children dress, play with—and some actually touch—occult things/dolls. Numerous unsuspecting and unguarded lives are endangered later on. Books about magic and sorcery are aggressively marketed as children's fantasies. Are they really? Not a few of the so-called innocent characters are actually full of goblin and dwarf spirits. When moviemakers depict them flying on brooms and casting spells, don't you think that those occult-affiliated movie moguls and bookmakers know what they are doing? What is the concealed message behind the pied piper? Satan has many Piped! I have cast out spirits of oppression (in affluent neighborhoods) that had hatched unto supposedly innocent dolls. About a year ago, a lady kept getting horrible nightmares whenever she slept in her child's room. She would awake suffocating and sweating profusely. She was advised to sell the house. I was invited to visit the house. As I entered the door, I sensed a frightened spiritual force. In the bedroom was a supposedly innocent doll received at Halloween.

I have since encountered similar and more terrifying incidents than the one with the Halloween doll. Parents need to be cautious and wise. There are millions of innocent toys, cloth and rubber dolls depicting genuinely innocent characters. However, anything connected to magic or occult symbols (festivals or seasons) is fair game. The eve of Halloween is not placed around All-Souls' night accidentally. It is hallowed for Lucifer.

CHAPTER 10C. GET THE CHIEF, GET HIM!

In a certain American state with an ugly foundation altar, you can carry a gun almost anywhere in the state except into a federal building or on an airline; yet their laws prohibit the reading of a Bible in a public school. Once, an Attorney General's wife called the press in anger "to spill the beans." We remember the Martha Mitchell incident. She was bound and gagged in her hotel room. No arrests were made. American Presidents that have been classified as "Traitors to the Cause" have been assassinated.

Within the past ten years, a brilliant man from Little Rock, with ties to the South and its plantation society, ran for President. Shortly after his nomination, a picture was taken with a lady who raised him as a child. She gleamed with pride next to him. The woman had Hebrew/African traits. Her big lips, pronounced nose, melanin-strong skin and grey curly hair were unmistakable. In the clubs, jokes circulated that this guy was a Moses: "Was his nanny his grandmother?" The resemblance between the two, the thickness of his lips and noses were the subjects of much banter and lots of jokes. One day, to top things off, his daughter who was shielded from the public, suddenly appeared on the cover of a magazine. Even though his wife had New England roots, the daughter had big lips and frizzy hair. On his inauguration night he leaned over and wrapped his big lips over a saxophone in the presence of a streetwise black reporter: "If that man isn't a brother then I am a member of the Klan," he joked. A pastor who overheard the comment retorted, "For Pete's sake keep that out of the press or else his Bathsheba, his Delilah or his Jezebel will be dispatched immediately." "Expect large scale appointments for Blacks and Jews," they howled. When he rewarded his supporters, who were mainly Afro-Americans and Jews, they accused him of being on a mission. They vowed to get him. They were obsessed with getting him: "Get him at any cost, get him." The very people and their friends that bound and gagged the Attorney General's wife spent millions and millions of taxpayer's dollars to get him. The demonic forces that were unleashed to bring him down were so strong that his Commerce Secretary became a casualty. Even though there was a big legal loophole in that whole impeachment charade, great lawyers were spiritually and legally blinded. Only after the intercession of certain pastors was the spiritual thing temporarily abated. Please pray for him. He needs prayers.

A tour bus stopped in front of a building in Harlem recently. The driver opened the door for a picture stop. "Here is the office of the former President of the United States, Bill Clinton." One Oriental male asked how come the place wasn't full of secret agents. A man that looked like a drunken vagrant off the street replied: "He ain't need none; he be one of us." Here is a not-so-funny thing. Pastors that were his most vocal critics, that were unforgiving, left their churches' altars exposed to invasions. Mark 11:25-26, "When ye stand praying forgive, if ye have ought against any; that your Father in heaven may forgive you your trespass."

Anyone truly moving with the gifts of the Holy Spirit should recognize a demonic attack when they see one. In Mathew 7:1, God warned us thusly, "Judge not that ye be not judged." There is a certain preacher who arrogantly prints his own Bibles and insists on television that Ham was cursed, in spite of the fact that the Torah and all accurate translations state that God blessed Noah and all his sons. Translations that are true and accurate instruct us to pray for our leaders. No mention is made of whether we like them or not. Instead of attacking the President on his broadcast every chance he gets, it would be wise to apply the True Word.

The thin line between charisma and pride is spiritual. Shebna in Isaiah 22 is an interesting case study of a charismatic man of God that was oblivious to Satan's moves. Satan defeated him with the spirit of pride. I referenced Shebna so that he and others like himself may understand why his bouts with the spirits of gluttony, "unforgiveness" and pride seem unending. God did not take away the gifts that He had given to Shebna. God removed him from the exalted position on His sacred altar. All three of those spirits are killers.

I once found myself in such a situation and was rebuked personally by the Lord. Here is something for the legal profession to ponder: The Attorney General or presiding judge ruled that President Clinton could not invoke his Presidential Immunity; he figuratively had to *disrobe* and appear as a *civilian*. In essence, he was not appearing in his presidential capacity. How can a person be ordered to appear as a common civilian and be tried for impeachable offences?

A CIVILIAN CANNOT BE IMPEACHED!

Is there then a symbiotic relationship between the spiritual climate of a country and its inherited altars? Can repairing and reclaiming the national altars reduce the number of rapes, murders, abortions and divorces in a country? Certainly! There is wisdom in the scripture, "Give to Caesar the things that are Caesar's and to God the things that are God's." Hence, the primary role of "The Church" in any country is to protect, repair or reclaim that nation's altars and not to throw away the stones. Father, forgive our brothers and sisters and cancel the curses that may have been brought on your altars by their "unforgiveness."

CHAPTER 10D. BROKEN BREACHES

Any established entity that engages in perpetual motion, began with a prime mover, (a positive spirit, person, place or thing). Every tangible or created thing had a foundation or commencement point: physical, spiritual or financial. Since we are creatures of choice, anything guided by us is subject to our directional selections. Over time, we choose either positive or negative directions. Here are some urgent spiritual warnings.

1) *ANY NATION THAT HAS OR HAD ITS HIGHEST ALTAR OR ALTARS PAYING HOMAGE TO A GODDESS (OR GODDESSES) IS INVITING A SPIRITUAL MARRIAGE THAT WILL EVENTUALLY TAKE PLACE.*

All countries that I have visited where the dominant religions engage in any of the above practices have serious entrenched witchcraft strongholds. Mass suicides and mass murders are not uncommon and much incense and libations have to be made available for the usurpers of their state altars. Many such countries have regular bloody upheavals determined NOT by men. The spiritual energies in those countries allow Satan easy access to podiums of power. Hopefully this manual will assist them in correcting their situations.

2) RELIGIONS THAT HAVE ALTARS (PHYSICAL OR SPIRITUAL) WITH GRAVEN IMAGES EXALTED TO ANY ENTITY, THEY AND THEIR MEMBERS WILL BE EXPOSED TO EXTREME BONDAGE EVENTUALLY.

As long as any of their custodians have unrepented sins, the altars will split. Three or more blood-related sins and the cracks become canyons that allow the entire assemblies to be controlled by Satan. Sad to say, many of the custodians of those altars sprinkle incense and mix concoctions that, contrary to their beliefs, actually strengthen usurping spirits. In the past, I have had occasions to cast out numberless demons in homes and places where shrines and statues of supposedly godly people were erected. The Spirit of the Living God led me to homes where I have had to cast out serious evil spirits and demons out of persons wearing rosaries around their necks, praying that the horrible nightmares they were experiencing would have abated. I have yet to see an evil spirit respect a statue, a rosary or any graven image for that matter.

Religious statues are either *inaccurate in their depictions* or are *carved in disobedience;* they help rather than hinder the abode of darkness. On four separate occasions I have had to cast demons out of altar custodians themselves. When believers fall into sin (Romans 6:12-18), their spiritual hedges become broken; they backslide and crucify the "Saviour all over again." So much for mythical teachings (Hebrews 4:6) like "Security of the believer" and "Demons cannot possess saved persons?" Oh yeah? I have been in pastors' conventions when God had directed that we form small prayer groups. I have to confess that I do not pray casually. On numerous occasions, spiritual nests were disturbed. Thank God they had been uprooted.

3) *RELIGIONS THAT HAVE FEMININE PRINCIPALS AS CHIEF ICONS HAVE ALTARS EXPOSED TO POWERFUL SPIRITS OF APOSTASY.*

There are two spirits that dwell in religious places only. They have the ability not only to sit undisturbed around the "praise" and "worship" but also to partake and influence the proceedings as well. Those two types of usurping spirits are the spirits of Apostasy and False Christ spirits. Their purposes are to replace the true foundations of altars with false ones. When God presented this schematic in my Damascus encounter between King David's burial place and the Melchizedek foundation, He revealed this scripture to me: "For this purpose was the Son of God manifest, to destroy the works of the Evil One." The mission statement of this schematic is to awaken all seed of Abraham from their spiritual slumber. When altars are usurped, Satan enshrines the myth of exclusion. That cements their myths that their usurped teachings are the only true teachings and also that their pure devotees must not mingle with other impure sheep.

If you are disconnected from the True Olive Tree, (the Zion church that was planted by Jeshua in Jerusalem) either your foundation or your workmanship is faulty. The olive tree incidentally sprouts best in stone or stony ground and grows into a mighty tree. Jeremiah 11: 16, The Lord called thy *name*, a green olive tree, fair and of goodly fruit...Verse 17...For the Lord of hosts planted thee." Neither the ancient Israelites redeemed from Egypt nor Jeshua practiced or preached "Doctrines of Exclusion." King Solomon (there was none, naturally conceived, wiser) in Proverbs 18:1 warned of the nature of persons that isolate themselves from true worshippers of God. Actually Solomon did not write all of the Proverbs. Lemeul and Agur were also writers. Most people like me actually give Solomon credit for all. Sorry Brother Lemeul and Brother Agur, many a church leader and president get credit for most things and ideas actually given by their advisors and by their wives.

CHAPTER 10E. FROM WHENCE THE STONES, ZION OR BABEL?

Occasional examinations of foundations will reveal ruptures—from hairline fractures to severe canyons. As in the natural, so it is in the spiritual. The stones in the spiritual are either from Zion or from Babel. If your foundation stone is Babelic, repairs are necessary otherwise your institution will be doomed to the eventual curse of Babel. If it is Zion, it is possible to believe that everything is all right. However, the word of God declares: "All have sinned and come short." All have shortcomings. It is possible that the workmanship is faulty. Make sure that your foundation flushes to "The Chief Cornerstone." If your organization pays homage to an exalted being and your foundation is faulty, look for a devout Caleb or Joshua first before you search for a David. Invite a powerful international crusade to break the spiritual ground first, so that those rivers (natural, spiritual and financial) can begin to flow into your country, your organization, or both. 1998 was the most recent Jubilee: we are in the first post-Jubilee season. Notice the "Temple of the Lord" was built only after the entire period of bondage years had been broken. Then they celebrated in the *first Shabbat season after Jubilee*. 430 plus 50 equals 480 years. So 480 years after the children of Israel left Egypt, they received meticulous instructions for the building of Solomon's Temple.

Here are a few things worthy of mention. David's son (Solomon) built the temple. The plans were given to David, his father—David did not build the house. In the records of 1st Kings 6:1, "No hammers, no axes, or any tools of iron were used at the building site." God prearranged all stones with no room for compromise, change, alteration or substitution. A mould was made; the chief cornerstone was laid in Zion for all chosen to measure up and fit snugly to. Since the principles of philosophical masonry have limited degrees, philosophical or esoteric masonry is "Not" the way. When stonemasons apply the finishing touches to the surfaces of stones, they set and harden with time. When damage occurs, oft-times they have to break down entire structures. With carpentry, repairs focus on specifically damaged lumber. Carpenters are first workers on construction sites with the formwork. They are usually the last workers doing the finished work. Who shall lumber on God's Holy Hill? Which carpenter could be pure enough to challenge all of God's enemies on earth for the right to plant an emblem on a wooden altar on God's Holy Hill?

14 generations after Abraham's seed killed Goliath, one of the ancient "Mighty men," a new era in spiritual warfare began. Since God's redemptive path is progressive, let us use *Spiritual Carpentry*, our esoteric slide rule to compute and to find that "The Special Branch Servant/Warrior/Shepherd/Messiah" in the Davidic line that must confront and defeat the father of all Goliaths. An esoteric Day from the *Master of Masters* is 1000 years or 14 generations. From Abraham to David is 14 generations; from David to the Babylonian captivity is 14 generations; from the Babylonian captivity add 14 generations and you arrive at the third esoteric day on which Satan the mathematician tried to kill all the Hebrew lads two years and under. Jeshua was born in Bethlehem on that day to a virgin—Isaiah 7:14, confirming Micah 5:2. He was crucified—Psalm 22 and Psalm 69, overcame the devil, died and resurrected—Psalm 68:18.

Those fulfilled prophecies among others are strong arguments that Jeshua son of Miriam is the Messiah, the one shepherd chosen to usher in all seed of Abraham, and of Gentiles also.

Spiritual Reconstruction Time. The Son of Jah, the contractor poured all the materials for the mould, hence the name—Jah and son. However, they are joined/merged into the same spiritual mission; hence the special name documented in the Library of Alexandria. The Greeks transposed and filed loads of things they did not comprehend in vaults called "Mythology." Thus Jason, the mythical figure was predestined to find the Golden Fleece. The middle wall of the temple must be broken down. It was prophesied that the two kingdoms would merge (northern and southern). In the process of time the Old and New Testament would become one. We will examine John's vision at Patmos later on.

It is written in Isaiah 11:10 that the *Anointed One* would emerge from the root of Jesse (seed of Abraham). Notice that even though Mary's womb had both Kingly and Priestly bloodlines, she was not the root of a line of Kings or Priests. Micah etched the words over 2700 years ago. Micah 5:2, "But thou Bethlehem ...though thou be little among the thousands of Judah, yet out of thee shall come forth unto me that is to *be ruler in Israel* whose goings forth have been from of old, and from everlasting." See the word of God prophesied by David in Psalm 110:4, "The Lord hath sworn and will not repent; Thou art a Priest forever after the order of Melchizedek." The Spiritual kingdom and the Physical kingdom would merge as per prophecy into one of *Kings and Priests* after the order of Melchizedek. There would be a better priesthood without foundational blemish, destined to be *everlasting*. That priesthood has a *prefoundation* and also a *postreconstructional* destiny.

Satan had already sent all of his thoroughbred spirits to war with King David; he knew that David was commissioned to bring forth the seed of deliverance. When those failed, Satan returned to headquarters and called his favourite foundation destroyer by name: "Adultery, Adultery, Adultery!" Faithful spirit that she is: she came forth in all her strength and glory in the midst of a battle. How could a technical warrior like David leave his men in battle to go take a breeze? I saw in a vision how Satan set up my buddy David. David's eyes were the first place of invasion. The Lord even arranged for a special wind of warning by letting a branch sway to hide Bathsheba. Satan then attacked his hearing. David was musically minded. When the sound of water splashing off her body amplified into his musical ears, Satan knew that he had him. When the princess adultery captured him, she walked with her favorite companion, murder. Never blink until the last bell rings. "It aint over till it's over."

ABORTION AND MURDER ARE TWIN-SPIRITS.

CHAPTER 10F. BRIDES OF CHOSEN SPIRITUAL MEN

Priests petition God on behalf of their flock. Chosen men/women of God, especially true prophets, convey the heart desires and mind of God to the faithful. God designed a litmus test for His chosen. Every man/woman that God calls to do His work should first be married. The main reason for this, as explained by Moses, Titus and Paul, is that they should first establish their ability to rule their houses well. Their relationships with their spouses will reflect their relationships with the "Brides of God" that they would represent. Hence there are adverse effects on men/women of God and or their ministries when "chosen" men/women of God marry divorced persons; God forbids such. All of "God's Chosen" would be afforded futuristic glimpses of the fruits of the assemblies they would be assigned to rule over. Scripture references are: Leviticus 21:7, Titus 1:5-9, 1st Timothy 3:2 and 5, 1ˢᵗ Corinthians 3:16-17, Titus chapters 1, 2 and 3, 1ˢᵗ Corinthians 6:9 and verses 15-20 also the entire book of Romans, particularly chapters 3 and 6. The shape of a human being is very significant. It is the physical manifestation of the "Temple of God." That is why He refers to His Church, Synagogue and or Temple as His bride.

The desire to defile the body of God's chosen bride (physical and spiritual) is Satan's obsession. That is why Satan seduced Eve. The teaching points for all churches, mosques, and synagogues are that Satan will go after *"ALL RELIGIONS."* He will bring doctrines contrary to God's word. Corporate worship is a must. During those periods, the Head must seek God for guidance in all matters. They must seek their Father who knows all, hears all, sees all and is all. They must seek (corporate) clarification on any word or doctrine that is unclear. Adam did not consult God about the "contrary word" that *"HIS WIFE"* received: Genesis 3:1. Since Eve was the first mould or prototype of the spiritual relationship between God and His spiritual house "hu-man" and His physical house/church/temple/synagogue, then countless spiritual wives will be led astray by contrary doctrines: 1 Timothy 4:1-3. Given that he successfully seduced Eve and through his agents destroyed the Temple of Solomon, next the chief adulterer will pursue all spiritual persuasions. By detailing the lives of "Brides of God's chosen men," we can learn more about the stalking styles of our perennial suitor. When God rebuilds His edenic earth, all "E^ts" must be free of physical and spiritual termites. All "E^ts" or trees as we say in English, must be grafted into the *"Pure Branch"* which in turn will root into the *"Tree of Life."*

The Torah bears record of women chosen to be brides of spiritual men. We must understand that it is possible for spirits to enter human beings. If we do not, then we cannot believe that Mary's conception was by the Holy God, who is Spirit. God cannot break His laws. God already gave men dominion over earth. If Eve did not allow the first evil spirit access, then those angels could not have left their heavenly abode to "go into the daughters of men" as per Genesis 6:2. In recent times, men and women that have broken free from satanic servitude, have been emboldened by God, and have found the strength to document their cases. There are numerous case studies of women that had been "chosen" by spirit men.

In fact I will document the testimony of one such person in a later chapter so that persons with similar experiences may know that they can share their testimonies. There might be others in desperate need of assistance also, afraid to come forward. Before I document that case study I will introduce readers to a Biblical reference in Jeremiah 44:19. That is a factual case of a powerful spirit that was exalted by the ancient Israelites by the name of Queen of Heaven, a spiritual reference for a "Bride" spirit.

Let us tackle some serious foundational misunderstandings. Inside the womb of Mary (wife of Joseph of Bethlehem Judea) was the foundation of the *restorative ministry* not the original plans. Inside of her womb were the genes of both priestly and kingly tribes. Joseph had Davidic ancestry. He was a carpenter. He gave the physical building plans to Jesus. Since Jeshua or Jesus' unusual birth was preordained, then His priesthood was prefoundational. *The Great Architect of the Universe* gave His spiritual building plans to Jeshua. Here is the evidence: John the Harbinger spent seven years around the wilderness of Judea introducing the impending reformation. All Jesus' brothers and sisters served in Jesus' ministry the same way Jonathan was happy to serve David. There were no recorded quarrels about inheritance. The foundation of the ministry seed in *Mary's womb* was the "Seed of the Promise" to Abraham. She was chosen among women. Interestingly enough, specifically selected women in the Bible figuratively and prophetically meant "Brides of God" or churches. Miriam or Mary the Mother of Jesus had both the genes of Levi and Judah in her loins. The Church that emerges out of the womb of Mary will be "Chosen" above all churches, because spiritual kings and priests shall come forth. It is written, "Many are called; few are chosen." Any church birthed by any of her seed would be able to have ordained elders functioning both as spiritual Kings and Priests. Since God's Temple always had an outer court and an inner court, God in His wisdom allowed Jeshua to be responsible for "The Inner Court" only. So any person or institution exalting the womb of Mary would have *only* outer court experiences and would have to make way for inner court experiences. Incidentally Mary was not born in Rome. She had no Gentile children. She had the restorative seed ministry in her womb. That is why Joseph could not have planted the seed. In addition to those, at a wedding feast in Cana, Mary laid the foundation for anyone who would ask her to beseech her son for favors: Do whatever "HE" (Jeshua) tells you to do. "Do the will of my Father" was the theme of Jeshua's messages. Another version—I have laid a foundation. I am the cornerstone. My Father and I are one spiritual structure. I am the bridge between this world and the perfected one. It is written: "I am the Way, the Truth and the Life."

There was an apparition at Fatima. Never in recorded history did God ever use *dead* female personages to deliver messages. Even the angelic beings documented in God's holy books have male features. Every prophet who ever encountered one, including your humble servant, has seen only (what appeared to be) male images. Territorial spirits are "*Thrones.*" Why would God establish the Jewish people and their language as "His Oracles" and then send a message excluding them? Regardless the source, treat any assumed "Message of Exclusion" with suspicion. To be perfectly honest, I am neither sure of the identity of the personage or the content of a supposedly "secret and exclusive prophecy?" If God indeed sent a dead female with a message to a particular church bride, then the message is obvious.

John saw a church in his prophetic vision: "A Church that did not know it was *dead.*" That message (not yet published) was allegedly delivered at Fatima. Just for the record, the first tomb of Mary the mother of Jesus has been, and is there even now in Jerusalem where the bloodline of King David ended. The second tomb of Mary is in France in the courtyard of a secret monastery with an insignificant headstone marked "Matri Deum." There are those that would not want to bring attention to the fact that the bloodline of Jesse is extinguished. Another group would not want Mary's Jerusalem's burial place publicized.

According to the witness of 1st John 5:7 and 8, Mary is not, nor has she ever been one of the three that bore witness on the earth or in heaven. If you exalt her as an intercessor, I will give you her reply and spare you the onslaught of demons that might invade any incorrectly erected and unguarded altars. John 2:5, "Do whatever He (Jesus) tells you!" In other words, follow all the laws. Do not add or subtract anything. If you own a catechism and you are substituting it for the complete word of God, you are committing a grave sin. Satan has regained authority over most earthly temples because of inaccurate teachers, lackadaisical custodians and the errors of King Solomon. That conclusion is underpinned by the legacies of Solomon's physical and spiritual houses.

CHAPTER 10G. HE CHASTENS THOSE HE LOVES

One day during a prolonged fast, I received a witness in my spirit to visit a friend that I had not seen for a long time. I was shown the person vividly wrapped in cords. I drove quickly to his house and met him there as shown. He did not feel like going to work that day. I explained that the visit was not social. I mentioned my perception of his serious spiritual difficulty. "Who is the lady that you grew up with (not your mother) an aunt? It appears that she died some years ago?" His eyes opened in amazement. "The ring that she left for you," I demanded "where is it?" He confessed all. After the second cleansing on the issue of iniquities, I told him of the need to confess all habitual sins, especially…all of a sudden, out of my mouth blared, "MUR-DER!" The Lord did not reveal that to me previously so when my mouth issued the word, in shock I turned it into a question. Now that was in the early days of my Deliverance Ministry. "Murder?" The Spirit of the Lord confirmed, "Murder as in abortion."

My friend is a very prominent person, choir member, and well respected in his church, community, jury foreman etc., so upon that revelation (before his reply) I was shocked. Uncontrollably he wept and confessed: "The lady you met here the last time. The one that I introduced to you as my sales agent, it was not true. She conceived," and in his exact words: "We got rid of it!" My immediate reply, "That 'it' young man, was a life and the Lord has you accountable for murder. I am sure you felt the anger in the voice spoken through me." After those demons got expelled and he started doing well financially, he got "Involved?" Majority opinion allows us to pick philosophies we like and to reject the rest. Picture an imperfect society with no punishment. Are we to assume that "Society" is correct in its amelioration of the word "adultery" into words like "involvement, affairs and flings?" Is God so good and merciful that He would not punish His children?" Hebrews 12:6, "For whom the Lord loveth He chasteneth, and *scourgeth* every son whom he receiveth."

I returned home, feeling good after that victory at my friend's house. Then the Spirit of the Lord chastened me sternly: "Did you hear what your friend just confessed?" Start with your sojourn in America." All of a sudden I was reviewing the iniquities of my entire sinful journeys as time rewound on a visual spool. "The prayers of both your grandmothers, those early stalwarts of the Pentecostal movement and those of your daughter came into agreement and prayed you out of 'Lodebar.' Where are those unborn brothers and sisters that your daughter never received? Where are the ones that pride and murder deprived her of? You killed them!" I cried hysterically for hours. Hebrews 12:6, He chastens those he loves.

Even though I thought that I confessed all my sins, I had glanced over the category of abortions previously. God did that deliberately. On a visit to a jail the weekend before, I was praying with a group of inmates. One who had committed a terrible murder had asked, after my teaching on ancestral curses, to pray for that curse to be broken on his life. His father was a whore-mongering adulterer and his stepmother died under mysterious circumstances. His grandfather was also a womanizer. He even went further; he was the sole participant in a crime of passion. The girl (that he was formerly engaged to) was a Christian. I have never read a commandment that thou shall sample the fruits first. If you rely on the Lord to choose instead of getting into a mess, many of you would not be messed up to begin with. **GOD DOES NOT BLESS MESS!**

Next in the prayer line was a young man, a backsliding lay preacher who physically fought with a Jezebel. She called the police. The judge received an "impulse," (synonym for *spiritual message*), so he confined the lay preacher to jail: 90 days for his first offence. When the backsliding lay preacher asked for prayers of agreement, the confessor of the crime of passion attempted to come forward. I erred. He had already repented, been faithful in the church services and had voluntarily asked God to renew his original right spirit. When he hesitated I should have chimed in with, "God washes sins as far as the east is from the west." Instead, I pretended that I did not see him and waited until one of my assistants was available. For that, God not only rebuked me, but humbled me also. In other words, "Who do I think I am?" In the eyes of God, I had committed more murders than all the inmates combined. He was gracious enough to pardon me; so who made me judge and jury for God? On my next prison visit, I replayed the experience whereby God rebuked me, as my testimony. I ended with the words "There is now no condemnation to those who are in Christ Jesus."

CHAPTER 11. FINDING/RECLAIMING OUR LOST TREASURES!

CHAPTER 11A. OPERATION RECLAIM

The Oracle or only true light, the lumber, the foundation stone and the pillars are all segments of the Messiah's temple according to the prototype of Solomon. A good thief would attempt to steal or to mimic every aspect of the building, especially the sacred things. Whoever the Messiah is, must come as a repairing light, true and strong branch, a tried and tested cornerstone and must be able to reside in the Holy of Holies as the accurate Oracle of the most High God. His pillars must fall, to be rebuilt.

During the ancient Stellar Mythos, much more ice covered the earth. The social structures of societies were different. There were only two classes of people: a minute Priest Class and a Hunter/Gatherer class. The first places on earth where *physical altars* were used to serve God were sacred (heavily wooded) groves (live trees). Man searched physically for the "E^ts of Life." I emphasized physical altars as opposed to intangible or remote ones like the stars. Those physical altars were usurped. God gave the dominion of earth to man. God does not bestow gifts and take them back. So since man transgressed, man must come to repair all the breaches: Isaiah 53. The earliest missionaries were commanded to tear down all ancient altars. They failed. The Levites failed. Israel and Judah failed.

America did not complete its task, as a result, the spirit under one surfaced and is using slick television advertisements about ancestral data to lure the unsuspecting. Every altar of God on earth had prior victories or setbacks. Those that had setbacks can rejoice now, since the sacrifice at Calvary released the power to reclaim "all lost or stolen." In God's spirit domain altars have either of two messages: a) victorious or b) vanquished. In Satan's domain: a) yearning to vanquish or b) vanquished. Remember that Moses threw down a rod (a formed *branch* from a dead tree). It was *transformed* into a serpent to *defeat all* of Pharaoh's serpents. Hence we can defeat Satan at his own game.

The first materials King Solomon received to build the house of the Lord were *cedars* from Lebanon. Within the Holy of Holies, the lumber was *Olive* from Jerusalem. Jesus was ordained to be the Branch/Rod/Light and Way. Unknown to Satan then, God had preplanned that His foundation stone would be in Zion. Satan pursued every *ancient grove* in pursuit of the "E^ts, or Tree of Life." The groves became polluted altars. God then ordained the erecting of stone altars, tangible altars of *naturally formed stones*. The altar of Solomon's Temple was made of perfectly formed, uncut stone. Satan pursued and threw down all the stones and columns of Solomon's Temple, in nervous anticipation of the arrival of the Chief Cornerstone of Zion. Since all the columns of Solomon's Temple have fallen down, then the Messiah's earthly house must follow the script. I hate to admit it but all the supposedly strong columns of the Messiah's Temple are fallen down or damaged also. If you disbelieve me, pick up the papers or put on your television. However repairs are possible. God then commenced the perfecting of human altars for His Spirit to redeem and to speak through. Since the righteous foundation had been laid, implementation of His fail-proof plan was next. Observe the pattern of the enemy. Let us compare the physical altars with our altars. A human can be described as: a temple in construction, a temple stolen, a temple neglected, a temple being destroyed, a temple being rebuilt, and or an imitation or false temple. In the Temple of Solomon, the two cherubim represent the prefaced word and the confirmed word. All temples must be reconstructed. They must have a before and after restitution pattern. Therefore any doctrine that cannot be prefaced in the patriarchal records should be questioned. Since the wives of covenant heirs are prophetic images of His future churches, Rebekah must have a spiritual counterpart. Isaac took Rebekah into his mother's tent to live with her. There must also be a connection between the "Old Covenant Carrier" and the "New Spiritual Vehicle." Although the "Rebekah" covenant has to be connected to the Sarah covenant, since Rebekah violated traditions and customs, of necessity we must look for all violations in Rebekah's legacy.

CHAPTER 11B. SPIRITUAL ENTRANCES

Our temples have two public dual-purpose (entrance/exit) doors "minds and mouths," two separate double-entry passages (eyes and ears) and one private "most holy" entrance. At times we see and hear both good and bad things. The natural temple had three sections: the outer court where all could enter, the inner court for the "Elect," and the "Holy of Holies." Once per year, the "One sanctified by God" could enter the Holy of Holies. In the first temple and every temple since made, there is one chief personality (good or bad). In the first temple, one chosen human could enter the most holy entrance and the spiritual entrance was ordained for God's Spirit. In other words the one God chooses as "husband or wife" only. If you do not know the location of your "Holy of Holies," you are in trouble. The Ark was covered, so was the Holy of Holies "behind The Veil." Those of you who want to bare it all in public for the entire armies of the U.S.A., Russia, NATO and Israel to view and or to march through especially on the Internet, here is a very subtle message for such as you, "Keep your demon-possessed altars to yourselves!" Most habitual and deliberate exhibitionists need serious deliverance.

Our minds are perennial battlefields. They are usually the first entrances. All thoughts or vibes *knock* first. Seek spiritual maturity and wisdom before you decide who or what is welcome in your temple. The same way you do not open your house to everyone who knocks on your doors, you have the right to deny access to intruders unless you have already been overpowered. Most spirits invade when body fluids are exchanged, in disobedience to established spiritual laws. Dirty oil wrecks engines and so do blemished body fluids.

Who the heck is Society? Did society make your temples and set the rules? Might in numbers never made anything right. Go search the historical records of Sodom. Speak to workers at hospitals that witness the horrors of people who are about to die in sinful states as they get glimpses of their eternal destinations. If persons could discern the spiritual aftermath of every allegedly pleasurable sexual act committed in disobedience, steel suits would be the hit. Look around at persons that "fell in" and then "fell out" with the person they fell in lust with. Some got bitter; others got promiscuous and others even hardened. Usually with each transfer of disobedient seed, moral standards dropped lower and lower. Is it coincidental that the more unmarried sexual encounters that people have, the more they fall away from God's teachings? Is it coincidental that the more adulteries, abortions and or murders that they commit, the more they rebel against Gods teachings? Point to any person that belongs to the third successive generation of obedient Godly families and if he or she is an example of Godly living also, you will see a person blessed in health, wealth and happiness unless he or she allowed Satan to pick his or her mate.

David defeated Israel's enemies. A Jezebel spirit knocked him down. He got up the way determined fighters do, repented, rebuilt his personal altars and went on from victory to victories. The teaching point here is this: you must get up and rebuild your temple otherwise Satan and his gang will eat your lunch. He will drive you insane; inflict your body, finances and ultimately your soul. That in a nutshell is his obsession.

Everyone should pay a visit to a nursing home or an institution for the aged. Observe the folks that have completed their contract time of 70 years. You will find only two types of persons. The first group will be at peace, enjoying the grace that God has extended to them. That group, more often than not, receives comfortable rest when they turn in to sleep. The other group often displays constant irritability. They rarely sleep well, as there are manifestations of restless personalities. We carry in our spiritual baggage the fruits of our life patterns. In physics we are taught that every action has an equal and opposite reaction. As it is in the natural, so shall it be in the spiritual. The difference between the natural and the spiritual is that in the spiritual, the consequences can be forgiven. Left unrepented they accumulate and manifest in personality deterioration, sicknesses or unrighteous departures. In the physical, we reap the consequences of disregard and carelessness in our immediate environment. Are we allowing ourselves to be bewitched into believing that we can break spiritual laws without consequences? Simply put, we eventually reap what we sow. We also pass our baggage on to our offspring—Exodus 34:6-7.

CHAPTER 11C. SACRIFICES REAL OR COUNTERFEIT?

Let us examine ourselves to see how often we mimic God's holy priests in wanton desecration a certain ordained sacrifice. While we are doing that, let us paraphrase David's words from Psalm 139:7-12. Is there a place in the universe to hide any thought or action from God? David lamented that not even in the bottom of the ocean could he escape God's scrutiny. God knows all and sees all.

The Real Sacrifice: Think of a lovely turkey on Thanksgiving Day. It is upturned on a plate to give pleasure to selected loved ones. In the book of Leviticus, a turtledove was an ordained "sin offering" sacrifice. Notice the way the anointed High Priest carefully removed the clothes—I mean the feathers, of the turtledove.

The Counterfeit Sacrifice: In England women are called birds. Is your altar desecrated? Men, here is a question, "Are you the High Priest, anointed to offer sacrifice pleasing to God, or an imposter making illegal fire like Nadab and Abihu?" Are you offering lewd sacrifices to Baal—Numbers 31:15-16. Twenty four thousand were destroyed during one day because of *fornication*. I wonder why that demon party was abruptly cancelled. Refer to Numbers 25:1-9 quoted by Paul in 1st Corinthians 10:6-8. Numbers 25:1, "Israel abode in *Shit*-tim and the people began to commit whoredom with the daughters of Moab." Verse 9, "Those that died in the plague were *twenty and four thousand*." I care not who you are, if you are engaging in whoredom you are in deep spiritual Shit-tim. Your contrary opinions are totally irrelevant. I am tired of casting out demons from people that I had previously forewarned. At one time, tiredness caused my impatience to digress into anger. I left a hospital refusing to pray for a person that was disturbing an entire wing with the noises of agony from AIDS' spirits. I had warned the person many times prior, about spiritual consequences that promiscuous lifestyles beget. At my home I was suddenly and angrily rebuked by the Spirit of the Living God, "Do you know how many times I sent persons to warn you when you were an *Emperor in the Kingdom of Sin?*" "Did your daughter stop praying for you? Did the blind lady who spoke to you that day, did she let you go when you tried to run away from my warnings back to your foolish ways and ideas?" I drove as fast as I could back to the hospital as Ezekiel Chapter 33, was spelled out to me. Sad to say, the person got healed miraculously and then fell back into sin—2nd Peter 2:20. I did not attend the funeral. That blood was not on my hands.

Jesus was crucified between two posts on the 14th day of Abib, the first month of the Hebrew calendar, identical to the way the Levites would kill the "unblemished lamb" between *two posts*, (not on a stake) outside the camp. At Jeshua's crucifixion there were two condemned men, one on each post at opposite sides of Jesus. Both of them (like all of us) received the gift of choice between *everlasting life and eternal damnation*. One made the *right choice*. The other one received the sentence of Psalm 55:15: "Let them go down quick into hell; for wickedness is in their dwellings and among them."

It is logical to assume that Miriam of Magdala (mistranslated as Mary Magdalene) did not get seven demons in her from discussing politics at the local bar. She obviously had some casual "*flings*" and "*affairs.*" Got the drift? By the way, since when did a society as patriarchal as that of ancient Israel begin to document ladies with surnames? Did not the scribes list the male forefathers first, then the siblings as sons and daughters of so and so? Are we to believe that there was a Mr. Magdalene of Hebrew antiquity that left zillions of generational curses for his lovely little daughter? Are you wondering why I do not include a clear step-by-step guide so that people can first check their altars for contamination? I just might do that and include some spiritual bleach.

First let us look at the way to safeguard ourselves after cleansing. Let us use Saul of Tarsus as an example. Saul of Tarsus a former murderer, after having his altars restored, spent time in solitude and in cleansing before even daring to go back near the jungle. After his conversion and restoration to "Paul," he was baptized with fire. That is a term used for "Being Chosen." Trust me, you do know when the *Spirit of the Lord* has baptized you. While incarcerated the first time in Rome, between 60 C.E. and 61 C.E. he wrote a letter of encouragement to the brethren at Ephesus. In the discourse labeled Ephesians, in the New Testament or New Testimonies of First Witnesses, Ephesians 6:12, he wrote: "We wrestle not against flesh and blood but against spiritual wickedness in high places, against *principalities* and *rulers of darkness.*" Paul had to know because he had numerous battles with them. That is why people like myself are called, first to engage in similar battles so that we can be new witnesses like the *Firstfruits* of witnesses and proclaim: "**We bear witness.**"

There are different types of prayers and there are different intensities. Intensity is not influenced by how hard or how long a person prays. The main ingredient is *the quality of the sacrifice.* Impure or insufficient sacrifices are ineffectual. The word of God declares: "The effectual fervent prayer of the righteous availeth much." Quality sacrificial prayer that is right and pleasing to God contains penitence, extreme sincerity, much faith, wisdom, cleanliness, persistence and follow-through. If we are functioning in 90 percent error-mode, it is logical to assume that many things we are doing, though we honestly believe we are right, are in fact fallacies and may eventually doom us.

It is written in Proverbs 16:25, "There is *a way that seemeth right* unto a man; but the end thereof are the ways of death." Examine the ways that Satan has connived all nations, many people, and most religious persuasions that somehow "their way" or "their philosophy" is the correct one. No wonder the main cities of the world are messed up; so many personal relationships are messed up, and so many church congregations messed up. Add to those the numberless spiritually induced diseases, classified as "incurable." Every time Satan induces a locality into a specific amount of corporate disobedience, a new disease is unleashed. We then have to serve the bondage time (years without the cure) until a Moses-discovery is made.

CHAPTER 11D. FALSE ACCREDITATION!

The Greeks were falsely credited with the invention of numerous things that existed for hundreds of years in other civilizations. We covered prior usages of mathematics, algebra and the square root in Egypt and Central America. People from Mainland China, with their 9000-plus years of unbroken history, invented visual and moral teaching tools for posterity. As time elapsed, the "moral and wise teachings" were called "Proverbs" and most recently—philosophies. The Chinese invented paper, writing, the compass, and used gunpowder mainly in their sacred ceremonies. Earliest inhabitants (some believed to have been survivors of a global catastrophe) recorded prior and prophetic events in an ancient alphabet. Amazingly, they referenced "Pangaea," the earliest name for the landmass that is now Africa. Fragmented versions of those gems are stored in verbal legends about the land of "Pan Gu." Mythological tales by Greeks are nothing new. Africa had their "Griots" that did the same thousands of years prior, and so did the "Ab-original" people of Australia. The Norse and the Vikings had similar verbal storerooms. Since we were not taught the foundation of philosophy, we had incorrectly given credit to Philo the Greek. We also gave intellectual reverence to the literary emissions from those considered as icons of Philosophy's Mt. Olympus. Since the main purpose of darkness (the encroacher) is to engulf unlit persons, places or things, wayward and contrary philosophies were the best spiritual wine that Satan released on thirsty minds. As a result, millions of homes are spiritual deserts. The occupants wasted years in *pursuit of invented wisdom*. Given that a person's philosophy determines his/her ultimate destiny, be sure to hang your hat and life on the correct one! As long as we function in concentric circles of finite wisdom, we will be outside the reach of fresh revelations. Then again, we must be sure that those revelations originate from God. Hence my Muslim brethren are battling this question: "How do we know the source of editorial inserts in the Holy Koran if we believe that Prophet Mohammed (whose words are enshrined in Sura 2:87) is the final prophet?" Sura 2:87, "We gave Moses the Book and followed him up with a succession of Messengers; we gave Jesus, the son of Mary, clear (signs) and strengthened him with the Holy Spirit."

No fresh revelation is ever released without some significant move towards true light, which in turn triggers true peace. True peace triggers true wisdom in the belly of the clock (whether we hate it or not) a land called Israel. Naturally Satan is busy selecting his team for the final script, which we can either hasten or hinder. Pilate admonished the Chief Priests for desiring to change the inscription on Jeshua's cross, "King of the Jews" with the same words I will repeat, "What is written is written." The King's decree cannot be changed!

CHAPTER 11E. RECENT PROPHETIC FULFILLMENT

Have you attended a local, regional or international convocation? Psalm 24:3, David wrote the requirements: "Who shall come into the Holy Hill of the Lord? Only those that have clean hands and pure hearts" double-cleansed as per Exodus 19:10 and 11. In 1998, Israel celebrated the first Jubilee after they became a nation. It was spiritually significant. One messianic Jew told me that every time he read Leviticus 25, when he was in bondage in the "Lands of the North," he wondered if the Lord would remember them. Now, the Soviet States have been disbanded, survivors have been able to commence their third "Exodus." The next prophecy he anxiously awaited was Zechariah 8:22-23. At that time he reported that Israel was isolated with few allies. "How would the nations gather to come up to Jerusalem and pray for her peace?" Not only did Zechariah say nations but *all the nations*. Lo and behold as Israel celebrated Rosh Hannah, I witnessed (I will not mention his portfolio or name) a member of cabinet laugh and weep for joy as he attended a dinner where over 1500 persons from over two hundred nations went to pray for the peace of Jerusalem. There were saints from at least 15 Arabic speaking nations. We all wept together, sang and prayed for peace. It was very touching. There were some serious shakings in the heavenlies. Israel was on high security alert during the entire convocation. Forty days after that, an "intent" to implement a peace accord was put in place. Satan is fighting that "intent" the same way he has fought everything else in the region. I mentioned those incidents as examples of different types of prayers, especially in this prophesied season of Jubilee.

There are prayers of genuine repentance that move the heart of God towards His mercy and favour. There are other prayers that stir His heart to anger against His enemies immediately. There are other prayers whereby God sets in motion the "process" of reconstruction, of healing, and or of deliverance pending completion of His assigned conditions. The processes of cleansing, forgiveness and repentance are the avenues whereby most hindrances/blockages are broken. There are also those prayers where God says forthrightly that He will not accept our prayers. Those times are mainly when our *hearts are not sincere*, when we have *unrepentant attitudes*, when we are in sinful lifestyles or where we are asking God to do something contrary to His word—Proverbs 15:29. To most bakers, his/her bread is the best: criticism good or bad is unwelcome. I witnessed the anger of the Lord manifest at the same convocation, as a delegation from a European nation presented their petitions before the Lord. Trust me; you really do not want to witness an occasion when God is angry. The entire convocation stopped. We fasted and went before Him a *second time* with prayers of intercession, then thanksgiving and praise. That nation was given a suspended sentence as the hand of God was stayed. The word of God is specific in that all have sinned and come short of His glory.

There are sins of commission and there are sins of omission. There are also attitudes' sins as per Matthew Chapter 5. One of my popular teaching and lecture topics is "Be unto God as His attitude" called "The Beatitudes." There are also sins of "unforgiveness." "Unforgiveness" is not only a grievous sin, it is a hindering sin. I will include two separate case examples that I witnessed personally: one, where a person had lost sight in both eyes and another where the person had been physically challenged after a long bout with AIDS.

In the latter case the person had lost the ability to walk. The legs became bent and rigid. I also saw that happen to a physically challenged lady. There were deep hatred and revenge conceived at an altar of Satan. After she genuinely asked for forgiveness, she received her breakthrough. In both cases, although they made general confessions, only after they confessed that they had deep-seated hatred, admitted their "unforgiveness" and closed the openings (serious anger and "unforgiveness" toward someone they held deep in their bellies) did they get healed.

The questions are: 1) "What the heck is sin anyway? 2) "Isn't the definition of sin a matter of opinion or interpretation?" Here is a little piece of advice. The manufacturers of vehicles prepare manuals. This daily wrestling match is not a casual game. This is serious; it is life and death. Believe me, not one hair on your head is yours. If you disbelieve me, then keep all your hairs forever! Read on!

CHAPTER 11F. EVE OF THE SHEAVES

If the spirit of adultery snatches your husband or your wife, follow my previous instructions for wilderness situations in Chapter 7. Make sure that you complete the necessary cleansing prayers first so that nothing can block your prayers. Pray for the release of him or her by name from those spirits of adultery. Call the prayer hotline I gave you and ask them to pray with you also. Never ever go to a witchcraft worker or to a psychic hotline; most are connected either indirectly or directly to satanic altars. Most of them need deliverance also; not to mention the numberless ones, which are completely fraudulent. A contact with any of them is a bond with a satanic altar and constitutes a serious spiritual breach—Isaiah 8-18-19 and Leviticus 19:31. Those contacts increase your spiritual problems 1000-fold. You have the rulebook—the Tanakh or Bible. Unfortunately, some coaches have not been properly trained. Coaches have been butt-kicked and beaten up. Know the enemy. Learn his weaknesses and fears. Study the book that has his history on earth documented. Listen to the teachings that are passed on to us by those who fight him daily. Many are willing to show us how to be perpetual overcomers. Most importantly, it is a tag team fight.

To touch your team member your hands must be spotless. It matters not how dirty you have been. There is only one type of spiritual bleach acceptable to God—the sanctified perfect-ed blood sacrifice of Ja-son. That Son as per Psalm 2, bloodline cleansed by His sinless mother and "impossible-to-sin Father" is now accessible after confession. That sacrifice as per Isaiah 53 sealed the covenant of Abraham and ushered in the New Covenant. Abraham's sacrifice had to have been confirmed according to *God's Law of Double Reference*. Since God is the Most Holy Spirit, only sinless cleansed blood can enter His Most Holy place to bond with Him. For God to bond with us, we also must be cleansed and blood-washed. There is only one way, and that is through full repentance. Exodus 19:10 gives insights into multiple cleansings. The significance of the second wash is listed for the benefit of pastors, backsliders or sinners that are at this point being convicted. Zechariah 3:3-4 highlight the second wash. First for errant pastors or backsliders, wherever you are, do a Jonah prayer. Dig deep into the bowels of your conscience; cry out from the sinful dungeons that you have dug yourselves into.

If I take off my shirt and wash it, even though it smells clean and looks fine to me, there are germs floating around it from the atmosphere or there might be perspiration stains. By adding heavier detergents, the persons that add extra cleansers most often receive a cleaner wash. Now there might be additional stains. Those persons that examine the garment in the light and spray on stain remover are study cases of the proper cleansing processes. Iniquities as per Exodus 34:6-7 are the stains. What if you are a person that had been in the world search-ing like I once was, and finally you heard your loving Father calling your spirit? Here is the prerequisite for restoration. Wherever you are—office, bathroom, or parking lot—look up to heaven and ask God to forgive you of all sins known/unknown, all sins of your mouth, mind, eyes, attitudes and sinful intents. Ask forgiveness for all infractions against families, friends and neighbors. Thank God for providing an everlasting living sacrifice named Jeshua who shed His blood for all. Thank God for including you in that sacrifice. Ask God to send His Holy

Spirit through Jeshua, to guide you through the "WAY" to His Holy Temple. For a more comprehensive cleansing, read Deuteronomy 27:15-26 and confess every act punishable by curses. Do those on behalf of yourself, your parents and parents' parents going back four generations. Someone must have committed at least many if not all. So confess all to be sure. Go over the Ten Commandments and confess all also. Since an offense in one creates a guilty verdict in all, confess all. Ask God to reveal the truth to you, since you have been blinded by a world of disobedience. Call a 24-hour prayer line for spiritual help and guidance. In the absence of a prayer line in your country, call out the name that shatters all spiritual darkness of this world. Call out to "Jesus or Jeshua" through God's restoration prayer package. Receive and cherish the greatest gift certificate on earth below.

MOST IMPORTANT PRAYER

Heavenly Father, I am not worthy to come into your presence because of misdeeds. I ask for total forgiveness of all my transgressions. I call upon the name of your special Son of Psalm 2. Jeshua, please help me! I believe that you were the seed of Isaac, chosen to redeem humankind. Show me the way, the truth and the law. I thank you for your complete redemption package, from which I can receive forgiveness from all of my misjudgments and sins. Exchange my sinful past for your sinless future. As pardon for my sins, I accept your suffering death, pre-ordained and predestined to be humankind's everlasting sacrifice. I ask to be in the *New Covenant*. Bond me to God, spiritually and mentally. Burn the files of my wanton past and remove every generational curse and every satanic contract on my life. I thank you for inserting my name in the *Lamb's Book of Life*. I renounce Satan, all of his works, hexes, diseases and evil habits. Heavenly Father, now that I am reborn (spiritually) please renew my mind, spirit and body. *Lead me into all truth, Amen.*

Satan feeling like a jilted lover will be revengeful seven times. Instill the provisions of Matthew 12:43 and 2nd Peter 2:20. Be reminded at all times that if you ever go back into sinful living, you will end up with seven times the oppression, seven times the depression, seven times the sicknesses and seven times the number of evil spirits that left. I have seen what transpired when former AIDS' patients revert to sinful living after receiving miraculous healings. The rapid transformation from bloom to immediate gloom was horrific. I cannot count the number of miracles I have witnessed after persons have said that prayer. The greatest miracle is the one that you can receive right now—freedom from all of Satan's contracts on your life, and this gift certificate—*Salvation*. Stay clean!

CHAPTER 12. CONCEALED FOUNDATIONAL CRACKS

Satan is the only being to have tasted Paradise and then be banished from it permanently. He is the world's angriest, most hateful, most jealous, most untruthful, most envious, most wicked and most bad-minded being there is. Paradise has zero tolerance for disobedience and discord. The absence of gravity in outer space should remind us that gravity and negative energies are concentrated on earth, en masse—Genesis 1:2. The earth is the spiritual courtroom of the universe. Satan is head prosecution attorney! His title in Revelation 12:10 is "Accuser of the Brethren." Carnal negative vibes/energies, situations of severe gravity and most maladies originate from him. They are his to dispense, as punishment to those found guilty. From Genesis 1:2-3, the Spirit of God already removed all negatives. In all 31 verses of Genesis 1 and the first 4 verses of Genesis 2, everything created was obedient and very good. Man's disobedience negated and continues to negate much good that was done in the beginning. This book will unveil Satan's armies and their plans. I will show you their patterns of attacking individuals, families, nations and their main targets—spiritual temples. Satan is a thief, a robber and a killer. His plans have always been to weaken altars and custodians until he can destroy them. We will examine a nation that he has engaged in perennial battles and then some damaged altars as per recorded history.

CHAPTER 12A. THE CRACKED FOUNDATION OF PALESTINIA: SPIRITUAL ROOTS

Gath, Ashdod, Ashkelon, Ekron, and Gaza were the five major cities of the Philistines. All were heavily fortified physically and spiritually. All had, and still have strong and evil territorial spirits surrounding them. On those ancient foundations, an altar was raised to Dagon. It was strengthened by the sacrilegious act of placing the Holy Ark of God in Ashdod (1st Samuel 5:1-7). Other altars were raised to the demon powers of Astarte, Melkart, and Baal. Figurines and statues were erected in their honour. In Judges 1:19, Israel's military branch, the tribe of Judah upon whom God bestowed other spiritual responsibilities, failed to uproot the Canaanite armies because of "their chariots of iron." In the end times, buried figurines will be found and adored as priceless museum pieces. Some will be conduits for ancient spirits. As soon as the corporate iniquities of the region become heavy enough, much blood will be spilled to strengthen the entrenched demonic forces. Question: Did the custodians of the tribes of Levi and Judah, or any of their seed, repent of those transgressions?

Why do you think the throwing of stones in the West Bank around Gaza has taken up so much attention and energy internationally? Satan is strengthening his ancient (altars) strongholds with his spirits of intolerance, greed, hate, anger and death. In Jericho also, there were five entrenched principalities. I mentioned those events to alert the unfamiliar that whenever Satan gets specifically involved in waves of violence in those regions he will use his five-fold plan of anger, hate, pride, "unforgiveness" and either (stubbornness, lies or distortion). Usually he will empower five pockets of hate and they will move together. Pay close attention to all news stories coming out of those localities to observe closely Satan's modus operandi. David took *five* stones with him for his sling when he confronted Goliath. The spiritual and esoteric significance of the stones must be noted. Goliath was from Gath. There were also *five* Lords of the Philistines. David had a stone for each one.

In Genesis 9:1, God blessed Noah and sons Ham, Shem, and Japheth. God did not proclaim an everlasting blessing on all of their seed. Having already blessed Ham, when Ham interfered with Noah's wife, God placed a curse on Canaan. That act of defilement established a spiritual precedent. Observe that the other sons placed a garment on both of their shoulders for a covering. The woman would represent the parent place of worship: *The Bride of the Living God.* The seed of the nations of Canaan would defile the true worship of JHVH. Out of the seed of Canaan sprang the Sidonians, the Jebusites, the Amorites, the Girgasites, the Hivites, the Arkites, the Sinites, the Arvadites, the Zemarites, and the Hamathites (Genesis 10:15-18). The seed of the aforementioned nations had prior generations of grove and idol worshippers. Some became perpetual enemies of ancient Israel.

So to answer the question posed by many of my friends in the region as to whether or not the just God was fair in sending His people to occupy a land that was already peopled: one reason given in God's word is that the inhabitants of the land were spiritual pollutants. God's orders were to destroy them. In Judges 1:20…God gave Hebron to Caleb…and he expelled the three sons of Anak. Judges1:18, "Judah took Gaza, Ashkelon, and Ekron, and the Lord was with Judah; he drove out the inhabitants of the mountain: but could not drive out the inhabitants of the *valley*." Judges1:2, "The children of Benjamin *did not* drive out *the Jebusites* that inhabited Jerusalem but the Jebusites dwell with the children of Benjamin in Jerusalem unto this day." Samuel recorded that prophecy over 2300 years ago. In Nehemiah 4:7-9, God warned Nehemiah that those inhabitants of Ashdod, inspired by Satan, tried to prevent the rebuilding of the temple wall. When that effort failed, they tried to mingle the seed. Observe how many of God's sacred altars are on that land. If they were not important Satan would not pursue them perennially. Therefore God cannot abandon that land. In Isaiah 43:1, God called the land Israel, His land. In Ezekiel 38:14, He promised to overturn **all her enemies in a "latter day" battle.** Since God already gave us the end time script, I will expose as much as possible, so that all can understand the spiritual energies behind the regions' upheavals.

Adjust all Timepieces! The information listed in this sector is inserted for your enlightenment. The epicenter of all spiritual clocks on earth is the land called Israel. In 1948 Israel became a nation and the countdown for the final prophecies began. Those should all come to fruition by 2018. That should be 1948 + 70 = 2018, a generation after the last Exodus. Calendars used by nations from the roots of ancient Babylon adjust to the Hebrew calendar every 50 years. 1998 (1948+50) was "New" Israel's first Jubilee. The significance of that date cannot be overlooked. There is a special three-year period whereby God Almighty calls "all the people" of nations that were under the Edict of King Ahasuerus (Esther 3:8 and Esther 1:1). They are called today: India, Pakistan, Turkey, Istanbul, Libya, Chad, Syria, Lebanon, Egypt, Palestine, Israel, Jordan and the entire Middle East, North Africa, to Ethiopia. Also included are "the remnants" of former plantations in the Americas and the dispersed from the islands of the sea of the Gentile nations of Antigua and Barbuda, Aruba to Trinidad and Tobago alphabetically also North/South Carolina, Brazil and Suriname. The three-year window (Jubilee of Leviticus 25) was from 1998 to 2001. Corroborating scriptures are Leviticus Chapter 25 in its entirety, Esther 1:1, Joel 3:20-21,

Genesis 10:4-6, Jeremiah 31:31-40, Jeremiah 3:18-19 and Isaiah Chapters 60 and 62.

Joel, Isaiah, Asaph, Daniel, Ezekiel and David were among God's messengers chosen to predict the times we are living in (1st Jubilee after the 1948 Exodus). In Leviticus Chapter 25, the requirements for achieving the promises of Jubilee commenced with forgiveness of debt, of wrongs etc. People need to scrutinize the spiritual structures of their institutions for cracks and past penetrations to make immediate repairs. If you classify yourself as victim or benefi-ciary, your responsibility is either to repent or to forgive. Any other action makes a person very vulnerable to heavier bondage. "Unforgiveness" is a hindering spirit. It is the main deterrent to receiving the healing power of God. I have witnessed numerous miraculous healings to diseases, considered incurable, with the words: "I repent and Father forgive ..."

Here are more roots of the Israel/Palestine conflict. Satan memorized the prophecies and had been trying with all his might to doom as many heirs as possible. As soon as a remnant returned to Israel first in 1882, 1917 (Balfour Declaration) and later on in 1948, he sprang into action. He recalled what happened when the seed of Isaac first crossed the Jordan. He remembered his losses under Joshua and Caleb. He remembered when the Jews returned un-der the "Decree of Cyrus." 1945 began to worry Satan. A tyrant that he planted on the world scene—a know hater of Jews, Adolph Hitler—had been defeated and subsequently killed. Four years prior, on May 5th, 1941 Crown Prince Regent Ras Tafari of Ethiopia (the Ethio-pian branch of Solomon's bloodline) defeated the last bastion of the power base of Rome, the armies of Mussolini. The creation of a Jewish state at the end of the maximum 430-year subjugation period was a strong third strike possibility. Satan began sowing serious seeds of division among the inhabitants of Palestinia. He knew that Palestinia was built on the very land called Canaan, a land covenanted with promises to God, spiritually rich and loaded with underground springs. The last things Satan wanted to contend with were battles against God's people on lands where God's most powerful altars stood—Psalm 122. Satan had to fortify his ancient bases. He could not allow the disharmony that existed in Rebekah's womb to heal. If all the occupants of the land had been in an obedient state, the mess in the region would not have existed today. The irony of the whole situation is that the two main occupants were seeds of Ishmael, Isaac, Esau and Jacob (Abraham's sons). Satan blinded the British also so that their land transfer was riddled with potential confusion. I would be remiss if I did not detail the Balfour declaration of November 2nd, 1917.

The Jews at the time of Ahaseurus consisted of all twelve tribes. Before 1917 the blend that lived in Palestinia consisted of Nomads (seed of Judah, Benjamin and Ephraim) Pilgrims, Christians, Arabs, Turks, and Jewish refugees: remnants of tribes as per Joshua 15 &16. The decree of Pope Fernan Martins 5th (to expel Jews during the 15th and 16th centuries) caused those that lived in Spain and Northern Europe to return to Jerusalem during the reign of the tolerant Ottomans—Isaiah 43:5-6. Ezekiel made that prophecy also in Ezekiel 11:17, "Thus saith the Lord God, I will even gather you from the people, and assemble you out of the countries where ye have been scattered, and I will give you the land of Israel." After the 400-year rule of the Ottomans ended, the British became supreme rulers in the land. At the end of World War 1, returnees got involved in preserving the Jewish language and her customs. Those that settled in nearby Arab dominated countries were *catching their tails*. Much bad blood existed between the seed of former brothers Isaac and Ishmael (to this day).

The Paris Peace Conference that convened after World War 1 began the current mess. The United Nations gave the League of Nations mandate to Britain to create a nation out of lands currently named Jordan, The West Bank, and Israel. The land was called Transjordan briefly.

By 1917, except for Jerusalem, the area around the Jordan valley regions that comprised the nation of Israel, including the West bank and Jordan, attracted mixtures of small farmers, herdsmen, and migratory nomads. Religious institutions and foreign consulates in Jerusalem lobbied and encouraged the United Nations to ensure that Jews would have a homeland. The Balfour Declaration of 1917 spelled out that:

1. Britain must create a national home for the Jewish people out of its territory Transjordan, without prejudice to the civil and religious rights of all non-Jewish occupants of the land.

2. Jewish immigration must be facilitated under suitable conditions.

3. They must re-position the scattered Jewish settlements to allow close proximity of Jews to one another on their new homeland.

4. The land should be called Palestine.

In spite of the aforementioned, Jews and Arabs lived in Transjordan under tense conditions for another 24 years with all policy, laws, land division and travel dictated by the United Nations mandate. Both believed that the other side was influencing the partitioning of the land, since no specified boundaries were placed in the Declaration.

CHAPTER 12B. ARABIC ROOTS

Over 4000 years ago, Moses recorded that not only would the seed of Esau and the seed of Ishmael intermarry, but also he gave us a preview of the two main branches of the Islamic religion and "brotherly intolerance" in Genesis 28:8-9. Pay attention to God's prophecies because when Satan is agitated, he makes angry outbursts and tries as hard as possible to fulfill them. Satan promised to attack and destroy religions by polluting truth; therefore all religions (barring none) need to see what doctrines will create brotherly intolerance. We must examine all conflicting passages. Satan's secret desires—*Isaiah 14:13, "I will exalt my throne above the stars of God. I will sit also upon the mount of the congregation, in the sides of the north."*

Let us examine spiritual roots of historical confrontations and then let us look at scriptural biases that incite confrontations. Examine the spiritual map. The British Government's files show the distribution of land ownership in Transjordan up to the year 1948 as follows: approximately 70 percent was owned by the British Government, 10 percent by Jews, 5 percent by Arabs, and the other 15 percent belonged to private absentee owners. Most of the absentee landlords were from Cairo, Beirut, Damascus and Rome. The Arabic population greeted the renewed interest in the Hebrew religion and language by returning Jewish refugees with nervousness and suspicion. The distribution of the Old Hebrew Law with emphasis on "Eye for an eye and a tooth for a tooth" would eventually lead to intolerance and it did. It became convenient to dismiss Jeshua and His doctrine on forgiveness as *guilt syndrome* perpetrated first by the Romans and later by their offspring, the British. The British sensing unease could not wait to get out, and be freed from—what they perceived to be—national ingratitude. At the same time, the Arab contingent had their own doctrines and their own language. They were not immune to Satan's interference. A Holy war in the name of Islam began to conceptualize.

Having believed Satan's lie that there are separate "races," large ethnocentrically religious groups take pains to establish a prophet of their ethnicity as "The One, True, and Only prophet."

That is in direct contradiction to God's word. God sent 40 prior messengers with cumulative prophecies and confirmations that His own kinfolk would reject "God's Chosen Messenger." That rejection would open the door for all others to be grafted into and receive God's redemptive package. I have seen no evidence in *God's Law of Double Reference*, or in the Holy Koran's forerunner, *The Torah*, that God wanted the seed of Ishmael to establish a new religion—in fact, just the opposite. "The Golden Fleece Found!" will highlight major discrepancies. Unlike Christianity, *Repentance and Forgiveness are not among Islam's 5 pillars of faith.*

Satan has lies and deceit for every situation. Satan knew that Ishmael's seed was due a blessing. After Mohammed died he sprang into action. Different schools of thought wrestled to insert their analyses for the Holy Koran. Here are *Suras*: the meanings are as obvious and plain as daylight. Sura 5, 48: "To thee (Jesus son of Mary mentioned in Sura 5, 46) we sent the Scripture in truth, confirming the scripture that came before it, and guarding it in safety." Sura 5, 46: "And in their footsteps we sent Jesus the son of Mary, confirming the Law that had come before him: We sent him the Gospel therein was guidance and light and confirmation of the law that had come before him: A guidance and an admonition to those who fear Allah." If the Holy Koran secured that Jesus was sent to *confirm* the *Law* and Mohammed was the seal, then who gave the *new instructions to unseal* and to change the Book? How could anyone but Satan have people misinterpret so plain and simple a message? Is the fact that one calls God, Allah, and the other calls Him, Jehovah, sufficient criteria for new and separate religions? How could any other than Satan convince a person that he or she had the right to take his or her own *life?* The meaning of the word contradicts that myth. At birth we are given a "Right Spirit" to ferry us on the journey of life to the "Destination of Truth"—Ezekiel 36:26-27. That spirit is an arranged loan. Our actions allow us either to find truth and everlasting happiness, or we will allow that spirit to be overcome by stronger spirits of hate, deception, lust, murder, envy or death. Those contrary spirits either rob us of life slowly or suddenly. In Ezekiel 11:19, God made this promise to those that receive His restorative package: "*I will put a new spirit within you.*" In the case with David, after he had sinned with Bathsheba, he begged the Lord in Psalm 51:10, "Create in me a clean heart, O God, and *renew a right spirit* within me." He could not have asked God to renew something, had he not messed it up in the first place. How could a person take a life that was not his to begin with? The spirits that convince people to do such things will exchange places with their *right spirits*. When seeking truth, never stake your life on a saying or a text that has no foundational precedent in the Torah.

Some of the greatest and most brilliant Muslims (the Kharijites, the Ismailiya, the Mutazilites and the Asherites) spent years studying and offering analyses of the Holy Koran. They were highly respected. They were among the few intellectual sects favored to fashion a code of conduct for all Muslims. If you read the Koran (and their evaluation) in its entirety, it is a book of worship benedictions and holy prayers to God exhorting Muslims to seek peace "not violence" with all men. It is emphatic: it exhorts followers of Messenger Mohammed to coexist with all men *peacefully*. Sad to say, many people that follow and believe verbal dictates, supposedly emanating from their faiths, never read the texts to ascertain if in fact what they are told is factual or mythical.

In the Book that Prophet Mohamed exhorted Muslims to seek for truth, Isaiah could not be clearer. Out of the lineage of Jesse shall be "One" that all Gentiles should seek. That one special messenger "In whom my (God's) soul delighteth," mentioned in the same Isaiah 42: 1, God promised to put His Spirit on Him. Prophet Mohammed confirmed the promise in Sura 2:87, that God had put His Spirit on Jesus. History has shown us that Satan's pattern is to use charismatic leaders who are able to manifest some truth, and then use power emanating from either a financial, philosophical or national altar to do the rest.

SOME TRUTH CANNOT BE ALL TRUTH AND IS THEREFORE PARTIAL TRUTH. SINCE PARTIAL TRUTH IS NOT ALL TRUTH, IT IS THEREFORE UNTRUTH.

Satan has successfully used that maxim to transpose religious zeal into philosophical zeal. He has caused much intolerance by changing religious ways of life from initially progressive searches for ultimate truth into arrogantly stagnant philosophical doctrines. Already Satan had convinced militants to insert maximum philosophical zeal to protect *their* sacred "New Way" at any cost. Supposedly, it was considered honourable to die protecting that "Way." Satan had and still has all players on a collision course. Every player had and still has a new identity and a new mission, all fueled by unyielding zeal. No one looked at peaceful coexistence.

Resentment against the British was strong from both Arab and Jewish residents; both felt that the British were favouring one ethnic group over the other. During those years, there was a steady flow of Jews fleeing Russia and Europe until the outbreak of the Second World War when the Aliyah door closed. Tensions between Jewish returnees and Arabic settlers mounted and inevitably major nationalistic skirmishes erupted until November 1947, when the U.N voted to partition Palestinia into two separate nations: one Arabic state and one Jewish state. Britain sliced the land from the Jordan Valley, giving Jordan as an Arab state and deciding that the rest should be a Jewish homeland. The main problem with the subdivision was that the Arabic-speaking Palestinian settlers wanted a separate homeland from that of Jordan. The ink was hardly dry on the accord before war broke out. Jordan grabbed a chunk and invited all Arab residents to be part of a bigger (All Arab) state with Jordan as its capital. Jordan's call for all the dispersed Palestinians sounded appealing. It was never prophesied to happen; so it did not happen.

800,000 Palestinian Arabs that were original residents in the Jewish designated area left for Jordan at the commencement of the war in 1948. On the other side of the coin, approximately 900,000 Jewish refugees migrated from neighbouring Arab states to Israel. After the war, there was a shift in destinies for both Palestinians and Jews. The Jews that arrived in Israel, impoverished and destitute, were welcomed and granted citizenship. By 1967, the Six-Day War saw a redesign of the map, with Israel regaining land that Jordan had annexed previously. The Jordanian residents soon found the nomadic ways and culture of the arriving Arabs much too difficult to absorb into theirs. They ended up treating the Palestinians as refugees. The United States of Arabia *was never formed*, leaving disgruntled and displaced Palestinian Arabs to this day. The nomadic Palestinians never felt welcomed in Jordan. In contrast, Israel granted amnesty to Palestinians that fought alongside Jordan, as long as they were willing to return to Israel after the war ended.

Why did the British divide Transjordan into two, instead of three, parcels of land; since there are three distinct and different nationalities? Did they assume that because all the Jews were focusing on one Jewish homeland that the Arabic Nomads of Transjordan would have had the same intentions? One organized group "seed of Esau" built a country named Jordan and promised the nomadic Palestinians a national base. It did not happen. The other group decided to covenant with a derivative of the Philistine name—Palestinia. They are the displaced Palestinians. Since then, Jews and Palestinians have been fighting to control the remaining droplet, with each side trying to convince the world that they are in fact the victims of injustices. In the meantime no one is reading *The Book*, which offers the spiritual roadmap for peace. Satan keeps blinding all sides with spirits of hate, "unforgiveness," intolerance, arrogance and death. Whenever I ask, "How is it that the Palestinian issue is muted when neighboring Arab States negotiate their borders with Israel?" Some argue that the Jewish returnees from America and Europe are polluted seed: "They marry Euro-Gentiles and even look like and behave like them." Others believe that they and imposters in Hollywood hatched a secret plot to discredit the original race, through movies, and the media. The evidence I found refuted such. Except for recent returnees, I found Hamitic Jews all over Israel and even represented graphically in Museums. Some truth is not all truth!

The Jews took a name that God gave to Jacob, "Israel," and renewed their covenant with Him. Even though Jacob had character blemishes, God did not cancel the blessings placed on him by his father, Isaac. *Esau*, though omitted from the covenant, was promised material blessings. He *was granted no messianic seed.* He was put in the desert with *one measure of refreshing*—a one-measure container. Since Israel succeeded with her call for returning refugees, others in the region became nervous as more and more waves of Jews returned to their new homeland, in accordance with God's edicts—Genesis 22:2, Genesis 22:14-18, Genesis 23:17-18, Genesis 25:5-6, Genesis 26:23-25, Genesis 35:1-7 and especially verses 10,11 and 12. Verse 10 reads, "Thy name is Jacob, thy name shall no more be called Jacob, but *Israel shall be thy name.* Verse 11, "I am God Almighty; be fruitful and multiply; a nation and a company of nations shall be of thee, and kings shall come out of thy loins." Verse 12, "The land, which I gave Abraham and Isaac, to thee I will give it *and to thy seed after thee will I give the land."*

That inheritance, a homeland according to ordinances made over 3500 years ago, is filled with redemptive hope, promises and serious blessings. Millions have died and will die for those hopes and promises. Satan had planned that for centuries and it is inevitable. Satan will influence the selection of leaders (in that region) who behave as if they eat gunpowder. Prophets can only forewarn with the hope of minimizing the carnage and hopefully have as many as possible redeemed from the curse of death, without the true knowledge of their God.

After Sarah died, Abraham had another wife named Keturah. She produced seed also. However Abraham already blessed his heir. By taking another wife, he confirmed God's foundational law of "Double reference" and also the prophetic significance of wives of chosen Patriarchs. *Of necessity, seed of Abraham would produce another religion after the Messiah arrived.* In Genesis 25:6, Abraham had concubines also: "Unto the sons of the concubines, which Abraham had, Abraham gave them gifts and sent them away from Isaac." In my travels I have met seed of Abraham also living in the same countries previewed in Esther 1:1, building shrines on, and around, strange doctrines. A word to the wise: A person's pursued philosophy will determine his or her ultimate destiny.

CHAPTER 12 C. THOSE (OTHER THAN UNCUT) STONES

During (what was classified as) the Dark Ages, corrupt altars at a large church institution magnetized power-hungry men and wedged them into positions of authority. The satanic network wooed and enticed men like Maffeo Barberi (a former Pope) with offices and titles. They engineered close marriages between church and state and decreed what could be printed and what could be thought. Any institution that interferes with your mind, your capacity to make independent sensible choices, and/or your freedom to speak/think independently, is contrary to the principles of God. All such institutions can be satanically influenced. Conversely, an institution, positioned as your covering authority, is obliged to steer its flock away from danger. Nonetheless, attempting to regulate mental dietary choices is a dangerous horse of a different colour. Spirits of "Domination" find it difficult to resist any enclave whereby much power and influence is concentrated. Eventually, without learned spiritual guardians, proper checks/balances, and a tough moral code, repeated attacks will crumble the institutions' custodians/altars, and or both. Such collapses have transmuted formerly progressive institutions into cults—often resulting in horrific deaths.

Between the 7th and the 15th centuries, the Muslim nations were world leaders in culture, education and sciences. The Byzantine peninsular, home of the Turkish Empire, was the centre of art, culture, learning, and much trade. Unlike the early Christian movement, which was nomadic, autocratic and secretive because of persecutions, the Muslim world flourished under openness, an outpouring of goodwill, educational encouragement, and religious tolerance. During those centuries, Europe was feudal and educationally backward, for the most part. When Christianity was kidnapped or annexed and its upright columns replaced, disharmony set in. Spiritually speaking, the Roman architectural attempted replacement of the Jerusalem foundation caused structural damage to the altar. That altar of stones—not supplied by God, not fitted jointly to the chief cornerstone—crumbled as referenced by Nehemiah. Rebuilding obstacles are in Nehemiah 2:9. Paul the apostle, assigned to bring the Gospel to the Gentiles, warned the Corinthian brethren in his letter chronicled as 1st Corinthians 3:11. "For other foundation can no man lay than that is laid, which is Jesus Christ." The really interesting part is in verse 12. "If any man build upon this foundation, gold, silver, precious stones, wood, hay, stubble, (13) every man's work shall be made manifest: for the day (revealed light) shall declare it because it shall be revealed by fire; and the fire shall try every man's work of what sort it is." As a result of the incongruence, what is called Christianity today is not what was practiced by the early churches in the first 5 chapters of Acts. In many cases today, Christianity represents an incongruent aggregate of reformed Judaism, autocratic Capitalism and Legalism. Microphones and television cameras have caused much "Flesh" to glory in the presence of God. Satan even has manciples disguised among disciples. Every church today can match the personality traits of each of Solomon's wives, princesses or concubines. There is none "without spot or wrinkle." Why is that so? It stands to reason: *none of Solomon's wives were virgins.* Simply put, the Messiah's house spiritual sojourn must follow the path of God's physical house on earth (the Temple that Solomon built). Prophecies of David, Micah, Zechariah, Isaiah, Jeremiah and Ezekiel point to a messianic kingdom that would be "torn down," yet rebuilt. Jeshua and His witnesses fulfilled most of those prophecies. The unfulfilled ones are looming, as per *John's vision on the isle of Patmos.* All of Jeshua's disciples were willing to die rather than deny what they had witnessed. In fact most of them, mainly Jews, died defending the *Good News.*

Europe borrowed the Hebrew law and used Greek Philosophy rather than the oracle of the *Most High God* for edification. To compound matters, the Roman and Grecian Empires evolved from the ashes of Babel, a city founded by a rebellious grandson of Ham—Nimrod. He was a mighty hunter, obsessed with making a name for himself. It is documented in the Tanakh, the Torah, and the Bible—his ways did not please God. His father (Cush) and his seed are recorded in Genesis 10:6-20. In those verses, countless rebellious and warmongering people of yesteryear are documented as offspring of that seed. Many were generational enemies of Israel and Judah: Nineveh, Accad, Asshur, Babel, and their seed, became the Jebusites, the Arvadites, the Philistines, and the Amorites. The spirits that influenced those national strongholds were, and still are on a confrontational course with God's redemptive plans for Israel and

Africa. Data in the Tanakh/the Bible should negate the myth that Anglo American prejudice was, and or is racially motivated especially since 80 or more percent of our "white" population "evolved" from that son of Noah (Ham) whose seed produced the blackest nations.

CHAPTER 12D. AN ANGLO-AMERICAN FOUNDATION

The Pillars on which Joseph Smith built his American based church appear to have been left from an open Druid altar in an Oak grove. The pillars of the formalized early European church were restructured on "New Stones." Those were stones not from God's spiritual temple of continuity as per David and Solomon, but blood-soaked stones of religious intolerance, incompatibility, substitution, and flawed doctrines of infallibility. There were also demonic doctrines of hate, superiority and spiritual alliances of church/state. "Doctrines of Substitution" meant that even though nothing should be added or subtracted from God's word, a subtracted form called a Catechism was introduced. Jesus himself taught us to give to Caesar the things that are Caesar's and to God the things that are God's. In other words, ensure that spiritually prudent custodians guard the highest spiritual altars. A constitution, though a declaration over a national altar, cannot be substituted for a moral code. From archaeological points of view (natural or spiritual) "new stones" form quickly and are brittle. They fall easily when hit.

CARNAL BEINGS OR THINGS CANNOT SAFEGUARD SACRED PROPERTY PROPERLY.

An American, named Joseph Smith, once strayed in the woods to an ancient ceremonial site, an Oak grove. To understand the seriousness of doing anything supposedly Godly at an ancient ceremonial site, read Judges 6:25- 30, 2nd Chronicles 15:16 and also 1st Kings 15:13.

In Deuteronomy 7:5 and Deuteronomy 12:3, God commanded that all ceremonial groves should be destroyed and burned. Exodus 34:13, "Ye shall destroy their altars, break their images, and cut down their groves." Smith allegedly sat at an abandoned Druid altar to pray. He had, by his own admission, one of the most vicious demonic attacks ever recorded; yet a large denomination in America reverences him as their foundation stone.

I will replay the encounter using his words. His testimony: "He was seized upon by an awesome terrible power which overcame him, and had such an astonishing influence over him that it *bound his tongue* so that *he could not speak*. It engulfed him in *darkness* to such an extent that he felt doom and destruction." Refer to my chapter on Alien Encounter and my Damascus experience for a full explanation of what transpired. God made sure that Mr. Smith used specific words that emanate from the realm of darkness so that in an appointed time, any prophet with the "Gift of Discernment" would know that the attack was definitely demonic. Anytime anyone commences praying to Almighty God and a thing (unseen) either stops his/her prayers or binds his/her tongue, take it from a person with years of experience in *Deliverance Ministries* it is a demonic attack. *Every tongue must be able to confess and praise God.* Isaiah 45:22, I am God. Verse 23, "Every knee shall bow, every tongue shall swear…" Every tongue must be able to affirm God's supremacy and Jeshua's authority unless hindered by evil spirits. The question beckons, Did Mr. Smith have his generational curses broken, since by his own admission he had a large spiritual opening?

I have witnessed evil spirits wrestle persons to attempt to stop them from saying, "Jesus is Lord." David taught us in Psalm 34:1, "I will bless the Lord at all times: his praise shall continually be in my mouth." Smith continued to verify that he finally got delivered from "the enemy that *bound him.*" Jacob wrestled with an angel but at no time was Jacob unable to communicate with his God. Jacob said, "I will not let you go until you bless me." Smith admitted it was the enemy. In Mr. Smith's autobiographical account labeled his testimonies, he admitted that the pressure from society was such that he slipped into a serious *state of depression* (demonic attacks in the realm of *depression*). The amazing thing about his experience is that the entire foundational process was centered on the tablets and not the *source* of the tablets. In the past, I have seen spirits envelop amulets and art pieces. Only after the bound person renounced having contact with a satanic altar did they get delivered. Exodus 34:14, "Thou shall worship no other god, for the Lord is a jealous God."

God gave the dominion of earth to man. God does not bestow gifts and take them back. So, since man transgressed, a man must come to repair the breach—Isaiah 53. Had God not given that task to man, when He sent His angel to destroy Sodom, He would have allowed His angel to destroy Satan's entire kingdom in one swoop. Since the days of Pentecost, we have been in the season of grace (as this period is called). The Spirit of the Lord began the revisiting season previously prophesied by Joel. There are times when he sends ministering spirits with empowering gifts through His redeemed Son. Jeshua is now the permanent intercessor. In times of spiritual battles He sends "The Angel of the Lord," Daniel 3:28 and Psalm 34:7. God's army is not dysfunctional. All the rebellious angels already signed on to Satan's army. They have brought and will bring messages to attempt to confuse and to negate all of God's corroborating prophecies. That is why God established His Law of Double-Reference and cautioned us: "To test the spirits to see if they are from God." I am not led at this juncture to give a description of what *The Angel of the Lord* looks like, except that he always has a sharp glittering sword at his right side. Pray to God that you never see him with his sword in his hand. Those are the personages God has ordained in this dispensation to contact and to speak to persons on earth. Other personages are intruding extraterrestrials from the satanic divide that can contact persons with ungodly spiritual openings—Psalm 91:5-6.

There is nothing abnormal about dreaming about a deceased loved one. On the other hand, attempting to reach that person through a spirit-medium is a sure recipe for contamination from a satanic altar. Isaiah 8:19, "And when they shall say unto you, Seek unto them that have familiar spirits, and unto wizards that peep, and that mutter, should not a people seek unto their God?" Leviticus 19:31, Regard not them that have familiar spirits, neither seek after wizards to be defiled by them. In Leviticus 20:27, a man or woman that hath a familiar spirit or that is a wizard shall be put to death. All decrees in the Book of Leviticus punishable unto death are foundational openings for spirits that carry sicknesses unto death. If a person is in a sinful state and God initiates the contact, there can be only one message: Repent!

One might ask, "What about Cornelius the Firstfruit Gentile convert?" He was fervent with his prayers to God and generous with alms giving. He paid his tithes and sought the Lord daily in prayer. *God sent His ministering angel to steer him to his earthly prophets* and confirmed his impending conversion. God then sent the same ministering angel to Peter. God always works through His appointed prophets/apostles and then confirms His word. God is not a God of confusion. God did not tell Cornelius to form a new church for the Gentiles. All Gentiles were to be grafted into the natural olive tree. That seemed to have been a big problem with the seed of Babylon. There is one cornerstone. Psalm 24 explained what Moses decreed; no one can enter the presence of God unless he/she has been sanctified. "Who shall enter His holy place? Those with clean hands and pure hearts..."

Let us source Mr. Smith's apparition. 2nd Corinthians 11:14 "Satan himself is transformed into an angel of light; (15) Therefore it is no great thing if *his ministers* also be transformed as the ministers of righteousness; whose end shall be according to their works." According to Mr. Smith, two supernatural personages approached him and told him that all churches were supposedly wrong. They would give the truth to him alone. In the book of John Chapters 14 and 15, it is very clear that while the Logos was on earth manifest in human form, there could have been only one manifestation. From the time the Logos arrived in the form of man, the turtledove sacrifices ceased. In the river Jordan the Logos appeared in the form of a dove and landed on Jeshua. There was a spiritual transfer of "the scepter" until Jeshua was surrendered unto death temporarily.

America was never connected to Israel. What I do know is that there is a fierce war being waged over its spiritual connection to Zion and its esoteric connection to ancient Babylon. God chose Zion for His chief cornerstone. Paul warned against contrary foundations and the consequences for such in 1st Corinthians 3:11-14. Paul should know since he was first given the authority to preach to the Gentiles. Since Paul was Jewish, God did not break His commandment that stated: "To the Jews were committed the Oracles of God." The God of Abraham's covenant was and forever is "omnipresent and invisible." Mr. Smith was not Jewish. It is obvious: since anyone remotely Jewish would know the purposes of the Holy Instruments—Urim and Thummim. They were *never fastened* to the breastplates of any of the High Priests. The breastplate of the High Priests had only stones that were ordained for the "Twelve Tribes." Adding insult to injury, the messenger, a Gentile named "Maroni," was neither recorded in the Torah/Tanakh nor mentioned by Jeshua or by any of the Firstfruit witnesses. God has never inscribed any message on a gold tablet. I will not spell out the reason in this book.

If you want to know the reason, examine Moses' account on the construction of Solomon's Temple. God used a specific substance for witnessing *the Law of Moses* at Mt. Sinai, and on the wall in front of Belshazzar of Babylon. Of the two branches carrying Joseph Smith's legacy, one branch believed that the tablets were inscribed in brass. The other believed that they were inscribed in gold. When the differences were first discovered, his disciples allegedly split into two separate factions. I believe the rifts exist through to this day. Paul's letter to the Corinthians explained that there could be no new tablets in 1st Corinthians 3:12. John the Apostle clarifies what he could have seen. "Not that anyone hath seen the Father, save he which is of God, he hath seen the father"—John 6:46. See the last segment of this book called Mystery of Mysteries for a complete revelation of that matter. The entire universe, including everything known/unknown, and visible/invisible, existed in the mind of God before He spoke matter into being; yet Mr. Smith allegedly saw not one, but two "European deities?" Score that as one of Satan's big victories. To this date, millions of Americans believe that the two "European looking men," allegedly seen by Mr. Smith were God and Jesus! Exodus 19:21 refutes such. John 4:24, "*God is spirit: and they that worship Him must worship Him in spirit and in truth.*"

NO HUMAN BEING HAS EYES BIG ENOUGH TO SEE ALL OF GOD, NOR COULD THEY BE RADIATION-PROOF ENOUGH TO GET SO CLOSE TO GOD.

The human transformer, the cloned of God (Jeshua) visited us. God, through all of His prophets, promised us one redeemer. Any other human vessel, pure or strong enough to carry the Spirit of God on a redemptive mission, would have to arrive first through a cleansed bloodline, purged through the wombs of Rebekah, through Rachel, through Mary, and accompanied by hundreds of prior prophecies. To all devotees of Mr. Smith, the genealogy of Jesus had been given, coded in Psalm 87. Rahab, Solomon and David were all extremely black people.

According to the Torah, your foundations have been weighed in the balance and found in need of serious remedial actions. I love the way that God conceals things for seasons to expose fallacies and inaccuracies. Since Satan has promised to pursue all of God's holy altars, it is very important to examine the spiritual foundations of your families, your cities, and your religious institutions. Pursuers of truth beware! Inaccurate theses in the name of God are the breeding grounds for false religions.

CHAPTER 12E. OPERATION WATER-SERPENT PROPHESIED

I have shown, in a previous chapter that Leviathan is mission-focused, water strong and water based. She has laid eggs in institutions, countries, and under respectable altars (Isaiah 14:6-9). If those eggs are not removed, through God's law of duplicity, doom will fall on all that qualify for a "double-portion." Just like wood–borne parasites, those spirits will cause and have caused powerful foundations to crumble. Revelation 18:1-18 need to be expounded upon. Verse 1 reported that the spirit that moves that mystery harlot sitteth among many waters. She had induced mighty persons in authority with her spirits of lust. Lust is a synonym for excessive desires/greed. The spirit was puffed up with *the blood of saints*. That spirit has a master plan to manipulate kingdoms into specific warfare. *That spirit had corrupted many multitudes and tongues.* It was entrenched in a power base, a city with blood on her foundations, which, prophetically "will be destroyed in one hour!"

God's laws of duplicity dictate that it happened to ancient Babylon; it will happen again to the entrenched base of the seed of Babylon, unless corrective steps are taken. The institutions that are most prone to that prophecy have the identical vision in all of their foundation books. However by rewriting and reducing them to subtracted versions called Catechisms, congregations are not inclined to ask questions pertaining to such. According to God's modus operandi, *He gives His word, seals it with action, and confirms it at least once more.*

I will expose that matriarchal spirit's infiltration of God's seat of power. First the builder of God's physical house on earth cracked the foundation by erecting a huge house for the daughter of Pharaoh: the second opening for the matriarchal spirit to penetrate, and germinate in the *Messiah's house on earth.* By allowing Athalia (2ndKings11:1-3) to hold Judah's scepter, the matriarchal spirit corrupted, and laid eggs under Israel's highest altar to *The Most High God.* Those eggs were strengthened with the removal of temple vessels to Babylon; then to Rome with Titus in 70 C.E. Later on, in complete detail, I shall examine the altars of that major city. The foundations of which conceal to this day, ritualized paganism, rivers of martyrs' blood, matriarchal adulation, satanic cults, and also spiritually tainted buildings and paintings. As we peel away layer by layer, the image and plan of the final Antichrist will be revealed.

When John recorded his vision, the Babylonian Empire had been destroyed already. He was careful to point out that the vision referred to a spirit entrenched in a power base. In Revelation 17:6, the spirit was responsible for the blood of Jesus' followers. In Revelation 18:6, a double portion of spiritual violence was the only remedy ordained for its demise. Since water is a desert destroyer, that spirit has the unusual ability to function *within the refreshing.* Esoterically speaking, that spirit targets religious foundations and is strengthened with body fluids spilled disobediently.

When John was on the island of Patmos, he saw a vision of a spiritual hot spot that had forged alliances between kings of the earth, businesses and churches. It had caused Jesus' witnesses to be martyred: "There was no repentance in her mouth." (Revelation 2 and Revelation 9)

God always finds a way to warn His people. God provides ample time for repentance. We are in the age of "Grace: we are Granted Reprieve and Amnesty on Condition (that we forsake) Evil." If we do not, then the demons that are entrenched, will cause such bondage to the custodians and the altars, that eventual destruction is inevitable. God always sends His prophets to fore-warn—Ezekiel 33:6.

CHAPTER 12F. UNSOLVED DEATH OF A POPE

Before the *First Crusade*, Islam was a regional and philosophical way of life. The 1st Crusade spread violence, superiority, death, and all the other demons that Satan had unleashed under that institutionalized banner. He succeeded in building partitions of hate between the seed of Abraham, His purposes, and the churches of the Roman provinces that taught that they were to replace God's people. It is very important to detail the first 100 years of Jeshua's ministry to show the accuracy of Solomon's Temple and the fulfillment of what was etched in clefts of the rock base by the Anointed One or Messiah. It is amazing how many millions have assumed *errone-ously* that the foundation Jerusalem church was in Rome.

The early churches built by Jesus' apostles were all under the jurisdiction of Elder James, of the Jerusalem base church up until 98C.E. or 99 C.E. Because of the persecution around Jerusalem, the headquarters moved to Antioch in Syria. The Eastern and Western Churches of Rome merged in 326 C.E. That coalition was an amalgamation of churches in Roman controlled provinces, directed to unite with the blessing of Constantine. Out of that 4th century union, the Roman Catholic Church was born. Besides those, there were a few monastic divisions, which were watered by the original bases of Jerusalem and Antioch. The carnage that followed Titus' destruction of Jerusalem forced them to function like most modern-day small town churches. Unlike the days of Paul when they were fed regularly with visits and letters of encouragement, they became scattered and retreated into remote caves. An organized fire could not reignite them until the winter of martyrdom had ceased. Those early remnants became the Greek, African and Russian Orthodox churches.

In the early stages of the structure of the Roman church, men with covetous eyes sought the choice seats of power. Eventually the persons that sat on those thrones were the greedy, the pow-erful, and the manipulative—in many cases, all three types. The ordinary folks were not involved in those major power struggles. In reality, many Catholics (including those on our research team) were oblivious to these facts until they saw tangible evidence. That segment of research took over 20 years. It brought a sense of relief to many, a sense of closure to some; filled in lots of missing pieces and finally revealed the truth. Not everyone handled the news and revelations gracefully. Some were embarrassed by the findings; others, bound by spirits of Apostasy, became more hardened.

A person of high rank from a European church leaked to our group—news that in Rome, one in supreme authority was contemplating the bold move of total disclosure. Unfortunately it stalled after his untimely death. John Paul lived an extremely pious life, was a fitness addict, trekked up mountains daily and maintained a strict healthy diet. He was nevertheless diagnosed as having died of natural causes and no known autopsy was performed. To this date, the death of a Pope John Paul is shrouded in mystery. He was not the first Pope to be stopped physically for fighting to uproot entrenched spirits from beneath the altar of the church. Two former Popes were assassinated for such: one held office from 813-820 C.E., Pope Leo V, and the other ruled the church from 842-867C.E., Pope Michael 111.

CHAPTER 13. BEHIND THE VEIL OF SECRECY/ SORCERY

Prior to the Protestant Reformation of 1520, "Secret Organizations" were the only intellectual causeway open to explore "other avenues of wisdom" outside of the accepted state/church-controlled "Schools of Thought." It was noised about that the formulae for the transmigration of souls could be discerned through alchemy. Alchemism, which predated formal chemistry, became a powerful lure in early England and France. To be an alchemist, it helped if one was a member of a secret organization. It was widely rumored that organized occult practices ferried over across the channel from primeval Europe to England. The tinkering with alchemism caused an increase in occult activities either accidentally or deliberately. The then powerful irascible church/state organizations outlawed all practices, real or imaginary. Any intellectually provocative or dissenting thesis was classified as supportive of the occult and therefore heretical. Clashes with the intellectuals of the time were frequent. One of the most noted occurred in Florence between Galileo and Maffeo Barberi or Pope Urban VIII in 1623.

How dare Galileo publish his theory—the sun was the centre of the universe—despite being advised that the autocratic church in Rome had a contrary opinion? During and after *The Inquisition*, established by Pope Gregory IX in 1233, under the system of spontaneous trials, it was very easy to accuse someone of being a witch. The punishment for conviction meant that the accused would be "bound on a stake" and "burnt alive." Joan of Arc was among those that suffered that fate. Even though there was no evidence whatsoever that Galileo was involved in either secret alchemy or any form of occultism, he had to sign a document of renunciation and face imprisonment instead of the dreaded torture for heresy or practicing witchcraft: "Death at the Stake." In 1415 *The Council of Constance* ordered John Huss (the religious reformer) burned at the stake. In a later chapter I will define in detail the nature of cults. I will spell out two forms of ritual killings only, since this book is not designed to enlarge the wisdom files of the twisted. Those *two* types have been known from yesteryear.

There is a large church organization that needs to fast and seek the wisdom of the Lord on the spiritual reason for a blatant "Sacrilegious Substitution." The word of God in Deuteronomy 4:2 is specific. Nothing must be added or subtracted from God's word. Jesus was more explicit; he warned that no person was allowed to change even a dot. Jesus knew the prophetic power, precision and "pelicost" nature of God's word. All major libraries recorded that until Titus sacked Jerusalem in 70 C.E., the Romans used crucifixion as their harshest form of punishment. After the Inquisition, the state-controlled religion decreed that anyone condemned as a witch should be burned "at the stake." There are stark spiritual and physical differences between the punishments of burning on a stake, the ritual death of impalement, and crucifixion. Since impalement is ritualistic and demonic in nature, one seriously needs to question why that organization would want to insert in all of its weekly magazines, religious books, and Bibles, that Jesus was *impaled*. I will detail as much information as possible to assist those who might be led astray accidentally or deliberately.

God and His language are so awesome. God foresaw all possible errors and mistranslations and concocted a perfect language. He then earmarked on a plan to perfect a people to a perfect lifestyle of obedience and blessings. For example: in Hebrew, God allowed the use of a plural word for "tree." The same word is used for "tree," and "wood." When English was invented, God made sure that "stake" was a singular noun. For starters, a person cannot be impaled on a tree. To make a stake, one has to sharpen a branch from an e^ts. Can anything be added to, or subtracted from God's word? Make up your minds; it is impossible for Jesus to have been impaled on a tree. All those that belong to organizations that portray Jesus tied to a stake like a pig to be barbecued, please access research from Israel and Rome on the way Romans crucified people on dead trees. Incidentally the Hebrew word for trees is (e^ts = branches) wood (a plural word). In Hebrew, the word for wood/tree and trees is the same. The obvious misunderstanding manifests in those publications where you state that Jesus was *impaled* between two posts. How can that possible? It is written in Galatians 3:13, "He became a curse for us." Death by crucifixion was considered a curse. The Old Testament precedent—For a sin offering, a lamb was *"slain"* between two posts. According to descriptions given in all English dictionaries—the implications in your Bibles and weekly magazines—Jesus was impaled between two posts is contradictory. Death by impalement is a ritualistic practice.

In spite of that, your organization's American base and overseas branches worldwide insert throughout your entire publishing network that Jesus was "Impaled on a tree." Incidentally, burning at the stake was a punishment for practitioners of "witchcraft" or heresy against a religion formed at the end of the 3rd century. One of the aforementioned is outlawed and defunct. Be precise and specific. I am praying that your eyes of understanding will be opened, as your international zeal in *witnessing* is wonderful. In addition, the chapter on "Mystery of Mysteries" should be a tremendous help to your organization. Also Psalm 122 and 132:4-17 encase God's restorative plans for Israel. Those, plus Luke 24:46-53, Romans 1:16 and also Romans 11:1 contradict your teachings that God abandoned Israel. Zechariah 8:3—"Thus saith the lord; I am returned unto Zion, and will dwell in the midst of Jerusalem: and Jerusalem shall be called a city of truth…" God's word (not yours) is His litmus test. In Genesis 3:1, Satan taught men to misinterpret God's word: "Hath God said?" The word of God is unambiguous: Nothing should be added or subtracted from His word.

ONE DOESN'T HAVE TO BE A MASTER TO KNOW THAT THE BRANCH CANNOT BE IMPALED ON A TREE!

CHAPTER 13A. THE IMPALING RITUAL

The spiritual backlash that occurred after Jesus' death, and the resulting darkness and earthquake that ensued frightened many away from continuing the practices of crucifixion. In the first century, being fed to the lions replaced crucifixion as Rome's main publicly disgraceful form of death. There are both physical and spiritual differences between crucifixion and impalement. English dictionaries describe the act of *impaling* as one of piercing a person on *one* sharpened stake through and through. Impaling is ritualistic. The act of gorging through a person with one thrust to ensure maximum expulsion of pressurized body fluids is demonic.

Records from primeval Europe unveil an increase in the ritualistic practice after the commencement of the 2nd millennium. Pope John XX11's decree of 1320 caused over 30,000 to be impaled. About the same number died in the slaughter of June 1099 at the hands of the monk Peter the Hermit. That is recorded in the annals of history as the *First Crusade*. In fact those *Crusaders* were given an official pardon in advance by Pope Urban 11. History recalled that the Crusaders not only impaled, but also practiced cannibalism. The news media and those churches were deafeningly silent for years on the sacrileges committed. The Roman army surrounded and trapped Jews and Christians in the synagogue in Jerusalem. While singing to a Jewish Messiah, they celebrated mass murder of His people, by burning the synagogue to the ground with the occupants (mostly Jewish Christians) trapped inside. History also made mention of another infamous monster, Vlad the Impaler. From his birth date to the date of his demise is recorded as 1431 to 1476. His nickname was Dracula (son of the dragon). During a six-year killing spree, that demonized person was responsible for 60,000 to 100,000 innovatively horrific deaths. His specialty was impalement. Since God's word is specific in that nothing should be added or subtracted from His word, I question the American organization again for implying impalement. Those breaches in their foundational altar have blocked them from receiving proper understanding as to how God used Jeshua as a human generator to give spiritual current to the masses.

Anyone who alters God's Word, injects his opinion over and above that of God's chosen prophets and publishes such is committing a sacrilege. Each word—its placement and its meaning—is precise and oft-times, prophetic. The Hebrew language is esoteric: forward, backward, sequentially, and/or diagonally, it can be translated—as long as the source is the unadulterated Hebrew texts. I have a serious problem with those who go beyond expounding on God's word—those that dare to mistranslate, change, add, or subtract from God's word. Eventually egotism and disobedience encourages you to insert biased opinions. Some hint that Ishmael received no blessing whatsoever. Others imply in print that Ham was cursed and therefore all black people received a curse from Ham. God changeth not. He already blessed Ham and his sons. The generational curse—for Ham interfering with Noah's lady when dad was drunk—became due on the spiritually-exposed seed, Canaan. Observe that Genesis 9:23 mentions "Laid a garment on both of their shoulders." They were both naked and drunk. Leviticus 18:8, "The nakedness of thy father's wife shalt thou not uncover; it is thy father's nakedness." Those curses last a maximum of four generations.

By the way, Ham's pigmentation came from his extremely tanned father Noah and so for that matter were 90+ percent of the people in the Old Testament. In any case, God blessed Ham and his sons. Who God blesses let no man curse. God blessed Noah who produced the black Hamites, the brown Semites and the "destined to evolve" Japhethites. Noah was mindful of the fact that God had already blessed him and his sons. Hence when Noah discovered the sacrilege of Ham in Genesis 9:25 his words were: "Cursed be Canaan." Noah's curse fell unto the grandson, Canaan and would last on his seed a maximum 280 years if they walked in disobedience. Ezekiel 18 expounds on generational curses. If you have been following God's pattern in this discourse so far, you will realize that there is esoteric significance to the sacrilege of Ham. I will list a few things that one can call coincidences or parallel events:

1. Early Rome and later England became places where being accused of occult practices by their churches meant immediate persecution, usually after phony trials.

2. Occultists need blood, semen, or both for their sacrifices—Leviticus 20:2-3, and 6.

3. Certain geometric patterns were and are utilized during occult practices.

4. Specific dates (called High-Energy times) were and are selected for Occult harvests.

5. The Atlantic Slave Trade provided all of the above.

CHAPTER 13B. THE ATLANTIC SLAVE TRADE, MYSTICAL ROOT

History books are littered with hints that the transatlantic slave trade was established for economic purposes to provide sources of cheap labour. We will look at a small portion (the spiritual root) of that foundation since it is impossible to examine the foundations of all that was recorded. Next we will examine some esoteric and prophetic source data. During the Atlantic Slave Trade, the merchants' home bases, the land from which they got their cargo and the lands where the slaves were taken to, constituted a triangle. The majority of persons that participated in different aspects of the slave trade were members of sinister organizations that had erected altars and regularly engaged in ritualistic practices. Preserved paintings held priceless by collectors show remnant of Judah, former Kings that swore to protect the sacred things of God, yoked like ploughs (like oxen in the fields) to the seed of all of Israel's former enemies. Deuteronomy 28:48, "Therefore shalt thou serve thine enemies which the Lord shall send against thee, in hunger, and in thirst, and in nakedness, and in want of all things: and he shall put a yoke of iron upon thy neck…"

All the people (except the preliminary hunters) that engaged in the purchasing, trafficking, forced breeding, rape, and mass murder of the slaves were of the ashes of the Babylonian Empire, and (as per prophecy) in turn grew into Greco/Roman seed. Judah was the "chosen" third generation to follow Moses. The archives in Israel show the tribe of Judah with a lion as its symbol. Their banner features a large-nosed black male depicting the *Conquering Lion of the Tribe of Judah*. They were given strict instructions to destroy all enemies of God before they inhabited the promised lands. Had Judah been obedient, neither Babylon nor its seeds—ancient Greece and Rome—could have become mighty nations of flawed philosophies, and spiritually-deficient world centres. The United States of Israel would have been a large blessed totally self-sufficient landmass, encompassing the Caspian regions, Greece, Turkey, the Gulf regions, India, Transjordan, and the continent of Africa.

Jeremiah prophesied that the tribe of Judah would not remember its heritage and it came to pass—Jeremiah 12:17, and Jeremiah 17:4. He foreknew that they would be dislodged from their prophetic calling. Just as the almug trees that fashioned the fine instruments for Solomon's Temple came from Ethiopia (Africa), remnants of that human lumber (hotly pursued by Satan) are lavishing the music industry with jazz, hip-hop, rap, reggae, cadence and calypso. *Few* have heeded their prophetic calling as worship leaders and gospel singers/musicians. Israel's Museums and department of Antiquities have many an artifact depicting the Afro/Hamitic, Afro/Semitic, and Afro/Japhethic features of their ancestors. Paintings of Abraham and Isaac on their way to the sacrificial site (base of Calvary) and many flasks and figurines of ancient Hebrews are unmistakably Negroid. The southern nations especially around the Gulf of Arabia are 60 to 80 percent Negroid. Since the tribes of Simeon, Judah and members of the Essenes had populated the southern regions of Israel (now called Massada and En-gedi), it was customary to trek back and forth to Ethiopia, which at that time included such countries as Sudan. When Josephus Flavius chronicled Israel's plight after the Roman siege from 66 C.E. to 70 C.E. he confirmed that Jews, who escaped the carnage and starvation, fled to Africa. According to his findings, the majority of the survivors fled to, and settled around Ethiopia and Sudan. The Ethiopians and the ancient Hebrews intermarried so frequently that they were, and are indistinguishable. Amos prophesied the intermarrying and settling. In Amos 9:7, God asked, "*Are ye not as children of the Ethiopians unto me, O children of Israel?*" They not only spoke a common language, but also looked very much alike. Moses' wife was an Ethiopian and so was the Eunuch who spoke to Evangelist Philip without a translator. In the court of Queen Esther was an Ethiopian also. The prophet Nahum elaborated on the closeness of both people and God's plan for both in the end times. There is a chapter commemorating the name of Queen

Esther in the Tanakh or Old Testament as it is called with serious prophetic implications. It details how God wants His bride (His church) to approach Him. It is also a very good source material to understand the period in Israel's history before the racial types got saturated.

Until the reign of king Ahasuerus (some believe that he was Artaxerses) India through Israel to Ethiopia were under the rule of Persia. Ethiopians, Indians, and Jews looked so much alike; at a glance, people could not differentiate one from the other. Esther 3:3 and 4, "Mordecai had not told them he was a Jew." They also spoke the same language.

When Esther was selected to be Queen, no one knew she was a Jew until she told the King that she would be included in the plot hatched by Haman the Agagite. To this day, the features of the inhabitants of India, the Ethiopians, and the Jews in the south of Israel are indistinguishable. The *seed* of the northern tribes that ended up in the Diaspora of Poland, Russia and Germany lost most of their melanin, but still retained their large noses and thick hair. Joseph's coat had "many (melamim) colours." By prophetic disclosure, the seed of Joseph would become multi-ethnic. Whenever entire nations are systematically snatched from their homelands and enslaved in lands of different Gentile tongues, as long as the enslaved people are not wiped out or assimilated, then their survival is the result of a prior prophetic decree. Their *enslavement* resulted from *generations of disobedience* to God's word. Their captivity would then be demonically engineered and there is a prescribed maximum allowable time for that bondage.

In the first chapter, I offered a detailed insight into the domain of darkness. There is a spirit from ancient times that is able to establish strongholds on nations that have incongruent spiritual philosophies. Whenever that happens, Satan can empower and usually empowers a war machine that is able to shed blood in the name of that "False Way." The spirits that control national and spiritual altars corporately are—Leviathan and "Babylon the Great" (see Revelation 17 and 18). Strengthened with sweat and "blood of God's people," they encroach and then spread their clouds of hate, which dissipate over "spiritually dry places," as false doctrines.

Only nations that broke their covenant to God can be enslaved in a foreign country (seed of Babylonian Empire) for 400 years and not be wiped out or totally assimilated. All covenant seed—that practiced corporate rebellion, and did not repent from sinful living, in spite of repeated warnings—their decreed punishment was sure. Unbroken generations of successive rebellion (mixed with idolatry) beget six generations of captivity and subjugation—speaking Gentile tongues in Gentile nations. Their covenanted *Oracle Powers* would be supplanted by *Babel utterances*. However, there is a maximum punishment time allotted. At the end of those subjugation times, serious woe would befall the oppressors and their seed, according to God's unfailing word. In God's mercy He allows a Shabbat for the 7th generation. As we hold up the canvas of Gentile history to spiritual scrutiny, we will realize that every seed of the Greco/Roman nations enslaved either tribes of the north or those of the south.

I want to point out something to all Hebrews. I don't care what you call yourselves today—Jews, Arabs, Indians, Americans or Black people. Whether or not you are Hamitic, Japhethic, or Semitic, there are institutions that thought they were excluding you from their memberships. God in His wisdom allowed nations to hide many of His people from becoming entangled in numerous so-called exclusive organizations (through an assumed doctrine of superiority) to prevent deeper spiritual tarnishing and to preserve remnants that repent to receive all of His promises.

History recorded that the Atlantic Slave traffickers considered the captured people as cargo and therefore inferior to them. What was the real reason that the planters, especially the married ones, made such a regular practice of having children with the slave women? If they were allegedly inferior, why would males (regarded as of the least procreative of nations) bring offspring through their seed? There are entire villages in Martinique, Guadeloupe, Saba, Antigua, Barbuda, Santo Domingo, Cuba, Haiti, Suriname and Brazil where the Creole mixes today are results of years of "seed mingling."

In the folklore of Savannah Georgia, Raleigh North Carolina, and many of the former slave plantations there are verbal tales that are replayed in every location that generally match textbooks' events of cruelty, rape and death, that accompanied the Atlantic Slave Trade. Most oral tales, especially the intricately spicy ones, are unrecorded. The best and most profound book I have read on the topic was one dictated by a previous slave to his grandson. That old man lived to be over 100 years. He was a buggy driver for the Governor of one the plantations on Antigua; so he had access to many a gossip. His humor was second to none. His book "To Shoot Hard Labour" described the life of Papa Sammy Smith 1877-1982.

His description of events during those times makes it an all time classic; it was written from a slave's actual experiences. He stated that the people of the plantations were very religious. The horses were given a day off on Sundays by the religious folks; so the slaves had to pull the buggies to church by hand. That was a big job; people would pay if they could for one of those jobs. Just the fact that they could dress in those fine long coats with the top hats and gloves made that job number one. However, not one record gave us any inkling about a sacrosanct topic: "The Legend of the Headless Horseman."

CHAPTER 13C. LEGEND OF THE HEADLESS HORSEMAN

One mysterious figure that kept resurfacing in legends throughout countries where the Atlantic Slave Trade flourished was that of the "Headless Horseman." I had to have the same story from more than 1 dozen sources before pursuing it. Old timers were scared to death to talk about that "gruesome goblin." After 20 years of piecing bits and pieces of information together about that shadowy figure, I will list the correlating and repetitious data that I found: (a) The figure always waited at crossroads. (b) The figure would snatch males at nights. (c) They were never seen again. (d) The figure appeared to be headless. (e.) The figure rode a dark horse. f) Horse and figure simultaneously appeared around All Souls Night.

I worked as an investigative reporter for years. Certain stories, though they may seem bizarre at first, really need careful scrutiny. Since most of my research in the first phases began with investigating mysteries in the supernatural, after a while, you learn to pay close attention to oft-repeated stories from different sources that are similar in nature and invoke extreme fear in the people that reluctantly relate them. There was an incident whereby the sister of a hospitalized woman swore that a curse had been placed on her sick sister. The hospitalized lady swore the same. How did they know? The sister related a story of a giant frog that blocked the entrance to the sick lady's door. Her sister moved to the left; the frog followed. She moved to the right; the frog followed. Finally her sister turned to run and the giant toad chased after and bit her. She became hospitalized. We had a royal laugh.

When so many eyewitnesses started showing up and swearing that it was true, I decided to ask the hospitalized lady a few questions:
Are you afraid of frogs and deathly so?
Are you interfering with someone's husband or boyfriend?
Do you have high blood pressure?
Are you very superstitious? Yes to all four ended that. That story could not fill a paragraph.

Startled Frog jumps! Woman with high blood pressure collapses. Fright, guilt and superstition were the culprits!

In the case with the headless horseman, the breakthrough occurred when I discovered that the headless horseman appeared around the eve of All Souls' Day. There is a traditional event that is celebrated very close to that night; it is called Halloween. Take an educated guess as to whom the eve is hallowed. Lots of paraphernalia on occult practices and witches are sold in stores during that period. Innocent children are paying homage to Satan and by association, are inadvertently touching some accursed things, which create direct spiritual bridges. Those breaches count towards future participation for second and third strike iniquities by future abortionists, adulterers, and psychic network pursuers. Read about touching the accursed things in Joshua 7:15. Not a few with wide-open ancestral bruises, end up demonized later on in life for attending some strange function on hallowed evening.

I had made a grim discovery that most large slave massacres took place behind the curtain of nightfall, on nights regarded worldwide as occult festival nights. Researchers need to make documentaries of the patterns of brutality found at large slave burial sites. Our careful observations of such sites revealed that bodies were buried facing a specific cardinal point. Compare that to what God directed Moses in Leviticus 1:11, "Moses shall kill it (the offering) on the… side of the altar." People (who are aware of occult practices) or curious Archaeologists can deduce why facing "Vega" was ritually selected. A mild and subtle interpretation was adapted and injected into the movie "The Tamarind Seed." There have been similar legends around plantations in the Caribbean and the Carolinas. Let us not forget that there were ordinances forbidding the slaves from reading and writing on most plantations. The Virginian slave Uncle John Vaspar was a notable exception. His master taught him to read. He was so good that he became a powerful preacher, attracting large crowds of both Plantocrats and slaves. Is it safe to assume that the foundation of his church was one of compromise? Did he ever preach on the sanctity of human life or about the equality of all men? Can you imagine the shock of many of his self-righteous brethren when they died and met the ultimate judge, a large-nosed, dark bronze-coloured, Nazarene?

There were numerous slaves very loyal to their masters, despite their payless plights. Lots of them really cared for their masters. Those were mainly the house slaves as opposed to the field hands. One incident similar to *The Tamarind Seed's* story is where a slave and others were accused of stealing their master's rum. The slave swore he neither did, nor would he allow anyone else to do so. The slave opined that in the past he had risked his life and would do so again for his master. An ultimatum was given. Find the rum by sundown or he and a gang of "field hands" would be killed. They were killed ritualistically around "All Souls' Night."

Public burnings and torture for anyone found practicing the occult arts or wizardry was a bit much for many families to bear—especially if one was a prominent person. On both sides of the Atlantic, those were common practices in the 15th and 16th centuries. Slavery provided perfect cover for all those who wanted to practice their arts undeterred. I find that the time of the massacres, the memberships in clandestine organizations, and the ritualistic nature of the sacrifices, somewhat conflicting, and negate what has been widely published: "*Cheap labour and profit were the sole motives for slavery.*" Slavery was unique in that slaves were the property of their owners. Here were seed of people that promised to be bondservants to God ending up as slaves to nations that were "sworn enemies of God." Slaves became chattel goods. An owner could buy, exchange, extinguish, sell, or prolong his seed. All seed that reneged on the promise to be a "Holy nation unto God," ended up under horrible havens of unrighteousness. Some sinister minded owners apparently used their perfect venues for ritualistic practices.

There was an ancient African secret organization that had links with the "*Tribe of Judah.*" They were called the "Coramante." Through an elaborate underground network of signs and unspoken messages they organized a large slave revolt on the isle of Antigua. The plan was to surround the annual society bash with fire and burn all at the headquarters of the British (Nelson's Dockyard). The ringleader was a *Master* by the name of Court. The Governor's ball was postponed and a neophyte by the name of Tomboy began sweating profusely. Tomboy's owner observed him using secret symbols. The owner, a member of the Golden Dawn, was privy to such knowledge. He "Petitioned" Tomboy, and true to the terms of his oath gave him all that he petitioned. Yet on the day of the mass executions, when Tomboy petitioned his British brothers for his life, they turned a blind eye. They ignored the "Mercy Plea," just as members of the Luminous Lud ignored the *petitioning of dying Jews in Germany*.

What alarmed and upset me most, was that I found consistent patterns of torture on slave plantations. Large slave massacres that coincided with nights of "High Energy," left spiritual fingerprints—hinting DNA of ritual killings. Those parallels raised eyebrows in our research departments. Manuals found at plantations had detailed instructions on Occultism. The instructions were not in Geez, Hebrew, or any ancient languages, but in the languages of the captor nations. I will pose some questions to challenge oft-repeated suppositions:

1.   Were the occult arts exported supposedly from Africa to all former plantation sites, or were the plantation sites rich practicing grounds for the occult arts?

2.   With reading outlawed to slaves before Emancipation, and no money available to them, where would they buy potions?

3.   Did any of the former apprentices that assisted their masters eventually carry on the arts after emancipation?

Year after year, mass killings occurred on the same dates. Evidence from such sites makes it a hard case to imply—mere coincidence. The people who planned the massacres were members of sinister organizations, whose primary universal tenet is that "Body fluids sacrificed on askew altars on *High Energy* dates engender power and financial rewards." History also recalls that the custom of forced breeding was done to increase the labour force cheaply, not exactly the way a cattle owner would increase his stock.

Let us examine the inaccuracies. Why take cargo from a large land where the Nile runs, ship them all the way to islands that traditionally suffer from drought? They then brought the cane roots from New Guinea and India. In America, the Caribbean and South America they refined the crop and then shipped the end product (sugar) back to Europe. It would have made better economic sense to establish large plantations on Africa, then to process the entire product and ship the sugar (a stone's throw from Africa) back to Europe. It would be too gruesome to rehash the atrocities of Gorè. I will say in one sentence: those things had been prophesied and they are and were ritualistic, purely and simply. See prophecies of Moses in his 5th book—Deuteronomy 28:49-50, and also verse 68. Moses prophesied in the 48-49th verses, "They shall serve thine enemies which the Lord shall send against thee, *in hunger, and in thirst, and in nakedness*...he shall put a *yoke of iron upon thy neck* until he have destroyed thee." Incidentally the ancient Hebrews spoke and understood the Egyptian language.

How interesting: the forefathers of the tribes of Judah and Israel promised that they and their generations would be yoked to God (covenanted). Since they broke that promise as spelled out above, they ended up *yoked by nations* that sprang *out of Babylon/Greece/Rome and their seed*. When the British/French/Spanish/Portuguese and Dutch captured the remnant, in the onset they spoke *no Gentile tongue*. Those that ended up in Germany, Poland and Russia did not speak the languages initially. Hence when Moses wrote in verse 49, "A nation whose tongue thou shall not understand," that explains the words of Genesis 10:4-6. The same Moses wrote that the islands of the sea of the Gentiles would be peopled by the seed of—Shem/Ham/Japheth; yet they would be dispersed. Then they would speak the languages of the Gentile nations. Notice the accurate prophecy of Deuteronomy 28:68—first to the North African transshipment point "Again with ships."

Although it has been established that North Africans first initiated the Atlantic Slave Trade, the Europeans expanded it. If individuals wanted to get into the rituals and did not have plantations full of slaves, they had to devise cunning ways to do so. They could not just steal a slave. That would have been the equivalent of stealing a luxury car today. First he would have to get easy and undeterred access to another person's unguarded chattel. The laws were rigid during the flourishing plantation era. Runaway slaves were ordered captured dead or alive—Deuteronomy 28:66. Runaway slaves knew that capture meant death. If someone could find a slave outside of a plantation at night he could be classified as a runaway and be killed.

Female slaves had separate living quarters from those of the males. A male who was attracted to a female slave had to be extremely discreet and careful. Most times the one he had his eyes on, was the one that "Massa" was stalking—Deuteronomy 28:30, "Thou shall betroth a wife, and another man shall lie with her: thou shalt build an house, and thou shalt not dwell therein: thou shalt plant a vineyard, and shall not gather grapes thereof." Since "Massa" had the pick of the crop, castration was the ideal punishment for a competing suitor. Birdcalls, coded messages and pebbles thrown on windows under the cover of night were common. The horses' barns provided ideal meeting spots. Abortions were regular to conceal those illicit dalliances. However "Massa's" children were encouraged. They usurped the pecking order and were automatically elevated to a privileged class.

Whenever messages had to be delivered between plantations, buggy drivers usually did so during the daytime. A buggy driver's position belonged to the most loyal of the slaves. As much as possible, buggy drivers would warn suitors of impending doom. Buggy drivers often got chickens, leftover booze and eggs for their understanding hearts and sympathetic attitudes. Prowlers would observe male slaves leaving the barns at ungodly hours. On specific nights, masked men would appear at crossroads attempting to snatch the wearied males. They would place hoods over their faces to conceal their identities. In the 16th and 17th centuries, plantations used lanterns. Electricity was non-existent. Today's scary movies were cartoons by comparison to tales of hooded forms with no head, appearing in the shadows of night to snatch wearied males—Deuteronomy 28:67. Eyewitnesses were few. Many males that survived an attempted attack had involuntary diarrhea. Some of those guys, after hours of strenuous exercise would outrun the ghastly hooded figures.

The speeds of the escaping slaves were legendary—Deuteronomy 28:65-66. What the captors did not know was that because they had forgotten their original Hebrew teachings, they had borrowed pagan beliefs—Deuteronomy 28:64. The encounter with a shadowy figure dressed in black in the dead of night made mockery of the myth that it is only recently men ran the 100-meter dash under 10 seconds. Desperation led to another risky situation: that of being on a horse and hoping it did not make giveaway noises. That apparently happened, according to oft-repeated stories. The combined form of hooded headless thing and beast draped in black, emitting a shrieking noise, caused barn doors to be entered while shut, with only the shape of a human as evidence that someone flew through them. Some females witnessed the desperate dashes as their frightened suitors saw the shadowy figures. Those oral traditions are the only records of 8-second 100-meter dashes—flashes of Olympic precedents subliminally recorded for posterity. Those feats laid the foundations for many of their descendants to hold world records (to this date) in sprint events. Some fell, were captured and died of fright. Those that were outrun by the horses and captured alive were never seen again.

Our exploration of mass graves at former slave plantations turned up tons of evidence of ritual killings. To assume that all of those were slaves caught by headless or hooded horsemen would be pure conjecture. The legends survive. Prophecies concerning the above are in Nahum 3:9, "Ethiopia and Egypt were her strength and it was infinite," and concerning the tribe of Judah, Nahum 1:15, "*Judah,* keep thy solemn feasts, observe thy vows." Nahum 3:10 "Yet she *went into captivity*: her young children were also dashed in pieces at the top of all the streets: and they cast lots for their honourable men, and *her great men* were *bound in chains.*" Joel 3:6, "*The children of Judah and of Jerusalem have ye sold.*" However, verse 18 states unequivocally, "It shall come to pass, in that day…(Verse 20), Judah shall dwell forever, and Jerusalem from generation to generation."

Scientists have determined that seeds that survive pestilences, famines, floods and the like are strife-resistant and are considered hybrid seeds. The two groups mentioned above have survived the following: slavery, captivity, genocide, famines, implantation of laboratory produced diseases, degradation, deprivation, hunger, spiritual/financial/physical rape, and even theft of—lands, religion, resources and labour. The Vandals, Slavs, Mormons, Saxons, Jebusites, Perizzites, Berbers, and Cretans have all disappeared.

An intelligence officer of a certain country gave us documents on experimental germ warfare. The serum was allegedly tested through vaccinations on the unsuspecting seed of Judah. Although the antidote failed, in spite of the cover-up and the "incurable disease" it allegedly produced, they (remnant of Judah) have survived because of God's promises. The decreed punishments and sufferings are God's specific promises to those backsliders that have worshipped other gods, or have committed abortions, sorceries, adulteries, fornications or any three of the above, habitually. Deuteronomy 28:35 foretold the plight of Judah's seed with the AIDS pandemic. One might argue that other people do those things and seemingly no obvious punishments befall them. Here are three logical reasons:

1. Judah and Israel covenanted with God and those others, who appear well, may be either promised beneficiaries of God's gifts of forgiveness, or they are spiritually dead.

2. Seed of only two tribes (Jeremiah 31:31) were selected for double-portion inheritances—beneficiaries of both Old and New Covenants—"The House of Israel and the House of Judah."

3. Whereas over 99 percent of their seed are ignorant of their double-portion inheritances, the best thief in the universe knows; he has targeted and is targeting their treasures.

CHAPTER 14. TRANSPOSITION OF PRINCIPLES

14A. SERIOUS COMPUTATION ERRORS

One of the most common errors to which modern intellectuals succumb, is the inability to equate ancient concepts, cultures, attitudes, mathematics, and customs with our own and vice versa. We omit a present conceptual value. In the telephone and cyber ages, messages take seconds. There were times when people lived and moved to a much slower pace. A smoke signal, a pigeon or the horse and carriage were the concords of yesteryear. News used to crawl or swim. Pollution was unheard of. Whereas we write on paper in the steel age and cut trees to do so and consider ourselves intelligent, people wrote on stone in the Stone Age and we classify them as primitive.

The Hebrew societies of yesteryear were so patriarchal, that rarely did temple priests or scribes document events regarding females. Adam had left thirteen generations on earth before he died. The only details of those families and their migrations that Moses recorded are from the male stems of Adam's family tree. The records of the first three generations consisted of the names of two male branches only. Then in Genesis 5 from verse 4, the documentation of the other ten generations are flicked over and listed by male siblings: "And *the days* of Adam after he had begotten Seth were eight hundred years…and he begat sons and *daughters*. All the days that Adam lived were 930 years and he died." Neither Noah nor any of his sons' wives are documented. All recorded events (regarding covenant seed-incubators) were prophetic moulds of future temples, synagogues, or churches. Mary represented the mould of the *Firstfruit New Covenant* church.

In January 11th 1988, Newsweek published a cover story to the effect that DNA samples of every major ethnic group on earth revealed—we are all genetically related to a melanin-strong female that lived in the North African region approximately 200,000 years ago. Since each race must have had origins and DNA, distinct and separate from other groups, why do we use such terms as different races? Is a brown horse a different category of horse from a white one?

If a person's colour differentiates his or her race, why stop there? Shouldn't short people be a different race from tall ones as in olden times? DNA research gives us an idea as to how idiotic we have been on those issues. Science now grudgingly affirms that there is one race. Here is a formula that would make Pythagoras squirm with envy. Past time, times everlasting time quotient, times 1000= total allocated human time. 7X33X1000= 231,000 years. Abraham had the everlasting time computation formula in code. Abraham had to wait 99 years or three esoteric days, for the seed of promise to germinate. The Day of the "Promised Seed," (time quotient) is 99 divided by 3 or 33 years.

When God calls His prophets, He bestows special gifts upon them. God's prophets are equipped with exponential or (Trans-universal) power. To the "Wise-Hearted" or Biblically wise, "One shall … a thousand." So to recap: *The Seven Stages* or Genesis Epochs are computed thusly—7 X 33X1000. A day in the life of "The Genesis Light" is 1000 years. Scientists did not invent that. Now you understand the meaning of what was placed in the Bible thousands of years ago. Here is another mystical revelation. In the book of Genesis in English (Moses first discourse) God created man after His (tselem) image (perfected spirit). God fashioned a vehicle to carry the soul of man. That vehicle became corrupted: so it would have to be returned to the factory, earth, in exchange for an incorruptible vehicle. Man fell from a perfected state because of disobedience and had to learn all over again. Man began in a state of perfection and wisdom; that is why Enoch could have built a city.

There was a time in the distant past when grafted species of evil humans roamed the earth. Ancient records indicate that an enormous deluge purged them. This current specie of Homo Erectus Sapiens has transgressed the Stellar and Lunar time periods. We are now in the Solar Mythos. The fact that six generations of purging had to have been undergone before our advent, makes mockery of the myth that we are on earth only 6000 years. Assyria, Israel, Egypt, China, and Africa have unbroken histories documented, that span over 9000 years.

In a later chapter we will examine computational errors of our predecessors. Some have computed time from distant periods using our current value systems. There are artifacts on earth left by remnants of those civilizations, which surpass anything achieved by this lot. So far the records of people who came from beyond the boundaries of this earth give us hope. They have manifested higher degrees of wisdom: Melchizedek and Jeshua. Their powers, aims, and teachings were all directed toward taking humankind back to an impeccant state. Hope lies also in the fact that all of their teachings indicate that their perfected state has a zero tolerance for error, flaws, and disobedience to divine laws and principles. Many that searched for the Messiah, looked for a man to come with carnal powers and a sharpened sword, killing enemies and establishing an earthly kingdom on the same earth that had been accursed. That limited expectation has left multitudes in frustration. However, when the shakings begin, woe to all falsehoods: the transformation and redemption of the earth will not be pleasant.

CHAPTER 14B. MICROSCOPIC AND MACROSCOPIC VIEWS OF RACIAL ORIGINS

In the true sense of the word, to qualify as an ethnic group, a select people must have dwelt on the same landmass for several unbroken generations. They must have had the same language, same customs and have been of the same geo-political origins. Different races MUST have different DNA groupings. When legal documents categorize one group as belonging to a race different from other human beings, they are actually treading on dangerous grounds legally. Your place of origin might determine your current ethnos but it has nothing to do with your race. All but a few dictionaries stress genetic links and ancestral ties as criteria for classification of "different races." However in their definitions, there are no differences between their meanings for races and those assigned for countries of origin, save for ethnicity. When you get to the bottom of the real issue, most of the scientific establishments seem to be implying that shading and various degrees of melanin created different races. How contradictory and silly! Scientists rely on facts gathered after research and trials. Their tests and trials show that there is no difference in DNA according to ethnicity. Their descriptions and portrayals of what is or is not considered a race is entirely wrong from a scientific point of view.

EACH RACE SHOULD HAVE ITS OWN SPECIFIC DNA, DISTINCT AND DIFFERENT FROM ANY OTHER.

SECRET FINDINGS:

1. Ancient libraries' records indicated that the uniqueness of an ethnic group lies in its ability to proliferate among others and retain dominant physical characteristics and traits.

2. An ethnic group has the ability to assimilate and enlarge itself through its military might, cultural domination, conquests and other people's subjugation.

A group of organizations that have sworn secrecy unto death took that information and instituted a programme of fragmental amalgamation. The "... Dawn and The ...Lod" are still around today. Even though they are not as influential as they were once, their legacies still manifest in the "Right by Might" philosophies that they export. Using fragmented wisdom from ancient civilizations, they have tried constantly and secretly to persuade nations (out of the ashes of Babylon, Rome and Greece) to forge alliances based on specific seed traits, military might and conquests. They had and have fueled wars, influenced financial markets, inserted governments and removed them. They have influenced church institutions and have been very instrumental in much of the misinformation that permeates worldwide. Most of their members were Atlantic Slave traders. Their unrighteous mammon is used today to affect the world's monetary systems and to select political leaders of their persuasions. Since each race must possess unique DNA and each ethnic group must have distinct countries of origin, when did France, Germany, England, America and most cold countries merge into a conglomeration called "Whiteland? Even though there is no such land as "Whiteland or Blackland," why do we imply that there are both black and white races?

It takes at least seven genetic mixes over time for a person to lose his or her melanin to become a white person. The same way the colour white is a derivative of other pigments, all so-called white people "evolved" from darker species. The irony of that whole mess is that descendants of those who created the myth sell skin lightening products to those who want to be lightened or bleached, and darkening products for those who want to be darkened. Both sides of the equation do the opposite of what they are supposed to believe. Is this our subconscious way of saying that we miss where we once were—one race of brown people mixing and intermarrying and are being hustled by some modern day Pied Pipers?

The migration of ancient Israel is a perfect example of such. In countries where seed of the original 12 tribes are found, their features to this day are Hamitic: brown or black. When they left Egypt, they were dark brown or extremely black people—Exodus 2:19. In the Kerala province of India, at least three waves of Jewish migrations survive. The Malabaris can trace their ancestry back to traders stranded after the destruction of the 2nd Temple in 70 C.E, through to the Babylonian exile of 586 B.C.E., back to traders that brought spices, tea and ivory during the reign of King Solomon. They are black in comparison to the brown Meshuhurarum Jewish descendants of slaves. Then there are the Paradesim seed of European Jews who reside close to the Kochangadi Synagogue. All three groups live harmoniously in India and trade around the Cochin archipelago. Since the last group is melanin-deficient and the other two groups are brown and black respectively, are they different races? Today there are Jews who are nationals of different countries; however they are still Jews. God has also ensured that regardless of which country they dwell, whom they intermarry, what efforts of elimination are concocted, that the seeds of Ham, Japheth, and Shem will retain their original ethnic identities. In essence, the word melanin actually originated from the Hebrew word "melamim" which means coat. Joseph's coat of many colours was God's way of telling us that the Jewish people would be enslaved and they would "EVOLVE" into people of different colours. The obvious question is—why are people with the most mixes called white and people with the least mixes called coloured? Since horses, cows and apes are mammals just like us humans, shouldn't the brown ones be labeled differently from the white ones?

SOME DAY, SOMEONE WILL FILE A LAWSUIT FOR USING THE TERM MIXED MARRIAGE SINCE THE IMPLICATIONS ARE SPIRITUALLY AND PHYSICALLY SINISTER.

CHAPTER 14C. MYSTERY OF EVOLUTION SOLVED

Billions of dollars have been spent trying to find the missing links in an incongruent chain called evolution. To date, no zebra has ever evolved into a horse or donkey; they reproduce *after their kind*. Here is evidence that has been concealed. Newsweek published the results of a scientific study where DNA from all nations or as we say "different races" were collected and analyzed. Published results in the January 11th 1988 issue revealed that:

ALL THE SO-CALLED RACES EVOLVED FROM A WOMAN OF AFRICAN ANCESTRY WHO LIVED APPROXIMATELY 200,000 YEARS AGO.

Notice the use of the pregnant word, "EVOLVED." The only evidence we have found of evolution in human species, is that people evolved from—brown to black, from brown to yellow and from yellow to "white" or melanin-lost. If there were separate races, white people would have white hair only. Yet we find the hair of black people turning white, and the hair of melanin-depleted people turning silver grey. All people are born pink, have red blood, pink gums, white teeth, and like cars come in varying colours and sizes. Hospitals have no means of discerning from which ethnic group they derived different samples of blood, saliva or excrement, if the samples are switched around. On the contrary: if a deer, a cow, a donkey, a sheep, a rabbit or a horse live on the same farm and eat the same grass daily, each animal will produce not only different types of dung but also they will consistently reproduce *after their own kind*.

Let us question the collective reasoning of "Evolutionists." The apes that God created (before He made humans) have an everlasting desire for leaves and fruit and reproduce after their own kind. So far, they never became curious for the taste of meat. Did a strain "evolve" into a carnivore, throw away its original fur and then grow it back in summer? Can you think of a better *name* than an *ape* to give to an animal that left its original state, evolved into an intelligent being supposedly and then reverted to its primordial state?

When horses of different colours mate and produce offspring of varying shades, the external changes do not engender reclassification of species. Since all mammals are governed by the same rules, it appears that "a secret school of philosophy" has to invent something as bizarre as "cloning" as a thread of hope on which to hang their tired and flawed theory. If we believe that human beings started as apes and evolved into higher beings, why has our collective behaviour regressed so drastically? Why have we supposedly stopped evolving? Birds have been around for hundreds of thousands of years and they are still flapping their wings. I would think by now that they would have come up with something new. With all the latest inventions and improvements to the natural diets of humans, are two feet really sufficient to carry us around after so many hundreds of thousands of years? When plausible answers couldn't be found, another myth was invented: the myth of reincarnation. Why would a dead granny that was a vegetarian and allergic to dogs return as a carnivore? I have yet to hear news of a rancher whose herd increased by itself after the death of a loved one.

I have been diving for years and I still have not figured out a way to recycle the air in my lungs the way that fish do with their gills. I do not know if we should laugh or feel sorry for those intellectual geeks. Millions of taxpayers' dollars are spent every year for the big "E" analyses. The proponents have surmised that ancient skulls of varying sizes found by archaeologists belonged to different species of humans. It would be interesting to find out how many hat makers send their children to study the *myth of evolution*. Who but an extremely arrogant, devious, rebellious, conniving and conceited being could attempt to manipulate people into believing that a questionable unproven theory of a finite man could falsify the infallible word of an infallible God? First light, Genesis 1, God spoke it in verse 24. God confirmed His word in verse 25. "God made every beast of the earth after his kind and every living creature after his kind." Maybe, just maybe there are boundaries set on this disobedient generation.

Societies love to invent and exalt fallible philosophies of finite men and to reject the tested and proven truisms of our just, fair, Holy God and accurate Oracle. Love neighbor as self. Love your "maximum" Creator with your whole heart and mind and strength. We believe that we are more important than others are. Based on what? We are all born naked and despite the fact that we cannot take any tangible thing with us when we die, everything in our coffins at the time of our demise will rot or be taken away. Most people on earth have an *invented way, an invented philosophy*, an invented truism and an invented lifestyle. Every good watch, clock, machine or vehicle comes with a schematic from the manufacturer. The ability or quality of a human vehicle hinges more on concealed traits than to external features. As we progress, it will become evident why Jeshua is so hated by carnally-minded people. His exemplary way of life exposed all fallacies and myths. He loved the poor and downtrodden. He taught that all of God's sheep are loved, once they become obedient.

Our God is the only manufacturer that cannot fail, fib, flounder or forget. Are we to assume that no schematic exists for the tested and proven, most intricately and wonderfully designed mechanism called universe? It would take a theory as warped and misguided as "Evolution" to twist a mind to such a degree as to conceive such a thought. *Is there one way/one truth* to shatter all falsehoods, to destroy all misconceptions, and to straighten all wrong paths?

CHAPTER 14D. GRADUAL ASCENT THEORY SHATTERED.

The assumption that the early man was primitive and that somehow we are rising to an intellectual apex is flattering. What perennial yardstick do we use to arrive at that? During The Stone Age, a large phallic shaped stone was carved and strategically placed at precise points where accurate calculations of the summer and winter solstices could be observed. Sites where accurate computations of the Vernal Equinoxes were recorded featured heavily in their secret ceremonies. The most prominent structure depicted what the Great Spirit Creator would use to impregnate a mortal woman made of earth. The unborn child in her belly would come at a time of crisis on the earth to bring peace and wisdom. Archaeologists have documented those as sites of "Phallic Worship." When I presented my findings to a certain university, their response was disbelief. Academics asked "Who taught them astronomy?" Here is an example of cultural transposition. Ancient and wise elders used the male/female principle to simplify their teachings; the chief force (sun) is masculine. The symbiotic light force, the moon (on which the sun is as codependent as a man to a woman) is feminine. When men and women are in conjugal harmony, babies are born. So when that harmony first existed between "Father

Sun and Mother Moon, Baby Earth" was born. The Vernal Equinox is that season when there is perfect harmony; hence we have equal days and equal nights. "Not bad for primitive people!" The event was so sacred that they fasted for forty days in preparation for that grand event. They then danced around the pole. Follow me slowly; I do not want to lose you. Count forty days after the Vernal Equinox and we end up in the month of May. Hence the name of the pole dances we celebrate only in May. In our modern times, intellectual organizations exclude female members for the identical reasons as the so-called primitive people.

THE ANCIENTS HELD SACRED IN DANCE, AND TRADITION, THE PROMISE THAT WAS GIVEN TO THE JEWS!

Ruins of past civilizations that we have yet to match with mathematics or architectural skills are negating the gradual ascent theory. History recorded the use of plastic surgery in India in 65B.C. Which father waits until his last child comes along to decide that he will make an educational investment in the last one? How would a natural father (without biological complications, age constraints, natural deterrents or debilitating illnesses in either mate) know which child would be last? Here is your dilemma; you say that God knows everything? Then God whose intelligence is proven far superior to that of humans would not make such a stupid assumption, since it is not consistent with His record. Therefore any "Doctrine of Superiority," just like our other doctrines, must be subject to scrutiny.

Careful observations of artifacts of antiquity reflect civilizations that rose and fell, and also records of men attempting to reclaim their lost Olympus. According to our current system of analysis, Egypt was a superior nation to that of the Hebrews before and after the first Exodus over 5000 years ago. Man's perception as to how important he is or is perceived to be, has no impact whatsoever on the plans of God. In fact many a past superior nation has disappeared and so-called primitive ones have survived *The Great Flood*, genocide, language transplant, prophet thefts and virus implants, you name it.

FOR A LIE TO LAST, THE TRUTH MUST BE CONCEALED AND DISTORTED FOR AS LONG AS POSSIBLE. IN FACT IF THE EVIDENCE COULD BE WIPED OUT ALTOGETHER THEN THE REPLACED FALLACIES MIGHT STAND.

No one who conceived such a beautifully complex device as this clock would allow a thief, an imposter and a liar to succeed. He might allow him for a while to say to the disobedient ones: "I told you so." There is only one way to come out of the mess. Jeshua, the son of Miriam, is the only person to have walked this earth to have completed and surpassed our litmus tests:

a.   He fulfilled prior prophecies by His birth.

b.   He fulfilled prior prophecies by His ministry.

c.   He fulfilled prior prophecies by His clear elaboration of the Gospel with signs, wonders, miracles, and His exemplary way of life.

d.   He fulfilled prior detailed prophecies of His death.

e.   He fulfilled the promise of God to be the firstfruit through the passage of death. "I am The Way, The Truth, and The Life." He is the grafted Branch. He is the blood-cleansed, "Firstfruit." God told Nehemiah that His desire is to dwell in the booths of His righteous children. He shared with Jeremiah the desire for His New Covenant.

In other words, there is no way other than the New Covenant. The old breakable covenant or contract (not law) is finished. Jeshua'a words: "No one comes to the Father who sent me but through me!" In other words, *follow me to the truth.* We will examine that heavy-duty statement.

BY THAT STATEMENT EITHER BILLIONS OF PEOPLE WILL BE RESCUED OR PERMANENTLY LOST IF THAT IS BLASPHEMY! CONVERSELY, IF THAT IS A MAXIM, MANY SHALL BE LOST WITHOUT THAT WISDOM.

On the same commemorative days, Jeshua became the embodiment of Israel's sacred feasts and in so doing brought to light the spiritual significance of them all.

CHAPTER 15. WHO WERE THE ANCIENT JEWS?

15A. TRIBES LOST OR CONCEALED?

Let us scrutinize the identity of the ancient Hebrews. If surveys were sent inquiring as to the identity of the remnant of the ancient Jews, most people outside of the Mediterranean and African regions might consider the Hasidic (Orthodox), to be the remnant prophesied by Isaiah. Please note that God pointed to all places where a remnant of the supposedly *Lost Tribes* are. Let me spell out the countries where former families are living and are fighting against their own brethren today. Isaiah 11:11, "And it shall come to pass that the Lord shall set his hand *'The second time.'*" Please take your Torah and circle every eleventh word. After you do that and you have any doubt as to the identity of the Lord, then you are really lost. He will lead the Gentiles because, "He came *unto his own* and his own *received Him not.*" Verse 10 tells what happens when the Messiah first came. Verse 10 previewed the end of the "Royal Bloodline." Isaiah 11:10, "In that day, there shall be a root of Jesse, which shall stand for an ensign of the people, to it *shall the Gentiles seek* and his…. shall be glorious."

The four most popular male Jews whom the Gentiles have sought: Alan Greenspan, Bruce Springsteen, Jerry Lewis, and Jeshua son of Mary. Which one do you assume Isaiah was referring to? Verse 11 continued with the list of the "remnant," *which shall be left.* The destinations are: Assyria, Egypt, Pathros (Upper Egypt), Cush (East, Central and West Africa to Ethiopia), Elam (Persia or Iran), Shinar (formerly Ur, Ugarit, Mesopotamia, and Elba to Damascus—ancient cities of Syria) from Hamath, and from "The Islands of the Sea," (as per Genesis 10: 4-6).

I will speak a prophetic word to a little island in the Caribbean Sea. That island is significant in that it has the shape of a man's head (begins and ends with the same letter and is of seven letters). The same applies to one in the shape of a foot. I will visit both island nations and give the rest of the prophetic messages in person. Thus said the Lord: "A remnant of my people (as per prophecy) lives there. I have blessed you and your seed with businesses. My reasons for sending you there are threefold:

1. to conceal a remnant,

2. for you to learn to live together like you did in ancient times as examples to others and

3. I have handpicked you because of the prayers of your parents. Sadly, mainly the young ones have replaced me with gods of silver and tin: casino chips, cars and money. I see all your doings."

*"RETURN TO YOUR FORMER STATE OF OBEDIENCE OTHERWISE THE
WOMBS OF MANY OF YOUR WIVES WILL BE SHUT UP. IN MY SEASON
WHEN I BEGIN MY SHAKINGS, THOSE WHO ARE DISOBEDIENT WILL
RECEIVE MY PLAGUES."*

Malachi 2:11-12, "Judah hath profaned the holiness of the Lord which he loved;" made a covenant "with the daughter of a strange god." The master and the scholar will be cut off. Moses, Malachi, Jeremiah, Joel and Nahum all prophesied Judah's plight and displacement. Nahum 3:9-10, "Ethiopia and Egypt were her strength and it was infinite. Put and Lubim were thy helpers. Yet she was carried away into captivity: Her young children were also dashed in pieces at the top of all the streets and they cast lots for her honourable men and all her great men were bound in chains." Before boarding the slave ships in Gorè, babies were plucked from the females and dashed against the rocks as per prophecy. Moses wrote in Exodus 12:38, "A mixed multitude went up also with them." Esther 1:1 gives a clear picture of the mixtures. India through Ethiopia housed a mixed multitude under Persian rule. They spoke a common language and intermarried frequently. Most of the people spoke Hebrew and Persian.

If a Scandinavian lived in Africa for 50 years, he would gain melanin. His seed would become brown. At the end of 100 years, his seed would be indistinguishable from that of any African. Jews the world over are remnant of 12 tribes, seed of Jacob. According to Genesis 48:1, Joseph's first two sons and from the third to the sixth generation of all the 12 tribes were born in Africa: Genesis 50:22. Let us confirm that by looking at how the ancient Jews described themselves. Samson had seven locks—Judges 16:19. Nahum 2:10, *The faces of them all gather blackness.* Job 30:30, my *skin is black.* Jeremiah 8:21, *I am black.* Lamentations 5:10…Our *skin was black like an oven* because of the excessive heat and famine. David, Absalom, Ezekiel, Elijah, Jeshua and Solomon all had the *same type of hair.* Ezekiel 8:3…took me by *one lock of mine head* and lifted me up between the earth and the heaven. Elijah had "coarse" not limp hair. Daniel 7:9, hair like wool, feet like burnt brass. Song of *Solomon* 5:11, "My locks are *bushy and black* like a raven (black bird)." They were describing how they looked after they and their parents lived in North Africa (Egypt) for 430 years and of their exposure to extreme arid conditions, sun and famine.

Ask Italian, Australian, British or French seafarers that have done any Trans-Pacific or Trans-Atlantic crossings by sailboat? If their destinations were the Caribbean or the Pacific, remarkable changes would occur to the skin and to the hair. By the time of their arrival, the sun would darken the person's complexion and the hair would curl (tighter) and thicken. Left uncombed, they would become "locks." It doesn't matter what he or she looked like before, the effects of the sun on skin and hair are the same. Look at the children of Europeans and Americans that live in those islands; as each generation gets darker, the sun thickens, hardens and coils the hair. Freeze those thought frames and then imagine a brown people that lived in a desert in Egypt, for four hundred and thirty years. Picture their seed. By the time they were ready to leave Egypt, it would be fair to say that they had difficulty seeing their hands at night. Their children and their children's children comprised seven generations of people encompassing every shade of brown and black. Most ended up black like ovens (according to their descriptions in Lamentations 5:10). Ethiopians lived among and married them. There should be no surprise that in spite of living in cold Russia and Germany for years, many still have their big noses, thick lips and frizzy hair. Moses' wife was an Ethiopian. Moreover, in Exodus 4:6, when Moses asked God for a miracle to persuade Pharaoh, God told him that his hand would turn "white." I doubt that Moses had ever seen a white person in his lifetime. Nowhere in The Torah did anyone mention seeing a white person unless it had to do with describing a leprous condition. In fact the Hebrew word in Exodus 4:6 is *"tsara"* (*leprous* as snow). It is also logical to assume that when they dwelt in Canaan by the Jordan Valley and primarily in Jerusalem, nothing drastic could have happened to bleach the well-tanned people who came out of Egypt.

Jeremiah recorded Israel's backsliding from their period of deliverance until their captivity. In Esther 3:8 and Esther 1:1, the roots of many allegedly "Lost Tribes of Israel" can be traced. Solomon died in 925 B.C.E. Since Israel was originally a nation of extremely burnt people, I will reproduce the identities of nations that conquered their lands during those periods from 920 B.C.E. to 580 B.C.E. Medes—the land of the Medes is Iran, previously called Persia. Sargon took some 30,000 of their people to the regions of Assyria, Chaldea and Babylon. Shalamaneser came through all the land and also took them away captive. Hoshea is the last king before Israel was led away into that captivity. Prophet Jeremiah recorded that entire episode in 2nd Kings. In the British Museum of Archaeology, London, there is an obelisk documented as belonging to the same Assyrian King Shalamaneser 111. Other archaeological finds in Syria from ancient civilizations (Elba to Damascus) document important events of that period accurately. Israel's ethnic history is a case study of how people "evolve" from the original brown and black to the modern shades. Hopefully this elaboration will destroy Satan's myths about different races. Those myths have seeded subtle cloning and caused much ethnic hate and strife. It is my hope that God's truth will set millions free, so that they may return to their ethnic origins: one race of God-filled people.

CHAPTER 15B. SCIENCE AND LITMUS COME HOME TO ROOST.

This chapter is one of the most important in this discourse. By using the discipline of science, we can see how Satan used misinformation, a seed from ancient Babylon—planted on a Gentile base—along with his hatred for God's people. He used all three to reduce and transform God's people and their resources from the mightiest to the most downtrodden. The Hebrew language is so prophetic that we can find the predestined paths of all of God's chosen people, their history, genealogy and the seed nations they would produce ultimately.

God foreknew that Satan would use every means possible to try to eliminate the seed of His covenant. So He concealed them in His "Word." The sons of Noah were Ham, Shem and Japheth. In Hebrew whenever the name Ham was given to a patriarch (as in Abraham) that person and his entire seed would be melanin-rich. Some would gain more and others would lose varying amounts of melanin. However, for the most part, they would remain melanin-strong. All of God's chosen warriors would digress from being mighty men to bondservants—Nahum 3:9-10, Jeremiah 3:17-19 and Ezekiel 27:10. The seed of Ham were Cush, Mizraim, Canaan and Phut. Phut produced the inhabitants that dwelt on the African north coast mainly between Ethiopia and Egypt and also Tyre and Sidon. Mizraim produced the Egyptians, and Canaan for the most part produced the Palestinians, Jordanians and most of ancient Israel especially those of Judah and Bethlehem (birthplace of the Messiah) and Jerusalem. Cush, another son, produced the Ethiopians. In Jeremiah 23:13 and Lamentations 5:10, the Ethiopians' dark skins would be distinguishing features.

Let us look at two multi-ethnic cities—London and New York. Both places are in the north temperate regions. They are seasonally cold, and the majority population is melanin-deficient or melanin-depleted. The minority is melanin-strong. Let us look at Israel. Most of the European and Russian transplants live around Tel Aviv and Jerusalem. The Nomadic and regional people live, for the most part around the Jordan Valley and the southern regions. Examine the features of the Nomadic and the southern Jews; they resemble the brown and melanin-strong black people of the Caribbean. How do you explain the fact that the Caribbean, a tropical country with majority melanin-strong (90% 400 years ago) evolved into melanin-depleted and melanin-deficient societies? Similarly the Hittite foundational British have lost their melanin; they have retained their Hamitic noses and ears. Today they are melanin-deficient. In the Caribbean, India and Pakistan the changes are due mainly to climate and inter-breeding. Those three countries reflect a mix similar to what Israel looked like 2000 years ago.

Israel has changed over the past 2000 years to reflect the appearance of the majority that have returned. Similarly New York and London are located in temperate regions (north latitude) an area that should be 100% melanin-deficient. The people from Samaria and Syria still have large noses and ears for the most part. Some seed today have "Evolved" into varying shades of brown and less brown. Their complexion is a reflection of the migratory patterns and intermarriages of their parents and grandparents and not to the demonically taught and oft-believed myth of "superior race." Facts really are that satanic seeds took God's plans for a "Theocracy" and established a counterfeit "Demon-cratic" system. Jesus started the "Theocratic" system by sharing food with the poor. The usurped system burns surplus food. Instead of God being head of a nation-government, Daniel told us there is a "Beast" substitute. Let us first find the spiritual foundation, and then show readers how Satan used a Babylonian beast-spirit (Unicorn) to attack the "Lion," the keeper of Judah's scepter.

Satan's first strategies were substitution and distortion. Rebekah changed the appearance of Jacob. Daniel foretold us—clusters of nations that would fight against God's people would have the shape of beasts. The symbol for the tribe of Judah is the "head of a lion." The features of that beast, native to Africa with its large nose and bushy hair, would also be stamped on lands where God placed His most powerful altars: Africa, Palestinia and Antigua, an isle of the sea. Later in the discourse, we will discover how God forewarned us that Satan would use the foundation of a Gentile church to dilute His word. Satan planned some real gems: (a) Eliminate all Jews (b) Mingle their seed (c) Eliminate their prophetic language (d) Change the features of the Messiah (e) Substitute the Messiah's teachings with doctrines of devils. In short, steal their wealth, lands, resources, religion and icon and set brother (seed) against (brother). In Deuteronomy 27:11-12, specific proclamations separated Levi, Simeon, Judah, Issachar, Joseph and Benjamin from the other tribes. It is obvious that those were more prone to intermarry. Persons that have access to Jewish esoteric traditions will notice that the office of Priesthood as confirmed by Moses had to be Aaron's descendants, the tribe of Levi. The hair or lock had to be able to curl naturally around the earlobes (like those of a lion). The hair and features of the Lemba, concealed in South Africa, confirm such.

In Leviticus 13:31-37, you were exempt from the temple if your hairs were to turn "from black." You would be readmitted if it turned back "black." People were never separated by colour but by tribal regions. The people from Media were the Medes. Those from Midian were the Midianites. Similarly a Gideonite came from Gideon. You would have been perceived as very silly if you applied our present-day prejudices in those times. For Noah to produce the black Hamites, either he or his wife was black. Since Shem and Japheth were Ham's brothers, it stands to reason that they were originally one race of black people and also those years of migrating and mixing caused their seed to lose some, none, or all of their melanin. Within black people, flat noses were considered blemishes in days of yore. Hamitic priests that had those blemishes were excluded from selection—Leviticus 21:18. Genesis 11:1—"The whole earth was one language and one speech." Score another one for DNA research confirming what was written over 4000 years ago.

Let us examine the genetic roots of two of David's sons. One of the locks of Absalom weighed almost five pounds. To prove that the hair of King Solomon, another of David's sons, was very frizzy and his skin was extremely burnt, refer to Song of Solomon 5:11…"His locks are bushy and black as a raven." Observe a translator struggling with his conscience in verse 10. In Hebrew, there is one popular word for the colour white as in cloth: "LABAN." True to the prophetically accurate nature of the Hebrew language, many of the seed of Laban that remained in Padan-aram (now Syria) intermarried Berbers and other northern people and have become a melanin-deficient population today. Descendants have married the seed of Vikings and inhabit Lebanon today. Many are "LABAN-ESE," or Lebanese. God is so brilliant that he preordained Lebanon and Syria to be right next door to Israel.

The word for dazzling like radiant is (TSACH). I find Wycliffe's translation of "tsach" for Solomon's poetic description of the perfect woman (symbolic reference to the perfected church) extremely strange. Ruddy in English is the same as Adamy in Hebrew. It means *"earth-coloured, brown or black."* Bible translators invented a word and called it *"ruddy"* when describing the word "adamy." We could stretch the meaning to include the colour oxblood. As each generation seed of Templars emerged, the meaning shifted from brown to red. They used red to describe David's complexion. In verse 10 of Song of Solomon, he is being poetic and describing that beautiful woman of his imaginations, which is "The perfect Bride of God." *She is dazzling and adamy*; yet we get in King James' translations: "white and ruddy," an obvious contradiction. Nowhere else in the King James Bible is this word TSACH used for colour. The irony here is that light compresses seven colours to achieve its dazzle. All English Bibles that I have found use one colour: "White" for brilliance in their Bible dictionaries. The subtle adjustments to certain words in English are not so "subtile" anymore. Let us examine the shift in meaning of the word: "adamy." In Hebrew the word means dark brown or earthy. When John Wycliffe did his translations of the Bible, he did not translate from the original Hebrew texts; he translated from Jerome's Latin Vulgate. Now that the *Dead Sea Scrolls* are found, we await new translations from Jewish, English, Arabic and American academics, to assess whether or not the first translations were shaded. So far, preliminary reports, though long in coming, indicate that there are no major differences in *historical data* from what we already have.

Let us rehash the plights of Tyndale and Bede, two Bible translators. William Tyndale's Bible was different. Tyndale sought the original Greek texts and ancient Hebrew manuscripts. He would not bow to officialdom's opinions. In his handwritten notes are the words: "shocking and disgraceful" and to date "No repentance was found in her mouth" for those acts. When word of his comments reached Officialdom in Rome, a decree was issued to burn as many of Tyndale's Bibles as could be found. The Roman ecclesiastical gentry made large acquisitions and those holy books were burned. They sought vigorously to find and murder Tyndale. Tyndale born in 1492 was martyred in 1536.

Bede's translations (not his original texts) show oxblood and red as meanings for "Adamy." A heifer was used for sacrifice. Even though the descriptive word in Hebrew is "Adamy," it is recorded as a *red* heifer. Believe it or not, the colour oxblood is derived from the dark brownish red-tinged blood of slain oxen. Jacob's soup was made with *lentils* and *venison*. Furthermore, the Hebrew texts offer a distinct prophetic picture of the ethnicity of Esau and his seed. One of the twins (Jacob) was described as lighter in appearance and the other was described as dark with hair rolled up like oats or as some would say, "Nappy Hair." How could they arrive at "red all over like a hairy garment" for Esau's description? Was God using His *Law of Double Reference* to give us a warning as to how the "Nappy Haired" man would be hunted for his inheritance? Would the smooth ones try to take his land, gold, oil, and diamonds by unfair means? Would the accurate translations create too much guilt? Instead, we ended up with Esau asking Jacob for some of his *red soup*. Since that would have sounded extremely silly, the translators have used the words: "red pottage." God planted specific words in Esau's mouth. He asked his brother for some of the soup that he *cooked*. Although venison (deer meat) is reddish brown, if they implied that the meat was red, the cooked soup could *not have been red*. The rams used for sacrifices though adamy are all now translated as *red rams*. I will show scripture references and also the accuracy of the Hebrew language in that it exposes fraud. Exodus 25:5...and Exodus 39:34...*ram skins* (dyed) red...there is no Hebrew word in the original text for dyed. They did it again by inserting "red" to explain how the ram skins became red. Exodus 26:14...a tent of *ram skins* (dyed) red. Translators inserted the word "dyed" to explain that the rams might be red instead of dark brown. They continued the idiocy by describing Esau (whose seed became the black Edomites) as being *red with coarse hair*. The Hebrew word for Esau is *Edom*. He and his seed dwelt in the land of Seir in the southernmost part of modern day Israel, where Jews with the most residual melanin live. Incidentally, David's complexion is now in all modern Bibles as a *red Jew* and *father of* one of *the blackest men* ever known.

Do those subliminal slurs reflect our inherent deficiencies? Such inaccurate depictions are among the main reasons that Muslims, Jews and Africans refute the "Messiahship" of Jesus. Some assert that if Jesus is the person portrayed in the Occident, it is impossible to proclaim that He is the Messiah. Song of Solomon 5:11 cannot be tampered with because Solomon said his skin was black as a raven and his hair was bushy. God in His wisdom had made Solomon extra black and had him compare his skin colour to that of a blackbird; otherwise we could have been reading about a red Solomon also.

JESUS IS THEREFORE WHO HE IS PORTRAYED TO BE AND NOT THE MESSIAH OR HE IS NOT WHO HE IS PORTRAYED TO BE AND HARD EVIDENCE THEN PROVES HIM TO BE THE MESSIAH.

CHAPTER 15C. MESSIAH'S BIRTHPLACE AND GENEALOGY.

God warned Jesus' parental guardians in a vision that Satan was making serious attempts to wipe out the promised seed. They were advised to go to Egypt. Hosea 11:1, "Out of Egypt will I call my son." Hosea dictated that prophecy some 700 to 800 years after the Israelites left Egypt and his use of future tense is self-explanatory. Mary and Joseph took infant Jesus there and were able to mingle with the dark-skinned Egyptians and not be recognized because both the Egyptians and the inhabitants of Canaan were the Hamitic seed of Mizraim. Let us not forget that Moses passed for an Egyptian for years. In fact he was perceived to be the son of Pharaoh's daughter by many. Examine the pyramids and the pigmentation of the ancient Egyptians. Mary had both the lineage of David and that of Levi in her veins. Those revelations are extremely important to unmask the slickest plot that Satan planned to unleash on humankind. I will put the vision by John—the transformed Jesus with feet like burnt brass—on hold until a later chapter.

PROPHETICALLY, KORAH THE PSALMIST RECORDED THE MESSIAH'S GENEALOGY AND HIS AWESOME ANOINTING IN PSALM 87.

Since the Psalmist listed the birthplace of the Messiah, we must search the Hebrew names and the towns mentioned to learn of His predestined ethnicity. In Psalm 87:4 are all His ancestral mixes. "I will make mention of Rahab and Babylon to them that know me." The previous four words refer to the "Keepers of Esoteric Wisdom." Verse 4…"Behold Philistia and Tyre" (Galilee) and with Ethiopia, *THIS MAN WAS BORN THERE.* One of His great matriarchs mentioned by name was Rahab, a much tanned lady who concealed God's holy prophets in Jericho. The Ethiopians mentioned in the text have looked the same from ever since. Psalm 87:7 has a very powerful pronouncement: "All my springs are in thee." Also Ezekiel made mention of a spiritual river in Ezekiel 47. The Seven ministering spirits that conduct and maintain the harmony of the *Most High God* will be touched on later. The mysteries of both the spiritual river and the ministering spirits are spelled out in verses 5 to 7 to show the "Wise-hearted" the authority and the anointing that would be placed on the Messiah. Undoubtedly, many people would be born there, but God issued a decree for *one special person* with that ethnic make-up. Verse 7, "All my springs are in thee." *All of God's springs would be in that person.* Any "dry place" would be shattered with His anointing. Along with the aforementioned, Michaiah prophesied in Micah 5:1-2 that of the thousands that would be living in Jerusalem after the absence of all Israel's Judges, one man of the tribe of *Judah* shall come forth, be born in *Bethlehem* and be ruler of Israel forever. That was a frightening prophecy! At a time when Israel had neither king nor judge, God would appoint a King, *not in Judah but in Bethlehem* to rule all Israel? Rastafarians believe that King was King Selassie. The Torah and the Holy Koran refute such—Sura 3, 45, "O Mary! Allah giveth thee glad tidings of a word from Him: his name will be Christ Jesus."

Can you imagine a child upon whom God decreed names such as Power, Wonder and Might? Isaiah previewed the redeeming powers of that "Special Child" with all of His accolades. In Isaiah 9:6, are attributes of the Messiah: wonder-worker, firstfruit, and might of God or *Mighty God.* We must examine the last name more closely as male Hebrew siblings are given their father's names as a prefix to theirs. JHVH God is Most Mighty God. According to Isaiah, the Most-Mighty God would sire a son and call Him, *Mighty God.* There is no way that child could have arrived unnoticed, since He would have a name like no other name. He would have authority and power unlike any other person that ever walked the earth. Samuel foretold the birth of that special seed to King David in 2nd Samuel 7:8-13. Then the Psalmist prophesied the declaration of the birth of that Son, the Messiah in Psalm 87. Samuel shared those prophetic messages with David—2nd Samuel 7:12-14. 2nd Samuel 7:12, "When thy days are fulfilled, and thou shalt sleep with thy fathers, I will set up thy *seed after thee* (which shall proceed out of thy bowels) and I will establish his kingdom." Verse 13, "He shall build a house for my name, and I will establish *the throne* of his kingdom *forever.* Verse 14 …I will be his father, and he shall be my son." Samuel bore witness to the prophetic echo of God's word by confirming the contents of Psalm 87 regarding the Messiah's genealogy. God in His wisdom knew that deceivers would attempt to change the appearance of the Messiah the same way that Rebekah changed the appearance of the seed heir. So, in 2nd Samuel 19:42, the ethnicity of the Messiah's tribe is recorded. The ministry, life of the Messiah and His genetic lineage, were all profiled in advance. Here is another revelation. The Messiah's house must match the physical house of Solomon in the spiritual architecture, lumber and workmanship to fulfill the prophetic echo-effect of God's word. In many cases in the Tanakh the words: "I have set my king upon my Holy Hill," are prophetic references to the Messiah—Psalm 2:6. Psalm 2:7, Thou art my Son, this day have I begotten thee. That verse was recorded not as *a decree*, but The Decree.

Micah 5:2-3, "Out of thee (Bethlehem) shall come forth he that is to be ruler in Israel *whose goings forth have been of old, from everlasting. He would stand in the majesty of the name of the Lord his God.*" Also Micah 5:5, "*His greatness would be until the ends of the earth.*" After His death and resurrection, Jesus gave a prophecy to one of His witnesses by the name of John. Amazingly, the only aspect of the detailed path of proliferation of a specific determined spirit is the Day in the not too distant future when the Lord's anger will be kindled to uproot all the eggs and tentacles of a particular spirit. Revelation 17 and 18 foretold the plight of all her hatchlings and her networks in their "Day of Doom."

Here is something very strange. Satan has convinced millions of people that dead people can come back to advise and warn loved ones. However, many of the same people would doubt that Jesus had broken the life/death cycle. Of all the predictions that are published annually supposedly from dead people to mediums, with over 90 percent wrong every year, the same people do not waiver in their beliefs that the dead can advise and warn. I do not have the space to record Revelation 18 entirely; nontheless, all are welcomed to read the Revelation of John as documented on the isle of Patmos around 96C.E. On record, Jeshua (who fulfilled prior prophecies about His unusual birth and temporary death) gave precise instructions to John two thousand years ago that have been on target so far. What a paradox!

CHAPTER 15D. STOLEN BIBLE VERSES ON WHICH RACISM WAS BUILT.

Any gift that Most-Holy Spirit God gives to us that we leave unprotected, Satan and any of his spirit thieves will take. If we are careless with any of God's sacred gifts, Satan has a license to steal, imitate, inflict, kill, and or to desecrate anything that God already blessed for us. Before touching the stolen verses, let me unmask two plans of the devil so that readers can identify either the source or the intent behind certain behavioural patterns. I will print the perennial plans of the devil. His unmasked plans are (1) To infiltrate, to confuse and to replace God's truths with "cloned lies" and (2) Having laid that foundation to demonize and kill all (if possible) in trespass so that he can inherit "That Lofty Exalted Position" by default. He would then be able to claim that God's children were not worthy. Oh yeah?

Custodians of surviving fragments from the ancient Libraries of Alexandria have agreed to mention his plans in public only under the code name of "BAHOMET." According to their legends, a prophet shall arise in the latter days. To Him shall the *Great Architect of the Universe* reveal all that is concealed. That prophet would find the solution to (a four thousand-year) unsolved riddle. By the way, "Ancient Civilizations" is my preferred study discipline. There are certain established criteria used for evaluation purposes in that field. Whenever hairs or portions of hairs were described for any civilization considered as ancient, the word "lock" inadvertently showed up. Civilizations from Sumer, Ugarit, Meroè and Nubia, now defunct, braided their hair in locks. By and large they were Negroid. The hair of all Levitical Priests had to curl in a lock naturally. To this day all Rabbis keep the hairs around their earlobes in the prescribed Horus Lock. I wonder why?

At the time of Jesus' birth, neither the Romans nor the Greeks in any large scale were converts to Judaism. There were Persians, Egyptians and Ethiopians who were married to Hebrew people. Others in search of enlightenment and wisdom had converted and pursued the All Knowing God of Abraham, Isaac and Jacob. Ancient records of Indo/Persians attest to that. Until Rome razed Palestine and Jerusalem in 70 C.E., Judaism was relatively small and according to today's classification, "ethnically confined." There were no classifications as "white races" or "black races" up to the time of Jesus' death. The people with little or no melanin were Greeks, Romans and Cretans, called "Gentiles." On the other side of the coin, the melanin-rich people were Jews, Cyrenians, Egyptians, Libyans and Ethiopians.

After the third Roman sponsored carnage of 1099, Satan's obsessive hatred of the Jews spread like fire over altars of *Usurped Theocracy*, allowing institutionalized racism, anger and anti-Semitism to follow in the wake of wars in captured nations. Since he forged a marriage between himself and a "corrupted church/state," he had a powerful vehicle, a secret "Bride." Scripture references are Revelation 17:3-7. Over time a secret doctrine surfaced, implying that two source tributaries fed the lake of humankind. Allegedly there were two different species of people: one group "evolved" from the apes. Their seed bore the Hamites, Semites and Japhethites. The other was "created" *from the mating of angels with the daughters of men.* Out of that group, allegedly sprang the Arians.

As silly as that sounds, so serious were the zealots that they actually mistranslated the Hebrew texts to reflect their beliefs. The Edenic record, Genesis 6:2: "The sons of God saw the daughters of men that they were *fair*; they took them wives of all which they chose." When angels mated with the sons of men, the inhabitants of the earth spoke one language and were all melanin-rich. In Eden because of its sinless state and because of the warm environment, residents wore no clothes originally. They had dark earth-coloured skins for suits. Later myths, ingrained over the altars of Rome's state-religion allowed the gentry to invent a "Babylonian spirit-polluted" adulterated religion that gave rise to racial intolerance.

Let us examine comfortable teachings that evolved from those myths:

1.   Jews killed Jesus. What nationality was the soldier that thrust the spear in Jesus' side?

2.   All of the followers of Jesus, including those who heard Him preach and those that were healed, did not accept Jesus: so they were not worthy of Him?

3.   Florentine painters could paint away His ethnicity?

4.   Ham (father of the dark Hamites) received a curse, contrary to what the Bible taught?

5.   The dark-skinned people killed Jesus; therefore all of their people were not worthy? I wonder, is it righteous to "hate" a supposedly "unrighteous people?"

While Satan was letting them believe that it was right to kill God's people, why was he not telling them that it was wrong to steal their gold, their diamonds, their labour and their religion? He simply blinded nations and religions with hateful doctrines, and as a result, "a new race" grew around "new doctrines" on new national headquarters. While on the isle of Patmos, John saw the extent of the deception. It was so severe; it would last until "The Eve of the Apocalypse." Did Satan's new headquarters set up a pure religion for a pure new race? Satan's disciples believed that up to today; so they built armies and began to purge the world. They used murder, mammon from stolen gold, stolen labour, false teachings and witchcraft.

Let us look at three Hebrew words: to^wb = a good thing or beautiful, ya^pha^h = bright and beautiful and ya^phe^h = beautiful. All three are used to reflect beauty. Solomon, one of the finest ancient poets used the last two extensively in his poems. Job, who had occasion to use the equivalent of the word FAIR, in describing the weather, used the Hebrew word za^ha^b. Literally the word means shimmering, golden or figuratively sunny. In every occasion when the word for beautiful was used to describe a human being, even though the Hebrew word (to^wb) was used to describe persons (in Genesis 6:2 and Esther 2:2, for "beautiful" virgins) in Jerome's Vulgate and subsequent translations, *fair* is substituted for beautiful. How clumsy it becomes when the language is shaded. Examine 1st Samuel 17:42 "ruddy" and a fair countenance. God is no respecter of persons. You make any change deliberate or otherwise to His word and His truth will expose all.

A Florentine group, with a specific agenda, wanted their opinions of two different types manifested. They used their influence to have all of Wycliffe's work edited to reflect their philosophical biases. God in His wisdom warned: "To the Jews were committed the Oracles of God." Put another way, His God-ordained language would reveal all truth. In the book of "Esther," the narrative used careful words to explain that from India to Ethiopia were under Persian rule. When the king summoned all the beautiful maidens, he could not distinguish between Jew, Indian, Persian or Ethiopian. Of course people were not ethnically labeled as is done today by occult-influenced organizations. The residents of India, the Indians, Ethiopians and southern Jews have retained their ancient features to date. I was shocked to find so much evidence as to how Satan engineered racial intolerance as a platform to drive wedges of hate between all tribes of Israel and seeds of ancient Rome/Greece—the Gentiles. Missionaries labouring in India in the 12th to 17th centuries died in frustration, as the gentry of successive Gentile nations were deaf to their requests for Bibles and teaching aids, as Indians were so hungry for the Gospel. Sad to say, "Lost Tribes" of Jews, denied access to their true word because of exported "myths of superiority," have invented substitute religions and are calling themselves Pakistanis and Indians, elevating altars to all forms of foreign gods just as God portended. We need to pray for the brothers and sisters of the world "Indian Evangelical teams" that have such difficulties attempting to rebuild and reclaim so many stolen altars.

How could we miss that prophecy about a special spirit that glues to political institutions, that glues to enclaves of power, whether those powers belong to huge religious institutions, armies and or persons of influence? The pattern is unmistakable; it searches out the charismatic ones, the oppressive ones: eventually their temporary adulation will lead to eventual destruction. A logical question to ask is why does it appear that the Gentiles are blessed en masse? The logical answer is that the question is loaded with illogical assumptions. The unrighteous mammon had been handed down to their seed. The secret "Babelists" stuck to their game plans. They destroy surplus food to keep export prices high. The monetary systems in the world are set to extract the riches from the seed of "The Tribes" towards the seed of the Gentiles by a rate structure, not based on resources, but by instructions allegedly emanating from occult-inspired institutions. They are obeying the spirit "Babylon the Great." What if within 40 days, all poor nations set up a league of underprivileged people? They then decide to prioritize trading and resources within their own territories? Within 40 days, every formerly rich country would either be paying them to go back to their former status or war would be declared on them. Without poor nations, there can be no rich ones. God preordained specific punishments for disobedient seed and it came to pass.

CHAPTER 15E. INSIGHT INTO THE ANCIENT OF DAYS.

Let us reexamine the mystery of who Jesus is, or was. Abraham, to whom the seed of promise was given, lived 99 years before that seed was sown. These are revelations for Masters incidentally. It takes *three* prophetic stages (or days) for the promise to manifest from darkness to light. In Egypt it took 3 days from the period of darkness to deliverance. From the cross, Jesus' crucifixion to His resurrection took 3 full days in the tomb: Thursday sunset to Friday sunrise; Friday sunset to Saturday sunrise; Saturday sunset to Sunday sunrise. On the morning of the "First day" He became the Firstfruit of the promised resurrection. Then "The Day of Manifestation" must be 3 divided into 99 or 33 years. "The Day of Fulfillment" which was predestined since ancient times, must complete 33 years to reveal the mystery of "The Ancient of Days." Obviously that "Day" must bring exceptional light: revelation, healing, exorcism, and at least reprieve from spiritual and ancestral darkness—Isaiah 53.

In the days of Ahaz, the son of Jotham, the son of Uzziah king of Judah, God commanded Prophet Isaiah (Isaiah 7:11) to tell Ahaz to ask for *a sign* of very important things *to come.* Isaiah's main assignment was to prophesy "the restoration to come." Isaiah 7:14 foretold the Messiah's name and also gave a spiritual description of His mother (very unusual to preview a matriarch in a patriarchal society). Most importantly, Isaiah 9:6 gave us His authority. "The Government (authority) shall be upon his shoulder and his name shall be called Wonderful, Counselor, Everlasting 'Father' (the Hebrew word is Branch or First fruit) Prince of Peace and Mighty God." Why would a child be called Mighty God, or Might of God? The seer Balaam the son of Beor foresaw Him as the "Star of Jacob" and the "Sceptre of Israel" while in a trance—Numbers 24:14-17.

Ancient Israel's society was built around Patriarchs. Any time a male was addressed, his parental bloodline was listed also. Isaiah was describing the perfect ancestral bloodline of the child. In Psalm 110:4 and Genesis 14:18 we were taught that Salem already had a king. God was careful to have His ancient scribes document that Melchizedek was the forerunner of the future nation priesthood. He was "King of Salem, as in Jeru-Salem." Unlearned men, not versed in ancient Hebrew ethnology, have actually mistranslated that passage in Isaiah to infer that the child would be God. Consider this: God has no restrictive traits, titles or boundaries. A king's domain ceases at the borders of his kingdom. God is! God who appoints and disappoints kings could not be a king, much less a prince! There is a pregnant word used in the prophetic verse of Psalm 2:7, "Thou art my Son; this day have I begotten thee." The important clue here is the word "begotten." Besides that, the word Son is capitalized. No way could that refer to David since David was born in and reigned in Judah and had full authority in his kingdom. That Son would have had someone in authority over Him. That Son was, and is to dwell on His holy hill, Zion. God is supreme!

Approximately 2000 years ago, a carpenter born in Bethlehem grew up in the region around Galilee. To escape the wrath of Herod, His mother and stepfather hid Him in Egypt. Jeshua fulfilled Psalm 80:8 and Isaiah 53:2, in that the child grew from a tender shoot into the "Branch" that was planted sacrificially on Mt. Moriah.

WILL I BE SATISFIED WITH THE BLOOD OF BULLS AND GOATS OR WILL I REQUIRE A BETTER SACRIFICE?

Jeremiah promised us that the better sacrifice and the New Covenant would not be messed up like the last one. Anytime disobedient children allow God's unstoppable plans to be shelved temporarily, serious woe would befall the covenant breakers. As we allowed God's eventual plans for a Theocracy to be delayed, we received a usurped "DEMONCRACY" as a very bitter substitute.

CHAPTER 15F. THE PATRIARCHAL FOUNDATION.

We saw from Moses' discourse that male beings from beyond the borders of the universe had mated with the daughters of men. There are male and female species of plants. The male papaya and the male avocado trees bear beautiful blossoms but no fruit. The female plants are the ones that produce fruit with seed after their kind. There are other trees that are "single-gendered plants only." The olive and a type of tropical plum are examples. They have no female plants, so bees cannot cross-pollinate those trees for them to produce fruit. From the single-gendered plant, a branch must be plucked and grafts made. So it is not beyond the realm of probability for God to father a redemptive Son. The questions now are: "Is Jesus the one who came and will come again?" Is He a prophet that came and we are awaiting the Messiah? Is He the first Messiah that came again the second time as Prophet Mohammed or King Tafari? Is Prophet Mohammed the one chosen for all Jews, Gentiles, and Arabs? Since the chosen *Branch* had to be able to receive numerous cuts and grafts, and only one was chosen to roll away the stone for the three flocks in Padan-aram, then "The One Chosen" must be of the seed of Isaac. By selecting that one male plant to be grafted, all future grafts, true and wild olives *must be grafted to the one true and chosen olive.*

God's concealed message is that by the time the Messiah was born, no more seed would be concealed in the wombs of any females of Levi. The male branch, chosen, had to have been from a Jewish "Olive Branch of Continuity." He would have been connected (with customs and teachings) to the *Law of Moses*. However that messianic stem would be able to be *grafted repeatedly.* The Messiah would have been single and produced no carnal seed. Let us search the *Law of Moses* to find the foundation of the spiritual graft. I will list the scripture—the significance will be highlighted in chapters "Mystery of the Three Flocks" and "Secrets of Rebekah's Womb"—Genesis 24:67. Rebekah became his wife, and he loved her. Isaac was comforted after his mother's death." If Sarah was meant to be the parent incubator (or tabernacle) then the Messiah's Tabernacle has to be bonded to the old law. Sandwiched between the three schools of thought—Islam, Judaism or Christianity—is the truth. Next, let us search for the seed of Isaac that was chosen to *roll away* the stone for the three flocks.

At the beginning of the first century, there was a physician companion of Paul the Apostle by the name of Luke. Almost every early Christian writer noted his educational and cultural background and penchant for fine details. Luke 24:1, "Upon the first day of the week, very early in the morning they (two previously mentioned ladies) came unto the sepulcher where Jesus was entombed under heavy Roman security." Verse 2, "They found *the stone rolled away* from the sepulcher." Luke then continued to relay the events concerning Jesus who was last seen dead and subsequently alive. If that event was a hoax, then I, who was one of the most cynical of cynics, have gone totally bananas. Not only that but we would have to condemn the Torah, The Koran, The Tanakh, and then destroy all the archaeological records and artifacts of at least 10 nations' museums. There was never a known case of a Hebrew attempting to steal a dead body. Their strict laws and customs explain the reasons. Besides the obvious, Jeshua's disciples became "the hunted." Luke's record is for posterity.

Why would the Romans crucify Jesus exactly the way that God prefigured it 490 (7x70) years in advance? Psalm 69:21 foretold that they would give Him gall and vinegar. Look at all those other prophecies about Jesus and His Ministry: Micah 5:2, His birthplace, Isaiah 11:10 entrance for the Gentiles: "He would be a Standard Bearer" to the Gentiles; exact details about His crucifixion in Psalm 22, Psalm 69 and Isaiah 53 from verse 2. In Zechariah 11:12, ransom price and rejection by His kin were all foretold by God's prophets that lived prior to Jesus' birth. Ezekiel 21 and 22 spelled out in prophetic detail what would happen—for prolonged generational disobedience (Ezekiel 22:30-31) and for "**Rejecting His Son**." Ezekiel 21:10 used stern words "contemneth," (casteth away or rejected) the rod of my son." In Ezekiel 21:14, the words (double punishment) are mentioned *three times* for *rejecting "His Son."* In Numbers 24:17 Balaam was entranced and previewed His authority.

To many Jews, the name of Jesus inflicts painful memories. Mention the name and some flinch and squirm. This messenger wants to add something new. I want you to puke! Satan has sown much confusion between all of Abraham's seed: those of the Freewoman—the tribes of the north, the tribes of the south—and the seed of Ishmael. How ironic it is that today, so many of the seed of Ishmael are intermarried with remnants of the 12 tribes; they are calling themselves by different names and are fighting for turf. Satanically inspired nations are kindling the fires of hatred by selling them armaments and by milking their resources. In Revelation 9:21 the state/church league and the spirit that sitteth on many waters, indulge in unrepented *sorceries, murders, thefts* and *fornications* until the end times.

Correspondence from "Early Church Fathers" shows that when the churches of the Roman provinces first tried to establish linkages with the early foundational churches of Jerusalem and Antioch, their efforts were rebuffed. The rejection and condemnation (centered on Rome's sponsored institutionalized bloodbaths) forged the surviving first stems along a geographical and spiritual divide. The first branches sprouted the Greek Orthodox, Russian Orthodox and the Ethiopian Orthodox churches, and the 3rd to 4th century grafts established a matriarchal foundation on a city of seven hills. John foretold those events while on the isle of Patmos in 98 C.E. Revelation 9:21, "neither repented they of their murders, nor of their sorceries…nor of their thefts." Had the church repented to the Inca, to the tribes of Simeon and Judah for the years of theft, hate and doctrines replacement theology? True, this current Pope closed his organization's Jubilee door in 1998, and made repentance in Israel for the carnage of 70 C.E and 1099 C.E. On the other hand, the oceans of murder stretched from the coasts of Gorè through to the plantations of the Suriname, Brazil in the South and to the Carolinas in the West. Why would John say that she repented *not* of her murders? The historical record of Rome's leaders is infested with assassinations. The Central and South Americans were slaughtered by their seed for their gold. Much of that gold is still on church steeples in Europe. God calls it the *unrighteous mammon*. That event, one of the "World's Most Guarded Secrets," is concealed around a series of inaccuracies. God is unveiling a lot of data today in "Spiritual Archaeology." Much of the hard Biblical evidence that was concealed is now coming to light. Some of those revelations will cause pain to the proud. Unless there is **Repentance and Forgiveness, there can be no Jubilee**. This has been appointed the first significant Jubilee. The physical Jubilee must happen first. The spiritual Jubilee is the one that Satan is deathly afraid of!

CHAPTER 15G. A HUMAN ALARM, DAY OF JUDGMENT.

Isaiah 42:1, "Behold my servant whom I uphold; mine elect in whom my soul delighteth; I have put *my spirit upon him; he shall bring forth judgment to the Gentiles.*"
42: 3…"He shall bring forth judgment unto *truth.*"
42: 4…"till he hath set judgment in the earth."
42: 4… "The isles shall wait for his law."
The Holy Koran confirms the above in two separate suras. In Sura 43, 61 Jesus is referred

to as the sign for the coming *Hour of Judgment* and in Sura 2:253 To Jesus the son of Mary we gave clear Signs and strengthened him with the Holy Spirit.

Whoever the Messiah is or was, He would have had a major impact on *TIME*. We have already established that the universe is a remarkable timepiece. In an earlier chapter I mentioned that the present is a bridge between crisscrossing realms past to future and future to past: from the unrevealed to the revealed. That is why God can reveal futuristic things to us through "His Chosen." Satan has been cast out and down so he has lateral knowledge and excellent files. There must be natural and spiritual "Harvests" and natural and spiritual feasts of "Purim." The Messiah has to be "Unleavened Bread, Sacrificial Lamb, Firstfruit, Pentecost, Shabbat, and Kinsman Redeemer." Anything less is not acceptable! His legacy must parallel the spiritual trek of the Israelites from the time of David to the Babylonian captivity. It would have been impossible for the Messiah to come—to what was then the most insignificant nation then—without major adjustments being made to Israel's natural, spiritual and historical clocks.

Here is food for the wise-hearted. We need to find out what relationship exists, if any, between God our Creator and His son (the repairer/redeemer) on: time, Israel's history, and Israel's sacred feasts. Since Jeshua dwelt in Jerusalem as per prophecies of Micah 5:2, Malachi 4:5-6, Isaiah 40:1-14, and His first exit was as per Daniel 9:24-27, we have had new international time references. All dates prior to His birth are B.C.E. and all dates after His first departure are referenced as C.E.

Since Jesus' birth and death, the following have been affected positively or adversely:

1. Judaism became the universal bond to hold a scattered and persecuted people worldwide.

2. Judaism and the Jews were transformed to centre of the rewound universal clock.

3. The provisions of the *New Covenant* of Jeremiah 31: 31 are being enjoyed.

4. Sacrifices of bulls and goats ceased immediately after His temporary exit. I dare anyone to offer the ancient sacrifices of bulls and goats in any temple in Israel. The veil of the temple was ripped at the time of His death. How come no one has put up a new veil? Is the world out of cloth?

Mohammed was the first seed of Abraham known to have answered God's call for a Theocracy. The indifferent Romans rebuffed Maimoniedes, one of Mohammed's mentors. As a result of their arrogance, Prophet Mohammed concentrated his efforts on reaching his kin scattered over the desert regions. He taught them to pray, to fast and to seek their God of Abraham, Isaac and Ishmael. He explained to them that God loved them as much as He loved Jews and Christians. God was not a God for some people only. God had and has the Nomads in His plans also. As his messages spread, intellectual improvement and blessings followed. An unprecedented period of enlightenment and knowledge ensued. Unfortunately after Mohammed's death, power struggles began. Satan could not allow his legacy to go untouched. Successors were assassinated. Different schools of thought wrestled for supremacy of their opinions—the usual spiritual attacks by the chief thief. Just like the original script, Abraham married Keturah after Sarah went to "sleep with her fathers." In Genesis 25:6, Abraham's concubines also bore seed, which he gave gifts and sent them away eastward. Genesis 25:5, "To Isaac he gave all that he had." Seed of Abraham went east and formed new religions after the "Sarah Temple" fell asleep. The Muslims can check their spiritual time clock and then compare the historical record to the schematic. All that I have done was to sketch history with a spiritual pencil. I will ask all of my Muslim friends, "Now that the world's spiritual clock is rewound, why has God's progressive clock apparently stopped and where do you want to be when the alarm rings?"

Before Jesus came on the scene the world could be divided into five major types of people:

a) Those that worshipped gods made with human hands. Oft-times, consciously or not they engaged in witchcraft and or practiced curious arts, magic or sorcery.

b) Those that worshipped things created from the first fruits of creation: animals, oaks, plants, rivers, reptiles and orbs etc.

c) Those that enslaved.

d) Those that were enslaved.

e) Seed of Abraham.

Men of wisdom from various parts of the world left teaching tools that we later called philosophies. Other sources—from nations that kept records, whether in stone, hieroglyphics, papyrus, scrolls or tablets—recounted sacrosanct ceremonies: to the Creator, some created god, or some form of ungodliness. Prior to Jesus' birth, the mode of worship of the one God of Abraham, Isaac, Ishmael, Noah, Solomon, and David was documented by the Hebrew prophets in a prophetic oracular medium—now called "Hebrew." The teachings were harmonious and continuous for hundreds of years. Archaeologists and other chroniclers have found evidence of counterfeit worship of demonic beings under altars of pagan gods and goddesses. Since Jesus came to confirm the Torah—as stated by Prophet Mohammed along with over 90 Koran verses—wisdom-deficient men have crossed the intellectual divide. Carnal minds have attempted to describe the most sacred things and as such have classified even pagan expressions as religion. Every ethnic group seems to be flaunting doctrines over their own "Ethnic altars."

The people who not only knew God, but sought Him, found Him and covenanted with Him were 12 tribes of Jews, and Satan has given them and their seed no respite. Mighty nations came and vanished. Prior to Jesus visit on earth, mankind groped in darkness searching for the "Truth." Since Jesus' first exit, new religious ways keep popping up in almost every nation with a "ME TOO MESSAGE." Let us apply a free and fair litmus test to filter satanic imitations from God-ordained truth. The challenge to find the lines of separation between cult, philosophy, religion and chosen path will be presented to you the reader. The evidence was found by meticulous detective work, after outlining the research guidelines for this material.

CHAPTER 15H. SECULAR DEFINITION OF RELIGION.

Dictionaries have established certain criteria on the definition of religion. What they all omit is the intangible altar or spiritual proclamation. With such broad and unregulated criteria, Satan has so many potential areas to invade. Let us examine the criteria established by institutions that classify as religions for registration purposes in their countries of origin. Here is a summary of their requirements:

1. Divine revelation.

2. Prior prophecy.

3. Shepherds (Pastors, Prophets, Elders, Bishops, and Priests).

4. Flock (Faithful Followers).

5. Sacrifice.

6. Sacraments.

7. Pilgrimage, Convocation.

8. Self-Denial.

9. Meditation.

10. Mysticism.

Any institution with a philosophical base, a tangible or an intangible altar, a shepherd, flocks, and an account of a divine revelation can qualify. Is there anyone in the secular world able to evaluate the source of a divine revelation or the sources of prophecies? Enough of the "yesterdayisms." The time has come to raise the bar. Satan is a spirit being. He *cannot* foretell events. He can hit and miss with predictions like most people, and if he gets any chance whatsoever he will take over the sacrifice. So I must publish a foolproof litmus test from a spiritual, as opposed to a secular perspective. If anyone is intentionally duping flock, the flock can discern the identity of the sacrifice-recipient, by the purity of the preparations or lack thereof, and the concealed spiritual messages. For all intents and purposes—as far as this concerned—"religion has to be pure and truthful" to avoid spiritual theft. God is not a God of confusion. By highlighting such incongruence and confusion among God's adherents, hopefully some remedial action will be taken.

A RELIGION HAS TO LINE UP WITH WHAT GOD GAVE TO MOSES IN THE WILDERNESS. SUBSTITUTES ARE UNACCEPTABLE.

Solomon built God's house on earth. The Messiah has to build God's spiritual house on earth from the original blueprint with identical problems and pitfalls. Therefore if a person is either a shepherd or a member of a flock that had one prior messenger and that messenger was prophet, scribe, shepherd, architect, builder and foundation stone all in one, an alarm bell should sound immediately. God gave one person the plan for *His Temple*. He appointed another to find the building materials. He set 12 pillars to function around His foundation stone. My question to all such would be, "Who revealed the original message to your first fruit prophet?" Who confirmed God's word? God always confirms His word. His Rama words are confirmed not by one, but by many prophets with signs of miracles and healings. In other words, is the seed connected to God's continuous plans or is it a disconnected seed?

From whence came the foundation stone? God specifically said that His foundation stone from the seed of Isaac would be laid in Zion (Isaiah 28:16). I make no apologies for God's word. The Holy Koran urged Muslims to study the "Book," which is "The Torah." The Torah, the Tanakh and the Bible are emphatic in that the special place for God's foundation stone is Zion. If the foundation stone is not in Zion, laid by Jeshua, then the foundation stone is altered. Once a spiritual foundation is altered, it is subject to penetration by Satan.

Everyone reading this should be able to apply him/herself to the schematic and analyze self, institution, and country:

1 . Enemy of Israel, positioned by Satan and an ancient spirit from Babylon for collision purposes.

2 . Northern 10 tribes: they were mixed, migratory, and scattered.

3 . Southern less mixed Judaic traits, the former hunter now the hunted.

4 . Seed of Ishmael.

5 . Stranger that co-mingled, connected by marriage or by assimilation.

6 . Gentile.

CHAPTER 15I. FINALLY A LITMUS TEST!

It is time to pull the plugs on the many hoaxes passed on to humankind in the guise of religions. If someone has a mystical experience, then separates himself/herself for a while, attracts followers and publishes a doctrine, is that enough to say it is a religion? Shouldn't there be distinctions between a religious pursuit, a religious experience and pure religion?

NEW LITMUS TEST FOR PURE RELIGION:

1 . Strict, devout in corporate prayer like many Muslims and a new breed of Christians called "Prayer Warriors."

2 . Corporately generous to their spiritual brothers and sisters like Muslims, most Salvation Army churches, *some*—not all, Christian denominational, Baptist and Pentecostal churches.

3 . Forgiving in principle, like the early Christians documented in the book of Acts, *some* born-again Christians called "Charismatics" and some members of denominational churches.

4 . Unwavering with code, commemorative holy days, accuracy of prophetic language and inheritance like the Jews of the Torah. Whoever merges those principles shall be blessed of house, family, country and altars.

5 . We must do more than worship an exalted being. In any case there are 30-foot statues. We must worship the most powerful and highest mentally, spiritually, and intellectually. As simple as the latter appears, think for a moment. If your God cannot be exalted above the natural, you are in trouble. If your God cannot hear you, teach you, instruct you, talk either to you or through messengers to you, then you are in serious trouble. You do not have God, but a toy.

6. There must be past and current witnesses supported by historical and archaeological data that testified to miraculous events done by or on behalf of the God that you worship.

7. Since any God who is superior to man must have more knowledge than man has, your God must be able to foretell the future in precise details.

8. I really have a problem with one-shot prophets. Evidence has to be confirmed. Events prophesied, fulfilled and reconfirmed is factual evidence.

9. A God that *can* foretell all events, fulfill them and cause them to be reconfirmed is a God worthy of exaltation, worship and praise. If your God does not meet those requirements and you have exalted spiritual imitations on any altar, whoever you are, you have built altars that will or already have been usurped. Any building dedicated to a god that does not meet the requirements of this chapter, not withstanding your identity and how educated you think you are, you *have created an altar of disobedience* and the *Lord of disobedience* will occupy it or has already inhabited it. Chances are that you will have to sprinkle incense and pour all sorts of spirit-enhancing libations to strengthen the spiritual usurpers.

Religion should not be simply worship of *a creator* since there are many creators. Pure and true religion must be solely and exclusively worship of the *Creator of the Universe*, The All Wise, and All Knowing invisible God. Hence we are forewarned from committing serious sacrileges by carving any image *whatsoever* for worship. Giving power bases to Satan by creating *altars in disobedience* knowingly or unknowingly is violating Exodus 20:1-17. The practice of a religion establishes a system of worship to an "Exalted Being." Calling the being God is not enough. In the pre-deluge days, spirits had taken over not only humans but their worship and their ceremonies also. In temples in Central America, they invaded the altars and had Inca and Maya priests worshipping them as gods. There were many gods carved and exalted in ancient Egypt also. Anything manifest is calculable and has limitations. The forces of cold, heat, propulsion, winds, energy, life and electricity—though expandable and finite—are invisible. We have evidence of their existence and manifestation of their powers. Omnipotent God, who created the universe with all the aforementioned, must be incalculable and therefore invisible to the natural eye. We also have evidence of His power, prophecies, voice, laws and prophets to confirm His Word.

Creator of the Universe, the God of Abraham, Moses, David, Jeshua and Mohammed, is God with precise laws that should have nothing added to or subtracted from *His Word*. Since all prime movers are positive entities and this "Prime Mover" speaks, moves, creates, and is all, then this prime mover is an ultra positive super being and since "IT" is for neuter gender, shouldn't we give our greatest respect to Him? The prophetic supra-gender is "El." As we progress we will search and then ask a very specific question. Does any adept of the Creator, follower, disciple, student or prophet have any other mandate whatsoever but to speak, teach and or transpose the accurate word into other languages? If any other entity wants to cut in on this deal, let it create its own universe with its own rules. I think that is fair. No wonder Jacob found three flocks when he went to Mesopotamia. He was deemed worthy to roll away the stone. The prophet that removed the stone to the well of truth for Jews, Gentiles, Arabs and Christians just happened to be of the last family (documented) that had both bloodlines of *Levi* and *Judah* in His veins. He brought no state religion. He expounded on the Law and taught us how to live and to be the law. His name is Jeshua!

OH YOU JUST HAPPENED TO DROP IN AND EXPECT US TO FOLLOW YOU?

Moses prophesied and performed miracles to show that it was God who sent him. Elijah defeated 450 prophets of Baal: one for each year of blinding and binding bondage that Satan releases. Elisha prophesied and performed miracles to show that God sent him. Jesus defeated blindness, paralysis, dumbness, hunger, and Satan himself. He brought exponential power principles to fruition: He multiplied 5 barley loaves and two fishes, the very principles that His Father used to build the universe. He defeated leprosy, the grave, and hell. He gave us a victorious precedent over permanent death. Present me with evidence that you can defeat all of Satan's demonic forces. Through His resurrection power and His name, all of Jeshua's true disciples can ask for and receive the same miracles, healings and power gifts. Any religion that cannot defeat Satan or his demons in this season is a spiritual football, waiting to be kicked by Satan.

CHAPTER 15J. VENGEANCE (FOR JUDAH AND ISRAEL) IS MINE SAYS THE LORD.

Here is data from Satan's most secret files. Prior to the time of Jesus' birth, the people that gave him serious trouble were Moses, Joshua, Elijah and David. All four were Hamitic Hebrews, large-nosed with dark brown skins. Since then, every time a powerful *tanned* leader arrived on the international scene, satanic agents and organizations immediately become extremely paranoid. The reason is that the identity of some presumably *Lost Tribes* was well concealed in the southwest corner of Solomon's Temple. Southwest of Israel are Panama, Central and South America and the Caribbean. A special secret lay in the foundation of Solomon's Temple. Solomon, one the blackest and richest men who lived, built the world's most elaborate structures. Solomon's Hamitic seed must follow his path and build with their treasures and labour, the ten toes of the "Beast" envisioned by Daniel. Everyone that reenacts Solomon's rituals must know that Solomon's Temple will be rebuilt. When that time comes, all imposters must submit. It is written:"The wealth (unrighteous mammon) of the wicked is laid up for the righteous." One day, Solomon's Hamitic seed will shake the kingdoms of this world, which are built on the backs of free labour, greed and injustice.

Whenever Satan sees a charismatic Hamite, he sends his best: Jezebel, pride, fornication, lust, adultery, murder, addiction and incarceration. To Moses he sent two off-speed pitches called *anger* and *intolerance*. Moses missed and was called for strike on both occasions. Elijah he got with *fear* (from Jezebel) and (judging) or condemning God's people. Joshua (the seed of the Name Jehovah is Salvation), he could not touch. He got David with *anger* and his darlings: *lust, adultery, and murder.* Every one of his lustful spirits took a bite out of Solomon, laying the foundation for every "secretly controlled" organization to expose and ridicule those seeds of Judah with spiritual openings. Rev. Jesse Jackson he disgraced with Lust. In 1996 all polls showed Colin Powell way ahead of William Clinton. He was spoken to quietly! Colin must have known that when you are spoken to and you disobey, the natural hedge of protection (as opposed to the spiritual hedge) becomes weak. Martin Luther and other charismatic leaders of the sixties in America were murder victims. God sent Martin Luther with messages of peace and repentance. America's national altar is now crevassed by his prophet's blood, blood of four kings (presidents) indigenous people's blood, blood from clandestine murders/wars, seed of Judah's blood and blood from millions of aborted babies.

During ancient times, when Jews were not permitted to own property and their books and belongings were confiscated, elders recited oral traditions. They constructed a dialect called Yiddish. In Deuteronomy 28:68, God forewarned that their seed would be enslaved and then transported by ships. Those enslaved from the south by ships had a similar fate on the plantations. They invented their own dialects. Those in the French speaking countries invented "Creole." Those in the Dutch speaking ones invented one they called Papiamento. Those in the English speaking ones invented a dialect they called Calypso English, or "Twang." There is also "Hip-Hop." Some of those dialects are also used in calypso, rap, cadence and mambo by displaced "Remnants of Judah." I have spent years researching and analyzing those so-called dialects. Imagine what would happen if they discovered their true history and their spiritual potential? Unfortunately, millions are deaf to their calling as prophetic worship leaders like Asaph and Korah. For centuries Satan had been deathly afraid of this new season of Purim. It has arrived: Shout *Purim Power!*

SATAN KNOWS THE POTENTIAL OF HYBRID SEED POWER OR PURIM POWER.

CHAPTER 15K. TRANSFORMATION THROUGH THE POWER OF PURIM.

The events revealed in this chapter have caused considerable amounts of pain and damage to the entire legacy of Jesus. Satan's implanted spirits of fear, arrogance, love of unrighteous mammon, lies and tainted blood have allowed him so wide a canyon that his Leviathan spirit enters churches at will, *even sideways.* None of Solomon's wives were virgins. Leviathan's wake has inflicted all churches with such spiritual blindness that God prophetically recorded the maxim: All have sinned and come short of God's Glory!

Prior to Constantine's mother becoming a Christian, national hostility to Christians and Christianity were part and parcel of Rome's decrees. To be more precise, Rome passed satanically engineered laws. By the time the former hostile establishment became transformed from persecutor to partner, capable teachers were already dead. Consequently, seed of former pagan nations were wrestling with understanding and interpreting God's dictates and His revelations. God used precise languages to teach the principles of obedience. On the other hand, Rome, a nation born out of generations of disobedience, was attempting to transpose a perfect language into imperfect media. It is more than likely that much was lost in the transfer and translation processes. Martin Luther found 99 major errors. In addition to those, the Old Testament (which established the setting up of The Law together with examples of persons who pleased God and those who disobeyed and displeased God) was eliminated from 90 percent of their teaching materials. In Paul's letter to Jewish converts living in Rome (prior to the decrees to expel Jews) he was instructed to address specific spiritual issues. The leadership of the Jerusalem church asked him to explain to the Roman Jews, God's restorative plans for humankind through His redeemer Jeshua. His letter, appropriately called Romans, is so prophetic in that every issue that the future *Roman State Religion* needed to understand was addressed prior by Paul to people who inhabited the same country 300 years earlier. In Romans 11:1, Paul asked, "Hath God cast away his people?" His answer to the same question: "God forbid, for I also am an Israelite."

In spite of the question and answer in Romans 11:1, later churches in Rome were the main exporters of serious false doctrines, especially that of *Replacement Theology.* To outline properly the prophetic fulfillment of Jesus' restorative mission on earth, I should do an entire book on the subject since the correlation between events of David's reign and the brief restorative attempts under Joshua as High Priest are important references. The precision of God establishing *His Law*, His sacrifices, and His mode of worship may have caused analytical difficulties in an era before automated printing was established. Today however, except for spiritual blindness, distortion, and concealment, there are no more excuses.

Every time Satan lays a trap for you and you turn the plan upside down, a powerful anointing is released in the form of deposits to you and your family's spiritual accounts. It is called "Purim Power!" Pastors and preachers start proclaiming it; begin shouting it from your pulpits: Purim Power! When you are heavily tempted or challenged to say or to do the wrong things, shout *Purim Power* and watch those demons scatter as fast as possible. Jeshua brought a double-portion of Purim Power to us. Instead of being tripped up by Satan's most powerful spirits, Jesus turned every one of them upside down. Purim Power was released! I feel like preaching as this heavy anointing has come upon me: *Purim Power!* Bishop Jakes, the day you preach this sermon, I proclaim from the lips of the Mighty God through me this moment, people will be healed just at the shouting of those words. Anger: In the temple in Jerusalem, Jesus upturned His tables of anger against those that were defiling His Father's house: Purim Power! Lust: Jesus, instead of being a victim, cast the seven demons out of Miriam of Magdala and converted her: Purim Power! Vengeance: Instead of killing His enemies He forgave them: "Father forgive them for they know not what they do." Conceit and selfishness: He unleashed the Power of Purim by preaching about the one who sent Him and described in detail "The One" who sent Him: Purim Power!

From the book that Mohammed instructed Muslims to seek, in Isaiah 43, God's chosen servant must open blind eyes and heal deaf people. Here is a four part litmus test for anyone that receives a vision to start a new religion:

1. Describe the one that sent you.

2. Show prior prophecies that you were previously announced.

3. Since no unannounced messengers are ever sent, show which prophecies you have fulfilled! List at least 7 prior prophecies that your redeemer has since fulfilled.

4. List at least the same number of miracles performed by your magi.

Carefully observe the extent of Satan's deception and slickness. Satan figured that some might see through his web of lies. Since Jesus is the one that passed all of God's ordained litmus tests, he had to find ways to distort the world's perception and understanding of Jesus. Satan's policies have been to get people to deny Jesus, dilute Jesus, wipe out Jesus, steal Jesus' followers, counterfeit Jesus, and/or all of the aforesaid. Jesus came to *confirm and to teach the Law*. Every time Satan got a person to misinterpret God's truth, he encouraged the birth of a "New Religion." Next in the sequence of inquiries, let us scrutinize Satan's behaviour towards Jesus' legacy. Why would Satan devote so much time attempting to eliminate the following?

1. Jesus' bloodline?

2. Jesus' spiritual church?

3 . Jesus' shepherds?

4 . Jesus' heritage?

5 . Any true image of Jesus?

6. Remnant of the tribe ordained to carry the scepter?

7. The prophetic nature of the Hebrew language?

8. The concealed wisdom in the Temple of Solomon?

In the Book of Esther, God has shown that even though He has given Satan a license to harm the disobedient, there are times when God has to show that bum who the real boss is. God released Purim Power for Mordecai against Haman the Agagite; hence the source of the word agitation. God overturned Mordecai's devious deeds. God always reads the hog's mind: no disrespect meant to hogs. By so doing, God always has time to forewarn us. Unfortunately, we have become disobedient and spiritually deaf. Jesus the Christ is Everlasting Purim! Jesus the Christ is a perpetually programmed Butt-kicking factory! His spiritual tools are in Ephesians 6:12.

Up to the time of Jesus' death, whenever blood was spilled ritually, disobediently or in murder, a trumpet would blow in Demon land. "Come all ye slurpers; take a gulp!" Can you imagine when the earth "Opened her mouth" (see Genesis 4:11) to receive that spilt blood when Jesus died? The blast from the spiritual shofar shouted: "Surprise, knock knock, look who is here?" Purim, Purim, Purim! Thank God for the spiritual power emanating from the Feast of Trumpets. There are times when the anointing manifests through the power of the *Word* on these pages. Glory! **SOUND THE SHOFAR SOMEBODY!**

Those who were referred to as Ashkenazi may recall in folklore a word called "Dybbuk." There is in my research files, reference to a film by the same name. Maybe some film archivist might want to research that and remake it. That is exactly how demons behave today when you are casting them out. That dybbuk was an evil spirit, which resided previously in a wicked person. That is so accurate. Evil spirits do not go home voluntarily. After they have delivered a person unto death, they don't even visit to receive their accolades: "They are scared of their homes."

Constant irritability or unexplainable restlessness in homes could be a sign of an evil presence or an evil visitor attempting to get in. Another thing that strikes terror into an evil spirit is when you begin to ask for Jesus' permission to send them to "The Pit." I have sent a few to preach to their kind. What do the scriptures say? "Every knee shall bow and every tongue confess." That is the assignment that I give to them: Go and do nothing else but terrify your kind with the proclamation of the Purim Power that "Jeshua is Lord!"

Dybbuk spoke through the bound person's throat. It also caused much discomfort and spiritual distress. I wish that someone would publish a new book on "Tales of Jewish Folklore." Those are not casually composed literary gems. They are concealed treasures about times when solace and hurt were stored in tradition by living libraries of people predestined to endure! There is a saying: "If you can't beat them join them." That is Satan's latest shot, his foundation for "The Antichrist."

CHAPTER 15L. OBEDIENT MESSENGER.

During the years spent compiling the research material for publication, I had frequent and unusual experiences. Like most people, I used to have spiritual attacks in my sleep. Unlearned people even believe that "Their spirits leave them" during those experiences. I was led to believe that they were nightmares. Let's be serious, with my pre-conversion carnal inclinations, which female horse would dare to enter my room at night naked, especially after penetrating my closed solid wooden door unnoticed? The attacks used to occur more often as my research tunneled deeper. The more I uncovered, the more the strange nocturnal visitations increased. The visitations were so predictable that one night I pretended to be asleep. I concealed a gun under my sheet and decided once and for all to solve the mysteries. I drowned all the lights in the building. Whatever could enter my locked door undeterred would have had to prove its bionic ability.

Years before, I opened my eyes during one such encounter and it took me fifty years to understand what I actually saw. Between those years, I convinced myself that I was having bad dreams. However to avoid possibly seeing anything like that again, I always slept on my belly (until 5 years ago). That night as I felt the intruder arrive by my bedside, I tried to retrieve the metal object in the dark. My hands could not move. I tried to shift first to the right side and then to the left side. I could do neither. The thing grabbed me. It had superhuman strength. I was livid. I fumed. The thing laughed an awful disdainful laugh. I swore silently as to what I was going to do. When it finally let me go I grabbed the metal object and squeezed it so hard that it cut through my index finger. When I put on the lights expecting to find a motionless form, all I found were holes in my bedroom door. I took at least half of an hour to cool down, and then I fell on my knees. I asked God to show me the truth. I wanted an explanation as to what was happening. I swore to find and publish the truth and nothing but the truth. In the middle of my prayers, a soft-spoken reassuring voice gave specific instructions, which I will rehash in the next two chapters. I became a messenger of obedience.

MY CALL AND MY MISSION.

I sat quietly in a Benny Hinn crusade as a hard-nosed reporter/skeptic. Why did he single me out of 7000 people and ask me to come to him? I whispered: "Who me; is this guy for real?" When the anointing fell on me, something supernatural happened that evening. I began hearing and seeing unnatural things. I told no one. I visited Eddie Long's church in Atlanta. I visited World Changers also as a hard-nosed reporter/skeptic. I concocted a test in my mind that no one other than our Creator God Almighty could have known. Before Creflo Dollar preached a word, he interrupted the service with "a message for someone" the answer to my prayers. I made a promise to go to Israel. In fact, I was on a specific spiritual mission and was directed to go there. Several missionaries that I met quite accidentally confirmed my mission and each one strengthened my conviction for going. I selected a programme for Israel and arrived two days before the rest of the group. The day I arrived, I went on a tour on which half of the participants were secret agents; so I exited through the Armenian Quarter and went to The Upper Room. **The Light spoke again:**

GO FIND MY LOST SHEEP. I HAVE ALWAYS CONCEALED A REMNANT OF MY PEOPLE. THEY HAVE BEEN IN BONDAGE FOR HUNDREDS OF YEARS; THEY KNOW NEITHER THEIR MIGHTY PAST NOR THE COVENANT OF THEIR FATHERS. THE ENEMY IS A BETTER KEEPER OF RECORDS THAN MY PEOPLE ARE UNFORTUNATELY. EVERY TIME I AM READY TO UNVEIL A NEW THING, MY ANOINTING IS RELEASED THROUGH MUSIC. FIND THE PLACE WHERE I HAVE UNLEASHED NEW MUSIC AND NEW INSTRUMENTS WITHIN THIS CURRENT JUBILEE AND YOU WILL FIND MY PEOPLE. SINCE I HAD ALREADY GIVEN THEM MY HOLY WORD, WHERE THEY RESIDE THEY HAVE INVENTED NEW LANGUAGES; YET I

HAVE CAUSED THEIR NEW LANGUAGES NOT TO BE PUBLISHED. WHEN YOU FIND THEM I WILL INCREASE YOUR MEASURE.

The experience was too overwhelming, so I returned a few days later. I confessed that the only place where new forms of music, new instruments and many spoken yet unpublished languages (that I knew) existed were in fact islands formerly controlled by the Gentile nations of France, England, Spain, America and Holland: Genesis 10:4-6. The Light appeared and spoke specific instructions to me—hence the revelations in this book.

CHAPTER 15M. ALIEN VISITORS AND A DAMASCUS ENCOUNTER!

When this project started, I found serious inconsistencies between God's established pattern of doing things and what Christians portrayed as factual. Ten years into the research, lots of us had gotten seriously disillusioned. Here we were from different religious persuasions peering into the foundations of our faiths. Prior to our finding the schematic, we had all clung to our beliefs based on countries of origin, comfort of peers, tradition, blind loyalty, and in many cases simply lack of choices. At first I had planned to flush out the truth with a hostile barrage of insinuations that someone was pulling a big hoax on the world by concealing more than what was revealed. I became a skeptic. A series of supernatural encounters forced me to answer a basic question:"Aren't you after the truth?"A challenge was given me. Walk spotlessly for 365 days and I would be led to the truth! That is figurative speech. I became a hermit; I fasted and searched. I spent meditative time in the deserts of Australia and Israel. At the end of the 365-day abstinence of all my worldly desires, a major breakthrough came.

I have encountered two supernatural personages. One spoke these words: "I came as a *carpenter* to show the people of the world how to *mend* their differences, *cut out* all falsehoods, *build* relationships and *fit together* the broken pieces of every structure that my Father has purposed." I then posed a question to that intruder into my stoic world: "What tool are we to use as a yardstick to measure truth?" The answer came faster than my question: "*My spirit level!*" The depth of the mechanism or term for that tool of carpentry did not hit me then, but now, Wow—in other words—my testimony, my living word! The strange thing about that encounter is that I needed a table and did not have the money; so I thought my mind was playing tricks on me. When He showed me a piece of wood and told me to travel with it, to my surprise there was a 4X4X36 piece of wood right behind me. Someone wanted a favour. The place where I went, I found three other pieces of 4 by 4's. I took them and gave a lift to a man, who needed to discard a piece of glass. Just as I volunteered to throw it away for him, I heard: "There is everything you need to build the table." I followed the instructions and built the most beautiful table.

The other personality was very strange. Where I slept one night I heard an argument outside. When I looked up through the ceiling window, I saw a huge bronzed coloured man with a sword on his right hip. His hand was resting on the sword at his right side. He looked down on me lying on my bed. I was not sleeping. It was not the first time I had seen that colossal being. I had seen that unusually tall man twice before in Jerusalem. I remembered our first, second and third encounters and on each episode his hand caressed the sword on his right hip. On every occasion he made it possible for my eyes of understanding to be opened more. On the street below I saw what I thought were three ladies and a man arguing. I went back to lie down when I realized the conversation was about me."Why should we risk going to (calling my name) this guy? You know how far he is climbing and what he is doing? Let us continue on our mission.

What if he awakens and attacks us as he has done to others before us?" Then a strange thing happened. I saw the head guy storm through my locked gate, through my closed door, through my solid wall towards where I was sleeping supposedly. As he approached, I leaped up in anger and out shouted the words, *"In the name of Jesus."* Just as I said that, he winced like a man who received a massive blow. I then had a sudden realization as to the identity of the personage. As he got up, he spun around to run and screamed *"The day you slip up, I will deal with you person-ally!"* He reached back and his hand brushed my neck as one implying that he would cut my throat. I had no choice; I was more determined than ever. I had to live an almost errorless life. The stakes were bigger than I thought. I had to complete the research and publish the findings. The rest of the conversation and other supernatural encounters will be detailed in sequels. "For this purpose the Son of God manifest: To destroy the works of the Evil one."

CHAPTER 16. OLD AND NEW COVENANTS.

CHAPTER 16A. THE OLD TESTAMENT FOUNDATION.

In Nehemiah 2nd chapter from verse 9, just as the Temple of God is rebuilt, Satan rose up agitation in Sanballat, Tobiah and Geshem to retard and to oppose the project. When Solomon had completed building the magnificent Temple of God, Satan rose up the identical types of spirits plus more. After King Solomon's death, a succession of wicked kings distressed God's people—1st Kings 8:10-18. After the human pillars of Jesus' ministry were martyred, a succession of warring armies invaded Israel for about 1000 years. It took the same time as in the Old Testament for the Leviathan influences to be disrupted (not yet removed) from under the altars of God's church. In 1054 C.E., the Orthodox churches of Africa and Asia (called today the Eastern Orthodox and the Ethiopian Orthodox Churches) expelled the Church of the Roman provinces from their then temporary alliance. Notice after Solomon's death only two kings of Israel did right in the sight of God. The data from that period is not trivial. Esoteric institutions of lesser degrees teach the importance of threes. The decreed stages from darkness to light, from "Bondage" to the "Promised Land," and from the unrevealed to the revealed can be decoded with the Fleece. Hence a day in the life of the Golden Fleece is 1000 years. Some calculate the *First Day* from 33 C.E. to 1054 C.E; others from 98 C.E. to 1099 C.E. Let us work backwards from Jesus' birth to the original covenant with Abraham and vice versa. From Abraham to David is 14 generations (roughly 1000 years); from David to the Babylonian captivity is 14 generations; from the Babylonian captivity add 14 generations and you arrive at a very significant crossroad: first Day of Jeshua—"Day of Redemption."

The Second Day or epoch was the day of the Moon dominated rituals of occult institutions and the international proliferation of them. The second millennium (1054 to 1948) saw the spread of a ritualized form of Judaism. Weak to lukewarm churches were born with little understanding of the word. The emphasis was placed on rituals and ceremonies as opposed to sound teachings. For the most part they lost the power gifts. The entire written word was substituted for a catechism. Inspired scriptures were supplanted by repetitions in a pagan tongue, a dead language called Latin. Deuteronomy 17:19 "Learn to fear the Lord his God, to keep all the words of the law and these statutes, to do them." The duration of the second Day could also be calculated from 1099 to 1948 or 1998. At times 50-year variations in computations appear. The reason is simple. We are using a Roman calendar. The Hebrew calendar is Lunar. *This (third) day* is the day of Justice, Jubilee, Purim, and Restitution. Woe to the stubborn! Every 50 years, the Roman calendar automatically adjusts to the Hebrew calendar. The third day began in 1998. The first spiritual week of years ends 2015.

It is unfair to blame Jesus for the plight of the Jews as many of our research team used to say. It is amazing when the real evidences started surfacing how many wept uncontrollably realizing that so many generations had missed these revelations. Isaiah foresaw the Messiah's sufferings in Isaiah 50:6-7. Also David, while "In the Spirit," on seeing the vision of Christ crucified both in Psalm 22 and also in Psalm 69:21, 22, 23, right through to verses 27, in anger proclaimed a curse on his seed for that deed yet to come.

The spiritually cracked foundation of Rome, on which *The Church* transferred, parallels the period of corrupt kings in Israel's history from the death of Solomon to the death of Jehoshaphat (1st Kings 11:43 to 1st Kings 22:50) B.C.E.1040-580=460 years. During the reign of Constantine, Rome had its first spiritual Jubilee. On the foundations of the churches of the provinces of Rome, what we call the Catholic Church was born. Moses received specific restoration plans as to how "Temples" should be rebuilt. The "stones" or "spiritual rock bases" had to come from the quarry in Jerusalem. Neither compromises, nor substitutions of His entire Laws for reduced versions called "Catechisms," were or are allowed.

The criteria to be "Chosen of God," as Kings and Priests are specified in Deuteronomy 17:14-20 and Deuteronomy 18:10-22. Similarly Jesus' ministry had the following precedents: Adonijah, one of David's sons, conspired with the army chief Joab and Abiathar the High Priest, to usurp *The Kingdom of David*. Emperor Constantine, a Bishop, and a wing of Jesus' church attempted to usurp the authority of the Antioch headquarters in the fourth century. I found no evidence to suggest that Peter had any intention of usurping the authority of Jerusalem in his lifetime. Take a look at his letter written from Babylon approximately 62 C.E. to 64C.E. 1st Peter 2:6, "Behold I lay in Zion a chief corner stone" (not in Rome). Psalm 122:3, "Jerusalem is builded as a city that is compact together whither the *Tribes of the Lord* go up unto the Testimony of Israel to give thanks unto the Name of the Lord." Psalm 132:13, "For the Lord hath chosen Zion; He hath desired it for habitation."

Verse 14, "This is my rest *forever!*" Verse 16, "I will also clothe her priests with salvation." Verse 17, "There I will make the horn of David to bud."

If you were an evil spirit that hated Jesus' guts, where would you antagonize daily and sow the most strife? Where would you stir up conflicting ideologies? What place would be in the news daily? Observe Psalm 118:22, "The stone which the builders refused is become the head stone of the corner." Notice how Satan used the same links. I will show that the development of the church of the *Western Provinces of Rome* mirrored prior events in the Tanakh. Before 7x70 years of the Israelites bondage in Egypt, their restoration came. Before 7x70 years after the Redeemer's time, Rome (that occupied Israel) collapsed. As soon as that serpent gets under the foundation of an altar, it will raise its ugly head from time to time as it is strengthened by blemished blood: 1st Kings 12:28-33. 1st Kings 14:22-26 prophetically warned the Occidental Church that its weak teachings, masturbations, acts of sodomy, lusts and murders will continually attack the altar until either of the following occurs:

1 .   The Serpent is cast out, like Elijah did by destroying its 450 eggs also, or

2 .   It produces "The Antichrist," which is its mission. Make sure that your foundation prophet/stone overcame at least five of Satan's evil spirits.

Rome spirituality mirrored the carnal footsteps of Jeroboam! Jeroboam of the tribe of Ephraim fulfilled prior prophecy by becoming ruler over the 10 northern Tribes. Solomon's "Seed" was ordained to rule Judah "the anointed" plus one other tribe: probably Simeon. Jeroboam's sacrifice was not pure; so the altar was ripped—1st Kings 13:1-5. The altars (set up in Rome) were not pure and were constantly ripped. Jeroboam set up two golden calves: One in *Dan*, the other in *Bethel*. Rome set up two principalities: *Rome of the East* (called Byzantium) and *Rome of the West*. Jeroboam appointed priests that were not in accordance with God's plans. Rome appointed priests "that substituted God's Laws." After 1054 C.E. the "Ten Kingdoms" that Daniel prophesied would grow out of the fractured "Beast" bonded to "The Western Churches" of Rome. Through the cracks in Jeroboam's altar, Omri's son Ahab married Jezebel and Leviathan entered. Rome's main altar exalted a matriarchal spirit in a doctrinal marriage also. Rome, the combined carnage of *The Crusades*, and the results of *Pope Gregory's Inquisition*—those same eggs germinated. However what was left of the Jerusalem church (first seed of Jesus) grew into the Eastern and African Orthodox churches. Pillars of that second stage church were Titus and Ignatius of Antioch.

The Churches of Asia remained under the authority of the Antioch church. They, just like those of the Eastern Orthodox and the African or Ethiopian Orthodox churches, refused to be associated with the diluted teachings of Rome and became the Greek Orthodox churches. The Upper Room, where Jesus and His disciples shared the "Last Supper" is still there in Jerusalem open for all to visit. I received the shock of my life when I visited it the first time. To the spiritually untrained it appears empty. As I entered, I was knocked down, but did not hurt myself on the cobble stone floor. I began staggering all over the place in the awesome presence of the Redeemer. He still churches there until the words of David printed in Psalm 24:9 are fulfilled "The King of Glory shall come in." The Messiah's legacy is therefore a spiritual reproduction of the historical plight of Israel.

16B. THE NEW TESTAMENT CONFIRMATION.
THE "DEUTER" OF DEUTERONOMY.

Titus the Apostle, first Bishop at Antioch succeeded James the chief pillar of the Jerusalem church. Titus' letter of appointment can be verified by reading Paul's letter to Titus in the New Testament. In Titus 1:5, we get a glimpse of how much authority Titus had: a) to set things in order in Crete b) to ordain elders in *every city* and c) to assign missions in Corinth. After the demonic assaults on Jerusalem began in 70 C.E., the Roman army under Titus (the son of Emperor Vespasian) carried away the sacred temple treasures, repeating the sacrileges that preceded Shishak's invasion of Jerusalem (1st Kings 14:26) and also those of the Babylonian Captivity of Judah.

Today in Rome, a marble fragment of the "Arch of Titus" depicts the Roman sacrilege over Jerusalem with a goddess in a chariot drawn by their *"Four Horsemen of the Apocalypse."* It is one of Rome's most revered relics—save the Coliseum. By the middle of the first century, the Church of Jerusalem had main branches in Carthage, Greece, Ethiopia, Alexandria, and Asia Minor. Jewish Christians, mostly elders that escaped the sacking and burning of Jerusalem circa 70 C.E. took refuge in Antioch. Titus became Bishop of "All Christian Churches," after the church headquarters moved to Antioch, Corinth. Titus was Bishop in Antioch from 67 C.E., until his death. By the 4th century, even though mass conversions took place in Rome, the Antioch and African branches rebuffed all offers to meet in Rome to mend differences. The envisioned alliance was not to be. The churches in Asia Minor, Greece and Northern Africa remained separate and became what we call today, the Greek, African, Russian and Ethiopian Orthodox churches. Initially there appears to have been a positive reaction to the concept of amalgamation. However after the repeat of atrocities under Peter the Hermit, (the 1st Crusade) all hopes of a merger were permanently dashed. Back in 61 C.E. the Apostle Paul "Churched" with converted Jews, mainly traders, who used to attend the annual pilgrimages from Rome to Jerusalem to observe her sacred feasts. From the inception of the word "Christian" in Antioch, to the end of the second century, the word "Christian," in Rome was synonymous with death or lions' food.

ATTACK ON THE STONES.

God's *Law of Double Reference* ensured that the carnal substitutions that Rebekah made would have a spiritual impact on the behaviour of the equivalent "Rebekah Church." 1st Corinthians 10:4 specifies that the special rock on which God built His church is Jesus. The Roman church disagrees. The Word of God is specific: a) There is "One" intercessor between God and man, "The Man" Christ Jesus. b) It is appointed for a man once to die and after that the judgment. Purgatory is an invention of a penetrated altar. Melchizedek, to whom *Father Abraham* paid tithes, laid the foundation for the Everlasting Priesthood. The foundation of Solomon's Temple was perfect, however the rest crumbled. Any ministry claiming infallibility is spiritually incongruent with the schematic of the *Temple of Solomon*. At the dedication of Solomon's Temple, his 1st prayer of thanksgiving was that: "Even the foreigner from distant lands may know you as Israel do." A 14-day feast followed.

Is there really a Trinity as such? Refer to Mystery of Mysteries for fresh revelations on the issue. Please join the debate. There is one God with His "Infallible Logion" or "Logos." Since we are to be reconciled to our God, a transformer is necessary. God allowed His "Logos" to become flesh to "step-up" humankind to Him. John Wayne played roles of soldier, cowboy and frontiersman. Does that make John Wayne three separate persons? The Logos appeared in "A Rock, A Branch, Water, Foundation Stone, Fire, Wind, Spirit, and Sanctified Human." Does it take a rocket scientist to figure out that God wants to reconstruct our temples spiritually? One person, Jeshua, fulfilled everything necessary for temple rebuilding purposes. Isn't a person a carnal being made with limitations? Is "Three Divine Persons" really accurate? God is "The Complete All," including the unrevealed, the complete spirit realm and the revealed.

For the first 100 years in Rome, there is no record of anyone seeing or hearing of a "Pope." In fact no such person or office existed. As the early congregation grew, Christians were called saints. All converts required baptism. The Church Elders, usually versed in Hebrew Laws were consecrated as Bishops. Jesus did not come to replace any of God's laws. On the contrary, He came to confirm them. Baptism always has been a symbolic gesture for washing away sins. For persons to receive God's redemptive package they must "repent first." For that reason, baptism is the symbolic act of them being washed or "forgiven." I have attended "Christenings." I have yet to hear a baby speak—much more to repent of sins. Baptizing a baby does not break unrepented ancestral curses. If a person desires someone to "stand in the gap" and request the breaking of generational curses on a minor, especially one born out of wedlock, there is one way only. That person has to act as surrogate before the Lord and repent of all of his/her individual sins, current and past, then those of parents and grandparents of the child on both sides regressing four generations. The procedure is not to be tampered with; it is called "Intercession." Jesus did something similar to that on behalf of the entire human race two thousand years ago. The exception being that Jeshua bore all of our sins so that when we repent we can receive the atonement that He made for all of us. A person, who assumes that he/she can break God's laws without any consequence, implies arrogance and superiority to God! The Foundation is "The Hebrew Law." The Repairer was sent to "repair the breach," not to replace or to substitute it (Isaiah 53).

All those who teach that God hath cast out His people need to read Romans 11:1. "Hath God cast away His people?" God gave the answer to David in Psalm 147:19, and to Paul in

Romans 11:1-5. Verse 5, "Even so at this present time also there is a remnant according to the election of grace..." All those who replace or substitute God's laws are in breach and have *come short* of God's Glory. Isaiah 40:1-14—there was only one being with direct Divine blood. He was not created but begotten. Micah 5:2: He came from the future and is described as "Everlasting." All other created beings are fallible; that is why we sin. God gave us a gift: choice. A myth of infallibility presumes that God would take back His gift. God's word says that all have sinned (not some) and fallen short of His Glory. God never contradicts His Word; neither can any animal, place or thing do so without consequence.

Simon was a good apostle/preacher, but a weak administrator. His "stony" temperament and penchant for speaking first and thinking afterwards caused him to be knocked down by Satan's soft-punching spirits called "Compromise, Fear and foot-loose Antichrist." Churches that exalt "Simon" as their foundation stone automatically inherit those same spirits. From the date of Paul's second imprisonment, through to the infamous "Fire of Rome" until the "Decree to expel all Jews," Peter the formerly fickle disciple never set foot in Rome save his pre-requested preference "to drink of the same cup of Jesus." The offices of "Popes" were instituted in the eleventh century, as a matter of fact, long after Simon's death. The Book of Acts states that the authority given to Jesus' disciples was threefold: 1. To Preach. 2. To heal the sick. 3. To cast out devils; not to forgive sins after death: in fact, just the opposite. "Confess your sins one to another." In other words, go to the person you have wronged, repent, seek forgiveness and make recompense. A person has to be alive to confess. If any priest has the power to promote anyone after death, then conduct all-night prayer vigils and empty all of hell. If God were to permit such folly, He would have to apologize to all those from Sodom and Gomorrah. Persons that did not confess before they died missed the boat period. Read the account of Lazarus and the rich man. Hell has an *"unbridgeable gulf!"*

Originally I had planned to leave "The First 100 Years of Errant Church History" for another book. However some documentation is necessary about foundational matters; otherwise people will imply that I am slinging mud. I will document the following:

1. The First 100 unbroken years of the early church of which James (brother of Jesus) was the first Bishop and Titus became his successor.

2. The First 100 years of churches around Antioch, Crete and Samaria.

3. The First 100 years of churches around Northern Africa.

4. The First 100 years of anti-Christian and anti-Semitic sentiments in Rome.

5. The First 100 years of "Absence of Church Buildings" in Rome.

6. The First 2 Years of "Churching" or "House Gatherings" in Rome.

7. The Leviathan Fury against the Early Church.

8. The Nest of "The Beast" or "Antichrist Spirit."

9. The First 100 years of non-existent Popes.

10. First 100 years of the "Church in Asia."

11. The First 100 years of documental errors in and around Rome.

I found a very important letter attributed to Barnabas. It is a very powerful document that shows the great divide between the attitudes of some of the brethren that originated around Rome and the Jews that maintained ancestral ties to the Hebrew patriarchs. The translation from Lightfoot is in English and might not be available and accessible until this book is released. Every now and then the prevailing condescending attitude surfaced. The fact that he thought it significant to compare the "complexion" of Jesus to that of the special ceremonial "red heifer," I attribute to the noticeable differences between the complexion of the Romans and those of the Jews. I hope and pray to God that the document remains intact. I will not support the opinions of a few commentators who believed Barnabas' letter implied any racism and as such it should have been omitted from any of the Bible Canons. All those cynics had to do were to visit the libraries and museums to confirm the abundance of melanin in the early church Elders: Barnabas, Ignatius and Saul of Tarsus. The people that were connected to the earliest churches were not identified by colour, but by countries of origin. In his discourse, Barnabas also pointed to the scapegoat as relating to Jesus, bearing the sins of the people. Roman painters could not justify portraying Jesus—first as Indian, then as Roman Gentile—if those data were part of the Bible. As a general rule, the different mixes of people were found primarily around Greece and Antioch (main cities) as opposed to Jerusalem, a Jewish conclave where the inhabitants resembled the people of India and Ethiopia today. May I remind you that Paul was mistaken for an Egyptian? My entire staff, my researchers and I have concluded that there existed a large measure of arrogance in the 2nd millennium Rome-controlled churches.

CHAPTER 16C. REFORMERS CHOSEN FOR A DOUBLE-PORTION!

Before I recap the first 100 years of the early Christian church, I must outline God's complete reformation package from previous blueprints. Here are important points to absorb. When followers of Jesus received "baptism for forgiveness of their sins," through the "Promised Seed," once redeemed, they were called "Saints." Jerusalem's synagogue and temple were still functioning at the beginning of the 1st century. Afterwards, Jesus' disciples used to "Church," that is, gather at various houses to fellowship, to encourage one another, and to teach one another how to understand the scriptures. They also assisted those in need financially. They continued to attend the synagogues to expound on the Law until they were banned. Since John the Harbinger was sent, the emphasis was placed on "baptism for the forgiveness of sins." As with every move of "Reformation," there are those that move forward and those that are left behind spiritually. As far back as the season of Israel's Judges, every one of God's seasons of reformation found the same conditions:

1 . The custodians of God's altars were battered and weakened.

2 . The restorative emphasis was on the priesthood. Isaiah 22:16-17 illustrates the origin of the terms, "The Curse of Shebna." "It is not by might or by power, but by My Spirit," saith the Lord.

3 . Unlike when men choose, when God selects, He selects people based on the "Attitude of their hearts," devotion, humility, obedience and how they run their homes.

4 . Those "Chosen" today are required both to "Lead the people," and to "Offer Sacrifices." In other words, they must perform the functions of kings and priests.

5 . Every reformer (when he is called) has to defeat enemies of Israel. In the Torah, the enemies were physical. Today they are spiritual: Ephesians 6:12.

6 . God is progressive. Every Reformer must have had a predecessor and must bring new messages for improving the spiritual walk of the flock.

7 . Reformers must be either natural or spiritual descendants of Abraham, through Isaac.

8 . Each reformer has to manifest that God prepared, empowered, and moulded him/her.

9 . Each reformer is progressive.

10 . Each person called must fulfill his/her Prophetic Mission.

First, I will list the foundational stones and then former reformers that God called to reconstruct the habitual directional shifts towards error:

1) Patriarchal foundations: Melchizedek, Noah, and Abraham.

2) Reformers: Joshua (son of Nun), Nehemiah, Jehoiada, David and Jeshua.

To perform the functions of both earthly leader and that of priest is no easy feat. Up to the end of the lineage of Jesse, any person attempting to offer unauthorized sacrifice before God or even touching the altar with unsanctified hands would be killed. Aaron's two sons (Abihu and Nadab) and also Uzziah, all three were killed for such sacrilege. Today our punishments are held in abeyance, giving us time to repent of our errors—that is through God's allowable mercy by Jeshua's sacrifice. We are allowed "Suspended Sentences."

ALL PRIESTS/PASTORS WHO ARE STANDING ON GOD'S ALTARS AFTER DOING ABOMINABLE THINGS, MEDITATE ON THAT SPECIAL PLACE OF TORMENT.

Psalm 55:15, Isaiah 5:14 and Isaiah 14:12, give a glimpse of the special place set aside for presumptuous priests and pastors. The oven in the Book of Daniel gives a nice clue. We were given examples of earthly leaders who got carried away by ambition and pride and took it upon themselves to offer illegal or tainted sacrifices before the Lord. In 2nd Chronicles 26:16, we see Uzziah overstepping his bounds and going beyond his anointing. I will touch on that when I detail the behavioral patterns of spirits. In 1st Kings 13:1-5 we see Jeroboam being prophesied against by a prophet for making unauthorized sacrifice to God. In 1st Samuel 13:8-14 we see Saul, Israel's first king overstepping his anointing and entering the temple to offer sacrifice. We know that was the beginning of the end for him. When God stopped communicating with him, he did the worse possible thing. He visited the "Altar of Satan" to consult the "Witch of Endor." All Psychic seekers need to read God's warning about such in Leviticus 19:31 and Isaiah 8:18-19.

Noah crossed over with "Eight Chosen." Abraham crossed over with a Firstfruit sacrifice, paid tithes to Melchizedek and sowed seeds of being born again by "circumcising his entire household." Moses crossed over with higher miracles, overcoming satanic forces. Joshua attained higher levels for bigger devils. He was reclothed, given new skins for the "New Wine." David and Nehemiah: One received the plans for the temple. The other acquired the instructions to rebuild. Jesus' restorative ministry started with eight missionaries like Noah, (12 disciples in all). The eight chosen missionaries were Paul, Simon, Matthew, Luke, John, Mark,

James, and Jude. Moses with 12 chieftains left from Mt. Sinai *150 miles north* to Kadesh-Barnea in the regions of *Tyre and Sidon*. Like Noah, "Eight chosen" churches began Jesus' ministry. The first fruits of Jesus' ministry led disciples *150 miles north* to the same regions of Tyre and Sidon where seven branch churches were, plus the base in Jerusalem. *Eight* were chosen: Philadelphia, Sardis, Ephesus, Pergamum, Laodicea, Thyatira, Smyrna and Jerusalem. The spiritual river took the identical path to that of Moses in the wilderness. Are these very unusual coincidences or is God extremely meticulous?

Churches from the Roman territories were destroyed, burnt, and Christians were martyred. In Zechariah 3:1, we find an interesting scene in which Joshua as High Priest is presented to the Lord for higher anointing after being "Chosen by God." It is interesting to note that at that higher step, Satan is presenting "Iniquities before God." In preceding chapters I showed that Satan keeps your files, those chronic sin files of your parents and the unrepented ones of your grandparents handed down to the third and fourth generations: Exodus 34:6-7. When God sanctifies you, you must be reclothed and reborn spiritually: Zechariah 3:1. The symbolism of discarding your old robes is akin to cutting off the foreskin for circumcision—the foundation seed of being born-again spiritually. It is a promise to shed all past sins.

NO ONE PUTS NEW WINE IN OLD SKINS!

Follow this important fact. When Jesus was on the cross, soldiers cast lots for His garments: Psalm 22:18. In Psalm 69:2, it was prophesied thusly: "They gave me gall for my meat and in thirst they gave me vinegar to drink." As David foretasted Jesus' death, God showed him that He would place a curse of "spiritual blindness" on His people in Psalm 69:22d-23:

LET THEIR TABLE BECOME A SNARE BEFORE THEM AND LET WHAT SHOULD HAVE BEEN FOR THEIR WELFARE LET IT BECOME A TRAP. LET THEIR EYES BE DARKENED THAT THEY SEE NOT.

Joshua the son of Nun received a prophetic name. In Hebrew we get a clearer picture of the Firstfruit of the anointed name. It is *Jehoshua or Jeshua*, as the Born-again Jews of today call Him. The meaning is *JESHUA IS SALVATION*. The early Greek texts transpose it and call Him *Iesous*, from which we derive *Jesus*, in English. The meaning is the same "God is Salvation," or God's complete redemption package is here. No wonder evil spirits and demons flee when they hear that name. When we utter the name of Jeshua "respectfully," We are actually saying: "The living God that manifests His love, grace, mercy and power to us is salvation!" The proclamation is praise to God. It is a very high praise acceptable to the Lord, as ordained in "The Book of Praises," Psalm 2. It is important to observe the power of the name "Jesus" overcoming satanic walls of resistance and to compare the obstacles Satan presented to the *Firstfruit* of the name Joshua. Compare also the obstacles that the Israelites encountered in the wildernesses of Moab and Sinai. As one does comparative analyses it is obvious that Jeshua overcame every spirit that had defeated the Israelites previously.

King David, while he was king, offered sacrifices of a priest and Jehoiada as a priest offered both: sacrifices and offered inspired leadership prior to his death. I included both as foundational examples to show that Jesus was walking in God-ordained plans for full reformation of His people. He functioned as king and priest and by so doing, confirmed God's law of double-reference concerning the Melchizedek priesthood of Psalm110. It is important to detail those things so that we can ascertain that God carefully laid out the foundation that Jesus was spiritually connected to. No one can stop God's ordained plans. God might allow delays and interruptions, the same way He allowed "His Light" to be interrupted in the beginning. Despite Satan's numerous attempts to prevent the "Seed of Promise" from being manifest, God's purposes always manifest in His specified times. Time and tide might not wait for man, but they are totally obedient to God. Having failed in his many attempts to have the seed stifled, Satan's emphasis shifted to confusion, distortion, and finally imitation and deceit in the form of The Antichrist. Here is a question for Satan. Why is Jeshua the only spiritual leader that you want to imitate? *Imitation is still the greatest form of adoration.* Since you wouldn't learn, I want you to memorize Isaiah 14:12.

CHAPTER 16D. THE MISSION AND FALL OF THE FIRST FELLER!

HOW THOU ART FALLEN FROM HEAVEN, LUCIFER, SON OF THE MORNING! HOW ART THOU CUT DOWN TO THE GROUND, WHICH DIDST WEAKEN THE NATIONS! FOR THOU HAST SAID IN THY HEART, I WILL ASCEND INTO HEAVEN. I WILL EXALT MY THRONE ABOVE THE STARS OF GOD. I WILL SIT ALSO UPON THE MOUNT OF THE CONGREGATION, IN THE SIDES OF THE NORTH. I WILL ASCEND ABOVE THE HEIGHTS OF THE CLOUDS; I WILL BE LIKE THE MOST HIGH. YET THOU SHALT BE BROUGHT DOWN TO HELL TO THE SIDES OF THE PIT— ISAIAH 14:12.

Here we see God reading Satan's mind, giving us a peek at his plans, and prophetically telling us about his outcome. It is important to look at that scripture from time to time to understand the plans of our enemy. The last pieces of information I want to submit with reference to the foundation on which Jesus stood, are errors of Jehoiada and David. I want to show the type of spirits that Satan unleashed against God's people in their victories and in their major defeats. In the case of David, the entire Old Testament is an attempt by Satan to eliminate not only the promised seed, but also the bloodline through which the seed would eventually come. Satan introduced seed polluting demons. He introduced Jezebel spirits and after Jezebel succeeded, he introduced murder. We covered those in earlier chapters.

What we will cover in this part is the 400 years that "The Ark" or presence of God was not in Israel. That is important to show how accurately Satan keeps files and his awareness of God's precision when it comes to time. We either already documented or will document in later chapters that the house of God could not be built in Rome for the first 100 years of Christianity. God is consistent. The church had to start in Israel first. Initially, profane hands could not touch the holy church. Those chosen had to desecrate both "Holy Altars" first before profane hands could access and interrupt the flow temporarily. During the interruption, the church would rest on the foundation of an enemy of Israel.

Gath, where Obed-Edom lived, where the Ark of God rested after being defiled, first was a Philistine city. The Ark was placed before Dagon. Let us find messianic references. Rome, where Jesus' church would rest after defilement and interruption was a former pagan city. The Messiah's church of necessity must move unto a tarnished enclave. The journey of the Ark did not begin in Gath; neither could the foundation of the church be in Rome. When the Ark was in Obed-Edom's house, he prospered. When Jesus' church rested in Rome, the nation prospered. In 2nd Samuel 6:12 is the precedent for the Gentiles being blessed. The Ark rested in the house of Obed-Edom (1st Chronicles 13:14) and the Lord blessed his house.

DAVID RETURNING FOR AND WITH THE ARK IS A PROPHETIC GLIMPSE OF JEWS BOTH THE NORTHERN TRIBES AND THE SOUTHERN TRIBES COMING INTO THE FULLNESS OF GOD`S PLAN AS PER PROPHECY, CALLED ALIYAH!

Since David succeeded on his second attempt, The Messiah must return to complete His "Finished Work" the Second Time. In 2nd Samuel 6:14—David wore a priestly garment. He also wore a linen ephod; he increased his sacrifices before God and God accepted his priestly functions. A new order of worship was introduced.

All folks left behind during the last reformation that turn up their noses against the "New Charismatic Order" of Worship need to ask God for forgiveness from the "Curse of Michal." Saul's daughter (David's wife) did just that when she observed David's exuberance. David laid the foundation for the dancing exuberantly before God when he retrieved His coveted presence. Nonetheless it is not possible to praise God on an ecstatic level unless you have His presence. Psalm 16:11 "In thy presence there is fullness of joy."

There are times when I am in homes interceding and weeping for sick persons. After they humbled themselves before God and repented, a miraculous transformation would take place. Within a twinkling of an eye everyone would begin to laugh. I have been in churches where the presence of God descends on the congregation and the same thing happens. Now do not get me wrong, it does not mean that every church that worships ecstatically is filled with the "Spirit of God." The fruits usually follow. The redeemed will cancel old habits. The merciful will be healed and delivered. Then their churches' membership will grow in leaps and bounds. As the presence of God returns to the earthly houses, evidence of His blessings will begin to manifest. Let us look closely at the opening sentence in 2nd Samuel 6:14, "David danced before the Lord with all his might." In verse 19, David sowed the first seed of Jesus breaking bread and feeding the multitude.

A "Matriarchal Spirit" seeks out bases of power in a country. She then hatches plots of murder to strengthen herself with one aim in view: to usurp the highest spiritual altar of that nation. We will examine the behaviour of that spirit that resided in the person of Jezebel. After hatching, her eggs become "trans-generational." 2nd Chronicles chapters 21 to 24 give a backdrop to the behaviour of a Jezebel spirit and its persistent nature: Jehoram, the son of Jehoshaphat married the daughter of Ahab and Jezebel. Observe 40 years of terror and dread that followed. He got wiped out but his wife survived. In 2nd Chronicles 22:12, he was so blinded spiritually that he ignored the warning of Prophet Elijah. The priest Jehoiada had to hide Joash, the seed of promise.

While Paul visited Ephesus on a missionary journey, sacrilegious worship was rampant. Ephesians paid homage to Diana, a deep-rooted "Demoness." Egypt had an Isis; there was an ancient one revered as Athagartis. Greece had "Ceres or Demeter." There was a "Queen Moo" and a host of others. It matters not what name is given to the female entity. Once a foundational altar is laid and a female icon is exalted, then spiritual blindness follows. Once saints are martyred there, Leviathan's altar is strengthened.

In most of early Europe we found a foundational goddess culture. God gave the everlasting uprooting remedy to Jehoiada. He arranged the "First Major Convocation." He organized the entire priesthood to rout out the Leviathan eggs. Jehoiada lived 130 years and was buried among the Kings. Notice how his kingly seed was protected, as precedent was laid to protect the Promised Seed. Anyone claiming to be the Messiah must meet all those preconditions. We then saw Mary and Joseph duplicating the protective roles by taking the child Jesus to Egypt to escape Herod's decree to wipe out "All children 2 years and under." There were three epochs or "Days" of darkness in Egypt before deliverance of the Seed of Promise. At Jesus' death there were *three days* of darkness before "The Promised Seed" came forth.

I could write five books explaining everything that Jesus did in his ministry as fulfillment of either a former prophecy, or the manifestation of the overcoming ability of one who received the gifts: "Priestly and Kingly Anointing." Satan can only make a move to overthrow a church, a nation, or a people when he has majority control of the altar shares. I have shown previously that he stays focused on his game plan. The first 100 years after a reformation is the most intense period of attacks. It means that as new seeds are sown, Satan unleashes more intense and experienced fighting spirits.

Deliverance is the next step after a prolonged state of subjugation or season of darkness. Egypt, Babylon, Medo-Persia and Rome come to mind as we reflect on previous foundations of bondage, occupation and persecution. All four foundations had eggs with the "Mission of Jezebel" stamped thereon. Check the subliminally packed export boxes: "Deviled eggs grade X." If Moses did not get up to a new level we would still be in bondage in Egypt.

The names for the wildernesses after Egypt appear to have been prophetic: Shur and Sin. Unfortunately, many people are extremely entangled and spiritually blinded in wildernesses by similar names. Satan promised out of his own mouth in June 1998: "I will pursue young people with unprecedented fury. The Internet is my toy. My energies are focused on those plus *the churches that I already own.*" 300 other witnesses and I heard those words.

After 430 years of silence in Egypt, God sent a deliverer. Observe God's 430 years of silence in Israel as per prophecy in Amos 8:11-12. Prior to John the Harbinger proclaiming the Good News that the Kingdom of Heaven was imminent, God last spoke to Israel through the prophet Malachi. In Malachi 3:1-5 God told Malachi to inform the people that he would send *His messenger* to His temple to *purge the Levites* and their offerings. Wow, that was an awesome promise given to the prophet. Then there was silence for about 430 years.

Let us look at the first 100 years of reformation from the transformation of the verb "to church" into the noun "church" and from the Priest-King Jesus, through to the church's first Elder, James the brother of Jesus. We will highlight James' handling of the first recorded inter-apostolic bickering and how he resolved it. Observe how *Simon and Paul* submitted to the chief Elder.

This chapter is being meticulously documented because careful scrutiny must be given to the second largest and also to the second most-pursued altar in the universe. Let me eliminate all those questions that I am picking up in the spirit as to which is the first. Refer to Psalm 24:1, "The Earth is the Lord's and the fullness thereof!" God foresaw Satan's intentions and gave us a peek in Isaiah 14:11-21. Verse 17 previewed the destruction that he hath leveled on the world through hate and war. So his first target is the earth and the "Fullness of the Earth." Drought is a curse. Sickness is a curse. Poverty is a curse. Entrenched misdirection is a curse. Spiritual blindness is a curse. Spiritual deafness is a curse. Let me quickly confirm those things from the scriptures before I get into the meat of this chapter. Then at the end I will insert one more concerning the behavioral patterns (the ping pong syndrome) of the most peripatetic of spirits.

Everyone that attends a church should make notes of the following. These are and were specific requirements for the priestly office. Moses recorded them as everlasting parables. That form of parable is transmissible from generation to generation. Since the enemy tries constantly to infiltrate weak believers, beware of God's warning that many are called, "Few are chosen."

That means that you have to be connected to God's purpose in manner and manifestation of His gifts: healings, miracles, teachings and versed in God's word. Leviticus 21:10-23: Levites came from the tribe of Levi, an inherited office. The translations of Leviticus 21:10-23 are as follows:

a)   You must know God's word and be in tune with His Kingdom's purposes.

b)   You must have spiritual covering and be in *His Covenant*.

c)   You must not be spiritually blind. d) You must not have a critical spirit.

e)   God's enemies cannot dwarf you. f) You must grow in God's wisdom/knowledge.

g)   You must neither be overambitious (extended limbs) nor lack good judgment (blemish in the eyes) nor have any shortcomings. Signs and wonders must follow.

In this dispensation you must be able to be both King and Priest.

CHAPTER 16E. THE MESSIAH'S CHURCH FIRST 100 YEARS.

In Psalm 132:13-14 and Psalm 122, God specified that Zion in Jerusalem would be His Holy habitation forever. Any church whose spiritual foundation is not in Zion is foreign to God's purpose. I am very sorry, I will not spend time and space to list them all. Satan has already bragged. I heard him myself. He is confident that he has not only churches but church administrations so choked that he calls them His. Thank God for *God' Redeemer* and *Everlasting Oracle*. God's chief cornerstone *is laid in Zion*. That was established and confirmed in the first century. There was no uprooting of the original cornerstone. All religious institutions planted in the 3rd 6th and 7th centuries and beyond, please study God's laws of double-reference and His consistency before more sacrileges are committed.

To fulfill the joint offices of King and Priest when Kings originated from Judah and Priests came from Levi would take divine intervention. To offer holy sacrifice, one had to be called and ordained by God. Jesus had to fulfill God's foundational precedents: "Star out of Jacob" and "Sceptre of Israel from Numbers 24:17. In Genesis 14:18 we see mention of something held sacrosanct by every ancient wise person: being called to the mystical office of King and Priest. God's redeeming Son would occupy that office, from which Melchizedek was the forerunner. Melchizedek offered the patriarch Abraham *bread and wine*. The dual-purpose foundation of *King of Peace* and *Priest of the Most High God (forever)* was established.

The First 100 years of Jesus' ministry that began with John brings us to 100 C.E. Jesus was not sent to start anything new. He was sent to "Repair" all that was breached as per Isaiah 53. Jesus did not introduce His restorative ministry, John announced the time of pending *Reformation*. That is why John is called John the Harbinger in Hebrew. Jesus ushered in *New Levels* of anointing *to conquer all devils* that previously defeated Israel. Jesus was throwing devils over cliffs, out of bodies and out of temples. When Satan introduced temple dwelling demons within people that had access to the Temples, Jesus threw them out.

WHEN PEOPLE ENTER GOD'S HOUSE WITH THEIR PET DEMONS DEEP WITHIN THEM, IT IS ONLY THE POWERFUL JESUS PRESENCE THAT CASTS THEM OUT.

The evil one that was in their midst (Judas) was unmasked and kicked out. When Jesus' presence is powerful in a house of God, demons become agitated. I bear witness. Put my testimonies to the test. Empty sin and false philosophies from God's house and introduce the same reformation package that Jesus brought and watch what happens.

When we add Jesus' 33 ministry years to John's 7 ministry years, the first 40 years was spent outfoxing Satan, confusing Satan, kicking Satan's butt every which way. Purim was confirmed. Read the book of Esther about Haman the agitator. Let us begin around 33 C.E. with the disciples churching in the Upper Room. They were in one accord. They had been set apart and sanctified. Let us recap some dates. Peter was in Jerusalem 33 C.E. in the Upper Room. Shortly after Peter's arrest and miraculous release he went to church in John (Mark) Marcus' house. Dorcas the maid was so astonished to see him that she ran and left him outside. Mark's mother and the church brethren told Peter to *report to James*—Acts 12:12-17. That James, brother of Jesus, was overseer of the Church in Jerusalem. Paul got converted and traveled to Corinth and Antioch 50 C.E. to 52 C.E. Paul then went to Macedonia, Colossae, Crete, and finally to Rome in chains 60 C.E. to 61 C.E Luke traveled with Paul on his third missionary journey: Acts 28:14. In Acts 28:30-31, for two years Paul churched in his own house 61 C.E. to 62 C.E. Peter left Jerusalem sometime between 61 C.E. and 62 C.E. for Babylon. Paul encountered Peter and rebuked him publicly at Corinth for his compromising attitude and double standards. James was in Jerusalem in 64 C.E. presiding over the first assembly when he summoned Paul and Peter to appear to resolve their conflicts concerning circumcision. Peter then left Jerusalem for Babylonia and Asia Minor. Shortly thereafter, serious anti-Christian sentiment spilled over from Rome into all its provinces. In 98 C.E. John wrote to the seven branch churches from the isle of Patmos. The seven that he addressed were: Ephesus, Smyrna, Pergamum, Thyatira, Sardis, Philadelphia and Laodicea. He then sent his report to the Elder James since Jerusalem was and always is the foundational headquarters of the God's church. The veil is now shredded and destroyed. Outer court and inner court is now merged into one office of "King and Priest—Psalm 110." Jeremiah 23:5, "Behold the days come, that I will raise unto David a righteous 'Branch' and a King shall reign and prosper, and shall execute judgment and justice in the earth." Verse 6, "In his days, Judah shall be saved, and Israel shall dwell safely: and this is his name whereby he shall be called 'The Lord Our Righteous.'"

CHAPTER 16F. SATAN, STILL LOOKING FOR BASES TO COVER.

Satan does not know the future. What he knows is that God does not fib. Whenever God says something, it comes to pass. Satan marks every base and tries as hard as possible to obstruct, to subvert, to frustrate, and to demolish whatever he can. As a result of his repeated questioning of what God hath said, millions have rejected the modern versions of Christianity. Custodians have presented "tarnished altars" and altered versions as unscathed and infallible, when in fact some of their teachings were *blood-soaked and profane.*

The only way to straighten out matters is to print this schematic. Let those (in breach) see their errors. Of course Satan is going to disquiet those persons with pet demons embedded deep within. God already showed me their "fumes" in visions. There are those people that love their religion more than they love God. God cannot speak to such. Spiritual blindness is a condition that harbours *vanity and pride*: both of them are in Satan's army.

There are times while fasting that I enter spiritual houses. On one such occasion an evil spirit was actually taunting me because of the "lofty place" where it was going to sit. There have been times when the Spirit of God directed me to leave houses, supposedly of God. There were other times when God commanded me to stay and to make contrary spirits uncomfortable. However nothing matches the feeling that you receive when the Spirit of God welcomes you. That occurred when I visited the following sites: Mt. Carmel where Elijah defeated the prophets of Baal, the ruins of the house where Simon Bar Jona used to church, the Upper Room, and churches that are pregnant with the presence and power of the Living God.

A European based organization has consistently implied that Jesus gave Simon permission to build a church, even though Simon the Apostle wrote in 1ˢᵗ Peter 2:6 that God placed His foundation in Zion. However their records even go as far as listing Simon the Apostle as the founder of their church. We have found the names of two people listed as successors to Simon to be erroneous. That is important to note, since up to the time of Simon's crucifixion he was attached to the base in Jerusalem over which James presided until his death. Also before Simon's arrest and crucifixion, he was neither in Rome nor was he ever a Bishop or a Pope. The house where Paul used to church in Rome had to be abandoned as well prior to Simon's death. Those believers that did not escape to Antioch and Ephesus like Priscilla and Aquila (Acts 18:26) were crucified or thrown to the lions. If they were Roman citizens, they were given a chance to renounce their faith publicly or be put to death. For at least 100 years after the death of Simon "Peter," there was neither church nor a Bishop or a Pope in Rome.

If a house of worship begins outside of Jerusalem, compare the teachings. If it compliments the Torah and its teachings in a progressive manner, check the reformation chart. If the organization begins outside of Jerusalem and it has a cornerstone that contradicts the Torah, find the section in this book that reproduces the Temple of Solomon and pick your category. Any cornerstone that contradicts the word of God is prone to harbour spirits that will eventually encourage Leviathan, Jezebel and or Antichrist to proliferate under its altars. In Romans 1:16, it is written that *The Gospel* came to the Jew first. The Torah reported that "He came unto His own and His own received Him not." Romans 3:2, "To them were committed the Oracles of God." God painfully established those words for good reasons. God looked into the corridors of time and saw those errors; so He carefully planted a second hand and a minute hand in His giant clock. Satan used nations to attempt to eliminate David's seed witnesses, but God kept a remnant to prove His word is His bond. Apply God's word. Check it to the last iota and the impossible becomes possible. With God, all things are possible. God called a people to be witnesses to His word and purpose. They cannot be replaced, displaced or substituted. Maschil of Ethan the Ezrahite scribe, writing in Psalm 89:4, "I have made a covenant with my chosen, I have sworn to David, my servant, Thy seed will I establish forever and build upon thy throne to all generations."

Having failed in his many attempts at eliminating David's seed, Satan's current plans include: intolerance, hatred, suspicion, selfishness, conceit and "xenophobia." Satan is trying a new twist. Already he has people in Israel redefining who is, or who is not a Jew. There is already the school of "It is I and not you who is a Jew." Today they use lineage from the mother and not from the father as in ancient times. *Hollywood and all the broadcast media have helped Satan tremendously. They forgot Pope Fernan Martin's decree:*

GO BACK TO AFRICA WHERE YOU ALL CAME FROM!

Shofar to the Diaspora! God stated that He would call a people that were not His people—Isaiah 11:10. They were the children of the former separated and neglected nations. The Jews (northern and southern tribes) used to be clannish. Over 80 percent of their marriages were within their tribes. When Satan got a chance to mingle their seed, God wiped them out. There is the school of thought that swallow the astute deception that if a Jew has money, his or her ancestry is outside of their Hamitic/Japhethic/Semitic lineage and consequently they are Caucasoid. That alone exposes the hoax. Children of the financially comfortable do not mind if they are perceived thusly and as such rush to marry "Other Types," completely ignorant of what promises are due in this season—Isaiah 11:11-16. People in the U.S.A. Diaspora wake-up! This social displacement philosophy of Satan is causing the spiritually blind to end up with seriously high divorce rates.

I will insert a prophetic quote from Jeremiah 23:1, "Woe unto the teachers/pastors that destroy and scatter the sheep of my pasture," saith the Lord. Verse 3, "I will gather the remnant of my flock out of all countries whither I have driven them and will bring them again to their folds, and they shall be fruitful and increase." In Isaiah 11:11, God gave a preview *of all of His scattered* that were included in His restorative plans. God specifically mentioned the locations where scattered and supposedly "lost sheep" are. He mentioned from Assyria, from Egypt, from Pathros, from Cush and Elam, (Africa) from Shinar, Hamath, and from the islands of the sea.

CHAPTER 16G. WORLD'S MOST PURSUED ENIGMA SOLVED!

Legend has it that only three men know the world's best kept secret. Within the ruins of Solomon's Temple is the world's most sought-after secret. The secret is buried in the north-west corner of a certain place? Or is it the southwest corner of a certain place? What are the nationalities of the men? Their identities will be revealed at *Jubilee* or is it Jubilus or Jubila or Jubilo or Jubilum? Hidden under the altars of a transplanted foundation is a guarded secret. It must be protected at any cost. To the north and west of Middle East the secret shall be hidden. A carpenter has the *tselem* (perfected spirit) restorative image/plan for *The Temple*. His identity is buried. He and Hiram have the same ancestry. It is amazing how many millions of people have died trying to solve that riddle. One was recently trying to get permission to see what is hidden in the foundations of a certain Masonic structure (literally). Psst! It is not in the Roissy Chapel! This book is full of clues as to the solution of one of the world's oldest unsolved riddles.

On the surface it may appear that the three men of the "Jubil" clan represent those chosen to handle the secret plans for the Holy Sanctuary. The stages to perfection would be more appropriate. The plans were given to David. Solomon built, flaws included. The Ark was not returned on its first attempt. At an appointed time, the "Wooden Ark" would return. *The Ark was made of wood.* The time frame for the solution of the riddle was prophesied. Israel became a nation in 1948. The first *Jubilee* was 1998. According to Leviticus 25, the Firstfruit Jubilee revelation is three years. So the "The Golden Fleece Found!" ought to be one of the first places that the solution would be revealed. The work on this book has now spanned over 20 years. But according to God's ordained plans, it could not be completed before 2001. The identity of the Master Builder has to be revealed first.

To the millions who searched in vain, all stones were to be fitted as per instructions. Since 90% of Solomon's Temple consisted of carpentry, I would like to end the world's longest wild goose chase by advising that He was the *Son of Man* (son/man not ma/son)—Psalm 80:17. Carefully examine Psalm 87 to see His parental planting. He and *Hiram* are Hebrew *Ham-ites*. His mother's name in Hebrew is Miriam. *WHOEVER SOLVES THIS FINDS THE FLEECE!* From The Golden Fleece, the causes of racial prejudice will be exposed. The foundation of the antichrist will be revealed. Keep your ears glued for a charismatic leader from the ashes of the Roman provinces to surface in the final season. As I recap past errors, observe the serpentine undercurrent of the one that accuses the brethren day and night. God appointed an unrighteous wicked spirit to be Man's accuser—Revelation 12:10. Of necessity, there must be a "Righteous Judge" that keeps records of every event. Moses advised us that God keeps our accounts for four generations—Exodus 34:6-7. Remember that Jezebel seeks a permanent foothold. She then sows her eggs through offspring and then starts a campaign of war and bloodshed. Then she exalts a matriarchal spirit that will invade church altars. Picture the spiritual risk involved when churches pray to the mother of a god. Who or what in the universe would seek to exalt itself above God? Isaiah 14:12, "O Lucifer, son of the morning, how art thou cut down to the ground, which did weaken the nations!" Verse 13 quotes his intentions: "I will exalt my throne *above* the stars of God: I will sit also upon the mount of the congregations of the *north*." God did not say of the south, west or the east.

When Christians were dragged to Rome to be martyred as entertainment for a demonized populace, their resolve inspired many. By the 2nd to 3rd centuries, Romans (not Jews) living in Rome (since Jews either fled or became lion food) started studying the Christian letters. Some that lived outside the area of carnage got converted and returned to Rome. Most notable from their own testimonies were those of Iraneus and Tertullian. The blood of saints on Rome's foundation bothers me. John, one of Jesus' disciples penned the Russian nuclear reactor's explosion 1900 years prior. He also forewarned us that Satan would transform a church "filled with martyrs' blood" into a "Mother of harlots." This book must show how God used the Temple of Solomon and the wives of *Chosen Patriarchs* to preview future churches. More so, Simon a sorcerer had been credited with building a foundation church in that city. If Satan already has a demonic-inspired foundation and gets a spiritually-flawed structure erected on it, then all he has to do is to keep strengthening the base with blemished body fluids. We must examine all aspects of the *Temple of Solomon* for more evidence.

CHAPTER 16H. LIGHTS OF THE FOURTH DAY.

The sun is assigned the role of primary energy source or light-giver in our solar system. The constellations are sources of reflective light. The stars and the moon are considered secondary sources of light. The constellations were assigned the regulatory fourth epoch. Witchcraft is based on secondary light principles. In the first century, a major light sprung out of Jerusalem. The second century saw major shedding of blood on God's holy foundation. The second/third centuries saw the churches' headquarters moving to Antioch with branches in Carthage. By the fourth century those who were churching in Rome started setting up secondary lights. Rome began having its own Bishops and heads of their branch churches. They tried to have Convocations. Those attempts failed. One was eventually held in Carthage. Finally with the help of Emperor Constantine, the churches of all Roman provinces were invited to a state-sponsored convocation. Out of that, a universal Roman church was born in 382 C.E.

Between 240 C.E. and 340 C.E. increased interest in the Christian Gospels caused Roman citizens to include Gospel teachings slowly and progressively in their schools. By the end of the third century a few of Rome's teaching facilities actually went through the complete metamorphosis from schools into churches. By the 4th century Christianity made an intellectual fashion statement in Rome. Prominent citizens, including Emperor Constantine became Christian converts. Churches were soon all over Roman provinces. From 382 to 1053 C.E. a fragile federation of the churches in Northern Africa, those in Rome, and those around the

Caspian Sea (Asia Minor) was attempted and finally forged.

During those approximately seven hundred years, the mammon of wars with the rich Turks threw weight behind Rome's quest for influential leadership. The absence of printing presses and telephones retarded the truth about the sponsorship role played by the church of the Roman provinces in the 1st Crusade from reaching those churches in Africa and Asia. The Pope had actually blessed the soldiers before they left. By 1054, the temporary and fragile alliance between the Eastern Orthodox churches and Western Churches of the provinces of Rome split apart. Monks in remote monasteries were slow to receive news and as a result many became isolated and lived hermitic lifestyles. By then, Europe had grown wealthy from the spoils of war acquired by Byzantine Rome. Rome then moved back to areas where they had expelled the Turks. Following the footsteps of Jeroboam who set up headquarters in Dan and Bethel, Rome had a Rome of the East and a Rome of the West. Pregnant with its avalanche of new wealth, the Church of Rome financed Latin translations of the Gospels. An organizational structure was set in place. Loose orders of monasteries and all the churches of Rome's provinces came under the powerful umbrella, the organizational base at Rome. Today that is known as The Roman Catholic Church. The revelations of their collusion in the Crusade against Jerusalem cemented the resolve of the African and Asian churches. They were convinced that their decision to secede to avoid additional spiritual contamination was the correct one. They remained separate to this day. From those original stems sprouted what are known today as Eastern, Greek, Russian and African Orthodox Churches. Since the Roman church was not formed until the 4th century, initially they were never part of the original church of James, Simon, John and Paul.

By the 4th century, Kings, Nobles and Bishops in Rome created a powerful alliance. Over the years they became "Infallible." If they decided that someone was a Pope, so it was. Since we reap what we sow, those organizations that were sown in arrogance, stupidity, false doctrines and murder will reap the same (double) unless they undergo serious wholesale cleansings. That is God's word not mine. Entrenched spirits do not budge under the first thrust. One national convocation or Day of Prayer will never eradicate all *Territorial Spirits*. If that were so, Jesus would not need to come back to "Complete the Finished work." David did not retrieve "The Ark" on his First Attempt. I will insert the prophecies for the skeptics. Revelation 18:6, "Reward her (the spirit of Babylon) even as she rewarded you, and double according to her works." The symbolism of the double wash in Exodus 19:10 was precisely to eliminate the double portion of iniquity. John forewarned us in Revelation 17:5-6 and Revelation 18:23-24.

In John's vision on Patmos, each church received a candle. He likened the returning Messiah to a bridegroom coming for His bride, a church without spot or wrinkle. John warned that either a religious institution or a spirit that engulfed one will be called Babylon the Great. In Revelation 18:23, "A light of a candle shall light no more in thee; and the voice of the bridegroom and of the bride shall be heard no more in thee: for thy merchants were the great men of the earth; for thy sorceries were all nations deceived. 24...In her was found the blood of prophets, and of saints, and of all that was slain upon the earth."

THE BOOK OF REVELATION STATES:
"RENDER UNTO BABYLON DOUBLE."
IN THE BOOK OF ESTHER,
"RENDER UNTO HAMAN DOUBLE MEASURE."

CHAPTER 16I. A CARPENTER'S PLANE.

People I know study what can be called philosophical masonry: how to build leadership. The problem with masonry is that all settings are in stone. Adjustments after buildings are completed are difficult. With physical and spiritual carpentry, where incongruity sets in, lumber can be planed to a smooth and accurate finish. Let us repair some spiritual lumber. During the reign of Emperor Claudius 41C.E. to 54 C.E., a decree was issued banishing "All Jews from Rome." Rome by the 1st century had conquered all of Ancient Greece and Europe from Spain in the west (called Gaul) through Northern Africa including Jerusalem (called Palestina) to the Asian coastal provinces. By the 1st Century, Jerusalem was a popular trading route, between north and south, east and west. Residents and traders for the most part spoke a form of Greek as the official language. A large population of Jews lived in Rome in the 1st Century. They were mainly traders, copyists, and tent makers. Regular pilgrimages to Jerusalem they made to observe the holy feasts. During Jesus' ministry the news of His miracle working powers and the clarity of His teachings caused thousands to be converted. There were no bookstores at the time. Copyists were in heavy demand to make handwritten copies of temple teachings. It became necessary to encourage the new converts, so the Elders of the church appointed Paul, Barnabas, Timothy, Mark, and Peter (all Jews) to visit and strengthen the converts. By 59 C.E., Paul landed in Rome as a prisoner. Mark and Luke were with him. Paul, a Roman citizen had appealed to Felix the Roman governor of Jerusalem to have his case heard before Caesar.

Paul was in Rome from 59 C.E. to 61 C.E. He had a serious complaint, so he referred the matter to *James the Elder,* who summoned Paul, Simon, and John *(all apostles)* to resolve the dispute. Simon was wrong. *James the Elder corrected Simon the apostle.* If Simon was a Pope and Popes are supposed to be infallible, Simon could have responded, "I have so decreed! So be it!" Simon the apostle was also married and Popes cannot marry. By Paul's second imprisonment, Rome burned under Nero 64 C.E. Satan convinced his spiritually blinded agents that the Jews were responsible. By 66 C.E., Rome attacked Jerusalem. Jews (mainly Christians) were targeted. When news of Nero's revengeful anger reached Jerusalem, Simon began to exhort and to encourage the brethren not to panic.

I am going to point out some details from the last letter Paul wrote from Rome just before the infamous fire. Paul and Peter were at the *First Convocation* in Jerusalem where Peter was deemed *inaccurate on the circumcision issue.* Peter left shortly thereafter for Babylon and other Asian towns to do damage control. God is definitely way above genius. Jesus' church was fallible and erred according to God's word that all have erred. Refer to the very first chapter of this book: given any chance, darkness will encroach upon light. If God's church is fallible, then whose church is not? Only Satan could encourage that teaching. I checked 35 names that Paul mentioned in his letter to the Roman brethren. He sent greetings and encouraged them in the faith. He also mentioned those who had done him serious wrong. None of the names in Paul's letter correspond with later reconstructed lists of Bishops or Popes. After the persecution of Steven, Peter, Paul and James by Herod (the Tetrarch), responsibility for church governance fell on John, Titus, Ignatius, Hermas and Barnabas who steered the flock. Without the source reservoir to nourish, feed and encourage them, seed of that original remnant borrowed doctrines from the later powerful Roman church. Isolated stems are (what we call today) the Eastern, Russian, Greek, Ethiopian and African Orthodox churches. I am detailing those things to show where the errors occurred.

God, in His wisdom had John record his vision at Patmos and then send copies to the first churches from Jerusalem. Hand copies were addressed to the seven churches that were in Asia. God is not a God of confusion. There were eight pioneers in Noah's Ark. If John had included Jerusalem in his letters and said eight churches, historians could have said Rome was the eighth church. Our All Wise, All Knowing God, had John address the letter with the authority of his Jerusalem base, to the Seven Churches that were in Asia.

THE CHURCH FROM WHICH ROMAN CHURCHES SPRANG WAS NEVER INFALLIBLE OR WAS IT? PETER THE APOSTLE ERRED AND WAS CORRECTED.

Handwritten copies of those epistles were discovered in caves in the south of Israel. Archaeologists have deduced that survivors of Titus' siege either hid them or that they were abandoned during their escape. Other parchments of Early Churches' letters have been found concealed in earthen jars in other wildernesses and caves of Judea and around Ethiopia. Those records attest to the closeness that existed and still continues to exist between Jews and Ethiopians. Philip, an early apostle/missionary expounded on the word to one of the Court of Queen Candice of Ethiopia and Philip baptized him. On the African West Coast, Peter raised Tabitha from the dead. When Ethiopia was struck with famine and civil war, the government of Israel sent charter flights for *"Her brother and sister Jews in Ethiopia."* The highway of brotherly love between the Ethiopians and Southern Tribes confirms Amos 9:7.

The "Far Right" began panicking and immediately their oracles, "their chosen media houses" started campaigns of "Misinformation." If only that highway could expand to include the Egyptians, Palestinians, Jordanians, Africans, Syrians and Indians etc. My next logical step is to ask—are readers going to agree with me in prayer for their restoration?

CHAPTER 16J. RECONSTRUCTING THE 1ST 100 YEARS OF ERRANT CHURCH HISTORY.

I examined the list of Popes supplied by a College of Cardinals, formally established in 1179. It has prompted me to set up a fund that offers U.S100, 000.00 for anyone who supplies proof that there was any Pope attached to a church in Rome before the year 100 C.E. If such existed it means that God's word is a lie. Scripture quotes, "Let God be true and every man be a liar." There are two main sources, which provide lists of "Fathers of the early Church." Strangely, none of the two document James as first Elder or first Bishop. It is a highly Romanized list with dozens of names of people that Rome martyred. A few Roman converts of high rank (martyred prior to the reign of Constantine) were assigned the titles of Pope. That alone certifies the inaccuracy of the list since the Roman Catholic Church was formed after Constantine became Emperor.

Both lists start off with a Peter who was Pope of a church in Rome from 32 C.E. to 67 C.E. That is disturbing. There was a magician named Simon Paeter. Church historians refer to him as Simon Magus. We searched all available pieces of evidence and found no Simon Magus. What we realized was the same error used to document the name of Maryam (Miriam) of Magdala. Maryam of Magdala over the years became Mary Magdalene. Magus is actually singular for *Magi*, something similar to our modern day psychics. Simon the magician became transposed over time into a fictional other person by the name of Simon Magus who was actually Simon Paeter. Secular records show the only Simon Paeter as a magician. He was beguiling people around Samaria and the surrounding Roman provinces around the 30's.

In Acts 8:9-22, that Simon had a run-in with Philip and some of Jesus' apostles. Secular historians recorded that he went to Rome and made a name for himself. He was hailed and given the title "Divine" by the same Christian-hating authorities that persecuted the apostles. Rome erected a statue in his honour. Simon the occultist was allowed to open a mystery school. He was obsessed with finding *the source* of the "New Wisdom" of the inferior Jewish non-citizens. He searched known pagan customs, cults on fertility, the roles of the matriarchal deities and the many Trinitarian cults of ancient Egypt, Mesopotamia and Babylon. On the other hand, *Simon Bar Jona* was sent to strengthen the churches in Asia Minor at the same time that the mysterious Pope Peter ruled in a city where Jews were banished. Jews wouldn't dare to appear in public. Roman citizenship guaranteed an accused Roman the right to a public appearance: a chance to renounce their religion publicly and be spared a horrible death. When Simon the apostle and John went to encourage the flock of Steven in Samaria, that *Paeter the false prophet* followed them around and offered money for their special healing gifts. Acts 8:19, "Whereupon he was blatantly rebuked for his blasphemy." Acts 8:21, "Thou hast neither part, nor lot in this matter, for thy heart is not right in the sight of God." Records in Rome alone imply that later on he converted to Christianity.

Here is something very strange: most of the early Christians were Jews and all that refused to deny Jesus were tortured to death. If that Simon had not publicly renounced Jesus, he would have died also. The logical question is this, even if he had converted, where would he have had time to study much more to qualify to teach the Hebrew law sufficiently to become a Bishop or a Pope? Was he martyred after his alleged conversion and became a Pope either before or after his death? Historical records in Rome testify that Simon (the Sorcerer) was in fact afforded the honour of setting up a debate centre. Archive files of Rome show that a Simon got permission to set up an "institution of learning." I intend to track down his whereabouts after he returned to Rome. That Simon could not have been Simon Bar Jona since 1st Corinthians 10:4-17 stated unequivocally: "The rock" on which the church where Simon and Paul functioned as apostles is Jesus the Christ; thus confirming Numbers 24:17.

Let us look at Satan's first attempt to kidnap and usurp the Temple Mount in Jerusalem. Antiochus Epiphanes IV 163 B.C.E., king of Syria declared Judaism illegal and commanded the Jews to desecrate their altar by sacrificing pigs to him. From then through to Titus's siege and then Hadrian's routing of Jerusalem in 130 C.E. and beyond, it is safe to say that Satan worked feverishly to sow conflicting ideological seeds on Jerusalem's spiritual base.

During Paul's missionary journeys, Rome was hostile to Jews. Although Claudius, who ruled from 41C.E. to 54 C.E., banished all Jews from Rome, there was a small group of migratory Jews living there prior to his reign. In 61 C.E., Paul sowed the apostolic seeds from his house in Rome. However, when Rome burned under Nero, Christians (whether Jew, Greek or Roman) became the hunted. That ban forced Aquila and Priscilla who churched with Paul in Rome, to relocate to Corinth—Acts 18:2.

All you have to do is to follow the history of Rome and figure out how much blood was shed either by her, or on the foundations set up for her. Next, read Revelation 18 and see why God asked John to expose and identify the mystery of "Babylon the Great." Please remember the Fleece's reference to Solomon's spiritual equivalent "wives, princesses and concubines." John's description uses the superlative for "biggest and worse" cases' scenario for one that was chosen yet became utterly defiled. John prophesied 2000 years ago that a trans-generational spirit would engulf and transform a chosen spiritual virgin into a "mother of harlots." That description is frightening. Mothers are able to bear fruit. So according to John's 2000-year prophecy that mother would have borne much seed. If left alone, many altars would be shackled and transformed into satanic strongholds of substitution. Since Jezebel and Leviathan have established serious strongholds under both state and religious foundations of ancient Rome, serious convocations are past due.

There is a person listed as second in succession to a Paeter that was head of an underground church in the 1st century. Questions immediately pop up. Were there Popes in the first century? Where was the church in Rome in the 1st century, allegedly "Poped" by a Peter? Those on our research team, reputable members of high rank of the church that held those myths sacrosanct and believed them to be factual, were shocked by our discoveries. After the findings, they went into periods of deep depression. Readers I am advising you, the main purpose of this exercise is to correct centuries of errors. The Word of God is unambiguous: "You shall know the truth and the truth shall set you free." It is better to discover the errors in your lifetime and receive the truth than to go to your graves having *spent years in error.*

Heads of churches around Asia Minor, North Africa and Jerusalem ordained men to preach and to teach the Gospel. The overseer of each church was a Bishop. The Chief Elder from the *base church in Jerusalem* had to confirm the recommendations from the apostles before anyone could be appointed to the "Office of Bishop." The apostles that were "sent from Jerusalem" with letters of "appointments" first had to send written progress reports by messengers. Upon their return they would report the events that took place on their missionary journeys in person. Search the chronicles of such apostles as Paul, Barnabas, John or Simon and their letters not only encouraged the converts but also supplied correlating data to the Jerusalem headquarters. Scripture reference is Acts 21:17.

Archaeo-historians like me have few sources to cross-reference data. What I have discovered over the past 20 years by critical analysis is that many of Rome's teachings—especially their *Doctrine of Infallibility*—do not pass the *Litmus Test* of God's *Law of Double Reference.* James, the first Bishop wrote a letter of encouragement to all the faithful. In James 5:13-15, he instructed the entire Christian congregation as to how to pray for the sick. Verse 14, "Is any sick among you? Let him call the elders of the Church; let them pray over him." Rome's repeated lack of understanding of the Gospels caused major "substitutions" of God's word. Instead of Elders praying for the sick, Rome introduced a form of divination; they presented dead Christians' bones to be touched. Supposedly every formerly sick person that got healed, touched a dead bone "believed to be from a holy person." That alone established the criterion for "sainthood." In contrast, the early church called living disciples that prayed for and gave to less fortunate brethren, "saints." Paul always gave reports of his various missionary journeys to the Jerusalem church. In Paul's letters—Romans 8:27, Romans 12:13, 1st Thessalonians 3:13, Ephesians 1:18 and Ephesians 4:12, he confirmed the requirements for sainthood as being a *living fervent follower of Jeshua.* One of the legacies of Constantine's state religion is that real or fake bones of dead Christians could participate in ritual prayers for the sick. As long as a sick got healed and that person said that they touched a dead bone, a graven image could be made of the dead and future prayers could be channeled through them. In essence that church established *dead intercessors.* That practice is strictly forbidden—Isaiah 38:18. Every one of the aforementioned is either blasphemous, in direct contradiction to the word of God, ritualistic, a demonic doctrine of substitution or all four.

Let us examine the process of retrieval of Christian bones. Christians were regularly rounded up and brought to the Coliseum in Rome for daily entertainment. Sympathizers, mainly Romans, had arranged secret burials for some. The reason I say some, let us be serious:

which Christian sympathizer would argue with lions over the rights to Christian bones. Assuming that you found some, how would you know which bones belonged to whom? A street hustle sprung up in those days—that of exhuming any bone and selling it as a Christian relic. In my many years in *Deliverance Ministering,* I have witnessed invasions of ritualistic things by evil spirits. Anything remotely ritualistic and spiritually incorrect can be attacked and magnetized. Bear in mind also the difficulties that surrounded Christianity within the first 100 years in Rome. Nero and Hadrian signed decrees of expulsion, death and burnings of all Jews and Christians' properties and persons between 65 C.E. to 85 C.E. Once you were fingered as a Christian convert, as many Jews were, you were selected as choice "tenderloin." Did that word evolve from the original reference "tender lion-food?"

Roman citizens were offered the opportunity to renounce their new faith publicly or to be put to death. House churches and teaching manuscripts were burnt and the erudite eradicated regularly. Where then could one from Rome study? It is logical to assume that highly unusual circumstances would permit Romans to study the Hebrew language and those complex Hebrew laws. Those circumstances could not pass unnoticed. Let us examine the evidence. When the Church of the Roman provinces replaced the Roman Empire as Europe's uniting force, all martyred Christians were referred to as saints. It is therefore highly improbable to find accurate records from the first century.

The title of Bishop was the official designation for chief parishioner "selected to baptize converts" until 382 C.E., when they were officially united (thanks to Emperor Constantine) under one supreme Bishop. Retrogressive lists were compiled later on. Numerous saints became bishops, and many bishops became Popes. For example, the "College of Cardinals" decided who would be selected to be on the list of Popes. In the Acts of the first Apostles, mention is made of the first Roman Gentiles that converted to Christianity: Cornelius, and Sergius Paulus. In Asia Minor, Paul and Barnabas had made appointments of *"older and wiser men"* to become elders, who were learned and *knew the Law.* When Paul was a prisoner in Rome, he was allowed to have his own house. That he used as a missionary base under the guidance and covering of the Jerusalem church. Other than that seed, no official church was set up in Rome in the first 100 years. That would explain why all "unchanged" original historical accounts document Asia Minor as the place where Romans like Justin Martyr, Polycarp, Polycrates, Iraneus, Tertullian and Eusubius received their conversions.

CHAPTER16K. THE FIRST 100 YEARS OF NON-EXISTENT POPES!

From the official list of Popes, Peter is listed from 32 C.E. to 61 C.E.—the same time that he was either in Jerusalem, in jail then miraculously released (Acts 12:7), in Joppa, Caesarea or on his way to Babylonia. During that time, followers of Jesus used "to church" in houses. After Peter's escape from prison, he went to the house of John Mark where they "churched." In Acts 12:17 he was told to report to the chief.

Linus or Lie-nus is listed as following someone called Peter. Linus' tenure of office is given from 67 C.E to 76 C.E. That is absolutely incorrect. James was the first Bishop. After the death of James, Titus became Bishop of the church in Antioch and absorbed the survivors of the Jerusalem church during and after the carnage of 70 C.E. We found one Linus in our twenty years of research. He was a well-wisher (encourager) mentioned casually as "one of the converts" by Paul in his letter to Timothy. Anyone can source that letter since it is recorded in detail in the New Testament as Paul's letter to Timothy (that was after Paul had been there in 61 C.E., and had converted some of the Jews who lived in Rome). Refer 2nd Timothy 4:21. In 64 C.E., Paul wrote from Jerusalem telling Timothy that he Paul received an appointment as "Apostle to the Gentiles." The terms of reference for his appointments in 2nd Timothy 1:11 are preacher, apostle, and teacher. Similarly, James appointed Peter as: preacher, apostle, and teacher (of Hebrew believers). Peter was Hebrew and Paul was a Greek Jew and a Roman citizen. Peter was shepherd to the flock that grazed around Jerusalem.

In Paul's letter to Timothy (who was among those Jews that fellowshipped or "churched" in Paul's house in Rome), Paul listed the most fervent of the flock: Priscilla and Aquila "churched" at the house of Onesiphorus. Erastus abode at Corinth and Trophimus at Miletum. In the second to last verse we observed him sending greetings from other flock (to the by- the-way-brethren): Eubulus, Prudens, *Linus* and Claudia. Then miraculously from the 11th to 12th centuries when the "College of Cardinals" compiled chronological lists, Linus was promoted posthumously from "Brethren of those who churched in Rome," to a Pope who succeeded another first Pope called Peter. It is believed that Linus was among the early martyrs. In spite of having no supporting evidence, Linus is listed as Pope in Rome from 67 C.E. to 76 C.E. when Nero's anger against Christians was hottest. The only place in Rome that an office of a pope could have been set up between 64 C.E. and 100 C.E. was at the Coliseum in the belly of lions. When Paul wrote that letter around 65 C.E., James was still head of the Church until 76 C.E.

Paul addressed a letter to the congregation in Rome from Jerusalem in 64 C.E. Of the forty or so names he sent either to welcome or (in four or five cases) to rebuke, he mentioned only Apellas and Rufus as Elders. Among those who covenanted with them, only those two were mentioned as "chosen." In fact I am going to quote a few extracts from that letter. In Paul's letter to the Roman brethren, Romans 16:17, Paul or Tertius (the copyist) warned the brethren: "Mark them that cause divisions and offences contrary to the doctrine, which ye have learned and avoid them." Please read the entire letter. Another of his letters, sent to the faithful at Corinth, is addressed to "All churches of the Gentiles," 1st Corinthians 16:4. Verse 5, "Likewise, greet the 'Church' that is in their house." Notice the designation given to Urbane, "helper." In verse 16 greetings are sent to the *House of Narcissus*.

God in His wisdom hid those names from the people who, later on, invented Popes' names. To tell the truth, had they used names such as mentioned in Paul's letter we would have had a much harder time unearthing evidence. Paul was very clear in Romans 1:5 the terms of reference, "Apostle to the Gentiles," and Peter was called "Apostle to the Jews" in Asia. That is why it was Paul's responsibility to strengthen those young disciples in Rome. There was a Cletus or Anacletus listed as Pope between 76 C.E. and 91 C.E.

Our research turned up patterns of error. Hegesippus did most of the documentation of names of Bishops for the early church files. The Coliseum of Rome was completed around 78 C.E. Christians, mostly the learned and eloquent were stars for the live entertainment. Many were given the chance to renounce their religion. That denial would allow their lives to be spared. Steadfastness meant death. The testimonies of Tertullian and the other Roman converts of the 2nd century make very good reading material. According to their own accounts, what impressed them and convinced them to study those newly copied Greek Gospels were the fervor and determination of the Christians to face death rather than to renounce the "New Wisdom" of the Jews. One such was Polycarp who was martyred in 155 C.E. after his clandestine visit to Rome to find out if in fact an Anicetus (not Anacletus) was polluting the gospels through a liberal school in Rome. Polycarp reported to the church's new headquarters in *An-*

tioch that the information was correct. Spies reported Polycarp.

St. Iraneus and Julius Africanus, whose chronological lists from 222 C.E. were used as source documents, actually derived their information from Esubius' same erroneous source. There is a new catalog floating around which identify St. Jerome as chronicler. If you research that thoroughly you will find out that St. Jerome's source is actually Eusebius.' The average life expectancy of a proclaimed Christian during the years of 76 C.E. to 91 C.E. in Rome was approximately 15 days. For a Christian, much more a highly visible person such as Bishop or Pope to survive for 15 years would have been in the archives of miracles.

CHAPTER 16L. MYSTERY OF THE TWIN POPE.

Were there Pope twins? Our research turned up two Clements of Antiquity. One is definitely real; the other one (through confusion of letters) seems to have been an earlier reproduction by people trying to fit together patterns and dates that they believed to be factual. As much as I would like to, I cannot attribute those inaccuracies to accidental errors. For example: I have been unable to solve a mystery surrounding two persons that appear to have been Popes simultaneously. Both were listed as heads of a Roman church in the latter part on the first century. On a "List of Popes" 88 C.E. to 97 C.E., we encountered the name St. Clement or Clemens. There was a Clement mentioned by Paul in Philippians 4:3. He was one of the church helpers at Caesarea Philippi. It is well known that John wrote his vision in 98 C.E. and James died around 75 C.E. How coincidental it is to list names of people whose tenure supposedly fit between those periods. When Rebekah faked Jacob's identification, God did not cancel His blessings on Jacob because of His covenant promise to Isaac. A seed of God's church had to follow God's law of duplicity. They had to commit fraud also. God also did not cancel His anointing because of His covenant promise to His Redeemer and human foundation stone that was established in Zion—Isaiah 28:16 (not Rome). On some lists of *Early Church Fathers*, there is a Pope called Pope Clement, St. Clement or St. Clemens depending on which list you search. Where he is not listed with successive Popes, instead of his birth date, a date of commencement of reign is given from 88 C.E. The date of death is listed as unknown. Did that vagueness gave rise to persons accidentally or otherwise assuming that Titus Flavius Clemens could have been a Pope? Let us be careful here. That Clemens' school of Gnosticism and Pantheism around the middle of the second century was a furnace of hostility to Justin Martyr and to Christianity.

In the Book of Acts, Chapter 13, Luke mentioned the names of the prophets and teachers: Barnabas, Niger (Simeon) and an African by the name of Lucius who hailed from Cyrene. Barnabas accompanied Paul while Sergius Paulus was deputy of Cyprus. So Paul was under the headship of James the Bishop of Jerusalem. Ignatius succeeded Titus. Both were Elders of the church of Antioch that absorbed the survivors of the Jerusalem church. Neither of them was demoted. Since Popes are over Bishops and neither of the Elders of Antioch were ever Popes, Clement or Clemens remains a mystery. However when this Clement or Clemens is listed on a list of Popes he is listed from 88 C.E. to 97 C.E. In those days the day of end of office and day of death coincided anyway. Allegedly, that Pope Clement was able to stay alive in Rome with its thirst for Coliseum live shows miraculously for nine years. How does one reconcile the name Pope Clement with the other list showing Cletus or Anacletus as Pope from 76 C.E to 91 C.E.?

There was also a Clement of Antioch (referred to as St. Clement) whose martyrdom was given as 164 C.E., but was not accorded a birth date. In chapter 26 of Clement's letter of "Appeal" we see why God in His wisdom had decreed that the priests should know the Law (not be a foreigner) knowledgeable of God's divine plan and purpose. That is why the "Wild Olive" was ordained to be grafted to the "Natural Branch" and not the other way around. Since the "Branch was planted in Jerusalem," Rome's claim for foundation rights have as much validity as those of America, India, Mecca and China. God already preordained that the wild olive tree (Gentile churches) would be grafted into the Jerusalem branch. From that "branch" planted in Zion, enlightened Elders would "be chosen" for the joint office of "King and Priest." Deuteronomy 17:14-17 list the requirements for God's kingly office. Ezekiel 44:15-31 encase the requirements to be God's chosen ministering priest. Verse 22, "Neither shall they take for their wives a widow nor her that is divorced." A wife of a prophet or chosen Messenger in the Torah translated into *future spiritual bride*. The prophetic meaning of Deuteronomy 17:17 and Ezekiel 44:22… No *chosen vessel* of God is allowed to form his own church otherwise he would be competing for God's bride! Wow! That is why only one wife was and is allowed: Leviticus 21:14 and Titus 1:6. Prophet Mohammed not only had more than one wife but also his first wife Khadija was widowed.

I find it strange that this Clement does not use the Biblical reference of the Book of Esther as precedent for Rome turning around and becoming a fruitful church, but uses instead the pagan-based reference of a phoenix bird rising from its ashes as a pretext for his argument. That is precisely the plan of the "Spirit of Babylon." His letter is, from what I can gather, a veiled attempt at an apology for the behaviour of Rome towards the Christians. The real intent of the letter is revealed in Chapter 56. He asked the churches of Rome to "Let us admonish and correct one another." In his 41st chapter he confirmed the headship of the church is in Jerusalem. I would like to include the letter in one of my sequels save the length. It is just too long. A copy of the same letter is in the headquarters of a large church in Rome. The letter is so vague in that there is nothing in it to indicate that the first Clement or Clemens wrote it except that it had been paraded as such. Here is another challenging piece of evidence that an early Clement or Clemens from Rome could not have written it. Jews mostly used to traffic and trade between Greece, Rome, Alexandria, and Jerusalem. They performed the elaborate tasks of copyists during safe times. Which Roman Christian would have approached a Jew to ask him to copy something in Hebrew when spies and informers were all around Rome and her provinces in the 1st century?

By the 3rd century, Roman citizens were becoming converts and since few Jews remained, Roman Christians were the ones being persecuted. They studied the gospels in Greece and Asia Minor; hence I believe that the letter was actually written by Clement of Alexandria. Here are my other reasons: 1. He had time to write a letter of appeal (similar to that of Justin Martyr) and 2. The fact that he referred to the authority in Jerusalem conforms to the format of the Churches of Asia Minor and Africa. That letter is not listed among "Bible Canons" but as "Apocryphal Works." It is too long (over 50 chapters) to be included in this book. The churches of Asia Minor never joined the Roman conglomeration long enough for St. Clement of Alexandria to have been considered a Pope.

In some lists he is referred to as *Clement of Antioch*. In Acts chapter 13, God directed Luke to document the names of the elders of the church at Antioch, which was a Roman province at the identical time that Clement was supposedly a Pope. While Luke addressed his letter to a Theophilus, James was head over all the churches. Acts 13:1, "There were in the church of Antioch certain prophets and teachers: Barnabas, Simeon (who was called Niger), Lucius of

Cyrene, and Manaen of the house of Herod the Tetrarch and **Saul**." In the second verse Luke told us what they were doing: "They ministered to the Lord." Why was Clement not among those who ministered? God in His wisdom always looks into the corridors of time. Since He is all wise and all knowing, He had Luke single out the names of the Elders so that in His Day of Revelation all dogma would either pass or fail the litmus test of truth. I rest my case; I will get the truth at whatever financial cost. U.S$100,000.00 for evidence confirming that anyone on the published "List of Popes" was either a Pope in the first century or that there was any person that held the office of Pope before 100 C.E.

I must say without prejudice that I was very impressed with the candor and methodical approach in which the Eastern Orthodox churches dealt with historical matters. When there was interruption through foreign invasions, they did not invent data to fill in missing pieces to claim continuity. Their accounts reflected what they knew as honestly and accurately as possible. When data was unknown or unavailable, they stated that. Evidence suggests that as a result of their being badly scarred by the behaviour of the Roman churches, they mirrored the attitudes of the survivors of the Jerusalem church. They became protective, ultra-conservative and totally resistant to any change whatsoever. Over centuries writers have labeled them "Clannish and Stagnant."

God already gave Isaiah the gravest of warnings. God prophesied through Isaiah that He would use the Gentiles after the Jews rejected His Messiah and He did. In God's wisdom He used the same church of the Western provinces of Rome to effectuate what He had arranged for Haman in the book of Esther. God did a Purim! As was done with the ancient Israelites, God sifted the seed while pruning the branches. God pruned. From the branch in Rome sprang the reform stems, *Protestantism*. From those stems sprang *Pentecostal Leaves*. The next growth is the one that Joel the prophet prophesied. *Sheaves* (churches without spots or wrinkles) are next. All those churches that are experiencing revival of the Pentecostal power had been warned by Paul "Boast not, against the branches." Pray for them instead: for the fullness of the Gentiles to come in. The Jews will then be led to jealousy.

1998 Jubilee saw descendants of Judah living in Gabon, West Africa, Central Africa, South America, and seed of "Lost Tribes" living in India, Uzbekistan, Jordan, Egypt, Palestine, Syria, China, together with hundreds of other nations coming to pray for peace in Jerusalem. I was there and witnessed what was foreseen in Zechariah 8:22-23. I bore witness to that and the prophecy of Isaiah in Isaiah 11:11, "It shall come to pass that in *that day*, the Lord shall set his hand again *The Second Time* to recover the remnant of his people which shall be left." Pray for the fulfillment of Isaiah 62:

JERUSALEM'S SALVATION SHALL BE LIKE A BLAZING TORCH.

CHAPTER 17. UNDERSTANDING BLOCKAGES.

The compilation of research data for this book took some 25 years. The file as to insight into the satanic divide should be at the end, technically. Yet I will list most of the data in the following chapter. The information should be relatively new to most readers. If you are unfamiliar with the contents, I propose that you read first, then after you have completed the book, read the chapter again. At the end, most of what you wrestled with should have become more palatable. I would like to admonish you however, that a person cannot be a spiritual conqueror unless he/she is sanctified through forgiveness and then drawn into "The Veil." You cannot be drawn into "The Veil" unless the Spirit of the Living God ushers you in. Adversely, there have been utterances from oracles "Not chosen by God" that have been accepted "en masse." There is "One Way to God's truth." Any time there is plurality of concepts or philosophies, then all elders need to fast and seek guidance from the Lord. For instance: How can two identical invisible spiritual entities plus one perfected purpose make three persons? The three that bear record, or bear witness in heaven are the invisible Father, Holy Spirit (spiritual comforter/connector) and God's word. All three are limitless. One is visible; two are invisible, therefore one manifest witness. The word became flesh to be the sin sacrifice. Since no flesh can glory in the presence of God, there is no carnal Son anymore. The Son now directs us into the Most Holy of Holies of wisdom. The Son is the "Door or Way" connected by God's Holy Spirit to His everlasting All. As per (entire Psalm 2) Psalm 2:12...Pay homage to the Son, lest he be angry and ye perish from *The Way*...blessed are all who put their trust in The Son. Verse 7 describes the Son begotten, not made and placed on *His holy hill* of Zion. The name Jeshua is spelled out in sequential letter code in Hebrew. God's word promises blessings upon those who trust in Him.

The Book—of Abraham, Isaac, Ishmael, Jacob and Esau—encases prophecies in Isaiah 60 and Isaiah 62 to the effect that Jews, Muslims and Christians will be reconciled in the one Messiah. Naturally before those prophecies can be fulfilled, all of Satan's damage must be repaired.

The Holy Koran highlights the seriousness of the "Gospels:"

1. "We gave Moses the Book and followed him up with a succession of Messengers; we gave Jesus the son of Mary clear signs and strengthened him:" Sura 2, 87. Here is proof from the words of the Holy Koran that all Arabic seed of Abraham are to study the Book of father Abraham, The Torah.

2. "O people of the Book, ye have nothing to stand upon until ye establish the Torah and the Gospel and what has been sent down to you from your Lord:" Sura 5, 68.

3. "To thee (Jesus son of Mary mentioned in Sura 5, 46) we sent the Scripture in truth, confirming the scripture that came before it, and guarding it in safety:" Sura 5, 48.

4. "And in their footsteps we sent Jesus the son of Mary, confirming the Law that had come

before him: We sent him the Gospel therein was guidance and light and confirmation of the law that had come before him: a guidance and an admonition to those who fear Allah:" Sura 5, 46.

After Prophet Mohammed died, severe power struggles ensued. Intellectual schools of thought were juggling for positions of dominance. By the time attention was directed towards preserving the Prophet's teachings, these groups were selected to fashion a spiritual code or Creed for Islam and to interpret and to preserve the prophet's visions and teachings. The Mutazilites, Kharijites and the Ismailiya sect of Shiah were among those selected. How much impact did the dominant Ismailiya's ("Secret Seven Sleepers") sect have on Sura 18? Were those scholars given sole responsibility to edit and to transpose the teachings of the Prophet?

Over time, litanies of prayers and devotions have been transformed into another regional and ethnic religion. God is not a divisive God. If we, His children, elect to separate ourselves into different clans that feed on intolerance, do not expect our perfect God to sanction such behaviour. I urge all my brothers and sisters to use the schematic to superimpose their religious doctrines in the same way that I have analyzed Christianity's 2000-year history. Whenever any doctrine is plotted against a true spirit level, accuracies or inaccuracies must manifest. True prophets do not take sides; they speak the mind of God. How then can a book confirm what preceded it unless there is harmony between the original and the later documents? Sura 19 documents events about Jesus' chaste mother and His early childhood. However verse 28 calls Mary the mother of Jesus, "Sister of Aaron." Aaron died about 1000 years before Mary's birth.

Mary is dead and so are Simon, Buddha, Bahaulla and every statue. They cannot intercede or bear witness! Psalm 88:10, "Shall the dead arise and praise thee?" Psalm 115:17, "The dead praise *not* the Lord, neither any that go down into silence." No seed of Abraham or anyone for that matter should be praying to or through any being carved in a graven image. It is an abomination to God. Show me a seed of Abraham who prays to or through any other spiritual witness and I will show you a poor person, a depressed person, a sick person, a demonized person or an unhappy person who in turn will produce the aforementioned seed. Dead saints do not, nor can they bear witness in heaven. Dead ceremonies cannot bear record or witness. Ecclesiastes 9:5, "The dead know not any thing, neither have they *any more a reward.*" Verse 6, "Their love and their hatred, and their envy is now perished." *Mary does not bear witness or record in heaven.*

It should bewilder a person if a psychic says that he or she established contact with a deceased relative. Since they do not bear witness in heaven, ask them, "Where do you bear witness?" Doesn't it appear strange that all persons that they supposedly contact made it? Acts 8:9-11 and verse 22, Acts 13:8-10 and Acts 19:13 explained such. In Acts 16:16-18, the word of God is clear in that there are two spiritual kingdoms: one under obedience to the Spirit of God. Fortune telling belongs to the other spirit types—occult spirits of divination.

I will recap Satan's biggest triumph and give a preview of the mould for obedience as opposed to our inherited disobedient history. Satan's biggest triumph had been that of enticing Solomon to have children with so many "strange women." Those acts established the foundations for weakening the *Bride of Christ* and strengthening the *Babel Beast* as per Daniel's vision in Daniel 2:31-34 and Revelation 17:12-13. The flip side picture of obedience is meat for another book, "Shape of a Man." No peeks yet; just one injection into your imagination. Imagine the "Proposed Theocracy of nations" as partially previewed in Esther 1:1, south to the farthest sea, a rich self-sufficient land speaking the prophetic language. The contents of this book would have been common knowledge. There would have been no sicknesses or diseases on that land. Instead of there being seed of "Twelve Brothers" keeping one another's flocks on a rich land of plenty, all sorts of "Demon-cracies" and "One Demonic Order" of philosophies are being peddled in the name of political solutions. Every false way hinders and blocks people from receiving God's eternal truth.

CHAPTER 17A. BEHIND ENEMY LINES!

Freeing persons from satanic strangleholds (whether via soul, body or spirit, oft-labeled as mind, body or soul) the teaching points are:

1. Tag team wrestling: a bound person is pinned by at least one, most times seven or more spiritual opponents in an uncomfortable corner. Detailed analyses and fighting styles of your opponents, and your always-accessible tag-partner will follow.

2. Pharaoh's behavior before Moses is a class example as to how demon spirits behave when they are challenged to *let God's people go*. By the way, they will only let go a person after a prolonged fight. When demons or evil spirits find a place to rest, (Satan has given them permission to invade any captured territory) they will fight with superhuman strength to stay away from that place of everlasting torment (the pit). Every week when I am on missionary tours I hear them crying, begging, bargaining not to be sent to the place of everlasting torment. If they are so deathly afraid of that place, why should I be careless and allow them access to my temple?

3. Imagine yourself in a relationship where you had been the dominant partner. All of a sudden that other person decided to end things. At that point, those things that controlled your mental and physical urges (the spirits of lust, control and domination) would invite ANGER to join the gang, followed by the spirits of rejection, hate, rape, jealousy or murder. All that spirits seek is one small opening.

4. Another example is that of an addict trying to get rid of a particular habit. The intruding spirits are able to invade a human body to acquire tastes for such things as tobacco, addictive drugs, alcohol and body fluids. Arrested minds, compare similar bondage situations.

5. Attempting to escape a prison alive in North Korea without any assistance.

6. A slave attempting to run away from a plantation on his or her own without any help.

7. A conceited or proud person trying to come to grips with humility.

8. Trying to be good and live righteously always—even when you think no one is looking.

9. Wrestling a lion, bear, or elephant alone and without training.

10. Trying to win this victory and reclaim any altar permanently without the "*Ja-son Schematic, The Authority,* and *The Word,*" the weapons and their skillful uses: "The Name" plus *GODSPEAK,* and *PELICOSTICITY.* Don't try to find the last two in a dictionary. Dictionaries have limits. "GODSPEAK" is the supernatural utterance possible when your body has been rededicated as a temple of the living God and you beget the "Obedient Oracle Utterance." The Greek word "*PELICOST*" means spiritual reach.

When you have climbed Jacob's ladder and have reached the top, you have overcome. Let us examine the progression of an overcomer, King David. He overcame rejection, progressed through the wilderness, shepherding, through to overcoming lion and bear spirits, then on to defeating Philistine (territorial spirits). In 2nd Samuel 7:14, David as king, was able to offer acceptable sacrifice to Almighty God. In other words, you can become "Chosen for the Order of Melchizedek" (Psalm 110) to be both king and priest. Asking a person to undertake those tasks without any supervision could be a prescription for disaster for many reasons. The most obvious is the possibility of an avalanche of uncontrolled evil spirits and demons flying all over the place invading the nearest open altars.

Imagine Satan having overcome an elder, a choir member, a minstrel in God's house, or a man (of God), luring him to a house of prostitution at the very moment that someone (who may have been in a backslidden state) received my detailed instructions on self-deliverance. What do you think would happen the next time that person stepped unto the podium? The second reason is that after deliverance, people need proper counseling. A person recently delivered (a freed hostage) that had allowed himself or herself to fall back into doing or touching accursed things, his/her plight would be seven times worse automatically.

That process was very nicely described by one of Jeshua's *Firstfruit* witnesses named Matthew in his discourse entitled Matthew 12:43…When an evil spirit comes out of a person, it goes through arid places seeking a resting place, finding none, it says: *I will return to my former abode, now swept clean and unoccupied, and it taketh seven more wicked than itself.* The point here is that a person who got delivered or as secular people like to say exorcised, that person needs to be taught how to be strengthened and to be spiritually filled.

Imagine me being irresponsible and printing every detail. Here is a better example: picture someone in a hospital getting convicted and going through unsupervised deliverance. The person in the next room whose spiritual passages were open would suddenly undergo personality changes as all those expelled demons rushed into the first *open passageway.* Inexperienced deliverance ministries that witness in hospitals have reported cases whereby a roommate absorbed the traits of a person that died the night before. Remember the words of the song, not the way Nat Cole sang it, but the way it was originally intended, "Demons rush in, where angels don't go?" In Moses' first book, Genesis, Satan was called a serpent. Since he lost his initial "covering" he has been forced to protect his silver cord with temporary earth suits: he sheds his skin often. His best spirits bond best to wriggling things. The description also matches his primary personality, his crooked physical and spiritual movements, his behaviour, his wrestling style, his stalking prowess and his ability to fight better in dry places. He is able to slip through unlit crevasses and remain unseen for long periods of time. All wildernesses suit him.

This manuscript will examine the following sayings: 1. *There is one true way through the wilderness of life, one truth to the place of perfect peace, one achievable everlasting life.* 2. *There is only one name that provides the authority, the way, the truth and the life—the anointed one of God, the Messiah.*

CHAPTER 17B. OUR ELUSIVE ENEMY'S SECRET FILES!

People commit spiritual transgressions because they are totally ignorant of the functioning of the spiritual world. Some have had what they call "weird or strange experiences." Here are results of surveys on that matter. Millions of people believe that there are good dead people and bad dead people, but the same people that believe, do not want to understand what makes some die good or bad. It is one of Satan's great tricks, that of *Concealment*. Once, I thought of fasting and asking the Lord to allow the spiritual divide to be opened so that all people could get a peek into the spiritual world. However, as I climb the ladder of wisdom, I have come to realize how unwise that would be. Millions would die instantly from fright. Millions would suffer other maladies. One evening, as I prayed for a young man hooked on cocaine, I asked him if he wanted to see the cause of his addiction. He dared me. In retrospect it was a bit irresponsible of me. I prayed for the Lord to grant his request. To date I feel guilty for what transpired. His hair turned white immediately. The last time I saw him he was running through the main street of a city screaming like a maniac.

Another asset that helps Satan is that of *arrogant assumption*. In Leviticus 10:2, Aaron's sons, Nadab and Abihu were presumptuous enough to believe that because they were sons of a priest they could break God's law. The word of God could not be clearer: He is no respecter of persons. We assume that because we are intelligent, because we have money or power or some other ego-induced myth, we can do as we please without consequence. Here is a good example: "It is our body, and we can do what we like with it." They assumed that they could do as they pleased with God's Altar: Nadab and Abihu were consumed instantly. Three times the same transgression today translates into an iniquity. It can be passed on to the third and fourth generation: Exodus 34:7. Anyone with three or more different types of blood transgressions might experience any of the following:

1.   Unprovoked mood or vocal eruptions.

2.   Choking or being wrestled during sleep by a stronger force—Psalm 91:5 and Job 34:20.

3.   Strange and unusually loud and uncomfortable growling in the abdomen even when not hungry. All three are symptoms. The same repetitious horrible dreams and nightmares should not be taken lightly seemingly as you felt a thing much stronger than you pin you to your bed as it forced in more squatters.

So you thought repetitious nightmares were simply bad dreams? At the moment, some of you reading this awake frightened at nights sweating profusely. On your beds are open scissors to form crosses. Some even hang rosaries over open Bibles hoping that the intruders will go away. The territorial spirit had just visited you and received permission from Satan to send a squatter or more into the very wide spiritual opening beneath your altar. Your spiritual résumé indicated that you had been a gracious host/hostess to some of his previous visitors by your presumptuous lifestyles. Every time you experience a night terror, the head "Honcho" or territorial spirit paid you a visit. I can hear the legalistic and self-righteous asking for proof. Proverbs 3:24, "When thou liest down, thou shalt not be afraid: yea, thou shalt lie down, and *thy sleep shall be sweet*. Job 34:20, "In a moment, they (unrighteous men) *shall die and the people shall be troubled at midnight*, and pass away." In other words, if you are righteous you should not be troubled from your sleep *ever*. If any spirit "troubles" your rest, then overcome it like Jacob did. Those that teach "*Security of the Believer*," need to read Isaiah 1:28-31 and 1st Samuel 16:14. A man that God anointed and chose, fell into sin *thrice*. God's "Right Spirit" left Saul and an *evil spirit entered him*.

The first time a person commits an offence—that is a first strike warning or "*Conviction*." An alarm goes off in the spiritual domain. The third strike allows your most secret files to be ferried across "A.S.N or All Spirits Network." We watch television and observe recorded and live events. Relatives that have passed to "*the beyond*," instantly their spirits witness live films of your atrocities. Satan distributes your films and files and you are fair game for the host of darkness. Unfortunately your dead parents cannot warn you anymore. Left unrepented, those files are available for the entire spiritual world to view. Your "hedge of protection" is immediately removed; your spiritual insurance policy would then lapse—Job 1:10.

Double-minded persons use "Once saved always saved" to lure unsuspecting away with lust. If they were correct, Satan would not tempt Christians. God has a message for such: "Get away from me, I never knew you." One such very prim and proper female elder walked into a deliverance meeting. She chimed in "Devil get out in Jesus' name." The demon that watched her star in private erotic encounters replied from the girl's belly: "You better tell the married man that was by your house last night to get out!" How foolish some of us are! We sneak into remote hotel rooms; we switch off lights and function in the dark to conceal our deeds. *No act goes unseen or unnoticed. Similarly no disobedient act goes unpunished.* Many men reading this are scheduled to have prostate cancer as punishment for more than three *secret flings* with other men's wives, or for their sneaking and doing things with someone other than their wives. Numerous cases of breast cancer have already been prescribed for iniquities already committed. Those of you reading this know that if your grandparents were around to witness your sickening lifestyles they would vomit. Some are feeling a deep sense of disgust. Immediately repent and change, not tomorrow or the next day but now! There is a right way of obedience and a wrong way of doing things. The wrong way leads to hurt, sickness and or even untimely death. Some reading this *"became curious,"* as they say. Some did it because they foolishly felt that no one knew their secrets—Psalm 139:7-10. For instance, Lesbianism and Homosexuality are the biggest silent transfusion stations for demonic activities. Every forbidden exchange of body fluids is a license for penetration of spirits' eggs—they hasten lung, breast and throat cancers, ovarian cysts, menstrual complications, strange blood related allergies; prostate cancers, AIDS, and hosts of other physical, spiritual and psychological maladies. Before each exchange, there is multiplication then distribution. Now you understand why so many supposedly hot relationships fail. If the spirit of lust chose either you or your mate, then a carnal selection was made. Trying to blend and control so many complex spiritual variables on your own while Satan is giving orders is almost impossible. As soon as that spirit brings a prettier, richer, more intelligent or lustier person that injects fresh urges, your mate will flirt and invite more spirits. It is a matter of time.

Attractions, not "agape-spirit-motivated" will root spiritual eggs of disobedience, each possessing traits temporarily shared. At the moment of pairing, like personalities enjoy each other or contrary personalities exchange hate. When the boss of disobedience, Satan, gives the next orders, they have to obey. If the order given is to move on, to deceive, to hurt, to aggravate or to shatter, then so it has to be. Believe it or not, abortion, murder, lesbianism, sodomy and rape leave strong residual spirit matter. I have actually heard spirits use the mouths of their victims to boast that they entered through rape. Now if those things plague you, you are far away and you want to do something immediately, read Psalm 35, Psalm 70 and then call the numbers listed.

Strewn along every wilderness of "SIN" are numberless sand dunes of wisdom to direct the lost to the nearest oases of forgiveness and truth. The "Lost" must first acknowledge their hapless plights; then cry out to God for assistance like Jonah did. From the bottom of your hearts, desperately cry to your heavenly Father for help. Ask Him to steer you in the right direction for assistance. Avoid lukewarm, weak or spiritually dead churches. Find a church that understands spiritual warfare. Deliverance can only be achieved fully in churches where the power of God is manifest through "The Gifts of the Holy Spirit."

Mr. Beckles might be a wonderful pipe organ player but his music is "not" one of the "Gifts of the Holy Spirit." There are wonderful hymns written by English gentry, long laid to rest. The lyrical lines are beautiful. Unfortunately they are "Not" among the gifts listed in 1ˢᵗ Corinthians 12. My job is to ensure that in addition to Mr. Beckles' music, in addition to Charles Wesley's hymns, "The Gifts and the Power" of the Holy Spirit manifest in every "Zion-yoked" church. Psalm 33:2-3, *Praise the Lord …sing unto Him a **new song**; play skillfully with a loud noise.* So if the young people's experience can be sung as testimonies "I've been a football to sin, but I'll be kicked around no more," God will allow them to dance with all their hearts like David did. Whether it is salsa, mambo, jazz, reggae or rock, God is neither a respecter of persons nor persons' music styles. I know that the *Pharisee spirit* will rise up to upset Mrs. Peebles. She will threaten to leave with all the ladies that make cakes for sale; so what? We enjoyed your cakes Mrs. Peebles! We are saved by grace not by works: it is not by might or by power of any personality or cakes or music or church building but by God's Spirit that runs His things.

THE GIFTS OF THE HOLY SPIRIT (HEALINGS, MIRACLES, RAMA PROPHETIC WORD) AND THE AUTHORITY AND LORDSHIP OF JESUS THE MESSIAH ARE GOD'S TOOLS.

If your body was yours as you have foolishly thought, how come you can only make it respond to the things where you have been given the "Right to choose?" Tell your hair to grow or to stop growing. Command your mouth to be odor free if you leave it unwashed for three or more days. I dare you not to blink. Go find your own air to breathe since you are so independent. Go concoct your own fresh mixture of air, since all those "inferior people" have been polluting this one. Find some new types of blood to put in your veins that diseases will run from. So how come when you allow the spirit of *REBELLION* to make a "wheelie" in your mind you have to speak and do everything it tells you to?

Oft-times when I sit in courtrooms listening to arguments from people who seek permission to end their marriages, I feel a sense of pain, not only for what Satan did to that couple but the spiritual liabilities willed on their children. Assuming that half of the accusations leveled by one party against the other were true, millions of spirits of hate, rejection, anger, lust, adultery, "unforgiveness," greed, homosexuality, lying, theft, fornication and addiction are already entrenched in one or both parties. If for any reason one or both parents of contesting parties had similar experiences, then the children would be the third generation to attract the spiritual traits. Preachers in America, England, Europe, Africa, etc., rescue the young!

MASSIVE CORPORATE DELIVERANCE MEETINGS AND CRUSADES FOR THE HURTING YOUNG ARE NEEDED URGENTLY.

CHAPTER 17C. HABITS THAT KILL GENERATIONS.

I feel led to list some habits that kill. Everyone can make up his or her own list. What is the big deal? Let us stray over to the other parameters of untapped wisdom, OK? Are we friends at this point or do you hate my guts? It really does not matter. It is written in God's word: "You shall know the truth and the truth shall set you free." I will do much better than simply providing a list of habits that kill. I will produce a list of habits that kill generations:

1 . Ignorance and lack of true wisdom.

2 . Presumptuous beliefs without supporting or correlating facts, simply stated—guess-work.

3 . Self-hypnosis by "Obtuse Meglomanitis" blinded by indescribable egotism: Conceit.

4 . Philosophies from usurped altars.

5 . Climbing askew steeples: in other words living to be noticed, as in Matthew 6.

6 . Misusing or misunderstanding the purposes of our bodies, souls and spirits.

7 . Playing chess with Satan by wrestling the serpent in his wilderness.

8 . Living without the true schematic. In other words, if you are living outside the tenets of this schematic you are dying slowly.

9 . Having mixed up priorities.

10 . Mistaking the counterfeit spirit of Lust for the spirit of Agape Love and passing those iniquities to your children and children's children up to four generations unknowingly as per Exodus 34:6-7.

It is easier to fight a serpent or snake in a forest than in a wilderness. In a forest, the following are easily accessible: sticks, stones, water, and trees to hide behind. In an arid and desolate place you are thirsty, weak, moving with no cover and the chances of dehydration are very strong. No tangible weapons are allowed or available. The slippery one, the slimy one is more comfortable there. He is a patient stalker. We are to seek our Father constantly for fresh manna and for fresh refreshing. When Hagar and the lad Ishmael were sent into the wilderness, Hagar only had "*one bottle of water.*" She cried out to God and He answered her prayer because of the promise *given to the father of the lad.* She had no promised incubating anointing. The prayers of any church formed out of the womb of Hagar would receive answers because of the "Promise to Father Abraham." That one bottle of water represents the "*Refreshing Promise for all seed.*" On his first appearance before the birth of the lad, the angel told *Hagar to go back and serve Sarah.* If you want more spiritual water or you want to climb higher, you have to return to "The Veil of Victory" through the womb of Mary until you find the *one male branch* capable of grafting all of the redeemed. God put all of His spiritual springs in Jeshua—Psalm 87:7.

Whereas finite men engage in exercises of futile frivolity by verbally challenging God's authority, none have even attempted to challenge Satan for his job. To have kept his for so long, Satan has to be very good at his job. According to prophecy, until Jesus' arrival, Satan controlled the turf undeterred. After the builder left, Satan's anger and deception machine went into overdrive. That is why you are to guard your altars where you are bequeathed strength and where you have your spiritual rights. Regularly check your habits. Habits determine traits and your traits determine spiritual personalities. Since Satan's plans are to grab as much turf as possible, let us examine the turf. *He that has the turf decides the rules!*

VERY IMPORTANT NOTES:

1 . The enemy has been fighting harder and longer than you have been doing.

2 . He has (in the natural) more strength than an untrained person has.

3. He is far brighter and smarter than you are.

4. He has the files of all your generations, those of your parents and grandparents.

5. He knows all of your generational curses, iniquities and weaknesses.

6. Most people know very little about him. If they did, their marriages, children and countries would not be so messed up.

7. His *Secret Service* is better equipped than the CIA and the FBI combined. His infiltrating agents have penetrated families, friends, news media, politicians, churches, universities, temples, countries, plus institutions of prominence and power. Added to those are unguarded altars and minds also.

8. Over eons, not only has he been able to persuade most people on earth (especially leaders of governments) to sponsor and provide venues for his biggest parties (called wars) but also he has made them pay for all transportation, food and drinks.

9. The highway called "the mind" is patrolled 24 hours non-stop by his armies and satellites. They rest not and his arsenal is innumerable.

10. They access persons easiest through body fluids—forbidden sacrifices offered on altars that God (not man) decreed to be His holy altars.

This book was not compiled in the sequence in which it is presented. There will be times when it appears that material is being repetitious. Those seemingly repetitious data more than likely are abrasive solvents to replace myths cemented over years and paraded as truths. *My desire is to unravel every satanic foundation by documenting all foretold events of deception.* The information given above can be stated in one sentence: Those are things that the Occident has latched on to—fragments of civilizations that rose and fell, yet failed to rise above 30 degrees.

OUR UNDERWEARS ARE VEILS.

CHAPTER 17D. EXTRATERRESTRIALS, FACT OR FICTION?

A diagram or illustration is necessary at this point. We all probably know by now that each orbital mass and each planet has its own highway or orbital path. Through the boundaries that they traverse, each has its own prescribed lane, so they do not bump into each other. They have their own prescribed space and unique characteristics. Beyond the limits of their combined borders I refer to as the universal boundary. Everything in this system of things is confined to specific domains with specific rules. In addition to the next chapter, the chapter "Beyond the Boundaries of the Universe" will reveal the movements of intruding extraterrestrial beings, their footprints, booty and carnage on our earth over eons.

We have been fascinated with the media blitz regarding extraterrestrials. The spiritual realm is the abode of extraterrestrials. There are two armies: one under the command of The *Creator of the Universe* and *His Anointed Lord*, and the other under the command of Satan. I have had encounters with both. The first things I observed about Satan were his restlessness and his impatience. Here is a little secret: he is so afraid of powerful people of God that he harbours obsessive hate and anger towards them. Whether you choose to believe or not, you had better take this information seriously.

Satan's team can be likened to a group of selfish AIDS-stricken people that want everyone else to share their torment and woes. They know that they are on borrowed time. Whenever there are seed openings, extraterrestrials of the satanic kingdom either enter to maim, kill, steal, destroy, and/or to inflict with sicknesses. They ferry through occultism, masturbation, sexual intercourse, lesbianism, bestiality, incest, pedophilia, and tinkering with new-age objects. They also magnetize Ouija boards, homosexuality, abortion, rape, "unforgiveness," addiction, adultery, hate, murder, and or deliberate ingestion of other persons' body fluids.

Those on the other team function harmoniously through God's Holy Spirit to warn us, advise us, and to teach us. They contact people after repentance, through: (1) the Holy Spirit of God, (2) through baptism (washing for forgiveness) and (3) Jesus' unblemished sanctified blood. Those are the only three "materials" that reach from the earth to "touch" or bear witness to our Eternal Spirit Father. Only then can we receive supernatural "Power Gifts" from the "One" that designed this intricate clock. No dead—doctrine, saint, statue or thing—can touch our Living God. God's appointed Lord personally draws adepts into "The Veil."

The Romans asked Josephus Flavius to chronicle the history of the Jews just after they razed the city of Jerusalem (the first time) around 70 C.E. Though called a turncoat, he classified Jesus as a miracle-worker that founded a sect of "Nazarene Rebels." Josephus also wrote that Jesus' followers scattered after His death, confirming Isaiah 50:6 and Isaiah 53:2-7, "*They shall kill the shepherd* and *scatter his flock*." Also, Psalm 69 and 22 explained how and why He should suffer. The prophesied time is recorded in (Nehemiah 2:1) 69 weeks of years from Nisan (April- 450 B.C., to the year ending April 33 C.E.) until the Messiah will be cut off in the 70th week of years which happened in 33 C.E. Daniel 9:24-27, "From the going forth of the word to restore and rebuild Jerusalem until the Messiah…"

Take into account the fact that the Roman calendar had not been invented yet; so weeks of years meant multiples of seven years. Hence on the Sabbath of the 69th week of years meant less than seven times years: in other words, seven times seventy minus seven (7x70-7=483 years). Nehemiah's prophetic season began about 455 B.C. and ended round 420 B.C. I will not try to affix a specific time to his prophecy since I am not sure. What I do know is that they were using the Hebrew (Lunar calendar). My research revealed that the prophecy occurred in the 20th year of the reign of Artaxerxes. When Daniel was in Babylon with the Jewish exiles his record of events was based on the Babylonian calendar. Those Prophets from Judah (Jeremiah and Nehemiah) would record events using Hebrew calendars. For example, the cultural differences produced an alleged four-year disparity when they tried reconciling the calendars. The reason is simple. Judah became a province of Babylon in 620 B.C. four years after Nebuchadnezzar became king (624 B.C.) The king was also assigned co-regent of the annexed province. For example: First co-regent year (under Jehoiakim) would be 620 B.C. in the Hebrew records and 624 B.C. on the Babylonian calendar. Every prophet from Jerusalem that recorded events used the date of the Jerusalem commencement. Whatever the specific date, or whatever calendar was used, the Messiah should have come and left by the first 40 years of the 1st century. Hundreds of Jewish witnesses died rather than renounce Jesus. Most of the prominent witnesses (except John) were murdered.

Let us try to fathom Satan. He tried for centuries to eliminate the seed. Satan knows that mortal men die; so he made numerous attempts to kill Jesus. However when Jesus died, a strange thing happened: Jesus brought with His resurrection, the hope of every person—

chiefly the chosen and obedient ones. For hundreds of years prior, institutions of the Highest Learning ritualistically dramatized man's eternal dream of surpassing the cycles of life and death. Most sought images of the Temple of Solomon for guidance. The Egyptian Priest Kings and the early Greeks were obsessed with discovering the "path" for the transmigration of souls. They tried desperately and failed to discern it. Some nations attempted the passage physically and others philosophically. Indians and Chinese tried the approach mystically and ended up with millions of abandoned and usurped altars all over their countries. Early North and South Americans repeatedly tried with rituals also, and failed. In Central and South America, blood sacrifices to "Principalities" concealed beneath those grotesque images have caused their national altars to be stolen. Since the Temple of Solomon is regarded as the world's foremost structural enigma, this book will unveil its tri-dimensional seed nature. Everything it bore, good or bad would manifest physically, spiritually and prophetically.

About 2000 years ago, Satan faced his most serious problem. On the same land where he (Satan) had suffered his biggest defeats, up jumped a lad with both the genes of Levi and Judah in His veins. He resisted sin and overcame every evil spirit, including Satan. Since he could not overcome Jesus spiritually, he tried his last shot, a carnal approach in a deadly chess game. At that point, he knew without a shadow of a doubt that he had to start counting backwards. A human had just completed every possible Hebrew feast and transmuted their spiritual powers to all that followed His examples and teachings. With all his evil might Satan targeted Jesus' witnesses and pursued them with relentless venom. After three hundred years of trying to wipe them out, instead of their numbers diminishing, they kept increasing with more zeal than ever. Satan decided that since he could not defeat them, then he would join them. That is what he has done, and to date that has been his best shot.

God's ordained scapegoat sacrifice on **Mt. Moriah** (Zion) took on special importance with the first substitution of "a lamb for Isaac, Abraham's first son." According to God's law of duplicity, a "Better Substitution" would have had to be made. Jesus was planted on a cross on the same **Mt. Moriah**. God allowed David's son to build His physical house on earth. God spoke through His prophets: "Out of Egypt have I called my son." "Thou art my Son, this day have I begotten thee." That is a very powerful revelation. Prophetically, David wrote in Psalm 2:6... Yet have I set my King on my **Holy Hill**, Zion. David would never have been presumptuous enough to assume that meant him. God sent Jeshua to "Repair the Breach" in Isaiah 53. Demons had badly breached and taken over so many physical and spiritual bodies that they had most of the earth in bondage. Readers, in response to your question: "You mean to tell us that the writer is thinking that some beings are trying to take over our bodies, minds and even our civilizations?" I have news for you. The costume designers and screenwriters in Hollywood are pretty close. In many cases "The Body Snatchers" have already invaded. "By and large there are billions in the spiritual world. Though mainly confined to the realm of the unseen (called invisible by many) at times they manifest ethereally and or in the forms of diseases."

Jesus exited as prophesied. He then released "Purim Power" to His first fruit witnesses. Today, when the schematic is applied, "Redeemed Man" has the same power to cast out all demons, to take authority over them and to determine their fate—most importantly. God is a God of order. Under His universally prescribed laws, "Dominion over Earth" was given to man. Extraterrestrials cannot function powerfully on earth except through "earthly vessels," not *spacecrafts*. Would God, who is an extraterrestrial, violate His own laws? When Jesus came in the flesh to redeem all lost territory for all generations, Satan took the opportunity to invite Jesus to his strongest domains: places where he had been winning and winning. He tried reverse psychology in the "desert." Would it not have been a permanent feather in Satan's kingdom, if through pride, Jesus had allowed Satan to usurp His authority as "The Bread of Life," by responding to Satan's first chess move? How about Satan's second move: Coveting the exalted place, the "Steeple of Wisdom, Truth and Understanding?" The third move was an all time classic to assume that all men who tread on earth are limited in focus just to the visible kingdoms. Since then, Satan hates Jesus with such a passion that given any chance, a demonized person will be highly perturbed at the mere mention of Jesus' name.

CHAPTER 17E. THE FIRST ALIEN INVASION?

Before God created the earth, spirits (sons of God's Agape Spirit) never saw a human body. A transient quarantine station was designed with positive and negative principles (time and energy mechanisms) called earth. When spirit men saw a woman for the first time, God's Agape was usurped by Lust. Since then spirits have licenses to invade body temples through body fluids that carry the nuclei of life—Genesis 6:2. Without that precedent, Jesus could not have been born through Mary.

Spirits are not terrestrial beings; they are extraterrestrial. I wish that Hollywood would use their correct names "Evil Spirits," instead of such euphemistic terms as space aliens and monsters. Satan was an anointed cherub before his fall. *He is an intruding alien!* Each domain has prescribed laws and boundaries. During Moses' challenge to Pharaoh, we observed Satan's access to certain types of crawling and creepy things on earth. Man, created for earth, was given dominion over the earth. Since pre-Edenic men can touch and contact humans, Satan was, and is able to sow "carnal knowledge and carnal seed"—in Eve and any willing human—up to this day (Genesis—3:7, 4:1, and 19:5). Eve's nuclei of life exchanged over an altar of disobedience allowed Satan a fair exchange. Since Eve did not guard her altar, he seduced his way by building a spiritual highway whereby access through body fluids is gained up to this day. I cannot but wonder if any part on man's anatomy reflects the original serpent-like personality of Satan. That one-eyed serpent look-alike is still spewing much sought-after body fluids as food for the bold and ugly. Whenever humans are careless with gifts from our Spirit Creator, any other spirit can pursue and or steal them. Any carelessly discarded semen will be stolen. To this day, the wiggle that he first taught Eve is the biggest exchange centre for disobedient eggs. Some hatch in the form of "incurable diseases." Others, in the form of worms and maggots await our sleep in death to have the rest of us—Genesis 3:14. Tadpoles, wrigglers, baby reptiles and semen have much in common. Their gestation periods are influenced by the moon's cycle. They are nourished in liquid before enlarging themselves on earth.

Numbers 13:33 is a perfect case study to enlighten us that spirits prefer earthen human vehicles to cruise around in. So many people have allowed their vehicles to be stolen that Satan and his team cruise around neighborhoods in stolen vehicles appearing quite humanly. He has many to choose from. Check the attitudes of some of the people you come in contact with daily. Goliath spirits are still around. I encounter them functioning as territorial spirits. Take an educated guess as to the spirit types he has assigned to many past and current world leaders? Satan, their Commander-in-chief, is assigned a quasi-permanent position on earth: man's accuser or *The Accuser of the Brethren.* In Revelation 9:1-20, Satan's legacy was prophesied and published. People need to pay attention to the messages contained in Ephesians 6:12. Paul advised us that in this spiritual war, we are not fighting against flesh and blood, but against wicked alien spirits.

Satan's armies are loaded with two main missile types "Spilled Blemished Blood" and "Stored up or pent-up bad blood." Blemished are fornication, adultery, masturbation, incest, murder, homosexuality, pedophilia, abortion, and witchcraft. Pent-up blood turns bad and blemished through anger, theft, "unforgiveness," hate, addiction, lust, rebellion, dishonesty and more. Daniel's vision of the "Beast" enlightened us to their base at Babel and strongholds in Babylon, Persia, Rome, and beyond. In Revelation 12:7-9, John received a peek at the first alien war between Michael and God's angels and Satan and his ungodly armies. In verse 8, John shared with us God's intolerance for sin, rebellion and evil in heaven. Though the defeated Satan was cast out, God removed neither his strength nor his power. God does not give gifts and take them back. In verse 17, John shared with us another of Satan's obsessions—to destroy the Church of the Messiah with falsehoods, lies, rebellions, counterfeits and sin.

CHAPTER 17F. THE RECLAIMED SCEPTER/BRANCH.

Moses recorded one of the most important prophecies in Genesis 49:10. The scepter of Judah, the symbol of the most powerful authority on earth (not some mythical lance of invincibility that Grail Seekers are pursuing), "shall not depart from Judah until Shiloh come; and unto him shall the gathering of the people be." That scepter cloaked with invincibility shall not be removed until Shiloh's visit. In other words, the seat of power that Satan is forever after will be entrusted to the tribe of Judah only, until the arrival of the Redeemer. That tribe was either concealed or destroyed by 70 C.E. God conceals a remnant always.

The lineage given in Psalm 87 indicates that only Jeshua, son of Mary qualifies to be the son of the virgin that fulfilled over 300 prior prophecies. That prophecy has another part. The custody of the real spiritual things of the most coveted altar shall not be with any other *than that seed of Judah*. Let us look at Psalm 49:10, "…Nor a lawgiver from between his feet, until Shiloh the Messiah come. Shiloh shall the gathering of the people be." That rod (branch) chosen to be the scepter of authority had to be uniquely carved. The tree from which the branch was chosen could only spring from Jerusalem, not Mecca, not India, not Rome or China because the only wood allowed within the Holy of Holies in the Temple of Solomon was the "Olive" from Jerusalem. It is the only tree or "èts" that can be grafted, bruised, cut, gashed severely and remain for long periods of drought and "not die."

It has the ability to be reborn. Whoever grafts into that *Special Branch*, will receive the power from the scepter as soon as they meet the requirements. By now it should be so obvious why Satan and all his earthly operatives consistently target the remnant of Judah. Be that as it may, my eternal Father is a warrior. To give us an insight into that aspect of His personality, God revealed one of His titles to us: *JEHOVAH SABAOTH*. Literally that means *God of Armies*. He is tired of wimpy children allowing thieves to steal their meals, their wisdom and their riches. Here is the deal. I am going to be direct as I possibly can. No more repairers! God sent judges, kings, earthly priests, and collectively they failed. The boss is angry. He sent His Son to retrieve all that was stolen. He left us a schematic. No more free lunches! Fight the good fight and redeem what is yours. If the spiritual treasures were not worth fighting for, Satan and his zillions of evil spirits and demons would not dedicate a full time 24-hour army to hunt them. Until Jeshua visited us to restore all usurped altars, Satan and his team had the upper hand. Since the *Conquering Lion of Judah* reclaimed the scepter of Judah, Satan's anger is kindled even hotter against all remnants of Judah. In Jeremiah 4:16 and 17 we learned that he assigned his most powerful spirits "the watchers" or "Fellers" against all ancient altars that should have been *guarded by Judah*. Those are the same spirits that were kicked down to earth with Satan. Take it from the writer who has met and fought them. They are persistent, but no match for the "Power" accessed through the "Unblemished Blood" of Jeshua. There are numerous nations with both concealed and exalted ceremonial altars. Unless those altars are uprooted—through corporate reception of the Messiah's redemption package and *National Days of Prayer and Fasting*—those nations' spiritual power bases belong to Satan. He is free to send pestilences, war, storms, famine, drought, diseases and malnutrition as long as they are vanquished.

Priests came from the tribe of Levi and kings from the tribe of Judah. David had the plans for building God's temple. Solomon built it. David was a king who performed priestly functions and was not killed for doing so. Let us examine God's law of Duplicity for the tree first, then the "Branch Chosen to be grafted." In Genesis 2:9 there are different types of trees: a) tree that was pleasant to look at, b) good for food, c) tree of knowledge of good and evil, and d) tree of life. That last tree "E^ts of Life," with seed to reproduce after its kind, was planted in the "Adamy" ground and every seed on earth evolved out of that tree. Genesis 1:12 refers to "The Tree," yielding sustenance whose seed was "in itself," (after his own kind). Since then, all earthlings sprouted from a seed planted by The Creator and are related.

Let us look for God's confirmation: Psalm 80:15, "And the vineyard which thy right hand hath planted and the branch that thou madest strong for thyself." To discover that which God planted in the vineyard, we must refer back to verse 8. Verse 8, "Thou hast brought a vine out of Egypt," not Europe. Verse 9, "Thou hast cast out the heathen and planted it. Thou preparedst room before it and caused it *to take deep root, and it filled the land.*" Zechariah 3:8, "Behold I bring forth my servant the Branch" (whose name is coded in the Tanakh). Zechariah 6:12, "Behold the man whose name is *THE BRANCH* and he shall grow up out of his place and he shall build the Temple of the Lord." Verse 13, "He shall build 'The Temple of the Lord' and *he shall bear the glory*, and shall sit and *rule upon his throne*; and he shall be a **priest upon his throne**: and the counsel of peace shall be between both."

Kings are assigned to rule. Would God allow a priest to rule His kingly office? Observe this man/branch; obviously He will be a natural and spiritual *carpenter*. He will be a king, allowed to function as a priest. He will build God's spiritual house from spiritual seeds implanted in Him. Zechariah wrote the prophecies long after David died. Then after Malachi there was a four hundred-year silence until John the Harbinger arrived in the wilderness of Judea. Over 300 prophecies stated that the "Branch" must be rejected, despised and smitten. Naturally, wherever the remnant of "Judah" lay hidden or concealed, they *MUST BE DESPISED SMITTEN AND REJECTED ALSO*. All natural branches of a particular tree must have at least some similarities to the main branch. Let us assume that the rejection of the Messiah had not been prophesied, then 400 years after Malachi, plus the 600 years to Mohammed would make *14 generations of silence*. Any wise Hebrew or custodian of the altar must have perceived that period. It could not pass unnoticed. All over Europe and Asia, churches were erected with altars paying homage to a female European as mother of a god. Statues were also placed on altars of churches in God's Holy Land. That sacrilege happened once before when Athalia sat on the seat of power in ancient Israel. In the ensuing period, desolation followed. In 622 C.E., 1000 years after Malachi, the only person of influence (seed of Abraham) to command an *army* over the very regions that Solomon once reigned was Mohammed. He was *not the Prince of Peace*, but became an army commander. Even Prophet Mohammed walked in God's Law of Duplicity.

After Sarah died, Abraham took another wife named Keturah. Keturah and Abraham's grandson was Sheba. According to Israel's predictive history, the relationship between the Queen of Sheba and Solomon, *and the seed that they bore* after *Solomon's physical Temple was built*, established the precedent for a religion to be born by Abraham's seed after the Messiah had built His spiritual house on earth. The African Orthodox, Rastafarianism, and Islam had to commence after the Messiah laid the foundation for God's spiritual house. In other words those religions could not have been born until *after the Messiah's first visit*. Since neither Keturah nor Sheba's queen were chosen seed incubators, none of those later religions could have been God's restorative brides. Isaiah told us that a human olive would suffer so that all righteous persons would be grafted into Him.

WHY ARE WE PORTRAYING A WIMPY-LOOKING EUROPEAN AS THE BRANCH?

Isaiah 50:6—He would be spat on and His hair torn and "thorned"...I gave my back to the smiters, and my cheeks to them that plucked off the hair: I hid not my face from the shame of the spitting. Matthew 27:30-31...and they spit on him...and mocked him. Isaiah 53, the process of the branch being cut and bruised, wounded, rejected, and led like a lamb to be slaughtered was prerecorded in precise detail. Verse 2 previewed...His growth from the ground as a tender shoot until the grafting was completed. The scepter is secure at the right hand of the altar of the Most High. Bow (humble yourself) and kiss the signet ring of the son of the king. Psalm 2...Kiss the Son, lest He be angry and ye perish from the *Way*... Blessed are they that put their trust in him.

JESUS' RESURRECTION WAS WITNESSED 1000 YEARS PRIOR IN PSALM 68.

Psalm 68:18, "Thou hast ascended on high, thou hast led captivity captive." Whenever you pray, if your altars are weak or taken over when you try to access the Father, it is the same as a person with a flashlight with dead batteries trying to signal an aeroplane overhead. He knows you are down there but His laws are the same. He is fed up and tired of rescuing His children only for them to return to the same things over and over again. We have been given the fight manual. Acknowledge: "We are more than conquerors" through His Son, Christ the Anointed one. Remove the erosion from the contact points. Recharge your batteries. Let your light so shine before men (animals, places or beastly things) that they may see your good works and glorify your heavenly Father. Prove it!

CHAPTER 17G. STARS OF THE TIMES VS. STAR TIME.

We place stars on a pavement in Hollywood. I have met persons that would pay (if they could) to have their star on the ground among those human stars in the "City of the Angels." I heard a commentator say without remorse "They are bigger than life." In the 10,000 years of documented history that is available for scrutiny, there is only one person whose entrance, temporary exit and life story is written in the heavens. Balaam was in a trance and proclaimed in Numbers 24:17, "I shall see him, but not now: I shall behold him, but not nigh: there shall come a *Star out of Jacob*, and a *Sceptre shall rise out of Israel*." A star heralded His arrival, Matthew 2:2; His temporary exit was ushered in by darkness: Luke 23:44. People need not look on any pavement to see His star, but within self or in a mirror. You will either see His light, or your preferred darkness.

Now folks let us be real. We line up for hours for an autograph from persons that make their livelihoods pretending that they are other people. Like any other profession, not all actors and actresses are wonderful humans. People adore them mainly for the inspiration, real or imaginary that they provide. Millions prefer illusions to reality. In the sports arena, wonderful men and women run after balls for a living. The subliminal chase, I assume, causes people to adore them to the point of worship. I have yet to see a ballplayer that causes the clouds to condense into rain to flow into the rivers or the rivers to flow into an ocean made salt so that it does not evaporate quickly. Slow evaporation without the salt leads pure water back to the clouds to the rain to the rivers again and again. I have yet to see an actress make a planet for the people they love with just the right mixture of air (nitrogen/oxygen etc) for us to breathe. We then breathe out carbon dioxide. Plants are allowed to breathe in carbon dioxide during the daytime and release oxygen when we are most active and to reverse the process at night. I have seen gods of stone; they cannot hear. They have never healed anyone and never sent a moral code. Some have to be invoked with "Bo or Bu" -ing. Thousands never uttered nor can they utter one word: yet people build elaborate shrines and altars to them. Trust me, no altar goes to waste. I operated a bar for years. Any woman that came in and got drunk to drown sorrows and casually hinted at carnal needs, "volunteers always were available."

It is my hope that altar-custodians in hundreds of countries will use the information contained in this discourse:

1. To begin a 24-hour worldwide watch in 2005 as a preamble to Numbers 29:1.

2. To have a worldwide month of confessions, forgiveness and reconciliatory prayers.

3. To share with the world how to retrieve all treasures and altars taken by Satan.

4. To reveal to all seekers of truth that if, through repentance and obedience we return to our rightful places, we can reclaim the power of the one true *Light of the World*. Instead of being temporary stars of the time, we can usher in a new season of "stars time."

In Moses' books, extraterrestrials (angels of Genesis 6:2 and 4) mated and accessed humans through body fluids. If Satan and other fallen (sons of Spirit God) can mate daughters of the sons of men, the most powerful Spirit God, must be able to produce the mightiest man. Why is it difficult to grasp that our all-knowing Spirit God can either speak things into existence or to bond to humans through cleansed body fluids? How do you think babies are born? The life seed was planted in the first garden where God gave the original command. It is still producing fruit: some obediently and in others disobediently, all carrying the traits of their fathers. Are we to assume that God has put limitations on what is possible or not? Isn't it written that with God, all things are possible?

He even fixes the clock. There is a famous saying: *Time and tide wait for no man*. Do you agree with that statement? Here is something to ponder. Since the moon affects tides, and time can only be adjusted outside the clock, anyone who can adjust the mechanisms of this "Universal Clock" had to have been trained by the maker himself. He must have received the schematic from the maker personally. Let us look at what direct witnesses had to say. Witnesses were fishermen, tax collectors and simple people, who had no background in astronomy or science. Mathew 8:24-26, "There arose a great tempest in the sea… (26) Then he arose and rebuked the winds and the sea; and there was a great calm." Mark 4:37, "There arose a great storm." Verse 39, "Peace be still, and the wind ceased and there was a great calm." Luke 8:23-25, "There came down a storm of wind on the lake…and they were in jeopardy… (25)…what manner of man is this! ...He commandeth even the winds and water and they obey Him." In the Psalms, David prophesied that it would happen—Psalm 107:29...He *maketh* the storm a clam; so the waves thereof are still. Notice that David did not use past tense. Mountains of evidence confirm that Jesus was and is superhuman. Comic book writers used esoteric references to mimic His super powers for years. They always portrayed Him rescuing the sick, helping the poor: subliminally they showed Him flying. As entertaining as they intended to make His sublime character, Leech Lucifer could only bruise His heel (in other words only cause temporary annoyance). Prior to the global deluge in the time of Noah, evil spirits (seed of the first alien invasion) had taken over, not only human vehicles, but their sacrifices also. By applying esoteric carpentry, preserved writings in Uxmal and Inca/Aztec edifices attest to such. A remnant of Noah's seed defeated an ancient spirit man, Goliath of Gath. Following the Davidic bloodline and the promises for Isaac's covenant seed, Jesus not only fulfilled over 300 prior prophecies and was born within precise prophetic timelines but also He taught us how to overcome Satan and all Goliaths.

A survey was once passed out to many college campuses asking which person that lived had the greatest impact on our way of life. Who was the greatest teacher? Who was the greatest philosopher? I could include: Which person do evil spirits fear the most? What shocked us all was the gap between the points Jesus got compared to those others mentioned. Before Jesus arrived on the scene, time was recorded as B.C. Since His first exit, time is recorded as C.E., or A.D; every Jubilee year after His first exit, Roman calendars synchronize with the Hebrew calendar.

What in heaven or in earth could let time and tide wait on, cater to and respond to? Obviously no ordinary human being could accomplish that. This man is not only unusually "awesome" but also the mere mention of His name strikes *terror* into the entire *Kingdom of Darkness*. Might he be the "Light of the world?" I hope that one day you get to meet someone, who has been *delivered* or (after being cleansed) you witness the *deliverance* process. After the experience, either of two things might happen: You might be scared out of your wits, or you will understand who or what Jesus means to us in these latter-day battles. Remember when the quarterback is on the line with one yard to go, whom do you call? That's the answer: Jeshua, the demon buster. When that "Light" is turned on, those who behaved like, and talked like they were tough are instantaneously reduced to wimps.

CHAPTER 18. SERIOUS FOUNDATIONAL ERRORS.

CHAPTER 18A. REMOVE ALL LEAVEN!

You might ask at this point, "How come churches never brought us to this level before?" Answer the question yourselves by analyzing the following scripture: *All (not some) have sinned and come short of the Glory of God.* Believe it or not, power corrupts and blinds many supposedly sensible people. It is amazing how many pastors, preachers and elders forget that God knows and sees everything. We are accountable for every spoken word and every action or inaction.

Haven't you observed men on TV, standing on an altar of self-righteousness refusing to forgive President Clinton? They need to read Leviticus chapter 25. Satan uses the vehicles of radio, television, and the pregnant pauses during sermons, when preachers leave the anointing to express "their opinions," to his full advantage. Railings, speaking badly against God's people, (other denominations) self-righteousness, pride and exaggerations for ratings sake are unleashed oft-times. Be cautioned that radio and television are not sanctified altars; they are secular media used by men and women of God for "Kingdom Purposes," sometimes.

Preachers, you are responsible for every act, every word spoken or delivered on that medium during your broadcasts. Then again, Rebekah had character blemishes. There is a kinsman redeemer. Even though some behave as though the seeds, the land, the vineyard (the church) the water (the anointing) and the flock (congregation) belong to them, the earthly shepherds are corporately responsible for the flock of each territory.

Moses was responsible for the sheep of his father-in-law. David was responsible for the sheep of his father. When the chief shepherd arrives, all pastors will be responsible collectively for the entire flocks of their nations. Jeremiah 50:6, "My people have been lost sheep; *their shepherds* have caused them to go astray." Observe who is held accountable! There are differences between those that "Can and those that are Able." Genesis 4:1-4. The (i) in Cain is silent. God foreknew that Americans would pronounce can as Cain. Those that behave like Cain are those who *can*. Those that behave like Abel are able. Hence the origin of the term "able-bodied." Bear in mind that God is Able, so to be Abel or Able is to be like God, in spirit and in truth.

Cain took some of his produce to God (as if he was doing God a favor). Abel took the first and the best to God. Those that are "Able" offer their first and best to God always. They press the right buttons; say and do the things that are pleasing to God. When God saw that Abel took the purest, the fattest and the one without blemish, Daddy must have smiled and said "This son has the mind of dad." He picked the image of the Fleece. Take into account that of all the millions of animals and creatures that God made, only four were deemed worthy for the sacrificial offerings in Leviticus chapter 1.

There are subliminal personality connections to the animals selected. The turtledove equates to modest, genuflecting types of preachers; the bull represented the confident charismatic preacher-types; the sure-footed goat can survive in arid and desolate places like most missionaries and street pastors, and then the gentle and obedient sheep. However all the blood (the carnality) had to be removed on the sacrificial altar.

Similarly God allows no leaven on His sacred altars. Exodus 12:19, "Whosoever eateth that which is leavened, even that soul shall be cut off." Also in Psalm 24:3, "Who shall ascend into the hill of the Lord, or who shall stand in His holy place?" Verse 4, "He that hath clean hands and a pure heart, who hath not lifted up his soul to vanity, nor sworn deceitfully:" (In other words those that are not living a lie). Galatians 5:9, "A little leaven leaveneth the whole lump." Judas knew, and worked with Jesus. Where is he now? Satan was an anointed cherub. In short he knows music, has his strengths, and maintains strongholds in music-connected entities. Whereas in David's era God's chosen warriors had to fight physically, the Messiah (referenced in the Tanakh) gave us new weapons of spiritual warfare. His witnesses like Simon and Paul recorded those accounts in Bibles: records of everlasting battles (greed, hate and envy) with a corrupt spiritual lawyer over a family's inheritance for the seed of Abraham: a bastard, an adopted and a spoilt rebellious child. I would suggest that you seek guidance and instructions before trying to master those new weapons.

One month ago, I walked into a church where the congregation was expecting me. The father of a youngster met me in the parking lot and asked me to hurry to the back office: the pastor needed me urgently. An usher relayed the same message. I went to his office and was asked by the pastor to help with a situation that began manifesting just as the praise began. He had to get ready for his sermon and did not want either the youngster who was a famous rock musician or his father who was very prominent, to be embarrassed. Very soon a demon began crying from inside the lad's belly in a really wimpy voice saying that he had helped the lad so much with numerous hit songs. He bragged that he had a good relationship with the lad; they had composed hits together and that he had planned to take the lad to the top of his art. I have encountered situations where the indwelling intruder *pretends* to display a liking for the person. Consider this fact: evil spirits have to obey their boss. Pastors do not be fooled by such antics. Allow no compromises. Within minutes, that formerly pleading demon began wrestling the youngster until the musician called the name of Jesus and His expressed mission on earth. "For this purpose was the son of God manifest to destroy the works of the evil one." That thing began choking the youngster.

Thank God he was not alone and in the midst of members of his church who had prior experience with deliverance. I would like to believe that the experience strengthened them. The victory was swift. I was due to leave the country the next day. I delayed for a week. The father was very happy and assured me that the lad was much better. The experience brought him, his wife, in fact all his family back to obedience. He renounced having sought satanic altars for help in acquiring his position of prominence. He then confessed all of his sins and the ancestral iniquities. Back to the question: "Why has this wisdom been blocked?"

Many an institution has had their light partially or fully blocked. Let us go right to the foundation error. It was God's intention to offer Israel a Theocracy, an unfailing loving God, giving leadership and providing perpetual blessings. Instead, Israel asked for a king like those of other nations. That was the biggest mistake ever made in the history of humankind, in my humble opinion. God's chosen wanted (and still want) to sit on a seat of power *giving instructions* that "they believe are from God," instead of *receiving* God's direct instructions. Some say brazenly, "God is my co-pilot."

CHAPTER 18B. BE CAREFUL WHAT YOU PRAY FOR!

Saul was Israel's first King. He allowed the kingly altar to be corrupted so badly after he visited a "Witch at Endor," laying the foundation for future "Kings and Rulers" of Israel's 12 Tribes to strengthen ties between the altars of divination and their exalted offices. Satan loves power. He enjoys manipulating and possessing rich, influential and powerful persons. Saul became "possessed with an evil spirit." It was David that chased away the evil spirit from Saul by playing his anointed harp. Saul also had spirits of envy, hatred, wrath and other squatters in him. Saul widened the doorway for Satan to advise God's anointed rulers. Here is something noteworthy. Jonathan, Saul's first son was born when his father was packed with demons. Satan figured that he had to put enough in Saul so that when his son became King he would be well fortified. Satan cannot read minds nor does he know God's plans. He knows scriptures and prophecies very well and he is good at meddling.

God had another plan. He had David anointed king. He first had David brought to Saul's house as Saul's understudy. Jonathan paid homage to David. Even though Jonathan was Saul's son, he loved David like his own brother. Even though Jesus was not Joseph the carpenter's son, Jesus' brothers like Jonathan happily served Him. Saul first loved David like his own son (first fruits of adoption of non-natural sons for the kingly office) before Satan's demons moved in. All Christians should read the entire chapter of 1st Samuel 15.

God had offered Israel a Theocracy whereby he would teach esoterically-deficient and finite men how to function in 360-degree wisdom potential. Israel asked instead for a conquered altar called kingship. "Give us a king like the other nations." They got Saul. In some African and Caribbean nations, locals have a saying to describe people who are "Unlucky." They say those persons are "Sauled." Disobedient is more appropriate. Your church boards are kingly offices and as such are prone to the advances from intruders. It is obvious that Satan has penetrated many.

I WOULD NOT LIKE TO REHASH THE PERSONALITIES OF THOSE THAT GRIN AND SMILE IN PUBLIC; YET THEIR PRIVATE LIVES ARE CONTROLLED WILDERNESSES.

Let us examine the words of Jeshua himself with regards to the times and the places from whence grafts should be made. Luke 24:46-53, Jeshua told His disciples that the *preaching* must commence in *Jerusalem in the temple.* The branch would have to be chopped from the Jerusalem temple tree, and planted in the earth for an appointed time. How then could any Christian church teach that the foundation of which Jesus himself said *began in Jerusalem* could have been in a city different from Jerusalem? Is there another counterfeit foundation? Since that church postulates its infallibility, we will have to examine that foundation statement carefully. The Book of Moses, Abraham and David is specific "ZION." Luke 24:46, the words of Jeshua himself, "Thus it is written and thus it behooved Christ to suffer and to rise from the dead the *Third Day;* and that repentance and remission of sins should be preached in his name among all nations, *beginning at Jerusalem.* 48...ye are witnesses of these things." Jeremiah 23 promises serious woe for bastard sheep and adopted shepherds that sow seeds of envy, hate and strife by teaching that God abandoned His people. Jeremiah 23:1, "Woe unto the pastors that destroy and scatter the sheep of my pasture."

The Olive Tree, when grafted, has to be nourished. If the graft then is per prophecy and according to the purposes of God, then no man, beast or thing can destroy His vineyard. Jeremiah 23:2-8 and Isaiah 35:1-10 wrote prophetically as to how the "Restoration" would take place. Any branch that is either disconnected or withered would be pruned. Confirmation can be found in Jesus' words noted in John 15:1, "I am the true vine, and *my Father is the husbandman*. 2) Every branch *in me* that beareth *not* fruit he taketh away: and every branch that beareth fruit he purgeth it, that it may bring forth more fruit."

The Lord has a chosen place and a "Chosen Branch" not many chosen places, nor many chosen branches. It is not Rome, Paris, San Francisco or New York. Isaiah prophesied even John's ministry. Read Isaiah 40:3. The schematic of Solomon's Temple allows us to highlight "Babel Slants" in religious institutions, nations and families. Proverbs 28:13 is specific: "He (priest, pastor, president, pope, parent or pagan) that covereth his sins shall not prosper." Pride, conceit, arrogance and self-righteousness are sins that plague persons that occupy seats of power. Regrettably, time constraints and lack of space allow me to select a few case studies only.

The contents of Isaiah 38:18 should destroy the myth that "Purgatory" is a place where the plight of dead people can be changed, after the fact. All those that teach such need serious prayers. Here is a small unselfish seed for all assemblies that really yearn for the truth. First pray for the peace of Jerusalem; then create a spiritual hot-link with the remnant that is responding to their prophetic calling. I will leak no secrets save to disclose that "The remnant of roughly 10,000 pastors and flock," the seed from at least 6 tribes are responding to prior prophecies. The Lord is specific in Isaiah 52 verses 7, 8 and 9. Verse 9, "Break forth into Joy; sing together ye waste places of *JERUSALEM*, for the Lord hath comforted his people, he hath redeemed *JERUSALEM*."

CHAPTER 18C. SATAN'S ARMY EXPOSED!

I need to do a dossier, a spiritual profile on Satan's army. Satan has so many spirits in his army that he does not handle every situation himself. He goes after certain types of big fish: those that can influence millions by their lifestyles and their powerful positions. By now you should have an idea where the concept of brainwashing originated. Here is insight into the structure of *his network*. Our minds are spiritual highways. There are spirits that constantly tempt you to say or to do things that merit punishments. There are others that will inflict your bodies and your circumstances when access is granted. All of them are under orders.

Every person, family or institution of power has at least two altars to safeguard and to protect. The national altar or podium of power is the nation's collective voice that speaks corporately into the spiritual world. The language of your moral code and the contents of your constitution translate into spiritual declarations. There are spirits that attach themselves to things and places. There are territorial spirits that take up command posts when the national altars of countries become weakened.

Space does not lend itself to showcase every nation's altars. Four locations: Israel, Rome, America and Africa will be used as case studies. As their spiritual battles are dramatized in these volumes, bear in mind that the purpose of this expensive exercise is not to cast blame, but to *repair Breaches*. Use those examples to wage spiritual warfare for your nations' altars. Plan annual days of prayers and fasting.

Muslims refer to evil spirits as Jinn. The difference between what we call *evil spirits* and *demons* is that the primary mission of a demon is to find an empty abode, inhabit it and to invite in as many minor or like spirits as possible. So a demon is a division commander. Spirits are assigned to places or things. They can attach themselves to any contact point where body fluids and secret potions were secreted. They bond easily to pendants that have been treated on satanic altars. Certain works of art that have occult symbols or messages are bonding agents also. Here is a shocking piece of news. A Rosary does not break a curse or a satanic attachment. I have witnessed cases whereby people hang them around their necks and in their homes to no avail. Only repentance first, plus Jesus' sanctified sacrificial blood, deemed acceptable to God (applied in faith) will redeem you.

The most common and most successful of his spirits are: spirits of *Pride, Vanity* and *Lust.* Those are group spirits. Lust for power, position and money; Lust for body fluids of fornication, rape, incest, adultery, masturbation, lesbianism, pedophilia, homosexuality, and evil conspicuence—all are in the same group. To persons who are actively involved in Deliverance Ministries, always mention "all those under the domain of the group names," and call out the categories. When conducting deliverance, *DO NOT BE IN A HURRY.* The person might be in pain and discomfort. Remember they took years getting themselves tangled up, so it takes time to unravel them. Next, treat the rope marks and then go after the *Roots of sins.* Do you recall Nebucadnezzar's infamous dream? Even though the tree (Babylon) was destroyed "its roots remained in the earth." In the 18th Chapter of Revelation, we find that the same root could be dislodged with a double measure of violence only.

All sins are punishable eventually. There are two main types of punishments for sins according to their categories: one of Reaction and the other of Delayed Action, the parent category for a prescribed time period of accumulated unrepentant actions.

1.   "DELAYED ACTION OR SUSPENDED SENTENCE."

The verdict was not yet due—Ecclesiastes 8:11. It takes three strikes for punishment to be administered either on the recipient or on his/her seed. If the recipient has a spiritual bank account, withdrawals are made until either forgiveness or punishment is transmuted. Left untreated those in the subcategory of "Oppression" can spread into the second group.
DOMAIN OF PRIDE, BOASTINGS, SELF-RIGHTEOUSNESS AND CONCEIT.
DOMAIN OF UNFORGIVENESS: ANGER, SPITE, HATRED, JEALOUSY AND RAGE.
DOMAIN OF MURDER: MURDER AND ABORTION.
DOMAIN OF DECEPTION: LIES, FORGERY, GREED, AND THEFT.
DOMAIN OF EVIL CONCUPISCENCE AND LUST (visual and carnal): *PEDOPHILIA, RAPE, HOMOSEXUALITY, LESBIANISM, FORNICATION, MASTURBATION, INCEST, ADULTERY, AND INGESTION OR ATTEMPTED INGESTION OF BODY FLUIDS.*
DOMAIN OF REBELLION, OPPRESSION, AND WITCHCRAFT: (**mind binding** **spirits**) *OCCULT, OUIJA, TRANSCENDENTAL MEDITATION, TAROT READING, DIVINATION, MANIPULATION, DOMINATION, PSYCHIC SPIRITISM, MIND CONTROL, PRIDE, FEAR, CHRONIC SLEEPLESSNESS AND EXTREME ANXIETY.*

2.   "REACTION" OR "BENEFICIARY OF DUE SENTENCE."

The sub-categories are "Possession and Infirmity"—the domain of most contracted (so-called) incurable diseases, certain types of blindness, and certain types of paralyses.
ARRESTED DEVELOPMENT and HEAVY uncontrollable ADDICTION are strong spirits.

Once I met a young lady that I fell deeply in love/lust with. Her father was a pastor. She moved to New York not knowing that as the daughter of a pastor or spiritually strong person POTENTIALLY, she would have been a prime target for the enemy. She had many gifts to inherit. She was the seed of prophets. For years my mother resigned herself to the myth that she and only she would she accept as her daughter-in-law. To this day my mother still has her picture on her make-up cabinet. The damsel had a fascination for Ouija boards. One night, while she was playing with one, I felt a strange presence. I was spiritually blind, so I knew not what it was. I snapped at her and demanded that she stop playing with it. Use this exercise to follow how spirits link up. I was accused of being very angry; I probably was. She felt hurt and rebuke (spirits of pride). She moved out. I decided I was not chasing after her (pride again).

She looked for, found and shared an apartment with a girl that was into all sorts of weird things. There were things in the house above the doors. One night we met for reconciliation. The things I had encountered that night (through the Ouija board) resurfaced. It began tugging both of us into a deep tunnel of darkness. I cried out like Jonah did for help. At the utterance of "JESUS!" the thing released its grip. Just then I heard the thing running away from us down the passageway with a clanking sound behind it. We were so afraid; we broke up. She moved to California. I moved also. It took me years to get over her. I pray God, heavenly Father, you know the young lady; you know my feelings for her were genuine at the time. I was walking in ignorance and so was she. Wherever she is, in remembrance for the works and service of her father and the prayers of your servant, I pray a Jonah salvation for her. "Your promises are yea and amen." The following two promises I would like to bring to your remembrance: a) that whatsoever I shall ask for in faith, you will grant and b) that the effectual, fervent prayer of the righteous availeth much. You know that I have voluntarily chosen to serve you and to offer this wisdom to those that are bound as I was. Please Holy Father, through the sacrifice of your Son and your grace and mercy, wherever she is, give her a divine revelation and rescue her now, in Jesus' mighty name I pray, Amen.

I was not comfortable with casual relationships. We worked together; we got very involved (notice the euphemisms for fornication and lust). When I met her she was living with another man. First we spoke daily: on the phone and in person. The first time we went out after work the attraction was so strong that it happened. We stayed out all night and we decided to live together immediately. She made the long goodbye phone call.

I always spoke out my intention to marry and to settle down. Satan had that on his file. His first plan of action was to send the spirit of FEAR. He got all Sanballats and Tobiah spirits to call her and ask her what she was doing. To appease the situation, we went for a lot of dinners and drinks so that the annoying calls would cease. The other guy got all her friends to call. Fear brought on addiction (mild) first to cigarettes and then to liquor. Addiction, fornication, lust and "occultism" were already entrenched. Satan would not be satisfied with those because he knew that we had deeply religious backgrounds. If we got married into a Holy Spirit-filled church that her father pastored at the time, he would lose two that had been careless with their large spiritual inheritances. So he sent Division Commanders to complete the job. Thank God for Purim. Through the power and principle of Purim, God turned Satan's plans around, Amen.

Before I touch the next segment, I will quote Moses. Exodus 18:11, "Now I know the Lord our God is greater than all gods," (with a little "g"). The word god by itself means exalted being. My ever-present, forgiving, loving, all conquering God is exaltation! The scripture is a testament to what I have decreed and will decree again and again and again, "I bear witness!" Since we are referencing Exodus (Moses' 2nd book), refer to Exodus 23:20. It is important because I will be dealing with the matter of Extraterrestrials in more detail. Some of you might be saying at this point, "My God, he has lost it." In 1st Samuel 19:9-10, the evil spirit that overpowered Saul changed his demeanor permanently.

CHAPTER 19. BEYOND OUR BOUNDARIES.

19A. HOME OF EXTRATERRESTRIALS.

The prefix "extra" means beyond or outside. Terra is a Latin word meaning earth. This chapter "Beyond our Boundaries" will deal with beings that dwelt or originated beyond the boundaries of our earth and heavens. God's word announces that "Though heaven and earth pass away" His word will stand. The record of His word also witnessed that His word is Life and that His word was made flesh. Since flesh was made from earth, when all flesh dies, His living word will stand in another domain beyond our boundaries.

Back to Exodus 23:20; I have not forgotten. There we encountered a "Ministering Spirit" sent from its heavenly abode or seventh heaven. "Behold I send an angel before thee to keep thee in thy way and to bring thee into the place, which I have prepared." Congregations take notes, God did not say a place; He said *The Place*. "*Beware of him and provoke him not.*" In Moses' first book Genesis 2:1…The heavens (plural) and singular earth and host of them were finished.

The steps to spiritual perfection are seven: six for building or sowing, and one for reaping or resting. Six of the seven epochs were set aside for building as follows:

1. From Ecclesiastes 3:15-16, the first epoch was infinity (before time was) the *Law* or *The All* was there. That is the seventh heaven, the realm of absolute and eternal wholeness or "Place of Eternal Rest." Since God is Alpha and Omega, the first and last is the same. Before the boundaries of the universe were set, there was absolute perfection, and beyond the boundaries lay the same—light, infinity (the seventh heaven) and wisdom—John 1:1.

Translators called that first epoch, "Day."

2. The second epoch or stage was that of polar opposites (Psalm 29:7) i.e., motion based on the *Law of Opposites, The Laws of Perpetuity*: movement/countermovement or (yin/yang) or from unrevealed to revealed. The formulation of time, space, dimensions and boundaries commenced. Limited civilizations out of the ashes of Babel call those epochs lateral days as opposed to *dimensional days* (Law of opposites), Genesis 1:6 and Psalm 29:3.

3. Third epoch: seed time/harvest time, reflective light, energy, long and short waves, wisdom, subconscious and conscious epoch—Daniel 2:22, period of gestation and insight (Genesis 1:12-13, *The Third Day* as in Isaiah 11:2 and John 1:9.

4. The Fourth Yowme: Note that the sun, moon and other orbs were not allocated their regulatory positions until *this time* frame (the 4th Yowme) was set up. The pre-atomic world of neutrons, electrons, atomic and sub-atomic particles—the nuclei of our plan-

etary systems became organized in this epoch. Then the constellations received their prescribed sequences. After the Sun, Moon, Mars, Mercury, Jupiter, Venus, and Saturn were assigned regulatory roles, then and only then did we have a system of repetitious time—Genesis 1:14-19.

5.   God set a separate gestation period for eggs of fish and birds different from that of mammals. The moon's cycle affects tidal motions and fluctuations. The regulatory cycle of the moon takes approx. 28 current days. *Jupiter's* different and multiple moons ushered in the 5th epoch. When it was Jupiter's turn to commence a constellation sequence, birds and fish hatched among us—Genesis 1:20-23. Those cycles could only take place after each orb was assigned its role and position.

6.   At the unveiling of new epochs, all orbs injected their unique influential fragrances on the primordial atmosphere. The brilliance and heat of the sun, contrasted with the fluctuating tidal temperamental cool of the moon plus mercurial injection into the arrows of Jupiter was so much that the next epoch in Genesis 1:24-31 (Venus epoch) had to have been pregnant with the pollen of Eros. Did you know that there is an asteroid named Eros that approaches to within 15 million miles of earth once every 44 years? What effect it had on the opposite sexes of mammals, when Venus ushered it in the first time? As above so below: rest follows those periods.

7.   A time arrived when Saturn's influence on the solar system allowed reasonable fluctuations on earth's atmospheric conditions. A complete revolution of the planet with its ten satellites takes approximately 29 1/2 years.

Whenever the Sun's position in the heavenlies is first, the day is called first or Sun's day or (Sunday). Similarly when the Moon's position becomes dominant in a 168-hour period (called a week) the day is called lundi (Moon day) or Monday. Hence Mardi is for Mars' dominant day, Mercredi (for Mercury's role, until we get to a Scandinavian mythological influence with Thor for (Thursday) or Mercury's ruling day and Fryer or Venus' day (Friday) to Saturday or Saturn's day. The Sun is the earth's primary manifest natural light force. People today assign a fixed time of 24 hours to its first light season and call it a day also. In other words are all epochs the same? What then is the three-month period of polar darkness called? How do we compute the Day of Jubilee, which comes around every 50 years? Wouldn't it be more accurate for people to teach that the world systems were set in place in one day since no boundaries were set, instead of six consecutive days of 24-hour durations?

In Genesis 1:5, God brought all trees, plants and herbs from beyond the boundaries of this earth. A seed grows into a plant. Those plants came from somewhere else already fully grown before they were put into the prepared ground. There is a place beyond earth's boundaries (Job 1:6 and Isaiah 14:12) from which place all disobedient spirits were expelled. Genesis 1:8 states that God planted the garden in Eden. Nowhere in Moses' discourse does it say that God made the earth in *Seven Sequential Days*. It is postulation by unwise men. If everything was done in seven sequential days, supposing that to be truth, then the rate of implantation could not have been at our current regulated time. The speed had to have been at macro pre-regulated time, or exponential time. Verse 8 confirms that. It did not say that God spoke a garden into existence. He planted the garden. He also brought seeds "before they were in the ground." In Moses' first Book called Bereshith in Hebrew, Genesis 3:5 confirms that there are exalted beings beyond our boundaries. All things that originated beyond our boundaries have had an existence before our time clock was set in motion. The confirmation is in Genesis 2:5, "God made …and every plant of the field before it was in the earth and every herb of the field before it grew…"

Prophet Isaiah wrote in Isaiah 14:12: "How thou art fallen (demoted) from heaven, O Lucifer, son of the morning, now thou art cut down to the ground (earth is a place of trial and preparation for eternal judgment) which did weaken the NATIONS." I will take the liberty to paraphrase Isaiah's preview of the downfall of his kingdom. In other words: *Look what you have come to. You lost it all through bad mind, envy, and greed. The power you fell with, plus your ability to create beautiful music, caused you to corrupt the nations. To you and all those that obeyed you and disobeyed God, it is very close to your season of everlasting doom. You boasted that you would exalt your power base above the stars of God. Lu Lu old chap, Jesus did not give up any ground. God set a trap for your sorry self. You had your fair chance to win him in an 'All or Nothing' game. Like so many at crap tables, the last thing you figured in your miserable spirit is that you would lose it all. When the adrenaline is at its peak, wisdom usually takes a back seat.* Up to the time of Jesus' ministry on earth, Satan and his armies had been invading bodies as they pleased. God finally sent a redeemer.

The "Excellent" kicked his butt ROYALLY and left a blueprint for all "Sons" that have been redeemed, "The everlasting recipe for 'ROYAL BUTT-KICKING.'" Just the mention of the name "Jesus" sends eternal fear throughout his entire network. I bear witness!

CHAPTER 19B. TESTIMONY OF A FORMER WITCH.

In a later chapter I will document a bit of Satan's history on earth plus the testimonies of a few that he recruited. Up to about 2000 years ago, Satan had not gotten a personal butt-kicking. I have had both the pleasure and displeasure to witness Satan manifest through a person. I have also heard several of his agents spill dirty secrets, deeds and plans of their boss during bouts of fright and anger. I have had extreme contentment also in hearing a detailed testimony of a lady who was the former head of a witch haven. She confessed to having being harassed by Satan and his demons, which swore revenge for what they called "a serious betrayal."

That lady before she was WASHED AND DELIVERED (spiritual terms for what is called exorcised) had a serious fascination with the occult. She would acquire all the occult books she could lay her hands on. She practiced all forms of the arts that she could learn. In truth and in fact she became so proficient that she and her works came to the attention of the satanic Commander in Chief. When Satan sent a senior witch to recruit her, she jumped at the opportunity. She excelled so quickly that she received his highest post. She had the ability to leave her physical body (astral travel). Finally he made her his bride. Her assigned task was to take an army of evil spirits to certain territories to penetrate churches that were weak and vulnerable. She confessed that she was obsessed with power. Satan is a bragger. I later verified that. He is very generous with money. He has the ability to take people's money and reward those who are loyal. She reported that Satan has the ability to take money away from spiritually unguarded people causing them to suffer unexplained losses. A former warlock corroborated her reports. She confirmed that spirits and demons travel mostly between the hours of 1.00 A.M and 4.00 A.M. People pray less during those hours. On the other hand, powerful prayers (by sanctified persons) short-circuit occult activities and their energies. One night they went to attack a pastor in his sleep. They had already weakened him with a lustful lady they planted in his church. As they entered his house, a child woke up and started to pray. This is what shocked the lady. She had her best demons and evil spirits with her. As soon as the little girl mentioned the name of Jesus, her best demons fell backwards (confirming the power of Jesus in Psalm 27:2) through the wall. She was left alone. She went to ask them what had happened. No way were they going back into the house until the girl stopped praying. She then did the unpardonable. She asked, "When the girl mentioned the name of Jesus why did you get so afraid?" They all scattered and warned her not to call that forbidden name in their presence again. Like a faithful wife she told her husband about the day's proceedings. When she mentioned the name of Jesus, Satan's anger exceeded the combined anger of all her troops combined. He was livid. She then started getting books and began reading secretly, to find out who Jesus was and why His name irritated Satan that much. One day he caught her reading a Bible. He beat the daylights out of her. She was beaten unconscious and woke up in a hospital.

The doctor was a born-again Christian and wondered about the strange marks that he saw. He did the right thing. He called his Holy Spirit-filled born-again pastor who had little experience in deliverance, but tremendous faith and skill in the application of the WORD. Her deliverance and her testimony were not easy. Satan sent one of his most powerful spirits the *Spirit of Suicide*. She attempted that seven times. She had a Damascus Encounter. The Spirit of the Lord told her, "I will save you and use you as one of my most powerful witnesses." That He did. Almighty God, please protect your servant. You know who she is. She has and is risking her life as she boldly confronts the kingdom of Satan and exposes its works. Protect her dear Father; cover her in faith with the redeemed sanctified blood of your Son, Jesus. I beg this of you in His mighty name. The demonic master plan will be unveiled later on in more detail, please read on.

CHAPTER 19C. MELCHIZEDEK.

God's redemption package is encoded in those two *Steeples of Wisdom*: "King," apex of man's podium of power and "Priest," apex of his spiritual office. We are to be the head and not the tail. On earth we are to be God's ambassadors living like kings. We must be pure and chosen *priests* to offer sacrifices to Him. Scholars that have viewed the original Greek Texts affirm that the book entitled "Hebrews" in the New Testament was among the same scrolls as Paul's letters from Rome, to Timothy. That would make sense because in verse 13 of Paul's second letter to Timothy (more personal in nature) Paul asked him to fetch his cloak and his parchments from Troas. The writer told the brethren that Timothy was expected to bring things back to him in Rome; both letters have the same farewell signature statements. In Hebrews 5:6 and Hebrews 7:1-21, he described the priesthood of Melchizedek with exceptional clarity. According to Paul's letter to the Hebrew brethren and confirmed by Moses in Genesis 14:18, that priesthood though a forerunner to the temporary Aaronic priesthood, was predestined to be everlasting. The Spirit of God prophesied through David in Psalm 110 about Jesus' restorative ministry. In verse 4, "Thou art a priest forever after the order of "Melchizedek." Observe that Melchizedek gave Abram *bread and wine*, a seed and tithe offering to father Abraham. That everlasting priesthood is for all of Abraham's children: natural, spiritual, Jew, Arab, Gentile and transformed pagan like me. God gave laws to the Levites and stipulated that those were for them and their generations. In Jeremiah 31:31, He promised a new unbreakable covenant to the next generations. In the Tanakh, God carefully pointed out that He would not select weak covenant partners like the first lot. The New Covenant could only be had, when they came into the "Land that God promised" them. Hebrews Chapters 9-10 are brilliant expositions.

What books are some Jews really reading? They became a nation in 1948; the flawed Aaronic priesthood extinguished after John the Harbinger died. Rabban Gamaliel taught that the Melchizedek Priesthood had no beginning or end. It was beyond the boundaries of the universe. Paul who had access to the Sanhedrin and was a zealot before his Damascus conversion would have been well schooled in those esoteric matters. Paul's letter to the Hebrew brethren (Hebrews Chapters 7 and 8) are musts for ministries intending to grow higher in God's wisdom. Please note that Melchizedek is referred to as a *MAN* without father or mother, (verse 3) a Firstfruit everlasting King and Priest. Melchizedek's Kingship and High Priestly offices are what the righteous ones on earth are called to. That office was ordained to be everlasting and was confirmed by Jesus: we have an everlasting intercessor before God. Reflect on the fact that David was one of the few kings in Israel's history allowed to offer sacrifice before God that He (God) accepted. Note how correctly the prophet, Isaiah 11:10 established that David was not the root of the tree from which Jesus became the "Branch." The patriarchal head was Jesse whose bloodline ended when Mary had her last son with Joseph.

When the veil of the Jerusalem Temple ripped in 33 C.E. it signified the end of the Old Covenant and the beginning of the New Covenant—Leviticus 23:12. That incorruptible scepter and that altar are in the custody of the Priesthood after the Order of Melchizedek. I wonder if you folks reading this, the ones that take your calling lightly and have allowed your altars to be tarnished, suddenly realize the seriousness of your deeds? Is there anything that God does not see or know as David once asked? You have to be seriously messed up to be a person of God and even dream to commit a sin. Backsliders beware of Hebrews 4:6.

WHEREVER YOU ARE RIGHT NOW YOU NEED TO FALL ON YOUR FACES AND CRY OUT BEFORE THE LORD YOUR GOD IN HUMBLE REPENTANCE LIKE JONAH DID.

A former witch got saved and did confess that her evil spirits would use masturbation, adultery, fornication, and homosexuality to trap altar custodians. If you are in a ministry that forbids marrying and there is need for a spouse, leave the ministry, get a spouse and be married. There are many international outreach-missionary organizations in which you and your spouse can continue to be useful. Paul wrote about such in 1st Corinthians 7:9, "But if they cannot contain, let them marry." 1st Timothy 4:1-3: "Now the Spirit speaketh expressly, that in *latter times* some *will depart from the faith*, giving heed to seducing spirits, and doctrines of devils: speaking lies in hypocrisy; having their conscience seared with a hot iron; forbidding to marry…" The priceless insurance that Christians receive lapses when we sin. Matthew 7:21-23 and Hebrews 4:6, Believers that backslid will not enter His rest. Romans 6, Romans 8:1-12 and Hebrews 10:26, "If we sin willfully after we have received the knowledge of the truth, there remaineth no more sacrifice for sins." Jeremiah 23:1, "Woe unto the pastors that destroy and scatter the sheep of my pasture, saith the Lord." Verse 2: "Ye have scattered my flock and driven them away and have not visited them. Behold I will visit upon you the evil of your doings saith the Lord." So much for such myths as "Security of Believers" that some teach. Jeremiah 23:11, "For the prophet and the priest are profane, yea in my house have I found their wickedness saith the Lord."

Let us shift from persons or things that arrived from beyond the borders, to those that went beyond our boundaries. The seventh generation of Adam produced *Enoch*, Genesis 5:24. The first fruit cycle years (7X70) or 490 years equals a perfect generation in God. "Enoch walked with God and he was not; for God took him." In other words those chosen to be "High Priests Forever" did not succumb to death. The prophet Elijah was translated.

Man's continuous search for extraterrestrials outside of our boundaries is endless:

1. This generation, like those of Babel cannot exceed God's prescribed bounds without consequences.

2. Major celestial orbs are spherical. The movie "2001 Space Odyssey" had serious subliminal messages. Take a string and travel as far as you can in a straight line upon a huge sphere. Eventually you are back to square one. The only ones allowed to pass "The Veil" are those selected to be High Priests forever, ministering to God in obedience, not arrogance. Those that do not (as we saw from those *fallen angels* that lost their exalted places) are permanently angry, frustrated, and wicked. We had better learn from the errors of the past.

Giving a list of the various spirit types without giving an insight into their behavioral patterns will not provide solutions. Some you already know. I will start by listing the slickest one: the one most misunderstood, Satan's trump card, the spirit of "Lust." First and foremost, the differences between "Love or Agape" and "Lust or Eros" need to be spelled out in graphic detail.

CHAPTER 19D. LOVE, AN AGELESS ENIGMA.

For centuries people have been confusing "Lust" for "Agape or Love." Agape is love that searches the inner being first; it is spiritual. Agape is a synonym for God-approved love. Since it is spiritually given and spiritually directed, agape is attracted to the "positive" spiritual qualities of a person. A person who possesses agape realizes that her/his body is a "Temple of the Living God." That temple is made with a sanctified *Holy of Holies* and only "The One" that passes the spiritual litmus test, sanctified by God to offer holy sacrifice, is permitted. Only one is chosen worthy, not the Russian Army, not the British Navy, not the U.S. Marines, not every person that "looks cute." Cute-ness is an outward appearance. Ask the one that placed the extra rib in you, "Whose rib do I have?" and men: "Where's my rib?"

Evil spirits love cute-looking people. Some of the prettiest and most attractive people die from AIDS, a spiritually induced disease. 90 percent of the people, from whom I cast out demons, are exceptionally attractive physically. The outward wrapping has no bearing on the person or personalities living inside. Agape, when sown in obedience, produces living fruit, called obedient offspring. Lust produces, disobedient seeds, which manifest in reckless offspring, sicknesses and spiritual death. Many "Cute" seed are the fruits of lust. That is why so many of their parents are divorced.

INSIGHT INTO THE BEING OR BEINGS THAT LIVE INSIDE!

Some "types" must be cast out with prayer and fasting. Others leave with simple repentance prayers and the "Will to Change" for the better—Psalm 51. Let us do a little quiz: A hoggish person has what type of temperament and what type of dominant spirit? An impatient person? A cantankerous person? A double-minded person? Instant playback is its specialty. It likes to reminisce on the past and is very difficult to detect. It hampers Christians a lot and is a chief cause of backsliding. That is why follow-up work is necessary. The list goes on ad infinitum! A rebellious person? A thieving person? A vile person? An envious person? An extremely jealous person? A wicked and hideous person? A conceited person? A proud puffed up person? A highly domineering person? A conniving and manipulative person? A gluttonous person?

An unkind person? An arrogant person? A flirty person?

Some cases are easy to recognize. Sorry they are not "Gay" they are "Sadly bound." The spirit or spirits once lived in a grandparent of a different gender, or were implanted after spiritual openings of rejection or hate set in, or were implanted by curiosity, ignorance, or most commonly by lust. Carefully examine the eyes of "bound" homosexuals and lesbians. When agitated, the spirits within them gleam and peer through the bound beings. In severe cases, the other personalities manifest traits of opposite genders.

The Kingdom of God (notice that a kingdom has rules) is based on three simple principles:

1. The principle of Sowing and Reaping. If you sow foolish choices, you reap confusion.

2. Loving the Creator and His precepts with all thy might and thy being.

3. Loving thy neighbour as self. Are you crazy you are asking?

How come you are choosy about selecting your physical neighbourhoods and careless with your spiritual ones? Make sure the person you choose is *kind-hearted*. Remember the meaning of personality.

Agape is charitable, is kind, envieth not, vaunted not itself, is not puffed up, doth not behave unseemingly, not selfish, (thinks about others besides self). Agape is not easily provoked, is not judgmental; it is truthful and honest. Warning! Agape is always hounded by Lust. Agape must find its equivalent, never the counterfeit Lust. Do not mistake Agape for "Lust," Satan's counterfeit spirit. Lust and its armies are the biggest destroyers of persons who were blessed with "Agape." After Lust injures, it brings along its friends: "unforgiveness," deceit, fornication, hurt, anger, murder and or adultery.

If you know you have "Agape" and there are a lot of very fine men and women who either do or did, beware of wolves in sheep clothing. Examine their inner personalities first (their traits, their demeanor and their behaviour). Their spiritual lights must shine before men/women. Observe their inner qualities first. Here is a fail-proof wisdom: never be alone in an environment with anyone where Satan can take advantage of that weak situation. There are situations when disobedient emotions cloud the time to think properly and soberly. Lust and love invoke the same emotions but with different consequences.

One is ordained over an "Altar of Obedience," the other is instigated over an "Altar of Disobedience" with inescapable consequences. Body fluids contain spirit energy. A man or woman desiring to spill or exchange body fluids over any altar in disobedience is consciously or unconsciously exchanging *obedient spirit* types for *disobedient spirit* types. Since the king of disobedience decides what spirits enter, is the chance worth taking? A simple translation of intent to mate by unmarried people is, *"MAY I IMPART SOME DISOBEDIENT SPIRITS INTO YOU?"*

Always fast and ask Almighty God if that person is the one? Do not get married to anyone before you go to a church that knows how to pray for the removal of generational curses and the canceling of iniquities of parents on both sides of the families (fathers and mothers) going back at least four generations. In fact in these volumes I will insert those prayers. Commit to memory: there is one rib missing from each man and it is planted in *one woman only*. Trying to find that rib by oneself will turn you dog-like. You will receive a canine personality sniffing under every skirt for the missing bone. Have you been to countries where men actually go up to a tree and water it like a dog? Dogs love wheels made of rubber (oozed from trees). Men usually go directly to the tree roots. In the Hebrew language the word for tree and the word for human is the same. Women, beware of "H.L.S.," the Hind Leg Syndrome—1ˢᵗ Kings 16:11, *DO NOT BE PEED ON!* Stop doing Satan's work by desecrating God's holy temples through disobedience. *Men, you will sniff until you die and not find the right one because the location of that bone has to be released spiritually.*

Pastors before you marry persons (after cleansing) ask God to re-programme both the man and the woman. Use Psalm 51 as a guide. Ask not only for a "right spirit" for both the man and the woman but also a matching bone and bone socket in faith. If the secret way to God's heart is agape, then God must confirm His word with an everlasting gift/sacrifice. John confirmed in John 3:16... For God so loved the world that He *gave* His only son. God confirmed what was prophesied in Psalm 2 and in Isaiah Chapter 53. That was recorded by Saul of Tarsus, called Paul, in his letter to the brethren at Corinth. Paul had visited them some 50 years after Jesus went beyond the boundaries of the universe to set things in order. Paul stayed almost two years encouraging the brethren. When he arrived at Ephesus, he observed the abundance of witchcraft (worshipping the goddess Diana). He delivered many and received a witness in his spirit to write the brethren at Corinth to follow up and encourage the flock (1ˢᵗ Corinthians 13). The "Follow-up" ministering is so important for nursing the young lambs back to strength and out of the grasp of stalking lions and other spiritual predators. May God help those weak shepherds! Agape does not wear off with time. On the contrary, Agape increases over time. As both parties grow together like trees planted by rivers of living water, they must prosper. The word of God will grant them power to proclaim and to come into agreement with proclamations that they make. They are blessed to bring forth "good fruit" in season; their leaves shall not wither and whatsoever they do as long as they are sown in obedience God will prosper them. You see why Satan attacks marriages so viciously? Where two or more are gathered in God's name, God is there also in the midst. Satan loathes God's gifts.

Anyone that has been bestowed with "Agape" and finds a similarly blessed person of the opposite sex, as long as they seek repentance for past sins and iniquities and jointly live in obedience, they will be blessed and blessed and blessed. Many reading this are not walking in the blessings because of past suspended sentences. Confess all transgressions and begin to enjoy your inheritances. Beware of the thief. Confirmation of the above can be found in the words of God's servant, David (see David's 1ˢᵗ Psalm). When God speaks, it is Law. If you allow those blessings to be blocked or stolen, it is because of ignorance. God said: "For the lack of wisdom my people perish." Deuteronomy chapter 28 lists all the promised blessings. Do not get into a mess because of flawed judgment and impatience, and then ask God to bless your mess. If before reading this you realized that you messed up, take into account that He is a loving and forgiving God. Trust me, if you are contrite (humble and really sorry) He will forgive you and give you another chance—Job 22:21-29.

Father, I confess all my unworthiness and seek permission to enter your throne to intercede for all those being convicted right now like I was on the day you convicted me. I am led by the Spirit of God to pray for someone that is bearing the pain and guilt of error right now. Your loving Father is 100% agape and merciful. There is none comparable. Find a quiet place as I send these prayers into the future to lead you back to safety. After you have confessed all your sins, seek forgiveness and absolution according to the one everlasting sacrifice of His dear Son, Jesus. Please accept their renouncing of Satan and redeem them back to you. Enter their names in the "Lamb's Book of Life." That initial prayer requires follow-up prayers to uproot "wilderness" situations. You need the Redeemer after Moses to take you through all wildernesses of "Sinn."

That has been the main problem with churches up to this time. Leaving Egypt is the beginning of the journey.

REDEMPTION PRAYER: PSALM 23.

The 23rd Psalm is not a recitation. It is not to be rattled off as prose. It is the summary of a two-way contract between God and humans, pointing us to His permanent Shepherd. It consists of salutation, conditions, terms and a preview of results. From verse 1 "The Lord is my shepherd." God promises to provide us with a shepherd to lead us from all of our mess: financial, sinful, spiritual, and generational; to take us from Lodebar to *The Promised Land*. Every promise of God has conditions attached. The green pastures metaphorically speak of when we have completed our part of the deal, when we have returned to utmost obedience like sheep. Spell out and confess all sins known and unknown. Confess sins committed with our mouths, eyes, ears, attitudes, and with God's temples—our bodies. Forgive all those that have hurt us first to receive God's forgiveness for us hurting Him. Ask for a permanent distaste for sinful habits and deeds so that we are led no more into temptation. Proclaim deliverance from evil by saying so with meaning and by adding "I renounce Satan and all his works. Jesus, thank you for your sacrifice! I appreciate you substituting your life for my sins, my sicknesses, and my iniquities. Please write my name in the Lamb's book of Life." Father send your "Royal steed" to receive those prayers. Now you qualify to be grafted into the dwelling of the house of the Lord forever.

Imagine the amount of bondage that will be broken when your entire families, churches, synagogues, temples and their entire congregations say and mean those prayers once per week. Do not be ashamed when tears of spiritual cleansing are poured out. Ask God to pardon your sins and to transform you through Jesus' acceptable blood sacrifice. Petition Him for cancellation of debts of "unforgiveness" and hurt; healing for diseases through His stripes and forgiveness of iniquities through His bruises (see Isaiah 53). Ask God to lead you to the right pasture so that you can be fed properly. See the list at the end of Chapter 7e.

God instituted a complete redemption package. In the canons of the Torah, "Grace" (in the eyes of God) was mentioned some 365 times. Grace or "Priestly anointing" was first given to Moses and later to the Levites to intercede for the errors of Adam—John 1, Hosea 4:6, and Hosea 5:6. The "Kingly Anointing" or "Gift of Righteousness" was sent through Jeshua to reclaim us back from prodigal sons to perfected spirit beings as in Romans 5:15-21. Hence confirming Psalm 110, that we are called to be "Kings and Priests" forever. We are now enfranchised to receive happiness, healings, riches and blessings in abundance.

19E. COVERT MARRIAGE WRECKER EXPOSED!

We were discussing the spirit of lust and how it tries to disguise itself as Agape by using itself, deception, and its own inability to be fulfilled. Lust must be obedient to its boss. Its mission is to proliferate and to sow seeds of anger and hate. It has a different focus. It is fickle like a bird. A bird does not sit on a tree and pick one fruit and eat it until it is satisfied. It picks one, then the next and then the next. That is its nature. Lust has the identical nature. Lust is a multi-faceted spirit. It is a groupie. It does not travel alone. It belongs to the domain of evil conspicuence. Rebellion, covetousness, selfishness and greed are part of its family. Those are Satan's faithful groupies. They are mission-focused. If they are not rooted out, eventually you will be another victim. Fowls and other earth-based birds display selfish attitudes. They mate on a first come, first served basis. Since "Lust" is empowered carnally, most pretty people are the seed of persons that were attracted to the "looks and carnal desires" of the opposite sex. Their true personalities are concealed. Sin has prevented many children of God from receiving the "Gift of discernment." If we all had that gift, we would run from 90 percent of the people that we are attracted to. What if we could only see what is inside many "perceived-to-be nice" people? The divorce statistics and prison records are minute samples (less than 1%) of those that Satan has already vanquished. If you and another person (of the opposite sex) really care for each other and want to make it into a responsible God-ordained union, you both have to be cleansed, spiritually, or "be spiritually reborn" to have a fighting chance. On your own, you are no match for Satan. Once you use any of his agents, they leave behind eggs that proliferate and spread like cockroaches, which become harder to eradicate as time elapses. You cannot fight them alone. They weakened the judges, the kings, the priests and the people of ancient Israel. They have and are weakening preachers, teachers, pastors, parents, serfs, kingdoms, nations and institutions. Satan has history and experience on his side. Jeremiah 50:6, "My people have been lost sheep; their shepherds have caused them to go astray, they have turned them away on the mountains…they have gone from mountain to hill… they have forgotten their resting place."

Think of how many people that appeared so happy together and you were impressed as to how happy they seemed, only to find out the contrary. Lust brought on fornication, masturbation and adultery into their lives to steal their souls. Lust is a counterfeit for Agape. Agape is the foundation for marriage, a blessed union. Lust is the foundation for "shacking up," a temporary resting place and proliferation point for demons of lust, fornication, masturbation, homosexuality, lesbianism and abortion/murder. Lust cannot be cast out with the sacrament of marriage; hence the high divorce rates. Wake up preachers: whenever couples present themselves for marriage, first check out their carnal history. Love is a spiritual asset. Find out if they have tried to find love carnally. If they did before marriage, then they had been incubation factories for the carnal counterfeit spirits: lust, fornication, masturbation, incest, homosexuality and or adultery. Reprogramme their "Lustometers." Ask them to repent for the sins of lust, masturbation, homosexuality, "unforgiveness," hate, and sins of attitudes. It is important to do the cleansings before they begin to have children. Removing the spirit load factor can eliminate serious problem-pregnancies and crib deaths. What do you think happens during pregnancies when mothers crave for dirt, soap, and strange things? Be smart. Let them know that since the habitual sins go to the 3rd and 4th generations and since they knew not what their ancestors did, they should confess *all* on behalf of themselves, their parents, and grandparents as far back as possible. Then break all generation curses, hexes and ordinances. Next, spiritually cleanse yourself and both parties and have them repent of all generational iniquities and transgressions. Then ask the Lord to break all ancestral and generational curses. That would be 1000 percent more effective than what is done today. It is not too late. Do the same cleansings for your assemblies; there are little girls with heavy voices and unusual physical development. There are also little boys that those spirits cannot wait to get into. *Those stalking types* previously camped in some grandma. Their voices shriek a bit too much. Arrange monthly large-scale corporate cleansings for your assemblies until you produce "Spotless brides for the Lord."

By doing those cleansings, future generations of potential rapists and murderers can be purged with these simple revelations. Murder statistics can be reduced significantly when ancestral curses and covenants of death are broken. Elders can cease wasting water in bath rituals by baptizing children. Instead they can stand in the gap and confess all sins on behalf of both sides' parents, grandparents of the child, and the great grand parents going back four generations of all sins known and unknown. What then is the motive behind a pastor or priest baptizing a child? What sin has the child committed? Water baptism is for the "Remission of sins committed by the person to be baptized!" Apostle Paul calls those "Doctrines of Demons" since they have no Biblical foundation and make no sense spiritually. Jesus was wounded for our transgressions; bruised for our iniquities and received stripes for all our diseases. Isaiah foretold all details in Isaiah 53. Some improve on the ridiculous by sprinkling the water. Please fast, seek the "Wisdom, Guidance and Presence of the Lord" and remove Satan from all ceremonies. Read Exodus 19:10-11 as examples of those cleansings. If you are a member of the clergy and you do those things, read John's book of Revelation. There is an immediate blessing for those that read it and those to whom it is read. Do the same to your entire assembly and or your executive or governing boards. There is much wisdom in the commandment for us to be reborn. We must go the potter's house figuratively and "Be born again." Even though Solomon's Temple was destroyed, God's redemption package affords us an exchanged sanctified temple. Find the unblemished lamb sacrifice acceptable to God; seek forgiveness and cash in on the promises.

If two obedient people make a promise over an altar of obedience, it has to be kept. If one or two partially obedient people make a promise, chances are, it will be broken. Partial obedience is not obedience. Since your teachers were partially obedient, and then the students were also, then the fruits of partial obedience are disobedience. Divorce is an act of disobedience!

CHAPTER 19F. PASSAGES THROUGH THE EARTH.

God, *Creator of the Universe*, sees and knows all aspects of the universal all. Since God is beyond the boundaries of the universe, and since He gave man dominion over earth, is God a welcome visitor or an intruder? God visits only sanctified persons, places and or things; so when man transgressed, God promised that His Spirit would not always reside with man—Genesis 6:3. There are millions willing to pay heavily for beliefs that human conduits who sit at satanic altars (called psychics) can guess the future correctly. My God, who answered me when I was searching for absolute truth, knows all things. God limited man's wisdom and understanding. If we want more, then go to the owner. God created the animals and beasts first, so that we can observe all their carnal ways. The dinosaurs are not around anymore. They ruled the carnal roost for years. Any system of survival based on supreme elevation by carnal might is transient. God put His Spirit in pieces of earth and called such Hu-man. Humans were right spirits in walking mud originally. We have digressed into wrong spirits with inflated egos.

In Zechariah 6:5-7 we can read about spirits ascending and descending the earth. When fornication or adultery is committed, spiritual caviar (called semen) is neatly wrapped in plastic (prophylactic) and discarded. Most times it falls to the ground. The equivalent happens whenever murder or abortion (same thing in the eyes of God) is committed. Let us take a spiritual journey to the first example of that in Moses 1st book, Genesis 4:10, "Abel's blood crieth unto God from the ground." Semen and blood have spirit energy. In verse 11: "The earth opens her mouth" to receive this blood. Human bodies are composed of earth; they have sacred altars also. Earth was created as a magnificent altar for humankind to be blessed and replenished. 1st Corinthians 10:26, "The earth is the Lord's and the fullness thereof!" That is why, when we surrender our original right spirit unto Glory, or we are taken out by disobedient ones, we have to surrender our earth suits. Ecclesiastes 12:7, "Then shall the dust return to the earth as it was: and the spirit shall return to God who gave it." In Job 1:7, Satan answered: "From going to and fro in the earth." The *"Living Earth" has spiritual passageways*! Just for the record, in every droplet of semen are millions of living eggs. Genesis 38:9-10—God killed Onan for spilling his semen on the ground and for disobedience. In Isaiah chapter 5:14, the more sins are committed, the more the spiritual door (hell) opens to release new waves of demons and evil spirits. After every elevation of corporate wantonness we have fresh releases of so-called "Incurable diseases." Isaiah 5:14, "Hell hath enlarged herself, and *opened her mouth* without measure." Verse 18, "Woe unto them that draw iniquity with chords of vanity and sin as if it were a cart rope." We must examine the behaviour of spirits as body fluids spilled in disobedience become free caviar for evil spirits.

Very strong urges occur as body-less spirits invade unguarded earthen altars and become strengthened. The strengths of those urges (spiritual hunger) cause most people to lose focus. They fail to comprehend the sources of those urges. Every surge of emotion, propelled by evil spirits, is instigated in *disobedience* to God's word. There is a party among evil spirits whenever they get spiritual eggs (wine and caviar). Do you now realize why God gets angry whenever fornication, homosexuality, masturbation, adultery and abortion are being committed? They create proliferation points for all foul spirits to get access and strength. Leviticus 20:10, "The adulterer and the adulteress" are punishable. Gay? Leviticus 20:13, "If a man also lie with a mankind as he lieth with a woman, both of them have committed an abomination. Their *blood* shall be upon them." Whenever an act God is accursed, that creates blemished blood. It attracts evil spirits. On the other side of the coin, if body fluids from "cleansed" persons are released in obedience, as ordained in marriage, purer and more powerful surges occur. Take a look back in time, when Moses offered the sanctified blood of bulls and goats, how it was able to keep the "Death Angel" away from the camp of the Israelites, Exodus 12:13. How much more forgiveness, power and grace is assigned to the most acceptable sacrifice? Observe what one of Jesus' followers witnessed in John 19:18, *Where they crucified him and two other with him, on either side one and Jesus in the midst.*

The instrument that struck the lethal blow became an obsession for a group called "The Grail Seekers." I have news for all such. Wherein Satan is obsessed with the instrument, he is deathly afraid of the ooze. That blood created and still creates immediate access to God. It offers the earth redemption and victory over Satan. What a time we live in! We do not have to purchase bulls and goats for sins' offerings as in times past. We atone by repentance and faith. I know that my sins' offerings would have cost me a fortune—Numbers 25:1-4, and verses 8-11.

All priests connected to churches in Rome or England need to read Paul's all generations prophetic letter to all shepherds of those churches—Romans 1 and 2. Read them at least once per week. There is one "Holy of Holies" and there is one way. *The Temple* is now sanctified with only one type of sacrifice pleasing to God. It must be holy, sanctified and without leaven. Our body is designed as a temple with an altar accessible through our "Holy of Holies." It will either be dominated by God's right spirit of Psalm 51 or by millions of contrary and evil spirits of oppression, depression, possession, addiction (for lust/power) and or infirmity. If we want to pursue the cleanest spiritual lifestyle as taught by Jeshua, it behooves us to obey all of God's laws including abstinence from spiritual conduits: toll-free psychic hotlines, prostitution houses, and things bonded to spirits of addiction.

CHAPTER 19G. TEST THE VIBES.

From the beginning, man was built with a brain that is compatible with God's H.S.P.O or God's "Holy Spirit Programme of Obedience." God's programme has been shelved for the most part and all types of substitutes have been tried. Fallible philosophies, arrogant assumptions, non-correlating and prophecy-deficient religious persuasions, all in the ambit of "Satan's Inspired" or "S.I" programme range. To date, the 2000-year-old H.S.P.O. has outlasted and bested all the rest and the best of their best.

Since the invention of the computer, a sort of electronic mind, the following programs have been used: FORTRAN, Cobal, Word, and Windows 95, 96, 97, 98, XP, Excel and more. There are natural and spiritual viruses. In the latter category are evil spirits. They stalk minds incessantly. It is their first and most often targeted area. Hence we are to monitor and check the sources of all vibes. Check the nature and type of your thoughts. Wisdom dictates, "Test the spirits, whether they be of God." Check their traits, obedient or disobedient. Beware of extreme mood fluctuations too suddenly. Manage your emotions. Spirits will try to take you off guard. Too happy, beware of accidents. Too sad, they try to depress you. Never allow prolonged sadness or loneliness to engulf your spirit. There are legitimate times of grief. Learn to be prayerful during those times. Take into account that evil spirits attack altars when they are most vulnerable or unguarded. Psalm 127:2, when you are in God's favour nothing can interfere with your sleep. As a person is nursed back to spiritual health, over time, he/she becomes really skilled at spotting the enemy's moves. A few chapters later we will examine in detail the entire network supreme command center, its long history, strategic strongholds and most importantly the next big trump card, "Operation Prime Clone."

Societies try with sincerity to establish pillars. Men and women of renown to whom the rest of the populace should emulate are usually chosen and exalted as icons. For the most part the exercise is honest and the intent honourable. However there is a giant megalomaniacal spiritual force that has an insatiable appetite for any exalted position. It targets any power base of influence so that it can sway minds (altars) of the masses. Often it or its agents stalk people that fit certain personality profiles and then work on those "targets" to establish spiritual hot links to mythical Mount Olympus. Once persons are exalted and emulated, Satan seeks them out of every organization. As long as a person is high-profile and charismatic, he exerts tremendous pressure to recruit those persons as his Pied Pipers. Pied Pipers must be conspicuous and tremendously influential. Shepherds, please differentiate between carnal zeal, spiritual zeal and the "Love-of-attention spirit." Spiritual zeal is unselfish. If you are so energized when you see the microphone or the camera that you hug the spotlight 90 percent of the time, be very careful of the curse of Shebna, Isaiah 22:14-20. The more you exalt yourself, the less of God you will achieve. Your spiritual hearing will diminish. The more you are obedient and humble, more of God's presence will manifest.

Rebekah had character blemishes. That is why God gave Paul instructions as to how to reconstruct His spiritual body in 1st Corinthians 12. Critical teachings and/or preachings, and/or subtle "Boastings against Older Branches" grieve God's Spirit. I have been in churches with large memberships and the head pastor reads the notices, leads the song services, preaches the messages, handles the altar calls and does counseling after the service. The personality checklists are in Matthew 5. Be careful that your assemblies are not being groomed to be extensions of your leaders' personalities. God does not give gifts and take them back. The manifestation of gifts in or through an individual is no indication that he/she is functioning in obedience to the will and or plan of God. After all, freshly cut lumber looks good. Lumber not checked regularly cannot endure the test of time and will become termite-ridden. In Exodus 34:6-7, be awakened to the fact that "Iniquities of Spiritual Brides," temples, synagogues and churches are computed up to four generations. Examine any bride that has been around for those multitudes of years: are there any without spots or wrinkles? The word of God foresaw it: There is *none* without spot or wrinkle.

CHAPTER 19H. AN ABANDONED ALTAR CALLED HOME.

Our species Homo Sapiens-Sapiens are mammals by nature and design. We nurse our young. By natural law, the females are designed to wean, physically comfort and groom the young—in short, to instill yin characteristics. The males are designed to instill security through bonding, building, and most importantly to propagate the female species through their yang capabilities. Let us go back to our schematic. Never lose sight of that. The plans for the building of the complete temple: soul, body and spirit must be handed down to the children. David *received* the plans. Solomon *built* the house. God Almighty drew the plans; His Firstfruit Son *received* the redemptive plans (Isaiah 53). Subsequently, all natural and grafted branches, must line up, or fit *plumb* to the carpenter's spirit level.

Scientists have only recently discovered that the earth and the organ called "skin" have similar chemical nuclei. Here is something interesting. When the chief *Architect of the Universe* fashioned Adam, did Adam not represent a grafted plant? Did Eve not represent a pruned vine? Try to detect the *sources* of disobedience. The eggs of disobedience, once sown, proliferated and were passed on. What if Eve was obedient like Mary? Physical death would never exist! When the first family arrived, Satan successfully penetrated the union of woman and man. He planted seeds of disobedience and confusion in the original family. From that day, our immune systems became compatible with that of the *father* of death, sickness, and rebellion. He uses the same seeds to sow confusion in small families, big ones called institutions and God's family called the church. He sows confusion, lies, and deceit. If fathers would exert as much energy defending "Home" as they do defending a barstool, a beer bottle, some expensively financed sex den or "Home Substitute," families would be so compatible. We would not leave so many altars unguarded for Satan and his gang to trample and devastate at will. The truth is that there are deep feelings of emptiness and boredom in millions of men and women. They are spiritually detached from the truth. Whatever myths they have been chasing have left very deep fjords of emptiness.

There is nothing known that can be compared to the foundational love of a parent. So it is both in the natural and much more so in the spiritual. Think of humans, being separated by rebellion and sin, trying to fill large spiritual canyons with temporary carnal substitutes. There are not enough beers or alcoholic drinks in the universe that can fill those voids.

There are not enough cigarettes, or drugs that can fill those voids.

There are not enough cars, clothes or food that can fill those voids.

There is not enough gold or jewelry that can fill those voids.

No amount of men/women can fill those voids. Here is a big surprise:

No amount of money can fill those voids.

GRAVEYARDS OF THE WORLD ARE FILLED WITH THE HEADSTONES OF
BILLIONS THAT DIED IN FRUSTRATION, BELIEVING ONE OR MORE OF
THE ABOVE.

I am going to list the five most macho things that any man can do to reach the apex of manhood or "Machismo." They are:

1. Rebuild his personal altar.

2. Rebuild the family's altar by getting rid of all generational curses of both sides of your parents and your wife's parents through corporate repentance.

3. Re-establish a spiritual hot-link with your created purpose through your Creator.

4. After you have completed those three, ask God to introduce you to the Way, Truth, and Everlasting Life.

5. Ask God to lead you and your family to the right Holy Spirit-filled church or to let the Holy Spirit lead and have His way in your church/synagogue or temple. Years of leaving those altars wide open and unprotected have allowed Satan to introduce Pied Pipers of ennui and emptiness. "You shall know the truth and the truth shall set you free!"

There is a not so subtle battle being raged visibly and invisibly for the control of as many minds as possible. The News Media play no small part in that. You would have assumed that "Wise-hearted Persons" would have pooled their resources to have daily newspapers dedicated towards freeing captured minds. Truth is that the other side has infiltrated political parties, news organizations and educational disciplines. Do you think it is accidental that there are more "Gays" than preachers featured on live shows?

A few years ago we were in shock when we read about the Jamestown massacre. What do we expect when we have allowed ourselves to function in 90 percent error-mode for so long? Another time the news blared out stories about the Camp Dravidian compound. In the meantime millions are lured away into wildernesses of uninhibited sex and drugs searching for their El Dorado. In the milieu are latest versions of Don Quixote, chasing windmills, convinced that they are giants. Isaiah 5:20 cautioned, "Woe unto them that call evil good, and call good evil; that put darkness for light and light for darkness." Verse 21, "Woe unto them that are wise in their own eyes, and prudent in their own sight." Unfortunately, we do not spend enough time either on research, or in searching for the truth; many assume that might is right. The "Aye's" might have it, but the "Aye's" do not necessarily have it right!

A few years ago someone decided that inserting the word "LIKE" in every sentence after the word "is" was hip. Try having a one and one conversation with a high school student from a metropolis. It is like this, it is like that with no illustration whatsoever just mythical references. Some pied piper decided it was cool to put a ring in his nose or tongue and bingo they follow. Who and to whom are their altars of sensible choices surrendered? Bodies are expensively leased luxury vehicles. I have heard Satan swear that his focus is on this young generation. During Abraham's time, fathers used to bless their children because they were in a position, poised to do so spiritually. How many of us are in such positions? We all need to rebuild our altars and revert back to our homes of truth and wisdom. Regrettably emptiness and unfulfillment have left many homes haunted places. Father cannot wait to leave home; mother cannot wait to leave home. Children cannot wait to leave home in search of Pied Pipers eager and willing to lead them astray.

CHAPTER 20. "OPERATION PRIME CLONE."

There is an ancient science from which philosophy was incorrectly grafted. I will only mention its name in coded reference. Their adepts were told that the truth is embedded in a "Special Stone." With the quantity of clandestine and secret institutions worldwide, where does one ask these questions: Is Satan real? Does Satan have a secret trump card? If so would God reveal Satan's hand or would we be taken by surprise?

20A. THE PHILOSOPHER'S STONE, FOUNDATION STONE OF TRUTH!

However, the Master of Masters or Chief Philosopher left a special "*BLACK STONE.*" Finding the Philosopher's Stone meant finding the ultimate in wisdom. The erudite of developing Europe tinkered with all possibilities of smelting and mixing of metals and ores. As a result they eventually discovered Chemistry. Hundreds of books have been written supposedly leaving clues to a mythical trail, through clefts of rock for the black stone of the Chief Philosopher. This evidence is needed to expose a major deception.

For hundreds of years churches in the Occident were unfamiliar with Hebrew customs and terms such as: "Discovering the nakedness of a father, passing through the needle's eye, and eating the forbidden fruit." Those have been the topics of some of the most ridiculous and among the most misunderstood sermons ever preached. The inaccuracies were direct results of Satan's injection of his spirits of pride, conceit, and arrogance to name a few. Those are introductory spirits. They are capable of penetrating small spiritual cracks. They also have the ability, over time, to widen the pivotal cracks for more powerful spirits to enter. The principle of cloning, hatched by Satan himself, is a fruit from the spirit of pride. God will reveal the real sinister plot behind cloning, Satan's latest trump card.

Ancient Rome, then a pagan nation, blamed the Christians for burning their city during Nero's tenure of office (a plot hatched by Satan himself). The nation turned to Christianity during the Byzantine Era. That move shook up Satan. He sprang into immediate action and then hatched his back-up plans. He filled Rome with debris of ancestral hate and arrogance. For the first 200 years of the past millennium, seven kings governed Rome. Satan controlled almost all of them. Rome had a vanquished altar base. His next plan was to desecrate and kidnap the most holy church base. His agents first stole the sacred temple treasures from Jerusalem. Then they allegedly stole the body of Mary, the last messianic seed-incubator and placed her corpse on their soil. "The dead will bury the dead." Next they tried to steal *the identity of the cornerstone.* Having gotten away with all the aforementioned, they separated themselves and their teachings from the original ones. By disconnecting their "Church" and teachings from the true spiritual foundation, they created a canyon for "Babelic infiltration." Strangely enough they do not deny that since they have publicized the fact that their church was built on the foundation of either the pillar "Peter" or the Samaritan "Simon." When Solomon built the largest house for Pharaoh's daughter, she helped to turn his heart away from God. The Gentile-equivalent church will turn away many. In almost 1700 years of unchanging existence, the Roman church of Paeter was built on one key scriptural reference. So if by chance that scripture was wrongly translated what then? Following historic parallels of God's people abandoning His perfect word, teachings and laws documented as Old Testament stat-utes, the inevitable always happens. Satan implants a matriarchal spirit to usurp God's throne. Be that as it may, decrees would have had to be established to make it impossible for the rank and file of all members to even think of scrutinizing any dogma and doctrine. Coincidentally, thousands were killed for questioning or examining their dogma and doctrines in the past. Over years, the Roman church deemed itself infallible. Penalties for violating that would bring immediate church-concocted curses of Heresy and Excommunication. Even though God or-dains progressive paths for His "Chosen" always, in the over 1666 years of existence, change is discouraged. Bishops in the Jerusalem church were encouraged to marry. Those of Rome *were forbidden to marry*. In the Jerusalem church, only adults old enough to repent of their sins were immersed for baptismal purposes. The Roman church sprinkled children with water poured on their foreheads for baptism. The Jerusalem church used the word, and prayed in God's ordained language. The Roman church uses a "catechism" substitute for the word and chants in a restricted tongue (Latin was not the colonies' language). The Jerusalem church prayed to God. The Roman church *prays to dead* Christians who they *claim* are in an after death exalted position to assist their parishioners. Martin Luther found 99 teachings of the Roman churches that were contrary to the Bible. Instead of correcting the errors, Martin and all that sided with the truth were ostracized. I will list a few scriptures for many of my friends who have altars in their houses praying through statues to dead saints: Psalm 115:17, "The dead praise *not* the Lord." Ecclesiastes 9:5, "The dead *know not* any thing."

The Jerusalem church knew that God *laid the true foundation stone in Zion*. The Roman based church *laid a founding stone on a Simon* called Peter 300 years after his death. In 1st Kings 8:1 and 2nd Chronicles 5:2, the city of David is Zion. Since God placed the "Foundation *Stone of Truth* in Zion," any foundation anywhere else cannot be truth. Simon was an apostle and one of the pillars of the Jerusalem church. Now follow me: Simon called Cephas was the son of Jona, no lineage with David. He was not "Chief Elder" nor was he the Bishop of the Jerusalem church, James was. Simon was taken to Rome once, to be martyred.

The Hebrew gospels detailed God's desire to send one greater than Elisha and a greater deliver than Moses. "The Excellent One" was predestined to improve on all of Moses' work. Peter was the first to acknowledge that publicly. Simon, when asked by Jesus in the book of Luke 9:19, "But whom say ye that I am?" Some said Elias; some said John the Baptist. In verse 20, the Spirit of God calls the acknowledgment a "Rama word, a word of wisdom, a word in season, or a specific revelation." Peter replied, "Thou art the Christ." On the foundation of that revelation, that "Rama Word," Jeshua said, "I will build my church." I was taught (incorrectly I might add) that Peter means rock and that was the rock (Peter) on which some church was supposed to be built. In 1st Corinthians 10:4, Paul explained that the spiritual "Rock" was Christ. Peter also lied and erred; as a result Peter was fallible. Fortunately, the deceit and sub-sequent cover-ups were prophesied.

I had a brief meeting with a soft-spoken man of unusual stature. I thought nothing of his unusual capabilities save the fact that he was able to take me through rock solid places and that his attire, his sword and sheath were *not modern*. I thought it was a vision. However when I encountered him twice after the first instance I realized it was no dream. I referenced the incident prior to rehashing events in Genesis 19:1-5 and also Luke 24:4. In those and every incident documented in the Torah, the Tanakh and New Testimonials (witnesses of

Jeshua), whenever angels visit us they are always as "Ancient Men from the future domain." God's witnesses described His angels. They were always "Men" with unusual powers. Since they resemble "The Ancient of Days," they always appear ancient. Allegedly, the Roman based church has not only found "petite modern women," but also species with wings that brought them messages. I searched prior prophecies about the Messiah, hoping to find a Roman connection. I found writings of prophets of old with specific references to the restorative ministry of the Messiah and His witnesses: Isaiah 11:10-11. Those prophecies refer to Jesus' all-inclusive ministry—especially for the dispersed and downtrodden. I found prophecies about Jesus' betrayal by Judas and the *price* of the betrayal, even where Judas would be buried but Judas was not mentioned by name. Judas' name appears through select numerical sequencing. Zechariah 11:1, "So they weighed my price thirty pieces of silver." In Psalm 41:9-12 are prerecorded prophecies that the *Messiah would be exalted in the presence of God forever* and that a friend would betray Him. Psalm 41:9, "My own familiar friend in *whom I trusted*, which did eat my bread (I have found no Hebrew customs whereby their kings would invite a friend for a casual dinner) hath lifted up his heel against me." Still I found no reference to Rome until I received insights from the blueprints of the Temple of Solomon, and the prophetic nature of spiritual brides: Rebekah and Miriam.

Rome disconnected itself spiritually from the city of David and then secured its temple on a foundation of martyrs' blood. Those doings have opened a large spiritual highway for the image of the imposter. I wonder what secret ingredients were factored in the composition of the philosopher's stone that caused its blackness. Ancient libraries emphasized that since the first covenant was given to Abra-ham, the Hamitic seed should sprout after its kind. Since Solomon, a Hamitic Hebrew built the Temple of God and he (Solomon) transgressed, then the repairs must be undergone by another Hamitic Hebrew to intercede for His kindred.

CHAPTER 20B. PREVIEW OF THE FINAL ANTICHRIST.

Rome occupied Israel. A distinction needs to be made between the Roman Empire, ancient Rome and the current city of Rome. The current city is inhabited with loads of wonderful and spiritually transformed people, including some on my research team. When I use the word Rome by itself, I am referring to the ancient spiritual base. So Romans believed they were superior to the Hebrews. As Rome grew into a center of learning and wisdom, out of her arose an elite class of thinkers that learned to covet mental exploits. Rome's system of mental, educational and human osmosis helped to strengthen her militarily and culturally.

A doctrine of presumed superiority had prevailed and followed all of Rome's seed into Western Civilizations to this day. The Romans had brown limp hair and long noses similar to those of the Greeks. The Ethiopians, Carthaginians, Moors, and Jews had broader faces, black woolly hair, broader noses and were tanned, for the most part. Herodotus recorded that the builders of the pyramids and Egyptian civilizations had "burnt skin and woolly hair." All of the scribes' references to their skin in the Torah or Old Testament used the same Hebrew words, either: "adom, adam or edom" meaning dark brown. When referring to their hair and themselves, they also used the same words as Moses in (Leviticus 13:31), Solomon in Songs 1:5, Elijah in 2nd Kings 1:8 (no Hebrew word found), and Jeremiah in Lamentations 5:10. The Hebrew word for burnt black "shachar" meaning "dusky or pitch black" is used when referring to night and coals. I have spent years with my Jewish and Arabic colleagues questioning whether translators who subscribed to the Arian myth deliberately coloured the language to support Rome's pre-eminence.

Let us understand that Roman-perceived superiority was not based on pigmentation since approximately 1/3 of the Roman senate was North African by the beginning of the 3rd century. Confirmation of those views can be found in the infamous remark made by the advancing Romans when they conquered what would become England. The first impression the Romans (that had African Generals and senators) formed was that the British were barbarians: "They are not even worthy to be our slaves." How ironic it is that as the vanquished became later victors and as the "Esoteric literature of Babel" surfaced, Rome's seed adopted the traits of Babel. Later on it became enshrined in the minds and doctrines of the new European elite that there were perhaps two different types of people: one *allegedly mated with angels* and produced the "Aryans" and the other type "Evolved" from the apes and produced brown, black and yellow people. Fact is, to date, the only solid evidence of evolution in people found is: The original brown man getting darker and "evolving" into the black man, and the same brown man losing melanin to "evolve" into the pale-skinned man.

God gave to ancient Israel's Hamitic/Semitic/Japhethic people, the choice of a Theocracy. They were to marry their "covenant people." Had they been obedient, an Oasis of obedient people would have colonized the complete self-sufficient landmass Africa, shaped like a human head. Unfortunately, the lands where remnants of most of the southern tribes have returned to are spiritual, physical, financial and political deserts for the most part. As a consequence of disobedience, the opposite "Bahomet" was birthed.

The remnant nations of the ashes of Babel, driven by the Fellers and their secret decrees have amalgamated all the dominant seeds of Gentile nations that "paled" into war loving people (Revelation 17: 12-13, and also verses 17 to 18) for the sworn purpose of building a "One World Government." Paleontologists have attempted to create other racial types based on "Mythical mumbo- jumbo of unsubstantiated theories." Unfortunately their theories have to be adjusted with each new discovery.

It is amazing how many teaching-aids students have used that were actually "Rama" words: *Paleolithic man existed before people began paling!* Be reminded that white is a colour arrived at by the subtraction of colours, breakdown of colours or through bleaching. One day a very powerful legal mind will sue the Government of the United States of America for millions of dollars for the classification of "white" on a document identifying that person's race. Having no foundation to prove such folly and fearing an avalanche of further lawsuits, only then will the nonsense stop.

When Roman citizens began to decipher the wisdom captured in secret writings, their people were taught that Mary and her son were Hamitic Hebrews. That period of respect for accuracy occurred when Constantine's mother became a Christian and used her influence to send emissaries to Jerusalem in search of truth. However a Florentine bunch of undesirables eventually seized control of the Vatican during the reign of Maffeo Barberi (Pope Urban II). At the onset, church paintings portrayed ethnic accuracy. The earliest paintings of Jeshua and His mother throughout Europe, Asia, Ethiopia, Crete, and Corinth show a well-tanned mother and child. That would make sense since the Hebrew Jeshua lived around the hottest parts of Israel (the Judaean desert regions) at the beginning of the first century. From the 11th century, Rome was, for the most part, a Christian nation that had acquired sacred gospels' parchments. As the paintings increased, Jeshua evolved into an Indian male. By the 15th century, an effeminate-looking Florentine model became the artistic standard-bearer by which Jeshua was depicted.

CHAPTER 21. THE KNIGHTS ARRIVED!

CHAPTER 21A. THE LIGHTS WAXED DIM.

The Templars were the first Gentiles to gain access to the secret documents of the Essenes and the Sanhedrin. The all knowing God repeated what was done at Babel. He confounded their abilities to understand wisdom above and beyond "Point 33." The disconnection grew unabated. Rome engineered major massacres against the Jewish people: first under Titus in 70 C.E. and then the *First Crusade* of the 11th century. The *First Crusade* was not only horrific but also it shattered the ethnic and religious tolerance that existed in Jerusalem then. Why does God get the blame when Satan kidnaps religious institutions and their leaders? There were eight Roman-sponsored religious crusades plus Gregory IX's Papal Inquisition culminating with the expulsion of the Jews from France and the confiscation of their property in 1306 by Philip IV. It did not end there. Satan is still obsessed with attempting to eradicate their seed. Jesus' teachings became disconnected eventually and replaced by rituals: doctrines of substitutions and replacement theology. One of the biggest injustices was to infer and that God had rejected His people. The doctrine of superiority was exported. Colonizers were blessed (sic) and given the right to take anything they found in lands of "inferior people." They took sacrosanct treasures. They took gold, lands, library parchments and people. All those brazen "thefts and murders" were sanctioned by institutions whose "altars" were so poignantly penetrated that in many parts of the world today, the words "Jesus" and "Christianity" are synonymous with theft and murder.

Just imagine that Jesus inherited the blame for Satan's misdeeds and Satan still had the gall to influence the teaching of infallibility by institutions that he already penetrated. The word of God is the only infallible utterance. It says, "All have sinned and come short of His Glory." It never said all, except one, because one is infallible. Stealing is a sin; killing is a sin. There are millions in Mexico hungry today because their stolen gold sits on top of institutions that Satan has penetrated. There are people in Africa hungry because thousands of church members worked them undeterred for 400 years without pay.

Columbus received permission to draw a line in the middle of the Atlantic Ocean. He was commanded to divide the lands on one side for Spain and those on the other side for Portugal. What followed his wake of blood, theft and rape, became a trail that Leviathan followed through men, and by men leaving diabolical eggs on the earth. They established foundations for spiritual strongholds, turning this beautiful sustainable planet into a haven for demons and brainwashed people. Columbus was a Pied Piper.

Initially, Roman armies burnt Christian and Hebrew texts indiscriminately. Over time, pagan teachings and myths diluted God's original teachings, replacing them (to this day) with rituals strictly forbidden in "God's infallible word." Satan knows that Jesus is his everlasting "Daymare" and Nightmare. He has already penetrated churches; set divisions among God's people, set Gentiles against Jews, Jews against Gentiles, Muslims against Christians, Muslims against Jews and vice versa. People are not only searching through his web of lies, but also there is a new breed learning to kick his butt. Millions believe that a seed of Judah, relative of one of the blackest Hamitic Hebrews that ever lived, King Solomon, somehow "Evolved!"

Currently, scientists that belong to certain organizations (secret and sinister in nature) are working on perfecting a human clone. A body is a vehicle for carrying either a right spirit or disobedient and contrary ones. I wonder which spirit Satan will select to plant in that body when a scientist produces the "Prized Clone?" What a wonderful way to deceive the world! We already have millions of pictures of an antichrist. Will Satan jump into the prized clone?

Subconsciously implanted in the minds of many, is the effeminate European image of Jesus. Didn't He discern that those billions of disobediently inaccurate portraits and statues would have been distributed about Him? Jesus warned that false Christs might fool even the elect. He also said: "I will come like a thief in the night."

If cable networks ever flash the breaking news of the portrayed Jesus in a metropolis and people, ignorant of the deception begin running towards Him, I would not be fooled! If your house, your office or your assembly has those pictures or statues exalted on altars, in disobedience to God's own word, you are exposing yourself and your entire household to the worse Pied Piper in history, the final antichrist. Exodus 20:4, "Thou shall not make unto thee *any* graven image, or any likeness of any thing that is in heaven above, or that is in the earth beneath." If you will stop buying them, they will stop making them.

There is nothing wrong with making crosses as long as they do not have a carved image on them. Jesus was naked on the cross; He was laid bare, stripped and striped in nakedness and shame for the world to know that He bore our griefs and our shame. Why are the seed of the people (that pushed a spear in His side and desecrated His teachings) parading as the Messiah a half-wrapped European? Is it a form of barefaced mockery?

CHAPTER 21B. LEVIATHAN, ITS PATH AND ITS EGGS!

The moon is a reflector of the sun's light. It is referred to as a feminine principle. *The Ancients* surmised that the primary mass, the sun broke into masses: sun/moon etc. They compared the symbiotic relationship between the sun and moon to a male/female union. The sun has yang principles; the moon has yin principles. Since yin represents the feminine principle I will refer at times to her. As we progress you will see why that is acceptable: her cycle is 28 days. The female specie of humankind has cycles that correspond to hers. The role assigned to the moon in the orbital sequence of things is to be the dominant orb in the *second slots* of sequential time. Hence, every 24-hour period following the commencement of a week, where the *sun* has the *dominant* slot called the day (the sun leads) or Sunday, the moon's slot is called the day of the moon (lundi or lunes from lunar or in English) Monday. Moses' first discourse, the Book of Genesis holds the first seeds of coded messages sown. Before *The Creator* placed the vehicle of time in the universe, all possible configurations for the moon ushering in the second cycle were calculated and measured from the first cycle to the last cycles. It was determined then, as it is now and ever will be, that every time the sun ushers in the first sequence of days it should be called Sunday. The next 24-hour period is and always will be called the Day of the Moon or Monday. The moon regulates the tides. Even though scientists are having a hard time finding water on its surface, the moon has a powerful effect on all oceans and seas. Without releasing more information than I have to at this point, let us refer to something that one of God's early prophets spoke. Refer with me if you will to Isaiah 27:1, "In that day, the Lord with his sore and great and strong sword shall punish Leviathan, that piercing serpent, even Leviathan that crooked serpent and he shall slay the dragon that is in the sea." John, one of Jesus' 12 first fruit witnesses, while on the island of Patmos, received a vision which is recorded in Revelation 16:5. He gave us a preview of "The Angel of the Waters."

For every earthly messenger that the Lord sends, He assigns a post of "Prophet, Messenger, Revealer or Restorer." There is one that Satan could not, nor cannot handle: "The Restorer." He was forced to come up with a counterfeit spirit. Picture Satan, a programmed destroyer, attempting to forge a counterfeit life-giver. It is obvious that the only angle he has to play is the false foundation image and deceit to go along with it. Once he can get the image duplicated, then simply reverse some sicknesses that he had previously placed on people in a large public arena and millions would be fooled. Satan has put in place an archetype to spread as much havoc over that assigned area. Leviathan is the satanic archetype. In Isaiah's prophecy, it is only during the "Epoch of Full Restoration" that awful spirit is crushed finally. Up to now, the spiritually weak guardians of our spiritual treasures allowed the satanic army to maintain strangleholds on people and nations.

Since all satanic spirits draw strength from body fluids, Leviathan draws strength from massacres. Satan purposefully tries to engineer mass sorceries that perpetrate huge blood sacrifices either overtly or covertly. Every descendant of the 12 tribes of Israel had and has in his veins God's contracted and covenanted blood. Satan naturally had to devise a master plan to capture representatives of all tribes—Deuteronomy 28:64. First he would attempt to weaken them, then lure them away from their rightful God with religious spirits and then take them into foreign lands with pagan cultures and habits. Since God desired their blood to bond with, Satan ensured that blood of both the seed of Israel and the seed of Judah were used in occult ceremonies to usurp their covenant bond—Leviticus 20:2 and 6.

Although some "Secrets behind the Atlantic Slave Trade and the Holocaust" were already penned, I must make a small reference to some well-established organizations today, whose members have manipulated God's flock into very sinister tasks (in the past). Since so many prominent people belong to modern versions of those institutions, I will make cursory mention only. Pied Pipers of yesteryear include Jim Jones, and Adolph Hitler. Hitler's membership in organizations "Secret and Sinister" in composition and memberships, allowed him access to spiritual hot-links that were ungodly in design and nature. There is a famous international bank, B.B.D.C.O., whose founders, brothers, were major slave traders. Ironically that bank is one of the largest banks in those countries where slavery flourished.

Now folks let us be civilized for a moment. If a baby is in a tub and something with a lot of germs fell in, throw out the water and save the baby. If the utensil is very dirty, throw out the utensil with the water and save the baby. If we had examined our foundational altars in the past, millions of us would never have been pied to satanic pipers. I will list the patterns of secret rituals that were done by the pipers of yesteryear to show how they allowed Leviathan to spread its eggs globally. By the way, all those events had not only been prophesied, but in precision, they have come to pass. Before I list the entire prophecies, I will list the prescribed punishments for the seed of the beneficiaries of "Unrighteous mammon."

CHAPTER 21C. A PRERECORDED SCRIPT.

The human river is forked. One shifts gradually towards ultimate obedience and another towards ultimate disobedience. Everyone (that ever lived) finishes the race at either of the two mouths—Daniel 12:2, "Many of them that sleep in the dust of the earth shall awake, some to everlasting life, and some to everlasting contempt." Additionally—Isaiah 5:14, "Hell hath enlarged herself, and opened her mouth without measure: and their glory, and their multitude, and their pomp, and he that rejoiceth, shall descend into it." To all formerly intellectual geeks that have failed to come up with solutions to support their unproven myths, the world has listened to your types for too long. I know you are going to hate this but the era of guessing is over! Since people often wonder why horrible things happen to seemingly "nice children" whose grandparents may not have repented nor received forgiveness from horrible atrocities that they may have committed, these revelations are timely.

News media ask: "Why did so and so have to die such a horrible death?" God is no respecter of persons. God cannot lie. When God says *he shall visit the iniquities on the children*, the children's children up to the third and fourth generation, God did not say, "maybe." It is not my fault that you received weak teachings from tarnished altars. Even though victim nations hold the membership majority in the United Nations, there is no official UN resolution on reparations for "Lost Tribes" that were enslaved and provided labour still unpaid, for over 400 years. Neither have I read of a motion tabled seeking compensation on behalf of the American Indians or the Mexicans. I have never read of those atrocities being included on their "List of Human Rights' Violations." To add insult to injuries already sustained, the fruits of their labours are still being manipulated by an unjust and unfair system of monetary value and exchange rigged to ensure that their meager resources are chiseled away. When college students ask during my lectures: "Why do nations pay fees to a UN organization that allows veto power to have precedent over people power?" The answer: "demon spirits" as per the prophecy in Jeremiah 4:16-17. You see why Bible reading is being outlawed again?

Let us seek the words of the Most Righteous Judge. God promised through Ezekiel, punishment to His people. They would be displaced into lands of heathen nations that would rule over them and steal their resources. Ezekiel 22:15, "I will scatter thee among the heathen." Verse 27, "Her princes in the midst of thee are like wolves ravening their prey, to shed blood, and to destroy souls, to get dishonest gain." Isaiah 5:20, "Woe unto them that call evil good, and good evil; that put darkness for light, and light for darkness; that put bitter for sweet, and sweet for bitter!" Isaiah 5:21-24 list the inevitable for all the evil that men devise behind their self-imposed 'Right by Might' philosophies. Verse 24, "Their blossom shall go to dust, because they have cast away the law of the Lord of hosts, and despised the word of the Holy One of Israel." Isaiah 13:11, "I will punish the world for their evil..."

THERE ARE PRECONDITIONS FOR GOD FIGHTING YOUR BATTLES AND MAKING RESTITUTION FOR YOU!

Deuteronomy 30:7, "The Lord thy God will put *all* these curses upon thine enemies, and them that hate thee and persecute thee." Verse 8, "Thou shall *return and obey the voice of the Lord* and do *all his commandments*, which I command thee." The verse ends with these two words: "This day," not tomorrow, not next week, but today, now and immediately.

I am going to print two sets of promises that the Lord made to the people of His covenant. The seriousness of that covenant could not be emphasized more. God consistently explained: The task you have vowed to perform, the gifts that He has promised and those special privileges, all have preconditions. This covenant is valuable. It is highly coveted. Do not take it for granted. In essence, if you remain faithful and obedient throughout your generations, every seed and seed's seed will be blessed forever. If you ever lose your marbles and break *God's*

Covenant, you, your children and children's children will regret the day that you were born. In other words, if God's chosen children become disobedient and lax, then others will sit in the covenant seats. Besides that, "when" those curses befall, do not say that you are in bad luck; say like I once did, "I am guilty." God will not restore what has been stolen or lost if you did not lose or have something stolen in the first place (see Joel 2:25).

So for those that have guarded well and will endure until the end, the blessings first: Deuteronomy 28—*IT SHALL COME TO PASS*. In other words, not maybe and not perhaps, it *shall* be so. It is spoken and it is written. I have put my seal through my prophet. It *shall* happen. "If you shall hearken diligently unto the voice of the Lord thy God to observe and to do *all*" not some, not when you feel like or if you feel like; then you and your generations shall be blessed. This is the deal no maybe about it. When you repent and seek forgiveness, always be assured of God's promises. *He will restore all:*

Verse 1, These Commandments which I command thee this day that the Lord thy God will set thee on high *above all the nations of the earth.*

Verse 2, "These blessings shall come to thee and overtake thee."

Verse 3, "Blessed shalt thou be in the city…and in the field." The lord promised blessings in health, wealth, goods, crops, and anything that your hands produce. *It would rain regularly on your crops.* You should "Lend and not Borrow." Here is the *only* precondition:

IF THOU SHALT HEARKEN UNTO THE VOICE OF THE LORD THY GOD.

As I write these things, focus on two countries: one called *Africa* and the one called *Israel.* I will explain later. In addition to drought, all manner of sicknesses and blindness, the curses are many, Deuteronomy 28:

Verse 32 says: Thy sons and daughters shall be *given unto another people* and thy eyes shall look and fail with longing for them all day long, (Atlantic Slave Trade) and there shall be *no might in thy hand.*

Verse 33… the fruit of thy land and thy labours shall a nation, which thou knowest not, eat up and thou shalt be only oppressed and crushed alway. Sic. "Is it mammon's fault, I.M.F.?"

Verse 35…The Lord shall smite thee in the knees and in the legs with a sore botch that cannot be healed from the sole of thy foot unto the top of thy head (AIDS foreseen).

Verse 36…The Lord shall bring thee and thy king which thou shall set over thee unto a nation which neither thou nor thy fathers have known; and there thou shall serve other gods, wood and stone (those that ended up from the gateway of Joppa to Haiti, Cuba and Santo Domingo). Thou shalt become a byword (Nigger and Hebe prophesied) an astonishment, a proverb among all nations whither the Lord shall lead thee.

Verse 38… Thou shalt carry much seed out into the field, and shalt gather but little in, for the locust (Ethiopia's plight) shall consume it.

Verse 39... Thou shalt plant vineyards, and dress them, but shalt neither drink of the wine, nor gather the grapes; for the worms shall eat them.

Verse 40... Thou shalt have olive trees throughout all thy coasts, but thou shalt not anoint thyself with the oil; for thine olive shall cast his fruit.

Verse 41... Thou shalt beget sons and daughters, but thou shalt not enjoy them; for they shall GO INTO CAPTIVITY.

Verse 42... All thy trees and fruit of thy land shall the locust consume.

Verse 43... The stranger that is within thee shall get up above thee very high and thou shalt come down very low (in thy own land) (Africa).

Verse 44... he shall lend to thee, and thou shalt not lend to him (the rise of such as the Barclay brothers prophesied)... he shall be the head, and thou shalt be the tail.

Before I print verse 45, I want this message to go to every person living south of En-gedi, south of Israel's most southern border, markedly countries of Ethiopia, Central Africa, North, East, West and South Africa. Hear me, ye scattered and so-called *Lost Tribes*. Satan has sent captor nations to reverse your heritage, confuse your tongue and steal your wealth. Your country is blessed with the most wealth in the world. You have the most diamonds, gold, bauxite, tantalite and the most natural energy reserves per capita in the world; yet you have fallen from the mightiest and richest to the poorest and among the lowest of nations. Mohammed, born in 570 C.E. was sent with revelations for "God's Theocracy." Mohammed was not of the lineage of Isaac. God's covenant seed was sent as a sacrifice for all. Your ancestors made a covenant with the God of Abraham, Isaac and Jacob (or Israel). Prophet Mohammed taught his people for about 22 years. In accordance with God's *Law of Double Reference*, the **Chosen Redeemer** must have a two-fold ministry representing the northern and southern tribes. That ministry must sow seeds of reconstruction over a 40-year period.

Deuteronomy 28 continued:

Verse 45... Moreover all these curses shall come upon thee and shall pursue thee until thou be destroyed, because thou hearkenedst not unto the voice of the Lord thy God, to keep His commandments and His statutes which He commanded thee.

Verse 46... They shall be upon thee for they *shall be a sign* and a wonder *upon thy seed forever!* The remnant that had been held captive in the west: If you repent and return to the Lord, then you will be pardoned and blessed. Those promises after the pardon are in Deuteronomy 30:3-6. Then you can say like I do, "I say bear witness."

Israel`s Kings from the tribe of Judah dwelt in the southernmost regions. In the 1st century, a remnant flock was blockaded at Massada. A remnant of the southern tribes and others fled across to Ethiopia and Sudan. Most were rounded up and exported via Joppa and Gorè. That is why Isaiah in chapter 49 referred specifically to those who dwelt in the isles of the sea: the seed of those exported. Let us first look at the Massada prophecy: Deuteronomy 28:53... And thou shalt eat the fruit of thine own body, the flesh of thy sons and thy daughters, which the lord thy God hath given thee, in the siege, and in the straitness, wherewith thine enemies shall distress thee. Here is another prophecy about those from the "South" that went to and through Africa: Jeremiah 13:19-20.

JEREMIAH 13:19, THE CITIES OF THE SOUTH SHALL BE SHUT UP AND NONE SHALL OPEN THEM. JUDAH SHALL BE CARRIED AWAY CAPTIVE.

In other words because the tribe of Judah was given the kingly anointing and their ancestral land was blessed in all blessings of permanent sustenance, if Judah disobeyed, then the seed of kings would end up as slaves. Those destined to wear royal apparel ended up naked. To emphasize that point, God made sure that He allowed Solomon to be one of the blackest men that ever lived. He also allowed him to build the most elaborate house ever built on earth. The message was simple: "Seed of Solomon, once you disobey me, you will be a byword." Instead of building houses for God, out of your predestined resources, seed of God's former enemies will cause you to build their houses for free. So *all* of Judah, not some, and "their seed of disobedience" as per Jeremiah 13:19, "Shall be wholly *carried away captive.*"

Verse 23 is a killer text. In other words none will expect you to escape this wrestling match with Leviathan. Verse 23, "Can the Ethiopian change his skin, or a leopard his spots?" God's warning: *THEN MAY YE ALSO DO GOOD!* In other words you better come to your senses. As long as the leopard is spotted, remnant of Judah will be recognized; they will either be obedient and prosperous, or disobedient and degraded noticeably. God's Son is the only one who can free you from your bondage. His name is not Buddha, Confucius, Mohammed, Krishna, Bahaullah, Smith or Peter. His name is Jeshua! It is written and prophesied. You will die in spiritual, mental or physical poverty and bondage unless you call and receive the complete "Redemption Package" from the "One Shepherd." The name means "God is Salvation" or Jeshua. If you reject the teachings or the redemption package of the *Prince of Peace*, you, your health, your mind, your wealth, your sleep, your family or and your nation will *KNOW NO PEACE!* Satan had been very successful in selling a programme of ethnic conceit. Somehow you were not important unless you had your own religion. I do not care how hard this is to swallow, God said, *One Shepherd* and there are over 1000 coded texts that spell out the name *JESHUA.* The final part of Jeremiah 13:23, "Then may ye also do good that are accustomed to do evil." This word is for those that have grown accustomed to their wildernesses: *Do you know that God has even promised to send rivers in your deserts to redeem all that the locusts and their caterpillars have eaten?* Help them dear Father!

CHAPTER 21D. THE POWER OF PARDON.

True to prophecy, descendants of God's holy people have been captured and scattered to triple invasions under seed of Rome and Babylon and to multiples of slavery at the hands of every Gentile nation. Many escaped into the south. A minority was strengthening other scattered flock and converts in Asia, Ephesus, Corinth, Galatia, Lystra, Derbe, Lycaonia, Tyre, Sidon, Joppa and Antioch. Pockets, formerly of the Pharisean and Sadducean sects went underground—Judges 1:21. Some of those escaped during Titus' slaughter of 70 C.E. and their seed after them suffered subsequent persecutions. The seed of those that were scattered through Macedonia and Corinth ended up in Europe. Out of those northern tribes, a remnant returned after the 1948 Exodus.

There have been times when custodians of God's altars make intercession on behalf of a nation and God destroys the satanic power bases. In the book of Esther, Mordecai beseeched God on behalf of all Jews and God answered. Nehemiah called a national convocation and God not only pardoned, but also promised to "dwell in their booths." God did the same for Moses on behalf of the ancient Israelites. There are millions that belong to nations whose spiritual scales are weighed heavily on the side of unrighteousness. America and several coun-tries in Europe have had spiritual foundations that were not exactly flattering. All it takes is one pastor willing to lead a "convocation of repentance" for God's redemptive power through *corporate pardon* to take effect. It is more effective when a pastor or pastors intercede before catastrophes (natural or otherwise) strike.

Twice I was among 1500 to 2000 persons from 200 nations that participated in spiritually restorative convocations for Jews, Arabs, and Christians. Many attended out of curiosity, they thought. God called them to His Holy Place to sow firstfruit seeds of reconciliation. At one such convocation, someone received a "Rama word." He asked that a symbolic gesture be made to ease the debt of poor nations that are being yoked. The gesture was symbolic. Since faith without works is dead, he asked delegates to sow a one dollar seed. Not one person benefiting from the fruits of unrighteous mammon responded publicly.

To go into the ancestral rainbow of what is now Europe would take up much space rehash-ing an instant replay syndrome. Let us say that there was a path of blood through war and conquest. A trail of blood, like a giant snake, seeped below the surfaces of modern-day Europe. There, one of the biggest human melting pots brewed: the foundation for mixing paint can be referenced. Mix seven or more and the colours break down. The same way the colour white is derived from an assortment of pigments, all so-called white people "evolved" from seed of at least seven darker nations. Seed of former Neolithic tribes mixing among the victors and vanquished of the ever-changing landscape saw the rise and fall of empires, as prophesied by Daniel. When Babylon was destroyed, its roots remained in the earth. Incidentally out of the roots of Babylon's Empire sprung seed nations of Europe. From the ruins of the Grecian Empire came the Romans and out of their ashes came the Dutch, British, French, Spanish, German and American nations. As a matter of fact, nearly all Gentile nations got involved in enslaving at least one of the tribes of Israel. That esoteric message was coded in the different characteristics of the twins in Rebekah's womb.

So we can say that out of North Africa's original belly came two sets of people, the ances-tral seed of twins in the womb of Rebekah (Esau and Jacob). The first one lost his birthright. Out of one came the lighter ones that pursued the birthright of the darker ones—sounds familiar? See how easy it is to check what is true and what is not? It has to agree with *God's schematic*. It is important to make some things clear at this point. The demonic virus did not affect all of the people that lived in Europe then. Neither were there all bad folks that came across the Atlantic looking for new homes. Some of those that arrived in the New England colonies with the Pilgrim Fathers and others that went west across America were decent folks. Their seed started some of the greatest revivals and healing ministries of all times.

This is not a time to rehash bitterness. This is not a time for anger, but time for repentance. Let us not forget that all have transgressed. It is the first Jubilee since Israel became a nation. We must release all pain by forgiving first, then confessing current and ancestral transgressions to receive recompense. Readers might be wondering which of those genes flow in their veins. Many know; many do not know. People have been intermarrying for hundreds and thousands of years. God is so great that when He selected me to do this task, first He made me trace my ancestry and Lo and behold He had planted both the seed of the oppressors and of the oppressed in my veins. So if I were to be disobedient, which portion of my body should I get angry with? God in His wisdom made sure that I could not get angry and dejected. Instead He put a "right spirit" within me. Double-portion boos to you Satan!

At this point many of you reading this (especially reclaimed pastors) will feel the presence of the Lord as you have never felt it before. Some of you might be groaning like a woman about to give birth. If the latter occurs, that is God's *Spirit of Travail*, like a pent-up fire, pained for years for the suffering of His people: Say the "Redemption Prayer" in chapter 19d.

CHAPTER 21E. EARLY WELL DIGGERS!

This is not a complete list nor was it meant to be such. To include all, I would have had to write volumes on the early Trailblazers. I will, however, single out people like Francis Asbury, Robert Sheffy, George Whitfield, George Oglethorpe, David Barnard, D.L. Moody, Charles Finney, Smith Wiggelsworth and Kathryn Kuhlman (to name a few).

On June 10th, 1859 from Yorkshire England (famous for puddings) in a little town called Menston or Meston, Smith Wigglesworth was born. He was one of the most humble and powerful preachers of modern times. He had gifts of healing and speaking in God's Holy Tongue. The Daily Mirror, a London based newspaper carried regular headlines about Smith's miraculous crusades. There is a school of thought that opines, "Speaking in tongues were signs for *the apostles* only." Here is a question for those that espouse such dogma. Have the apostles ceased? You are partially right, since the 12 that Jesus called were Firstfruit witnesses. However, those of us "Chosen" witnesses are prophesying, healing the sick, speaking in different tongues, and most importantly casting out demons in the name and authority of Jesus. Wigglesworth made front-page headline news in the London Daily Mail many times from May 16th 1913. Newspapers between Canada and the U.S.A. carried his healing headlines from 1914 onwards. People were "slain" (appearing drunk) under the anointing of the Holy Spirit in his meetings. There are even reported and documented cases where he prayed for persons that had been certified as dead by the medical profession. After those prayers, God miraculously brought them back to life. Smith Wigglesworth had large crusades all over the world and traveled to Africa, Asia and then Europe, where they arrested him. The charge was that he was practicing medicine without a license. Imagine: some of the same doctors that certified the healing of their former patients—remember they had so-called incurable diseases—turned around and gave evidence against him. Wiggelsworth was arrested for impersonating a doctor: "Jesus the same yesterday, today and forever." He healed yesterday, since He gave His disciples power to do the same today, I, one of His disciples and anyone else called to this obedient ministry, will do the same today and forevermore. I bear witness that as long as you live a life in obedience, have faith in God's *Holy Word* and claim the redemption package of His Son, you will be able to perform the same miracles as Jeshua's disciples did, in His authority. I have no idea if Smith was related to the famous theologian Michael Wiggelsworth 1631-1705. I believe that Smith Wigglesworth died in the same year that I was born. Father, give me his anointing, double!

Lester Sumrall is not with us anymore. He died within the past Jubilee season. He was one of the best devils-casting-out preachers of all time. Serious preachers need to get as many books as possible on those great people of God to learn more about the measure of faith they had. Likewise Kathryn Kuhlman was one of the most impact-making modern day preachers. Her anointing was so powerful that she did not have to lay hands on people for them to be healed. She was born on a farm on May 9th 1907 in Missouri, U.S.A. In Denver and Idaho she had some of the biggest healing crusades in the early 20th century. She had many radio ministries, conducted numerous world tours and crusades. She died on February 20th 1976.

I am going to chronicle her life in two separate segments in a later book. I will show that God and His word are inseparable. I will document her life up to the point when she met and "covenanted" with a divorced man and the period afterwards. I will show you just as the Lord did to Shebna in Isaiah 22, when the Lord gives spiritual gifts, He does not take back His gifts or His promises. *God is no respecter of persons.* He will chasten those that He loves. I have witnessed incidences where Satan uses breaches in ministries to enter and to sow confusion. I will not get into debates as to how, when, and if divorce is permissible. However, in the in the Old Covenant, God gave specifics to Moses as to whom a priest could marry. Since we have a better covenant with a *better High Priest,* of course our standards must be higher, not lower. Let me search for instructions from Elders of the *Jerusalem Church for All Apostles,* called to the "Body of Christ." Since the mantle of the first Elder James fell on Titus, let us examine the letter confirming Titus' appointment. It contains the requirements under the New Covenant to be "Chosen" for a high office in the Body of Christ: Titus 1:5 to the end of the 3rd chapter. In Titus 1:6, an Elder has to be blameless and be married to one husband or one wife. Do not add or subtract from God's word. It does not say one at a time. 1st Timothy chapter 3 confirms what I have been revealing all along. The spiritual *types* of spouses and seeds of chosen vessels affect related ministries. Under the New Covenant, to be selected for highest offices, the examples you set in the homes are the main criteria for selection: 1st Timothy 3:11-12.

Don't get upset with me; argue with God. He hates divorce. If he allowed divorce He would have cast out Israel. Instead he confided to Jeremiah that He yearns for the day when she will return to her faithful husband. So if God hates divorce, here is a diplomatic question: Who in blazes are you? Find me any preacher who exalts his opinions above that of God and has dared to marry if he is divorced or if his wife is a divorcee. I will show you a man or woman with constant repetitious battles or who has all sorts of problems with family, money, and or health: from unexplainable allergies to blindness and more. God is no respecter of persons. If you disobey, you pay! What do you do if you are in that predicament? Ask the Lord to forgive you for not asking Him to select your spouse and then ask for original ribs to be returned and rib sockets to be replaced in faith. If you ask God to perform a task He cannot err. Your roles in the church cannot be primary roles. That is God's word not mine.

There is a warrior that had ploughed deserts of Africa for decades. Brother Reinhardt has dug wells, too numerous to mention. In America is a man who stays forever young. He is a living example of God's promise to mount us up with wings like eagles. He is one of America's perennial Holy-Spirit-filled preachers that have been butt-kicking Satan for over 50 years. I am talking about R.W. Shambach. As of August 1999 when editing of this book commenced, he was still preaching, casting out demons and leading people back to the Lord.

I would need an entire book to write about Robert Shula. I would need a series of books just to catalogue the accomplishments of Rev. Billy Graham. Heavenly Father, please preserve those ageless "Well-diggers." My short list includes Brother Shambach, Bro. E.V.Hill, Brother Maurice Cerullo, Oral Roberts, Brother and Sister Kenneth Hagin, Brother Paul and Sister Jan Crouch, Sister Dale Evans and all the early and current sowers. Wrap them in your cloak of invincibility the way you did for Enoch; this I ask you directly, plus all those reading this—please confirm, in Jesus' name, Amen. I could include hundreds more. I just wanted to touch those that were still kicking Satan's butt after 50 years or had done some serious damage to his kingdom before the Lord took them.

I am asking all that are nourished in the "Wild Olive Tree" to pray for Israel's corporate repentance. Can you imagine that with such evidence of God's power manifesting through the seed of former rebellious nations, many in Israel are still blinded to the fact that all the above could have happened only because they rejected the *Branch* that was sent to them? Out of that rejected branch, a graft was planted in Rome. In spite of all the filth and porous soils, the above fruits have come forth. I have been fortunate enough to be able to pray to the same God that Daniel, David, Elijah, Elisha, Jeshua, Moses, Nehemiah, Prophet Mohammed, and Solomon prayed. I have prayed to God together with seed of Jacob, Esau, Judah, Benjamin, Moab, Simeon, and also Gentile seeds of Greece and Rome. In every instance, whereby we humbled and cleansed ourselves and sought God's plans and purposes corporately, He responded positively. We were not presumptuous by surmising that God approved everything that we did simply because we organized events in the name of God or His Son. We sought His guidance first. "In all your ways acknowledge Him and He will direct your paths." I hope I am reaching someone right now: *YOU CANNOT IMPRESS GOD!*

There are thousands of religious programmes organized all over the world. How many confess collectively and seek pardons for their sins and iniquities of past generations' sins before they petition God? In some instances it is as if God is made after our own likeness and not the other way around. Am I the only person to have attended "A Programme" where you got the distinct impression that certain persons, by their conduct and attitude, projected themselves to be more important than others? My personal opinion is that arrogance and conceit in the body of Christ are two of Satan's best weapons.

CHAPTER 21F. SEASONS OF JOY AND SEASONS OF DOOM.

Poets and songwriters often use the words gloom and doom to rhyme with moon. There are God-ordained seasons to commemorate positive and negative events, past victories and past defeats. Those are not figments of imaginations. Sorcery, occultism and witchcraft draw energies from moon symbols, moonstones and rituals associated with moon seasons. Halloween is within 24 hours of *All Souls Night*, a night when most "demonically-inspired sacrifices" are staged either deliberately or accidentally (supposedly).

ISRAEL HAS SEVEN APPOINTED HOLY FEASTS.

1) Passover was and is commemorated (Leviticus 23:4-6) on the 14th day of the first month of Abib on the Hebrew calendar, usually between March/April on the Roman calendar.

2) Feast of Unleavened Bread (Leviticus 23:6-8) is the 15th day of the first month of Abib. This began on the day following the Passover through seven days.

3) Firstfruits, Weeks, Pentecost or Harvest were celebrated 50 days from the 15th of Nisan to the 6th Day of Sivan (May/June): Leviticus 23:10-21 and Deuteronomy 16:9-11, sixth of Sivan or 49 days from 22nd of April. For that Place of Promise, the first and best (tithes) belong to the Lord, 1st Corinthians 15:20-23.

4) Feast of Purim 14th/15th Adar (March/April- Esther 9:20-22 & 26-28).

5) Feast of Trumpets: Leviticus 23:23-25 celebrated the 1st Day of seventh month of Tishri (September /October).

6) Day of Atonement: Leviticus 23:27 is the 10th of the seventh month of Tishri on the Hebrew calendar, (September/October) is a day of prayer, fasting and atonement.

7) Feast of Tabernacles or Booths: Leviticus 23:34 celebrated on the 15th through to the

21st of the seventh month.

The occult world also has its related feasts. All Souls Night is when Leviathan, through murder and witchcraft, brings in the "Occult Harvest." I will not publish a complete list of those dates nor the seasons for obvious reasons. Whenever any sin is committed on a particular feast day, that is "punishable by death" or is called "accursed" by God, the earth opens her mouth and releases strong demonic spirits. Oft-times, wars and genocidal acts are satanically engineered. Almost all the large "Slave Massacres" ever held on plantations from the Carolinas to the Caribbean, just happened to occur on what occult circles classify as "High-Energy" nights. Coincidentally or otherwise, Jews across Europe were massacred at the hands of a demonic dictator on certain "High Energy" times also. Get the drift? For instance between the 17th of Tammuz and the 9th of Av on the Hebrew Calendars, God's people have had the most severe onslaughts. Pastors/Priests need to transpose the dates to modern times to pray and fast between the periods of intense attacks. I will "not" transpose the dates for obvious reasons. The following events took place during those two periods:

a). Moses smashed the Tablets (Ten Commandments).

b). An idol was placed on the altar of the Temple in Jerusalem.

c). The Temple was desecrated by the burning of the Torah.

d). Daily Sacrifices ceased.

e). The Babylonians destroyed the Holy Temple.

f). The Romans under Titus destroyed the Holy Temple again.

g). The Jews, particularly the seed of Judah were massacred at Massada.

h). Rome replaced God's Holy Temple (2nd Temple) with a pagan shrine.

i). The Genocide of the First Crusade occurred.

j). Jews were expelled by Royal Decrees from England, France and Spain "back to Africa" between the 14th to the 16th centuries.

k). The Polish Massacre, World Wars 1 & 2 and the 1st Gulf War happened during the same seasons also.

l). Most of the large slave massacres occurred during the same periods. Be forewarned:

THE BATTLE OF ARMAGGEDDON WILL COMMENCE DURING THOSE DATES.

As I mentioned before, the role of the selected Pied Piper is to use his or her charismatic charm to lead the altar-stolen to be pied. Now is not time for blame. Had we not neglected reading and performing His Word, and had we been better guardians, billions would not have been led astray. On set dates, prayer warriors need to bombard hell with all-night warfare. Too many in the Body of Christ have fallen asleep. We need to have prayer chains. Psalm 122: 6 exhorts us: "Pray for the peace of Jerusalem: they shall prosper that love thee."

CHAPTER 21G. ALL UNDER THE MICROSCOPE!

There are descendants of tribes that resided in Arabic countries, along with 14 of our original researchers, who believed Mohammed to have been the last prophet. When our research began, we decided to abandon our biases and to dig *critically* for the truth. We searched all published, available and accessible creeds' materials. Since the Christians were the least learned among the team and did not know where to go for the truth, at first we wrote them off as imposters. However when we referred back to our mandate, we were rebuked for rushing to judge before all data was gathered. However after the first five years, we narrowed our searches to those creeds with ancestral links to Abraham. Lots of others were relegated to the categories of philosophies. Some purely and simply were ritualistic transplants.

ON EXAMINING THE FOUNDATION OF ISLAM, WE DISCOVERED THE FOLLOWING ABOUT PROPHET MOHAMMED. WE WILL PRINT IT EXACTLY AS IS RECORDED. THE DISCOVERIES OF THOSE SPIRITUAL KEYS ARE IMPORTANT. ONE OF THE SIGNS THAT FOLLOW CHOSEN MEN OF GOD IS THAT THE WIVES THEY CHOOSE REFLECT THEIR SPIRITUAL LEGACIES. MOHAMMED'S FIRST WIFE WAS PREVIOUSLY MARRIED. A RELIGIOUS INSTITUTION LEFT AS THE PROPHET'S LEGACY MUST HAVE BEEN "MARRIED" BEFORE. MOHAMMED DID NOT GROW UP WITH HIS FATHER. HIS FATHER DIED BEFORE HIS BIRTH. ABRAHAM'S SON (WITH THE MAID HAGAR) ISHMAEL WAS BLESSED BY ABRAHAM AND SENT AWAY AT 19. ABRAHAM WAS NOT WITH HIM WHEN HE GREW TO MATURITY. NEITHER WAS THE COVENANT PLACED WITH THE SEED OF THE BONDWOMAN BUT WITH THE SEED OF SARAH (HIS WIFE) GENESIS 17:19, GENESIS 18:1 AND GENESIS 21:2-3. THE PROMISED SEED WAS ISAAC. PRECISELY THE PROPHET ISAIAH IN ISAIAH 51 SPELLED THAT OUT. ISAIAH 51:1, "LOOK UNTO THE ROCK…" ISAIAH 51: 2, "LOOK UNTO ABRAHAM YOUR FATHER AND UNTO SARAH THAT BARE YOU; FOR I CALLED HIM ALONE, AND BLESSED HIM AND INCREASED HIM."

Ishmael was promised to be head of a mighty nation; that is the Arab world. The prophet (Joel chapter 3) recorded the post restoration prophecy for those regions. God also promised a theocracy and the Arab nations got it. Mohammed's researchers searched the Tanakh and the early Christian texts for data. His researchers and friends were Christian slaves, monks and Jews. None of them found any evidence that God broke His covenant with Isaac. Therefore God never abandoned Israel. In fact Israel was likened to an unfaithful wife who transgressed from a chaste virgin to a horrible harlot: Jeremiah 3:20. God lamented but promised to forgive her and welcome her back. In Isaiah 49, God promised to restore Israel. In the previous chapter, God gives details: In a time when the house of Jacob settles in the land ordained, ancient hateful spirits will encourage spiritually conflicting philosophies to set **brother against brother** and the Prince of Peace will intervene: Isaiah 48-49. The Ismaili and Kharijites' philosophies need to be scrutinized.

Sarah's womb can be likened to the earthly womb called Africa. Africa (had every land attached to her when she was called Pangaea). Africa had every nation and tongue in her. Out of Isaac and Rebekah, the seeds of Judah and Levi germinated through Jacob (not Esau). To date, I cannot find any historical proofs why Jerusalem could have been considered as a Muslim holy site. From the Torah, which Mohammed taught Muslims to seek, is Psalm 147:19, "God **shows** his word unto Jacob, his statutes and his judgments unto Israel."

Up to the time of Mohammed's death, Jerusalem was a Christian city. No Muslim was allowed to pray facing a Christian city. Jerusalem could not have been perceived as a Muslim holy site when a Christian church (St. Catherine's) that was subsequently razed, had occupied the site where the Dome of the Rock is situated. In Psalm 137:7-9, God promised Israel that He will punish the seed of Edom (especially religious zealots from Iraq/Iran daughters of Babylon) for shedding blood on His Holy City, Jerusalem. In Joel 3:21 and Psalm 122, God outlined that Jerusalem would be His place of restoration, His Holy City; it will be a city of peace and praise. None of His scriptures authorize any new religious foundation on His Holy City; in fact He forbade such in Psalm 132:4-14. In those, God emphatically stated thousands of years before Jerusalem was founded, that He would not rest until He established His holy habitation in Zion. He singled out Ephratah: Bethlehem, the birthplace of Jesus as the place where "We will go into His tabernacles: we will worship at His footstool." Then in verses 10-11, He specifies the Davidic line as His anointed from which the righteous priests must not stray. Verse 11, "Out of the fruit of thy (David's) body will I set upon thy throne." Verse 12, "If thy seed keep my covenant and my testimony that *I shall teach them*, their children shall also sit upon thy throne for evermore." Verse 13, "For the Lord hath chosen Zion; he hath desired it for his habitation." Verse 14, "This is my rest for ever: here will I dwell; for I have desired it." Since God gave His Law to Moses personally, those religions that got their messages from angels do have serious problems. Unfortunately weak altar custodians allowed Leviathan to lure all the descendants of the "Tribe of Judah" to lands with usurped altars, where rituals were performed habitually. Like most reptiles, they drag you into their places of strength. Leviathan took in her wake implements from strange altars.

As a result of Leviathan enticing seed of "Lost Tribes" in India to abort their female fetuses, more males than females are being born. India is one of the countries where scanning pregnant females is used for preferential gender selection. Those who understand spiritual warfare need to war against the cravings for spiritual caviar in that nation. Gunpowder was used on the altars of ancient temples in the Far East. Cocaine or a derivative was used in ancient ceremonies. Many who think that they are using it for fun and kicks are rudely awakened. Intruders from the spirit world—like the genie in a bottle—say: "Thanks for letting me out. Now, you and I are bonded." Cocaine and other mind-enhancing drugs are conduits. They establish direct links to satanic altars. Things connected to you create insatiable urges because they have oppressed you, depressed you or possessed you. Since minds are highways, lots of "Experimenters" end up in traffic jams and serious accidental write-offs. I have met those, displaced from the tribe of Judah who grow marijuana and call it "Tampi" and also "Kali." Stop calling it Kali, since Kali is the name of a spirit. In ceremonies, she is referenced as a goddess responsible for fertility and destruction. Many that smoke and chant, "Blessed be Kali" then "Flex" or fornicate under its influence end up with lots of children out of wedlock. Those seeds, sown in disobedience around recreated ceremonies (whether you know it or not) are playing into Satan's trap. You are decreeing maladies and jail sentences unto the youths. Parents that touched accursed things (Joshua 7:12) need to have their generational curses broken. I will close out with the words from Isaiah 27:1. "In that day, the Lord with his sore and strong sword shall punish Leviathan the piercing serpent, even Leviathan that crooked serpent; and He shall slay the dragon that is in the sea."

CHAPTER 21H. MANY MORE BORE WITNESS!

As a modern day witness for the Lord at a time such as this, it is so easy to see that God had prepared a schematic for every possible situation: an eternal acid test to mirror lifestyles, philosophies and doctrines. I have searched for and found correlation between original Hebrew texts and documents written by Jesus' witnesses. I have met many that bear witness to Jeshua's Good News. To list the current ones is impossible since I do not know them all. Anyway, I will make mention of a few household names in America who were miraculously healed and went on to be great witnesses. Three of them are Oral Roberts, founder of the university, which bears his name, Lester Sumrall and Kenneth Hagin. All have been miraculously clutched from the jaws of death and have lived to give great testimonies.

From 1948 to 1955 my grandmother and three other ladies walked nightly to a little preschool building in a small town. Whereas most people would pull down their shutters by 6.00 P.M. every night, my grandmother and her gang would have praise and worship from 5.30 P.M. until 9.00 P.M. Little boys used to spread rumors that the dead walked at night. We believed that was the reason adults insisted on toddlers going to sleep by 6.00 P.M. sharp. As a child I was a mischief-maker and full of adventure; so I asked my grandmother to attend church with her. There was no electricity in the little preschool building. They all carried antique hurricane lamps. How important I felt, that a tiny tot was able to stay out after 6.00 P.M. I could report to all the children in nursery school as it was called then. In those days the boys played by themselves. The sissies (as girls were called because they cried so much) played by themselves. They did silly things like skip rope and played with dolls. Boys flew kites, made wooden scooters and played "Cowboys and Indians."

The first night you should have seen me. At 5.00 P.M. when we left, all my little friends with eyes wide open peered from my neighbours' houses to see if I was crazy enough to venture out into the ways of the walking dead. I was a hero. I attended and enjoyed the entire service. Energy bubbled up so much as I filled the oil lamps. To this day I have a problem when I go to those sweet little churches where they sing "A little oil in my lamp to keep me burning." I would blare out as hard as I can, "Plenty oil" because that is what I used to do. I poured lots of oil in those lamps. Since the Kingdom of God is based on sowing and reaping, I sowed plenty oil. I never completed filling the lamps. By the time the singing began and grandma and her friends started with their tambourines, the building rocked. Those 60 and 70-year-old mommas were not kidding. They danced and they sweat. After two hours of peeking between my fingers while singing and seeing nothing, I fell asleep.

In those days the ladies put a lot of starch in their long dresses. They also walked erect. They learned to walk uprightly by practicing the techniques for proper posture. They would place books on their heads as they practiced walking in a "prim and proper manner." Their sisters and neighbours evaluated each other while looking in tall mirrors. On the other side of the coin, young men would not dare to select a lady who could not speak or walk properly. On the way home I got as close to grandma as possible. There were large stretches with overhanging trees where there were no streetlights. As we walked I heard those swishing footsteps behind us. I asked grandma to stop. The footsteps stopped. "Let us speed up grandma so that I can go to the toilet, I begged." Grandma obliged; the steps grew quicker. How perceptive were the grandmas. She rebuked me; preached to me. "God did not give you a spirit of fear, but power, love and a sound mind!" Thank you so much grandma, especially for those early prayers. Can you imagine the disappointment on the faces of those youngsters when I had nothing to report? I slept all day Saturday, the next day. I am laughing hysterically at this point as I reflect on a song that my cousin and I used to sing. Only when I became an adult I realized the words were "Hold the Fort, for I am coming." For years, we blared out "Hold the fowl foot, I am coming."

Those nightly praise and worship sessions 50 years ago were the first places that I saw people "Slain" in the Holy Spirit. In Numbers 20:6, Moses and Aaron fell on their faces "slain." I assumed that to have been a normal reaction whenever anyone prayed. Unfortunately, after grandma died, my guardian was embarrassed by the way grandma praised the Lord; she took me to a church where all the aristocrats attended. It was considered embarrassing "The way grandma worshipped." I hate admitting it, but members of my family are still religiously "bound" to this day. I pray to God that the love for the ceremonies ahead of substance and the yoke of "Religion" will be broken from them. Father please remove the "Spirit of Blindness" from the eyes of "Believers," especially those in my family and may they realize that it is not the building, nor any other carnal thing, but by your "Spirit." Anyway, God made me a special promise. Since His promises are Yea and Amen I will say both.

CHAPTER 21I. THE VISION.

My grandfather was a rugged shipwright. He had Irish blood in his veins and the blood of Judah's clan also. Every time I was top of my class, which was every exam I took until after my father died, I would get a gift. That was usually a custom-made boat together with perks. The perks included the privilege of going to the docks to meet the fishermen. I even got to go on their boats, to sail out of the harbour with them and or to return on the tugboats. Grandpa knew all the boat people. Today many shipwrights in that little village still talk about and remember him. I never heard Grandpa swear or curse. He, like most macho men, believed the salvation of their wives was sufficient for them. His sermon was simple: "The Bottle is man's best friend."

The only time I ever saw him frown, was on a day that either his wife or any of his five daughters would prepare fish broth and did not fill the pot with broth. "How can fish drown in a pot?" He would ask. "If fish can't drown in the ocean, why presuppose that they can drown in my broth?" Grandkids learned to intercede on behalf of Grandma. His pleasure meant either invitations to the docks or matinee tickets. It came as no surprise that up to his death, a bachelor son, one of my two uncles (allegedly there was a third I never met) was very much his boy. He boxed, was a great swimmer and carried a steady 250 pounds of solid mass. He idolized everything "Macho;" he drank, smoke and cursed daily. He never got married.

At seventy-two years of age, my uncle fell sick for the first time in his life. I flew to the small place to see him. I witnessed to him and was surprised to see how ready he was to receive Jesus into his life. There was a Holy Spirit-filled church in the neighborhood. I told him that Zacchaeus laid the precedent for zeal in this "Era of Grace." He went out of his way, and *climbed to unusual heights* to meet his Redeemer. In the preceding spiritual season, a person had to await the "spiritual stirring-up of the waters." In that season, it was only the first person that rushed in, would receive healing or deliverance when the anointing started. That "stirring-up" today is called the altar called or altar call. That spiritual shofar signals that the spiritual waters are stirred up in the heavens and that God wants to sterilize some formerly lost souls; He wants to heal some formerly stricken persons and or He wants to redeem some lost sheep.

I told my Uncle he had to do a "Zacchaeus." What happened next floored me. As he went to the altar, right in front on the worship team, up jumped three ladies dressed in 1950's dresses in the year 1998. Those ladies wore long old-fashioned dresses. All had tambourines in their hands. They danced those young choir ladies to shame. I was impressed with their energies, so I leaned forward to get a better view. The strange thing is that those ladies were the only ones dressed in white and wearing nametags. As I closed my eyes for a minute something strange happened. When I closed my eyes I could still see the podium, but only those ladies. I opened my eyes and there they were again. My grandmother had died over fifty years ago. The last time I had seen her or any of that pioneering gang was approximately 50 years prior. I had already forgotten their names. When I reopened my eyes they all disappeared. What was the significance of that vision?

My uncle that legendary macho who had been to a church the first time in 60-plus years was openly crying. What a beautiful sight to see tears of redemption. When he returned, for some strange reason I did not reveal what I saw; instead I asked him who Miss Tanner was and who Miss Davis was. As I recalled the names, he said to me, "When you were a little boy, those ladies used to come for you every night to take you to services such as this one." Just then the anointing awakened. To be honest I do not know what I saw or imagined I saw.

Whenever a supernatural event occurs to me I like to check it out to see if there is a Biblical precedent. If by the time I complete this book and I find one, I will surely advise you all. I might add that the only witness I have is the one that counts, The Spirit of the Lord witnessed to my spirit that the heavens were opened and I was accorded a seat on His "Time" bridge.

I was directed to 2nd Samuel 5:23-24. That is a case and point when someone on earth had the honour of seeing the heavens opened to reveal things from the great beyond. He also referred me to John when He took John back and forward in time while on Patmos. I record these testimonies because many people reading this are in line to receive similar and even better gifts. I am advising you not to be careless with the treasures of heaven. This book has been put together over several years and not without peril. These testimonies have been brought to you with a great amount of sacrifice.

CHAPTER 22. SECRETS OF REBEKAH'S WOMB.

22A. PHYSICAL HEIRS.

Let us briefly but carefully perform an analytical post mortem on Rebekah, to see what prophetic seeds were sown in her. Since all seeds germinate in earthen wombs, *bear in mind that wives of chosen heirs influence spiritual fruit.* Whatever fruit she bore would have an impact, positive or negative on (1) The Seed of Promise and (2) The nation of nations promised. It will not take a rocket scientist to figure out that the seed must manifest first before the nation is formed. If we follow God's pattern or consistency of purpose, we should be able to find a process of purging nations, purging of people, purging of families, and purging of a specific family to produce the sanctified seed. Out of a spiritually sterilized hybrid seed God expects spiritually organic fruits. The Biblical flood was the first physical cleansing of nations with water. Water-cleansing alone could not purge entrenched mental warps. Similarly *baptism by water alone* cannot cut it today. Abraham represented the physically purged family root; however his seed had spiritual blemishes. Judah represented the purged army; yet spiritual flaws sprouted. Levi represented the purged priesthood and David represented the purged stem. In every case, the same being (Satan) tarnished the cradles. It had to take a sinless branch with a flawless philosophy to be resown as hybrid seed for Jews, Christians, Muslims and Gentiles. God's instructions to Abraham were specific. Thou shall not take a wife to thy son Isaac of the daughters of the Canaanites in whose land thou dwellest. Go unto thy father's house and to his kindred and take a wife (in other words, a woman chosen for the promised purpose of God). Rebekah was Gentile, so the future seed must be of Hebrew and grafted Gentile stock. While we're on the subject, the womb of Mary produced the last known seed of both *Judah and Levi* and not one of her children did any fighting. The one who is the standard bearer of the Melchizedec priesthood preached love, repentance, peace and forgiveness. People that Satan beguiled into believing that they are fighting wars in the name of God, better fast and ask the God of Abraham, Isaac, Moses and Jeshua: "In the name of which god am I fighting?" Since the person that God sent as "Prince of Peace" came and exited, first instance—

"NATIONS THAT ARE INTOLERANT TO THE TEACHINGS OF THE PRINCE OF PEACE HAVE NO PEACE."

Isaac was 40 years when he took *Rebekah* to wife. Genesis 26:21, Isaac entreated the Lord for his wife because she was barren. God already showed us with his father Abraham, that any matter concerning the promised seed had to conform to a specific timetable. The Davidic Ministry was birthed on a 40-year foundation. The *Messianic Ministry* must also have a 40-year foundation. Every seed of Abraham that pursues the ultimate truth must seek the identical time of travail, a 40-year spiritual gestation cycle. Esau also waited 40 years for a wife, so his seed also must seek the 40-year spiritual foundation. The Holy Koran mentions that God had bestowed the book first on Moses and that God caused Jesus to follow. Sura 5:46, "And in their footsteps we sent Jesus the son of Mary, confirming the law that had come before Him:

we sent him the Gospel; therein was guidance and light, and confirmation of the law that had come before him."

3500 years ago Moses gave us historical precedents for most of today's problems: disobedience. In Genesis 26:34-35, Esau did not entreat God for his wife; instead he married Judith the daughter of Beeri and Bashemath the daughter of Elon, both Hittites (seed of Ham through his second son Heth). There would then be an inherent inclination for spiritual seeds of Esau to be watered by the Hittite genetic rivers of ancestral rebellion and revenge. There must also be two main expressions of worship to God, born outside of God's prescribed instructions. Incidentally, the two main branches of Prophet Mohammed's legacy are Shiites and Sunnis. Genesis 25:23…a) Two nations are in thy womb, and b) Two manner of people shall be separated from thy bowels. One (of the nations) shall be stronger than the other, and b) the elder (the ones that emerged first) shall serve the younger. Hence the saying, "The first shall be last and the last shall be first."

Jacob and Esau, though twins were as different temperamentally as they were physically. Prophetically, both would produce different seed (physically and spiritually). We can observe some of their generational seed traits, since God gave us a peek at Laban's personality. I will highlight the physical and temperamental differences between Jacob and Esau. *Jacob* was not immune to getting by with his wits. He was a good talker. *Jacob* could buy and sell just about anything. He would more than likely live in (tents) cities. Esau was more inclined to be successful around arid regions. He would be successful in his hunting (for oil), gold, pearls and diamonds. Jacob would be more successful buying and selling the diamonds. Jacob would be a good lawyer, actor, entertainer and salesman. Because Jacob was inclined to dwell in the northern and cooler regions, *Jacob* would become smoother and lighter in complexion. *Esau* would become more adaptable to arid conditions and would end up darker with considerable more melanin.

CHAPTER 22B. SPIRITUAL HEIRS.

The Temple that Solomon built had a Holy Place and a Most Holy Place. The Tabernacle had the Levitical priesthood with limited ordained sacrifices. Add to your notes that any passage in a Psalm that had a prior reference from another prophet—that points to a New Testament stipulation. Psalm 40:6, prophetically recorded: "Burnt offering and sin offering hast thou *not* required." God also spoke this message through the prophet Isaiah. Isaiah 1:13, "Bring no more vain oblations; incense is an abomination unto me; the new moons and *Sabbaths*, the calling of assemblies, I cannot away with; it is an iniquity, even the solemn meeting." Since Solomon's Temple would be older than the Messiah's temple, the *older would serve the younger.* It so happens that the Old Testament did prophesy the events of the New Testament and the New Testament confirms the Old. The New Testament packaged the understanding of the scriptures into two clear messages: 1. Love the Lord, thy God with thy whole heart, thy whole soul, and thy whole strength. 2. Love neighbour as thyself. Observe: 1) People who enjoy hate and strife, cannot grip the Messiah's message of Agape. 2) Hate justifies their selfishness and anger. 3) Devilish minds cannot love; they influence other people who love the same God to reject His pure and simple message:

LOVE GOD FERVENTLY AND LOVE YOUR NEIGHBOUR UNSELFISHLY.

Jesus' church has a *foundation* of love, healings, blessings, and of collecting from the rich to give to the poor. Jesus threw out scoundrels from the house of God when He was on earth. He is the same in temperament and zeal yesterday, today and forever. I will say simply that His church has moved a long way from His teachings. Jesus' church had a zero tolerance for sin that is why so many signs and wonders followed the believers. All sicknesses disappeared. Instead of us having the Light manifest powerfully in all of His churches to fulfill "the greater works than those," they are mere shadows of things past.

Miriam or Mary the mother of Jeshua or Jesus had both the bloodlines of Levi and Judah in her veins. Her children: James, Jude, Joses, Johanna and Simon functioned in Jesus' ministry. James functioned as an "Elder" and Jude as an apostle. Since the wombs of wives chosen to carry David's seed prophetically mirror future temples or churches, the ministry out of the loins of Mary must have kingly and priestly offices rolled into one. The older way would be confined to the wilderness. The newer (way) would dwell in the promised (tent) tabernacle. The newer would be far from perfect. Hustlers and connivers would be under the tents, but God would tolerate such (for a while) because of His covenant. That in no way infers that God would negate His word by not punishing transgressors. On the contrary, He chastens those that He loves.

Rebekah, the second seed incubator matriarch, connived with Jacob so that Jacob would receive the birthright of his older twin. The Roman church (Gentile matriarch) plucked a branch from the Antioch church, changed the identity of Jeshua and told the world that they had the birthright. They taught that they were the only true church and therefore *infallible*. As is the case with all cracked spiritual foundations, Satan ran sideways through their churches the same way he made minced meat out of several Levites, judges and kings of the ancient Hebrews. He did another "Babel." He infiltrated from peasant to Pope in most of the religious institutions that have been around for more than 50 years. Notwithstanding their conniving (after much purging) God preserved the promised seed of Rebekah, to bring forth the *firstfruit*, Jeshua—the purged tree out of Miriam. From the flawed branches of the Roman church, God pruned, and is still pruning. Instead of identifying the reasons for the spreading of spiritual mildew and for hating each other, brothers keep on fighting brothers.

For the past 2000 years, God has been raising up reformers to bring corrections to the Babelic slants in His church. Solomon previously laid down the seeds for spiritual disobedience. He as a king had no "Queens" but a very unusual assortment of "wives," also "princesses" and "concubines." The role of a princess is to be subordinate to higher female authority. In a spiritual sense, that would equate to branch churches. Prophetically that would mean that the Messiah's church would be unique in that there would be denominations with numerous branches and stems under separate head churches. At the junctures where they parted, the divisive spirits caused the establishment to reject them and they ended up carving new branches, fulfilling the blueprints of both: *The Temple of Solomon and the womb of Rebekah.* Solomon built the biggest house for the daughter of Pharaoh. Statues and incense adorned all of Pharaoh's houses. The largest of the Messiah's churches would have lots of **incense, statues and Gentile influences**. The next phase of the tree is the sheaves.

In Genesis 25:23-28, written over 4000 years ago, God foresaw that there would be mistrust and spiritual tensions between ethnic groups and religions: verse 23, "...two nations and two manner of people ..." Verse 28...Isaac loved Esau, but Rebekah loved Jacob the younger. One of the twins represented the New Covenant expression of the Temple and the other represented the Old Covenant era. The old was exclusively Hebrew. Since Rebekah was of mixed ancestry, there would be mixed incubation in the womb of the New Covenant participants.

Ancient Israel was pleasing to God mainly during David's reign. The woman or bride of the Gentile-inclusive church is more pleasing in worship and sacrifices. God decreed that the inclusion of the Gentiles would bring *the Jews to jealousy.*

"YOU HOOO, IS ANYBODY OUT THERE? ADMIT IT, GOD SAID YOU WOULD BE JEALOUS AND GOD CANNOT LIE."

If some in Israel really want to challenge the messianic fulfillment of Jeshua, I dare them to install a king to sit on David's throne. Dare to have a priest go into a temple to offer sacrifices to God. Have both events televised so that we can see if God accepts the sacrifices. Don't sit in some corner and whisper your denial of Jesus the Messiah. Put your old sacrifices to the test. *Reenact Elijah's test!* I would be more than happy to participate.

CHAPTER 22C. MYSTERY OF THE THREE FLOCKS SOLVED!

Moses penned Genesis Chapter 29 over four thousand years ago. He was an obedient servant merely documenting the plight of Jacob, the son of Isaac as he attempted to flee from the wrath of his twin brother Esau, whom he twice swindled. As the story progressed, his father Isaac entreated Jacob to use the occasion to go to Padan-aram (an ancient city in the vicinity of Mesopotamia, Abraham's homeland) to seek a wife of his kindred.

Isaac *did not* send Jacob off before he blessed him. Additionally, he bestowed upon him the triple blessings that he personally received from his father Abraham: multiplication, fruitfulness and land for him and his seed after him. Genesis 28:4…and give thee the blessing of Abraham to thee and to thy seed with thee that thou mayest inherit the land wherein thou art a stranger which God gave to Abraham. Over three thousand years ago various idols' worshippers occupied the land. God gave the seed of Jacob instructions for *all such* to be *destroyed* later on. Moses hadn't the foggiest idea about what he documented. He received a prophetic peek at future history. Moses was afforded a foretaste: the historical and spiritual foundations of the mightiest religious and land conflicts the world would ever know. Jacob's journey into Haran was a prophetic glimpse of "The Hope" for humankind. The journey was perilous. God used that journey to conceal (from the chief thief), His path, His plan and His only solution to the conflicts that would ensue. Any other plan other than what God decreed would be doomed to failure. To avoid duplication, I will squeeze some grapes of discovery, using the waters prophesied by the same Ezekiel in chapter 47. That wine is too rich, blessed and abundant to imbibe selfishly. May God bless those that find the Path, The Way, and also those who drink the waters of this well of prophecy.

The three flocks at the well of Haran would represent the spiritual flocks of the seed of Abraham: Jews, Christians and Muslims. Observe that *the stone* (covering the well) could not be rolled away until all the flocks were in. Genesis 29:8, Jacob was *chosen* to roll away the *stone.* How could a man come into the midst of shepherds and roll away the stone? I am sure many people who write and conduct research arrive at a particular juncture whereby a specific discovery is the lynchpin that creams the cake.

All of our researchers felt compelled to take a serious look at whether on not there would be one shepherd as prophesied by Moses, David, Ezekiel, Isaiah and Asaph. Would there ever be harmony among the flocks? Would we ever drink together? We were hungry to see if our God, who was so careful to lay such a precise and detailed foundation, would leave us an incomplete script. We searched the Koran, the Torah and the Bible for answers. We searched critically for the fulfillment of Ezekiel 34:23, "I will set one shepherd over them." Isaiah 42:1-2, also spoke of one servant that would minister to Gentiles. In verse 7, additionally, He would cause the blind to see. To find that one shepherd, ethnological retrogression was necessary. Seeds of Isaac sown in the womb of Rebekah, through her son Jacob, planted into the womb of Rachel had to be scrutinized for every clue. We scrutinized from their births to their deaths, and from their personalities to their lifestyles.

Miriam the mother of Jeshua was the last documented female of the bloodline of Jacob: at that time, a family among the world's most Patriarchal. Her firstfruit son, Jeshua, (born in the same Ephratah, Bethlehem, where Rachel travailed and died in childbirth) was a stunning revelation. Not only did the prophet Micah prophesy it, but also at the time of Rachel's death, Rachel brought forth the lad Benjamin, the *only direct offspring* of Jacob to be born in the land promised. *Only one shepherd seed* was *planted* in Bethlehem.

Ecclesiastes 12:11, "The words of the wise...are given from *one shepherd*." Psalm 80:1, "Oh *Shepherd* of Israel..." Observe the capital use of the word Shepherd. In verse 15 of Psalm 80, "The Shepherd" is also referred to as "The Branch" that thou hast made strong for thyself. In verse 17, Asaph the prophetic worship leader of David asks God to let His hand be upon the man of "Thy right hand, upon the Son of man whom thou madest strong for thyself." Could Asaph, speaking under the unction of God, have any idea of the spiritual significance of what he prophesied: "*A man between the two cherubims*" on the *right* hand of God, a branch cut down destined to be the Shepherd of Israel? We found more evidence at the hands of Ezekiel the Prophet and confirming evidence even in the Holy Koran.

After Nebuchadnezzar captured Jerusalem approximately 2700 years ago, one of the sons of the Levites, Ezekiel, wrote thusly, long after David's death. In verses 22-24 of the 34th chapter of Ezekiel these words can be found. Ezekiel 34:22, "Therefore *will I save my flock* and they shall no more be prey; and *I will judge* between cattle and cattle." Verse 23, "I will set 'One Shepherd' over them and he *shall feed them* even my servant David." Verse 24, "I the Lord will be their God and my servant David a *prince* among them." Let us back up here: David was a king who united both kingdoms. David came from Judah, as was the decree for Kings. He reigned 7 years in Hebron and 33 in Israel.

Why would Ezekiel speak of a dead king to become a prince especially when in the next verse Ezekiel quotes God as saying that He would make with them a covenant of peace? Since Ezekiel was and is regarded as one of the mightiest prophets who ever lived, it is obvious that he was speaking of a future event. Melchizedek, the forerunner of the Everlasting Priesthood was "King of Peace." Since the designated shepherd would be a "Prince" to serve on earth, humility has to be one of His hallmarks. We concluded that God was prophesying about the Davidic bloodline. Similarly in Psalm 16, David was referencing "The Excellent" in whom God placed "all His delight." The one called "The Excellent" (in verse 10, would break the barrier of death. Of the ancient Hebrew sects, the Pharisees and the Sadducees, the former believed in the resurrection of the dead. According to texts in the Holy Koran, Prophet Mohammed and Muslims share similar beliefs. Sura 19,33,34, "Peace is upon me the day of my birth, and the day of my death, and the day of my being raised up alive." Since the previous reference in Sura 19, 15 mentioned Zechariah, John the Baptist and the "Annunciation" to Miriam, our research team had no difficulty identifying the "Firstfruit."

The Messiah was predestined to be the firstfruit of the resurrection. So the Messiah whenever He arrived *had to die temporarily* and then exit to return again. Coded in the Psalms are End-times/New Testament messages. Psalm 122:1-9, Jerusalem is where God has planted

His Ladder of Jacob with His fiercest spiritual guardians over His holiest altars. He commands His messianic church to pray strengthening prayers around them. In the Gospel of John, John recorded an incident where Jeshua was prophesying as to how He would die and the purpose of His death. It is recorded in John 10:11…that He *would lay down His life for His sheep*. That made no sense to John at the time. However, after Jesus' death He fulfilled what was prophesied by Isaiah the prophet in detail in Isaiah 53:7…*He is brought as a lamb to the slaughter*. David in Psalm 22 prophesied the exact details as to how He would die. It came to pass. Sura 4,158, Allah raised Him (Jesus mentioned in 157) up unto himself.

It is amazing how clearly all the Holy Books of the seed of Abraham proclaim the same shepherd. Since God's unadulterated word is absolute truth, and He gave His perfect language to "A Special Spiritual Seed" to protect and to plant, two things automatically become clear: 1. All persons seeking truth must find His teachings and the persons that can translate His teachings accurately, and 2. The greatest thief in the universe would try to influence change, substitutions, divisions, death and destructions. Is it coincidental that all of the above have happened and are happening?

CHAPTER 23. SPIRITUAL AGGREGATES.

23A. UNICORN OF BABEL VS. LION OF JUDAH.

As a result of ancient Rome establishing an exalted altar out of the shards of vanquished nations, the seeds of Rome (Western Civilizations) were literally and figuratively born in darkness. The first guardian of the "Everlasting Priesthood" was Melchizedek. He was called to teach. As a teacher of the Law of *The Creator* or *Great Architect of the Universe*, he had to possess access to 360 degrees of wisdom.

King Solomon was given the plans for building the House of God on earth; he was anointed with esoteric access. The Host of darkness sought him. The wisdom that Solomon obtained was not from the building, but from the *Builder*. Since people have tried and failed to reconstruct Solomon's Temple with the hope of extracting wisdom by osmosis, I will recap three stages of the construction only. My aim is to show not only the level of our inherited wisdom deficiencies but also, that had we been walking in the path of true wisdom, the leaders of the Occident would have been able to proclaim: "We have improved the quality of life for all!" The real question is, "Have we really done so?"

Picture a civilization of really wise people understanding the complete meaning of "Honour thy Father and thy Mother." Do you really think that the Sahara would be sending giant dust storms annually across the Atlantic accelerating the greenhouse effect? Redirecting 1/10th the military budget of nations into new waterways and dams would eliminate drought and seasonal flooding globally.

ALL WISDOM ABOVE 33 DEGREES COMES FROM THE CREATOR ONLY.

Today people that live in civilizations formed from the ashes of fragmented kingdoms of Greece/Rome call themselves masters because they possess a mere 29 to 30 degrees and are given an honourary three. Let us understand clearly that all people living on earth today had ancestors that came out of lands around North Africa. The first people on earth all had burnt skins and woolly hair, or what we call today "coloured features". Ham, Shem and Japheth, children of Noah were all ancient melanin-rich people and so were all of their descendants up to approximately 5000 years ago, when climatic changes and "cross-breeding" produced dramatic differences externally. In the Book of Genesis (Bereshith in Hebrew) is recorded the ancestry of all the nations we call today: Egypt, Africa, Israel, Iraq, Libya, Tunisia, Algeria, and Syria. All emerged from three brothers (sons of Noah) Shem, Ham and Japheth.

Their prophetic names reflect the changes that would take place in their offspring and the destinations of their descendants. Over time those that lived in cold regions lightened and others that lived in tropical regions darkened. Hair curls and thickens with constant exposure to the sun. In extreme cases it bundles into woolly locks. As the continents fragmented, the seed of the surviving people retained their original features to this day; for example: the Ab-original people of Australia, the Ainu of Japan, the Ethiopians and the Dogon. King James' translators describe the ancients as "red or ruddy." The Hebrew word is Adam or Edom meaning earthy, dark-coloured or brown. Could we stretch the meaning to "oxblood- brown?" Then again God says not to add or to subtract anything from His *Word*.

Until recent times, the whole world consisted of Indian looking people. Both the seed of Judah and that of Esau dwelt south of Israel around the Jordan valley and the Red Sea. Genesis 10 not only identified the seeds of sons that would people the world, but also those that would remain around a particular region of Africa and become more burnt because of excessive sun. Solomon mentioned that his extremely burnt skin was due to excesses of the sun. Song of Solomon 1:6, "I am black because the sun hath looked upon me."

The Hamites, the Cushites, and the seed of—Mizraim, Phut, and Canaan remained in sun-baked conditions. Except for invasions and intermarriages, up to this day, they have maintained either original or residual melanin. In 1ˢᵗ Chronicles 16:18, the translation of the original scroll reads:

> ## "UNTO THEE (DAVID) WILL I GIVE THE LAND OF CANAAN, THE LOT OF YOUR INHERITANCE; WHEN YE WERE FEW, EVEN A FEW, AND STRANGERS IN IT." NO ONE CAN FIGHT AGAINST GOD'S PLANS AND WIN, NOT EVER!

THE FORMER LAND OF CANAAN IS THE OFT-DISPUTED LAND CALLED ISRAEL.

In Genesis 10:4-5, Deuteronomy 28:20-68 and Psalm 44:11-14, Moses identified the seed that would be enslaved and shipped to the islands of the sea as slaves. In Psalm 44:11 is a prophetic look at Judeo/African slavery: verse 11 …thou hast given us like sheep appointed for meat; thou hast scattered us among the heathen. Verse 12…Thou sellest thy people for nought and dost not increase thy wealth by their price. Verses 13 and 14 prophesied all the derogatory names they would be called. Some are in code; others are as plain as the alphabet. Those to be restored by oracular decree: Isaiah 11:11, "The Remnant" in the islands of the sea, *Egypt, Israel, Assyria* and all of Northern Africa were prophesied to be reconciled when the Messiah returned the "Second Time." Genesis 10:5, "By these were the Isles of the Gentiles divided by their lands."

The seeds of Rome colonized the islands of the sea with inhabitants of allegedly *Lost Tribes of Israel* and enslaved them. As a result, Hispaniola, Puerto Rico and Cuba, are Spanish. Guadeloupe, Martinique, Marie-Galante and Sint Martin are French. Curacao, Aruba, Bonaire and half of Saint Maarten are Dutch. St. Thomas and St Croix are American. Antigua/Barbuda, Anguilla, St. Kitts, Montserrat, Nevis, Grenada, St. Lucia, Dominica, St. Vincent, The Bahamas, Trinidad and Tobago, Barbados and Guyana are English. They still speak the Gentiles tongues to this day.

Genesis 10:7-19, list the projected paths of all major players on earth and the ultimate destinations of the entire seed of the brothers Shem, Ham, Japheth: the countries of Assyria, Egypt, Africa, Libya, Jordan, Iraq, Israel, Ethiopia, Sudan and Niger. Verses 21-32 detail the ultimate destinations of all seed. The image of the spiritual house that the Messiah would build on earth (reflecting Solomon's spiritual weaknesses until the time of Restoration) was concealed in the physical House of David. The birth and destruction of the Messiah's House on earth were foreseen and prerecorded in Psalm 80. Psalm 80:8, "He would be *hidden* and brought out of *Egypt as a little shoot*." Verse 11, His ministry would *spread far and* wide by land and sea. Verse 12, The Shepherd of verse 1 would have His *hedges* broken. Verse 16 foretold *destruction* for His *vineyard*. Similarly, every seed church of the Messiah although destined to possess structural flaws should display the fruits of the Oracle of God. God gave Solomon rest on all sides from his enemies. Therefore the foundation and the finished work must be *peace with all men* and brethren, unselfishness, wisdom, fullness of grace and truth, blessed beyond measure (flock and shepherds not shepherds only) and over abundance of righteousness and joy.

ANYONE POSSESSING TRUE WISDOM MUST KNOW, BY DIVINE REVELATION, THAT THE TEMPLE THAT SOLOMON BUILT IN WOOD, STONE AND PRECIOUS STONES WAS A TYPE AND SHADOW OF THINGS TO COME.

CHAPTER 23B. SOLOMON'S TEMPLE.

PREVIEW OF THE MESSIAH'S HOUSE ON EARTH.

Prior to man's trek on earth, God made decrees in heaven. Amongst them He established that:

1. He would allow "His Chosen Seed" to build His physical temple on earth.

2. He would allow "His Chosen Seed" to build His spiritual headquarters on Zion.

3. He would ordain one servant to be His "Shepherd" and His chosen redeeming workman. That kinsman redeemer would be His foundation stone. All of the redeemed would have to fit *plumb* into that selected, yet concealed graft. He would have to be a spiritual and physical carpenter. That man would have to be the Special Branch chosen to be cut and to be bruised. To Him must all the elect be grafted. He would be God's Oracle and His Special Son. Since Satan was there when the decrees were made, and God wants His true worship to be offered from *His Chosen Temple*, true to Satan's nature, he would have to invent counterfeits. Hence, there is only one person in 500 billion that could fulfill all of the above. That person would have to fulfill hundreds of prior prophecies and have wrought mightiest miracles in His Father's name. That person would be the Special Son through whom God's true worship must be directed, to be purged, to be acceptable to God. **FIND HIM!**

Satan over the years has exalted men that he wanted to be adorned and worshipped. He enticed men to present graven images of wood and stone and he convinced men that they should worship them. He also presented man-made and inaccurate oracles: they all received audiences. God designed a foolproof acid test: God placed over 300 prophecies in the Tanakh and the Torah pointing to whom, when, and where the Messiah would build His spiritual house. His disciples were foretold. The specific number of weeks of years from a prophesied time that He would appear, His genealogy and where He would be born were all foretold. For example: in Psalm 87:1, His (God's) foundation is in Zion and the mightiest Himself shall establish her (verse 5). *This Man* (whose genealogy is hinted) was born there. The only person in history (so far) whose ancestry fits the prophetic lineage is Jeshua or Jesus "The Anointed." David was told to record the identical prophecy in Psalm 2:6-7. At the time when God decreed that His Kings must come from Judah and His Priests from the tribe of Levi, David was commanded to record the coming of a king—He would be God's Son—called to rule from

Zion (His holy hill). This was not just listed as a decree but *The Decree*. That son was not listed as a son but *My Son* (Capitalized). That Son would be "begotten" and anointed to rule over His spiritual house. 1ˢᵗ Chronicles 22:10, the instructions that Solomon received from His God: He shall build a house for my name and He *shall be my son*, and *I shall be His Father* and *I will* establish the throne of His kingdom over Israel *forever*. Solomon's Temple, physical house of David, Architect/Creator = God. Messiah's House must match that structure in design, plan and execution, since one was a prototype and the same Architect designed both. The rebuilt house must of necessity be of living stones and living lumber. The work must begin and end with *Spiritual Carpentry*.

The widely circulated modern and ancient copies of the Holy Koran give a host of references where Jesus is specifically referred to as Christ or (Messiah). From Bell's translations, the Fluegel editions and the Medina editions to the most recent ones sponsored by the Government of Syria, correlating suras (more so than less) attach primary importance and seriousness to Jesus' spiritual mission on earth:

1. Sura 2, 87: "We gave Moses the Book and followed him up with a succession of Messengers; we gave Jesus the son of Mary clear signs and strengthened him with the Holy Spirit."

2. Sura 3, 45: Behold the angels said, "O Mary! Allah giveth thee glad tidings of a **Word** from Him: **his name will be Christ Jesus. The son of Mary held in honour in this world and the Hereafter and of those nearest to Allah.**"

3. Sura 5, 44 and 46: We formerly sent Noah and Abraham, appointed the prophetic office and the Book to their posterity; in their footsteps we caused Jesus son of Mary to follow, and we gave him the Gospel: therein was *guidance and light*, and *confirmation of the Law* that had come before him: a guidance and an admonition to those who fear Allah. Those words are repeated in Sura 3, 46.

4. Peace is upon me the day of my birth, and the day of my death, and the day of my *being raised up alive*: Sura 19, 33. Is Sura 19, 15 the same?

5. Sura 3:55, "O Jesus, I am going to bring thy term to an end and raise thee to myself, and purify thee from those who have disbelieved; *I am going to set those who have followed thee above those that have disbelieved until the day of resurrection.*"

6. Sura 5,110, "O Jesus son of Mary, recount my favour to thee and thy mother. Behold I strengthened thee with the **Holy Spirit** so that thou didst speak to the people in infancy and in maturity. Behold I taught thee **The Book**, Wisdom, Law and the Gospel…and thou didst **heal those born blind, and lepers** by my leave, and behold thou **didst bring forth the dead** by my leave."

The three that bear witness on the earth are water, blood and the *spirit*. In the time of Noah, God used water as the cleanser for the first sanctification on earth to select "His Chosen." After that the *seed* of Abraham was *chosen* for a special *Covenant*. The *foreskin of Isaac* was the firstfruit of *human blood* acceptable to God. Jeshua's sacrificial death is either "*THE ACCEPTABLE SACRIFICE FOR THE NEW COVENANT,*" or we are in deep trouble. God's pattern is to set procedures into sequences as follows: three then a half rest, then another three before a whole rest. John, Jeshua's forerunner, brought the baptism by water. Jeshua fulfilled

Isaiah 53, and released baptism by the Spirit.

Jeshua, true to Suras in the Koran, brought the confirmation of all the symbolisms of the Tanakh. Jeshua's ministry brought the three: Water baptism, His perfected blood sacrifice and the *Baptism of the Holy Spirit*. According to God's law of double-reference, if Jeshua (Jesus) was chosen as the acceptable sacrifice to fulfill the prophesied redemption package for humankind, then Jeshua should also be confirmed as "a witness in heaven also." The Levites offered the unblemished lamb, and it bore witness of an acceptable sacrifice to God. Isaac was accepted before a lamb was offered as surrogate. The Messiah must be offered on the 14th of Nisan as per Hebrew custom. Coincidentally or prophetically, Jeshua was crucified on the 14th of Nisan.

In approximately 100 verses, the Holy Koran affirms that God sent Jeshua to confirm the Hebrew Laws. Among them "Moses had brought the Torah for the Jews, but Jesus brought the Gospel and the (fulfillment), or evidences, his teachings, miracles, and grace of his life." By now it should be evident why Koran translators prior to 1970 used the word *Messiah* instead of *Christ*.

CHAPTER 23C. 100 MUSLIM VERSES IDENTIFY JESUS THE CHRIST.

Six Patriarchs are singled out in the Holy Koran. One of the six, Jeshua, Jesus or Isa is mentioned in over 30 Suras and referenced in over 90 verses in the Koran as God's Word, His messenger, or His servant to confirm the Law. The six referenced are classified as follows:

1. Adam   chosen of God   Safiy Allah.

2. Noah   prophet of God   Nabi Allah.

3. Abraham   friend of God   Kahlil Allah.

4. Moses   spokesperson of God   Kalim Allah.

5. Mohammed   seal of God   Khatam Allah.

6. Jesus   word of God   Kalima Allah.

Jesus is also referred to as the sign for the coming *Hour of Judgment*: Sura 43, 61.

The Torah, the Tanakh and the Bible document encounters between God and His chosen witnesses: Adam, Noah, Enoch, Moses, Abraham, Isaac, Jacob, Samuel, David, Solomon, Daniel, Isaiah, Jeremiah and many others. The Tanakh and the Bible document all those plus the ones of Jeshua and His witnesses. Sura 2, 253, God strengthened Jesus with His Holy Spirit. Isaiah 11:2 predicted that all of God's ministering spirits including His Holy Spirit would be upon Jesus. Isaiah the prophet also wrote the following prophecy concerning the Messiah. Isaiah 42:1, "Behold my servant (singular noun) whom I uphold, mine elect, in whom my soul delighteth; I have put my Spirit upon him: he shall bring forth judgment to the Gentiles. Verse 4... He shall not be discouraged until *he set judgment* in the earth and the isles of the sea wait for his law." God would give tremendous power on earth to the Messiah. Isaiah continued to describe some of the power He would have. Isaiah 42:7...To **open the eyes of the blind**, to set the captives free...In chapter 53 Isaiah described in detail how the Messiah would be offered as a lamb to be slaughtered. He would also bring the new sacrifice. Isaiah 42:9, "Behold the former things are come to pass, and *new things* do I declare; before they spring forth I tell you of them." Coincidentally, after the crucifixion of Jeshua, the surrogate blood sacrifices ceased and the spiritual counterpart to the Temple of Solomon was born. One of Jeshua's disciples and witnesses, John recorded in John 3:16, "God so loved the world that He gave his only begotten Son that whosoever believeth in him should not perish but have everlasting life."

In Hebrew Moses is Moshe; in Arabic he is Musa, and Yeshua is Yasu. It is not unusual to find Jesus referred to as Isa in Arabic texts. Jesus was called Yasu in Syrac and followers of His who dwelt in monasteries in the 6th century were called Isaniya. Are those the believers referenced in Sura 3, 52? In Sura 3, 52 Jesus is reported questioning disciples: "Who will be my helpers?" After volunteering, they said: "We believe in Allah, and do thou bear witness that we are Muslims." Since Islam was born in the 7th century, our Muslim researchers were puzzled since the Holy Koran quotes Jesus as putting that question to the disciples.

JESUS IS GIVEN THE FOLLOWING SEVEN TITLES IN THE HOLY KORAN:

1. PROPHET OF GOD.	4. CHRIST.	7. WITNESS.
2. WORD OF GOD.	5. SIGN.	
3. SERVANT OF GOD.	6. MESSENGER.	

Muslim scholars interpret Mohammed's instructions to "Seal and secure" his vision that he was in essence "The Seal." However, "The Torah," the parent book of The Koran, The Bible and the *Tanakh*, all have Daniel's scriptures. Torah references are Daniel 9:23-27. Verse 24, "Seal up the *vision and prophecy*, and to anoint the most holy." Verse 25, "Know therefore and understand, that from the going forth of the commandment to restore and build Jerusalem unto the Messiah the Prince, (the exact time) shall be sixty-nine weeks of years." Verse 27 not only foretold the time that the Messiah would be cut off, but also that the Messiah would confirm the covenant. So the Torah, the Tanakh and the Bible all foretold the exact time Jeshua, or Yasu, or Ioshua, or Yeshua, or Jesus would arrive and leave and it came to pass. Critical or analytical examinations of all of Jeshua's teachings arrive at the same conclusions:

1. All of us are impure and we must confess our sins before we seek God's favour.

2. We cannot profess love for God unless we love our neighbours and our enemies.

Failure to enforce the above will give us a "Religious way that seems right, but the end thereof is death."

Whoever God sends as Messiah, of necessity, must be familiar with physical and spiritual building principles. Since the first person to build the formwork on a job site is a carpenter, and the last usually to do the finish work is also a carpenter, the Messiah should be familiar with physical and spiritual carpentry. Which of God's chosen messengers taught us how to *hammer* out differences peacefully, how to *repair* our breaches, how to *mend* torn lives, how to *reconstruct* broken homes, how to *patch* up differences with all people and to *build* lasting relationships with our neighbours? The arrow simply keeps pointing to the one prophesied from Zoroaster to Micah: Jeshua of Nazareth, a physical and spiritual carpenter. All teachers of wisdom use His spirit level as a tool to mirror lives, attitudes and knowledge of God's word. 2nd Chronicles 8:16: "Now all the work of Solomon was prepared unto *the day* of the *foundation* of the house of the Lord and until *it was finished*. So the house of the Lord was perfected." In the sentence before the last one, three parts are highlighted. Each of the parts has reconstruction principles and very deep esoteric meanings. The last chapters of this book hold important keys. Solomon even recorded the mission statement of the Messiah and what His ministry would evince. To eliminate duplication that information can be found under chapters "Mystery of Mysteries" and "Wisdom above 33 degrees." Solomon did not live a perfect life. Even though he constructed a beautiful house for the Lord, it was destroyed.

The *foundation of the Temple of Solomon was perfect*, since God designed it and all the stones were preconstructed. The Messiah must set a perfect example of pious living. His spiritual house must also have a *perfect foundation*; the columns and precious stones must be scattered; yet the *finish* must be perfect. Be that as it may, the physical temple is not yet rebuilt. If a spiritual structure has a flawed or cracked foundation, spiritual repairs are past due. There are enough detailed instructions contained within these pages as to how to repair those breaches.

CHAPTER 23D. TWO TYPES OF BUILDING WORKERS.

Under Solomon, the kingdom was divided into twelve tribes: 10 northern plus one of Judah and one of Benjamin. The distance between Mt. Sinai and Kadesh-Barnea is not only identical to the distance between Tyre and Sidon from Jerusalem but the direction is the same. Those that teach replacement theology need to observe that the willing-hearted did not replace the wise-hearted. They assisted with the work. The 10 nations that rose out of the ashes of the Babylonian Empire produced the churches of the Western provinces of Rome, which became a formalized church after 300 C.E. The Eastern Orthodox and the African Orthodox first and second branches followed specific preordained paths also.

From the central point of Jerusalem, the spiritual building spread first to Tyre and Sidon (north), just as the natural building materials arrived through Hiram to Solomon. Even Moses constructed the Tabernacle under God's instructions. Moses had two types of people on his construction site:

1. Wise-hearted: chosen and privileged workers on the Tabernacle.

2. Willing-hearted (wild-olive) privileged contributors to the work.

There were two types of workers on Solomon's Temple:

1. Chosen from Jerusalem, Tyre, Sidon, (Lebanon), and North Africa.

2. *Foreign* contributors for the *third* part of the Building only.

THE MESSIAH'S SPIRITUAL HOUSE FROM THE SPIRITUAL OLIVE BRANCH.

ORIGINAL OLIVE Chosen: All first tier disciples were from Jerusalem. Tyre and Sidon were 1st century churches. Peter introduced "The Gospels" to Joppa and Philip took the teachings to Ethiopia. 1st Kings Chapter 5, the fir trees came from Sidon. Carthage (North Africa and Joppa of the African West Coast formerly in Ancient Lebanon and Ethiopia had seeds planted between the first and second centuries).

WILD OLIVE Foreigners (Gentiles) from Ephesus/ Athens/Corinth/Asia Minor. Assimilated workers came from fragments of Babylonian Empire (third century).

The third tier Messiah churches came from Rome of the East and Rome of the West. The uncut stones were from Jerusalem, not America, not Rome, not Mecca. Next we will do a spiritual transposition to discover the prophetic significance of the building materials.

CHAPTER 23E. THE LUMBER FOR THE MESSIAH'S TEMPLE.

The lumber used to build Solomon's Temple required knowledge of the finest carpentry. Since the wood would be exposed to the elements, the lumber had to be tough to withstand choppings, cuttings, whippings, burnings, and shavings and must be able to last for ages. About 90 percent of the structure was in wood. The trees used were pomegranate, fir, cedar, palm, almug, and olive. Within the Occident are millions of people, graded by degrees, regarded as wisdom-filled because they study the "Masonry of the Temple of Solomon." Their aims supposedly are to learn by Osmosis. Since no more than *10 percent of the building was Masonry*, it is logical that students would acquire a maximum of *10 percent wisdom potential*. That should not be surprising. The stones were uncut. *No Masonry* at all was required on the building. The stonework had to conform to the specific design. The *pomegranate*, abundant around Jerusalem was worn ornamentally in the attire of the Levites (Exodus 28:33-34). The *fir tree* is the emblem of nobility (Isaiah 41:19). *Palms* were used symbolically in the Feast of Tabernacles (Nehemiah 8:15 and Leviticus 23:40). In John 12:13, they were laid at the feet of Jesus before His triumphant ride into Jerusalem. The *cedars*, which came from Lebanon, were shipped through the African northeast coast of Joppa where the Tribe of Dan settled (1st Kings 5:9-10).

The early African Hebrews lived all over Israel: (Judah's plight, Jeremiah 13:19-25), Jerusalem (Psalm 87), Cyrene in Libya (Matthew 27:32), and Joppa (Acts 9:38-43). Those chapters of Acts mentioned early church building in African Joppa where together with Gorè, most of the human lumber were shipped to build the empires of America, Holland, France, England and Spain. God promised His hidden remnant that on His "Day of Redemption," they would receive full *REPARATION*: Jeremiah 15:11-15 and Jeremiah 50:20 are among numerous other scriptural decrees. Observe how history follows a script already written for Israel.

The Egyptians enslaved the Jews and became wealthy from the 400-plus years of free labour. When the "Day of Reparation" arrived, all past due monies had to be paid. Follow the parallels. Out of the ashes of the Babylonian Empire arose seeds: Greece through Rome. Out of the ashes of Rome arose seeds: England through America. Many did the same things. They became wealthy out of hundreds of years of free labor. When the "Day of Reparation comes" the promise of "The wealth of the wicked laid up for the righteous," *has to be fulfilled*. Anytime a beneficiary nation of unrighteous mammon hesitates, reneges on payments or procrastinates with restitution, God automatically destroys that nation.

Let us take a look at references to Hamitic people that made regular pilgrimages to Jerusalem. Acts 8:26-27, "Philip, arise and go toward the south unto the way that goeth down from Jerusalem unto Gaza, which is the desert. (27) Behold a man of Ethiopia, a Eunuch of great authority under Candace, Queen of the Ethiopians, who had charge over all her treasure, and had come to Jerusalem to worship." There was a major desert road between Jerusalem and the Ethiopian provinces, which included Libya, Sudan and its ancient city Axum (called Aksum). The Queen of Sheba, who paid the first and biggest tithes to Solomon (to sow spiritual seed into God's house in 1st Kings 10:2-10) traveled that road before. Ironically it was the same road that was used to rescue a remnant of Judah after 70 C.E. Although the natural road may have been hidden through centuries of political realignments, "The Learned" of Israel used the spiritual road to fetch their brothers (Amos 9:7) that survived the civil war.

Why did David list Ethiopia with places that the Messiah would call His earthly home? Psalm 87 listed the habitation of the Messiah on earth as Philistia (Jerusalem) and Galilee (Tyre) with Ethiopia. I will give three reasons—two from the Tanakh and one from past history to expose the entrenched lie of Satan and his imminent antichrist:

1. Between 850 B.C. and 650 B.C. the Ethiopian Empire included Upper and Lower Egypt and territories: Palestinia/Jerusalem, Arabia, through Persia to India. Egypt regained control of Jerusalem briefly when Pharaoh Necho appointed Jehoiakim king of Judah. In 625 B.C. Nebuchadnezzar defeated Pharaoh Necho. The Babylonian captivity followed; then that of Persia was next. For that reason, in Esther 1:1, when Persia conquered the same Israelites (about 200 years later) the Ethiopians, Jews and Indians were indistinguishable ethnically and linguistically.

2. Solomon identified himself with the sun-baked Ethiopians in Song of Solomon 1:6. Jeremiah 13:23 asks, "Can the Ethiopian change his skin?" That question was asked in the same Chapter 13 where Jeremiah prophesied that sun-baked Judah would go to Ethiopia. Many would end up shipped as slaves, (those that remained); their land would be a desolate waste—Jeremiah 13:14-19. Verse19, "The cities of the south shall be shut up, and none shall open them: *Judah* shall be carried away captive." It is very important to note that the curses of famine, captivity, loss of identity and or death would follow all seed. In Babylon when Daniel was enslaved he received the slave name: Beltshazzar. His friend Hananiah, also of the tribe of Judah, was given the pagan name of Shadrach; his friend Mishael was given the name Meshach and Azariah was changed to Abednego. Remnants of Judah, shipped to the Caribbean, America and Brazil have had their names changed to Winston, Cleofoster, Edison, Pierre and the like. Israel's largest and most powerful tribe, Judah, consisted of at least 90% Hamitic Hebrews.

3. The tents of Kedar and the curtains of Solomon's house were black like sacks full of hair. Song of Solomon 1:5...I am black...as the curtains ... and the tents of Kedar. The fact that Simon of the former Ethiopian province of Cyrene was "chosen" to carry the cross of Jeshua, hinted that the Hamitic Ethiopians would suffer physically at the hands of the seed of Rome until the 'Day of Redemption.' In other words, the spirit that directed Babylon is the same spirit that drove Rome and her seed to pursue and try to eliminate the "12 Tribes of Israel," notably Judah. Therefore the secret testing of serum and antidote, the failures and cover-ups resulting in the AIDS pandemic, were the continuous plans of that demonic script. Every place where the remnant went, the seed of Babylon pursued them: India, Africa, the Guyanas, the Americas and the Caribbean. They were forced to make brick and sugar things necessary to *build and sweeten* "The Empires" in the vision of Daniel 2:42-43.

The deepest esoteric message intimated by Solomon is that a Hamitic Hebrew built the wealthiest and grandest house on earth. Hamitic Hebrews would be used to build the wealthiest kingdoms on earth. Since Solomon disobeyed God by marrying women out of covenant, seed of Judah would abandon the chosen virgin and go after other "spiritual wives." As punishment, Fellers from pre-Babylonian times (Jeremiah 4:16-17) would pursue Solomon's seed to steal all of their temple treasures until they became upturned from being the wealthiest to the poorest citizens. Their gold would be stolen. Their diamonds would be stolen. Their silver would be stolen. Their lands would be stolen. Their spiritual house would be destroyed. It came to pass. David declared that the spiritual house would survive despite attempts at elimination.

The 1st century believers' gatherings and the Jerusalem church were under the headship of

James the brother of Jesus. From 65 C.E., to 100 C.E., there were neither teaching facilities in Rome (to explain the Hebrew Law) nor was there a person who could live for more than 15 days that called him/herself Christian. They were neither allowed alive, nor permitted to own property in Rome until the end of the 3rd century. Follow the parallels. When Moses was building "The Tabernacle," people were bringing more than what was needed to build the Tabernacle. Similarly, there were more "willing-hearted than wise-hearted" workers. On the construction site of Solomon's Temple, there were more foreign labourers than skilled workers there. The Messiah's spiritual house had more assimilated workers (Gentile) than "Chosen" contractors, not because of scarcity but the fact that nearly all the chosen ones were killed. Observe the promise from Moses, through David through Jeshua to date. God's house and the power it carries will be with us as long as we are obedient. We can be Kings and Priests, (Psalm:110) willing-hearted and wise-hearted. At this moment, God is instructing me to re-send this prophetic message to the leaders and to the people of Lebanon.

"IS IT NOT YET A LITTLE WHILE AND LEBANON SHALL BE TURNED INTO A FRUITFUL FIELD AND THE FRUITFUL FIELD BE ESTEEMED AS A FOREST?"—ISAIAH 29:17,

The first lumber for Solomon's Temple came from Lebanon. The first place the Ark of God rested after David recaptured it was Kardesh-Barnea in Lebanon. Jesus' first churches outside Jerusalem were planted in Tyre and Sidon also in what is now Lebanon. If Bethlehem and Lebanon do not have massive revivals, then Satan can claim bragging rights over God.

1st Kings Chapter 6 told us where the support, the materials and some of the workmen came from. Hiram (king of Tyre) confirmed that God's house could *Not* be built until God had delivered His people, in stages:

1. The deliverance rite.

2. The baptismal rite.

3. The resurrection rite. Observe the three stages (yowme or days): subjugation, wilderness, through to promised land. That is the precedent for the Pentecostal movement deriving the symbolic 2nd and 3rd cleansing for deliverance purposes—blood from His wounds, stripes, and bruises—more wisdom: blood, water and *The Spirit*.

Every place from whence Hiram brought lumber for the *Temple of Solomon*, branches of Jesus' church sprouted. No materials came from Rome; so it was impossible for Rome to have had either a foundation church or a hand in the early labour. It was contrary to the foundational wisdom of God, concealed in the plans of Solomon's Temple. Hiram also sent lumber to David in advance for the work on God's house. John the Baptist (or Harbinger) also sent spiritual lumber to Jeshua for His ministry. Coded in the building of Solomon's Temple is the path of the Messiah, and every detail from His foundation to the *Second Coming* or prophesied reconstruction period. It is important to note that a temple can only be reconstructed if it suffered Babelism in the first place. So a "Remnant Seed" of the original builders (who knew the plans) must be there during reconstruction to correct what had gone askew. Let us see why no foreigner could work on the first court of Solomon's Temple.

It is written: "To the Jews were committed the Oracles of God." The 12 chosen disciples were all Jews. Hiram's levy of workers was sent *from* Jerusalem according to the schematic: the balusters around the second courtyard in the *Temple of Solomon* had signs "warning the profane." Therefore, James' letter to the *12 Tribes* is a prophetic fulfillment of Jesus' ministry, in according to the blueprint of Solomon's Temple. The trees that came from Jerusalem for Solomon's Temple were "Olive, Pomegranate and Palm." Notice the location of the olive trees: "Within the Oracle the 'Two Cherubim' were made of Olive Tree." The fact that Jesus spake forgiveness of sins and people became spiritually clean means that He "*Has*" the Spirit of God in Him. God does not bestow gifts and take them back. God gave Him the "Water" of Ezekiel 47, the Spirit (Isaiah 11:2) and the Blood for the New Covenant previewed in Jeremiah 31:31-33. Every time He decreed healing, all curses became broken and all diseases disappeared. Since Jeshua is the only person to carry God's three earthen witnessing tools, the schematic confirms that Jeshua has "Oracle Power" and is God's *Chosen Vessel and Messiah*. He carries the three that bear witness: blood, water and *The Spirit*.

In 1st Kings 10:11, the Ethiopians' roles in the beginning and in the messianic seasons were accurately foretold. The *almug trees* were placed in the pillars and those trees are no more. The first churches in Ethiopia and Asia Minor were persecuted into oblivion and erroneous teachings forced their seed to reject the Western "doctrines of men." At the construction of Solomon's Temple when the workforce was complete, ten months were spent abroad and two months in Jerusalem. We covered in an earlier chapter that Jerusalem had a base church, which sprouted branches in Africa and Asia Minor after the genocide of 70 C.E. Solomon's chief officer was over the work, just as James was over the work in Jerusalem.

Solomon appointed 12 princes from various provinces including one from Moab, one of Israel's known enemies. By appointing a traitor as one of His princes, the Messiah's Ministry would have had a traitor in the midst also. Hence Judas fulfilled his prophetic calling. Jesus' missionary work was built on a foundation of twelve apostles. After the backsliding of Judas from the 12, Jesus was left with eleven to complete His work. Anger towards Jesus was centered on the fact that a "Master" gave those revelations to serfs. Here was a "Master" in the true sense of the word, humble, cool, not ostentatious, releasing all that wisdom to fishermen and worse yet, making it available to the "Profane," perceived as "Chosen."

That assessment is incorrect. Jesus did all that God commanded. Jesus' chosen followers were according to prophecy. Every prophet of God that had been previously sent had problems with the stubbornness of the masses. Had it not been for inherent stubbornness, we would not have been able to reconstruct a common point of historical, geographical, and architectural reference. On record, every restorative prophet got ticked because of Israel's stubbornness. Elijah in 1st Kings 18:21, "How long shall ye be of two opinions? If the Lord be God then follow Him, if Baal then follow Baal." Joshua 24:15, "If it seems evil unto you to serve the Lord, choose you this day whom ye shall serve." Moses warned in Deuteronomy 31:27, "For I know thy rebellion and thy stiff neck." David retorted in Psalm 78:8 "A stubborn and rebellious generation." Isaiah 30:1 says, "Woe to the rebellious children."

The Book of Isaiah with its 66 chapters was a type and shadow of the Bible's 66 books. In those chapters Israel was continually warned that her inherent stubbornness, rebellion and idolatry would cause her—generations of woe. However God promised to send "His Son." Isaiah 9:6-7 and Psalm 2 were confirmed in Matthew Chapter 1. His "Shepherd" of Isaiah 40:11 was confirmed in Matthew 9:36. His Redeemer of Isaiah 61 was fulfilled in Luke 7:22. His Sacrificial Lamb of Isaiah 53 was confirmed in Matthew 27:26. Most importantly, His door for both Jews and Gentiles in Isaiah 42:1-2 was confirmed in Matthew 12:17-21. In Jeremiah 4:17, God spoke through His prophet: "She (Israel) has been rebellious towards me." That is so vexing to God that He gave us 1st Samuel 15:23, "For rebellion is as the sin of witchcraft."

1st Kings 6:7, "No compromise was permitted in the Law" during construction. Nothing could be added or subtracted from the law, Deuteronomy 4:2. The stones were uncut. The "Oracle, The Excellent" predestined by God, spoke: "I am the Way/Truth/Life." From that "Oracle of God" would utterances be given to the natural and grafted "Olive." The door in the middle chamber was on the right side, not the wrong side; there is one way, one truth and one life and that is the "Right Way." Satan knows it and he is deathly afraid of that maxim being resown into both the natural and the grafted olive. Verse 22, "The whole altar that was by the Oracle, he overlaid with gold." 1st Kings 6:19, "The oracle he prepared in the house within, to set there the ark of the covenant of the Lord." It is the awesome presence of the Lord that consecrates a house, not the application of a particular name. Without the presence of God, all you have is shell with an altar up for grabs or an usurped altar, a proliferation point for the following spirits that are assigned altar usurpers: Jezebel, Leviathan, False-Christ and Antichrist. Once I encountered an evil spirit that identified itself as "High Priest." The confrontational conversation was brief unfortunately.

THE DOORS OF THE ORACLE WERE MADE OF OLIVE TREE.
THE DOORS OF THE TEMPLE POSTS WERE OF OLIVE TREE.

CHAPTER 23F. THE FOUNDATION ROCK/STONE.

Olive oil is pure gold in spiritual value and colour. In the book of Exodus, God gave Moses specific instructions for making anointing oil. The references are Exodus 30:23-38. At Jesus' birth and at His death, every precious spice mentioned was given. Every one of the olive trees used in the construction of Solomon's Temple came from Jerusalem. Any organization boasting of their foundation stone coming from any place other than Jerusalem, or from the dual Hebrew lineages of Judah and Levi, must require critical analysis.

Isaiah 2:3, Out of Zion shall go forth the Law and the word of the Lord from Jerusalem, not Mecca, not America, not Rome, not China, not India, not Japan, not Korea or Persia. Let me advise millions that ceremonially recreate the magnificent Temple. When you build golden or brazen altars, an announcement is signaled in the heavenlies. I will go no further but to ask a rhetorical question: "out of the thousands of altars built over the centuries, how many do you think escaped corruption?"

I will trace the historical path of the "Rock" that was chosen as the chief cornerstone. In Deuteronomy, the Rock (capitalized) is lightly esteemed. Deuteronomy 32:15 … lightly esteemed the Rock of His (Jeshurun) salvation. In 1st Samuel 2:2, Hannah prayed…neither is there any rock, like our God. In 2nd Samuel 23:3, we get a clearer picture of the special rock. The God of Israel spoke: "The Rock of Israel spake to me, He that ruleth over men, must be just, ruling in the fear of the God." Those words cannot be taken lightly because David uttered them just before his death, foretelling who the Messiah would be. "The Rock" is not only capitalized, but the name is spelled out in code in the Hebrew Tanakh. Psalm 95:1, commands us to make a joyful noise unto to Him (*the Rock of our Salvation*). Daniel 2:34, Redemption was promised through the Rock. The rock/stone smote the Beast. Daniel 2:36 "The stone that was cut without hands that smote the image became a great mountain and filled the whole earth." That is very interesting given that all the war machines since Daniel's time have come and gone as per prophecy except the last ones mentioned: the Anglo-American feet of iron and clay. Daniel 2:28 and Daniel 2:43-44 decreed that out from the seed of the former Roman

Empire would the "World Deceiver" appear in the "latter days." To make a bold statement to the imposters of the Occident, Muslims planted a cornerstone in Jerusalem. In other words, that stone will not be removed until the correct stone (the only stone to unify Africans, Jews, Arabs, and Gentiles into uncompromising truth) returns.

European neophytes that pursued wisdom experimentally heard of a rock with all wisdom and all truth that encased a spirit level to test all philosophies. Millions in early Europe and England pursued a mythical philosopher's black stone. The numerous mixes of metals, the trials and errors of the searches are stored in the foundations of Alchemy and Chemistry.

AS LONG AS EUROPEANS KEEP DEPICTING A EUROPEAN STONE AS A SACRILEGIOUS ORNAMENT IN THEIR CHURCHES, THAT STONE PLACED BY MUSLIMS WILL BECOME THE WEST'S NIGHTMARE!

Daniel in Daniel 2:34 prophesied that a stone cut out without hands would smite the beast that was made of iron and clay and utterly destroy the beast and its image. Observe if you may, Satan's attempt to find and smite (first) that Rock. In Exodus 17:6, only a chosen priest could get close enough to the Anointed to touch, much more to "smite" that Rock. The Rock was predestined to be smitten: "And thou (Moses) shall smite the Rock." Numbers 20:11, "He smote the Rock twice." Deuteronomy 32:4… "He is the Rock, his work is perfect… for all his ways are judgment; a God of truth and without iniquity, just and right is he." In the previous verse it reads, I will publish the NAME. In the Tanakh His name is coded in Hebrew. The second smiting: Matthew 26:65, "The High priest rent his clothes." Verse 67, "Then did they spit on his face and others smote him." The Rock has a name and the name of the "Rock" that became the chief cornerstone was not Peter. Isaiah 53 the entire chapter foretells the identity of the Rock. His trial before Pilate was foretold. Peter could not be a cornerstone because of his appointment as Pillar to the spiritual house from which the Chief cornerstone was laid. Is it reported that Mohammed was sent to "Seal the Book" that was already written? He was sent to rescue his brothers that were under Byzantine occupation.

David received the plans. His son built. The Messiah and God would have an unprecedented *close relationship*. The churches' relationship with the Messiah would mirror the patterns of behaviour of Solomon's wives because the spouses of David and Solomon were of such prophetic significance. Since Satan overcame Eve and the custodians of the Old Temple, he would target every aspect of the spiritual structure relentlessly. Solomon had hundreds of wives, princesses and concubines; none of them were virgins. The Messiah's spiritual house must also have hundreds of spiritual wives competing for attention. The seed heir, Solomon, came through a Gentile named Bathsheba. Solomon was born after David repented. The Messiah's house would have a Jerusalem foundation or base, but the branches would be through a Gentile base that would reflect Bathsheba's characteristics and *traits*. Bathsheba was someone else's wife. She would not be God's original choice; she would come into the purpose of God on a Gentile foundation of *deceit, lust and murder*. Those churches would incubate in a Gentile womb. Most of the children would sprout from the union of pagan Gentile and seed of the chosen through much hatred, war, power-struggles and the like.

The Jerusalem church headed by Jesus' brother James, had eight original branches: seven in Asia and North Africa and one in Jerusalem. David's 8 wives mirror the 8 churches that John addressed in 98 C.E. Two of David's wives had royal lineages: (1) Michal, Saul's daughter and (2) Maacah the daughter of King Talmai of Geshur, mother of Absalom: 2nd Samuel 3:2. The other 6 wives were (3) Ahinoam from Jezreel, the mother of Amnon, (4) Abigail the Carmelite the mother of Chileab, (5) Hagghith the mother of Adonijah, (6) Abital, (7) Eglah the mother of Itheram, and finally (8) Bathsheba *the mother of Solomon.*

God took Bathsheba's first child through an adulterous union with David. The first house church in Rome seeded by Paul in 60 C.E. to 61 C.E. was killed, burnt and all the flock martyred. Rome could not get a Christian church until the seed of the Jerusalem church had sprung. Absalom tried to covet the throne from Solomon. An Absalom spirit used the decree of Hadrian as a weapon to fuel the attempt to wipe out the infant church.

Titus succeeded James as Elder of the Jerusalem based church. After the siege that followed the persecution of 70 C.E., the church headquarters moved to Antioch. Ignatius succeeded Titus in 105 C.E., and became Bishop of Antioch. Ignatius was torn to pieces by lions in 116 C.E. Jerusalem plus the seven churches addressed by John from Patmos mirrored the first 200 years of Rome's export-oriented anti-Semitism. By the third generation of David, his seed was more than 90 percent Gentiles. The third generations of Christian churches were mostly Gentiles except for those Jews in Axum and around Asia Minor.

Solomon had a relationship with the Queen of Sheba: 1stKings 10:13. Records in Ethiopia affirm that the union produced a son called Menelik. That seed sprouted past emperors and kings of Ethiopia—among them, Menelik 2nd 1889 to 1913 and King Tafari Makonnen (Emperor Haile Selassie), who defeated Mussolini's army in Addis Ababa, in May 1941. Here is a message for Rastafarians living in the United States, England, Europe, Jamaica and other Caribbean isles. Contact any Ethiopian Embassy and confirm the following data on Emperor Selassie. I will print an excerpt from historical records and from his family's letters.

"King Tafari was an ardent Christian believer who urged Ethiopians, in many of his speeches to pursue Christianity so that his nation could be blessed. He was an exemplary father and husband who practiced the principles he besought. He was admired in political circles for his staunch Christian behaviour."

Sheba was not "the wife" or even "a wife" of Solomon: she could *not* have brought forth the promised seed Messiah. I recently met a grandson of the late Emperor, also a born-again Christian, who was appalled to discover that "Brethren" were revering the Emperor as the founder of a religion. In 1st Kings 10:13, The Tanakh mentioned that the Queen of Sheba took back the teachings to the people of Ethiopia. Since she allegedly bore Ethiopian seed from Solomon after his temple was built, it did not surprise us to find Ethiopian pilgrims traveling to Jerusalem to commemorate the solemn feasts. One such, a Eunuch from the court of Queen Candace sought guidance from Philip the Evangelist of the Jerusalem church (Acts 8:26-40).

Examine the behavior of Christian churches; they mirror the behavior of the hundreds of wives and concubines of Solomon. The Ethiopian Orthodox Church would have its spiritual equivalent and as such, would carry the spiritual legacy of the Queen of Sheba. Whereas the almug trees played a significant part in the initial Temple, Ethiopian churches have the same spiritual parallel with the Jerusalem church. Since Solomon gave her the true wisdom, then her seed must pursue Solomon's seed heir, "The Prince of Peace" for the same true wisdom.

CHAPTER 23G. CUSTOM-BUILT.

The Messiah's spiritual house on earth has to fulfill God's assigned prophetic path. Isaiah 42:1-6, "I will put my spirit upon him: he shall bring forth judgment to the Gentiles." The seed of former Gentile nations would carry the messianic torch. David's first child with Bathsheba was stillborn. Paul's first missionary house for Gentiles in Rome was stillborn also. The Messiah's

Jerusalem church was not only destroyed, but its "human pillars" were murdered mercilessly. Let us seek prior references in the Word. 1st Kings 15 from verses 25 to end of chapter 26 is a prophetic period covering everything that happened after Solomon built the *House of the Lord*. Solomon through to Ahab's marriage to Jezebel is a physical prototype of Jesus' ministry up to the time that the same matriarchal spirit grabbed a huge altar in Rome. Rome's errant church history is coded in a Tower in Italy. It tilts.

Members of a clandestine group out of Florence maneuvered themselves into positions of influence in a large Western church. Mary, the mother of Jesus had been replaced by another Mary in occult rituals under cornerstones of major edifices that their members built. That Mary was the focus of ritualistic ceremonies with a head, taught by their faithful as belonging to John the Baptist. It matters not whether the head was that of John or not; what matters is that there are several wide open altars under buildings in Rome and other European cities ripe for all spirits of Apostasy to enter. As soon as any contrary doctrine or deed is ritualized over those sites, then Satan's alarm rings. Every time an altar custodian partakes in blood related offenses on any of the sites: masturbation, homosexuality, fornication or adultery, those edifices become strongholds for the spirit of *Babylon the Great*.

Occult shops openly sell statues of the "European depicted-Mary" in the same neighborhoods where Satan has infiltrated majestic structures. Former Satanists, now transformed/delivered, not only gave corroborating testimonies but also have written books about such. It is not surprising to hear people in churches where that spirit dwells chanting to a Mary, *mother of a god*. John prophesied that on the isle of Patmos. According to his account, only in the 18th Chapter of Revelation was *that spirit* uprooted. Early Roman converts, not particularly versed in the word came across references to a "Queen of Heaven" in the Torah. Since most early nations previously worshipped matriarchal entities: Ceres, Asthoreth, Athena, Demeter, Diana, Isis and Vesta, Satan conned them into believing that somehow Jesus' mother would be accepted for that role. The Law is specific: Nothing must be added or subtracted: Deuteronomy 4:2, "Ye shall not add unto the word, which I command you, neither shall, ye diminish ought from it." Let us see what has happened as a result of that infraction. Jeremiah 44:17-25 show clearly that there is a powerful matriarchal spirit by the name of the "Queen of Heaven." In the 7th chapter of the same Jeremiah in the 18th verse, God warns His seed in Africa and Jerusalem about the dangers of the Romans' incorrect interpretations of the Law. God told Jeremiah they provoked him to anger. Those who were the assigned custodians would have foreign missionaries giving them watered down versions laden with inaccuracies. I showed in a previous chapter what happens when a person erects an altar and the place where the altar is erected becomes tarnished. Sooner or later, that altar becomes engulfed. I once entered a church in Israel where supposedly Peter's palm is imprinted on a rock. As I entered, the Spirit of the Living God spoke sternly to me as follows. "Do not partake in this. Leave immediately. Pay no homage to the created, only to The Creator!" To add insult to injury, someone sent a prayer chain letter as one of those spam emails in my mailbox. No doubt the person's intentions were birthed in sincerity since he requested that the incantation be circulated. It was a prayer to a winged European lady, called mother of a god and "Queen of Heaven." The message boasted—just like the ladies did in Jeremiah 44:17 that when they burned incense to the same goddess called "Queen of Heaven"—all prayers would be answered.

"OH HOLY MOTHER OF GOD, QUEEN OF HEAVEN AND EARTH?"

The mother of Jesus had the following other children: Jude, Johanna, Joses, Simon and

James. The lady portrayed is not only called a virgin but their faithful are told so. Ancient testimonies record that she was a virgin prior to Jesus' birth. The Bible and the Tanakh state that she had *other* children after Jesus' unusual birth. Millions of people pray daily to a woman called Mary, who is alleged to be the mother of a god. That means that the lady is *exalted on an intangible altar.*

Here lies serious danger. Thousands of such things are mailed daily. At a glance the lady is first referred to as mother of the Son of God. A few sentences later she is called mother of God and then later on "Queen of heaven." God's word states that Mary was Jesus' mother. Hebrews 2:9, "We see Jesus, who was made a little lower than the angels for the suffering of death, crowned with glory and honour; that by the grace of God should taste death for every man." This is a prime example of how half-truths and inaccuracies entice blasphemy.

The "Queen of Heaven" is a powerful spirit that Satan will unleash at a set time in the not too distant future when sufficient sacrifices are offered to the exalted goddess. In the book of Jeremiah, Jeremiah 7:18-19 God promised us that He would become furious for those acts. Let those with eyes to see and ears to hear discern the danger. I was asked to say the prayers enclosed; then to send the sacrilege to a prescribed minimum number of people and I would be blessed. I was told not to break the chain. If the only prerequisite for my blessing was to send a prayer, then a redeemer would not have been necessary. Sad to say, the prayer is filled with blasphemy!

John, one of Jeshua's apostles, directed us to the *chosen* witnesses in *heaven* and *earth*. 1st John 5:7, "There are three that bear witness in heaven: Father, the Word and the Holy Spirit." They are one and the same. In the earth, they are the Spirit, the water and the blood. The three are in agreement (harmony). All three are for various *degrees of cleansing*. We already established that Jeshua carried all three. The gospels preface no other real or imaginary person. I will once again prove the prophetic parallels between wives of men selected by God and future churches. Abraham and *Sarah* served the Lord faithfully. Sarai was barren. She did not conceive until she was transformed to Sarah. She produced the *seed Isaac* that Abraham was willing to sacrifice. *Until ancient Old Covenant Tabernacles are transformed into New Testament churches, barrenness will prevail!* Mary's womb produced a promised seed sacrifice also. None of the matriarchs were revered. Their significance lay in them being chosen to bring forth *covenant seed*. Mary died and was buried in Jerusalem. Genesis 49:31 foretold the place of transformation from the Old to the New Covenant.

The mother of Constantine commenced a process of restoring religious sites in Jerusalem and its environs. The Papacy blessed and commissioned The Knights Templars as Rome's "Holy Army for a Holy Mission." They were granted absolution in advance from any sins committed during their secret missions. Can you imagine that? Not all details of the missions of the "Holy Armies" were published. However I found classified letters from Templars worried about plots to kidnap Mary's body for ritualistic purposes. The Knights Templars allegedly moved Mary's body from its original site to a courtyard in an Abby. The body is entombed in the first former Roman province to have a state-sanctioned Christian church. I do not think it wise to release a picture of the headstone. I have no reason to disclose its location. I will however remind the perpetrators that their act could not have been secretive because it was prophesied thousands of years, prior. Since Mary's body was moved to a Roman province, it meant that the church from the womb of Mary would be moved to Roman provinces also. The same former Roman province received the first Roman church. None can deceive God.

The history of the veneration of Mary is frightening. As saints were martyred, mourning led to collection of relics. The very practice was prophetically etched in code in the building of the Temple of Solomon. By the third outward movement of the church, relics and images would replace the cherubims. 1st Kings 6:29, "And he carved all the walls (not the inner sanctum) of the house round about *with carved figures of cherubims* and *palm trees.*" Hustlers began marketing everything as Saints' relics. Shrines began popping up with relics and later statues of deceased saints. Mary was not martyred. She died and was first buried in Jerusalem. I visited her first tomb.

By the fifth century, festivities to Mary mother of Jeshua replaced all early European cults to female goddesses. Her title soon changed to mother of (a) god. Her birth was celebrated. Around 1850 her birth took on religious overtones and she became a *Perpetual Virgin* even though the witnesses of Jeshua's ministry recorded that she had other sons and daughters. The date of her death was removed from all records and replaced by some fictional account of her being transfigured to heaven. In the 1950's that myth was accepted as dogma not to be questioned because of another myth of infallibility. By 1955 artists all over Europe were carving statues of a European woman who was supposedly exalted as "Queen of Heaven" in strict violation to God's laws and scriptures. Let us examine the specific commandment. Exodus 20:3, "Thou shall not have any gods before me." Exodus 20:4, "Thou shall not make unto thee likeness of any graven image, or any likeness of any thing that is in the heaven above, or that is in the earth beneath, or that is in the water under the earth."

LITTLE WAFFLES (ROUND CAKES), INCENSE, AND WINE OFFERED AROUND AN ALTAR RAISED TO THE QUEEN OF HEAVEN WILL STRENGTHEN A MATRIARCHAL SPIRIT.

God told Jeremiah to warn the people that when they burn incense before a spirit called Queen of Heaven that the punishment is a generational curse up to "a day of revelation and repentance." Jeremiah 44:19…and when we burned incense to the queen of heaven and poured out drink offerings to her, did we make her cakes to worship her. Jeremiah warned in verses 21-23. Jeremiah 44:21, "The incense that you burned …22 the Lord could no longer bear, because of the evil of your doings." Verse 23, "Because you burned incense and because ye have sinned against the Lord and have not obeyed the voice of the lord, nor walked in his law, nor in his statutes, nor in his testimonies, therefore this evil is happened unto you *as at this day.*" Notice that the curse is up to this day.

I know that in many cases the people who buy statues are ignorant of inherent dangers. However, as soon as you place them on an altar and anyone in that house or building commits adultery, fornication, masturbation, incest, abortion or homosexuality, *that place becomes a demonic base potentially.* That is the manner in which Satan penetrates churches and their headquarters. I know people that can relate to what I am conveying. I have cast out demons on at least four occasions where the persons dwelt in houses along with an ungodly presence, even though there were statues, crucifixes and candles also. In one case, the person, though wearing a rosary around her neck, was attacked physically and spiritually.

Priests and pastors who host crusades in Haiti, Santo Domingo, Mexico and Columbia—among others—can attest to such. If a person's physical body (a temple of God) allows evil penetration, no amount of holy water, incense or statues will get the spirits to leave. I do not know if in an earlier period those things were sufficient and that spirits became stronger as churches weakened. I honesty believe that some moviemakers with little or no experience in deliverance ministries thought up such. Why should that be? This book should at least alert you as to God's wisdom in the decree. 1st Samuel 15:22, "For to obey is greater than sacrifice," and 1st Samuel 15:23, "Rebellion is as a sin of witchcraft."

Why should that be? Aren't they sacred objects? Let us reflect on the wisdom of God. Didn't God say not to carve any graven image? Didn't God look down the corridors of time and see adulterers, masturbators, and occultists carving and building altar things? Did He not mention in the Psalms that you must have clean hands and pure hearts to come near His sacred places? Did you know that 99 percent of the church statues carved are artistically wrong and against God's specific commandments? By deduction, they are carved in error and rebellion. Hence they assist rather than hinder witchcraft spirits. Since *rebellion is as a sin of witchcraft*, most statues attract evil spirits as soon as sin and rebellion enter the house, church or place where they are erected. Churches that erect statues on dissonant or cracked altars attract spirits of Leviathan, Apostasy and eggs of "*Babylon the Great.*"

Since God's vision for His church was that of a "chaste virgin," any spirit that could turn a church over centuries into a "Harlot"—in the eyes of God—needs serious and urgent remedial action. Those are not my words but the word that God gave to John in a vision. They can be found in Revelation Chapters 17 and 18. Shrines in countries placed in lush gardens with flowing water and chimes are havens for *False Christ* spirits. In the appointed time, nations that have "Spirits of Apostasy" exalted over their nations will join forces and make war with God's covenanted people. Ezekiel 38:1-23, Jeremiah 25:15-29 and Daniel 2:41-45 echo the same prophetic pronouncements about worrisome wars against Israel. Those spirits must obey their leader, Satan. Apostasy is a strong spirit that seduces people into exalting *their religious doctrines* above God's word. God's word must be preeminent over any exalted way. According to God's progression of seed incubators, Noah's wife was not even mentioned. The wives of Abraham, Ishmael, Esau, Jacob and David previewed the progression or digression of His spiritual brides and concubines. Mary was chosen above all women to bring forth the messianic seed, so that churches out of her loins should manifest the spiritual fruits of the messianic mission: John described one of the churches, "mother of harlots." There are, have been, and will continue to be fallible shepherds doomed and damned because they thought that their doctrines were infallible.

I DO NOT CARE WHAT SOME FALLIBLE SHEPHERD (WHO BELIEVED HIS TEACHINGS INFALLIBLE) TAUGHT YOU. GOD PROMISED TO PUNISH EVERY SHEPHERD WHO LEADS HIS SHEEP ASTRAY.

CHAPTER 23H. SPIRITUAL PARALLELS WITH HISTORY.

After the 1st Crusade—another generation of years passed and Israel had not obeyed the "Trumpet of Jubilee"—the curse of backsliding occurred. That was vividly described by two of Jesus' witnesses: Simon in 2nd Peter 2:20 and Matthew. Matthew 12:43…When the unclean spirit leaves a person, it visits dry places looking for a resting place; finding none, it returns to its former abode and the last state is worse than the former. People who work in deliverance ministries can attest to such. You cast out spirits from a person in a country; they say everything is OK and they go back to a sinful life. You return to that country or city and their parents or spouses are hunting for you begging you to come urgently. As you enter, the same spirits you had cast out are there with a bigger gang. Yes they confess that they went back and did the accursed things (Joshua 7:12). Every backsliding case brings harsher punishment to a person, church, synagogue, temple or country.

1st Kings14, from verse 21 records the horrific period from Solomon's sons Rehoboam through to Jehoiakim (whose name was changed to Zedekiah during the Babylonian captivity) and from Jeroboam until the rule of Hosea in Israel. Ahab (the son of Omri) took the throne and married Jezebel causing the *matriarchal spirit* to take stronger root in God's house. Follow the determination of that spirit. In Numbers 25, we found Israel just after deliverance, targeted and captured by backsliding spirits. The *Jezebel Spirit* then as now, *pursues the Priesthood*. She targeted the priestly altars. In verse 6, one of the priests of Israel came and brought a Midianitish woman in the sight of Moses. He was about to take her into his tent to exchange demonic gifts. Then Phineas the grandson of Aaron (Eleazer's son) took a javelin and thrust both of them through. He confirmed the scripture, "Without the shedding of blood, there is no remission of sins." Because of the zeal of Phineas (one of God's Temple custodians) and the "Blood witness," the plague halted. It did not start there.

Satan first seduced Eve to plant his demonic seed. God purged the land through the flood of Noah, the equivalent of the baptismal rite or "Water" witness. The wife of Potiphar tried to give to Joseph demonic gifts when he was *Governor of Egypt*. Then Samson allowed Delilah to exchange evil spirits with him and set the pattern for matriarchal spirits to bind, blind and then to enslave God's chosen. Custodians of God's house that scoff at spiritual warfare are the spiritual equivalent to comedians parading in the house of God. Enough is enough! Satan sent numberless troops of demons after Solomon knowing that:

1.   Solomon had the chosen seed in his loins.

2.   Solomon had the plans.

3.   Solomon's actions would help or hinder the entire spiritual house of God on earth.

Take into consideration that a king could write his own laws; if a king wanted 1000 wives, all he had to do was to sign a decree. However he could *not break God's laws without consequence*. Plan a: send faithful Jezebel. That spirit passed on through her child Athaliah. She was great in Delilah. When she gets control, just like a serpent, she binds and blinds. In Babylon, Zedekiah was bound and blinded. Samson was bound and blinded. Those are serious spiritual statements. Captured children of Judah during the "Atlantic Slave Trade" were bound (physically and spiritually) and their languages were removed. Trans-generational spirits bind one generation and then blind their seed from the truth. Slaves were forbidden to read (spiritual blindness). How many people know that Zedekiah was the same Hamitic Hebrew named Jehoiakim, the last king of Judah? Got the hinted demonic message? Millions of Jews in the Diaspora changed their names. Some Hamites, even today, whose pigmentation (melanin) faded, know not, or choose not to know their identities.

Solomon not only married Pharaoh's daughter (1st Kings 3:1), contaminated and exposed God's highest altar, but sampled every Jezebel spirit that was sent under a skirt. He disobeyed God's highest decree: *"Abstain from pagan women."* Men and women of God, please choose spiritual soul mates. Here is a secret right out of hell: Seed of Judah are called *"Lost Tribes"* because of their love for carnal women. You see why Satan sends the same Jezebel spirits to the seed of Judah? Why change winners?

WOMEN COVENANTED TO CHOSEN MEN WERE FORETOKENS OF CHURCH DESTINIES.

The Eastern Orthodox (Greek and Russian) branches remained isolated and markedly stagnant. The Roman branches ended up with matriarchal spirits under their altars. The African branch, save for a dormant wing, almost got wiped out. Let us look at scriptures—2nd Kings 8:18, 25-28, 2nd Kings 11:1-20, 2nd Chronicles 22: 1-12, 23:1-21, 2nd Chronicles 24:7—and preview the behavioural pattern of a Jezebel spirit. We can learn from Athalia. The eggs of a matriarchal spirit are: war, plunder, slavery and death. The answer is "A Holy Convocation" of militant priests, like David (a king who performed priestly functions) Elijah and Elisha and the repairer of the breach, Jeshua.

In the Tanakh is recorded a prophetic observation of God's spiritual house—Proverbs 9:1, "Wisdom hath builded her house; she hath hewn out Seven Pillars." King Solomon advised us that the spirit of wisdom would be on *God's Spiritual House* in Jerusalem. The imposter set up a national altar in a city that has "Vesta" as a matriarchal spirit. The city has *seven* hills and the blood of saints crying beneath her altar.

We are commanded: "Speak to the Mountains!" Hello, that mountain echo is meant for the Wise-hearted! At least one more of God's prophets would echo the prophecy that the "Spirit of Wisdom" would be on God's spiritual house. Isaiah 11:1, "There shall come forth a rod out of the stem of Jesse, and a *Branch* shall grow out of his roots." (1) The Spirit of the Lord shall rest upon Him (2) The Spirit of Wisdom, (3) The Spirit of Understanding, (4) The Spirit of Council, (5) The Spirit of Might or Power, (6) The Spirit of Knowledge and (7) The Spirit of Fear of the Lord. Isaiah added to the prophecy of Solomon: a special man would be ultra wise, sinless and spotless. Verse 4, "With righteousness shall He judge the poor, and reprove with equity for the meek of the earth." John on the isle of Patmos wrote to seven churches (the same seven spiritual forests) established by the firstfruit apostles on the identical Jerusalem foundation from which Solomon got the lumber for the physical house. Note that the seven spiritual forests correspond with the seven physical forests of Solomon's Temple. None came from Rome.

CHAPTER 231. THE WORLD'S GRAVEST TRANSLATION ERROR!

Who in heaven or earth for that matter was called Simon Peter? The name would suggest that such a person would have had a father by the name of Peter and that the child being a male son would have been called Simon. Such a person *could not* have been Hebrew. There was no one of Chaldean, Hebrew or Greek ancestry in any of the gospels by such a surname. Simon son of Jona was married. No record that surfaced so far indicates that he had any children. A Simon Peter or Paeter is alleged to have been head of a Roman church *thirty years* before Paul set up the first house church in Rome. Hence it is impossible for that person to have been Simon son of Jona.

In the archives of early Roman history there is a Simon Paeter or Praeter, referenced by Justin Martyr in his letter entitled "Apology." I believe "No Apology" would have been more appropriate since he said in essence that Christians make no apology for wanting to die for what they have witnessed.

Justin Martyr contrasted the Christian martyrs' factual experiences as Godly and the Roman doctrines as ungodly and devilish. Since Justin's apology was his defense against charges that Christians, by converting to Christianity were in fact aspiring to exalt a king to overthrow Roman authority (and state gods), Justin was defending himself against the insurrectionist charge. Since the entire defense is almost 30 pages long, I will extract only the part about a Simon Paeter.

"After Christ's ascension into heaven, the devils put forth certain men who said that they themselves were gods and those men were not only not persecuted by you (Rome) but even deemed worthy of honours. There was a Samaritan named Simon Paeter. He was a native of the village of Gitto. In the reign of Claudius Caesar and in your royal city of Rome, he did mighty acts of magic by virtue of the art of devils operating in him. He was considered a god and as a god, was honoured by you with a statue erected on the Tiber River between two bridges and bore the inscription in the language of Rome "Simoni Deo Sancto," Simon the holy god." The surname "Paeter" is now edited out of copies of the original letters. Justin the first Roman martyr described the blasphemy in detail.

SIMON SON OF JONA WAS NEVER CALLED PETER WHEN HE WAS ALIVE!

Simon, Cephas—one of the twelve uncut stones from Jerusalem—was not the chief cornerstone. When responding to a question that Jesus put to him, Simon replied: "Thou art the Christ, son of the Living God." In other words, Thou art the Anointed One. Jeshua replied: "Thou art Simon." That reply came when some wanted to go after dead works: dead burying dead. Upon the revelation or the word of knowledge: "I will build my church." That error has caused millions worldwide to be led astray and must be corrected and proven without a shadow of doubt. The Hebrew words: *tsuwr*, *cela* and *challamiysh* mean solid mass or refuge. They were used as synonyms for the Rock that followed the children of Israel. In all Greek translations there are three words that are translated as rock in English: one is *lithos* meaning stone or rock and the second is *petra*, a feminine noun. The third is *tsuwr*, meaning refuge. How could Jeshua plant a church on another foundation? He could only perform the will of His Father. The Father already established a sure foundation. If they were correct, Simon would have been called Simon Lithos. Neither England nor its language was birthed until at least 1000 years later. Jeshua assigned a nickname of "Kephas" to Simon. All the translators assign two meanings to that word—personality types: steadfast or headstrong. Both actually describe Simon's temperament. Simon's personalities ranged from *impatient*, fearful and compromising to *headstrong* and backsliding. In the Gospel of Mark in the 3rd chapter was documented the reforming principle of Jeshua's ministry: "*To be able to be reborn.*" His chosen were fishermen, tax collectors etc., in other words—a cross-section of the community of the day. Their professions equate to spiritual significance for Jeshua's ministry work. Believers are called to be "Fishers of men," collectors of the unrighteous mammon, teachers and healers of the sick. Mark described their personalities in Mark 3:16-19. In Mark 3:16 lay one of the world's greatest inaccuracies. The Greek word "epikaleomai" lists as meanings: to refer to, to invoke, to nickname or to entitle. The main root from Greek is found in "kaleo" which means to refer to. It is obvious that the translators chose: "entitled" instead of "nicknamed." That might explain how they arrived at "*surnamed Peter*" in Mark 3:16.

To add more evidence—Jeshua called the sons of Zebedee "brunte" or "bremo:" the translations—"loud" or "roaring;" the personality trait is "belligerent." How do you graduate from a reference to a surname? I will give an example of what was done: There was an American V.P., whose first name was Dan. The American press nicknamed him "Potato." Calling Simon "Simon Peter" is the same as saying that the name of the former V.P. is "Dan Potato" or "Dan Tuber." Using the same logic, should not the Zebedee boys be called James and John Brunte or Bremo? The Qumran scrolls will clarify all mistranslations! Do not forget that the Hebrew society was rigidly patriarchal. Surnames were recorded as sons of the fathers' names. No one could change a surname. You were born into a certain lineage and that was that. Simon is Simon Bar Jona or Simon son of Jona. If, as is alleged that Simon's surname was changed, then just before Jeshua's exit would He have asked Simon, "Simon son of Jona, lovest thou me more than these?" See John 21:15.

Simon the disciple, until his death, was under the jurisdiction of James the Elder. I would like to see Bede's original translation of Matthew 16:16-18. In Matthew 16:18, interestingly enough the response is not "Upon you," but upon *"That..."* Upon the response of the previous revelation or "Rama Word" concerning "The Rock" which is Jeshua, a "Rock of Offence" to some Jews. Upon that "Cornerstone" I will build my church. Paul is explicit in his letter to the Corinthians in 1st Corinthians 10:4 whereby that "Rock" is Jeshua the anointed. Jesus asked them to secure the "Word of Knowledge" until the appropriate time in verse 20. Notice how Satan jumped on the saying and immediately began working on Simon—so much so, that three verses later, Jesus had to rebuke Satan for penetrating Simon's mind. Satan was so convinced that Simon might receive some divine appointment, that he placed *a spirit of antichrist* on his highway (the mind) by getting him to deny Jesus. To this day, churches that misunderstand the significance of Jeshua's "everlasting sacrifice" and do not accept His redemption package in totality, harbour spirits of antichrist under their altars.

In August 1998 upon leaving the Upper Room in Jerusalem, I was surprised to encounter the same spirit that attacked Simon. It was only after a severe battle (spiritual) in the streets just in front of the Armenian quarter that I received the full revelations about the inner secrets of *Solomon's Temple*. In other words, I had to overcome that Goliath. Had I not attacked that particular spirit, this wisdom would have been sealed until another prophet was either chosen or the nations would have been subjected to more bondage.

Earlier I emphasized the esoteric importance of a particular rock that followed the Children of Israel and how that *Rock* first had to be smitten by a High Priest before any profane person could have touched it. Moses smote the "Rock" in anger *twice*. Isaiah prophesied that the Rock had to be smitten. If Caiphas the High Priest did not smite Jesus first, what do you think would have happened to the Roman soldiers who touched *The Lord's anointed?* Let us follow the path of the rock in the New Testament as recorded by Matthew. The Greek word is "petra." It means *Rock* mass or mass of rock. References to that rock are as follows: Matthew 7:24...which built his house upon a rock. Matthew 7:25...for it was founded upon a rock. Matthew 16:18 upon the same identical Greek word, I will build my church.

The three Greek words for rock are used interchangeably and liberally. One of the most famous translators tried to distinguish *lithos* from *petra*. He felt that lithos more accurately meant a stumbling stone and that *petra* should have been a bigger rock. However the same translator used *petra* to refer to the stone of stumbling instead of either lithos or tsuwr. How else could the misguided "Peter" of the rock myth of Rome last, unless they consistently used the homonym petra? If down the road, out of a dead language called Latin, was constructed the same meaning in English, whatever meanings are assigned after the fact have nothing to do with the facts.

Jesus used the word on many occasions. Paul recorded in Romans 9:33...Behold I lay in *Zion* (not Rome) a chief cornerstone and a "Rock of offence," and whosoever believeth on *HIM* shall not be ashamed. What a dirty low blow that is, to imply that the "Rock" could mean Peter. The English language was not even invented then. I rest my case. That is a classic case of people who knew not the law, attempting to teach the Law. Imagine the millions of people who died in sin. They believed that a church founded on a contrary rock had some mythical power of infallibility and could pray them into everlasting glory after they died. Satan must be having not just a field day but field centuries.

CHAPTER 24. ACCEPTABLE MYTHS/CONTRARY FACTS!

CHAPTER 24A. THE WORD IS THEOCRACY.

1st Kings 3:12 reads thusly: (God speaking to King Solomon), "So that there was none like thee before thee, neither shall any (king) arise like unto thee." Verse 13 is even more emphatic: "There shall not be any among the kings like unto thee all thy days." Had it not been prophesied, no sensible person could convince me that the Jews were looking for the Messiah to come with physical building principles to uproot physical things. Isaiah promised that the Messiah would come to repair the breaches; be wounded for our transgressions; bruised for our iniquities and by His stripes we would be healed from diseases. I bear witness that the Messiah brought our complete redemption package.

The time of the arrival and the time of the Messiah's departure had been preordained: Daniel 9:23-26, within 69x7=483 years. In Daniel 9:27, Daniel told us that within 70 years, the Messiah would confirm the covenant. However before the 70-year period ended, the sacrifices would cease; the city and the sanctuary would be destroyed. The prophecy was born in the third year of the reign of King Cyrus' rule over Babylon. Cyrus' invasion of Babylon commenced in October 539 B.C.E. That would mean that the prophecy was given in 536 B.C.E. The time was predestined to begin from the "Going forth of the word to rebuild Jerusalem."

Ezra recorded that word in the 7th year of Artaxerxes' reign. The request to rebuild the temple was granted in 457 B.C.E. Ezra 7:13-28 detailed the decree. Four hundred eighty three years after that would end in 29 C.E. The Messiah was predestined to be born in the 69th week of years (according to prophecies of Daniel and Ezra) and be cut off in the 70th week (Ezra 7:18) by 29 C.E. The Messiah had to die between 30 C.E. and 99 C.E.

Beware O Israel! For more than 400 years before the prophesied time of the Messiah, "NO PROPHET SPOKE TO YOU." Here is a question: what could have been so serious, that by 70 C.E. God allowed every surviving Jew—from tribes north to south—including the concealed remnant, to be enslaved, killed, or dispersed? The scriptures give the answers. Ezekiel 21:7-10 portrays God running out of patience, especially for rejecting "the rod of my Son;" Psalm 78:56-60 records that their unfaithfulness would provoke Him to remove from among them, the "Tabernacle of Shiloh." The consequence: Nahum 3:9-10 and Psalm 78:61, God delivered **His strength** into captivity, and **His glory** into the enemy's hand. The entire ministry of the Messiah and His forerunner John the Harbinger are coded in Hebrew in the 32nd Chapter of Deuteronomy. The name of the Messiah is coded in the Hebrew version of Deuteronomy 32:3—"I will publish *the name* of the Lord: ascribe ye greatness unto our God." 32:4, "He is the Rock, his work is perfect: for all his ways are judgment: a God of truth and without iniquity, just and right is he." Verse 21, "I will move them to jealousy with those **which are not a people**; I will provoke them to anger with a **foolish nation**."

The same way that Daniel—a prophet loved by God—was chosen to reveal the history of all the Babel-seed-nations to follow, John—a disciple whom Jesus loved—was chosen to prophesy about the history of nations and their plights after 70 C.E. In the book of Revelation, not only is the history of the world coded two thousand years prior to its unfolding, but also that of the *Messianic Kingdom*. The real danger exists: when Jewish Zealots with generational stubbornness ask for a Messiah other than Jeshua. During the time of Israel's longest occupation (under Rome from 64 B.C. to 395 C.E.) Jeshua was born. At that time Rome controlled approximately 50% of the developed world. Light is born from darkness. Rejecting that light and asking for a better light is equivalent to asking God for greater darkness first. "The Chosen" of God keep rejecting God's king and asking for a *king like other nations*. He might grant your request *again*. Pilate wrote a decree on the cross of Jeshua: "Jeshua King of the Jews." The king's decree cannot be changed. To amend a decree of the king, a new decree must be given. Those decrees must be given by kings—either their own, or those of captor nations. Since it is impossible for Israel to have another physical king to sit on David's throne, you are begging for greater captivity. Beware O Israel! This prophet of God is giving you a serious warning: **YOU WILL BRING UPON YOURSELF THE GREATEST CAPTIVITY EVER.** Satan, ever so willing to assist with any rebellious plot, will send you a false prophet that you will cling to. Satan himself will enter the body of the Antichrist. How will you find out? When armies and nations on earth surround you and bestow upon you, harsher bondage than the combined oppression of Rome, Babylon, Assyria and Persia—then, when a remnant begs for mercy, the same Messiah will return to defeat the "Unicorn." Please confirm that I am not the first prophet to warn you about that. Daniel did—Daniel 2:34; John did also—Revelation 18.

CHAPTER 24B. BAHOMET AND THE UNICORN EXPOSED!

The word of God states that nothing should be added or subtracted from His Law or Word. In many instances "The Tempter" encouraged persons to insert "their opinions." The Tanakh says in over 300 instances that the Messiah would arrive and be rejected by His own. That rejection opened the "Door of Adoption" for the Gentiles. Picture this: the seed of Gentiles that received the "gift of adoption" have institutionalized a hate machine against all covenant seed of Abraham. Wild Olives boast against the original branches! The word of God states: "He came unto his own and his own received him not."

The Hamitic/Japhethic Hebrews that laid the foundations of the Messiah's spiritual house were ritually killed. Demon-possessed usurpers removed the leadership. Figuratively, they "cut off the mane," or Hamitic head of the Lion of the *Tribe of Judah* and replaced it with a wimpy-looking European substitute. In so doing, they institutionalized racial intolerance. They also institutionalized strife, hatred and poverty for the seed of brothers: Shem, Ham and Japheth. They venerated a goddess in the form of a matriarchal spirit that dwelt under a usurped religious foundation and called her a mother of a god. By that process, they were able to deceive at least 25% of the world into believing that the substituted European model's head is that of Jeshua, the Hamitic Hebrew.

Unfortunately, only a few among the wise Africans, Jews, and Arabs who know the truth resisted the spirits of intolerance and remained closely knit and inseparable. Those that steer the economic power base called Hollywood should be ashamed of themselves for allowing Satan to use them to peddle his filth and lies to the public time after time. When they are not implying that it is fine to use your bodies as toilet paper, they inject satanic slants in over 90 percent of their movies. The men that resemble David, Samson, Elijah, Mohammed, and

Solomon are always killed in their movies. I cannot understand why Jews, Africans, Asians and Arabs spend their monies supporting Satan's message that he hates them and would use anything possible to wipe them out. Satan is not only sowing hate seeds against you all, but you are paying for it as well? No wonder the word of God proclaims, "For lack of wisdom my people perish."

THE WORLD'S MOST GUARDED SECRET, HELD BY EVERY SECRET ORGANIZATION IS CODE-NAMED BAHOMET.

There is no physical head in the Roissy Chapel! Those organizations with the sealed box—supposedly containing the head of "John"—are upholding instead a usurped altar bonded to the supreme demonic authority. Their mission is to control world governments through ultra right-wing organizations. Their predestined purpose is to create a:

ONE WORLD POWER BASE OUT OF THE SEED OF BABYLON.

THERE IS A POEM IN ENGLAND WITH AN UPSIDE DOWN ESOTERIC MESSAGE; IT GOES LIKE THIS:

THE LION AND THE UNICORN FIGHTING FOR THE CROWN, THE LION CHASED THE UNICORN ALL AROUND THE TOWN.

The truth is that the lion—which represents "The Guardian of the Tribe of Judah"—would be pursued perennially by the "spirit energies" that propel the seed of Babylon, until the end of this age. The Unicorn, a demonic beast with one horn (Daniel 2:34-36) represents the desire of an occult base, to have one long "Horn" to replace and control the treasures of Judah. The nations of the "Unicorn or Beast" "discovered Africa and the lands of Judah" (in the isles of the sea by way of the Gentile nations), as mentioned by Moses in Genesis 10. Job 39:10-11 gave an insight into the personality of the Unicorn.

My team was not the first to have discovered that. Daniel prophesied that it would come to pass and it did. Other researchers have documented the secret intent of the sponsors of the American Founding Fathers. To this day, only a privileged few in America know the occult origins and secret plans of the European Order that sponsored America's nurturing and spiritual mission. Heads of nations openly champion the causes of the *New World Order*. The truth, verified by history, is that the Unicorn, true to the personality of its satanic icon, has robbed, raped, murdered and pursued the Lion all over the world. John 10:10 reads: "The thief cometh to rob, kill and to destroy." Unicorn-inspired armies and nations stole lands, gold, diamonds, labour and priceless artifacts, now being held in every major museum.

Before the dawn of the 18th century, Florentine societies were the most influential and richest of all Anglo-Americans' societies. Because of the Florentine links with the powerful church, Stonemasons played second fiddle in the orchestra of prominence. The popular school of thought was that there were two species of humans: one from angels mating with sons of men, supposedly producing a strain of blue-blooded mortals that were predestined to control commerce and power; the other from evolved apes which produced Jews, Arabs, Chinese, Japanese, Indians and Africans. Supposedly there were "Primitive" ones from "Primates" and the "Chosen," that left a thoroughbred remnant with blue blood.

To be an Archaeologist in the 20th century, one not only had to be brilliant and learned, but also be a member of powerful organizations. That was necessary to secure sponsorship and also to uphold the rules of sensitivity and adherence to established rules of protocol. As artifacts were unearthed from past advanced civilizations, it became increasingly evident that all the noses from the early inhabitants were broad and that their lips were pronounced. Three decrees were issued: 1. To appease the gentry, civilizations more than 6000 years had to be referenced covertly. 2. Civilizations over 6000 years had to be studied and classified separately as Ancient Civilizations. 3. All their related history and data were to be classified as prehistoric and sketchy.

Ancient noses of statues and statuettes appear to have been carelessly or accidentally handled. For years, modern archaeological students wondered out loud at the ability of Roman and Greek noses for the most part to remain intact until secret diaries of Napoleon were found. Napoleon was taught that a monument existed in Egypt paying tribute to the "Chosen" people on earth. It was the Great Sphinx of Gizeh. Blinded by the demons of incongruent ideologies and illogical zeal, when he saw a "broad nose" on the monument in 1799, he attempted to blow off the nose with cannonballs. One of his Templars advised him to return to France to seek the truth from someone versed in Ancient Wisdom principles. "The Truth," confided the Master "is that you are the one committing the sacrilege, Napoleon. The Kings and Queens of Europe do not have 'Blue Blood' and are not predestined to rule inferior mortals. European nations established a line of kings, copied from the tribe of Judah's ancient system. Their kings were blood-related. The face of sphinx is identical to the displayed insignia in Judah's flag and it also mirrors the features of the *Lion of the Tribe of Judah*."

All European kings supposedly descended from the mating of angels with the daughters of men, producing an Arian race with "Blue Blood." Incidentally the seed of brothers Shem, Ham and Japheth, Negroid sons of the Noah sired the entire earth. Science confirmed that all people have residual genes from a Negro female—Newsweek January 11th, 1988. It was during his crusade in Africa before the Great Sphinx of Gizeh that Napoleon (1769 to 1821) was rudely awakened to the revelation that the "Exalted in Europe" had no blue blood and that they were institutionalized in theory to support another myth. That revelation, along with ceaseless money woes and unaffordable bread prices, was the final spark that ignited the French Revolution. History recorded what happened to Royals during the French Revolution (a fate that secret societies ordain for infidels). As a "Shofar" of God, I have some advice for a European based religious institution. Apologies made recently were valiant and timely. However faith alone cannot transfer the wealth of the wicked that worked God's people without pay for 400-plus years. Inca gold still adorns your church steeples. Faith without works is dead. Remember what happened to Achan when he hid the accursed thing within the camp of the Israelites? Read also the instructions that God gave in Joel 1:13-15.

The real motive for the 1st Gulf War is sketchy. Was it based on greed? All wars are birthed in wombs of hatred, intolerance, greed, and or doctrines of superiority. The Arabs decided that they would determine the price for their oil. The *Standard Bearer* of the New World Order then called for war. The real reason that oil triggers occult-inspired institutions to create excuses for war shall remain classified. Were the daily occult consultations in the White House in the past accidental? Now Satan has managed to place most of his major players on the world stage for the eventual showdown. We will either postpone it or hasten it after America's presidential elections. Recently, by manipulating a president who never had his generational curses broken, Satan was able to trap him with adultery, his card winning spirit. Having killed young Kennedy (a fly in the ointment), Satan used the media to set the stage for his hand-picked. Members of the party that bound Martha Mitchell in a hotel room are all saints. He used pastors whom he controls with sins of "unforgiveness" to spread a thinly disguised plan of prejudice, as intolerance for sin. Satan now has the world stage set with some of the most uncompromising and antagonistic people occupying podiums of power.

Why was there such confusion in Florida during America's Bush/Gore-2000 elections? Some Jewish historians believe that the curse on America, bestowed at the same seaports in Florida that refused the Jewish people aboard the St. Louis ship, was revisited and strengthened by the occultists in the region. In Dade and other neighbouring Miami communities reside the seed of many who burned the remnant of Judah during nights of high occult energy. The St. Louis was refused permission to land with Jews fleeing persecution in Nazi occupied Germany. All the coastguards along Florida's seacoast received the words that were spoken into being, "Deny them access!" America was that your third strike? 1. You worked the seed of Judah for four hundred years without pay. 2. By denying the seed of the northern tribes permission to land, all on the St. Louis ship were massacred when they returned to Germany one Jubilee season ago. 3. You strengthened the altars of prejudice, hate, intolerance and theft against God's people again. It is my duty to include as many transgressions as possible so that pastors can identify and target those spirits when a national convocation is called: "For lack of wisdom, my people perish."

Since the Knights Templar laid eggs of replacement ethnology and replacement theology, their seed continues to follow their footsteps by doing the same things to this day. For instance, church groups that sprung from the Roman/Florentine moulds conduct tours to the Holy Land. Few stop at Israel's Museum of Antiquities on their itineraries. Here is another stunning revelation. Eve allowed Satan to enter her Holy of Holies and defile her temple, mingling the seed and producing a "race of giants," Genesis 6:2-4. Subsequently, angels received the green light to "mate with the daughters of men" along with the "right" to enter the bodies of human beings. The practice has not ceased. Since there are those angels obedient to God and those obedient to Satan, anytime humans join the "League of Disobedient Beings" they are open to involuntary spiritual penetration. Satan is waiting for that coveted mould, the cloned substitute.

CHAPTER 24C. ALL THINGS WORK TOGETHER.

Since breaking free from the cycle of ignorance perpetrated by unlearned men, I trust the wisdom of the All Knowing God wholly. It marvels me how much foreknowledge and foresight is available through Him. God's ability to use any situation for His purpose anytime and anyplace is what makes the processes of repentance and recommitment so powerful. For instance: Egypt, Assyria and Africa are not only the natural wombs of the earth, but also everything of major spiritual, archaeological and ethnological significance to God is birthed from those wombs. Israel, you are eternally bonded to Egypt, Lebanon, Syria, Arabia and Africa physically, ancestrally and spiritually. Mathematics was used by the early Egyptians to calculate the inundations of the Nile. The Priests of Egypt had their scribes write and record their data (etched in hieroglyphics) 5000 to 10,000 years ago, while what we call Europe was emerging out of the darkness called the Neolithic era. As much as people would like to believe that the Messiah could be born in Europe, He had to have been born in the lands called "The Cradle of Civilization" or "Womb of the Earth."

Ishmael was sent away with his mother Hagar, not because she was Egyptian but because she was the bondwoman. The banishment of Hagar affects females in societies influenced by the seed of Ishmael. To this day, that "spirit" affects the female seed of Ishmael. The "spirit of rejection" ferments the system of female exclusion in that area. It needs to be bound. Abraham blessed Ishmael—so *the seed of Ishmael is blessed* also. Egypt provided refuge for Israel in the time of Joseph and saved God's people from famine. They taught and preserved Moses. They preserved the infant Jesus from death. Later on in the 7th century, descendants of Ishmael heard that a "Matriarchal Spirit" had exalted itself with power over all Jerusalem and Arabia. It had massacred and subjugated God's people and desecrated temple treasures also. Out of deep conviction, Prophet Mohammed searched for and found knowledge of his great-greater-greatest-grandfather Abraham. He found that the features of the Hamitic messenger that brought back the Spirit of God to man was replaced by that of a wimpy looking European. He also noticed strange teachings brought back to his country by former pagan nations. A European lady as mother of a god, plus some invented doctrine of three Gods was a bit much for an enlightened and "Chosen seed of Abraham" to swallow. The sacrilege was too unbearable; someone had to act.

Judah was already dispersed to Ethiopia and the desert regions. Israel was raided, crushed, and "had a woman ruling over her"—2nd Kings 11:3. The matriarchal spirit (Queen of heaven like the legendary count) had taken a bite out of God's people and had liked the taste of their blood. The Muslim armies liberated their brethren from complete genocide. How ironic it is that a lion (the symbol of the tribe of Judah) was chosen by the seed of Babylon to effectuate most of the damage to the chosen contractors. People (who could neither read nor understand the law) were substituting their own versions. It is written in 1st Peter 5:8—"The devil, as a roaring lion, walketh about, seeking whom he may devour..." For almost 300 years of the 1st century C.E. he did so literally in Rome. David asked for deliverance so that the lion would not tear his soul. Psalm 7:1-2, "Deliver me: lest *he* tear my soul like a lion."

According to the files on history, after people are captured, enslaved and taken to foreign lands afar, they are often flogged, raped, tortured and eventually wiped out. Their disappearance is a result of harsh working conditions, and/or assimilation through loss of culture, language, and/or identity. The only people (privileged enough) to endure that deprivation for 400-plus years and still survive, are the Jewish people and the African people. History has shown that only people chosen of God that have broken His covenant for a double portion season of years, end up with that particular prophesied plight. That decree, in Ezekiel 21:10-14, given to ancient Israel, is a specific punishment for generations of backsliding. Coincidentally, every place where the seed of Israel and Judah lived, that plight befell them.

God never allows His people to be in subjugation or to be held captive for more than seven generations of years continuously. God always sends a deliverer. If there is none among His people, then He will miraculously find one—even among the captors themselves. Here are some examples: The first captivity in Egypt lasted over 400 years.

Approximately 720 B.C. to 536 B.C.—Israel's Assyrian captivity.

586 B.C. to 516 B.C.—Judah's 70 years in Babylon visioned in Jeremiah 29:10.

597 B.C. to 167 B.C.—Maccabbeean and Hasmonean subjugation periods.

323 B.C. to 198 B.C.—Ptolemaic rule.

64 B.C. to 395 C.E.—The Roman occupation lasted less than 490 years.

From the beginning of the 7th century to the end of the 19th century, the Arabs, the Romans the Egyptians, the Turkish Muslims' armies and the British wrestled with Jerusalem's occupation. From the 16th and 17th centuries, the Anglo-American occupation of a remnant will continue either to the "Day of Reparation" or Day of Divine Judgment. Some pundits believe that *floods* or *earthquakes* like those we saw recently in Turkey and Japan will topple large cities according to their interpretation of Isaiah 30:25. The Hebrew word for extremely large building is translated as a tower.

> *"THERE SHALL BE UPON EVERY HIGH MOUNTAIN AND UPON EVERY HIGH HILL, RIVERS AND STREAMS OF WATERS IN THE DAY OF THE GREAT SLAUGHTER, WHEN THE TOWERS FALL."*

The use of the plural word "towers" as opposed to "cities" is worrisome and could intimate more than one mishap. If water is used in the esoteric sense it could mean period of great spiritual purging or cleansing. God always used Isaiah to forewarn specific things. I believe nations such as France with its Eiffel Tower, and America with its Empire State building, the Sears Towers—among others, should be monitored since sinister minds have already included busy thoroughfares (such as the Twin Towers) as targets for mass destruction.

In the Tanakh, war mongering countries were oft-times characterized as beasts. Nations have emblems and flags artistically designed with deep rooted meanings. In 66 C.E., the Jewish revolt against Rome began and lasted 6 years. 66 years later in 132 C.E., the second revolt lasted three years, at which time Hadrian rebuilt Jerusalem as a Roman city and forbade Jews to enter its environs. That decree was issued in 135 C.E. This is God's law of duplicity in that John in the Book of Revelation confirmed what Daniel foresaw and prophesied. The same nations that were involved in the foundations of the image of the beast are the ones that *will* form *the league* from which the Antichrist will acquire its power base. Isaiah's 66 books warned prophetically of those events and told us who would have been sent to repair the breach. Daniel advised us that a Jekyll and Hyde personality-type would arise from the ashes of ancient Rome and control immense power in the *Unicorn* through a loosely aligned military alliance. The nations in the beast would resemble a mixture of "iron and clay." The smooth talking leader will be highly embraced by certain churches: Revelation 17 and 18 and Daniel 2:33. Countries connected by incongruent spiritual energies will introduce a "New World Order" controlling commerce and the world's monetary systems by amalgamations and mega-mergers. Advanced technology will work to humankind's detriment. Ancient monetary systems will be replaced by supposedly hassle-free paperless systems. Environmentalists will endorse the system for giving trees much needed respite. Behind the surge of convenient systems, sinister minds **will be** maneuvering to control absolute power by manipulating the ideologies and the resources of nations. Satan cannot resist such an opportunity (Revelation 13) with so much power concentrated in the hands of so few people. He will do it again. There will be a "winner takes all" clash for ideological supremacy. In Hebrew each letter has a numerical equivalent. His name = 666.

Follow the history of every country where offshoots from the tribe of Judah resided. Observe those that went south and married their North African cousins and those that left by ships from Joppa. Count the years of their captivity from the Atlantic Slave Trade to their successive independence dates. Those that have returned to the God of their covenant, those in the Bahamas, Bermuda and other places of obedience have either claimed their promises already (Isaiah 60:6-7, 12 and 14) or are about to receive their Jubilee. God always conceals a remnant of His people. They cannot be wiped out or ever be destroyed.

CHAPTER 24D. WHO WAS OR IS CALLED THE BLACK MADONNA?

By summing up the prophecies encased in Revelation 18, Satan is on the verge of another major victory. Satan and his army are afforded no creative powers on earth. They have come to steal, kill and destroy. Let us examine his biggest trump card so far—the foundation of what he is attempting to forge and mimic. John, one of Jeshua's disciples advised us that the tectonic energies behind the development of the Anglo/American countries is underpinned by the same spirit that Daniel mentioned thousands of years before. To test the purpose and extent of that major deception, we will go back to the prepared base, a city where sufficient sacrifices were made to ancient goddesses. Such a city (which never had its ancient altars destroyed) would be spiritually rich for "The Usurper." That perfect setting would be targeted over time with skillful deception, eventual substitution and theft of important spiritual truths.

The Etruscans were to Rome what the early Quakers were to America. The indigenous people they were not. South of the river Tiber lived the Latins (shepherds and farmers) from the ancient village Latium. History records that when the Sabines arrived in Europe about 3000 years ago, they encountered dark-skinned people whom archaeologists believe traveled upwards from Africa after the Sahara became parched over 10,000 years ago.

The foundation of the city of Rome is spiritually identical to the foundation of the church formed there in the late third century in many ways. The primary patron of the city of Rome was a goddess called Vesta. A temple to her honour was built around the late second century B.C. It is supposed to have been designed by Hermodoros of Salamis.

WAS THERE EVER A EUROPEAN-LOOKING MIRIAM OR JESHUA?

The portrait so revered by millions was a Florentine model. He was reputed to have been an effeminate looking relative of one of the church painters. Other painters copied the subliminally implanted image: Titian and Hoffman—to name a few. In fact 90 percent of the painters of the Occident placed erroneous and graven images on church altars. Those that erected statues of the artistically inaccurate and effeminate icon in their churches have experienced severe satanic penetration (no pun intended) and spirits of homosexuality run rampant through their clergy. Those infractions and findings were presented to a person of severe influence in Rome. All indications were that he was making serious efforts to correct the wrongs of yesteryear. Those in his inner circle believed that the disclosures would have had disastrous effects on the credibility of his church institution. His death came suddenly and inexplicably.

In churches in Rome today and in branches the world over, statues and portraits depicting a European lady are exalted on spiritual and physical altars. From the 11th century up to now, members of that church believe that she is the mother of Jesus. How could that be? The lady is European. Jesus' mother is of mixed Afro-Hebrew origin. In the Book of Lamentations, after the tribe of *Judah* was carried away captive, Jeremiah recorded the agony of the tribe of Judah (Lamentations 5:7) of which seed Mary sprang. Lamentations 5:8, Because of the sins of our fathers, we have borne their iniquities. Servants have ruled over us. Verse 9, "We got our bread with the perils of our lives, and because of the sword of the wilderness." Verse 10, "Our skin was black like an oven (because of the terrible famine)."

Before the 1st Crusade, the first churches in Rome and her provinces had Mary the mother of Jesus and her son shown as Afro-Judaic and for good reasons since Jesus' sayings implied that most of the people of His day were burnt in appearance. Least evolved people (Hamitic/Semitic/Japhethic) for the most part, have black hair. Their hairs change with age to white. Recently evolved people (or white people as some prefer) have for the most part—brown, blond, red and some have black hair. When those hairs change, they change to grey. So in most cases with age and stress, black hairs change from black to white and the hairs of white people

change from brown, red, or blond to grey. Jesus' words in Matthew 5:36, "Neither shalt thou swear by thy head, because thou canst not make one hair white or black."
Jesus did not say red or brown, or blond, or silver/grey. Also in the Book of Revelation, the vision of John at Patmos in Revelation 6:12…the sun became black as sacks full of hair.

THE ROOTS OF RACIAL HATRED ARE SPIRITUAL!

The beginning of the 20th century saw the complete taking over of paintings and sculptures. Then the Legend of Bahomet was born. Prior to the discovery of secret writings by the Knights Templars and their subsequent influence on Roman architecture, paintings and selection of Popes, all paintings of Jesus and His mother were portrayed as Afro/Hebrew. On December 28th, 1952, the American Association for the Advancement of Science assembled a group of prominent scholars to ascertain the identity of Mary and her Son, since artistic inaccuracies were observed. As a result, in 1985, Ian Begg allegedly published the results of a survey showing that 65% of the earliest paintings had Mary (Madonna) mother of Jeshua painted as black. All early Madonna and child paintings and sculptures in Poland, England, and Marseilles were found to have had distinct African features. Strangely enough the loudest critics belonged to a church that has its foundation stone in Rome. They decreed that they would not correct the inaccuracies on the popularly received paintings of the Florentine painters and models despite the evidentiary findings: "They were infallible."

In the early seventh century, Mohammed received a vision. Since the remnant in Israel had not heard the Trumpet of Jubilee, Mohammed was called to fill a spiritual leadership void. Debaters can argue as to whether or not he was sent as a retriever or usurper. Mohammed and his followers protected many "Tribes" from ignorance and total destruction and provided a place of refuge to this day whereby a brotherly hand "according to prophecy" will eventually be extended, after falsehoods are spiritually purged through either "Water, God's Spirit or Blood," 1st John 5:8. Fruits and seeds were exchanged between Pharaoh and Joseph and Jacob and Pharaoh. Genesis 47:10, "Jacob blessed Pharaoh." As a result, Egypt's perpetual blessing is guaranteed. Here is Egypt's prophecy. Residents of your nation that are blinded and controlled by *contrary religious spirits will wage a massive civil war in your land*. After your spiritual elders hold a national convocation of repentance and drive out all the evil spirits encamped in your nation, then the *Lord of Hosts* will use that as your spiritual Purim. In that day, there will be *wholesale salvation, deliverance and healing in your land*. In Isaiah 19:25 God proclaimed: "Blessed be Egypt my people, Assyria the works of my hands and Israel my inheritance." Miriam and her son took refuge in Egypt unnoticed. In respect for the wisdom of God, had He done it any other way, there would have been no reason for the final reconciliation of the Lost Sheep when the "One True Shepherd" returns.

Warning: Under no circumstances at all should any person even dream to perceive that I was sent to form any new religion or philosophy. I am a feathery funnel to the wind of wisdom. Not only was I called, but also chosen *to teach*, to instruct and to return the spirit level firstly to the houses of Judah and Israel. Equally and more importantly to find and present the same to "The Lost Tribes" (especially those in India and Pakistan), to Africa (home of most of Abraham's seed, those of Ketura and Hagar in particular), to Egypt, Assyria, Lebanon and other Arab nations. Those of "The Wild Olive Tree" are included as per prior prophecies.

Isaiah foretold that the Messiah would be "The Repairer" of everything breached. There have always been and always will be generational curses in the world until the *Day of Judgment*. The Messiah had to come as a man in a sinless form to present His pure unleavened body as a living sacrifice, holy unto God. He had to overcome sin, curses, death, Satan, hell, suffering, rejection, affliction and wounds. After His transfiguration He achieved immortality. At His crucifixion He was shown His earthly mother and brethren and His message was and still is: "*My brethren are those that do the will of my father.*"

The word of God decrees, "Thou shall carve no graven image." God is the sum of things made, unmade, visible and invisible, governed by His "Divine Principles." Since all earthly Mary's born are by God, if anyone prays to a mother of a god, they are disobeying one of God's commandments, period. Whether they know it or not, like it or not, they are paying homage to a matriarchal spirit that had already laid its foundation under an askew altar. Since God himself forbade it and God makes no exceptions to His Laws, those altars are incongruent and disobedient. If no corrective measures are taken, be forewarned about that spirit. That spirit according to God's word through John 2000 years ago in Revelation 17:5, was that it would turn that "*Bride of God*" from a desired virgin to a "*Mother of harlots.*" It is not my fault that you have been studying condensed and minimized translations and chanting in a pagan tongue instead of God's ordained language. It is not accidental that out of the ashes of that dead language, (Latin) arose other "Babelic" utterances. The Word of God is firm and sure. It does not waiver. Had you been reading and understanding *HIS WORD* you would have realized that all your Catechism does is to blind you from God's true complete living word. It is written—nothing must be added or subtracted from His word. A catechism is a subtraction of "The Word" according to God's own word. John went even further to predict that God would put out the light of her candle—Revelation 18:23-24.

If God is so specific as to have witnesses testify that the very hairs on our heads are known to Him, how can the Roman church, from a nation not chosen, not schooled in the law, advise their flock contrary to Deuteronomy Chapter 28? Curses *WILL* follow anyone who breaks the laws of God. How could they teach that they "not chosen, but of the adoption" have the power to grade sins because of their perceived severity? The next question would be: "Who granted them those errant powers?" The next chapter is overdue. It will make many people upset. There are thousands of priests that are frustrated, suicidal and are committing sins on a regular basis. A lot of their members are hell-bound because of teachings that are neither accurate nor scriptural. It is better that you get upset with me and have a chance to get it right than to die in error like numberless predecessors. *All that I am doing is revealing an ancient schematic that highlights the unfailing nature and prophetic accuracy of God's indelible word. With it we can find the missing strand in the chords of nations, families and institutions. We already know our physical history and our ancestral history. From the spiritual strand we can contrast Satan's determined plan to God's prophetic redemptive purposes for us.* If you really feel the need to get angry, then get angry with yourself, not with me. God's Bibles have been around for centuries.

MILLIONS OF GOD'S HOLY BIBLES GATHER DUST IN THE SAME HOTEL ROOMS FREQUENTED BY EVILDOERS.

At this point I would like to thank certain Bishops. I cannot thank you publicly and I know that you will understand. The frustration that you and predecessors before you had faced when you discovered the truth and were unable to receive a receptive ear is not unprecedented. For over 1000 years attempts had been made to correct those same errors with no success. There was a Pope who was bold enough to attempt the changes from within. He was in an appointed position to correct the changes and declared his intent to do so. He died suddenly of natural causes allegedly. May his soul rest in peace! Your churches need to arrange national convocations to reclaim the altars of your adopted nations and churches. You need to *do a spiritual Purim before it is too late!*

CHAPTER 25. ALTAR ON THE THIRD TIER.

CHAPTER 25A. HE IS UNDER OUR FEET!

In September 2000, I flew to Israel and sailed to the Yigal Allon Center. I left for Kibbutz Ginosar to examine the historic Galilean boat. What a revelation that was. Based on my experience there, I am going to make a prophetic statement. One day in the not too distant future, someone in a wheelchair with enough faith will touch that boat and be healed. I looked for and found nails in the boat about 2000 years old. All those who argue that Jesus could not have been nailed because there were no nails then are silenced forever. I touched the boat and was "slain" instantly. I then received more visions about the spiritual altars of Rome.

Rome is called the city of seven hills after those on the left of the Tiber River. Rome is the capital of Italy, which coincidentally, is shaped like a foot. That foot shape was of major significance to occultists of yesteryear. In Judges 1:6, there is a story of Adoni-Bezek. Those enlightened enough will recognize the type of spirits that roamed in the first five verses of Judges in the first chapter. Toes have nails. Hands and feet are the only parts of the body that have nails. Since Bible verses have multiple meanings let's search below the foot of Rome. As a foundation city, all spiritual cracks need to be repaired.

Early Roman history is sketchy. We noted earlier that when the Sabines arrived about 3000 years ago that they encountered brown people whom archaeologists believe traveled upwards from Africa after North Africa parched into the Sahara over 10,000 years ago. The migratory Sabines built trading towns. It is difficult to tell whether Palatine was a separate trading town or whether villagers from Latium had married the conquered Sabines and the dialectic merger had produced Palatine as a derivative of Latium. What is certain is that from the Bronze Age they had a state religion whose head was called Pontifex Maximus from which we derive the word Pontificate. In the earlier part of the former century, the Roman armies raided philosophical warehouses and took Empiricism, Epicureanism and Mithraism for adoption. They designed state deities (big shot gods) and little shot gods to handle domestic affairs. Like Greece before them, they were creating deities of the "thought processes," spirits of heavy oppression or mind binding spirits—some of the most powerful types.

They created their own Mount Olympus, invented 12 altars and assigned names to all but one. Male and female deities they created. Among them, Jupiter, Juno, Neptune, Mercury, Mars and Venus—those later became names of orbs in our solar system. They also had Ceres, Diana, Minerva, Ester and Vesta dedicated to female personalities. Over the past two thousand years, those altars had been and are being used by occult organizations to pay homage to the aforementioned spirit-connected "types."

A person called Helen was allegedly married in an occult ceremony to one named Simon. That ceremony is reenacted frequently today with a human head of a person known or unknown. Every time that ceremony is performed, body fluids are exchanged to commemorate the *union of their founders*. The body fluids, when used for ritual purposes, strengthen the evil forces that control those altars. Incidentally the mythical Roman *Queen of Heaven* was called Juno.

In Rome, there are two popular images that adorn paintings of Mary. One allegedly depicts the Mary of Magdala and another that is supposed to be a virgin mother of a god. Allegedly, Lorenzo Da Medici's wealthy family sponsored one mould, and supposedly, Leonardo Da Vinci commissioned the other. Mary, Jesus' mother had the following children after her subsequent marriage to Joseph: James, Jude, Simon, Joses and a sister named Johannes or Johanna. Mary or Miriam was serving as a temple virgin when she was chosen. Had not the unusual nature of her conception been foretold "while she was an espoused virgin," she would have been stoned. She was a temple virgin at the time of her conception. That offense would have been too great for God to ignore. Since she was already espoused, any spiritual church seed from her womb would have been espoused also.

She and her eventual husband would have to be temporary caretakers of the child Jeshua. Since Mary had both the genealogy of Levi and Judah in her loins, her son would have a better priesthood than that of Levi (*King and Priest* of Psalm 110:4). God spoke through David. Psalm 110:1, "The Lord (God) said unto my Lord, (notice the capital letters) Sit thou at my right hand until I make thy enemies thy footstool." The seat at the right hand of God is reserved for the Messiah, God's *firstfruit* Son. In an episode when Mary, Jesus' earthly mother was asked to intercede for them in John 2nd chapter, her response was recorded for posterity: "Do whatever He tells you!" It is the same response anyone will receive that prays to her for any intercession. In other words, I have no power to change things ordained by God. I am merely an earthen vessel chosen by God and for that honour I am privileged. Also in Luke 8:20 when told, "Thy mother and thy brethren stand without desiring to see thee," Jesus replied in verse 21, "My mother and my brethren are those who hear the word of God and do it." In other words, my life is a spiritual confirmation of the New Covenant and promised ministry custodians of Kings and Priests. God will select whom He chooses by His grace and mercy. In essence God will transform those battered altars of Judah and Levi. They will be hereditary no more. God's *Law of Double Reference* allows anyone to compare major doctrines against His prophetic Word, for veracity or lack thereof. In 1st Kings 2:27-35, when a covenant partner sent a petition through the mother of God's anointed "temple builder," that person was killed.

Roman state religion always had a vacant altar. Rome, guided by its state-adopted philosophies, instituted a system of bestowing divine honours upon their imperial leaders after they died. Julius Caesar was elevated to Mt. Olympus after his murder. Christians refused to bow to the state spirits that dwelt under the altars of Rome. By the end of the third century, through the *Power of Purim*, Christianity became Rome's state religion. At the end of the last millennium, the Roman church formally organized a "College of Cardinals." People who died 1000 years before the offices of Popes were invented were posthumously assigned Pope titles. In respect for those who died for the faith, a list of martyrs was kept. The name was adopted from one Justin Martyr, (100 C.E. to 165 C.E.) a 2nd century writer and researcher who became a convert in North Africa. He was believed to have been the first Roman Christian to be *martyred*. The list was later extended to include the earliest Christians who died in Rome. As the lists were upgraded, titles of offices were assigned arbitrarily. Some became bishops and others became Popes. Most people assumed that the lists are correct. The Emperor's decree was simple: all Christian sympathizers, converts and followers were ordered captured and fed to lions. Can you imagine a zealot standing there recording a successive list of Popes who were consumed? Who would want to be the next Pope? Where would they study? Who would they minister to?

John received a vision on the isle of Patmos. He saw the matriarchal spirit and wrote about such in Revelation 17:3, "I saw a woman sit upon a scarlet beast, full of names of blasphemy, having seven heads and ten horns." Revelation 17:6—"And I saw *the woman* drunken with the blood of saints and with the martyrs of Jesus." Notice the distinction in verse 6, "Woman." 2000 years ago—in Revelation 17:9-10—John prophesied and foresaw the nations that would be formed out of the ashes of the Roman Empire. Those have been fulfilled. Verse 9: The seven heads are "Seven Mountains" on which the woman sitteth.

God uses "The feminine principle" to reference a future spiritual house or "Bride" of God.

The imposter will naturally try to establish a counterfeit house for "The Bride of Satan" his matriarchal spirit. Just for the record, there are seven peaks by the Tiber River in the city of Rome. Can Satan take the vacant seat held for Appollyon? Jesus' ministry was centered on 12 living stone pillars called: "apostles." Have Rome's 12 erected altars to thrones and principalities become spiritual antennae to thrones and principalities?

WILL SATAN OCCUPY THE VACANT SEAT OF APPOLLO, TRANSFORM IT INTO APPOLYON'S SEAT AND REIGN HAVOC AS THE ANTICHRIST?

Paul under his assigned authority had made it clear to all that churched in Rome in Romans 3:2, "Unto the Jews were committed the Oracles of God." Jews have a God-ordained language; they were trained in God-ordained laws, and they were and still are everlasting witnesses and partakers to God's Covenant. If you have a problem with that, go argue with God. Whether you like the Jews or not, are tolerant of them or not, comprehend them or not, their traditions are sacred and their customs are sacred. Their *Covenant* and *land* with God's *most sacred altars* are most sacred. Take an educated guess as to who is manipulating the daily violence in the Holy Land?

Everyone else spiritually connected to Jeshua is of the *WILD OLIVE TREE*: they were grafted. That is why God told us "Boast not against the branches" in Romans 11:18. In John's end-time vision, God made provisions for representatives from each of the 12 tribes. Some are living under Arabic names and countries, others as Indians and Pakistanis. According to provisions already spelled out in God's redemptive package "a remnant" will miraculously receive His transforming grace and mercy.

GENERATIONAL STUBBORNNESS.

There is no secret that tons of those that have coined their own perceptions as to who is a Jew and who is covenanted and why, have inherited generational stubbornness. All of God's major prophets and witnesses called them from "stiff-necked to rebellious."

Abraham was of the Chaldean region. Many of the remnants of the northern tribes are returning to modern Israel as per prophecy. Most Libyans, Syrians, Lebanese, Moroccans, and Sudanese are of mixed Hebrew ancestry. True, some that lived in the northern Diaspora kept the customs, languages and traditions. Except for the Lemba in South Africa and the Falasha in Ethiopia, the majority of those from the southern regions inhabit new lands under different nationalities. Satan knew well what God promised—a man of the lineage of Abraham would seriously wound him in the head—Genesis 3:15. God told him that the Hamitic/Japhethic/Semitic people should be his fiercest enemies. The most Satan had, (unless they became rebellious generationally) was a license to bruise their heels. Satan was destined to be *beneath their feet*. Since God's elect were predestined to be exalted above him and his minions at all times, the most Satan's armies could inflict were bruises to their feet figuratively and spiritually. Satan's replacement theology and replacement ethnology drove such a wedge between

Arab and Jewish former brothers that they are on a perpetual spiritual and physical collision course. One is teaching "An eye for an Eye;" the other "A Jihad."

Satan knew that the solution is entrenched in the teachings of the Messiah: "Do good to those that hate you and love thine enemy as thyself." He could not prevail against the early church, evidenced by the witnesses in the first 15 chapters of Acts. So by chapter 16, he got dissension to enter. By the third century, he had a blood soaked altar, false teachings and a demonic base to dispense falsehoods all over the world. John identified the specific female principle or spirit in Revelation 18, as Babylon the Great. Some churches teach that they are first and that they are the foundational head. Even if all books could have been destroyed, Italy has been and still is in the shape of a foot.

Anyone can use this thesis to repair the breaches of their families, countries and or spiritual organizations. I might appear repetitious but certain points need to be reprinted for emphasis. I want to unravel the demonic plot behind racial hatred once and for all. The 400-year old anti-Jew, anti-Arab, and anti-African, media-encouraged doctrine is a subtle plot birthed by organizations with occult leanings. It had been implanted, cultivated and encouraged by large satanic-influenced organizations that are as active today as in the Templars' days. The spirits that agitate and harvest such need to be *"booted out."*

CHAPTER 25B. STONES TO BE REPAIRED!

The Church of Rome shifted from a sure foundation to columns of Biblical inaccuracies. Over time, their teachings were neither embedded in the indelible law espoused by Jeshua or His firstfruit witnesses nor do they have precedence in the Torah. Isaiah 45:20, Assemble yourselves and come, ye that are escaped of the nations for they have no knowledge that set up the wood of the graven image and pray to a god that cannot save.

In the 18th chapter of Revelation and the 20th verse, God promised to avenge the deaths of His holy apostles and prophets. John mentioned that God's churches have candlesticks. In verse 23 of the same Chapter 18, John warned that the light of *a candle would shine no more.* John prophesied that all nations on earth *would be deceived.* I hate to admit it, but inaccurate teachings detailed in these volumes have been transplanted all over the world.

However I am not going to assume that any person or organization is above correction. It is recorded in Colossians 3:25, "He that doeth wrong shall receive for the wrong which he hath done." There is no respect of persons. In spite of the aforementioned scriptures, the same church invented "the myth of purgatory."

Paul was given the responsibility to be the overseer of churches founded in Gentile nations. 2nd Timothy 1:11 documented Paul's offices: preacher, apostle and teacher of the Gentiles. Any elder of a Gentile region (Rome included) would first have to undergo apprenticeship. They would then have to travel and understudy an apostle/teacher like Paul while getting to know the church brethren, then return to Jerusalem to receive the *"RIGHT HAND OF FELLOW-SHIP,"* before being appointed as deacon or bishop. In Satan's kingdom you get promoted immediately. All you have to do is to be disobedient to God's word. The Romans, by the way, were Gentiles, so they were under Paul's authority. Under the mandate from the head of the church in Jerusalem (the Elder James) Paul's letter (sent with Timothy) contained guidance for office holders: 1st Timothy 1:3. In those epistles addressed to Timothy, there were two understudies being trained by Paul: Timothy and Marcus or John Mark. Paul told Timothy to stay in Ephesus to strengthen the early churches. Converts, not grounded sufficiently in the law/word, were bringing teachings that were biblically incorrect. Since printing was not yet invented, copying had to be done by the hands of Jews that knew the *Law*. Paul outlined that leaders must first be chosen by the base church or through his authority to consecrate Elders. First, they had to undertake apprenticeship, before becoming a deacon, and before graduating hopefully to a bishop or head of a house church. Verse 3, "Charge some that they teach no other doctrine." Verse 4, "Neither give heed to fables and endless genealogies which minister questions rather than godly edifying which is in faith: so do."

Paul prophesied that *a church* would invent papal legacies and other foundation myths. In Chapter 3, Timothy is given instructions and requirements for holy offices. "If a man desires the office of a bishop, he must be: (a) blameless and (b) married. He must be the husband of *one wife* (there are no words saying, at a time), vigilant and sober." Churches must read the entire chapter in detail. No wonder so many churches are lukewarm.

Church altars have been cracked and weakened through disobedience. Instead of being obedient, they mislead with such foolishness as telling members that:

1. Demons aren't around today. Test these instructions: call a national day of prayer, fasting, cleansing, repentance and forgiveness and see how many burdens get lifted.

2. Speaking in tongues and miracles are questionable. They are not; they are God-ordained.

3. Purgatory: John recorded Jesus' teaching to negate the myth of purgatory in John 5:28-29: "The hour is coming, in which all that are in the graves shall hear his voice and shall come forth; they that have done good, unto the resurrection of life; and they that have done evil, unto the resurrection of damnation." John 5:30, "I can, on my own self do nothing: as I hear I judge: and my judgment is just; because I seek not my own will, but the will of the Father which hath sent me."

4. Security of a believer is dealt with in 2nd Timothy 2:15-18, 2nd Timothy 3:7-9, 2nd Peter 2:20, 1st Kings 13:1-24 and Matthew 12:43. God does not contradict His word.

If *The Redeemer* can only reclaim what He was sent to redeem under the mandate of the Law of Moses and change nothing, how can Gentile followers pray someone out of purgatory? Wisdom can also be gained from Luke's record of Lazarus and the rich man. Luke 16:26, "Between us and you there is a great gulf fixed: so that they which would pass from hence to you cannot; neither can they pass to us, that would come from thence." In Revelation 20:10, after Satan deceives nations into a final genocidal war against God's people, he will be cast into "the lake of fire and brimstone, where the beast and the false prophet are, and shall be tormented day and night *for ever and ever.*"

Compare 1st Timothy Chapter 3 with the requirements given to Moses. Has God weakened His requirements for holy offices? Ezekiel 44 outlines God's laws for His "chosen priests." Ezekiel 44:21, "Neither shall any priest drink wine when they enter the inner court." That is the same as 1st Timothy 3: 3. Remember two of Aaron's sons (Abihu and Nadab) were killed for doing that. Ezekiel 44:22, "Neither shall they marry a divorced woman," are parallel sentiments to 1st Timothy 3:2 and 11. Verses 23, "They shall teach my people the difference between the holy and the profane," are mirrored in 1st Timothy 3:6 and 1st Timothy 5:17. 1st Timothy 4:3: "Never forbid to marry!" It is better to marry than to burn. Those that live double-lives and serve on pulpits are destined to burn unless those homosexual, lesbian, masturbation, fornication, adultery and presumptuous spirits are cast out.

HOW CAN YOU BE ON GOD'S HOLY ALTARS TOUCHING SACRED THINGS? SEEK DELIVERANCE NOW BEFORE THE LORD MAKES YOU A PUBLIC EXAMPLE. IT IS WRITTEN: JUDGMENT BEGINS IN THE HOUSE OF THE LORD.

I am asking Christians worldwide to join me in prayers for 40 consecutive days for the purging of God's holy altars, especially those in London's South End that operate their sodomite dungeons. We need to repent between the horns of the altar for all such sins and also for sins of apostasy to be removed from God's churches. There are too many brazen people engaging in presumptuous sins. David asked a rhetorical question: "Is there anywhere that he could hide from God?" Let this be cemented in your mental computer: "Judgment begins in the house of the Lord."

Another fable being distributed and taught is that there are venial sins and mortal sins. Folks, that is a doctrine of demons. The head of the Jerusalem church—James the Elder—in his letter documented as James 2:10, instructed Peter, Paul, the disciples and all the churches that taught Christ's doctrines. It reads: "Whosoever shall keep the whole law and offend in one part, he is guilty of all." Then in the next verse he spelled out the rest: "If a man broke one of the 10 commandments of Moses he broke all." What can be clearer than that? One commandment says, "Thou shall not steal." How can anyone teach that stealing is venial? How could anyone think that the receipt of unrighteous mammon and the theft of gold from poor people in Mexico and Central America are venial and falsely teach such also? There is no "Unction" extreme enough to change God's laws.

Can you imagine that the Conquistadors were pardoned in advance for murdering God's people? Matthew, one of Jeshua's disciples is even more specific: Matthew 5:17-19. Verse 17, "Think not that I have come to destroy the Law, or the prophets; I am come NOT to destroy, but to fulfill." Verse 18, "I say unto you, till heaven and earth pass, one jot or one tittle shall in no wise pass from the law, till all be fulfilled." Verse 19, "Whosoever shall break *one of these* least commandments, and shall teach men so, he shall be called least in the kingdom of heaven." Matthew 5:19b, "But whosoever shall do and teach them (the laws) shall be called great in the kingdom of heaven." I dare to ask such, because the word of God declares that I will be rewarded for living and teaching the Law.

CHURCHES WILL NOT HAVE MIRACULOUS SIGNS AND WONDERS WITH FALSE TEACHINGS, DAMAGED ALTARS AND DISOBEDIENT ELDERS.

CHAPTER 25C. A CLOSE LOOK AT PHILOSOPHY.

Philosophy is the euphemistic term for the invented wisdom of fallible men. Since the mind is a direct highway to the unrevealed or spiritual kingdoms, philosophy can originate from either side of the spiritual divide. Car manufacturers tested prototypes many times prior to producing their road-worthy versions. In every major country, highways are plastered with user-friendly signs to assist drivers with easy access between points. The signs are general indicators. One can still get lost or miss his or her ultimate destination in either the natural or in the spiritual worlds. Whereas for natural highways, the planners established rules and regulations for proper usage, philosophers invented theories and rules as they went along.

Transported fragments of Egyptian wisdom influenced the Greek pioneering philosophers. Since that root influenced over 50 percent of the thinking of the Occident, the first 1000 years of Western mental underdevelopment have caused some serious askew and Babelic patterns true to prophecy. Rome was the first country to import Greek philosophy on a whole-sale basis, flaws and all. When *The Crusaders* returned with fresh seeds of enlightenment, it was discovered that there was, in fact, a philosopher's litmus test. The Templars, and the others that ruled the intellectual roost, called it the Philosopher's Stone. Hundreds of years prior, all across Europe, graves were filled with corpses of men who died in vain attempting to find the "One True Path or Way."

In Justin Martyr's "Apologies for Christians" or "Apologies," he asked his Roman brethren about Simon the sorcerer. Simon the occultist was allowed to open a mystery school in Rome. It appears that some practices (like incense burning and the erecting of statues) seeped across from teachings in the mystery school of Simon Paeter "the occultist." Justin Martyr and Poly-carp questioned such things plus the changing of the 14th of the seventh month sacred feast to coincide with that of the fertility cult of Estair—now called Easter. Both were killed like thousands of others for the truth. Paul forewarned in Romans 1:22-25. Verse 22, "Professing themselves to be wise, they became fools (23) and changed the glory of the incorruptible God into an image made like to *corruptible man* and to birds and four footed beasts (idols and stat-ues). (25) They changed the truth of God into a lie."

Physical wildernesses are bereft of trees. Billions of trees have *died* to produce tons of pa-per on which are printed the mental mishaps, tragedies, and occasional temporary successes of myth-seekers and their trails of fantasy. Some searched in vain for "The Philosopher's Black Stone," others searched for a "mythical lance," and later on, others searched for a mythical head under the code name "BAHOMET." Ladies and Gentlemen, wildernesses, graveyards, archae-ology, history and incongruent religions either pained for, or bore witness to the one proph-esied to find the "stone." There is a prescribed limit to the physical pursuit of wisdom. The first head that found the stone had to be sacrificed for the stone. The stone itself had to be broken. The adjoining pillars had to be sacrificed. Looking for "a sacrificed head" or the fragments of the defunct physical structure of Solomon has not been, nor will it be the way. I will release the key to all the above mysteries. That key will open the door of truth and end those searches. I cannot take credit for finding the stone neither will I, since the name of the one destined to find the stone had been prophesied in Isaiah 40:3.

Zacharias (a temple priest) and his wife (a former temple virgin, Elizabeth of the Tribe of Levi) had a son by the name of John. John traveled in the wilderness. His ministry was *en-tirely in the wilderness*, proclaiming the Good News that the "Stone of Truth" of Psalm 87 was revealed. In verse 11 (Isaiah 40) Isaiah foretold the messianic mission, "He shall feed his *flock* like a shepherd; he shall gather the *Lambs*." The Templars and their brethren recite (in rhyme) the plight of a band whose pursuit for the "Stone of Truth" ended across the burning sands of Arabia. Since there is an esoteric link between man and tree, the prophecy of the one branch and the one stone could either mean a fossilized tree or a Master skilled in both masonry and carpentry. We studied *known principles* where finite men left dead trails. Whereas sediments from the old seabed harden into sand-coloured stones over vast expanses of time and the right conditions, ancient trees/branches harden into *dark* stone.

What are the odds that one person could fulfill the following: God's Oracle, redemptive Son born of a virgin, first light, firstfruit, hybrid seed, bread of life, carpenter, branch, teacher, prophet, magi, sacrificial lamb, time-adjuster, door and foundation stone? For that person to have the apex of all philosophies, He would have to be a "Living Fossil." Let us search prior prophecies first. The only vehicle that could do all of the above is a sterilized all-inclusive temple. God's redemptive plan (*for all*) stipulates that His former flawed temple would be reconstructed without blemish or wrinkle like a virgin reborn. The chosen Messiah/Shepherd must be the embodiment of every Jewish feast: Passover, Purim, Unleavened Bread, First-fruits, Pentecost, Jubilee, Booths, and Advent or Sabbath.

Unlike any philosopher past or future, that "Chosen Vessel," according to prophecy must have God's words in His mouth: so He must transcend philosophy. He would in fact be a super prophet! Again we must search the books of Abraham, Isaac, Noah, Moses and Prophet Mohammed. God dictated the qualities of the Messiah to Moses in Deuteronomy 18:18. "I will raise them up a Prophet (notice the capital letters) from *among their brethren*, like unto thee, and will put my words in his mouth; and he shall speak unto them *all* that I command him." Verse 19…and it shall come to pass, that whosoever will not hearken unto my words, *which he shall speak in my name*, I will require it of him." Jeremiah 8:20, "The *harvest* is past (1948+50=1998), the summer is ended and *we are not saved*." Verse 21, "For the hurt of the *Daughter* of *my people am I hurt*; **I am black**." I wonder why Satan's agents are so bent on eradicating all traces of Judah's and the Messiah's lineage and ethnicity.

The odds are so phenomenal that no one could fulfill all the above unless God had decreed it. We searched astronomy and found that a star heralded the birth of that virgin's son. We searched the ruins of the *Spiritual Temple of Solomon*: the builder was a spiritual carpenter, not a mason. Undoubtedly He brought to us the world's most effective philosophy for peace, love and harmonious living. We searched the foundation of the Roman church and discovered that it was a graft from the Jerusalem branch as had been prophesied. All that is left is the search for the philosopher's stone and the prophecy for the Muslim nations. If we find both, then we would have completed the 360° search to ascertain if the philosopher's stone is God's *spirit level of truth*, by which every doctrine, philosophy or way can be gauged.

Here is the litmus test. Both man and tree were born out of the earth. If in fact the "tree of life," concealed in paradise, released its spiritual pollen—then anything else created out of the ground would be able to "produce after its kind." Healing properties would be rooted in special plants that received "spiritual pollen" from the "tree of life" to heal sick and dying people. So whoever the messianic seed is, that person must first come from "eternity," transcend time and lead the way for all others to be transformed into "Living Temples of God." That person would have to be a Jew: "To the Jews were committed the Oracles of God." I am not being funny with the following questions: "Which Jew could be so unselfish to suffer and die for Muslims, Jews, Christians and all sinners? Which Jew could practice, teach and live that level of *FORGIVENESS FOR ALL?* Which person who ever lived on this earth could be the physical embodiment of all the attributes of God? He actually personified the hidden meanings of all the Hebrew feasts. Everything for the reconstruction of the perfect temple was perfected and manifest through *HIM*. The èts/lumber became earth/flesh. The Oracle became flesh. The door, the bread, the foundation stone and the feasts: Purim, Pentecost, Shabbat etc., they all became flesh and dwelt among us.

CHAPTER 25D. SPIRITUAL ARCHAEOLOGY.

I am an amateur archaeologist. I am allowed to search for fossils and to examine stone fragments for evidentiary materials. God foreknew that many metaphysical disciplines do not allow self-scrutiny. Obey instructions, period. In the book of the Levites, one of the main duties of a chosen king of God is that we are to examine His records for fresh wisdom. God encourages us to study His parchments. They have been documented already. However, according to the highest minds of our civilizations, there is only one stone deemed capable of accessing the apex of wisdom. By deduction and by a process of gradual elimination, the one that keeps surfacing, "that name above every other name, Jeshua," needs genetic, ethnological and archaeological scrutiny for the ten thousandth time. Since it was prophesied that an early foundation church would attempt to pull off a hoax by changing His identity, we must examine His genetic roots in detail. This sort of meticulous research is necessary, not to encourage street corner arguments, but to expose the world's biggest demonic hoax once and for all. God told us in His word that "The very elect will be fooled" by that hoax.

It is amazing how many people today believe that Jeshua, seed of one of the blackest men who ever lived, somehow became a blue-eyed Jew, long before the Jews migrated to cold countries or began marrying Berbers and Gentiles. As a youngster, His parents were able to mingle among dark-skinned Egyptians and not be recognized. Some might argue that God provided supernatural protection for Him; so we have to dig deeper. Whatever synonym they use in English to describe the "Adamy" David, we know that King Solomon (his son) had both parents of *Hamitic* ancestry since his hair was like date clusters, he was black like a black bird and one of his sons had "dread locks." Just coincidentally, the following women that are in Jeshua's ancestral mix: Tamar, Rahab, Ruth and Bathsheba were Hamites. So it is more than logical that Mary and Joseph looked like the dark-skinned Egyptians and were also Hamitic: most of their ancestors were born in Egypt—Genesis 50:22-23.

Since Rebekah used lies and deception (change of appearance and of pigmentation) to covet the seed promise, we need to examine the extent of *the lies* and *the deceptions*. Since lies reflect inaccurate speech, and lies were used to strengthen the deception, we must examine the language of the "Church" for false translations of words that supported the deception. Since the opposite of black is white, and the word of God faileth never, we will search the words used for both "Black and White." The Hebrew words: "shachor, kamar, (qedar) or kedar," all refer to the colour black. Though some of the words are used to reflect the colour of things like horses or hair, one of the words used to identify pigmentation "Qadar" got its prophetic root from the name of one of Ishmael's sons. The derivative "qedar" means ashy, whereas "qadar" means dark-coloured or black. "Shachor" has been used to describe the colour of "black" horses. In Jeremiah 8:21, the prophet used the word "shachor" to describe his skin colour. Whereas "kamar" means to be blackened, we find Jeremiah using "kamar" to describe the effects of the sun on their already black skin when they had been in the extreme heat for prolonged periods. Lamentations 5:10, "kamar" like an oven.

There is a Hebrew word for radiance (brilliance of light or wisdom). In the Tanakh, it is used in all instances to reflect spiritual glowing, birth of wisdom or Glory of the Lord. The word is "tsach." Greeks lost their melanin through generational mixes. They were called Gentiles. The Romans (also melanin-deficient) were called Gentiles too. There are two Hebrew words for "white." Laban is used to describe things like cloth or horses. The other one is *TSARA* pronounced *TSAWRAH* means to peel or to shed skin. To most Hebrews of yore, access to or contact with European looking people was infrequent. In Acts 21:38, the Roman captain of the castle mistook Saul of Tarsus for an Egyptian. Only after the Roman occupation and the establishment of Jerusalem as a religious and trading center did the average person encounter Greeks or Romans, who were and are still Caucasian Gentiles. So rare in fact was the encounter that to the average Hebrew, a person who peeled white had some sort of skin disease, like a famous black American pop singer. In fact the Hebrew word for white like skin is the same word for leprous. Every instance in which we encountered the word leprous, we found use of the word "Tsara:" Exodus 4:6, Numbers 12:10, Leviticus 13:44, 2nd Kings 7:3 and 2nd Chronicles 26:20. With no precedent at all for "tsach" to be used for white as in colour, why would translators for the Roman church have "white and ruddy" an obviously contradictory term, instead of "brilliant and adamy" except that it had been prophesied?

Since prophets refer to God's church as *His Bride*, why would a translator imply that the perfect Bride of God was leprous? To fix that, the *Bride of God* has been translated as "White and ruddy" and the chief among ten thousand to this day. Since by deduction, Jeshua is all the above (plus the "Hamitic Jew" who is portrayed as an "Evolved Roman") all according to prior prophecies, we are left with *His philosophy* as the last thread of evidence to find. Branches must first die before being transformed into stone. Jeshua not only became the chief cornerstone, but the philosophers' stone of truth. Jeshua penned the ultimate litmus test. Follow instructions and watch poverty disappear; watch hatred and injustices disappear. The question is—can we? Since Satan has stolen philosophies, minds, hearts, souls, families and countries, are we big enough to meet the challenge of the *Ancient of Days*?

THOU SHALT LOVE THE LORD THY GOD WITH THY WHOLE HEART, MIND, SOUL AND STRENGTH; LOVE THY NEIGHBOUR AS THY SELF.

CHAPTER 25E. A CLOSE LOOK AT PURGATORY.

Dante Alighieri—1265 to 1321—was a Roman playwright and a great admirer of Virgil. Virgil is known for such Latin mythical love stories as Orpheus and Uridice. Serious analysis of the works of Virgil would reveal his philosophical foundation to be artificial. Moses' records of ancient Hebrew sacrifices compared the acceptance of sanctified blood sacrifices of surrogate bulls and goats to that of *nectar in the nostrils* of God. Virgil's upside down teaching was that stuffing bees into the belly of bulls produced the formula for nectar. According to God's spiritual teachings, we are not purged and transformed into His nectar by going physically into the belly of a bull, but by going spiritually into the bosom of His sanctified lamb. We are not sanctified by works: Ephesians 2:9.

In Dante Alighieri`s masterpiece "Divine Comedy," there are three allegorical figures: Inferno, Paradiso and Purgatorio. Domenico Michelino was contracted to make a pictorial representation of that "Divine Comedy" (1465). That painting is displayed on prominent places of worship in Rome today. If you look closely at Roman paintings of purgatory we see an exact reproduction of the Tower of Babel. On top of the three church steeples are demonic-looking sculptured figures and figurines. The only one that has a vacant altar is the one that resembles the Basilica. It has an abandoned altar. I want citizens of France, England and America to give critical analysis and scrutiny to all elevated shrines also. When you arrange your national days of Repentance and Reconciliation, all altars' custodians can visit and pray at sites that offer satanic refuge deliberately or accidentally in order to cancel their energies and satanic covenants. Refer to prior prophecy by Daniel in Daniel 2:34.

Are there references by God's prophets to purgatory? Isaiah 38:18, "For the grave cannot praise thee, death cannot celebrate thee: they that go down to the pit cannot hope for thy truth." Exodus 32:33, *Whosoever hath (on completion of days of life) sinned against me, him will I blot out of my book.* The word of God specifically declares that nothing should be added or subtracted from the Law. Deuteronomy 17:19; 28:58; 31:12 and 32:46, as those scriptures are examined they forcefully state that "all the words of the Law" must be observed. The inclusive clause is extended to men, women, and strangers within thy gates. Deuteronomy 29:29 summarizes best "Secret things belong unto the Lord, but those things which are revealed belong to *us* and our *children forever* that we may do *all* the words *of this law*." Over the years, we critically studied the teachings of Jeshua. What we concluded was no different from hundreds of survey results. Of all the people that ever lived, by far He is the greatest expounder of the Hebrew Law. In the Torah, there are 613 laws separate from the 63 in the Mishna. The greatest irony is that every one of Jeshua's apostles warned the faithful to refrain from "doctrines of men." Others spoke of those that would forbid men to marry, introducing "doctrines of demons." In truth, any doctrine that men insert without prior referencing and confirmation through God's filtering process could be demonically inspired. Paul wrote in Colossians 2:8, "Beware lest any man spoil you through 'Philosophy' and vain deceit after the tradition of men, after the rudiments of the world and not after Christ."

The teaching on purgatory implies that a person on earth has the authority to usurp God's word. It is written in Hebrews 9:27, "It is appointed a man, once to die and after that judgment." In the parable of the rich man and Lazarus, Abraham was asked to send a message of warning to the rich man's family. The unbridgeable gulf between both zones is clearly described. The reason I took the time to detail this prophecy is for self-scrutiny. Self-scrutiny is extremely difficult if you are in a wilderness. Please call a solemn fast for all the members of your church boards. Treat the process as if it is the first instance that you are being called to the Lord. Ask for the forgiveness of known and unknown sins committed with your eyes, ears, mouths, hearts, minds, bodies and attitudes. Ask for forgiveness of known and unknown iniquities on behalf of you, your parents and grandparents as far back as ordinances were kept. Ask for forgiveness of unintentional sins, attitudinal sins, unknown and known sins; emphasize *murder* committed during *unjust wars*. Ask God to let truth and wisdom reign over your church, assembly, synagogue, temple, your flock and your nation.

The thing that groans my spirit is that weak, lukewarm, dead, and false teachings are really assisting Satan with his work. Think of the enormous number of people today that were once vibrant pre-teens who loved God. Weak teachers, imposters and hypocritical leaders changed many into a perverse flock. Today we are trying to apply BAND-AIDS as solutions to all the problems that we have inherited as a result of generations of spiritual recklessness. The perennial problems of our age all have spiritual roots. Pay little attention to those smooth-talking, cliché- releasing gurus. Does a paint job make a vehicle run better?

CHAPTER 26. APOCALYPSE: HISTORY OF THE WORLD AND CHURCHES PROPHESIED!

Solomon had hundreds of wives, princesses and concubines. The Messiah's spiritual house must have hundreds of churches all competing for the attention of the KING. Correspondingly, we have no records as to which one Solomon loved most. Records indicate that many were *not* pleasing to God but were of the flesh. The one that Solomon built the most elaborate house for—was far removed from the knowledge of the true God. The largest Christian church according to the schematic must be spiritually inaccurate. The Muslim nations built a Theocracy and according to prophecy many will be reconciled by the time the Messiah returns the second time. God gave Daniel a vision of a beast and used the interpretation to forecast 2000 years of history. People had ignored the prophecies of John until millennium fever hit the globe. All of a sudden, the so-called skeptics were not so skeptical anymore. Psychics and gurus made so many foolish predictions in the past that the only tested and proven prophetic document, the Bible was sought after. Secular magazines were sold out whenever any issues referring to Jesus and end-time prophecies were published. The most quoted was John's vision on Patmos. He prophesied that *seven types* of churches would emerge from Jeshua's base. One type of church would be prone to penetration by the same Jezebel spirit that I have been describing and exposing all along. Jezebel has to usurp the national altar first. God instructs all His custodians to spiritually sterilize any land before erecting His sacred altars. In Numbers 33:52, God warned: "Drive out all the...of the land and destroy all their molten images and pluck down all their high places." Hence the solutions to most national problems are already given to vigilant and spiritually strong leaders.

Rome is a city built on seven peaks by the Tiber River. If Constantine and his fellow citizens chose Rome as headquarters for their religion, why weren't the defunct altars destroyed? In Deuteronomy 20:17, Israel first had to drive out the Jebusites, Amorites, Perizzites and others. Constantine established a state religion on the site of martyrs' blood and where goddess spirits and those that launched the *Scepter of the Unicorn* congregate. If those spirits are not expelled, the plight of Revelation 17 and 18 will befall all. Revelation 17:6-9 referenced that the seven heads are seven mountains on which the woman sitteth. In Revelation 17, Daniel foretold the foundational history of the Anglo/American world.

TOOLS FOR RESTORATION!

In Jeremiah Chapter 3, God's house is likened to an unfaithful wife that had run after demonic men. Verse 1, "If a man put away his wife and she go from him, and become another man's, shall he return unto her again? Shall not the land be greatly polluted? But thou hast played the harlot with many lovers; yet return again unto me!" God is saying that He will forgive her of her unfaithfulness. Verse 7...I said after she had done all these things. Turn thou unto me (in other words, come back, God will forgive you) but she returned not. And her treacherous sister Judah saw it. Verse 8, ...I saw, when for all the causes whereby backsliding Israel committed adultery, I had put her away and given her a bill of divorce; yet her treacherous sister Judah feared not, but went and played the harlot also. Verse 9 …It came to pass through the lightness of her whoredom, that she defiled the land and committed adultery with *stones* and with *stocks*.

Children of Abraham that dwell in **The West**, there was a time when your forefathers were paying homage to Baal because they thought it was Baal that blessed their crops. God told Elijah to warn His people. He caused it not to rain for three years. This prophet is warning you again. It is not the condominiums, the stock market or the hoarding of precious stones that are bringing you your wealth. It is your grieving husband Jehovah Tzidkenu. First you must get rid of all those false altars in Africa, in Haiti, in Cuba, in Brazil, in Guadeloupe, in Martinique, Miami, California, India, New York, Iran, Egypt, Paris, Rome, Iraq, Pakistan and all the occult-strengthened bases of the world.

The stones also represent the psychics and other false religions that you are dabbling with. To those of the house of Judah that escaped or were concealed in the land in the south, those abominable stones represent the false religions that are all over your lands, causing the land of the south (**Africa**) to become a desolate waste. Jeremiah 8:19, "Why hath (the house of Judah) provoked me with their graven images and with strange vanities?" Verse 20. The harvest (Jubilee) is past, the summer is ended, and we are not saved. God's Spirit groans through the mouth of the land. Verse 21: "For the hurt of the *daughter of my people* am I hurt. **I am black.**" In Isaiah 11:10-11, Isaiah prophesied the Gentiles' inclusion, and the Messiah's *Second Coming* for His remnant of all tribes. In truth and in fact, he foretold that the Messiah would come first to His own people. In Ezekiel 21:20-32, their rejection would cause hardship, their demotion and the rise of formerly poor and downtrodden Gentile nations over them. Ingratitude, greed and spirits-induced war would cause them to attack God's people once too often. Then the Messiah would return the second time (Isaiah 11:11).

2nd Coming: Verse 11, "The Lord shall set His hand the second time to recover the remnant of His people that shall be left from Assyria and from Egypt and Pathros (Upper Egypt), and Cush (Ethiopia) and Elam and Shinar and from Hamath and from the islands of the sea." After you have returned to obedience, here is the promise of the Lord: Jeremiah 50:20. Jeremiah 50:20: "In those days (after we have repented) saith the Lord, the iniquity of Israel shall be sought for and there shall be none, and the sins of Judah, and there shall be none found, for I shall pardon whom I reserve." In the Caribbean islands of the sea are people from every nation in the Middle East intermarrying, trading and coexisting just as they did in times of antiquity. I stood once in one of those islands and wept with joy as I watched Syrians, Lebanese, Jews, Gentiles, and Africans at a wedding. What a rainbow of joy the future must be! I later found out that some 30 to 40% of all the above groups intermarry regularly on that particular island and they and their beautiful children are serious Christians. I wonder how many of them knew that God designed it specifically that way to fulfill His prophecies, especially the ones spelled out in Isaiah 11:11, Isaiah 60:6-10 and verses13-14.

CHAPTER 26A. FIRST TYPE OF CHURCH: THE CHURCH THAT LEFT ITS FIRST LOVE.

God is Agape. The *first type of* **church**—Revelation 2: 1-7, "The Church that left its first love" is one that has substituted God's word for some contrary doctrine (doctrine of demons) not enshrined in the Tanakh or expounded upon by the *firstfruit* witnesses. God and His word are one. Some worship their building and or positions of eminence. Close examination of many church boards reveals that Nepotism, Cronyism, and even Fascism are practiced. Religious Socialism was enshrined by the first church as a means towards ensuring adequate distribution to the poor. Has "Give and it shall be given unto you been replaced by bring and it shall be taken from you?" That substitution has left many Christians poor as mice. God is getting ready to shake many silent egotists from their Mount Olympus. Every so often pastors need to be reminded that it is God's church; He has one assigned kinsman redeemer. Remember this: judgment begins in the house of the Lord. If Switzerland could seek the wisdom of the Lord and set up their country on Godly principles, how is it that so many churches are finding those areas so difficult? The elected members of Switzerland's Parliament choose a governing seven from among their ranks—called "Bundesrat"—that take turns at the helm to steer their country's political course. What is wrong with having every competent senior and reputable member that tithes consistently for seven years rotate positions on your church boards? Even though Kings could decree whatever they were led to, God assigned prophets to warn them of the two possible sins they could commit: Idolatry and Rebellion. Many have multifaceted positions. Many would like to be prophet, overseer, teacher, preacher, marriage counselor and Board Chairperson. They need to be reminded that those are not exalted power bases but spiritual positions as outlined carefully in 1st Corinthians 12 and Exodus 18:25-26. The Spirit of the Lord witnessed to me that He abhors the "Biggie Biggie" carnal attitudes of persons (especially holders of important position) in the Body of Christ. It is one of the biggest hindrances to skeptics receiving salvation. It would be prudent to fast and seek the wisdom of God as to who should hold His holy offices the way the Catholic Churches selected their popes in the 20th and 21st centuries. If a daughter or son of an Elder receives an interest-free loan to finance a car dealership, book deal, movie, or any other private venture, the funds must be repaid. Tithes must also be paid to the same church that sprang the loan in the first place on all revenue received including sales of assets derived according to Biblical law. Except for payment of services and labour, God's assets cannot be used for the personal enrichment of anyone, regardless of his or her position. I have seen position holders get cut down prematurely with serious maladies for such infractions. Many churches were built on the sacrifices of hard working and countless poor folks. As custodians of the Lord's business you need to be wise and prudent. Many of the so-called independent churches have serious problems accepting and dealing with those matters properly. Read the book of Acts and observe how far from the "First Church" principles you have strayed.

CHAPTER 26B. SECOND TYPE OF CHURCH: THE CHURCH THAT WAS POOR, YET RICH.

In general terms, Revelation 2:8-11 would refer to types like The Salvation Army and The Seventh Day Adventist Churches. They have ploughed on humbly and taught their flock well. Whereas the former is unmatched in works of charity, the latter has established clinics, health stores, provided income, schools for her flock, Bible schools, book stores, given generously to charity and has taught many churches the importance of tithing. However one of the above has not fully understood the Biblical principle "The Spirit of the law." I am going to make a prophetic statement here. After the next and imminent Reformation, that church will undergo a major change. One segment will explode with miracles, signs, wonders, healings and gifts of the Holy Spirit. In other words, what happened to the Baptists will be relived. One branch of that church will have a mass movement of the Holy Spirit, just like in the days of Pentecost (as prophesied by the prophet Joel). After each *Reformation* or season of God, a quiet, humble shepherd receives higher promotion: (Joshua after Moses, David after Saul, Elisha after Elijah and Jeshua after John). The Pentecostal movement to the Charismatic movement: there have always been fresh shoots from a slow growing or seemingly dying branch. The remnant segment will miss the importance of the Spirit of the Law. The surpassing of Advent by Pentecost as the more important feast will be missed.

Legalism or fleshy arguments confound, bind and blind minds. There are many Sabbaths unto the Lord. Six of the seven epochs of time were set aside for building, sowing and planting. One of them God ordained for His Rest, Atonement, Purim, Passover or Jubilee. Six were set aside for labouring or sowing and then God's rest. Even though God gave man a gift of choice, no human can be totally stupid: a maximum of 6/7 of the human will, substance, and time can be devoted to carnality or stupidity. The other 1/7 is sovereign: for repentance, forgiveness, restitution or conversely for surrender unto death. Even when Satan has captured a person's consciousness, that 1/7 sovereign place/altar is a lifeline from God's *grace and mercy* to minds and or immune systems. The first and the best are for the Lord. So which is the first and which is the best? Since the Old Covenant Sabbaths were computed on the Hebrew lunar calendar—witnessed by the temporary Aaronic priesthood—God promised a new and better covenant. The Sabbaths (plural) you shall (observe) keep... for it is a sign between you and me *throughout your generations*... Notice until the generations of the Levites (Exodus 31:13). Then Romans 10:4 and Romans 8:2-17 explained the better sacrifice that was promised: the better covenant and naturally the better commemorative feast day. Levites were assigned temporary custody of the sanctuary. Notice the pregnant word temporary (Daniel 12:11). If you disagree with my use of the word, you should not enter the Holy of Holies unless you are a Levite—otherwise you should be put to death. You are either a Levite still offering the blood of bulls and goats under the Old Covenant by *the Letter of the Law (Daniel 9:27)* or you are under the Melchizedek office under the Spirit of the Law. In Matthew 12:1-12, Jesus chided persons that liked to make doctrines of the "Sabbath." He warned those—and everyone else that Pharisee spirits would engulf in the future—that the keeping of the Sabbath was a surrogate law until the manifestation arrived. He, Jesus was that manifestation; therefore He is Lord of the Sabbath of the New Covenant. Jesus asked the "Sabbath-types" if Levites did servile work when they ministered in the Temple on the Sabbath. Similarly Jesus broke corn (the symbol of Firstfruits) on the Sabbath. If you are upholding the Letter of the Law, you can only fast and pray, not preach on the Sabbath. Refer to Galatians 3:11-13. Psalm 110:4 confirms that the Priesthood of Melchizedek is established *forever* and Exodus 31:13 established that Sabbaths shall be a sign between the Levitical priesthood and God for "Their Generations." Jeremiah 31:31 states: "Behold the days come, saith the Lord that I will make a New Covenant with the house of Israel and with the house of Judah." Verse 32, "Not according to the covenant that I made with their fathers in the day that I took them out of the land of Egypt; which covenant they brake, although I was husband unto them." The New Covenant of verse 33: "I will put my law into their inward parts, write it in their hearts, and will be their God and they shall be my people, saith the lord: For I will forgive their iniquity, and I will remember their sin no more."

Ponder this also: every person has a birthday. It commences on a specific day of the week and on a specific date. How many times do the commemorative day and date synchronize with the original day and date? Fact is, every year the actual day changes as one celebrates the event on a specific date as opposed to the day on which the event occurred. Why then do we want to commemorate a particular day on our spiritually incongruent Roman calendar and then wonder why we cannot get three days from our incorrectly assigned "Good Friday" to our fixed "Resurrection Sunday?" According to the source decrees in Leviticus 23:5-7, why then do we want to pick a fixed Sabbath day on the incompatible Roman calendar?

There are churches that build a complete legalistic doctrine as to which day on Julius Caesar's incongruent Roman calendar is the Sabbath Day and not only postulate a veneer of correctness, but argue vociferously that all others are wrong. In the 23rd chapter of Leviticus, God gave a list of Sabbaths. One extremely holy Sabbath could not be celebrated until the Israelites came into the land that God ordained for them (Leviticus 23:7 and verses 10-11). In verse 21, God previewed that His "New and Everlasting" Sabbath should be celebrated on the first day of the week (Leviticus 23:24-25). That new Sabbath would be the commemoration of the Firstfruit festival on the first day of the week: Leviticus 23:20-25 and Exodus 22:29. The new offering for the new Sabbath is previewed in Leviticus 23:16-17 to celebrate the New Covenant mentioned in Jeremiah 31:31.

In the days of Jeremiah, all tribes functioned under the lunar calendar and all Jews dwelt in one place. Today however, people are scattered in many different time zones. Suppose we were still functioning under the *Letter of the Law?* People in Japan would be in breach and so would the Californians and Australians also. The time and energy spent on legalism had been prophesied by Paul when he addressed the matter in Colossians 2:16 thusly, "Let no man therefore judge you in meat, or in drink, or in respect of an holyday, or of the new moon, or of the Sabbath days." Hosea prophesied that the ancient customs, observations of the Sabbaths and new moons would cease—Hosea 2:11. In Hebrews 10:12-16, the better sacrifice (everlasting) had been fulfilled. In Colossians 2:17, Paul confirmed that the Sabbath was a *shadow* of things to come, but the *body* is of Christ. Most importantly, the word for "Day" in Hebrew means period, revelation (new beginning), or coming forth from the dark, "Yowme." Pay more attention to the "Manifestation," the "Event" and the "Fulfillment" of the Day in the Day that the firstfruit "YOWME" became flesh, to bring all flesh from darkness to His "light"—Hebrews 4: 4-7. Like the old atonement offering to God, through repentance and forgiveness, we offer ourselves as living sacrifices through our Everlasting High Priest from our since-cleansed and sterilized human temples.

CHAPTER 26C. THIRD TYPE OF CHURCH: THE COMPROMISING CHURCH.

Revelation 2: 12-17—countless churches fall into this category. Their institutions are run compromisingly instead of being run like a Theocracy. Some allow remarried (1st Corinthians 7:11 and verse 27) men and women to serve as elders. Refer to Romans 7:2-3 and then 1st Timothy 3:1-7, "If ye desire the office of Bishop or Elder…" Remember that God's ways are higher than man's ways. Psalm 24 warns about profaning God's holy altar. Serving and singing with spiritually clean mouths, clean hearts and right attitudes are more important to God than dressing in spotless garments. If appearing or looking holy is only a façade, beware of God's anger. God sees all and knows all. Psalm 24:3, "Who shall dwell in the Holy Hill of the Lord?" Some neither teach nor preach on the prophecies encased in the Book of Revelation. Others do not teach on the curses attached to adultery, lesbianism, rape, incest, fornication, homosexuality and masturbation for fear of offending themselves and their members. Their children see and know their hypocrisy—assume that all Christians are the same and become turned off.

There is a particular scripture recorded in Mathew 7:21-23 for such as those: "Not everyone that saith unto me, Lord, Lord, shall enter the Kingdom of Heaven." Unfortunately many decision-makers on the third type of church preside over spiritually tarnished and cracked altars: teachings that emanate from their spiritual rostra have been polluted. They have shifted their priorities. They have deviated from "knowing and being the word" to emphasizing the importance of their buildings, their choirs, their apparel, their roles in society and or how other members perceive them. Their members' allegiances are to their "Churches." God is a distant and secondary figure. They are married to their traditions. Members work hard to climb their social ladders and all outsiders are supposedly jealous of them. Some not only believe but also imply that God understands the weaknesses of men/women to such an extent that some mythical forgiveness room in heaven is never full—2nd Timothy 3:5-9. To many, their perceived image in society is more important than how they are to God, who knows all and sees all. I have cast out more demons from those pretending church-types than I have from homosexuals and ex-cocaine addicts combined. Those can be likened to secret agents that are being used behind enemy lines. Tons of unassuming and "nice" people become demonized because of presumptuous sins. Nadab and Abihu were presumptuous. David's deep dread of such are recorded in Psalm 19:9-13. Read Romans 6:1-2, Romans 6:12-13 and 22-23. Some repeat the devil's words exactly: Once saved always saved. God's unfailing warnings: "I will chasten whom I love." Jeremiah 23:1, "Woe be unto pastors who destroy and scatter the sheep of my pasture." You are the custodians of God's sheep. Beware of the words in Matthew 7:21-23, "I never knew you: depart from me."

CHAPTER 26D. FOURTH TYPE OF CHURCH: THE CHURCH WITH A JEZEBEL SPIRIT.

Revelation 2:18-29: That type of church has doctrines that contradict the word of God. They are easily recognizable since they are blinded into clannishness. That type of church usually tells its members "They are the only true church." They publish their own books as substitutes for God's word. Romans 2:17… "Behold thou art called a Jew, and restest in the Law. Verse 18… Being instructed out of the law. Verse 24… For the name of God is blasphemed among the Gentiles through you, as it is written. Verse 25… For circumcision verily profiteth, if thou keep the law, but if thou be a breaker of the law, thy circumcision is made uncircumcision."

Solomon had 700 wives plus princesses and concubines. None were virgins. He did not build the concubines any houses. Neither their foundations, nor their teachings emanate from Solomon's Temple. They have another Oracle. Some have had no forerunners, no prior prophecy and no notice of arrival. One day God decided to surprise His people by sending a Messenger *not during His ordained seasons* or at His prescribed times? Those organizations usually have laws that differ from the Laws of Moses, Isaac and Jesus. Some see evil spirits and believe that God sent them. A classic example is one that was founded in America. Their founder is supposedly the only person in history to have seen all of God. Allegedly they received revelation that cannot be prefaced in the Torah. Picture this! God, the sum of things known, unknown, visible and invisible cloned a generator (Jesus) pure and powerful to hold His Spirit. It has been recorded that no one can see the whole of God and live.

GOD'S LIGHT, PRESENCE AND POWER ARE TOO LARGE AND AWESOME:
THAT PERSON WOULD BURN INTO OBLIVION.

At the end of our transformation, we are to be reconciled with "The Whole." Yet, one Mr. Smith supposedly saw both Jesus and God and that is the foundation of their teaching. I have news for all misled people:

1. Where the personage of Jesus is, so is the Spirit Father: John 6:46.

2. Neither the Tanakh, nor any stone from Jerusalem fits their foundational stone. Check doctrines carefully against the schematic.

The sad thing about the fourth type of church is that Satan allows them access to lots of money and well-educated sales people. Thank God for His power of Purim. I am asking for 1 billion praying people worldwide to begin the process of binding "False-Christ Spirits and Jezebel Spirits" from all of God's churches. If we commence praying without ceasing for spiritual enlightenment and removal of spiritual blindness from the day this book is released, those spirits of darkness will be vanquished and the Light of Glory shall break forth.

CHAPTER 26E. THE FIFTH TYPE OF CHURCH:

THE CHURCH THAT DID NOT KNOW IT WAS DEAD: REVELATION 3:1-6.

David's first child with Bathsheba was born dead. Was the death of Prophet Mohammed's two sons also a similar fate for marrying another's wife—violating Ezekiel 44:22 and Leviticus 21:14? There are sites around Lystra, Derbe, Ephesus and many others where Jesus' disciples planted churches that died. Then again, there is a type of church that does not know that it is dead. There is no power in the worship; they have never seen a miracle performed and most likely take sicknesses and premature deaths for granted. In this category are churches that do the same things day in, day out, according to ancient traditions. Not a few adorn ornamental outfits and have elaborate ceremonies. Please be reminded that God brought forth prophets, priests, kings and judges before He brought forth reformers. The Tree of Life planted in Jerusalem over 2000 years ago cannot die. If your songs and worship are not progressive, your branch needs pruning—Revelation 3:1-6. Psalm 33:3, "Sing unto Him a new song..."

CHAPTER 26F. THE SIXTH TYPE OF CHURCH: THE CHURCH WITH AN OPEN DOOR.

Revelation 3:7-13, "What you open cannot be shut; what you shut cannot be opened." That type of church I will call "Present Truth." Those churches are highly obedient and are manifesting the gifts of the Holy Spirit. God is releasing His restorative anointing upon them. They administer God's works according to the dictates of 1st Corinthians Chapters 12, 13 and 14. They manifest the Agape love of God, through His sanctified Son. Some (not all) denominational churches and some Pentecostal churches fall into that category. That category is not labeled denominationally. I have found "Holy Spirit-filled" Baptist (as opposed to Water-Baptist) churches also in that category. In those churches, the teachings line up with the scriptures and they are manifesting the fruits of the Holy Spirit. In those cases they got to that spiritual apex after they received and put in practice the wisdom of the crucified sacrificial lamb (Jeshua) and have claimed His atonement, death, resurrection and promised gifts. There are also isolated convents with faithful Nuns that live pious and obedient lives away from sin and contamination. They are hearing from God, speaking in tongues and are witnessing signs, wonders and miracles also. Recall that Rebekah told Isaac to let the sins fall on her only.

I am led by the Lord to make two prophecies here before I list the seventh church. The Spirit of the Lord told me to proclaim that Edom and Ishmael will be saved. As I received that word, I ran to a map to see where Edom is and it is not on the current map. However, an ancient map revealed that its ashes are in Jordan. Glory Be to God! Jordan you are called prophetically! The lord will bless you and rivers of fresh wisdom shall spring from your deserts. Syria, I am proclaiming your refreshing also. The Spirit of the Living God refused to let me type another word unless I proclaim the deliverance of Syria. Glory be to God! Well, do I hear millions saying amen and coming in agreement?

CHAPTER 26G. THE SEVENTH TYPE OF CHURCH: THE LUKEWARM CHURCH.

There were numerous organizational churches that were great pioneers and very productive before the advent of the 1967 Six-Day War. One cannot ignore the parallels between seasons in Israel and those in the Messiah's church. God moves in Israel first. Similarly, there were others that were doing well before 1948. Those churches have allowed their altars to be weakened. Revelation 3:14-22 speak of the lukewarm church. There are "Water Baptists and Holy Spirit Baptists." John was a Water-Baptist. His ministry started and ended in the wilderness and lasted 7 years. He cast out no devils; he had no healings and no miracles. However, like Hiram, he produced living lumber for the future Temple. Water-Baptists behave the same way. They have great start-up ministries and are fantastic teachers of the youth. For the spiritually young to mature from milk to meat, they have to find spirit-filled shepherds or be grabbed by spiritual wolves or bears. The sad thing about that group is that instead of doing like Hannah and praying for the spiritual desert to spring forth, many are grieving the Holy Spirit by denying God's presence. Ephesians 4:30 confirms that. I have had many occasions to meet privately and pray a few of them and their spouses through deliverances fully. One that I prayed for used to preach and teach that church groups invented modern cases with demons for dramatic purposes until he saw what surfaced. Sad to say, some that I have prayed for (that have been delivered) have never gone back to their churches to testify about their deliverance. Their district leaders would kick them out. Anyway I am encouraged to see positive changes in the Holy Spirit-filled ones. Their teachings and services are more intense spiritually and there are marked increases in their churches' membership, confirming God's word, "It is not by might, nor by power, but by my Spirit says the Lord." The word of the Lord reveals "You are redeemed by the blood of the lamb and the words of your testimony." Unfortunately, others are still bound by legalism. People from that group are the only ones that I have been called to help and are deathly afraid of proclaiming the Good News of their deliverance. God help them! Please pray for them.

Neophytes have difficulty comprehending spiritual matters. How can they understand that when you have the presence of the Lord (the Ark) you behave like David and "Dance with all your might?" Many in that category turn up their "Saulish" noses like Micah did when she saw David (under the anointing) in the presence of the *Ark of God* and instantly became barren setting prophetic precedents for spiritually barren churches. All in that category need to follow the example of Apollos from Egypt in Acts 18:25-27. Every lukewarm church can be transformed through the words that God revealed in this discourse. Let us clearly understand what is being stated here. Not all Pentecostal churches are spirit-filled and not all denominational churches are lukewarm. There are denominational churches that provide wonderful faith-based teachers and teachings particularly for families. However to meet the spiritual challenges in this ever-increasing sinful world, what God has said and is continually stating is that higher levels are required to challenge the bolder devils. Had churches not digressed into the lukewarm category so-called Christian nations would not have been allowing the legalization of marriages between same sex beings. Also singers, musicians and teachers who violate the commands of Psalm 24 would not be permitted in God's Holy Place. Since our bodies are temples of God, there are bodies similar in spiritual types to the churches John saw in his vision. The billion-dollar question is what are we going to do?

CHAPTER 27. WITHOUT THE SHEDDING OF BLOOD.

CHAPTER 27A. RED RIVER OF DEATH AND PLAGUES.

Without the shedding of blood there shall be no remission of sins. What was Paul alluding to, in his letter to the Hebrew brethren? Incidentally, the Qumran Scrolls will reveal that "Hebrews" in the New Testament is one of Paul's letters. In Hebrews 9:22, Paul explained that almost all transgressions by the law are purged with blood. God had ordained sin offerings under the *Levitical Law*. Let us check that historically and spiritually. The book of Esther in the Tanakh demonstrates the tremendous power of Purim. At times, while on missionary journeys, I am reminded of ways that we baited mice. Mice food was laced with poisons. Remember that spirits are attracted to body fluids that echo with the nuclei of life. Whenever millions rush (in) to take blood of saints, spirits are repelled through the power of "Purim." Pharaoh's armies were filled with demonic spirits of hate and anger. Under Titus in 70 C.E. millions came with his armies. Rome was "Purimized." 30,000 were martyred in the 16th century before Martin Luther got his breakthrough. Ethiopia is undergoing one of the largest genocidal atrocities as I am writing this. I will issue this decree: "Ethiopia my child, you have suffered enough for not being vigilant when your sister Israel played the harlot." Jeremiah first spoke those words to you in Jeremiah 3:1-21. Isaiah 11:11 told us where the remnant would be concealed. Repent and you shall be a fruitful vine. You paid the biggest tithes to Solomon through Sheba just after his temple was built; you will receive the biggest harvest in the latter days. Remember your sister Israel came to your assistance in your distress during the civil war; do not forget her when you are reconciled! Be comforted in that God promised that Ethiopia will be saved.

In 1054 the Eastern Orthodox Churches cancelled plans for a permanent merger with the Roman churches. In essence they checked the advance of Leviathan. About 450 years later (less than 7 generations of years) many bound sheep got delivered under a shepherd named Martin Luther. Prior to 1517 the Leviathan spirit that lodged itself under the altars of Rome had caused over 30,000 people to be martyred or killed. In that year Martin Luther found over 100 abuses of indulgences and *erroneous teachings*. Unfortunately the leadership was too arrogant to accept the Bible as the law of God. They declared themselves "Infallible." They were divine. From those types of errors above, we put in remembrance the words of Deuteronomy 7:1. It is clearly stated that before any new spiritual ground can be claimed for the Lord, there are seven mighty types of oppressive spirits that must be expelled. Of all that left Egypt, only Joshua and Caleb made it to the Promised Land. At the end of the first 100 years, it was shown that only two types of churches had been victorious.

Observe that the "Hebrew-ness" of God's word dictates duplicity for clarification and emphasis. Since every stone of Solomon's magnificent temple was thrown down, then every living pillar that constructed the Messiah's house—Peter, Steven, John, Paul, Philip, James and thousands of early human stones were destroyed. It also meant that human treasures (Lost Tribes) must fall away and come short of His glory, to such an extent that they would either be killed or be carried away into captivity until deliverers were sent. Anytime a "Big Fish" spirit or "Leviathan" spirit enslaves God's people, the first thing it does is to bring false teachings. After that, count 7 generations of years. Never forget that Satan is a good mathematician and strategist. First he tries to wipe out all the teachers of the Law and then the witnesses. He follows a script that was already written. Two sets of plagues usually follow nations that do such: In Egypt, the firstborn children were lost and then all the host of Pharaoh, his horsemen together with his chariots—Exodus 14:28. Notice how Satan abandons his people after they do his dirty work.

There is another very important point I want to make here. The Lord established the Law of Duplicity to negate any assumption of accidental happenings to what He has decreed. An accident can happen. A force known or unknown is usually involved whenever two or more identical situations occur to the same people. On the wall on a temple in Karnak (Thebes) there is a relief with relevant hieroglyphic showing Egyptian King Shishak's invasion when he took away the treasures of the king's house in Jerusalem (recorded in 1st Kings 14:25-26) under the weakened altar of Rehoboam—seed of Solomon. Seed of Jesus' ministry, must end up bound, killed or enslaved, paralleling the historical path of the legacy of Solomon.

CHAPTER 27B. DIVINE JUDGMENT AS PER PROPHECY!

Habakkuk 2:3, "The vision (Revelation 18:6) is yet for an appointed time." It speaks of the end and will not prove false, though it linger, wait for it. It will certainly come. Habakkuk 2:8, "Because thou hast spoiled many nations, all the remnant of the people shall spoil thee, because of men's blood, and for the violence of the land, of the city, and all that dwell therein." Habakkuk 2:9, "Woe to him that coveteth an evil covetousness to his house, that he may set his nest on high…" Habakkuk 2:12 "Woe to him that buildeth a town with blood, and establisheth a city by iniquity." The God of Justice sees all.

Titus' army sacked Jerusalem in 70 C.E. In 452 C.E., there was a great outbreak of fever in the north of Italy. Bubonic plague surfaced at the end of the reign of Justinian in Byzantium 543 C.E. to 545 C.E. Rome had another severe attack towards the end of the 6th century. Even though the Roman Empire collapsed approximately 400 years later, provinces as far away as England received the same punishment 664 C.E. to 684 C.E. July 15th 1099 The Crusaders sacked Jerusalem. On May 29th 1453, Byzantine Rome's headquarters Constantinople fell to the Turks under Mohammed the Conqueror.

The spirit that engulfed Rome resurfaced through the national altars of England, France, Spain, Holland and America. They enslaved God's people and worked them without pay for 400 to 430 years. A large remnant of the Tribe of Judah ended up in North America, a land already tainted with the blood of original occupants. It is fair to say that by the time the seed of Judah arrived, a large portion of the inhabitants (especially persons in positions of power) had many punishable generational sins of hate, greed and murder. Added to that, persons who funded America's War of Independence were of the "Enclave of Bahomet." They transposed and cemented the foundations of the "One World Government." When Rome held the Scepter of the Unicorn, it had a senate, a Capitolina, and the largest military machine in those times. An eagle was its insignia. Whenever that demonic plot resurfaces, God miraculously intervenes and halts the spirit of Babel from exalting the Unicorn's machine of war, plunder and death after a maximum number of years. On October 12ᵗʰ, 1492, Columbus landed in America. The Pilgrims followed in 1620. Let us apply God's unfailing words of Habakkuk 2:10-12. We already saw that Rome received a double portion of punishment for its misdeeds. The Masonic Orders across Europe met and advised all their brethren about specific prophesied punishment as per Habakkuk 2:12. Their members in England heeded the call and blew the trumpet of warning about an upcoming 400-year jubilee season beginning in 1898. Under no circumstances were their members to hold any more slaves. So on August 23ʳᵈ, 1833 Slavery was officially abolished in all of Britain's colonies. According to Leviticus 25, no nation on earth can enslave God's people for 400 years and escape punishment during His period of Jubilee. The severity of the punishment would depend on the extent of the crime in God's eyes and not by the perceptions of fallible men.

In 1850 Henry Clay was successful at legislating compromises into the U.S. Constitution to allow breaches for "equality of all men." Secret Societies' members in America were of two opinions. All Ancient Orders except the "Lod" and "Golden Dawn" decided to heed the warning. However members of the latter two, markedly around Mississippi, Alabama and Louisiana were covenanted to the "Oath of Bahomet." They secretly argued that the American constitution was at loggerheads with their *sworn oath*. Members were able to persuade other *brethren* of Florida, Georgia, Texas, Virginia, Tennessee, Arkansas and North Carolina, to break away from the "Union" and form their own Confederate Government. On March 7ᵗʰ, 1857, their "brethren," through the *Dred Scott Decision*, ruled that the *Missouri Compromise* was unconstitutional. They then hanged the abolitionist John Brown on December 2ⁿᵈ, 1859. On February 22ⁿᵈ, 1862, they formed their own Confederacy and appointed Jefferson Davis as president.

The ten states that formed the Confederacy fought against the states in the Northern Union from 1861 to 1865. Even though the Union defeated them, they swore a permanent "brotherhood" to ensure that their collective will be enshrined on the presidency of the United States. Although slavery was officially abolished in the United States on Dec. 18ᵗʰ 1865, so far, neither indigenous Americans nor the remnants of Judah have seen the light of day under the 14ᵗʰ Amendment. Worse yet, the rebel states were readmitted without renouncing their secret oath. They also kept a remnant (of Judah) enslaved. The spiritual tug-of-war that exists in America is fueled by contrasting declarations between participants of "The Oath of Bahomet" and those of the Oath of 1776. The participants of 1776 swore to uphold "One nation under God and freedom/justice for all." At the end of this chapter, we will keep score of the spiritual damage done to America's main altar. Today there are antagonists in the U.S.A., manipulated by a select spirit type attempting to have the "Constitution" interpreted as "under gods."

A 37-year-young American general, George Custer, had a wonderful opportunity to break ancestral curses on his homeland. He could have sought a meeting with congress to ask for provisions, as outlined in the 14ᵗʰ amendment of July 28ᵗʰ, 1868 to be offered to Sitting Bull, chief of the Sioux, for lands taken in arrogance and greed. Had seasons of *restitution, repentance and forgiveness* been birthed, "The Power of Purim" would have overflowed the land. Instead of going on to be one of America's most brilliant statesmen, young Custer lost his life at the Battle of Little Big Horn on June 25ᵗʰ, 1876. More blood, hate and revenge engulfed the land. The period of revenge and bloodshed that followed (culminating in the death of Sitting Bull on December 15ᵗʰ, 1890) has been glorified and justified by moviemakers and historians alike.

Since the trumpet was sounded in 1833, a Jubilee has not passed without two American

Presidents either dying in office or an attempt being made on one of their lives. The President is the custodian of America's highest physical altar.

RECAP OF AMERICA'S SPIRITUAL PLIGHT FROM 1834 TO 2000.

Died prematurely in Office:		Assassinated:	
1. William Henry Harrison	1841.		
2. Zachary Taylor	1850.	1. Abraham Lincoln murdered	1865.
3. Warren G. Harding	1923.	2. James Garfield murdered	1881.
4. Franklin D. Roosevelt	1945.	3. William McKinley murdered	1901.
5. Richard Nixon's *political* death	1974.	4. John F. Kennedy murdered	1963.

ASSASSINATIONS ATTEMPTED:

Ronald Reagan survived an assassination attempt on March 30th, 1981. William Jefferson Clinton survived two assassination attempts. One person fired several shots through a balcony where they thought that Clinton was sitting. The other allegedly resulted in the death of his Commerce Secretary. Both attempts occurred prior to the year 2000.

NATIONS OF THE BEAST IN DANIEL'S VISION.

Judgment continued against the seed of the Roman Empire in 1917, and 1945 to 1947. Millions upon millions of Spanish, French, English, Dutch, Germans, and Americans lost their lives through the scourge of those world wars and hunger and stress following the wake of those disasters plus the collapse of the stock market (*first time*). Remember *God's Laws of Duplicity* for Babelic punishment. Revelation 18:6—"Reward her even as she (Babylon and her seed), and double according to her works." Verse 8, "Therefore shall her plagues come in one day: death, mourning and famine. The Lord God judgeth her."

The prognosis for the countries that profited from the mammon of slavery within the next twenty years or so does not look good. Russia, which played its part in the enslavement of seed of the northern tribes, already received a double portion of judgment. Woe unto her or any nation for that matter, if they join forces with attackers against Israel as prophesied by Daniel. Woe unto those who sell their deadly weapons to Abraham's seed and stir up strife among those in Africa, India, the Arab nations and Israel. Woe had been prophesied to fall on many stock markets swollen with unrighteous mammon. Woe will also fall on the churches that invest God's money in any mammon market instead of setting up their own cooperatives to find work for God's people. Again the Black Death plagues of the 14th century were divine retribution for the carnage of 1099 as per prophecy. God proclaimed it. His word cannot return void.

DUPLICITY.

In 1290 Edward 1 expelled the Jews from England. In 1306 Philip IV not only confiscated the Jews' properties, but expelled those from France as well. In the records of the Roman church, that Philip IV is called "Fair Philip." That was not meant to be funny. In 1346 and 1347 the citizens of the former Roman provinces were attacked with plagues. In 1360 and 1370 plagues struck again. Children and adults died like flies. History blames rats from the Far East for their sicknesses and called it the "Bubonic Plague." I think not.

Under Jehoiachim's rule, Nebuchadnezzar enslaved Judah. Nations of America and Europe are fragmented seeds of that empire. Man and the shape of a man have specific spiritual meanings. Since the "Beast" depicts a spiritual conglomeration of nations glued by war and "Bahomet-driven power," we need to ensure that too much power is not entrusted to any political figure from those regions. According to prophecy, someone will emerge from that region singing a song of peace but with a chorus of war in his heart. He and a sidekick will deceive many. He will be very charismatic. We are so privileged in that we have access to one everlasting sacrifice: we can receive forgiveness through genuine repentance or receive the decree of Daniel 2:35.

CHAPTER 28. THE REAL PRIZE IS THE NEW TEMPLE.

CHAPTER 28A. URGENT WARNING!

I grew up and spent quality years around mature folks. Some of their sayings are gems. An all-time favourite, which we will adopt right now is—"To be forewarned is to be forearmed."

Throughout history, God never rained judgment on any nation before first sending His prophets to forewarn them. Even God runs out of patience eventually. The fact that God would reveal so many mysteries at such a significant time (the season of the first major Jubilee) cannot be taken lightly. Even though most of the following events were planned secretly, they were all prophesied. The foundation seeds of cloning for the antichrist were sown in secret by institutions that used their power and influence to do the following:

1. Arrange marriages of churches and states and exalt a woman for over 1600 years as "mother of a god" on the same site where martyrs were sacrificed.

2. Sponsor paintings, sculptures and buildings of most churches in early Europe. In so doing, they ensured that demonically inspired shrines were placed over their altars.

3. Strengthen demonic foundations of those churches, by culturing an atmosphere for the proliferation of the following spirits: homosexuality, murder, theft, and false doctrines.

4. Invent a thesis for creating a new race out of fragmented nations of the ashes of the Roman Empire, based on doctrines of right by might.

5. Conceal real truths behind myths and legends, releasing as clues only the coded name "Bahomet" and that "Three" held those secrets.

6. Control world monetary systems with mammon from the Incas' gold and from the Atlantic Slave trade.

7. Steer the Occident's political directions, philosophies and its war machinery.

8. Influence Hollywood, Western print and broadcast media by brazenly promoting the demonic gospel of The New World Order: "Replace the Lion with the Unicorn."

9. Test a dangerous lab disease on a remnant of Judah and then blame its proliferation on green monkeys when the antidote failed.

2nd Samuel 3:1 reads, "There was a long war between the House of David and the House of Saul. David waxed greater and greater and *the house of Saul waxed weaker and weaker.*" Saul's house had an altar that Satan usurped. All who teach that men of God cannot be demonized need to examine their own altars. God in His mercy has given us all a final chance either to repent or to receive His wrath. Let us share the observation of David as he looked prophetically in time revealing the nature of the occupants under the altars of the houses of Saul in these prophesied times in 2nd Samuel 23:6. I should add that expounding on previously unrevealed matters is painstaking work. Thankfully, God's power and wisdom impact and encourage me towards absolute obedience. Rejoice: God's "Logos" is now preserved in Hebrew, a prophetic language with trans-generational power and precision.

David had left many things for posterity just before his death. I thank God for mine. Those who wish to know what David left for me, first ask God to open your eyes of understanding. May God reveal to whom He so chooseth, and conceal from whom He so desireth. Let us first read verse 6, "The sons of Belial shall be all of them as thorns thrust away, because they cannot be taken with (human) hands." Also in 2nd Samuel 23:7, "The man that touches them must be fenced with iron and the staff of a spear; and they shall be utterly burned with fire in the same place." Verse 8 to the end gives an insight into the apex of the ancient kingly offices. We have dual offices and exponential power potential.

A nation that controlled over 50 percent of the then developing world left no legacy of its spoken language in any of its former provinces. Classical pieces and literary works remain. God did not allow their language to be spoken easily. It quickly died as a language medium. Out of the dead language (Latin) arose many languages. English is one of the languages that sprouted out of Latin. Since its root (Latin) amplifies Roman thought processes, it is medium of double-speak. For example: the subject of the subject is subject to the subject of the *"subject"* subject. English has the ability to expand annually. English also defies linguistic law in that it has 26 instead of 24 characters. In order to decipher coded names, if one is not a "Master," it is difficult to find the hidden meanings. For example: a person without specific training would not be able to get the entire message from a name like Leonardo Da Vinci. However with knowledge of the proper condensation and pairings of letters, it becomes so evident that he was destined to have something to do with *THE VATICAN IN ROME.* Nero was predestined to be of primary importance in Rome.

IT APPEARS THAT GOD NOT ONLY CRUSHED THE ROMAN WAR MACHINE BUT ITS LANGUAGE AS WELL.

Jesus was not a priest after the order of Levi but after the "Order of Melchizedek." The fact that father Abraham paid tithes to a futuristic ministry, meant that the everlasting priesthood was predestined to have access to much more than the known 33 degrees of wisdom. No blemishes are allowed within that Veil. One cannot throw pearls to swine. *The Spirit of God* chooses *custodians* of *this order.* All prior priests and custodians had pledged to protect their sacred altars. Many allowed Satan to widen from cracks to canyons. Sundry members assumed that their Friday night secret pledges and the names of their organizations were sufficient to enshrine perpetual holiness. It is amazing how many thousands of such Satan grounded into spiritual minced meat. Sad to say, I have met many custodians who "talk the esoteric talk but don't walk the spiritual walk." Altars elevated to beings known or unknown become fair game for Satan. Over time hundreds of thousands of altars of churches, countries, institutions of wisdom, politics and finance have been totally controlled by the Kingdom of Satan. Thousands of years ago he bragged that he would do such. Isaiah recorded those utterances so that we can receive insights into his mind-set. Isaiah 14:13, "I will exalt my throne above the stars of God: I will sit upon the mount of congregations, in the sides of the north." Verse 12 shows the extent of the damage already done. "The nations did weaken." Verse 16, is that really the one that did "Shake the kingdoms…?"

Since the days of Isaiah Satan had set his sights on the coveted altar of Psalm 24:1. "The earth is the Lord's and the fullness thereof." I once watched a man who was highly demonized. He grabbed the microphone on a stage and beat his chest like King Kong. When the heavens opened up, I had an awful vision. The Spirit of the Lord is ready to do a new thing: first repentance, then deliverance, sterilization and then reconstruction.

CHAPTER 28B. CAN THE TREE OF LIFE DIE?

The first of Moses' five books is a book of seed wisdom: first fruits written in coded format. In the second chapter, the things, containers or beings out of this earth, which produce fruit "èts," and seed "after their kind" in English are classified as trees. In the second chapter it is obvious that there are four basic types of trees. All came out of the ground. Two types had to be watered literally: (1) pleasant to the sight (flowering and decorative) and (2) good for food (fruit trees). (3) Another type is planted spiritually through the mind: that figurative tree of knowledge (of carnal things/good and evil). That "tree" is planted first through the mind and then conceived through a material/carnal medium. Seeds sown through carnal knowledge can proliferate and reproduce "after their own kind," bearing carnal fruits. Man was "formed" out of the ground. 4. The same way God allows cross-pollination to take place between "èts" today, in the Garden of Eden He had a special tree that seeded all living containers out of the ground. It is capable of producing "after its own kind," that master-tree is called "The Tree of Life" in Genesis 2:9.

Here is the genesis of the "èts of carnal knowledge." Satan sowed some seed (knowledge of good and evil). Eve received it in disobedience. Genesis 4:1, "Adam (knew) his wife and she conceived." Genesis 4:17, "Cain knew his wife (carnal seed) and she conceived." She bore human fruit capable of producing after its own kind. Carnal knowledge first invaded the original garden through disobedience. The following germinating incubators or gardens are identified: earth, mind (spirit incubator) and woman, all have abilities to produce fruit. The fertilizers are: water, blood and "The Spirit." 1st John 5:8, "Three that bear witness on earth: the Spirit, the water and the blood."

1st Fertilizer: Genesis 2:10, "A river went out of Eden to water the garden." That river provides: gold, onyx stones and bdellium. That river of self-sufficiency waters Ethiopia, Assyria and the regions around the Euphrates. The 2nd fertilizer was tarnished; so the earth became accursed. Genesis 4:11, "Now thou are cursed from the earth, which hath opened her mouth to receive thy brother's blood from thy hand." Then in John 19:34 we read, "One of the soldiers with a spear pierced his side and forthwith came out blood and water." Let us review what Prophet Zechariah had foretold in Zechariah 12:10. "I will pour upon the house of David and upon the inhabitants of Jerusalem—the spirit of grace and of supplications: and they shall look upon me whom they have pierced, and they shall mourn for him as one mourneth for his own son, and shall be in bitterness for his firstborn." Also David recorded in Psalm 22:16, "They pierced my hands and my feet." Verse 14, "I am poured out like water." John 19:28, "I thirst."

GOD, OUR ALL WISE, ALL KNOWING, SUPER POSITIVE CREATOR WOULD BEGET A MALE FIRST FRUIT. HE WOULD PLANT THAT PURE MALE FIRST FRUIT WITH A REDEMPTIVE SEED THAT COULD ONLY BE NOURISHED BY HIS SPECIAL BLOOD. THE MALE OLIVE TREE WOULD BE BRUISED, WOUNDED AND LEFT TO DIE. ONLY GERM-FREE, VIRUS-FREE,

AND SINLESS GRAFTS WOULD THE FATHER ACCEPT FOR HIS TIMELESS GARDEN.

Why is that so important? God established a patriarchal society for His chosen people, not through absentmindedness but because of His ultimate wisdom. Now the *third fertilizer* is God's Spirit. We have to find the magnet or spiritual connector. Since spirits communicate through blood and bad spirits cannot touch or bond with redemptive cleansed blood, *the third fertilizer* is The Holy Spirit of God: His grace and mercy allows us to be reborn. How then do we find an invisible God?

Since "He" speaks, we have to find His voice; find His everlasting, perennial and supernatural Oracle. John 14:6, "I am the Way," confirming the words of Psalm 2:12 (road to the Father) the *Truth*, and the (key to everlasting) *Life*. No man cometh to the Father but by (understood) this Oracle/Logos, which I bring you. John 14:7, Jesus explains the Logos. If you see Jesus, you see the presence of the Father. Why is that so? If you hear the voice of a loved one nearby, it means that the person is either close-by or accessible in presence or recorded word. Read John 14:7. John 14:16, "I will pray the Father and he shall give you the Comforter (the Spirit of truth)." Verse 26 of John 14, "But the Comforter, which is the Holy Spirit (the indwelling spiritual presence to God) which the Father will send in my name, he shall teach you all things." The rest of the chapter is a must. Here is a perfect example of God's far superior wisdom to that of man.

Translators of the Koran struggled with the meaning of comforter. In older versions of the Koran the word used is "ahmadu." Some translators implied that Jesus was referring to Prophet Mohammed as the comforter. In John 14:16, the word is derived from the Greek word "parakletos" or intercessor. The only person in the Holy Koran that the "Spirit of God" is bestowed upon is Jeshua. God is specific in that He decreed "To the Jews were committed the Oracles of God." The Koran is unambiguous that Jeshua or Isa is the confirmation of the Torah, which preceded Him. Even though quotations from at least four Christian Gospels are in the Koran, there are insertions which cloud or question the same insertions. John Chapters 14 and 15 are expositions of The Logos—the best I have read in my 25 years of research. After the fall of man, God removed His Spirit from residing perpetually in humankind, allowing us to be *replanted* into the ground from which we came. Had God not removed His perpetual spirit, we would be able to live forever with all of our carnality. Only after rebirth can we partake of the tree of perpetuity or "ets of Life:" Genesis 3:19 and Genesis 3:22.

The seed must be *sterilized* through the resurrection promise of rebirth. Since man (who was given dominion over the earth) had lost his eminence, a man had to reclaim all that was lost to allow his fellowmen and women the *gift of everlasting life*. All four holy books—the Holy Koran, the Torah, the Tanakh, and the Bible teach on the hope of the Resurrection. On the earth, there are the worlds of the seen and of the unseen: matter and energy. There is a spirit world and a carnal world. God's Oracle must have "Everlasting" capabilities. By inference, when God first featured His Oracle, that Oracle "must" have had a pre-human existence and must have a post-human exit. It stands to reason that God's Oracle must be spotless, error-free and "pelicost" (pack tremendous power).

God cannot break His own rules. If earth is the domain of man and spirits need earthly bodies in this domain, then God had to choose a sinless seed. There could have been only one sinless body connector. Our God is original. Sura 19, 33: "Peace is upon me the day of my birth, and the day of my death, and the day of my being raised up alive." Since other verses mentioned: Zechariah, the "Annunciation," Miriam and John the Baptist in the same Sura 19, our research team had no difficulty identifying the Firstfruit. Prophet Mohammed had no problem identifying the Firstfruit. Sura 3, 55, "O Jesus, I will take thee and raise thee to myself, and clear thee of those who blaspheme; *I will make those who followed thee superior to those who reject faith, to the Day of Resurrection...*" Sura 3, 56, "As to those who reject faith, I will punish them with a terrible agony in this world and in the hereafter." The Tanakh and the Bible report Romans 3:23. Translation: All have sinned and come short of God's glory: wisdom, knowledge, understanding, promises and completeness of God.

Is it a coincidence that Abraham was willing to offer his firstborn son Isaac, as a witness to God's covenant (Genesis 22:2) on Mt. Moriah? Is it also a coincidence that God promised us a seed through David to plant as "His" King on His holy hill? Since Solomon built his temple on Mt. Moriah (2nd Chronicles 3:1) after David died, is it also a coincidence that Jeshua is the last male seed with both lineages of Levi and Judah? Is it a coincidence that Jeshua is also the only seed of Abraham to have been planted on a tree in Mt. Moriah? In addition to those, Abraham's sacrifice on the same hill was unto his generations and the covenant of Jeremiah 31:31 was forever. Doesn't it make sense that any sterilized seed planted on God's Holy Hill in sinless blood must be His everlasting sacrifice and an everlasting witness to His everlasting covenant? We must perform the covenant promise of Psalm 2—"Kiss the Son, less he be angry." Since Jews were never allowed to touch the dead, that king must reign forever!

The contents of John 1:1 have confused believers. "In the beginning was the "Logion" or "Word" and the Word was with God, and the Word was God. Before time, space and matter there was spirit. Most Holy Spirit God, and not yet manifest word, = spirit oracle or (infinity of) God. God is the only spirit with creative capabilities. Whenever spirit matter becomes flesh, it changes. God cannot change. He can create and decree: Isaiah 44:24. Whatever He decrees, becomes manifest. The moment it becomes manifest, it exits the spirit world; receives God's transforming capabilities, and permanent change occurs. He told Joel that in His select time, He would pour out His Spirit on all flesh. In the beginning, He poured out His Spirit. He allowed periods of darkness. Pssst! God has a spirit of judgment. Thank God that I have been saved from it. Hopefully my next chapter will remove clouds of confusion.

CHAPTER 29. MYSTERY OF MYSTERIES!

CHAPTER 29A. WHAT OR WHO IS THE HOLY SPIRIT?

Spirits are pre-human beings. They can inhabit animals, places or things. Jesus told us not to call any one holy but God. It is God's premiere nature. So according to the greatest teacher who ever lived, the designation of Holy Spirit distinguishes that spirit from any other spirit in that it belongs to God. What is His or its role in the spirit realm? Since God is 1st and a Spirit, why is "The Holy Spirit" called a third person?

At least 80 percent of Christians have varying degrees of knowledge on that subject. Responses to questions on that matter range from the sensible to the idiotic. A proper analysis could not be had without first finding the "Golden Fleece" and by applying the spirit level to spiritual things. These things must be cemented in your microprocessor/your mind: God is not just a spirit, but The Most Holy Spirit (1st Corinthians 2:12, and John 4:24, God is "a" spirit…). God is not third or second, but first (Isaiah 44:6, I am the first, and the last and beside me there is no God. God is (full stop). OK. I will elaborate. God is the sum of all concepts, things and beings: known and unknown, visible and invisible—Isaiah 44:24, "El Hosiem." Spirits penetrate matter and time. In Psalm 139:7, David asked a rhetorical question: "Whither shall I go from thy spirit? Whither shall I flee from thy presence? Verse 8…If I ascend into heaven, thou art there. If I make my bed in hell, behold thou art there." David described the omnipresence of *God's Spirit*. God removes His presence from unsanctified places—those of sin, bondage or torment—unless He intends to cast judgment or to transform (the place or the people) by sanctification. God did not go to Egypt for the Israelites, He sent His prophet Moses. God visits desecrated places for judgment unless His people are ready to repent and to re-establish a corporate covenant relationship with Him. God's ordained place for His children is a place of promise, fulfillment and bliss—A Promised Land. Zechariah 12:10 is spelled out in detail and confirmed in John chapters 14 and 15. However if your eyes, minds and spirits are not transformed, the *GIANTS* will remain. See all giants as grasshoppers and chase them out permanently! *THERE ARE NO FREE LUNCHES!*

When the children of Israel were in bondage in Egypt, God was far away from them. 400-plus years before Jeshua arrived, "no prophet spoke to them." Then John appeared in the wilderness of Judea with good news. He offered "water baptism." Then Jesus brought the blood sacrifice of atonement for sins and the "promise" of substitution for a better sacrifice than that first offered by Abraham. Please note—Abraham did not offer the sacrifice of the seed of the bondwoman, but the seed of the ordained union through Sarah, and his name was Isaac. Scripture references are Genesis 22:2-18. When the children of Israel were ready to offer sacrifices of prayers, praises and thanksgiving acceptable to God, God's Spirit met their sacrifices. It is written, "He inhabits the praises of the righteous."

Closer to obedience—God's tabernacle was built. After a while His tabernacle began to be desecrated. God told Nehemiah that He desireth to dwell in booths with His people. In other words, Daddy desires to go camping with His children: Nehemiah 8:13-18. Will any father camp with repeatedly rude or rebellious children? I think not. God was not confined to the tabernacle, but the tabernacle was a place where God communed with His people. Every time Jesus spoke, the Spirit of God (the Logos) manifest in Him and then He brought the *Word*: John 14:10. 2nd Corinthians 3:17…The Lord is that Spirit. After Jesus' death, His Glorified body was translated with the *Spirit of God* to heavenly places: 1st Peter 3:18. After Jesus was glorified, *His carnal body is no more*; His carnal robe has no significance any more; those are all discarded or dead things (dead works). We cannot be saved by works: there is no more baby Jesus. Paying homage to a baby at Christmas is missing the essence of His being and purposes completely. We are to mirror ourselves after His teachings.

Examine self! Ask the questions: Are we spiritual babes? Have we progressed not just to conquerors, but more than conquerors? Are we still carrying crosses of our parents and grand-parents, crosses of deep-rooted prejudices and intolerance, crosses of habitual lying, cheating on our taxes or cheating customs' duties? Can our attitudes pass the litmus tests of Matthew 5? Have we buried our old carnal selves with all of our crosses and are now reborn? Then we must follow His spirit level! His spirit being was transformed like a mighty generator, dispensing power to those chosen to be kings and priests.

Jesus exists with the Spirit of God in heavenly places as a perfected being. He was re-sown into the womb of the earth. In so doing He confirmed figuratively and literally what He preached, "We must be born again!" The Holy Spirit in this age is the equivalent of electricity from a huge power plant through a transformer (Jesus) to us the tents. He wants us to have **"His light of the World."** The source of energy is God, a super positive entity. Since in this pagan language we have only positive, feminine and neuter genders, pick one. God forgive us for limiting you to a gender. There is no more carnal Jesus. Jesus exists with the Spirit of God as His Logos, the promised seed—reborn, as part and parcel of the promised whole. Since the *Tree of Life* was chosen to carry the "Ark of God," our God would have to be dead for that power to cease. Jesus is only temporarily separated from "His Chosen" because of sin and time. When the time of individual or corporate redemption draws nigh, the magnetic energy will be so strong from that powerful transformer, that all deemed worthy will be sucked up to the source like nails to a magnet SHOOSH! Confirming scriptures can be found in 1st Thessalonians 4:17.

Is there a Holy Trinity or is there a Holy Whole? The *two* agree. The Spirit Father and the Son are now inseparable: John 14:28… "I go unto the Father because my Father is *greater* than I." His Spirit is what connects the selected (firstfruit) and chosen. When you pray to or through the Holy Spirit, where is your sacrifice? He will accept no more bulls and goats. You need Jeshua's sacrifice (Psalm 2) to intercede for you. When you pray to the Father (Spirit and Holy God) again make sure you have been cleansed and that your sacrifice is pure. You have to go through His only accepted sacrifice. I know this is hard for people with pride to do. You must repent and seek forgiveness; otherwise you are wasting words. 1st Timothy 2:5, There is one God, and one intercessor between God and man, the Man, Christ Jesus. Hebrews 2:9 confirms that Jesus was "A little lower than the angels (mainly) for the suffering of death." Since death is a spirit, if we propose that Jesus was God, then Satan would have serious bragging rights. God specifically allowed Matthew to record an incident in Matthew 8:24, so that in this particular "Day of Revelation," the doubters can compare those events with the words of Psalm 121:4, "He that keepeth Israel, shall neither slumber nor sleep." God is not a man and never was. God's word tells us that *man was created a little lower than the angels*. God is spirit, limitless, indefinable and immeasurable. His Spirit indwells cleansed temples. Since human bodies are vehicles for spirits, any human that is "transformed," spiritually reborn or grafted to the pure olive, then he/she is part and parcel of the Temple of God with His oracle/sacrifice—the Messiah. God the Father and God the Spirit is obviously one and the same. Whose spirit do you think God the Spirit is?

The so-called primitive people understood and taught the truth with simple illustrations, prior to their altars became corrupted. The sun, they taught, is the chief source of light—like the Father with the big eye to see all; He has a big nose to perceive all and a big head to know all. Even though the big Sun is away from them, its light illuminated them, while they were in the light. That, my friends, is the doctrine of the "One-Eyed Horus." The doctrine of the one-eyed Horus can be found etched in hieroglyphic everywhere that humankind lived during the Stellar Mythos. Notice the proximity of the so-called phallic stone and its prominence in all of their ceremonial sites. How could you teach students that they were worshipping their procreative parts? There was usually only one giant mass exalted on a slab adjacent to a **normal** sized female at all sites. How is it that my translations of the messages in stone relate that they taught that the *Great Architect of the Universe* would one day come into an ordinary female and the seed of that union would usher in an age of wisdom? Those so-called primitive people knew that what was in the pregnant female could not have been the same as the source of the impregnation, so there was a large distinction between the source of the seed and the seed to be conceived. We called them primitive for that? Our so-called wise are the superior mortals? By their very actions, their seed to this day also believe themselves to be superior. The question begs to be asked superior to whom? To allow the myth to last, the perpetrators of that fallacy had to add another fallacy that somehow God rejected His people and somehow they became less than human? God, who foresees all, allowed the northern tribes to suffer their humiliation first. Then He blessed their seed even though many are still rebellious. Those of 'The South' are approaching the end of their "Tribulation Age."

Is the Father, the Son and Holy Spirit the same? There is one God, JHVH, the Creator of all. God is not just a spirit: He is spirit, holy, and the Father of all—including Jesus. So God is the Holy Father. Since God gave every seed a right or comforting spirit at birth (Psalm 51) then all comforting spirits originate from our Father, God. Like the colours in a rainbow, they are connected to the Father as one. When we receive our "sonship" and renew our right spirit, it becomes holy or comforting. So the *Most Comforting Spirit* belongs to God. So if God is the Father of all, how can you ask if God has a Holy Spirit or a Holy Son? Would God share himself out? He has not one son, but many sons, and daughters. The Logos, "Debiyr" in Hebrew, His firstfruit Son was begotten before the foundation of the world. In Malachi 2:10, "Fathership" is God's chief characteristic, "Have we not all one father? Hath not one God created us? Why do we deal treacherously one man against his brother by profaning the covenant of our fathers?" God's supreme nature or title is God. Jeshua is Son of God and so are we through the redemption seed; therefore technically Jeshua is Jeshua Ben-God (John 6:46). In English they would say Godson or God Jr. The *Word of God* foretold that He would be called "Wonderful, Counselor, Mighty God and the Prince of Peace." The word did not say *He would be God: just that He would be called Might of God or Mighty God.* To draw on a simple illustration, Al Gore junior is called Gore like his father. Jeshua was not merely His name but His mission statement. His prophetic everlasting message from Hebrew is: "God is Salvation." His accompanying witness, John, who received a prophetic gift like Daniel, called Him "Logion" (in the Greek language) in John 1:14.

John used three Greek words to describe Jeshua as He is called: (1) "Logion" John 1:14, translated as *Word* in English. John 1:1 "Logos" from the Greek verb lego means to put together. Another meaning is to assemble as in speech or words. Luminaries use the Hebrew word "Omer" whenever referring to God's prophetic utterance. (2) Parakletos is translated into English in John 14:16 as Comforter or Intercessor. Solomon used the Hebrew word "Nacham" in Ecclesiastes 4:1 and the word is used as a synonym for intercessor. (3) John 1:9 "Phos" from the Greek word "phoa" means, "to shine." However the word is more used in reference to wisdom than artificial light. The right English word should have been Luminary. Daniel used the Hebrew word "Nehiyr" to reference spiritual light in Daniel 2:22. Daniel was boasting about the greatness of his God. He changeth the times and seasons (Verse 21) and in 22, He (God) revealeth the deep and secret things; He knoweth what is in the darkness and the "Light" dwelleth in Him. That light is the spiritual *Living True Light*.

Both Daniel and John were called to be "Shabbat" witnesses (witnesses at the end of Ages). John testified that the promised *Age of Wisdom* had arrived through the Luminary or anointed one. Since there never was or never will be a loving father who has been or is displeased with the deportment of his totally obedient son, then which father would object to his son being called by his name? Most times we are so proud. Jesus always referenced the Father who sent Him. John 12:46… I am come, a *light* unto the world, that whosoever believeth ON Me (not in me): in other words—on the Word, the Logos—should not abide in darkness. The 49th verse of John 12 …I have spoken not of myself, but the Father which sent me; He gave me a commandment (decree) what I should say and what I should speak. Jesus proclaimed that His words were spoken by *divine decree from God*. John 13:16 …neither is He that is sent greater than He that sent him. The Oracle cannot be greater than the source. Jesus himself confirmed that. John 14:28, *"My Father is greater than I."*

The Holy Spirit was *never a man* and cannot be limited to such, although He (from the limited masculine gender) can inhabit any place person or thing. Since God is living and positive, the Logos or Spirit of God is referred to as "He." God's Spirit is a living powerful expression and extension of himself. In response to: "How can you say, show us the Father?" John 14:10, "Believest thou not that I am in the Father, and the Father in me?" John 14:10 "The words that I speak unto you I speak not of myself: but the Father that dwelleth in me, he doeth the works." That confirms why every word Jesus spoke was "Law" or collaborating scripture. He became the Ark of the "New Covenant" of Jeremiah 31:31. Verse 11, "Believe me that I am in the *Father*, and the *Father in me*." Churches have mistranslated the previous sentence to imply that since Jesus had the Spirit of God in Him that He was God. I am not writing on my own: God is impacting and imparting through me—Daniel 11:32, "The people that know their God shall do exploits." Jeshua said that the words (within Him) are from the Living God. I can't heal people: God's Spirit through Jesus does that—Acts 1:8. God is omnipresent; He was and is always spirit. Jeshua was and is His "Chosen Vessel." God is spirit, the Holy All. Isaiah 11:2, The "Seven Ministering" or "Comforter" Spirits that complement the perfect Godhead were prophesied to rest upon Jeshua His chosen vessel.

JESHUA IS THE ONLY PERSON THAT GOD USED AS A VESSEL FOR HIS SEVEN.

Isaiah Chapter 11:1, There shall come forth a rod from the stem of Jesse (not root) and a Branch shall grow out of His roots. Verse 2…(A) The Spirit of the Lord shall rest upon Him, (B) the Spirit of Wisdom, (C) Spirit of Understanding: Proverbs 9:10 (knowing God's will and purpose) (D) the Spirit of Counsel and (E) The Spirit of Power or Might. The Spirit of Power "The Comforter" had to await the "Rest" or completion of God's task. It is the enabling spirit or "Oracle Power" that Jeshua promised to send after His resurrection. Today, it enables us to proclaim and to prophesy. The other two are, (F) the Spirit of Knowledge (foreknowledge of things we call that today "Rama Word.") and (G) the Spirit of the Fear of the Lord. To receive all is to receive the harmony of God: His absolute righteous personality.

I have yet to encounter anywhere else whereby God had promised anyone His spirit of utmost understanding and authority and the spirit of knowledge and fear of the Lord. In Isaiah 11:3-9, Isaiah explained the fruits of that spirit. In verse 10 is a clear description of the only person ever promised that gift. I will paraphrase because God specifically revealed the importance of those scriptures to me.

Verse 3.   Immediate understanding of God's purposes and His will. He would neither judge nor reprove from His own intuition. Everything He doeth is of God. WOW!

Verse 4.   He would judge both the meek and the mighty, differentiating between neither.

Verse 5.   He would be most righteous and most faithful.

Verse 6.   He would be an everlasting monument of peace.

Verses 7-9. He would possess the teachings and wisdom FOR ALL to achieve fullness of knowledge, peace and blessings.

Verse 10.   He would be of the last known and recorded bloodline of Jesse. The Gentiles would also seek Him. All who find Him, His knowledge, His blessings and His gifts of the above spirits shall have God's glorious rest—Acts 1:8.

The vision God gave to me as to the functions of the previous *Seven Spirits* was also given to John on Patmos isle in Revelation 1:4 and also to the prophet Zechariah. Revelation 1:4— "From the *Seven Spirits*, which are before his throne." In Zechariah 3:9 is also the vision of the above: "For behold the stone that I have laid before *Joshua*; upon *one stone* shall be *seven eyes*: behold I will engrave the graving thereof." The previous verse: Verse 8 "Behold I bring forth my servant the BRANCH." Find the power in the engraved and encoded name!

CHAPTER 29B. INSIGHT INTO THE DIVINE NATURE OF GOD.

This statement has to be understood without reservation: *God has no carnal nature.* No flesh can glory in the presence of God. Through centuries of purging, God predestined a human vessel perfectly sterilized to receive His "Holy" nature or Holy Spirit. Upon completion of that task, God returned the "Tree of Life to Jeshua." God changes not. Psst, "The transformer is step-down, not step-up!" Man can receive God's divine nature, not the other way around. God abhors carnality. Since the occidental transplants of Christianity have attempted to trivialize, reduce and limit God's ability (not intentionally perhaps), respect for God among millions of followers has diminished and leaves a lot to be desired.

Taking off lights and hiding to do evil is really insulting to God's wisdom and omnipresent nature. God not only sees all and knows all, but He sees and knows all of our secret thoughts as well—Psalm 139:7-12. He can also show those thoughts to "His Chosen."

The Hebrew language is perfect, prophetic and pure. It is the only language with a special supra-gender. God had, in times past given us insights as to *His Divine Personality or Divine Nature*. Before the *Great Deluge* (in the time of Noah) and prior to the spiritual coup at Babel when the earth had one language, all patriarchs referenced God as "The ALL." During those times, when man's unclean actions became unbearable, God prevented those with unclean lips from uttering His name. As the people of the earth fragmented, some could not get further than "The" or "El." Every place where history recorded that men sunk because of misdeeds, we saw "El" used alone. The obedient remnant always added a more reverent addition:

1. EL ADONAI (Creator or Father) Supreme Ruler...Joshua 3:11.

2. EL SHADDAI, He who dwells in exalted places...Exodus 6:3 and Genesis 17:1-2.

3. EL ELYON, Most High God...Numbers 24:16, Genesis14:18-20 and Psalm 18:13.

4. EL OLAM, Eternal, Everlasting God... Psalm 90:1-2, Genesis 21:33 and Isaiah 26:4.

5. EL BERITH, Covenant keeper...Judges 8:34.

6. EL ROI, The Only God who sees, hears and responds to His people...Genesis 16:13.

7. EL ELOHIM, The Alpha/Omega, God of totality and infinity...Genesis 1:26-27.

8. EL HOSIEM, Redeemer ...Isaiah 44:24.

9. JEHOVAH NISSI (Banner)...Exodus 17:15 and Acts 4:12.

10. JEHOVAH RAPHA (HEALER)...Exodus 15:26 last verse.

11. JEHOVAH TSIDKENU, Righteous God...Jeremiah 23:6.

12. JEHOVAH SHAPHAT (Judge)...Genesis 18:25.

13. JEHOVAH M'KADDESH (He that Sanctifies)...Exodus 31:13.

14. JEHOVAH GIREH (Provider)...Genesis 22:14 and Matthew 14:17-21.

15. JEHOVAH SHALOM (Peace)...Judges 6:24.

16. JEHOVAH SHAMMAH (Omnipresent)...Ezekiel 48:35

17. JEHOVAH ROHE (Ra-ah) (Shepherd)...Psalm 23:1.

18. JEHOVAH SABAOTH... (Genesis 17:3, Exodus 34:8), Supreme Godhead, Captain of the Hosts: Joshua 5:14 and Jeremiah 11:20. The last one should frighten those misguided youths that ring bells, wear ponytails, lift up a man, bow to him and call him Supreme Godhead.

God confirms His word. Early tradition omitted vowels in the name of God. Post Babel languages are more audio-oriented. Shout JHVH, the confirmed echo is JSHVH. Psalm 2 reveals the meaning of the "S" as in JA-SON, the Golden Fleece, not fleeces! So because God has given us insight into His personalities, which manifest through His Firstfruit, does that mean that each personality is a God? In Genesis 1:26, for (alpha/omega) the plural Hebrew word "Elohim" is used, verse 27 specifies, "Made in His image."

Where then is the Biblical evidence for the Trinity? Isaiah 44:24 should dispel every doubt: "I am the Lord that maketh all things, that stretcheth forth the heavens alone, that spreadeth abroad the earth *by myself.*" Isaiah 44:26, "That confirmeth the word of his servant." Each ministering spirit or "Comforter" is part and parcel of God's nature. The shepherds in the Occident have deprived most churches of the wisdom of the other ministering spirits. As a result, Christianity functioned during the past 1900 years, bereft of God's full teachings. Did the Jerusalem church sanction wars or bless armies to kill children of God? Did they teach that (sic) superior children could kill inferior ones without punishment?

The Old Testament sacrifices were forerunners to the *Everlasting Covenant* and the *Everlasting Sacrifice!* Was the sacrifice and God ever the same? Did not God receive back the accepted sacrifice to himself? Are we teaching underhandedly that the God who is all, who never slumbers nor sleeps, who cannot *fail*, or *change* can be mocked, spat on, be disrespected and can contradict His Word? As a result of erroneous doctrines, Satan has turned the Church of the Occident into a spiritual football! Jeshua confirmed that only God (His Father) knows everything and is the only one worthy to be called "Master." Since Jeshua is reconnected to the Spirit of God, then He and the Logos/God's Spirit are "nailed," interconnected and inseparable. There is an inseparable interconnection: Jeshua to God.

The previous revelation had the most profound effect on the entire research team. We took a year's Sabbatical. Is the electricity on your utility pole disconnected from the power plant? John revealed the wisdom thusly, "There are three that bear witness in the earth: water, spirit and blood." Just before Jesus' death, after He inquired, "Eloi, Eloi, la-ma sabach'-tha-ni?" "My God, my God, why hast thou forsaken me?" He spake *not* another word. The Logos (Living Word) exited. It is amazing; no one could find any utterance from Jeshua anywhere about anything but Oracle utterances. We were looking for the moment that the Logos left Him and we located it.

Matthew 28:19… Assuming that the translation to English is correct, which the Dead Sea Scrolls will reveal, then there is no foundational basis for any Trinity here because the word name is used as a synonym for authority. Paul explained that God is a God of order. That was elaborated on when he wrote to the brethren at Corinth: 1st Corinthians 11: 3, "The head (authority) over woman is the man, and the *head* (authority) over Christ is the *Father God*." Examine Matthew 28:19…Go ye therefore and teach all nations, baptizing them in *the name* (not names) in other words in the authority of: *the Father, the Son, and of the Holy Spirit.*

Spirits communicate through altars. Building an altar in one's home, office, sacrosanct organization or temple automatically sends signals to the spiritual realm. Your personal altars are pursued daily by the chief thief. Moses recorded that "In the Beginning," God spoke the world into being. God the Spirit had to create the world through His Logos and also from Ex-Nihilo, the unseen or spirit realm. Genesis 1:2, "Darkness was upon the face of the deep." Genesis 1:3…God said, "Let there be light, and there was light." Whenever a man speaks, his words ring echoes of themselves. God is the source of The Word. When God spoke the Word, the Word became an echo of himself. "Light, come forth!" That is translated as, "God said, let there be light." In all fullness: "Let there be Revelation, Understanding, Truth, Wisdom, Happiness, Sustenance, Repentance, Forgiveness, Grace, Mercy, and Everlasting Life also." God's word cannot return void.

Had God not given us the gift of choice, would God have invented the "Rest" mechanism called "Time?" God has set His times and seasons. In Ecclesiastes 3:1-8, there is a time or season for everything. In the beginning God set His time for decrees, and then He allowed times of "darkness or wilderness." After every three epochs, God calls a half rest and after the next three, or seventh "Yowme," He calls a complete rest or season. During those times, we have choices of sowing or reaping—obedience or disobedience.

All seasons belong to God. The duration of each new season of revelation or rebellion is called "Yowme" or Day. Lamentably, churches that celebrate a particular "Yowme" have not moved on to fresh revelations. Lord, lead such out of wildernesses. In every wilderness He gives fresh manna or revelation daily. Since God's words are *Life*, the "Echo Word" became matter, life, light and all the aforementioned. His word cannot return void. The Logos became flesh and dwelt among us. The Logos became the embodiment of every Hebrew Feast. The Logos came into the domain of man not to break the rules, but as man, to reclaim and to redeem all that man lost. Now man has the ability to possess the attributes and promises of God. Wherever the Logos is, the Spirit of God is also. The Tree of Life has fashioned the New Ark!

In Psalm 80, Asaph accurately forecast Jeshua's restorative mission. He would be a special man concealed (as a youth) in Egypt—the Oracle that lay between two cherubims in the Temple of Solomon; He would come as the *Shepherd* and a vine to be planted, spread, plucked and temporarily destroyed. Recorded in verse 17 thousands of years prior: "Let thy hand be upon the man of thy right hand, upon the son of man whom thou madest strong for thyself."

CHAPTER 29C. PROPHECY OF THE ONE SHEPHERD.

Why then would God emphasize one special shepherd? Who could fit the bill as a special shepherd for all of God's sheep? That shepherd would have had to be concealed in Egypt, die for all sheep and have fulfilled prior prophecies of Moses in Genesis 49:24. Isaiah 53:7, "He is brought as a lamb to the slaughter." Ezekiel 34:23, "I will set *one shepherd over them*, and he shall feed them, even my servant David; he shall feed them, and he shall be their shepherd." Ecclesiastes 12:11, "The words of the wise are as goads and nails fastened by the 'Masters of the Assemblies,' which are given from 'One Shepherd.'" Those prophecies were fulfilled as per John, quoting Jeshua prophesying about His imminent death. John 10:11, "I am the good shepherd: the good shepherd giveth his life for the sheep." Also mentioning the return of the Anointed one the second time, Simon's letter to early churches in Asia listed as 1st Peter 5:4, "When the chief shepherd shall appear." God has stored New Testament prophecies in the Psalms. In Psalm 99, "The Shepherd" is referred to as The Lord. Masters are called to teach; shepherds are called to lead flocks, therefore Master/Shepherd?

The Oracle in the house of Solomon rested between two cherubim. In Exodus 25:18-22, "Thou shalt make two cherubims…19…make one cherub on the one end, and the other cherub on the other end: even of the mercy seat shall ye make the cherubims …Verse 20, "The cherubims shall stretch forth their mighty wings on high, covering the mercy seat with their wings, and their faces shall look one to another; towards the mercy seat shall the faces of the cherubims be." Verse 21, "Thou shalt put the mercy seat above upon the ark; and in the ark thou shall put the testimony that I shall give thee."

Are these mere coincidences or are they part of God's divine plan that His Logos was first put in the Ark of testimony? 2. After the Logos became flesh, the Ark of the Covenant disappeared from the earth. Within the plan of the Temple of Solomon was recorded for all to see the power that was given to the Son. In the 99th Psalm the first verse reads "The Lord reigneth, let the people tremble: he sitteth between the cherubims; let the earth be moved." The power of that Oracle trembles the entire earth. As mankind digressed, God's Spirit departed from him. The Spirit of God only inhabits, dwells, and connects to heavenly or sanctified places, Psalm 24:3. God gave man dominion over all the earth. God does not bequeath gifts and take them back. The prophetic message was coded in the names of the seed of Adam. Patriarchal root names concealed the message of the Messiah. Look at the "pelicost" prophetic power of names of the male heads of each generation from Adam to Noah.

Adam (earth), Seth (manifest) Enos (mortal) Cainan (the tabernacle) Mahalaleel (blessed of God or praise of God) Jared (shall descend) Enoch (anoint) Methuselah (his painful death/sacrifice shall bear/bring) Lamech (those swallowed up or lost) Noah (rest/comfort). To put it simply, "*God shall anoint and send down to earth a transformed human tabernacle. He shall be blessed and consecrated for His purpose. He shall bear sorrows, grief and death; so that the lost shall find rest in Him.*" The first Adam allowed the first temple, the human lumber and the sacred vessels to be tarnished. In the new Adam or Messiah is the complete redemptive package for humankind. The first Adam allowed desecration to his missing rib. As that rib got tarnished, so did every temple, synagogue, tabernacle, church and even…institutions.

God sent a better redeemer than Moses: Deuteronomy 18:18-19. Jeshua was certain to be ridiculed and mocked (Psalm 22) for our "mockery of God." God promised us forgiveness through *His grace and mercy*. He who is Holy and Spirit had to choose a *sinless* body of *His own likeness and image*, to receive the shame, sin, guilt, and mockery back to Him for pardon. Genesis 49:23, "The soldiers/archers have sorely grieved him, and pierced him, and hated him. 24…but his bow abode in strength; and the arms of his hands were made strong by the hands of the mighty God of Jacob from thence is The Shepherd, the Stone of Israel." Jeshua came not to change the law, but to "repair" all that was breached—Isaiah 53. He was baptized and He attended a wedding. Whereas the Levitical laws dealt with cleansing the priest, people and temple, through Jeshua's everlasting sinless blood sacrifice we can receive God's restorative package for one repentant exchange factor: Psalm 24:3-4.

There are new shepherds trying to feed starving children for years. In contrast, thousands of executives are fed by those visual advertisements of starving children in Africa with flies in their noses. The cost of one advertisement alone could feed 50,000 of the same starving children. Jeshua used love and His supernatural power to allow five barley loaves and two fishes to feed thousands. If churches, nations and all so-called charitable institutions really had Jesus' love in their hearts, they could use $2.00, yes two dollars to feed millions. How is that possible? Most charitable institutions and church organizations with world outreach ministries have toll-free numbers. Calls to the ones that do not have such, cost $1.25 approximately. With the other .75 cents call your representatives in the U.S. Government. Tell him/her to arrange for some of the aforementioned institutions to pick up the surplus food that they burn monthly or you will vote them out of office. Within 40 days, world poverty will end. The sad thing is that the world is saturated with Satan's energy.

Every time man relinquished his authority over a specific domain, intruding spiritual forces overthrew man and took control. Carnal energy overruled spiritual energy. The kings of Israel failed for the most part. The judges (of Israel) failed for the most part. Jeshua was victorious. Had Jeshua been selfish, would there have been any hope for us unless we tackled the beasts and aliens ourselves? The history (of the progression or regression) of organized religion for the past two thousand years reflects the advances and pitfalls of ancient Israel. We are coming to the end of the *Tabernacle Age*. People like to dress up and to appear holy by visiting his/her tabernacle. It is not the visit to a particular tabernacle or the singing that makes you holy. Some people are living double lives and are still visiting His holy places. Anyone can impress the ignorant that he /she is sanctified and worthy and has the Spirit of God in him/her. However God is not fooled; He is not mocked.

The Muslims take special care in teaching the importance of respecting their private temples (bodies) and their created temples (Mosques). Look what Satan has done to us. Are we not all Abraham's seed? So if our private temple is sacred, are not all of our brothers' temples sacred also? The Logos draws us to "The Veil" with messages of love and forgiveness. Money cannot buy such. Without that closeness to our Holy Father, we are empty. In the Islamic religion, there are 99 Arabic names describing God's nature. Here are two questions for all Muslim scholars—which one is repetitious? Which two are missing? The two most powerful and important names of God's eternal nature are missing: 1. FATHER, AND 2. LOVE. To receive "Sonship" and Agape we have to chase away "unforgiveness" and hate.

The Dawn of this "Age of Truth" and God's camping season frightens many. The Spirit of God is selecting the tents and tabernacles that He finds sanctified and are causing miraculous signs, wonders and healings to manifest. It is so easy for a person who has not the Spirit of God, evidenced by His gifts, to deny the presence of God in another. That is a sin and grievous to the Holy Spirit for two reasons. 1. Grieving the Spirit of God is unpardonable blasphemy. 2. There is an immediate and everlasting curse. Judge not less ye yourself be judged. Simply put, if you are not sure, then ask God. If you cannot hear from your Father, you might not yet be seated in heavenly places; your spiritual ear might be blocked or your faith might be weak through doubt and disbelief. So fast and seek forgiveness for the causes of the blockage and ask again. Arrogance, vanity, conceit, fear and sin impair spiritual connections to God. Here is another secret. You cannot get through to the Father except through wisdom, repentance, forgiveness, and through *His Living Logos*. To get through, first you need to say the prayers of restoration in these volumes.

CHAPTER 29D. SCRUTINY OF THE TRINITY.

The concept of plural deities is rooted in paganism. Is there one God in three persons? Was God ever a person? If we cannot understand God's package, how can we teach what we do not understand? For two thousand years, men have wrestled with spiritual matters and have injected their opinions. All answers are in God's word. Since personality means spiritual nature and God is omnipresent, He can give His divine nature to "His Chosen." No gift from God relinquishes or changes either His omnipresent nature or His Divine spirit nature. The concept of a Trinity as decreed at Nicea is that there is one God in three divine persons. First of all let us remember that some truth is not ALL truth. There is one God! The first part of the statement is true! God has no limits; that is why He is invisible. The teaching on the Trinity has many contradictions. God is not a man, since men are finite, formed, made, begotten, visible, can hurt and be killed.

Moses explained that neither God, nor the one referred to as the Son of Man can lie. Moses expounded that the Oracle of God can only proclaim what God hath decreed. Numbers 23: 19, "God is not a man, that he should lie; neither the son of man that he should repent..." God is spirit, not just a spirit. God is holy, spirit, complete, incalculable, infinite and therefore invisible. For any spirit to be manifest on earth, it has to have a vehicle to carry it around. The Father, who is Creator, created all things and all men. The Father was never a person. The human body is created as a temple for God. Temples either worship God or they worship the devil. There are no spiritual grey areas. That was God's plan in the beginning and it will be His purpose in the end, when we are transformed. The Father (so immeasurable and incalculable that He is perpetually invisible) that created all flesh, never became flesh: flesh is carnal, limited, temporary, and designed to be a transitory vehicle in the quarantine station called earth. The Father is forever spirit. The Father is Holy. Since there are unholy spirits, The Holy Spirit is the connector/conduit to the Father's fountain. John explained that. On the other hand most people misinterpret His message. Those who are translating the Dead Sea scrolls should scrutinize those scriptures. In fact they should pay close attention to all scriptures that have caused major differences in interpretations.

By now readers should have become more familiar with Satan's methods. If he enticed anyone into error initially, he would use the very error as spiritual virus seeds. As soon as sensible debate begins on those issues, Satan stirs up antagonists. Misunderstandings of spiritual matters give Satan billions of seeds of hate. Some misquote 1ˢᵗ John 5:7, "For there are three that bear record *in heaven, the Father, the Word and the Holy Spirit and these three are one.*" Three spiritual conduits to the one God, is not stating the same as three persons in one God. The invisible spirit Father is the Invisible God. The Holy Spirit as opposed to an unholy spirit connects spiritual sons. Purged man connects first to God's eternal sacrifice. When we pass the litmus test, we connect through God's Holy Spirit to our *Most Holy Spirit Father*. In God's domain, each of His ministering spirits has a purpose and a name: their names define their purposes. The Spirit of Might cannot give understanding or vice-versa. Do not forget that God is omnipresent. Father and His Holy Spirit are connected. They are in harmony and they are one. The *Father* and His *Living Word* are one. One manifests to confirm God. They are always in agreement; that is why God cannot lie, since He speaks things into being. Read carefully, it does not say *three persons*.

1ˢᵗ John 5:8, "There are *three* that bear witness *in the earth*, the spirit, the water and the blood and these *three are in harmony*." They are not persons: "they agree in one." If there was a Trinity why then did Paul who was empowered to teach and preach to the Gentiles omit teaching that? Why did the Elders of the Jerusalem church neglect to teach that? In fact their teachings are to the contrary: Paul proclaimed a curse on all that teach any other doctrine and it came to pass. Galatians 1:8-9, "Though we, or an angel from heaven preach any other gospel (doctrine) unto you that you have received, let him be accursed." Neither Rome nor any country or institution has any authority to teach any *New Doctrine*. Inventions of new doctrines bring Paul's curse and death follows. A nation that establishes a doctrine different from the "Doctrine of Everlasting Life" upon its national altar, invites a *Covenant of Death*, and blood flows unabated. I have neither the time nor space to list the curses that followed the invented doctrines from the fourth century to our present season of Jubilee.

Aristhanus was one of the early proponents of the Trinity doctrine. His big discovery was that Jesus had two natures: one human and one divine. Whoopee! Aren't we all—until we fall into continual sin? Did not Paul (in Colossians 1, Romans 7:23, Philippians 3:3, 1ˢᵗ Corinthians 8:6 and James (in James 5) write extensively about the war that rages in our members? The carnal nature fights the spiritual nature constantly! Is not that one of Jesus' greatest victories for us that indeed we, like Him, can conquer our carnality? Paul is so clear about the mission of the Son (predestined of Psalm 2). In 1ˢᵗ Corinthians 8:6…"To us, there is but *one God*, the Father, of whom are all things and we in him; and one Lord Jesus Christ, *by whom are all things*, and we by him." In other words, God is all. He placed His firstborn son *in charge of all*. *He* created Him to filter, to purge and to discard those that do not line up with His "Spirit Level" or Living Word. God's Holy Spirit receives those that pass Jeshua's litmus test. In other words, "*The Resurrection*

Firstfruit" has to say: "Dad, this person has been successfully screened and redeemed;" then God's Holy Spirit reconnects that person to God.

Jesus was born carnal to overcome all carnality. His very witnesses recorded "In all points He was tempted"—Hebrews 4:15. God cannot be tempted—James 1:13. The son of someone cannot be that someone (John 17:3-5). An entity that is part of a whole cannot be the whole. Jesus slept, hungered, was thirsty, was smitten and died (all carnal attributes). Jesus, on earth had two eyes, two ears, one nose, one head and one body. *God has all eyes, ears, mouths, all bodies and minds!* If all who work at 1600 Pennsylvania Avenue are in the White House—that is not the same as saying that the White House is in all those at 1600 Pennsylvania Avenue. There is a step, a front door and balconies in the White House. The step, the door and the balconies are not the White House. The Spirit of God encases all attributes of God. They include Logos, comforters—His grace, truth, knowledge, wisdom, understanding, might, power, connector or way to His all—His restitution programme, and His judgment; for example: 6+4+2=12. Twelve (to the infinite degree) represents the whole, which represents God. God is His chosen (His Holy Spirit Selected Realm) plus His discarded. In the beginning was perfection= God. After the end, there will be perfection= God. I am the Alpha and the Omega. Matter + Spirit realm = God. Even though there seems to be separation between God's spirit realm and matter, they are connected because God is *omnipresent.* We know that all matter originates from the spirit realm or domain of the unseen and not the other way around.

All we have to do is to observe the birth of a child. Here is another major subdivision by God. God = Logos+Infinity or Complete Spirit realm. Bad matter + Rebellious spirit realm+ Good matter+ Obedient Spirit realm = God. Where then is the Spirit of God in the previous equation. The obvious answer is between the good matters and the spirit realm. In between are God's judgment, His will and His divine plan. The Spirit of God is the *connector of all good things,* people, promises, places and situations plus His judgment for the disobedient. 1st Corinthians 6:17, He that is joined to the Lord is spirit. Hence we should have a better understanding of John 1. In the beginning was the *Word* and the *Word* was with God and the *Word* was God. Another translation: In the beginning was the Logos and the Logos was with God and the Logos was God. Since God is Alpha and Omega, God has the first and last say and is the first and final word. That is why it is written: *"Though heaven and earth pass away, my word will stand!"* What a reassuring revelation!

Why has that given carnal men such trouble? Heavens and earth had not been created yet. God is and has always been spirit, connected to all holiness. God is and has always been *omnipresent.* So the invisible omnipresent God always had and has His decree-proclaiming Oracle capacity. God and His word are inseparable. That is why whatever God proclaimed and proclaims, has to be. Before God ever sent forth *His Word, His Word* was in Him and with Him. Obviously, the Oracle of God is connected to the *omnipresent invisible* God. He changeth not. The *invisible God* and *manifest oracle was and is one* (John 17:5). Here is an example. Place a pencil alone on a table. How many items are there? Shouldn't the answer be one? The correct answer should be one pencil and billions of germs, molecules and particles. However since the germs are invisible the answer is one. Why? A unit has to be manifest to be a unit. He that keepeth Israel can neither slumber nor sleep! God was never someone, but the sum, THE ALL-ENCOMPASSING ALL. God gave us an insightful glimpse of that in the first verse of Genesis—Genesis 1:1. Whenever references are made to God's infinite greatness, might or power, a plural attribute "Elohim" is ordained.

I AM GOD; I CHANGE NOT. THE PERFECTED WHOLE REMAINS PERFECTED!

CARNAL MINDS STOP TRYING TO CREATE A GOD AFTER YOUR OWN LIKENESS OR LIKING!

As contradictory as the following appears, I must elaborate on the not so obvious. The Father and the Father are not two but one, since there is only one Father of all. Any magnitude of invisible entities still remains invisible. The previous statement affirms the omnipresent nature of our invisible God. The Father and the Father is one. The invisible Father, invisible Holy Spirit is one. The invisible Spirit, omnipresent Father and the visible Son must be one.

If I improve until I live my life to perfection, can I have the invisible, omnipresent God in me? The answer is definitely yes. If then the redemptive Son hath completed His redemptive purpose, then the sacrifice is acceptable and is in the nostrils of God. The Son is now redeemed spirit man. When we give money to God's house, when we place our tithes and offerings into the collection plate, does the money go to the plate? So if we pray to the Son, our prayers must go through His unseen nostrils to the invisible Holy Father. Hence we have been forewarned from calling any *man* "Holy Father;" it is sacrilegious. God's Holy Spirit's role on earth is one of the three (conduits) that confirm God's presence, power and essence. The three that bear witness in heaven: Father, Word and Holy Spirit. Since they are all invisible, we need the cloned generator—the chosen firstborn—Psalm 89:27. God's Holy Spirit does the following for us:

1. Gives us access to, and knowledge of God—Daniel 11:32 and Ephesians 2:18.

2. Brings embrace, power and gifts from God—1st Corinthians 12 and Acts 1:8.

3. Purges our Babelic utterances and filters our worship—Romans 8:26 and John 4:24.

4. Brings to us our "Certificate of Sonship" from Jesus—Isaiah 11:1-11and Romans 8:14.

Isaiah 42:1 identified God's special servant. Isaiah 42:6, "I the Lord have called thee (the servant of verse 1) in righteousness, and will hold thine hand, and **will keep thee, and give thee for a covenant of the people**, for a **light of the Gentiles**; Verse 7, **to open the blind eyes**." We either accept Jesus' everlasting participatory sacrifice or we must be prepared to improve on it and hope that God will accept it after we are finished.

CHAPTER 29E. REDEEMED MAN, IMAGE OF THE INVISIBLE GOD.

Head: God is head of all and is all. His Eyes: 2nd Chronicles 16:9 …The eyes of the Lord run to and fro throughout the whole earth, to shew himself strong in behalf of them whose heart is perfect towards Him. Neck/Throat/Mouth is His Oracle—Genesis 1:3-5 and John 1:9. Hands—Psalm 95:5, "His hands formed the dry land." God gave every man a right spirit. He created spirits first. God does not bestow gifts and take them back. A multitude of spirits decided to follow Satan. They became permanent evil spirits. Would God have left himself out of the sharing? Wouldn't God assign the Most Holy Spirit to himself? What then is the image of the invisible God? Genesis 1:27, "Let us make *Man* in our own image, in the image of God created he him." The rebuilt Messiah's church must have the same attitude, pure mind, attire and shape of a chaste virgin. It must have the shape of a human—with God as head, prophets as eyes, the elders as ears, the junior pastors should function as the neck, the ushers as shoulders, ministries as the hands and feet; the members as the body. There are churches shaped like giraffes, horses and the like—with very long necks, long bodies and no shoulders. The outline given in 1st Corinthians 12 is for the shape of a human. The shape of all perfected and glorified things will be like glorious churches—temples of worship, shaped like humans. They have to be in harmony: hence one head—singing and speaking in one accord—decreeing all truth. The shape of a human vessel is profound in spiritual significance. As a potential temple of the living God, a human has a most powerful altar that the chief thief knows about and covets daily.

The first decree on earth was that God's Logos come forth. His Logos (perfect *Oracle or Light*) came forth and took form in the image of God. Since the image of God is the shape of a man, the first fruit of the image of God must have been the form of His Son: John 1:7-9. Earth is the domain of man. Let us make man in our own image. That was an esoteric echo. *Temples be ye perfect* or Temples be holy, as I am holy. If the first temple was not His perfect light or essence, then God failed in His purpose. There is a spiritual relationship between the shape of a man and that of a sanctified temple. When the Spirit of God pronounced Jesus at His baptism at the hands of John, His words: "This is my beloved Son."

There are no three divine persons. It is a doctrine of men, foolish men who knew not the word. God, over time, dwelt in the perfected body of His Son. Jeshua is now back to the future in the perfected spirit whole. He holds a "spirit level" to which all humankind will be judged. Psalm 2:1-2 was written specifically for this time: "Why do the heathen rage and the people imagine a vain thing?" Verse 2, "The kings of the earth set themselves, and the rulers take counsel together, against the Lord, and against his anointed..." Bear in mind that kings came from Judah. Verse 6, "Yet I have set my king upon my holy hill of Zion." Verse 7, "I will declare the decree: The Lord hath said unto me, thou art my Son" ...This day have I *begotten thee...* I will give thee the heathen (Gentile nations) for thine inheritance and the uttermost parts of the earth for thy possession. Since the earth is the Lord's and the fullness thereof—Psalm 24:1—then this Son will be given *all power and authority* by divine decree. We covered earlier that a double reference in a Psalm prophetically mirrors a future event.

In Psalm 2, an address is made to *all rulers of the earth*—kings and judges. "Be wise now therefore ye kings; be instructed ye judges of the earth. Serve the Lord with fear and rejoice with trembling." In Hebrew the word na^shaq, pronounced "naw-shaq" means to bond with or touch closely. In English translations it is used as a synonym for the verb to kiss. In the days of David, the office of kingship was no informal office. The only time a person could kiss a king in public would have been after every rule of protocol had been established. The person would have had to await the king's permission to kneel first. The scepter would have been placed in a position to indicate acceptance of the visit, and then *ONLY* the signet ring could be kissed. That command in Psalm 2:12 must have raised the eyebrows of those zealots of yesteryear. "*Kiss the Son* lest he be angry and ye perish from the way, when his wrath is kindled but a little. Blessed are they that put their trust in Him." In John 5:30, there is a direct quote from Jeshua: "I can of my own self do nothing; as I hear I judge: and my judgment is just; because I seek not *mine own will but the will of the Father*, which hath sent me." John 5:23... "That all men should honour the Son, even as they honour the Father. He that honoureth not *the Son* honoured not *the Father*." God told David in that same Psalm 2, that the Son is *the Way; the Way is to God*. For centuries men have searched for ways through the cycle of life and death. Those exploits are concealed in esoteric circles under "passages through the afterlife" and "transmigration of souls." John 5:24...He that heareth my word (Logos) and believeth on Him (notice He did not say "IT") that sent me, hath everlasting life, and shall not come into condemnation, but is passed from death unto life. John 10:9, "I am the door" is recorded as a quote from Jeshua confirming what was spoken by the prophet Isaiah in Isaiah 22:22-25 as to who would be the door and the location of the key that guarded the Fleece.

The treasures for the spiritual house of David were closely guarded from the chief thief. Isaiah 22:22, "The key of the house of David will I lay upon his shoulder; he shall open and he shall shut, and none shall open." Verse 23, "I will fasten him as a nail in a sure place and *he shall be a glorious throne to his father's house.*" Verse 24, "They shall hang upon him (not it) all the glory of his father's house, the offering and the issue, all the vessels of small quantity, from the vessels of cups, even to all the vessels of flagons." Verse 25, "In that day saith the Lord, shall the nail that is fastened in the sure place be removed, and cut down, and fall, and the burden that was upon it shall be cut off; the Lord hath spoken it."

The Son was a human vehicle for bringing the Logos and is now connected to The Logos. In other words, we humans are invited to be part of the Logos family, not bastards, but re-planted sterilized sons and daughters of the everlasting family of God. The Holy Spirit is the connector from Jesus to our Spirit Father God. God is not a person but a divine whole. Like a tree in a mangrove swamp we have the choice of being reconciled back to the parent plant or to reject nourishment forever. The Messiah himself told us that He hath not yet completed His finished work. Jacob was told that the stone could not be removed until all the flocks were in. Since Jacob was allowed to roll away the stone in the first instance, we must await the return of Jacob's seed for the completion of the finished work. When the work is finished, then the Son will be the permanent finished work of the refurbished temple of God. The Son is now God's Everlasting Oracle. Should we begin to give Him praises? Obviously! God decreed it in Psalm 2. Although part of a whole is not the whole, there is one path or one way to the whole of God. The Hebrew translation of the coded name or way is Jeshua. Hence when Daniel was granted a peek into the "future," he saw the redeemed light after the elimination of all spiritual darkness; he saw one "like the son of man." After the work was finished, the whole shone forth as one: the image of the past "shadow" and future "redeemed light" merged into one: 1st John 2:8 and Daniel 7:13-14. Genesis 1:5, "The evening *and* the morning were the first (yowme) day," the first (including the firstfruit Alpha/Omega) and the best belong to God.

CHAPTER 30. BEYOND THE PLATEAU OF RELEASED WISDOM.

CHAPTER 30A. WISDOM ABOVE 33 DEGREES!

Here is an esoteric chart. I will try to have a website set up at the completion of this book. Test your level of wisdom: By the year 2000, mankind's journey on earth would have been 230,982 years in my opinion. 2001 would be 230,983… 2018 would complete 231,000 years. Much evidence of those former years lay preserved under arctic ice at both ends of the poles. Piri Reis and Habagood's copies of pre-12th century maps show Queen Maud's land and other arctic regions ice-free and with rivers. The fact that the levels of polar ice have not increased might indicate that something in the magnitude of a global flood could have set the ice ceilings. Stonehenge, the monoliths of Easter Island and some man-made sub-Atlantic structures that I have seen, attest to those former years. Excessive carnality, influenced by the "Fellers," attributed to the demise of those civilizations—Genesis 6:4-12. Easter Island and four Caribbean islands I have surveyed—they appear to be residual masses from large landmasses that broke up. The carved heads that survived reflect the features of the former occupants.

MORE WISDOM.

Can a lion can hold a person that is perpendicular to the ground and draw him or her upward with its paw only? I posed the question to show those of lesser degrees that only the perfect master—*the one with 360 degrees*—can welcome anyone within The Veil. The Sphinx bears all the symbolisms of the Master of masters. His features are Hamitic. The symbol of the tribe of Judah is the head of a Hamitic man, or conquering lion of the tribe of Judah. A *lion's firm grip* affords and affirms the welcome. Archaeologists claim that the symbol for the tribe of Judah is a lion's head. Some say that the symbol is the head of a bear. Others say it is the head of an *ancient man*. The unfailing lion's sure steady grip for all the lost is *The Hand of the Conquering Lion of the Tribe of Judah*. The hand that greets you must be pierced—Psalm 22:16, "They pierced my hands and my feet." King David prophetically recorded those words. In Isaiah 1:11, he etched "To what purpose is the multitude of your sacrifices unto me? I am full of the *burnt offerings* of rams, and the fat of fed beasts; …I delight not in the blood of bullocks, or of lambs or of he-goats." Verse 13, "Bring no more vain oblations; incense is an abomination unto me; the new moons and *Sabbaths,* the calling of assemblies, I cannot away with…it is an iniquity, even the solemn meeting." To this day, assemblies are making a big deal over their rituals, or their preference for Sabbaths (dead works). All pastors need to read up to verses 15 from the first chapter of Isaiah weekly. Incidentally the altar of Calvary, from whence the cross of Jeshua was nailed, is on Mount Moriah. 1st Chronicles 22:3, "David prepared iron in abundance for the nails for the doors of the gates and for the joinings."

There is only one reference ever documented as to the identity of "The Ancient of Days."

Before I recap Daniel's vision, flash back to my solution to the 100-year college riddle as to which came first—the chicken or the egg. God hoisted the *Time Bridge* and figuratively Daniel saw the egg superimposed over the first chicken. Daniel recorded the vision he received while in Babylon during the first year of the reign of King Belshazzar. Incidentally, Archaeologists have already found inscriptions and cuneiform cylinders confirming the aforementioned. Daniel 7:13-14, "I (Daniel) saw in the night visions, and behold one like *the son of man* came with the clouds of heaven, and came to the *Ancient of Days* and they brought him near before him. Verse 14, There was given him dominion, and glory, and his kingdom that shall not be destroyed." According to the interpretation given for verses 17 and 18, those events have been partially fulfilled. The rise of the rulers of the Western Hemisphere had been accurately predicted and it came to pass. Verse 18 is yet to happen. The saints of the Most High shall take the kingdom, and possess the kingdom forever, even forever and ever. Since all the wisest people on earth memorize every aspect of the Temple that Solomon built, I will recap the important stages in the pre-planning of the construction. They had been listed in "Seven Progressive Stages:" 1) the foundation 2) the lumber 3) the victuals or provisions 4) the oracle 5) the altar 6) the door 7) and the nails for the door.

Isaiah 28:16, "Behold I lay in Zion for a foundation a stone, a tried stone, a precious corner stone, a sure foundation: he that believeth shall not make haste." Zechariah 3:8, "Behold I bring forth my servant the *Branch*." Isaiah 7:14, "Behold a virgin shall conceive, and bear a son, and shall call his name Immanuel." One of the names of God is Jehovah Jireh, my provider. Jesus took 5 barley loaves and two fishes and fed over 5000. Sorry Rastafarians, He is not Selassie. Haile Selassie was a born-again Christian who built numerous Christian churches in Ethiopia. I had the privilege of meeting a grandson of his. He is also a Christian convert, serving the one sacrificed at Calvary—*the Conquering Lion of the Tribe of Judah*—Jeshua. Napoleon visited the Pyramids of Egypt in search of that wisdom.

TRANSLATION OF THE ABOVE:

The failure to find the information in the previous chapter has caused more people to die of frustration than all the known killers combined. Imagine the cumulative figure if I include the numbers of so-called learned men who have died in wars and other demonically motivated conflicts because of the lack of understanding of the above. Forced slavery, racial prejudice, and every forged doctrine emanated out of the darkness that covered the things revealed herein. So in fairness to those that the establishments have considered "lesser mortals," I am ordered to disclose the ultimate secret. Over time, the imposter realized that the ultimate had been misunderstood and had caused unsuspecting men to invent a "Sophisticated Secret" which NONE of the so-called guardians ever knew. Had they known what the shrewdly supplanted secret was, they might *not* have guarded it. By default, the imposter had an interconnected altar of power in most deceived countries to receive homage to an unknown head that would eventually usher in "The New World Order." By bending philosophies, controlling their economies and their wars, the unknown head could only belong to one being. Unsuspecting men have paid homage to an unknown power. From the dawn of the Templars' Jerusalem invasion, to this date is almost 1000 years. Since the unsuspecting could not ask these questions, I will ask these two for you. Who is the supreme master of your secret altars? Why would God hide His supreme wisdom when He sent the only tried and tested vehicle to bestow the Golden Fleece upon all men? The tireless, ageless thief tried first:

1. To pollute the garden.

2. To kill the seed.

3. To prevent the branch from being grafted. The last two defeated him. Having polluted the ground, next he went after and polluted the first human "Seed Germinator." He figured that all the other seed would have been polluted. God in His wisdom arranged for all corrupted seed to be replanted in blood acceptable to Him. Then the spiritual grafting would take place. The thief cannot go to the altar where the grafting takes place. The Egyptians sought such a place by carnal means and their dead mummies are still there. The Greeks sought that place through philosophy. Many Americans believe they can get there with mammon. In fact a misguided church has caused millions to be lost by their teachings that somehow you can buy your way there through an "Indulgence." Supposedly, one of their chosen can pray you there after you are dead. The amount of falsehoods—taught and dispensed—makes me want to scream. No wonder the chief thief showed up in person one night threatening me: *THE DAY YOU BACKSLIDE, I PERSONALLY WILL CUT YOUR THROAT.* He then proceeded to brag and to name for me ALL the mighty men and women whom he had brought down with sex, deceit, money, power and printed confusion. He then bragged about his ability to wield influence in religious institutions that he controls, including one that I..."Before I explain, I must disclose the *Mission Statement* (Promised Restitution Plans) and meaning of the name of the Messiah.

CHAPTER 30B. MISSION STATEMENT OF THE MESSIAH.

Jeshua means God is Salvation. The Messiah's name is *His* mission statement. His name is spiritual authority and God's redemption plans: Immanuel, or God with us. The carnal Jeshua is no more. The translated being is the link to God through the Holy Spirit. 2nd John 1:9, "He that abideth in the doctrine of Christ, he hath both the Father and the Son." So far, among thousands of people worldwide who believe in the Creator, the only ones encountered in over 25 years of research who profess to have had a personal relationship with our God are those who have been ushered in the Veil. All were purged first before they came through the "One Door and True Light," whose name (authority) is above every name, translated: God is Salvation, Jeshua. How do we know that they spoke the truth? They manifest spiritual gifts and fruits of the Holy Spirit and they manifest the anointing of spiritual "Kings and Priests." Then again, I have encountered persons who have gone into unholy sanctuaries, who believe that they have met the true light. Sad to say they have met other lights, which will be described in detail in other volumes. For all those that have searched for, or are searching for the Messiah, be advised that Jeshua, Yasu, Jesus or Iosious is not only the first to have taught the way, the resurrection and how to achieve them, but is welcoming those who are "Chosen." I can now say, "I Bear Witness!"

His everlasting incorruptible sacrifice is affordable to all to reconcile us with our Creator through humility, repentance and forgiveness. Ecclesiastes 12:1, "Remember now thy Creator in the days of thy youth, while the evil days come not, nor the years draw nigh." In other words, before you become engulfed in sin, be reconciled to the Holy One. Ecclesiastes 12:5-7 gives us a foretaste of *THE PROMISE OF RESURRECTION.* Verse 5 lists the signs of impending death and verse 7 spells out the hope of resurrection: "Then shall the dust return to the earth as it was, and the spirit shall return to God who gave it." No mention is made of recycling spirits (no reincarnation).

The Messiah's identity: the Carpenter, the Logos and the Shepherd shall be nailed together, as the work is *"FINISHED."* The Carpenter's finished work will bring *all to judgment.* Ecclesiastes 12:10-14 contain the *WISDOM* of the centuries that have eluded man. They were recorded by the wisest man (born of natural conception) who ever lived. They could not be revealed until someone was invited within the veil to receive them at a specific time. In verse 10, "The *preacher* sought to find out acceptable *words* and that which was written was upright, even *words of truth."* In other words, Masters over the years have searched for those truths. Then the keeper of the Seal, the Logos who met me and invited me into *The Veil*, gave me the confirmation of His Word.

Solomon confirmed the "Word" in Ecclesiastes 12. Ecclesiastes 12:11, "The words of the wise are as goads (spiritual instructions) as nails fastened by the *Masters* of Assemblies, which are *given* from *one shepherd."* Verse 12, "My son be admonished, (be warned) of making many books there is no end; and much study is a weariness of the flesh." John 10:9 "I am the door" a quote from Jeshua. You will not find *the door* through philosophy or any other discipline; only by the *One True Confirming Logos.* In John 19:30, Jeshua's last words on the cross are: "It *is finished."* The Carpenter's Finished Work: Ecclesiastes 12:13, "Let us hear the conclusion of the whole matter: *Fear God and keep his commandments, this is the whole duty of man."*

Judgment: Ecclesiastes 12:14, "God shall bring *every work into judgment*, with every secret thing, whether it be good, or whether it be evil." Jeremiah 9:7, "I will melt them, and try them." 1st Corinthians 3:13—Paul elaborated similarly to the brethren at Corinth…the fire shall try every man's work. John received the visions of *Western Civilizations.* Revelation 3:10…to try them that dwell upon the earth. Jeshua since fulfilled the following:

a). Chosen vessel for the Spirit of God. Isaiah 11:2, Isaiah 42:1.

b). Oracle of God in the discourse of John.

c). Healer, Prophet, Magi, King and Priest. Isaiah 42:6-7.

d). Repairer of the breach. Isaiah 53.

e). Sacrificial lamb. Psalm 22.

f). Example of pious living. Isaiah 11:4.

g). Carpenter and much more; the defense rests.

Since Solomon built houses for all of his wives, when the Messiah arrived on earth the spiritual house had to parallel the path that Solomon traveled. Now that 99 percent of the prophecies have been fulfilled, it is time for the whole truth to be known.

The body that Jeshua used while on earth is translated. Like Enoch before him, like Moses, like Elijah—they are all translated beyond the boundaries of our universe. God sent *His Son* to show us the only way through "The Veil." Jeshua's former body is now a transformed spiritual magnet that draws pure, clean, forgiven and spiritually sterilized beings. Since it is a spirit/man, it is masculine gender. Jeshua now connects through the Holy Spirit to our Father and Creator. Many Christians mistranslate Hebrews 1:8, "But unto the Son, he said, Thy throne, O God, is forever and ever." Paul in his letter to the Hebrew brethren was quoting Psalm 45:6, written by the Sons of Korah (all 288 of them were prophetic worship leaders).

Follow the rules of the translators; lower case letters denote the quotes of the Tanakh or the Old Testament. The words of Jeshua are usually written in red letters. Since the words of Psalm 45 are not in red and are inserted in lower case letters, they were a direct quote from Paul from the Psalm. Therefore you cannot assume that Jesus was referring to himself as God chiefly because Jeshua did not speak them. The Roman church made that grave error and built an entire doctrine on that and similar errors. It was also easy for them to assume that—since so many regions had Trinitarian deities—they should have their own.

God is not foolish. He did not give Rome any authority to be His Oracle. In fact God prevented her language from being spoken en masse. Although it was used mainly in their literary arts, classical pieces, state letters and official documents, it was neither exported like the languages of other conquerors nor caressed in Rome's colonies as an everyday language.

CHAPTER 30C. THE HIDDEN KEY IN MUSIC.

Let us take a look at the keys on a piano. We will use the key of C for our reference. The notes in tonal sequence are as follows: C, D, E, E, G, A, B, then up to another C, an octave higher. Notice that the note of C begins and ends the scale; however the ending note is exactly one octave higher. The ending C note ends one scale and begins a new one—an octave higher. The sequence of notes represents the scale of C and all songs composed use similar or adjoining scales to encompass all the notes within. So a scale can be called a musical home for any given sequence of notes. There are seven ministering spirits that connect to the Spirit of God—one spiritual octave higher. Refer to the prophetic vision in Revelation 1: 4.

"Grace to you (seven churches in Asia) and peace from him which is, and which was, and which is to come, and from the seven spirits, which are before His throne." The seven spirits minister to the one that David prophesied would sit on the throne forever in Psalm 2. They are in total harmony. Harmony is obviously very important to *The Creator*. He detests disharmony or confusion. All the notes are comfortable in their respective scales. In the key of God, notice that the Seven Spirits minister to the Son, so the Son is the chord. Every time the Romans (to whom were not committed the Oracles of God) erred in their discordant translations, much confusion followed. In addition to fulfilling hundreds of prior prophecies, Jeshua is not only "The Golden Fleece" and God's spirit level, but His tuning fork as well.

Spirits are body-less beings. Each spirit in the harmonic key of Jeshua comforts the recipient. That is why when we praise Him, our praises go directly to God. Here is proof. In John 14:16 the translators use the word "Another" preceding the "Comforter," as follows: "I will pray the Father, and he shall give you (another) Comforter to abide with you forever." That is the newer translation. However the King James Bible translates, "And he shall give you another Comforter that he may abide with you forever." With that version, the proponents of the Trinity argued that the other means another *person* of the Godhead. The myth, which lasted almost two thousand years, can be dispelled immediately with the following facts: 1. God never was a man, since God creates all men and God changes not. "God is a Spirit and they that worship him must worship him in *Spirit* and in truth." The Greek word from which they derived "another" is allelon, the plural form of allelouia, which literally means praise to Jah. Consequently, allelon is used for praises from us to you or from "ourselves." That would make sense; since Jeshua was uttering those words. So, as root in the spiritual chord, He would be saying "ourselves" (from us, or appointed from us). Those were also esoteric praises uttered by the Essenes wherever the seven spirits were referenced in word. It is more evident that the early Romans were esoteric dunces.

Let us search for the preceding prophecy in the Tanakh—documented in Isaiah 11:1. "There shall come forth a rod out of the stem of Jesse, and a Branch shall grow out of his roots."

Verse 2…and the *spirit of the Lord* shall rest upon him,
> the spirit of counsel,
> the spirit of understanding,
> the spirit of wisdom,
> the spirit of might (or power),
> the spirit of knowledge,
> the spirit of fear of the Lord, alleluia!

Isaiah promised us that the Messiah (the chord of God) would be in total harmony with the Spirit of God, the higher spiritual note in harmony with His ministering spirits. Let us take a look at our redemptive spiritual chord when we become harmonious in God through absolute obedience. First, we must find our root—the perfect pitch. Let us begin with Jeshua: tested, proven, sinless, obedient, meek, loving, wise, and extremely generous.
Isaiah gave us the full meaning of His punishment in Isaiah 53.

His wounds are for:	1.	Transgressions.
His bruises:	2.	Iniquities.
His chastisement:	3.	Peace.
His stripes:	4.	Healings.
His blood (sacrifice):	5.	Sin Offering (unblemished lamb sanctifies us).
His blood:	6.	Deliverance.
His blood:	7.	Access to the Father (within The Veil).

Once we repent; we have an eternal sacrifice, which grants us forgiveness, access and sanctification. Once we are sanctified, our praises become the most powerful weapons available. Conversely, if we are sources of gossip-spreading or have been sowing discord in our assemblies, we must repent and cease from doing such things. Psalm 22 is a prophetic peek at Jeshua's complete suffering for our redemption package. Verse 3 tells us that the Messiah is *The Holy Chord* through whom God will inhabit righteous praises.

30D. THE MINISTRY OF MUSIC!

The second best musician currently touring the earth is Satan. He was *an anointed cherub* connected to the music ministry in heaven before he lost his heavenly job permanently. He was, is, and will continue to be over ambitious and frustrated. Any being that reached heaven and got permanent eviction papers has to be the most frustrated being ever. Ezekiel 28:13 gives a description of Satan before he came to earth. "Thou hast been in Eden, the garden of God; every precious stone was thy covering (and they are listed) …the workmanship of *thy tabrets* and of *thy pipes* was prepared in thee in the day that thou was created." When God gives you a gift and you mess it up, He does not take back the gift. Satan still has his music prowess. Hence, music is a powerful force that connects to the spirit domain. It can be used to praise Almighty God or to praise Satan. It should come as no surprise that as one plays certain hard rock and heavy metal music backwards and very slowly over amplified frequencies, subliminally implanted words such as, "I Love Satan" can be heard distinctly.

Let us inspect Ezekiel 28:14-16. Verse 14, "Thou art the anointed cherub that covereth and

I have set thee so; thou wast upon the holy mountain of God; thou hast walked up and down in the midst of the stones of fire. Verse 15...Thou wast perfect in thy ways from the day that thou wast created, *till iniquity* was found in thee. Verse 16...by the multitude of thy merchandise they have filled the midst of thee with violence, and *thou hast sinned.* Therefore I will cast thee as profane out of the mountain of God and I will destroy thee, O covering cherub, from the midst of the 'Stones of Fire.'" Observe how "Pride" had caused that embittered being to forfeit any future role or participation in the perfected sterilized, plague-less future. In John's end time vision, Revelation 12:10—"For the accuser of the brethren is cast down, which accused them before our God day and night"—His new assignments include being the accuser of the brethren and the right to attract to himself and to his domain of the damned, all puffed up and haughty people. No proud person can glory in God's presence. The list includes those believed infallible and above the law. Those types became laws unto themselves: *name, position, title, looks, worth or position does not impress God. They are all perishable.* Ezekiel 28:17, "Thy heart was lifted up because of thy beauty, thou hast corrupted thy wisdom by reason of thy brightness..."

I WILL CAST THEE TO THE (EARTH) GROUND. I WILL LAY THEE BEFORE KINGS, THAT THEY MAY BEHOLD THEE.

Every time I attend Pentecostal services in Israel, as the choirs begin and the ladies start to dance, I fall to the ground under the anointing. The precedent was established by David in 1st Chronicles 16:37-43. Whenever worship is sanctified, the presence of God is so awesome that people get healed and delivered. Psalm 22:3—God inhabits the praises of both His physically and spiritually chosen. I bear witness to both! David revealed the Firstfruit promise of "King and Priest" in Psalm 110, and John confirmed it in Revelation 1: 6—"Hath made us kings and priests unto God our Father."

At this moment I am receiving a horrible vision of despicable acts among loads of people in worship ministries and pastors also ministering on the holy altar of God while living double lives. Some are internationally recognized singers and musicians. Thousands of organists, singers, piano players, drummers and musicians who play and sing in churches are involved. I am going to call out the spirits (by name) that are corrupting the holy sanctuary and have you bound: Homosexuality, Fornication, Lesbianism, Adultery, Masturbation, Incest, and Addiction. Oh my God, the list is so long. Satan has targeted you for so long, that you are addicted to particular sins. I am warning you! Repent and seek deliverance now. Proverbs 28:13, "He that covereth his sins shall not prosper," spiritually or physically. Diseases that you are not aware of are already implanted. God is merciful. If you repent and turn from your evil ways, He will forgive your sins and heal you both of your addictions and of your diseases. Forty days after the release of this book and you continue in your iniquity, you will fall on your faces in the midst of your congregations and the spirits that have you bound will *make an open show for all to see. I proclaim it in Jeshua's name.*

30E. THE KEY OF WORSHIP.

Approximately two years prior to the birth of Jeshua, an *Ancient Order of Jews*—who had access to Jewish oral traditions—began searching for the Messiah. The Essenes, as they were called, carefully analyzed His teachings. They observed His many miracles and concluded that no one could perform miracles in the name of God and fulfill so many prophecies unless He was sent from God. Shortly after Jesus' death and the persecution that followed at the hands of the Romans, they retreated to secret caves in the area of Massada. In those secluded locations they were able to practice an extremely strict form of Christianity. Their traditionally secretive lifestyle caused later historians to assess them as clannish. Since all of their members were very erudite, they studied and practiced what Jeshua taught among them. The Essenes were esoterically enlightened. Their fervor, abstinence, purity of life and worship took them up to an unprecedented level of worship. It was not unusual for many of their brethren to see Jacob's ladder during their hours of pure worship. They chanted the Psalms. When the Roman gentry found their scrolls, they were unable to comprehend their writings. Records in Rome simply state that they were extremely pious and clannish. Only since the discovery of the Dead Sea Scrolls (which The Essenes allegedly hid) have translators begun to pay serious attention to their passages. Their records mention angels ascending and descending and joining their worship.

Our group of researchers has analyzed Christianity's checkered path over the past 2000 years. It has paralleled the paths of 1) Solomon and his seed and 2) Israel's journeys from Egypt through the wildernesses. Since a mixed multitude followed the ancient Israelites and all three flocks were promised one shepherd, it is logical that we had to search all accounts of the other two flocks. Since the demise of the Essenes, that level of worship that they experienced has only now begun to be experienced in a few spiritual assemblies. Sterilized assemblies (especially those in Africa and China) are experiencing that level of anointing.

Since none of Solomon's wives were virgins, we haven't found any 100% virgin or perfect churches. People have to be spotless for the worship to be righteous. Since Christianity was founded on principles of forgiveness and love, for the final prophecies concerning the "Fullness of the Gentiles" to come in, we have to find all that God included in that broad basket. We must find and forgive all that we have wronged. The Muslim seed of Abraham and God's prophetic plans for them also in the end times are of primary importance. The Muslims need to be forgiven for selling their brothers and initiating the Atlantic Slave Trade, so that the seeds of love and repentance can be sown corporately in their lives. An Arab/Christian Convocation of reconciliation and repentance can accomplish that. Christians of Africa, (North, Central and South) America, and the Caribbean should be included to break the yokes of hostility and rejection.

While the majority of Christians have witnessed the regression of their worship from the high standard set by the Essenes to that form of ritualized superficial recitations, Muslims in general have been consistent with their reverence for worship of God. Had Solomon been an obedient and pious shepherd, Satan would not have been able to interfere with the flocks. Prophet Mohammed would have been a reformer like Martin Luther. There could have been a reconciling convocation eradicating ritualistic substitutes and returning two flocks to the promise of—Gentiles bringing the Jews to jealousy. Can you picture the billions of angels that would ascend and descend from the *Ladder of Jacob* during the worship at such Convocations? Satan would go absolutely ballistic. Guess who would be brought to extreme jealousy by that? Psst, it had been prophesied. How can there be harmony in God's house when there is disharmony among the flocks? If the Shepherd is the Prince of Peace, shouldn't all three flocks eat of the *Tree of Peace* in harmony?

CHAPTER 30F. GOD'S PROMISES AND REDEMPTIVE PLANS FOR MUSLIMS.

There are promises mainly for Ishmael and his seed and Esau and his seed. By and large there are countries that are predominately Muslim and their primary religion is the religion of Islam. Those countries have been established as per prior prophecy. The birth of Islam was also prophesied. Since by definition Islam is the religion of Muslims, I will seek the words of Islam's foundation stone, Prophet Mohammed. Prophet Mohammed was of the seed of Abraham *through Ishmael*. He was a *trader*, not a *carpenter*. He was first married at 25. He was not born in Bethlehem, nor did his ministry span 40 years in Jerusalem. His first wife was a *widow*: that fact meant that any religious teaching emanating from him *would not* and *could not* be an original by divine decree. His spiritual legacy had to commence from a *religion* that was spiritually *widowed*. Had the former bridegroom disappeared? No direct communication or contact in His temple since John did 2000 years ago? Malachi was the last prophet that communicated with Israel corporately before John did. He never said he was the Messiah. *Prophet Mohammed testified as to the identity of the Messiah*. No real child of God could ever disobey God. By definition, to be a child of God you have to be obedient to God. Since the primary spokesperson for Islam is Prophet Mohammed, any Muslim who considers himself a child of God has to search the prophet's legacy for the directive as to where to find the prophecies of God for all of His people.

Covenant partners—who ever spoke disparaging words against Muslims, or doubted that they are God's people—*need to repent* of that immediately or as soon as possible thereafter for Muslims to receive the redemptive purposes of God. Prophet Mohammed never had access to a Koran. It was printed after his death. I will give the name of the book and the name of the Prophet that he directed Muslims to search: "The Book of Abraham, Noah, Moses and Jeshua." The "Book" that the Koran mentions has prophecies for all Muslims. We will be obedient and search that book for those prophecies.

THE PROMISES FOR ALL SEED OF ISHMAEL AND ISAAC ARE TO BE FOUND IN THE BOOK OF ISHMAEL, ISAAC, JACOB, ESAU AND FATHER ABRAHAM—THE TORAH.

About 2500 years ago, these words were recorded In the Torah. Psalm 118:22—"The stone, which the builders refused, is become the head stone of the corner." Prophet Mohammed's kindred did not reject him. His birth and death were not prophesied. Many of Jeshua's promises are as plain as the alphabet. Others would have required the publishing of this book to decode. God was specific in that He issued two prophetic paths: One for the Muslim nations, and another for the faith of Islam. In the Tanakh, the Torah and the Bible, the habitations of Ishmael and his seed were predestined to be the abodes of future Muslim nations. Such is the prophetic accuracy of the Torah. Genesis 21:12-21, is the genesis of the Muslim nations. In verse 13, God made a promise to Abraham for the child Ishmael: "Also of the son of (Hagar) the bondwoman I will make a nation."

Cain was born before Abel but because of the obedient heart of Abel, God selected Abel's sacrifice over that of Cain. Esau the firstborn of Abraham was genetically part Egyptian. He *had a disobedient heart*. In verse 19 of Genesis 17, God promised His covenant seed to his younger brother Isaac. However, in verse 20, God promised to make a *great nation* out of *the seed of Ishmael*. Until the seed of promise was sown, God *did not* prophesy *a religious covenant for Ishmael*. By prophetic appointment, since Esau and Jacob emerged out of the same womb, that of *Rebekah*, the Islamic religion had to be born out of the Hebrew religion and it came to pass. Esau was older than Jacob. God predestined the formation of *Arab* "nations" before the "the nation of Israel" came into being. Remember the wives of men chosen by God represent spiritual tabernacles. Since God only made a promise of "a mighty nation" to Ishmael through his father Abraham, in this book I will not detail all the paths of Ishmael's seed save those that were married to the seed of Esau.

The *promises* to Esau possess spiritual clout for the Arab and Muslim nations. Should a religion born out of the connected promises of God to Abraham through Isaac, through Isaac's promised seed, cause spiritual disconnection from God? God is too precise not to have forewarned of such. We searched and found prior prophecies. Genesis 25:21 was covered previously in the Secrets of Rebekah's Womb. In verses 6-9 of Genesis 28, we unearthed the root-foundation of Islam as a religion. In verse 9 as soon as Esau pursued Mahalath the daughter of Ishmael, the foundation of Islam was laid. Ishmael was conceived out of Abraham and Sarah's disobedience and impatience. When he was born, his mother (Hagar) felt "*abandonment and rejection.*" Esau went after the daughter of Ishmael because he felt rejected, betrayed and abandoned. Esau disobeyed the directive from God. His wife was sought through disobedience. Unlike Jacob, he did not seek his father—Isaac's advice or his blessing. In Genesis 26:34, Esau took Judith the daughter of Beeri (Hittite) and Bashemath the daughter of Elon (Hittite) for wives—more acts of rebellion as recorded in Genesis 26:35. God has proved time and time again that many things we do are born in disobedience. However God has made provisions for us by His redemptive plans, by His mercy and because of the covenant with our fathers.

Since Isaac had the messianic seed and God did not choose Esau's wives; then they (Esau's spiritual and physical wives) would have no messianic inheritance. The marriage between Esau and Mahalath the daughter of Ishmael meant that many of their seed would embrace Islam. There would be paternal emptiness also. The three wives of Esau give insight into the future branches of Islam: Sunnis, Shiites and the Kharijites. The omission of the two names of God in the Koran that deal with *fatherhood* and *love* reflect spiritual voids. Brothers and sisters, we need to pray for our Muslim brothers and sisters. The relationship of God to His redeemed sanctuary can be likened (better than) to that of man to his beloved wife. Women are *not* allowed in Moslem mosques. Readers who are not aware, that is not attributed to machismo, but to respect for God, the Holy and righteous spirit, decreeing that only sanctified blood be allowed in His sanctuary. Since there was one blood sacrifice deemed everlastingly acceptable to God, churches that accept Jesus' fulfillment of those promises have no such fear or worry. Jeshua had women ministering to Him. He preached *Love and Forgiveness!*

Esau and Ishmael's offspring also married Isaac's seed. By prophetic decree, the majority inhabited the southern regions of Israel. Those of Esau's Hittite wives ended up in African nations. Some of them got caught in the Atlantic slave trade. The greater majority had established separate nations whose promises were decreed in advance to their ultimate destinations. Ethiopia, Egypt, Lebanon and Assyria have had specific promises for their nations. Those that remained with their spiritual wells still covered had been identified by prior prophecies. Those destined to receive the latter-day prophecy of reconciliation, were identified by the prophet Isaiah in the 60th chapter of the Book of Isaiah—all the seed of Esau, Isaac, Jacob and Abraham. From verses 6-9, "*All shall come and show forth the praises of the Lord, those of Midian, Ephah, Sheba, Kedar, Naiboth and those residing in the isles.*" All mentioned are offspring of Esau. In verse 3 God began by prophesying through Isaiah that the Gentiles shall come to His light. The entire chapter 60 deals with reconciliation of the three flocks. The Midianites married the Moabites (Numbers 22:4) and settled around Jordan and Assyria. Moses married one of the daughters of a Midianite priest, Jethro. Here is a 4000-year-old quote from the priest of Midian, Jehtro, in Exodus 18:10-11. Verse 10, "Blessed be the Lord who hath delivered you out of the hand of the Egyptians and out of the hand of Pharaoh." Verse 11, "Now I know that the Lord is greater than all gods." 1st Kings 10:1-13 recalls the queen of Sheba's royal visit to Jerusalem's King Solomon. According to Ethiopian records, her son with Solomon bore the Tafari lineage. Most of them settled in Ethiopia and Sudan. Kedar produced nomadic rulers as referenced by Jeremiah 49:28-29. God made a prophecy for this remnant and it will come to pass.

Psalm 120, though recorded over 3000 years ago, the fulfillment has begun already. It is important to note that God prophesied that Satan would target specific people and beguile them with a false religious zeal "For a while" until a specific time when they will hunger and thirst for the truth. Psalm 120 singled out that offspring to show that whatever religion they would adopt, that the imposition would be *for a while*.

Verse 1, In my distress, I cried unto the lord, and He heard me.

Verse 2, Deliver my soul from lying lips and from a *deceitful tongue*.

Verse 3, What shall be done unto thee, *Thou false tongue*?

Verse 5, Woe is me, that I sojourn in **Mesech**, that I dwell in the tents (Bedouin) of Kedar!

Verse 6, My soul hath *long dwelt* with him *that hateth peace*.

Verse 7, *I am for peace but when I speak they are for war*. Since God prophesied that they would hunger for the truth, they will find the truth. Many of "those remnants" were enslaved and settled in the islands of the sea of the Gentile nations now called the Caribbean. Lots of their seed are producing mighty reggae gospel albums. Some from Ethiopia have *returned* to *Israel* and are working as missionaries. Others married the seed of Japheth and dwelt in Russia for a while. According to that prophecy they shall hunger for and receive the truth. Who then was that precious foundation stone upon which spiritual harmony is decreed? Who came as teacher, shepherd, priest, king, redeemer and firstfruit of the promise of resurrection? Who then is the Branch that is capitalized? Let us check Zechariah 3:8…for behold I will bring forth my servant the Branch. For behold the stone that I have laid before Joshua, upon *one stone* shall be *seven eyes*. To understand the vision of Zechariah 4:1-14, the meaning of the golden candlestick and the seven lamps, John the revealer explained the vision in precise detail in Revelation Chapters 2 and 3. Since the sequel to this book begins with the comparisons of both Zechariah's vision and that of John, I will simply say, "To be continued."

Next, let us scan (together) the master plan of Satan as directed towards Jews, Arabs, African descendants of both, and the most recently evolved of the Gentile nations. Satan is a thief, liar, destroyer and killer. Whenever Satan gets a footing, then his traits follow. Where he is entrenched, that is his aim: to kill, to steal, to rob, to destroy and to set enmity among those nations by a system of dividing and conquering—then deceit and even denial follows. At the center of this, or dismantler of his evil plot, is the teaching of Jesus. The Jews of yesteryear preached "An eye for an eye." Arab zealots argued that a jihad (holy war is justified.) According to Psalm 120:6-7, a philosophy of hatred and "unforgiveness" would cause them to search for, and find "The truth and path to peace." We must find and reveal the source of that hateful philosophy.

Around 760 C.E., the Ismailiya Secret Society got a foothold in Arab countries. They were very educated. "Druses and Assassins" held key positions of influence in the sect. Among the nomads, most of which were illiterate, they were held in high esteem. They established a philosophy that the seventh born from Ishmael should be set aside for greatness. They, along with the Asherites, the Mutazilites and the Kharijites were among the groups selected to evaluate Prophet Mohammed's revelations and to fashion a moral code for Muslims. The Kharijites on the other hand, held very Orthodox beliefs; among which—Death to anyone that violates their established principles—is primary. History records the power struggles that resulted in assassinations to some of Prophet Mohammed's successors. The displaced Gentiles have wrapped themselves into many false philosophies. Who else but Satan could influence people that arrived last on earth to assume that they must be first in all things? Satan has put in place a formula for everlasting conflict, "unforgiveness," death, rape, war, plunder, and greed. The Messiah teaches:

LOVE THY ENEMY. WOW! DO GOOD TO THEM THAT HATE YOU... WOW... FORGIVE!!!

There are four basic types of Jews:

1. Those that *knew* and died for their knowledge, to be "Born again to The Truth."

2. Those that had to fulfill the prophecy of the "Stiff-necked."

3. Those that know and are spiritually "Reborn," (the remnant as per prophecy).

4. Those still in bondage. Many are predestined to receive "The Truth."

There are the same types in the Arab nations.
There are the same types in the African nations.
There are the same types in the Gentile nations. However, many will receive God's judgment for being agents of the satanic master plan.

Had the Messiah and His teachings been accepted, there would have been no such thing as racial prejudice, war, discovering of lands, or spiritual captivity. Woe to those that do not ingest the words of Matthew 7:21. Many so-called shepherds, bound by the spirits of pride, weak teachings, the love of attention that propels some on the pulpits of arrogance, jealousy, greed, lust for power, money and fleshy glorying, their hell will be hotter because they **led God's sheep astray.**

The oft-foretold Messiah was predestined to be the rejected and crucified sacrificial lamb. Satan would love to believe that he engineered that. It has always been Satan's plan to exalt himself above the nations of the earth. Even though the event was prophesied, Satan did not dream to imagine what Jesus' passage would mean for him "beyond time." Trust me, he has an idea; that is why he tries to trap billions with falsehoods. Unfortunately, the most stubborn people are affected by his stubborn mind binding spirits. Those spirits *oppress* and then try to possess. They operate from an external base in the same manner that powerful radio and television stations work. They beam directly to captive minds. Since they are externally based, they are able to communicate with entire networks of spirits. People previously diagnosed as "crazy or schizophrenic," and have received deliverance, know what I am talking about. In addition to those extreme cases, people become "possessed" when—as a result of murder, occult practices, homosexuality or lesbianism, abortion, incest, paedophilia, adultery, fornication, masturbation or any "third strike occasion"—body fluids are released in disobedience to God's word. Humankind has made a 360-degree circle. We need to examine our collective alpha to determine our corporate omega. God is purity without limit. God waited until the earth collected enough excreta from dinosaurs and all the animals that lived on earth. When the earth's composition was 100% recycled garbage and dung, then He made man. From all that filth, He put His spirit in us. Without His light, His truth, His righteousness and His purity, His right Spirit will exit. Whenever the altar called man is unprotected, we return to our original cesspool. Spirits of a feather cling together.

To the houses of Judah and Israel, both spiritual and physical, we are the privileged. We are living in a time such as this, when our heavenly Father has chosen an earthly vessel such as I, a former persecuting, murdering zealot—who had been taken to the potter's house—to warn you. *Do not let your inheritance be stolen any longer.* May God reveal His true wisdom to you and may you have the strength to treasure and keep the same.

Prophetic Word: Out of the ashes of the former Roman Empire a leader will rise, whose meteoric climb will astonish the general public. Look for these traits: The church of the Western provinces will embrace him as one to unify the ancient Holy Roman Empire. By the time he escalates in the eyes of the world, his resemblance to what they thought was the messianic image would draw many lost to him with his charismatic zeal. This man will be involved in brokering a solution to the so-called Middle East Crisis. *Finis coronat opus!*

2000-year old letter found! I will print this letter written by a loving Father whose children wondered far off. Many are lost in strange lands with strange customs. His letter took over twenty five hundred years to reach you, who are the seed of the original M.I.A's. As more and more people use the computer as a research tool, more gems like these will be put together.

TO MY HUMAN RAINBOWS, THE CHILDREN OF THE WORLD:

You may not know me, but I know everything about you.	**Psalm 139:1.**
I know when you sit down, and when you rise up.	**Psalm 139:2.**
I am familiar with all your ways.	**Psalm 139:3.**
Even the very hairs upon your head are numbered.	Matthew 10: 29-31.
You were made in my image.	Genesis 1:27.
In me, you live and move and have my being.	Acts 17:28.
You are all my offspring.	Acts 17:28.
I knew you even before you were conceived.	Jeremiah 1:4-5.
I chose you when I planned creation.	Ephesians 1:11-12.
You were not a mistake,	**Psalm 139:15.**
All your days are written in my book.	**Psalm 139:16.**
I predetermined your births and your nationalities.	Acts 17:26.
You were fearfully and wonderfully made.	**Psalm 139:14.**
I planted you all in your mothers' wombs.	**Psalm 139:13.**
I brought you forth on the days that you were born.	**Psalm 71:6.**
Those who do not know me have misrepresented me.	John 8:41-44.
I am not distant or angry; I desire to lavish you with my love.	1st John 3:1.
Simply because you are my children and I am your father,	1st John 3:1.
I am the complete expression of love.	1st John 4:16.
I will offer you much more than your earthly fathers.	Matthew 7:11.
I am the perfect Father.	Matthew 5:48.
Every good gift that you receive comes from my hand.	James 1:17.
I am your provider and I will meet all of your needs.	Matthew 6:31-33.
I am always only a prayer away.	Jeremiah 29:12.
My plan for your future is total restoration.	Jeremiah 29:11.

I love you with an everlasting love.	Jeremiah 31:3.
My thoughts towards you are more than sand.	**Psalm 139:17-18.**
I rejoice over you with singing.	Zephaniah 3:17.
I will never stop doing good for you.	Jeremiah 32:40.
You are my treasured possessions.	Exodus 19:5.
I desire to establish you with all my heart and all my soul.	Jeremiah 32:41.
I want to show you great and marvelous things.	Jeremiah 33:3.
If you seek me with all your heart, you will find me.	Deuteronomy 4:29.
Delight in me and I will give you the desires of your heart.	**Psalm 37:4.**
I rejoice when you give and receive my good gifts.	Philippians 2:17.
I am able to do more for you than you can imagine.	Ephesians 3:20.
I am your greatest encourager.	2nd Thessalonians2:16-17.
I am also your Father who comforts you in all troubles.	2nd Corinthians 1:3-4.
When you are brokenhearted, I am close to you.	**Psalm 34:18.**
As a shepherd carries a lamb, I will carry you close to my heart.	Isaiah 40:11.
One day I will wipe away every tear from your eyes.	Revelation 21:3-4.
I will take away all the pains you have suffered on this earth.	Revelation 21:3-4.
I am your Father and I love you even as I love my son Jeshua.	John 17:23.
For in Jeshua, my love for you is revealed.	John 17:26.
He is the perfect representation of my being.	Hebrews 1:3.
He came to demonstrate that I am for you, not against you.	Romans 8:31.
To tell you, you can receive forgiveness for your sins.	2nd Corinthians 5:18.
Jeshua died so that you and I can be reconciled.	2nd Corinthians 5:19.
The sacrificial lamb's death was the ultimate unselfish love for all.	1st John 4:10.
Receive the gift of my Son (Repentance/Salvation); you'll receive me.	1st John 2:23.
Abide in obedience and nothing will separate you from my love.	Romans 8:38-39.
Give up sin; return to me. There will be great rejoicing in heaven over you-	Luke 15:7.
I gave my first and best to gain your love.	Romans 8:31-32.
I have always been Father, and will always be Father.	Ephesians 3:14-15.
My question is: Will you be my obedient children?	John 1:12-13.
I am waiting for you.	Luke 15:11-32.

FROM: GOD ALMIGHTY, YOUR LOVING FATHER ALWAYS.

COMPLETE TABLE OF CONTENTS

ISBN 1-4120-4319-0